Reproduced on the cover: Two views of architect Alfredo De Vido's own vacation home on Long Island illustrate the qualities that, for him, make up a very personal lifespace. The dramatic three-story interior reveals an interest in soaring vertical space. De Vido designed most of the furniture himself to create a unified overall effect. See also Fig. 476. *(Photographs: Ezra Stoller © ESTO)*

Inside Today's Home

Inside Today's Home

fourth edition

Ray Faulkner
Emeritus Professor, Stanford University
Sarah Faulkner

Holt, Rinehart and Winston

New York Chicago San Francisco Atlanta
Dallas Montreal Toronto London Sydney

Editor Rita Gilbert
Picture Editor Joan Curtis
Associate Editor James Hoekema
Production Supervisor Sandra Baker
Production Assistants Patricia Kearney, Faye Laffer
Designer Marlene Rothkin Vine

Figs. 5, 33, 200, 540, 655, Plate 4 from *Handmade Houses: A Guide to the
 Woodbutcher's Art* by Art Boericke and Barry Shapiro. Copyright © 1973
 by Arthur Boericke. Reprinted by permission of Scrimshaw Press, San Francisco.
Fig. 128 from *House & Garden Garden Guide*. Copyright © 1958, 1960, 1962, 1963,
 1964, 1965, 1966, 1967, 1968 by The Condé Nast Publications, Inc.
Fig. 470 from *The Personal House* by Betty Alswang and Amber Hiken. Copyright
 © 1961, Whitney Library of Design.
Figs. 528–530, 572, 573, 577 adapted from *Nomadic Furniture* by James Hennessey
 and Victor Papanek. Copyright © 1973 by Victor J. Papanek and James Hennessey.
 Adapted by permission of Pantheon Books, a Division of Random House, Inc.
Fig. 703 from *Cluster Development* by William H. Whyte. Copyright © 1964,
 American Conservation Association.

Library of Congress Cataloging in Publication Data

Faulkner, Ray Nelson.
Inside today's home.

1. Interior decoration.
I. Faulkner, Sarah, joint author.
II. Title.
NK2110.F38 1975   747'.8'8   74-11832

College ISBN: 0-03-089480-8
Trade ISBN: 0-03-089714-9

Composition and camera work by York Graphic Services, Inc., Pennsylvania
Color separations by Solzer & Hail, Inc., San Francisco
Color printing by Lehigh Press Lithographers, New Jersey
Printing and binding by Capital City Press, Vermont
789 138 9 8 7 6 5 4

Preface

The purpose of INSIDE TODAY'S HOME is to inform and delight—through images and ideas—all those interested in designing and personalizing their own homes. The underlying premise of the book is that the character of a home emerges from, expresses, and fulfills the personalities and lifestyles of its occupants. Thus, after much deliberation we chose the word "lifespace" to signify the kind of environment so totally in harmony with its inhabitants that it not only sustains but actually enriches life.

Through the previous three editions of INSIDE TODAY'S HOME we had endeavored always to keep the material as up to date as possible, in terms of both concrete information and general outlook. As we began work on this fourth edition, however, it soon became evident that an unusually complete and basic revision would be necessary. Styles and tastes inevitably change over a period of years, and these changes have a considerable effect on all areas of aesthetic expression, including the design of interiors. But beyond these superficial developments are more fundamental concerns that emerged during the decade of the seventies and that will profoundly influence home design for years to come. These factors include a marked increase in the diversity of lifestyles practiced today; new ways of structuring the family and the role relationships of its members; and above all a growing awareness of limitations in our world—limitations of space in which to spread out, of natural resources and energy supplies, of our environment's ability to absorb our wastes.

In response to these currents, we have attempted to discuss the special qualities, advantages, and design considerations inherent in all kinds of homes—from the tiny studio apartment to the multiroom house, from the prefabricated modular unit to the custom-designed dwelling, from the planned community home to the handbuilt cabin in the woods, from the brand-new structure to the renovated treasure, from the city loft to the country farm, from the mobile home to the huge megastructure, from the tepee to the geodesic dome. No longer can we address ourselves exclusively to the "housewife" as keeper of the home, for while many families retain the traditional work divisions, others have fragmented the task of household maintenance to spread the labor and allow each member to do what he or she does best. Our approach to environmental questions has been integral; throughout the text, wherever appropriate, we have dealt with the intelligent uses of energy and with the sensible application of materials from their sources through their utilization to their eventual return to the environment. More specifically, we have included sections on solar energy, on construction of homes to achieve natural climate control, and on recycling of materials—even whole houses.

As basic living patterns change, so does their outward expression. Of the 840 black-and-white illustrations in this book, more than 90 percent are new to the fourth edition, and all of the 61 full-color plates were chosen specifically for this revision. We believe that their size, fidelity of reproduction, and thorough integration with the text make them truly useful examples to support the written material, as well as strikingly beautiful decoration on the printed page.

Three completely new chapters have been added to this edition of INSIDE TODAY'S HOME. Chapter 1, "Personal Lifespace," sets the tenor of the whole book, with its brief outline of the social, cultural, psychological, and environmental factors that contribute to making our homes what they are. Chapter 7, "The Nature of Design," examines the fundamental role played by this elusive process in every facet of our lives, and discusses the ways in which design has adapted to a technological age. Chapter 25, "Modern Traditions," summarizes the history of architectural and interior design in the 20th century.

Overall, INSIDE TODAY'S HOME is organized in six parts. Part I, "Creating a Lifespace," begins with a general introduction to the concept of a home as a bubble of space that sustains and protects. The section proceeds to deal in turn with group spaces in which family and friends gather; private spaces where the individual can enjoy tranquility and solitude; and support spaces that provide for food and its preparation, the care and perhaps creation of clothing, and general household maintenance. The support systems of lighting, heating, cooling, and ventilation form the subject of one whole chapter, which also explores new and experimental energy sources. A final chapter treats the organization of space in the architectural plan.

Part II, "Design and Color," approaches the question of design from both a general and a specific point of view. After a broad discussion of design theory, it undertakes to outline the individual elements and principles of design, especially as they apply to the home. The chapter on color ranges from an introduction to color theory through the very concrete problem of choosing and carrying through a color scheme in the home.

Part III examines the qualities inherent in the various materials available today, from traditional clay and brick to 20th-century plastics and reinforced concrete. Part IV, "Major Elements," isolates particular segments of the home for special attention. Part V moves outside the home to consider first the architectural shell that defines interior space, next the immediate surroundings and landscape, and finally the community and the broader environment. This part concludes with a brief discussion of what we may expect to see in lifespaces of the future.

The home of today is not an isolated phenomenon but an amalgam of—and progression from—styles, tastes, and ideas of the past. Thus, we have included as Part VI a brief history of interior design from the Renaissance to the present, stressing throughout that the character of the home during each period was an expression of the social, cultural, political, and economic factors that then prevailed.

INSIDE TODAY'S HOME recognizes that the design of a living space is much more than a cosmetic attention to "furnishing" or "beautifying" rooms. Home design may, in fact, be among the most basic concerns of all of us, for it touches each human being and provides the springboard—the point of origin—for every one of life's endeavors.

Acknowledgments

The list of those whose help made this edition possible is very long; it has been a mutually reinforcing group whose efforts went far beyond the expected or anticipated. For expert professional advice, we are indebted first to Professor Victoria Brin of the Department of Home Economics, San Fernando Valley State College, who undertook a very complete analysis of the third edition of INSIDE TODAY'S HOME with a view toward improving this revision. Her comments were unusually helpful in stimulating us to fresh ways of considering the material.

Professor Cory Millican of Cornell University's College of Human Ecology generated many of the ideas now found in the design chapters and reviewed all the historical material in Part VI. Victor K. Thompson, Emeritus Professor of Architecture at Stanford University, served as our consultant on architectural plans and residential architecture in general, contributing much of the material in Part V. Many of the teachers who have used INSIDE TODAY'S HOME in their classes were generous enough to answer our exhaustive questionnaire, and their comments are reflected in the fourth edition.

A book that treats visual material depends for its quality on the excellence of the illustrations. We have been exceptionally fortunate in gaining access to many beautiful photographs, both black and white and color, and we wish to thank the many individuals and firms who supplied them. We are particularly indebted to photographers Morley Baer, John T. Hill, Philip L. Molten, Robert Perron, Julius Shulman, and Ezra Stoller who opened their files and allowed us to choose freely, thus giving us access to hundreds of extraordinary photographs, many of which had never before been published.

For the staff at Holt, Rinehart and Winston who collaborated on this edition, our enthusiasm is limitless. Our editor Rita Gilbert dedicated more than a year of her life to the project and really should be listed as coauthor, so great have been her contributions in the development of ideas, actual writing of manuscript, selection of illustrations, and above all relentless moral support. Joan Curtis brought to the acquisition of photographs and permissions her special brilliance, compounded of taste, persistence, organization, broad knowledge, hard work, and wit; we could not have made this beautiful book without her. James Hoekema combined absolute meticulousness and unflagging delight in reorganizing the historical chapters, in preparing the summary chapter dealing with modern styles, and in his considerable reworking of the material in Part V. The elegant design and intelligent page-by-page layout of the book were the work of Marlene Rothkin Vine, who perfectly supports our contention that aesthetics and function are compatible. Patricia Kearney and Faye Laffer manipulated endless production details; Sandra Baker coordinated the efforts of suppliers and worried constantly about the schedule; and Dorothy Lewis prepared a thorough and workable index. Our publisher W. Kenney Withers presided benignly and unflappably over the whole operation. Finally, to Dan W. Wheeler, once our editor and still our friend, go the special thanks due one who convinced us to undertake the staggering task of this revision.

Friends and relatives also helped us in various ways. Arbie Farmer kept track for many months of our voluminous lists of possible illustrations, cross-referencing them for easier control. And our sons, Jim, John, Pat, and Bill have once again lived through a book revision, a process that has practically paralleled their lives. To them go our thanks for providing the day-to-day support that enabled us to carry through on the project, not only by buoying up our spirits when necessary but also by supplying many of the insights into contemporary lifestyles. Jim and Pat also pitched in and worked on some of the chapters. All four are cause and effect, and the book is dedicated to them.

Stanford, California   R.F.
February 1975   S.F.

Contents

Creating a Lifespace

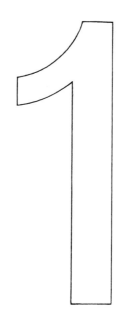

1 Personal Lifespace

A lifespace is a shelter that protects and encourages the fullest development of each individual's potentialities. Just as each life is at the same time personal and part of a larger society, each lifespace will be both individual and part of the total environment. Although we cannot cut ourselves off entirely from interaction with the environment (nor would most of us want to), we can each create a haven—an area and an aura in which the life forces within us can enjoy the peace and the stimulation necessary to come to full flower.

Central to the concept of a lifespace is the idea of *territoriality*. One's territory is that portion of the universe that is one's own, that engenders feelings of belonging, safety, and comfortable familiarity. Countless disputes and even wars have arisen over the "own" territory of a particular group. Anthropologist Edward T. Hall has written: "To have a territory is to have one of the essential components of life; to lack one is one of the most precarious of all conditions."

Not only should each household establish a territory of its own—implicit in the home or lifespace—but each individual should have a particular territory that remains inviolate to others. In the affluent household, each member may claim rights to a whole bedroom or study; less sumptuous arrangements could provide a special corner or simply a chair that belongs to one person and one person only. Hall points out a situation familiar to most of us. A guest enters the house and heads for the most comfortable chair. Approaching it, he hesitates. The host insists the visitor take that particular chair—and then throughout the encounter remains vaguely annoyed that a stranger has usurped *his* territory.[1]

The popularity of the monogram suggests how important this sense of ownership is to the human psyche. A world of increasing mechanization, of unfathomable billions of people reinforces the need for individual territoriality. The possession of a special chair, a special towel, even a special place at the dinner table carves out a segment of infinity that is uniquely one's own. Extended to encompass the area in which one lives, this is a lifespace.

According to the demands of their inhabitants, lifespaces can be wildly divergent in character. A lifespace may be large or small, temporary or permanent, on the ground, above it, or below it; it might be a studio apartment, a mansion,

---

[1] All notes to the text will be found in a special section on page 592.

opposite: 1. A two-story well above this dining room-gallery creates dramatic vertical space in an Oregon house designed by Campbell-Yost & Partners. Tall, narrow panes in the double window wall, as well as the rows of framed prints, help to emphasize the impression of soaring height. (*Photograph: Julius Shulman*)

a houseboat, a dome, a condominium, a mobile home, a commune, a tent—or even a house (Fig. 2). But in spite of the seemingly limitless variety, certain influences do guide us in the creation of a lifespace.

Biology dictates what our basic needs are: shelter from the elements and from intruders, physical rest, and nourishment.

Culture dictates generally how we will fulfill those needs—with a roof and walls to enclose us, places to recline our bodies, and facilities for preparing food.

Personality dictates what those need-fulfilling elements will look like, how they will be arranged, what will be their particular character.

Of the three, biology is both the most rigid and easiest to understand. Human beings cannot survive without food or sleep and will not endure for long in the absence of protection from rain and snow, cold and wind, sun and insects.

A much more complex term, *culture* refers to the system wherein a group of people—a *society*—share certain value perceptions; that is, there are common ways of doing things, common notions of right and wrong, common ideas about how things ought to be. An American child, while still quite young, generally learns to shake hands upon greeting people outside his or her immediate circle; a Japanese child learns to bow. Each of these types of behavior is "normal" for the culture in which it takes place.

Personality, of course, characterizes the individual rather than the group. It is the way in which each person realizes a special identity by learning to color the system without violating it. Personality is "the real me." A simple example will illustrate the interaction between culture and personality. Western culture decrees that, when one appears in public, certain portions of the anatomy must

2. Conventional materials, handled with imagination, shape the free, sculptural forms of this unique home in Oklahoma. Herb Greene, architect. (*Photograph: Julius Shulman*)

3. The classic Japanese house has sliding doors and panels that can be closed or opened to structure the interior spaces as needed over the course of the day.

be covered. Further, our culture delimits several degrees of modesty for different situations. The brief bikini that would go unnoticed on a beach would be shocking—in other words, a violation of cultural norms—on a downtown street. Yet within these standards what marvelous variety of expression we can find on any beach or street! No two costumes are alike in design, color, or fabric. We might say, then, that culture makes us comfortable or secure in our way of life, while personality enriches it.

In a homogeneous culture, where most people's values, tastes, goals, and ideas are similar, notions of what constitutes a home are fairly uniform. Yet the concept of a home, or even a house, that many of us take for granted is by no means universal. Anthropologist Margaret Mead has written:

> Ideally, even the appearance of a house should come to one as a new, fresh impression. In a sense it should come to one as a surprise that there are houses and that they are square or round or oval, that they do or do not have walls, that they let in the sun or keep out the wind or rain, that people do or do not cook or eat in a dwelling house. . . One can take nothing for granted.[2]

Considered in this context, we might say that the typical Western dwelling consists of a *multipurpose house* with *single-purpose rooms.* Traditionally in our culture, all the functions of daily life except working are performed within one structure—sleeping, preparing food, eating, cleaning the body, entertaining, and so on. Yet within this multipurpose structure, we have most often assigned specific regions to each of these activities and called them bedroom, kitchen, dining room, bathroom, living room. A separate structure, named office or factory perhaps, serves as the "working house." In other cultures, however, quite different arrangements may be seen as normal.

The classic Japanese home, for example, is a multipurpose house with multipurpose rooms (Fig. 3). Spaces are not demarcated permanently by walls; instead, screens or sliding panels that can be closed or opened easily adapt the space to

4. The New York loft owned by painter Frank Stella is a vast open space well adapted to displaying his collection of modern art. "Rooms" are created by arranging furniture on a square of rug or around a raised seating platform. See also Fig. 482. (*Photograph: John T. Hill*)

5. A collection of separate "houselets," private but companionable, constitute a home in the country. Individual units of such a multihouse dwelling could be built as inclination, time, and money allowed. (*Photograph: Barry Shapiro, from* Handmade Houses)

changing needs over the course of the day. What is by day the "eating room" or the "living room" becomes at night, with the addition of mats, the "sleeping room." Conversely, in parts of the South Seas we encounter single-purpose houses; the principal family dwelling serves for sleeping, while cooking and eating are done communally in a separate "cooking house."

In recent years more and more households in the United States have broken free of the boxes-within-a-box formula to create lifespaces suited to their individual needs. The studio apartment or loft is not very different in concept from the Japanese house and embodies the same goal in its planning: the most flexible utilization of space (Fig. 4). And one family in California satisfied their desire for maximum light, ventilation, and privacy by building a cluster of small, single-purpose houses for dining, bathing, and sleeping that together make up a family dwelling complex (Fig. 5).

right: **Plate 1.** Warm, sunny colors and a profusion of patterns can create a cozy environment to offset the depressing effect of a damp, chilly climate. Seymour Avigdor, designer. See page 11. (*Photograph: John T. Hill*)

below: **Plate 2.** A New Haven home combines striking modern architecture with mellow antique furnishings. White walls act as a perfect foil to the curves and vivid upholstery of the sofas. Caswell Cooke, architect. See page 12. (*Photograph: John T. Hill*)

Factors in Planning a Lifespace

Culture and personality are both broad, general terms. In order to understand them in relation to a particular group or individual, we generally list a number of attributes and characterize the unique expression of them. To describe a culture, we might consider its religious system, its moral code, the degree of isolation or cooperation among family groups, its mode of recreation. Samoan culture is typified by a belief in magic and ritual, relatively permissive sexual mores, communal cooking and working arrangements, a preoccupation with formalized dance, and so on. Similarly, in order to describe a lifespace, we can list several factors and then characterize the way in which a given household has responded to them. Among these factors are climate, location, mobility, people, lifestyle, psychology, and taste.

Climate

We might expect that a house built in North Dakota would have solid walls, tight insulation, and provision for adequate heat; that a house built in Florida would have protection from the sun, a cooling system, and screening against insects. But beyond these specific physical considerations, it is possible to create an *atmosphere* of "warmth," of "cool," of "snugness," or of "airiness." The living room of a house in Vermont (Fig. 6), meant for winter weekends, accomplishes just such a goal. Knotty pine throughout the interior lends a feeling of warmth and solidity in an area where heavy winter snows are common. The thick plush rug and comfortable built-in seating contribute to the sense of snugness. Of course, the fireplace, too, plays a role in keeping the occupants warm, not just in actual heat generated but psychologically as well. Nearly everyone recognizes the special feeling of security one can get when sitting before a roaring fire on a cold, wet night.

The thick-walled, light-colored houses of the American Southwest—as of most Mediterranean countries—have the same purpose, in reverse. Just as wood is considered to be a "warm" material, so adobe and stucco are "cool" materials, blocking the transmission of heat with their thickness and reflecting sunlight

right: 6. Warm natural materials—knotty pine, plush carpeting, and bright upholstery fabrics—create an aura of snugness in a Vermont ski house. Hobart Betts, architect. (*Photograph: Norman McGrath*)

opposite above: Plate 3. An antebellum house in Savannah was given a new life with imaginative renovation. Salvaged furniture, rejuvenated with new paint and upholstery, plus modern graphics provide a contemporary look. See page 22. (*Photograph: Elliot Erwitt, Magnum Photos*)

opposite below: Plate 4. The dining room of Art Boericke's handmade house continues the rustic, very personal quality of the exterior (Fig. 33). Old but sturdy furnishings, reused lumber, and found objects add up to a warm and inviting lifespace. See page 27. (*Photograph: Barry Shapiro, from* Handmade Houses)

left: 7. Cool, elegant furnishings and effects seem most at home in a formal city apartment or townhouse. (*Photograph: Morley Baer*)

above: 8. A rustic, country atmosphere defies what might have been a depressing location in this Chicago basement apartment designed by owner Don Konz. (*Photograph: Hedrich-Blessing*)

below: 9. If it is thoughtfully planned, a country house can be as elegant and sophisticated as the owner wishes, yet still blend with its surroundings. Myron Goldfinger, architect. (*Photograph: Norman McGrath*)

10. Many elements contribute to the special local character of this Santa Fe home—thick adobe walls, rugged beamed ceiling, wideboard floors, and country furnishings. The owners gradually acquired both building materials and artifacts in their travels. Nathaniel Owing, architect. See also Fig. 35. *(Copyright © O. R. Cabanban 1974)*

outward by their pastel colors. A home decorated in light colors and containing broad areas of uncluttered space will make its owners *feel* cooler to the point that they actually *are* cooler.

People who live in chill, wet climates, such as that of London, may choose to counteract the depressing psychological effects of the weather by the way in which they decorate their homes. Warm colors—reds, oranges, yellows—and in general patterns and colors that delight the eye can bring the quality of sunshine indoors regardless of its presence outside (Pl. 1, p. 7).

Location

Whether a home is in the country, the suburbs, or the city will certainly have some effect on its character. A city apartment, occupied for most of the year, seems to lend itself more readily to traditional, relatively expensive furnishings than does a vacation home (Fig. 7). But this effect need not be so rigidly dictatorial as some might think. No rules demand that a city apartment be formal, or that a house in the woods be countrified.

The living room pictured in Figure 8 forms part of a basement apartment in central Chicago. Previously a commercial laundry, the space was filled with pipes, electrical lines, water meters, and gas mains. To dispel the industrial image and create a more human atmosphere, the owner filled the room with mellow old furniture, soft textures, and a profusion of growing plants. Exposed brick walls and wood beams (which conceal the pipes) augment the rustic quality.

Figure 9 illustrates a sleekly modern, rather sophisticated living room such as we might expect to find in a townhouse or city apartment. Actually, it forms part of a cement-block carriage house built in the early 1900s on a large country estate. In converting the carriage house into a residence, the owners and their architect maintained the rural charm of the exterior yet made of the inside a bright, contemporary lifespace.

Both of these examples would seem to controvert the quality of their locations. A house in Santa Fe, however, exploits to the fullest the character of old New Mexico (Fig. 10), with its thick adobe walls, rough-hewn beams, and unfinished wideboard floors. Furniture and artifacts reflect the dual influences of the Southwest Indians and Spanish missionaries. Regardless of the approach—harmonious contrast or true authenticity—location will nearly always affect the mood of a home.

Mobility

When location becomes a question not of putting down roots for a lifetime but of planning a temporary or semipermanent lifespace, the outlook must be more flexible. As we all know, Americans are rather a restless people; one out of every five households packs up and moves to a new location each year—some only around the corner, many clear across the country. The increasing popularity of mobile homes suggests that people are less willing to commit themselves irrevocably to living in one place forever.

The family that owns a houseful of traditional furniture certainly might not want to throw it all out and start afresh upon moving into a modern home. The challenge then becomes one of making the old furniture fit gracefully into a new environment. Plate 2 (p. 7) shows how one family accomplished this. The house itself is strikingly contemporary, with flat white walls, varied ceiling heights, and a bright airiness enhanced by broad areas of glass; the furniture is traditional and quite formal. Yet there is no jarring sensation of grandmother wearing a space suit. Rather, the two elements settle together comfortably and in such a way that each heightens the drama of the other.

Several other furnishing possibilities exist for the household that anticipates spending only a short time in one place. Some people have made a science out of "scavenging"—that is, collecting old furniture for nothing or next to nothing and restoring it to furnish their homes (Fig. 11). Salvation Army outlets, junk shops, garage sales, even the street where trash is left for collection offer treasures for the canny scavenger. In rural areas the country auction or barn sale serves a similar purpose. Often such discarded pieces need only a coat of paint, or the removal of old layers of paint, to give them a second life. Then, because little or no money has been invested, the furniture can either be sold to incoming tenants or simply left behind when the household moves to new quarters.

For those who prefer brand-new, contemporary furniture, paper suggests an inexpensive way to provide for essential pieces of equipment—such as chairs, tables,

11. Recycled materials belie their age in this strikingly contemporary New Haven apartment designed by owners Andrus Burr and Peter Rose. The old table top rests on a new base of heavy plywood, chairs get a fresh coat of bright paint, and empty wine bottles without labels, serve as decoration. (*Photograph: John T. Hill*)

right: 12. A lounge chair made of cardboard is not only inexpensive to buy but light enough to be readily moved across the room or across the country. Frank O. Gehry, designer. (*Courtesy Easy Edges*)

below right: 13. Demountable furniture has long been a favorite wherever mobility is important. The "Colonial" chair is a descendant of British military campaign furniture prized for its stowability. (*Courtesy Stendig, Inc.*)

and desks—in a temporary home. Scarcely one's image of "cardboard" furniture, the lounge chair in Figure 12 was made by laminating together layers of corrugated cardboard. The resulting chair is very strong and surprisingly comfortable. More conventional in design, the chair reproduced as Figure 13 affords great portability, since it can be disassembled completely. The pieces occupy very little space and could be moved with ease.

Of course, the ultimate in mobility motivates those who carry their possessions—or, in fact, their lifespaces—with them when they move, in a trailer or camper. Fitted with kitchen appliances, bathroom fixtures, often quite comfortable sleeping and living areas, a wide variety of mobile homes offer the possibility of moving to a new location almost at will. Degrees of mobility range from the entirely self-contained camper with chemical toilet plus water and gas tanks; through the unit that requires hookups with external plumbing, electricity, and gas; to the most elaborate mobile homes that often are set upon foundations and extended with roofed terraces. Although mass produced, such accommodations present the same opportunity for personalization as any other lifespace.

People

The number and relationships of people who comprise a household must be a primary factor in planning a lifespace in order that the needs of each individual, and of the group as a whole, can be met. Anthropologist Paul Bohannan defines the household as: ". . . a group of people who live together and form a functioning domestic unit. They may or may not constitute a family, and if they do, it may or may not be a simple nuclear family."[3] Clearly, this definition encompasses a great variety of living arrangements: the single person household; two or more people who are not related; two or more people who are related by blood; the married couple; the nuclear family (husband, wife, and their children); the extended family (a nuclear family plus grandparents and/or uncles, aunts, cousins, and so on); the commune. Even this list is not exhaustive; the addition of long-term or short-term guests brings yet another variable.

Optimally, a lifespace planned for more than one person should provide just the degree of privacy and just the degree of interaction with others that each member desires. In addition, each individual should have at least a small portion

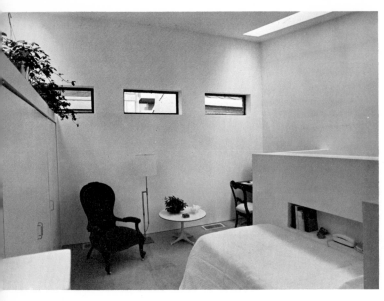

14–16. Decorator Betsy McCue planned two very different but compatible environments for herself and her mother, designer Mary Epstein, in the Philadelphia house the two women share.

above: 14. Miss McCue's bedroom complements her personality and serves as a haven in which to retreat from her busy life. The Victorian chair emphasizes the simplicity of the space and its furnishings. (*Photograph: Stephen Hill*)

right: 15. Mrs. Epstein chose to surround herself with old family furnishings, piling design on intricate design. A strict centering of the bed within the space unifies the arrangement. (*Photograph: Stephen Hill*)

below: 16. A cross-section of the Epstein-McCue house demonstrates how space has been manipulated to afford each woman privacy. The entire lower floor is a rental apartment.

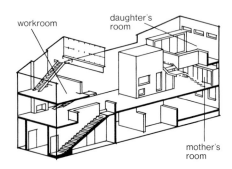

of space that expresses and extends his or her own personality. Decorator Betsy McCue conceived such an arrangement for herself and her mother, designer Mary Epstein (Figs. 14–16). The house is a converted stable in Philadelphia, of which the upper two stories comprise the Epstein-McCue residence. Miss McCue's bedroom-balcony, on the topmost level, is stark white, with broad, simple planes and a spartan bed. Mrs. Epstein's sleeping area below features a massive 19th-century four-poster bed, plus a happy mixture of colorful patterns in the bedspread, chair seat, and rugs. The stairs leading upward, covered in fragments of Oriental carpets, connect the two bedrooms, but the arrangement of spaces and partition walls allows each woman to maintain sufficient privacy.

Another element related to the people who comprise a household is the daily cycle that each maintains. For example, the classic nuclear-family routine might consist of rising, breakfast, husband going to work, children leaving for school, wife setting about her daily tasks, children returning from school and going out to play, husband returning from work, dinner, leisure activities, retiring for the night. Since no individual's daily cycle conflicts seriously with any other, an overall harmony prevails, and no special arrangements need be made in planning the home. But if two members of the household have conflicting schedules—if, for example, one works by day and the other by night, or if one maintains an office or studio in the home while the other pursues dissimilar activities—the lifespace must somehow accommodate both.

Lifestyle

Lifestyle is a nebulous term that could be defined in many different contexts. But for purposes of planning a lifespace, we might consider it to mean the portion of time devoted to various activities in the home. For instance, some households regard the home simply as a place to eat and sleep, with all other pursuits—recreation, work, and so on—undertaken elsewhere. This type of lifestyle might characterize the single-person household or the family who are much involved in community activities. Other families enjoy a considerable homelife that centers around sociable family meals, games or hobbies, and group amusements. Still others do a great deal of entertaining in the home, from small dinners to elaborate cocktail parties, the latter possibly having a quasi-business purpose. Finally, there are many households in which one or more members work full time in the home. The well-planned space will provide for whichever of these variables dominates the lifestyle.

The first lifestyle—that which considers the home a "base of operations"—makes few demands: it requires only a quiet and comfortable place to sleep, plus simple facilities for cooking and consuming food. The second, maintained by the family with many home activities, indicates a place for the household to gather—a living room or family room—as well as special provision for whatever the typical pursuits are (a game room, sewing area, workshop, studio, or whatever). Depending upon the scale of entertaining to be done, the third lifestyle may be satisfied by a generous living-dining area or even a huge center for social gatherings such as that illustrated in Figure 19.

The work area in architect Peter Samton's home (Fig. 17) shows how successfully a rather small space can be adapted to a home office. Here there is ample

17. A small home office can be delineated and partially segregated by built-in furnishings, yet still remain accessible and responsive to the life around it. Peter Samton, owner-architect. See also Figs. 30, 31, 161. (*Photograph: David Hirsch*)

right: 18. The small living room of this country cottage, with its overstuffed furniture, ruffled curtains, and floral patterns, would delight anyone whose ideal lifespace is a snug, secure nest. John Maurer, designer. (*Photograph: Robert Perron*)

below: 19. A Connecticut house built for people who entertain often and on a grand scale features an immense group space divided subtly into pavilions by means of varied ceiling heights, columns, and furniture arrangement. Donald Mallow, architect. (*Photograph: Norman McGrath*)

work space and storage, as well as unlimited light from the sloping glass ceiling. A comfortable chair in one corner and the tiny balcony offer the opportunity of quiet respite from work, while many potted plants help to dispel the cold office atmosphere.

Psychology

Claustrophobia—the fear of enclosed spaces—affects many people to some degree. In its mildest form it causes discomfort when the body is physically confined or when the individual is caught in the center of a tightly packed crowd of people. Serious claustrophobes feel great anxiety in small rooms and cannot tolerate elevators or telephone booths at all. The opposite phenomenon, agoraphobia, describes a fear of being in or crossing open spaces. In the absence of walls or other confining fixtures, the agoraphobe experiences a feeling of great insecurity.

Such factors deserve consideration in planning a lifespace. For many people, the living room illustrated in Figure 18 would be a safe, secure haven. It is a nest, cozy and comfortable because of its very smallness (it is only 12 feet square), the solid walls and low ceiling, the snug, overstuffed furniture. A markedly claustrophobic individual, however, might view such a room as a prison, feeling trapped until escape was possible.

The person who craves open space, broad vistas, and lack of confinement would delight in the house reproduced as Figure 19. Its huge living area, conceived in terms of four pavilions, soars to double-story height at one end. Clerestory windows under the ceiling augment the window walls in unifying the house with the out-of-doors. Such an enormous space could easily resemble an airplane hanger, but the architect has humanized it and created interest by varying the ceiling heights, by the pavilion effect, and by the subtle demarcation of areas through furniture placement. Of course, this house would not satisfy the individual who requires the psychological protection of a "nest."

A good compromise between the conflicting desires for "nest" and "vista" would be the inclusion of both in the same house. Indeed, many homes built today choose this solution. Group spaces, where the household gathers or guests are entertained (see Chap. 2), feature high ceilings and an easy flow between major sections, such as living room, dining area, and kitchen. But private spaces (see Chap.3)—meant for sleeping, reading, quiet tête-à-têtes, or whatever—are smaller; they have solid walls, lowered ceilings, and fewer windows. Thus they provide a sense of snugness and security. The house in Figure 36 offers both types of environment within the group living space itself—a wide open area plus a "cave" to one side.

Taste

Among the most revealing indices of personality is taste, which we can define as the particular likes and dislikes of an individual. Questions of taste are familiar to us from everyday experience—a preference for beef over lamb, blue over yellow, roses over chrysanthemums. Such preferences are almost impossible to explain, drawing as they do upon a lifetime of diverse influences. Moreover, many of our tastes are absorbed in the acculturation process. Going beyond the individual, we might speak of a "group taste" whenever significant portions of a society share a liking for some particular thing not popular in other societies. An affinity for sports of pageantry or rituals like the tea ceremony could be considered manifestations of group taste in particular cultures. For the most part, though, when we speak of taste we mean that of the individual, that which expresses personality. And taste is perhaps the single most important factor in determining what a lifespace will look like.

A comparison of Figures 20 and 21 shows how dramatically personal a room can be because of the tastes of its owners. The kitchen-dining area in Figure 20

left: 20. The kitchen of painter Alfonso Ossorio's Long Island house reflects the owner's joy in "things." Shunning closed cupboards altogether, he has made of food and the implements used to prepare it objects of delight for their colors, shapes, and textures. (*Photograph: Norman McGrath*)

below: 21. A drastically Minimal living room in New York subverts everything to the owners' art collection, which becomes the only focus of attention. Bil Ehrlich, owner-architect. (*Photograph: Norman McGrath*)

is an extravagant feast for the eyes, a bazaar of colors and shapes and textures crammed into every possible corner. Obviously, the owner of this house feels most at home surrounded by the comfort and clutter of "things" left out in view. Many people share such a taste for objects that carry special associations or that simply delight the senses.

An opposite extreme of taste created the utterly pristine living room reproduced in Figure 21. Walls, floors, and ceiling are all painted white; there are no windows to permit a glimpse of the intrusive cityscape. Even the furniture, which has been reduced to the barest essentials, is white and streamlined. The owners' overriding interest in art caused them to plan an "oasis" in which paintings and sculpture

22–26. Three houses occupied by Philip Johnson over a period of three decades show an evolution in the architect's personal taste.

above: 22. One of the earliest houses built according to the International Style in the United States, Johnson's Cambridge house of 1942 presaged his combined interest in openness and precision.

right: 23. The living room of Johnson's Cambridge house is precise and formal, dominated by squares and rectangles. (*Photograph: Ezra Stoller © ESTO*)

would be the *only* focus of attention. Taking their cue from the Minimal artists, they feel that "the more you eliminate from your life the more you realize you really didn't need it at all."

These two examples are extremes; most people would not want their homes to be either so stark or so rich. Nevertheless, they do illustrate how important a role personal taste plays in designing a lifespace that is successful for the individuals who will occupy it. If we were to transpose the owners of these two homes—to persuade them to exchange environments—each would certainly be uncomfortable.

Taste is not a constant, unvarying phenomenon but may change considerably over the lifetime of an individual. The house one furnishes at the age of forty will probably look quite different from the one planned at age twenty. It would be an oversimplification, however, to assume that personal taste gradually "improves," becomes increasingly refined, and perhaps becomes more conservative with advancing age. A great many factors—daily experiences, travels, new circles of friends, changing fashions in general, to name but a few—affect the development of taste, and this development is not necessarily an "improvement." It is merely different.

Even great designers experience fluctuating tastes. In the early 1940s the famed architect Philip Johnson planned a house for himself in Cambridge, Massachusetts (Figs. 22, 23). Marked by an austere, almost mathematical regularity, the house features flat planes and right angles, with the virtual exclusion of curves and diagonals. A glass wall forms one entire side of the house, but the whole is encased in a high, unbroken wall to ensure privacy. Furniture echoes the lines of the house in its overall square contours, as well as in the rigid rectangularity of its placement.

Then, in 1949 Johnson built the famous "glass box" as part of his own living complex in New Canaan, Connecticut (Figs. 24, 25). Almost a direct reversal of the Cambridge house, this structure brings the solid wall *inside* the glass enclosure to surround the bathroom—the only private space in the house. Every other portion of the home, including the bedroom, is open to the lawn. Despite his introduction of the circular wall around the bath, Johnson still maintained his preference for strict regularity. All furniture—much of which came directly from the Cambridge house—is arranged in precise, formal rectangles. The principal seating group has been even more rigidly confined on its squared island of carpet.

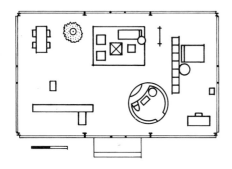

above left: 24. Johnson's Glass House of 1949 represents the epitome of his preferences for strict regularity and openness. See also Fig. 841.

above right: 25. In the living area of the Glass House, precision of placement and detail contrasts with the natural forms seen through glass walls on all four sides. (*Photograph: Ezra Stoller* © *ESTO*)

left: 26. By the 1970s Philip Johnson had begun to explore the possibilities for mobility in space. All furnishings in this converted carriage house are mounted on wheels, so that their arrangement can be altered at will. (*Photograph: The New York Times / Gene Maggio*)

Recently, Johnson moved into a converted carriage house in New York which he designed in 1950 (Fig. 26). He made no changes in the architecture but merely painted the walls white and removed the curtains. But in a dramatic departure from his previous taste for geometric order, Johnson put all the furniture on wheels—chairs, tables, everything. "Now there's no fixed place for the furnishings," he explains. "Everything gets moved around at will—you yank a chair here or there and it works."

These examples will serve to illustrate a basic concept of taste—and perhaps of human nature: Changing one's outlook now and then provides both stimulation and refreshment.

Goals in Planning a Lifespace

In discussing the factors that influence the planning of a lifespace, we emphasized specific needs of the individual or group. Yet it would be possible to design a house that fulfills each of these requirements perfectly and still does not provide a satisfying home. What, then, are the qualities that turn a house into a lifespace? What constitutes "good" home design?

A chair is well designed if it:

☐ gives comfortable support, thereby fulfilling its requirement of utility
☐ is worth the original cost, plus the time, energy, and money necessary for its maintenance; in short, if it is economical
☐ gives pleasure when seen or touched; that is, if it is beautiful
☐ suits the individual or group so well that it "belongs" in the home yet at the same time has special qualities of its own; in short, if it has character

The design of a lifespace, then, has four goals: **utility, economy, beauty,** and **character.**

Utility

Everyone wants a lifespace that "works" effectively, that serves the purposes for which it was intended—space that is planned for all group activities; chairs that earn the floor space they take; storage that is convenient and accessible; lighting, heating, and plumbing that do their jobs. Overemphasis on the utilitarian can, of course, lead to a laboratory-like coldness, but such excesses in no way diminish the primary importance of having our homes serve us well.

Economy

Economy refers to the management of human, material, monetary, and environmental resources. **Human resources** consist of abilities, plus time and energy. Because each person's productivity is influenced by the environment in which he or she works and relaxes, sound economy makes this environment as pleasant as possible. Those who garden are happier and accomplish more if they have convenient work centers, and certainly good cooks deserve well-planned kitchens. Labor-saving devices have contributed much to providing time and energy for life-enhancing avocations. Still, one can negate this advantage with poor planning, for example, by having a kitchen arranged in such a way that preparation of a meal requires twice as many steps as necessary. In building, buying, or renting space, one must consider how much time will be required for its maintenance and how much time is desired for other activities.

Material resources include all the things that have been purchased or received as gifts. It is regrettably easy to overlook some of them and to rush unthinkingly to buy a new object when, with a little repair and adaptation, something already owned would do as well or perhaps even better.

The economy of **monetary resources** will vary widely from household to household, depending upon relative affluence and individual priorities. Generally speaking, however, a system of using money wisely justifies the little time it takes to plan and follow. Even when financial resources are virtually unlimited, it makes no sense to buy haphazardly with no thought for an overall plan, because all the "mistakes" and excess purchases will have to be either disposed of or stored. Each purchase should contribute its full share to the total organization. It should be worth what is paid for it and not cost more than one can reasonably afford. Furthermore, it should be remembered that cost is both original and continuing. A long-wearing, easily maintained carpet with a high price tag may, in the long run, be a better investment than a less expensive one that is not durable or easily kept. Similarly, the advantages of wall-to-wall carpeting must be weighed against the possibility of moving to new quarters, in which case the carpet would probably need to be abandoned.

Concern over the conservation of **natural resources** is growing rapidly as we become aware of our great and too often unthinking impact on the environment. Ecological economy should underlie all our decisions and may well change our way of life fundamentally in the years to come. We have much to learn about this field, and choices are not always easy to make. Just as it is hard to determine which detergents are the least likely to pollute the environment—or, on the other hand, poison an inquisitive child—so it is hard to decide whether a chair, for example, should be made of wood or plastic. Wooden objects have a long life, can be refinished many times, and when they are no longer useful are readily reabsorbed into the environment; but our forests are being depleted, and for the first time in the history of the United States wood has become scarce and expensive. Plastics are relatively cheap to produce, but many are made from petroleum; also, a plastic object can be at the same time beyond repair and indestructible—that is, nonbiodegradable. Such ecological factors will concern us at all levels of home planning—from the choice of materials in furnishings and accessories; to the kind and amount of heating, cooling, and lighting we should use; to the components, types, and placement of our housing. Because these concerns have only recently attracted attention, and because the choices are so basic and controversial, we can point out only *some* of the issues as we discuss other aspects of creating a lifespace.

As suggested above, one type of conservation—sound economy from both a financial and an ecological point of view—consists of giving things a second life, making old objects serve new purposes. This principle can apply at many different levels, from accessories and furnishings through whole houses. Plate 3 (p. 8) pictures the living room of a house originally built in 1848 in Savannah. Before its present owners rescued it, it had become run-down and was considered un-salable. Now, a little money and much imagination have transformed it into a bright, contemporary lifespace. The old sofa was upholstered in a vivid yellow fabric; additional seating consists of salvaged church pews lacquered shocking pink. Modern paintings and graphics combine with the rejuvenated furniture to create a charming, happy effect.

Beauty

A much-abused word, beauty has fallen somewhat out of favor in aesthetic discussions; we refer rather to something as being striking, satisfying, attractive, appealing, effective, successful, and the like. But considered subjectively, we can speak of beauty as that which pleases the senses and lifts the spirits of a particular individual.

Two kinds of beauty—each appropriate to the people who live with it and to the geographical setting involved—are shown in Figures 27 and 28. Lofty, serene space dominates the living area of a house in New York City (Fig. 27). Its rectangularity is defined and given character by careful proportioning of forms

above: 27. Volume—intensified by quiet color and activated by changes in levels and textures—is the chief ingredient responsible for the beauty of architect Paul Rudolph's urban lifespace. See also Plate 22, p. 146. (*Photograph: Ezra Stoller © ESTO*)

right: 28. In a house designer Kipp Stewart planned for his own family, the love of natural materials and an active but comfortable lifestyle shape the criteria of beauty. (*Photograph: Morley Baer*)

and precision of angles. Series of levels, some broad, some narrow, ascend in asymmetrical sequence and intensify the impression of volume implicit in the three-story height, turning that volume into a great internal sculpture. Broad steps lead up to the dining space, intimately placed under an overhanging balcony. All surfaces are fairly smooth, white or light gray in color (except for the dark slate floor; Pl. 22, p. 146). This monochromatic scheme is highlighted by the sparkle of glass and metal, the shock of color in paintings and plants. Both the furniture itself and its placement acknowledge a formal rectangularity, but the built-in sitting sill around the room and the wide steps lend themselves to more informal use of the space. All these ingredients combine to achieve an elegant, sculptural beauty.

Very different in character but equally effective is the large, almost square living space of a house in California's Carmel Valley (Fig. 28). Despite the large glass openings, the major focus of the room is inward. We can sense the owners' delight in the look and feel of materials, in the warmth of colors, in the pure sense of structure. Clearly they have considered the actions of people, whether sitting and talking in front of the fire or working in the studio areas. The basic materials—adobe walls topped by a rough-cut pine ceiling, pine paving blocks, hand-woven fabrics—retain much of their natural character. This house typifies another kind of beauty—that of naturalism. Materials are permitted to reveal as much of their natural structure as possible, formed and shaped only enough to fulfill their functions. The rugged, informal character of this room contrasts strikingly with the tranquil, highly ordered spaciousness of the New York house.

Character

The quality that differentiates one home from another and expresses the personality of its owners is vital. While we can analyze a room to determine the components of its beauty, in the end the real determinant is the people whom it serves as a lifespace. No one wants a home to have the generalized aura of a hotel bedroom or lobby. Individuality—and therefore character—ensues almost automatically when a home is allowed to grow naturally from its inhabitants' interests and preferences. It develops most convincingly from fundamental lifestyles, not from acquiring the latest fashion in accessories. However, in our mass-production age, the quest for individuality is often overstressed, resulting in a shallow, self-conscious desire to be different—and different in a different way every few years. The result may be nothing more than a houseful of impersonal decorator's touches.

The two houses just discussed, in New York and California, exhibit character in their own ways. Both are based on a theme of rectangularity, but the vastly different results make us aware of the role played by needs and preferences, tastes and personalities, of the owners. A lifespace will have character if it is imbued with the individual qualities of its inhabitants.

Utility, economy, beauty, and **character** are as closely related as the warp and woof of a textile. None can be completely dissociated from the others and retain full significance. On the other hand, it is difficult to consider all these factors simultaneously. In choosing certain items—such as draperies, rugs, chairs, or beds—utility and/or economy may take precedence. Once they have been established, beauty and character can be taken into account. However, in selecting purely decorative objects, beauty and character will probably be the first considerations. Each factor must be balanced against the others.

Personalizing a Space

Most of us, when we move into a new home, occupy a preexisting structure; relatively few have the opportunity to design and build a dwelling from the ground up. Consequently, even before we begin to plan an environment, a number of decisions have been made for us: orientation toward the sun, total size of the enclosure, placement of walls and doors, and arrangement of rooms. Some of these can of course be changed, but such drastic alterations are very expensive and may be impossible in an apartment or condominium. Having chosen a space that most nearly meets their requirements, then, most people will accommodate themselves to its major outlines. Still, we can exercise much control over the quality of the homes we inhabit, both in the initial choice of a living space and in the shaping of it afterward.

Many degrees of flexibility present themselves in personalizing a space. One can personalize an apartment or house, completely remodel an existing house, individually design a structure to be built by contractors, or even construct a house by hand.

The residents of a highrise rental apartment in Philadelphia (Fig. 29) are active, vital people who entertain frequently and informally and have two young children. In their large, rectangular box of a living room they decided to "let plants, flowers, people, sky, color, and texture take the limelight, while casting the furniture in a background role." Although they like built-in furniture, they concluded that it was too expensive and permanent for a rented apartment. Instead, they chose multipurpose furnishings that can be reversed, rearranged, or removed to other quarters. A collection of polyurethane cushions of various sizes and shapes comprise a supersofa adaptable to sitting, lounging, or sleeping according to the way the units are disposed. Opposite the sofa a row of three tables provides space for a formal dinner party or work surface for large-scale projects. The tables can be separated for more intimate dining or games. An entire wall of movable shelf units at one end of the room stores books, a stereo system, and dining equipment. The magnificent view over the city provided by two window walls is softened by many plants, which also serve to cut glare. What began as an impersonal oblong space has been thoughtfully planned to work effectively and at the same time reflect the lifestyle of its owners.

Architect Peter Samton, whose work area was illustrated in Figure 17, took extravagant steps to personalize—and modernize—a hundred-year-old brownstone in New York (Fig. 30). Characteristic of such structures, the house had small windows that did little to light the space, and the interior, 80 feet deep, was divided

29. Flexibility is the keynote of this high-rise apartment living room in Philadelphia. The major furnishings consist of a collection of cushions that form a "supersofa" and a long table in three sections. Both units can be rearranged to create various combinations. (*Photograph: John T. Hill, Courtesy American Home Magazine*)

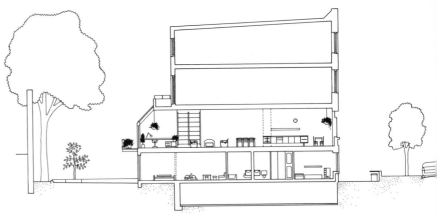

left: 30. A view of the rear façade shows how architect Peter Samton both added and reshaped space in remodeling his townhouse (see also Fig. 17). The work area is above, the play space below. (*Photograph: David Hirsch*)

above: 31. A cross section of the Samton townhouse demonstrates how interior walls have been ripped out to leave a floor-through space filled with light and air. Built-in storage units serve as partial dividers for the various areas. See also Fig. 161.

above: 32. This Montreal house was designed specifically to allow for informal, free-flowing use of large group space. Victor Pros, architect. See also Fig. 498. (*Photograph: Julius Shulman*)

left: 33. A basic interest in recycling can lead to unique resolutions. Art Boericke ''handmade'' his own house from ingenuity and scraps, the latter including pieces from a dentist's office, a shipyard, an army barracks, and a high school gymnasium. In the process he achieved not only personal satisfaction but a very personal house. See also Plate 4, p. 8. (*Photograph: Barry Shapiro, from* Handmade Houses)

into a series of small rooms. The owner knocked out many of the constricting interior walls and most of the rear façade on the first two floors (Fig. 31). Window walls and a skylight now flood the house with light; large, open areas seem to flow outdoors to a brick-paved patio and a small balcony. Taking the old brownstone, then, only as a starting point, Samton molded its space and personalized it specifically for his family.

The house shown in Figure 32 was designed for a family who often entertain large groups of people. A huge two-section living room, visually divided by the unique wooden supports and varied ceiling heights, allows many people to move about easily as conversation groups fluctuate. Ample seating is augmented by the carpeted hearth lowered one step from the floor level.

The ultimate in personalized space is the house designed and built by an individual. For the house pictured in Figure 33 and Plate 4 (p. 8), the owner-builder sought materials with character—old weathered woods that had stood the test of time. Using totally salvaged materials served two purposes: It saved the builder a great deal of money and at the same time made good use of raw materials that would otherwise have been scrap. In creating this very personal lifespace, the principles of utility, economy, beauty, and character were coalesced into a very happy balance.

Personalizing a space, obviously, occurs on many levels. When one occupies a hotel or motel room for a single night, the space may seem alien, even threatening, until one's own things are scattered about—hairbrush and comb, clock, purse or pocket contents, and so on. Even a toothbrush in the bathroom can make a neutral space seem personal, if only temporarily. Carried to its greatest extent, the personalizing of a lifespace can both provide peace and security for the individual and serve as an extension of the personality in the eyes of others.

Creating a Lifespace

The foregoing discussion was couched mainly in abstractions and general principles. Having acknowledged all the qualities that go into creating a successful lifespace, the reader might well ask, "But where do I start?" Like any problem, that of planning a lifespace to satisfy all the elements described above can be approached by segmenting it and dealing with a single aspect at a time. One possible system for creating a personal space would be to follow the six steps listed below.

Inventory present possessions, then list expected additions. Listing in an orderly manner all that you now own is an easy but strategic first step. Such a list provides a surprising index of both personality and resources. Especially revealing is the miscellany related to a household's interests—books and magazines, musical instruments, stereo equipment, television, sports gear, or paintings and sculpture. Making a careful inventory, perhaps at three- or five-year intervals, alerts you to what and how much you possess, where and how often each object is used, how fully it is enjoyed, and where it is stored. Possessions help make homelife more satisfying, provided their upkeep does not become a burden or the pursuit of them overshadow more important concerns. They should be used and cherished but not allowed to mold an artificial way of living or become merely status symbols.

List preferred activities. Individuals differ markedly in the hobbies or work they enjoy, and the lifespace should reflect this diversity. Some activities, such as group conversation or reading, require no special equipment other than comfortable seats, appropriate light, and protection from disconcerting noise. Other pursuits, like weaving and cabinetmaking, demand special provisions. Listing your possessions and activities lays the groundwork for the next stages of planning.

Decide on the general character of your home. Each room, chair, textile, artifact—any object we could name—has a definite personality of its own. Each not only expresses, but leads toward, a way of living. Beyond these are an almost infinite number of personalities, basic ideas, or themes around which a home can grow. A conference to discuss the group's and each individual's likes and dislikes, goals, and aspirations can be an illuminating experience. Within this framework, there will be varied ways of fulfilling the desired ends. The lifespace that is planned to slavishly follow current fashion, that copies a theme someone else has found successful, or that forces the household to conform to an arbitrarily conceived idea will not prove satisfactory in the long run. Rather, you should seek to understand the nature of the household, its members, and their way of life, then allow the space to develop around these elements.

Learn the ways and means of achieving the desired character. You can start by simply looking, listening, and touching. Then ask questions and make comparisons to help develop a vocabulary, a reservoir of ideas, and some guiding principles. Sources of inspiration and enlightenment are legion: stores, museums, motion pictures and television, your present home, the homes of friends, exhibition houses, books, magazines, and newspapers.

A good beginning is to investigate a single aspect of the total situation with some thoroughness. For example, you might concentrate on seating equipment. The variety is amazing: seating can be for one person or for two or more; fixed or movable; hard or soft, high or low, with or without backs or arms; of wood, fabric, cane, metal, plastic, or stone. It can be cheap or costly, easy or difficult to maintain, sturdy or fragile in construction. Its shape might be rectangular, curved, even triangular or free form, and it can be ornamented or plain. Size ranges over a considerable spectrum, as does weight. Character varies from formal to informal, relaxing to activating, unusual to commonplace. The list could go on indefinitely. To narrow it down, you should consider *who* will sit on a particular piece of furniture (large person, small person, child; agile person, stiff person); *where* it will be placed; and *what* that person will be doing when sitting in it (reading, eating, talking, watching television, and so on). The same system could be applied to any other type of equipment.

Consider finances. Costs—original and continuing—can never be ignored. How much is available for spending? Over what period of time? What expenditures will give the greatest satisfaction? There is no single way to solve the problem of wise initial spending, but the following suggestions outline one possible system:

□ Buy a few good basic objects, such as beds, comfortable seating, or durable, attractive storage chests that can be used flexibly. Or, concentrate spending on one extravagant item that gives special delight, such as a Navajo or Oriental rug, a piece of handcrafted or antique furniture (Fig. 34).
□ Fill in with frankly inexpensive, perhaps temporary things, such as cane or plastic chairs, large pillows, area rugs, and colorful accessories.
□ If even moderate expenditure is beyond the budget, let imagination substitute for money by converting unexpected objects into usable furnishings (Fig. 35).
□ Avoid buying expensive items that are not quite right—not really excellent in design, structure, or material—but that cost too much to be discarded later.

In short, hit high and low in the beginning, fill in the scale as you go along. As tastes evolve and needs become more definite, the general character of a home often changes. While avoiding commonplace furnishings, also think twice about those pieces so aggressively individualistic that they will fit into only one kind of environment.

Continually remember the desired goal. It is surprisingly hard to keep in mind what you set out to achieve, surprisingly easy to alter your course without realizing it. Irresistible bargains, impulse buying, or simply failing to hold fast to a plan can gradually lead you away from what you intended. To be sure, it may be necessary to change ideas. Economic conditions, size of household, and tastes all fluctuate. When such changes occur, make intelligent, considered modifications again with an overall program in mind. And, if you discover that you are moving away from the effect you originally intended, it may be that your plan was wrong for you in the first place.

Creating a personal lifespace requires far more than deciding on a color scheme or selecting and arranging furniture. The roots of a good home lie in the occupants' needs and wishes, tastes, and lifestyle; its major expression is the plan and the architectural shell that shape space for living. Furthermore, the full development of a home spills out into the landscape and the community beyond.

The following chapters isolate certain aspects of the home for particular consideration—group spaces, private spaces, support spaces, and support systems. A final chapter in this part focuses on ways in which these various elements can be organized to formulate the overall plan.

For many years studies in home design concentrated on achieving maximum efficiency. Time-motion studies and technical advances approached the home as though it were a laboratory. Of course, these aspects of design are important, and research continues. Now, however, attention is also being directed to emotional and spiritual factors. Concern with the effects on human interaction of new ways of shaping, furnishing, and coloring homes, even of heating and lighting, has begun to catch up with technical expertise. With an unparalleled array of potentialities at our command, we can create homes that are, in the words of architect Richard Neutra, "soul anchorages."

left: 34. One extravagant purchase—such as a pair of old stained glass windows too wonderful to do without—can be the design focus of a whole room. Raymond Zambrano, architect. (*Photograph: Philip L. Molten*)

above: 35. An uninhibited imagination can see the possibilities of new life in objects that have outlived their original purposes. The bedframe in this Santa Fe house is part of an old fence. See also Fig. 10. (*Copyright © O. R. Cabanban 1974*)

Group
Spaces

The group spaces in any home are the areas where members of the household gather and where friends are entertained. They provide an atmosphere for such activities as general conversation, games, parties, listening to or making music, eating, and small children's play. Most homes throughout history have included such communal gathering places in which the entire household could assemble for recreation, companionship, and often warmth. In medieval England the "great hall" of a castle or house functioned as a group space, perhaps being the only room that was adequately heated. American families of the 17th and 18th centuries typically congregated in the kitchen, drawn, no doubt, by the triple sensory pleasures of warmth, delicious aromas, and freshly cooked food—all conducive to easy companionship. For the same reasons, the kitchen in many a home today serves as a magnet for the entire family. Comparatively recently, however, new kinds of activities have become important in family life—reading, watching television, listening to music, and pursuing home crafts or hobbies. All of these make different demands on the group spaces in the home, demands that architectural design is only beginning to satisfy.

The emphasis given to each group activity varies from individual to individual and from household to household. Furthermore, our priorities inevitably change as the years pass. The group space that, for example, makes ample provision for children's play will assume a different character when those children are grown. Because none but the very wealthy can accommodate all kinds of activities equally well—it is a rare house that offers, say, a smoking room, a billiard room, a music room, and so forth—most of us must decide carefully which group pursuits are most important, then plan accordingly. A logical first step is to consider specific group activities, as well as the environment and equipment desirable for each, and then to design the group space so that it will best meet these requirements.

Group Entertainment and Leisure

One level of a house near Seattle was conceived as multipurpose group space (Figs. 36, 37). An impressive feature is the clear definition given areas appropriate for various entertainment and leisure activities within the overall open atmosphere. In portions designed for large parties, the windows and ceiling rise dramatically to a two-story height. Here, as the plan shows (Fig. 38), people can move about freely, can pass out through a door in the window wall to a projecting deck or

36–38. Changes in ceiling and floor levels demarcate different kinds of group spaces in the Lauren Studebaker house, Mercer Island, Wash. Wendell H. Lovett, architect.

left: 36. The wide-open, multistory space focusing on the fireplace seems ideal for large and gregarious parties. (*Photograph: Christian Staub*)

below right: 37. Small groups of people would naturally gravitate toward the cave for more intimate conversations, to watch television, or to listen to music. (*Photograph: Christian Staub*)

below left: 38. The plan of the Studebaker house indicates further the openness that has been controlled by the flow of space around center dividers.

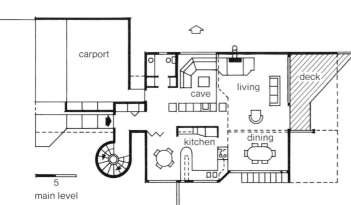

back into the more protected areas. To one side of the space is a "cave" where a few people might gather for informal eating or to watch television. Its ceiling is low, the windows relatively small and inset in the walls to create an atmosphere of intimacy. Because the cave is depressed one step and shielded by the projecting fireplace, it acquires even further coziness. Throughout this group space the open circulation plan affords alternate routes between points, but there is no cross circulation through the work areas of the kitchen or the sitting area of the cave.

In plan and execution this group space serves the various activities that characterize the lifestyle of the household.

Conversation

Far and away the most pervasive group activity is conversation, an exchange so much a part of life that we tend to take it for granted. Human beings communicate, both verbally and by nonverbal signals. Conversation may be seen as the amalgam of these forms of communication—a pleasant dialogue among family and friends. Obviously, we can and do converse in any part of the home. But the most natural settings for group interaction are those group spaces where people congregate—the living and dining areas. The elements conducive to easy conversation are:

□ **Space** sufficient for the usual number of people who are present. A person in an easy chair, for example, needs a space 3 feet wide by $2\frac{1}{3}$ feet deep, but with the legs extended a tall person may need a space 5 feet deep.

□ **Comfortable seats** for each participant; a minimum of one good seat for each permanent member of the household and additional ones to accommodate guests.

□ **Arrangement of seats** and tables in a generally circular or elliptical pattern so that each person can look at others easily and talk without shouting. This arrangement should be ready for group conversation without moving furniture. A diameter of 8 to 10 feet across the seating area has proved the most desirable in typical situations.

□ **Light** of moderate intensity with highlights at strategic points.

□ **Surfaces**—tables, shelves, and so on—on which to put things.

Conversation thrives in a warm, friendly atmosphere if the architecture, furnishings, and accessories are spirited but not overpowering, if distractions are minimized, and if sounds are softened. The "cave" in the Studebaker house (Fig. 37) seems to meet these criteria perfectly. It would draw in by its intimacy a few people to sit on the built-in couches; others would perch on the step down into the area to fill out the circular pattern that encourages participation in discussions. Moving outside the cave, another group could gather in an elliptical configuration provided by the freestanding couch, easy chair, and hearth—perhaps for more open-ended conversations. Dark slate gray and bright red cushions, plus the natural tones of the lowered wood ceiling and surrounding cabinets give warmth to the cave; in the open section, the dark gray pile rug provides a solid foundation for the soaring lightness of the walls and ceiling.

Group conversation is also the normal accompaniment of meals, because the furniture and its arrangements afford ideal conditions for an hour or so. The open dining area of the Studebaker house (Fig. 38) is demarcated by a lowered beam; its oval table helps to draw the diners into communication. On the other side of the kitchen a round table provides space for smaller groups, while a folding wall offers greater seclusion if it is desired.

Terraces and patios are also natural conversation centers when they offer good seating and some degree of shelter.

Reading

Some fortunate people can read with total concentration even in the most trying circumstances—noise, people talking, movement back and forth around them. But most of us, when we settle down for a quiet hour or an evening with a book, would prefer a more tranquil environment. The essentials are:

□ **Seating** that is resilient but not soporific, that gives adequate support to the back (and to the neck and arms as well for maximum comfort)

- **Light** coming over one shoulder, either moderately strong daylight or artifical light that illumines the room and concentrates fairly intense but diffused light on the reading material
- **Security** from distracting sights, sounds, and household traffic

Beyond these minimum amenities, we might add nearby tables or other surfaces, accessible shelves to hold books and magazines, and enough space to stretch the eyes occasionally. Such conditions, which are adequate for more or less casual reading, can be achieved easily in the typical living room. If, however, one or more members of the family often do serious or technical reading, they may require greater seclusion, and a bedroom or study should be planned appropriately.

Music

For many Americans today, music is an integral part of life, as natural as eating or sleeping. Its source may be simply a small radio or television, but more and more in recent years music in the home has become centered on a complex arrangement of stereo components that require considerable space. Further, the space must be kept flexible, because the number and shape of the elements change as new designs become available and as the listeners' sophistication increases.

At the same time, greater numbers of people enjoy creating their own music. Small instruments, such as guitars, pose few problems, but the placement of a piano is a major design consideration. It can be flat against a wall or at a right angle, in the latter case helping to demarcate a partially segregated area. More serious musicians may want a separate music center in a corner, an alcove, or even a whole room, where everything can be kept together and out of the way of other activities. Such an arrangement would be especially necessary when several instruments are involved or when they are hooked up to amplifiers—a combination that occupies quite a bit of space and produces a staggering volume of sound.

Optimum conditions for listening to music depend on what the particular listeners want. For many people, conditions similar to those recommended for group conversation or quiet reading will suffice—comfortable seating, moderate illumination, and a minimum of distractions. But committed musicians who have an intense concern for the quality of sound will demand further refinements. Although the quality can be no better than that produced by the instruments and performers or by the stereo equipment, several factors—notably the arrangement, composition, and shape of a room—can enhance or detract from the production of ultimate quality.

- **Seating** should be arranged so that the listeners hear a balanced projection from the instruments or from multiple speakers.
- **Space** can be shaped to enhance the sound. Experts have long known that musical sounds have a finer quality in rooms whose opposite surfaces are not parallel to each other or in which the space is broken up in some way.
- **Materials** often are chosen and placed for their acoustical qualities. In acoustical terms, materials are classified as sound-reflecting or "live" if they bounce the sound, as does plaster or glass; and as sound-absorbing or "dead" if they soak up sound, as do heavy draperies, rugs, books, cork, or other so-called acoustical materials. An excess of live materials gives strident amplification and reverberation; the converse, having too many dead surfaces, robs music of its brilliance. Studies have also determined that, for best results, live surfaces should be opposite dead sufaces.

Many of the devices that improve acoustical quality have been incorporated in the living room planned by interior designer Eve Frankl, whose husband, Michael Pollen, is a pianist and conductor (Fig. 39). Placed before a storage wall

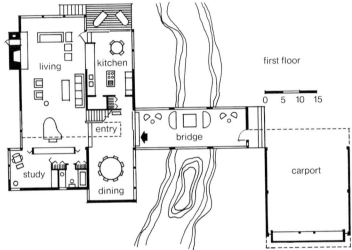

left: 39. A living room designed for live musical performances should meet as many of the criteria for good acoustics as possible: a combination of live surfaces to bounce sound and dense ones to absorb reverberations, both properly placed for their sound-enhancing qualities. Eve Frankl, interior designer; George Van Geldern, architect. (*Photograph: Ezra Stoller* © *ESTO*)

below: 40. The plan shows the flexibility of space for accommodating large or small audiences.

at the inner end of a long living area, the piano is protected from sudden temperature changes that might affect the strings and hammers. An overhanging balcony at this end of the room, plus a slanting wood surface above a glass wall at the opposite end, answer the requirement for contradictory opposing surfaces and break up the space for good sound quality. Rugs, deep upholstered seating and pillows, and a bookshelf-storage wall balance sound-absorbing materials against the live surfaces of plaster and glass walls. As the plan shows (Fig. 40), sufficient seating is provided for a small group of listeners, but plenty of open area leaves the potential for a larger audience, who could sit on the floor or on specially set up chairs. Good lighting is suspended above the piano for reading music, and enough space has been left for other instrumentalists to participate in an evening of chamber music.

The acoustical problems related to placement of stereo speakers involve a science beyond the scope of this book. In general, however, speakers perform best when they are mounted in or placed against a live wall facing a dead one. The exact placement of the speakers to achieve a well-balanced quality of sound will depend on the size of the room and the positions of the listeners, among other factors. For convenience and freedom from vibration, the tuner and record player or tape deck should be separated from the speakers so that the operator can get the desired balance, a feat next to impossible when the speakers are close by. Adequate storage space for a growing library of records and tapes will help to maintain them in good condition.

Television, Movies, and Slides

Bringing the theater, cinema, concert hall, sports field, and even the classroom into the home has altered patterns of both leisure and homelife markedly. Television especially, but also movies and slides, have become important sources of home entertainment. Major considerations for these activities are good seating, control of light and sound, and protection for those who do not care to participate.

    □ **Seating** requirements are much like those for conversation, except that the seating should be arranged within a 60-degree angle of the screen to avoid distortion. Easily moved or swivel chairs offer flexibility; backrests or cushions on the floor increase a room's seating capacity, while long lounges accommodate viewers in a variety of positions.
    □ **Height of screen** should be as near eye level as possible.
    □ **Lighting** of low intensity is necessary especially for watching television, but the light should shine neither on the screen nor in the viewers' eyes.
    □ **Acoustical control** is similar to that for music.

Although still cumbersome, especially in depth, television receivers can be put in many places, depending upon the lifestyle of the household and its members. Living rooms and family rooms are perhaps the most typical locations, but television sets, possibly small second ones, also appear in bedrooms and kitchens. If they are mounted in walls, television receivers can be treated as part of the wall design or hidden behind doors. Where feasible, they can be positioned to face more than one room. Mounted on a portable stand, a television set can be pushed from place to place as it is needed, but this precludes permanent hookup with an outside antenna.

Screens for movies or slides fold easily for storage when they are not in use. However, the family for which home projection is an important activity should consider a permanently mounted screen that disappears behind a valance or other fixture near the ceiling.

Quiet Indoor Games

Cards, checkers, and chess require concentration. A well-illuminated table about $2\frac{1}{4}$ feet high, plus moderately high, straight chairs, all arranged in a spot free from distractions, will provide the most relaxing accommodations for the players. Folding card tables or the new lower dining tables and dining chairs—set up in the living, dining, or family space—suffice for most households. However, serious gamesters may want a table and chairs permanently and suitably placed.

Active Indoor Entertainment

Dancing, ping-pong, pool, and other such vigorous games require plenty of space, a durable floor, and furniture that can be pushed out of the way. A family room—and, increasingly, community group spaces (Fig. 54)—can offer an ideal location.

Outdoor Entertainment

The urge to get a little closer to nature is deeply embedded in most of us. Even in the cities, more and more apartments boast outdoor terraces, albeit quite small but giving a semblance of expansion into the out-of-doors. For those fortunate enough to live in more spacious quarters, an outdoor room—which may be called a deck, terrace, patio, or porch—is a logical extension of the indoor group space (Fig. 49). When well conceived, it can augment the usable entertainment area.

left: 41. Apartments and condominiums can be designed to provide as much as possible for outdoor living, with terraces and decks sheltered from those of the neighbors. John O'Brien and John Armstrong, architects. (*Photograph: Philip L. Molten*)

right: 42. This Vancouver, B.C., house offers several degrees of privacy and interaction for various outdoor activities. Arthur Erickson, architect. See also Pl. 59, p. 451. (*Photograph: Ezra Stoller © ESTO*)

For an apartment housing project built on a steep site in California (Fig. 41), the architects enlarged the entrance deck of each unit to provide space for outdoor sitting, dining, or perhaps barbecuing. Changes in levels between the apartments, as well as protecting walls, provide a measure of privacy while allowing the tenants to enjoy the tree-studded site.

Outdoor games, such as croquet and badminton, or swimming, tennis, and other sports, require still more space and convenient storage for the necessary equipment. In many of the newer housing developments, playgrounds for children and outdoor community facilities for everyone expand the individual living areas and provide welcome breathing space on otherwise crowded sites (Figs. 53, 55).

The frequency with which outdoor space is enjoyed depends on the durability and dryness of the underfoot surfaces, the protection from wind, the privacy given by fences or hedges, the safety for young children, and the comfort with which some can rest while others expend their energies. For the house in Figure 42, the architect designed a series of terraces as extensions of interior space to allow a variety of outdoor living experiences—from sunbathing on a protected balcony, to dining or relaxing in sun or shade, to active sport in the swimming pool.

Small Children's Activities

The needs of small children range from boisterous play to quiet reflection; from eagerness to join others of their own age to desire for solitude; from wanting to be with the family to carefully avoiding it. Basic elements of a child's play area are the following:

- □ **Space** adequate for the discharge of abundant energy
- □ **Convenience** to a toilet and to the outdoors, as well as to the kitchen or home office for adult supervision
- □ **Surfaces** and fixtures—walls, floors, and furniture—that can take punishment gracefully and lend themselves to change
- □ **Light, warmth,** and **fresh air** conducive to healthy young bodies

Ideally, all this should be segregated from what, it is hoped, will be the quieter portions of the house.

Clearly, a living room is unsuitable for a permanent play space, and the dining area is only slightly better. A kitchen has the requisite durability, but even without children's play it is usually the most intensively used room in the house and moreover contains the household's greatest assembly of potential hazards. In older houses attics and basements served as playrooms for children, but these were often cold, dark, damp, and far from any supervising eye. Garages and carports have obvious disadvantages. This leaves two major solutions.

A family room, particularly if it is located off the kitchen or outside the children's bedrooms, can be an ideal play space during the day, transformed into a general group leisure area in the evening (Pl. 8, p. 42). Furnishings in a family room are generally less "formal" than in the group entertainment space and may be more durable as well. Too, such rooms often serve for storage of games and sporting gear and frequently house the television set and other audio-visual equipment.

The children's bedrooms themselves, or an area adjacent to them, may make excellent play spaces, because they already are, or should be, planned for the children to make into their own territories. A widened bedroom hallway can be both economical and efficient; the bedrooms might open into a multipurpose room (Fig. 43) or combine with each other to provide a space large enough for playroom, library, museum, and hobby center as well as study and retreat.

Although it is desirable to have a children's play space within the home, many small houses and apartments cannot offer even a modest area that meets the above criteria. This limitation is one of the reasons for the inclusion of community leisure facilities in large-scale housing developments, a feature that is becoming ever more popular. Group entertainment spaces, which often serve adults as well as children, are considered later in the chapter.

Dining with Family and Friends

Eating is a lively part of group living, for meals are often one of the few daily events that bring an entire household together with a single purpose. In all kinds of communal societies, including religious communities, meals typically are taken by the group as a whole, even though other facets of daily life may be kept separate. Of course, group meals serve a practical purpose as well as a social one. It is not much more difficult to cook for forty than it is for four, but it may be extremely tedious and time-consuming to prepare and clean up after ten meals for four each.

Entertainment of friends almost always involves the consumption of food, ranging from a simple snack with tea or cocktails up through the multicourse dinner. Nearly every society recognizes the offering of food as the standard token of hospitality to guests. Just why this is so remains unclear; perhaps it is simply a carryover from the days when settlements were much farther apart and travelers,

43. Space designed for active play of youngsters is a free-for-all multipurpose area that can change as children grow older to suit their evolving needs. Stanley Salzman of Edelman and Salzman, architect. (*Photograph © Maris [ESTO]*)

left: **44.** This open group space provides for several different eating arrangements, from breakfast at stools placed before the built-in counter, through more formal meals at the dining table, to light snacks around the coffee table. Mayers & Schiff, architects. (*Photograph: Maris/Semel*)

above right: 45. An amorphous kitchen-dining-living space brings the preparation and consumption of meals fully into the group living pattern. (*Photograph: Darrow M. Watt*)

right: 46. Indoor and outdoor group spaces merge harmoniously in this greenhouse-dining room. The huge window wall can be opened completely by drawing back sliding glass doors that vanish into hidden channels. Anton Mueller, architect. (*Photograph: Julius Shulman*)

upon reaching their destinations, genuinely needed sustenance. In any event, the sense of well being that accompanies a good meal unquestionably contributes to pleasant relationships and conviviality.

The traditional multipurpose house with single-purpose rooms, common in the United States through the early part of this century, generally set aside one enclosed space, called "dining room," in which all meals with the possible exception of breakfast were taken. Frequently, this room had no other purpose *but* dining. Even today many families enjoy the specialness of a separate dining room which creates a particular atmosphere for meals. However, with increasing interest in flexible space, fewer and fewer households are willing to set aside for eating a completely isolated space that will be used for only about three hours a day.

Just how open or closed the dining space should be depends in large part on the amount of room available and on the lifestyle of the family. In many homes, instead of one totally separated dining room, there are two or more dining spaces that merge into other areas and that can be used as circumstances indicate. The Studebaker house (Fig. 38), for example, offers the oval table for major group meals, the smaller round table for less formal eating, and the potential for light snacks in the cave. Similarly, the house illustrated in Figure 44 provides a permanent dining space off the living room, plus a built-in countertop with stools for breakfast or other simple meals.

When planning dining situations, we should first consider individual living patterns, then requirements for eating in general, and finally the specific needs for meals of different types. The essentials are:

□ **Surfaces** on which to put food and utensils, usually 27 to 30 inches high, but lower when indicated or desired. The age and physical condition of various group members are important here: limber young people can be happy at low tables that would be uncomfortable for many older people; small children are safer and more content at child-size tables.

□ **Seats** giving comfortable, usually upright support, such as chairs, stools, built-in or movable benches, or sitting platforms, scaled to the height of the table.

□ **Light,** natural and artificial, that illumines food and table without glare.

□ **Ventilation** free of drafts.

To these essentials we quickly add that *convenience to kitchen and dish storage* saves energy, *freedom from excessive noise* calms nerves and helps digestion, and *pleasant surroundings and table settings* raises spirits. A few of the many ways of planning dining space are shown in Figures 44 to 50 and Plates 4 to 6. Chapter 4 includes illustrations of well-designed facilities for eating in the kitchen; Chapter 6 shows the many ways in which dining can be integrated into the total house plan; and Chapter 16 takes up selection and arrangement of dining furniture.

Family Sit-Down Meals   Because they generally represent the most common situation, family sit-down meals deserve first attention. For these there should be one adequately large, relatively permanent space planned so that the table can be prepared, the seating arranged, the meal served and eaten, and the table cleared with minimum interference to and from other activities. The dining area illustrated in Figure 45 answers these criteria beautifully and yet remains integrated with the rest of the group space. Here kitchen, dining area, and living room flow easily into one another; two or more cooks can work comfortably in the kitchen, but the dining area is still partially secluded from the sitting space.

Holiday Celebrations   Important family events occur so seldom that the necessary space can rarely be reserved for them alone. This suggests a dining area with at least one side opening to another part of the house or to the out-of-doors, permitting the celebration area to extend as the number of participants increases. The dining space in Figure 46 occupies what is almost a greenhouse—a glass-roofed area filled with potted plants. Sliding glass doors that disappear into channels in the outside walls open this area completely to the terrace, where there is a second table. For holiday meals this family could set up a long table to bridge the indoor-outdoor space.

Formal Meals   The family that entertains frequently with rather formal dinners may want a completely separate dining space (Pl. 5, opposite) in order that the table can be set in advance, the guests will receive a pleasant surprise with the table setting, the meal can proceed without interruption from other activities, and the table will be screened when the meal is over.

Buffet Meals   Like self-service grocery stores and cafeterias, buffet meals permit us to see what we are getting and to enjoy the fun of choosing from an array of foods. Also, they simplify the labor of serving food and make it possible to use the entire group space for eating—all of which leads to a lively informality. If buffet meals are to be handled often and successfully, cafeteria procedures suggest a number of guidelines: good carrying trays, not-too-precious dishes and glassware, service counters near the kitchen, traffic paths that avoid collisions between tray-laden people, convenient places to sit and to rest the food. The dining space in Figures 47 and 48 would serve well for buffet meals, since it opens to both the outside deck and the living room. Built-in buffet cupboards on one side of the dining area pivot 90 degrees to merge the living and dining spaces.

Snacks and Quick Meals   Some families rarely eat "meals" at all but rather maintain a lifestyle that calls for a series of snacks, for one or a few people, at frequent intervals throughout the day. When members of the household function on different time schedules, mealtimes will inevitably vary. The primary goals in planning space for eating, then, will be speed and economy of effort, but a minimum of interference with other activities is also important. Counters and stools

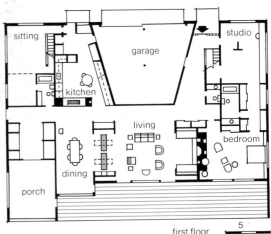

left: 47. A separate dining room provides a fresh and pleasant area specifically designed for serving and eating meals. In this room built-in cupboards hold tableware and linen and act as serving counters. A small breakfast for one or two would be delightful in the bay window. Judith Chafee, architect; Christina A. Bloom, interior decorator. See also Figs. 49, 420, 423; Plate 57, p. 436. (*Photograph: Ezra Stoller* © *ESTO*)

below: 48. The serving cupboards pivot 90 degrees to open the dining area to the living room.

first floor

above: Plate 5. When families entertain often with large dinner parties, their lifestyles may warrant a completely separate and permanent dining space. Here traditional furnishings and modern architecture combine for an elegant effect. See page 40. (*Photograph: Robert Perron*)

right: Plate 6. In most households today, dining space must fulfill more than one role. When not in use for meals, this handsome room doubles as a library-study. George Hartman and Ann Hartman, designers. See page 43. (*Photograph: Robert C. Lautman*)

left: **Plate 7.** A sensitive demarcation of different areas—created by varying levels, structural members, and furniture placement—can prevent a large, open group space from seeming barnlike, even in a converted barn. James McNair, designer. See page 45. (*Photograph: John T. Hill*)

below: **Plate 8.** Plenty of open space and sturdy, easy-care furniture make this family room suitable to the activities of both children and adults. See page 46. (*Photograph: Robert Perron*)

adjacent to the cooking area of the kitchen often work well. A small dining table and chairs near a supplementary quick-meal-preparation unit can be most helpful in reducing congestion in the kitchen proper.

Outdoor Meals   Eating routines benefit greatly from a refreshing change of surroundings, a different type of food, another eating pattern. In all parts of the country outdoor meals could be much more frequent if they were planned with the same attention given to their indoor counterparts. At its best, outdoor eating takes place in an appropriately furnished space near the kitchen or barbecue. Firm paving, a protecting roof, screening from insects, solid enclosure on two or three sides with garden fences or hedges on the others well justify their cost (Fig. 49). But of course, even without all this, picnics and barbecues can be happy affairs in which all members of the household and their guests can participate, actively or as spectators, in the fun of cooking, serving, eating, and even cleanup.

Small Children's Meals   A central part of family life, the meals consumed by small children represent an educational situation that is often poorly handled. We might as well acknowledge that eating is both an adventure and a problem for small children. They will play, experiment, and make rather gruesome mistakes. Common sense suggests providing a place—preferably in the kitchen, playroom, or family room—where children can spill or scatter food on durable, easy-to-clean surfaces. But at an early age children want to eat with adults and quite rightly object to conditions midway between those for grownups and those for household pets. Again, the design of the house, as well as the way it is finished and furnished, strongly affects the way this problem can be handled.

Because dining space functions for only short periods during the day, many newer houses are designed in such a way that the dining area has a dual role. For example, in a small remodeled house in Georgetown (Pl. 6, p. 41), the dining space is equally a library, with a bookcase wall and the table serving for reading or study when it is not needed for meals. In a New Hampshire vacation house (Fig. 50) dining space has been created in what is essentially a widened hallway connecting the living room and the kitchen. Between meals it would be a likely spot for games or just sitting and talking on the comfortable built-in bench.

Planning for Group Living

After considering the character and demands of specific group activities, we can formulate several generalizations useful in planning.

Many group activities occur in more than one part of the house and grounds. We can eat in the dining or living area, in the family room, on the patio. Conversation is enjoyed everywhere, and music often pervades the remotest corners of the home. Thus, planning today is more a matter of organizing space for activities than of arranging "rooms."

Group pursuits fall into four general categories in terms of noise and movement. The full development of each type is best realized when the home is appropriately zoned.

□ **Quiet, sedentary activities,** such as reading, conversation, and predominantly cerebral games, involve little physical movement. They produce minimum noise but suffer greatly from distractions, which suggests grouping them in a quiet zone of the dwelling.

□ **Noisy, sedentary activities**—eating, watching television, listening to music— deserve an acoustically controlled part of the group space that is more or less separated from those areas where tranquillity is desired.

□ **Moderately noisy, mobile activities,** such as adult parties, generally imply constantly changing groupings and noise levels, suggesting space that allows an easy flow of movement and some separation from quiet zones.

□ **Noisy, mobile activities,** children's play and physical games, take as much space as can be found. They may interfere with other home pursuits and are hard on furnishings, floors, and walls. Play or family rooms and the outdoors are logical centers.

Planning for group living demands that everyone's needs and desires be considered and realized insofar as possible, if the plan is to work. The steps suggested in Chapter 1 for creating a lifespace (pp. 27–29) are applicable.

50. A dining space can perform several functions. In this house it is used for circulation, but the placement of the table off to one side and linked to a built-in bench would also encourage its emergence as a secondary group-gathering spot. Huygens and Tappé, architects. (*Photograph: Lisanti, Inc.*)

51. A large central "box" separates this studio apartment into different sections for sleeping, eating, and group activities. Peter Hoppner, designer. (*Photograph: Louis Reens*)

The multiplicity of lifestyles and lifespaces available today both simplify and complicate the problem of providing for viable group spaces—simplify because there can be no single "right" solution, complicate because there is so much to choose from. We shall consider three different kinds of group spaces: those that coexist with private spaces, in a one-room apartment or loft; those that share a larger dwelling with private spaces; and those that exist quite outside the dwelling—community group spaces.

Single-Room Group Spaces

In a one-room apartment, group and private living necessarily share the same space. By visually separating areas and varying levels, we can design even this limited space to accommodate different activities. The room in Figure 51 cleverly provides for separated sitting, sleeping, eating, and work areas by means of the central all-in-one unit. Because it is impossible to see the entire room from any one vantage point, different portions of it take on a feeling of separateness.

Group Spaces Inside the Home

Basically two options present themselves in designing the group space for a home. It can be one large open area, suitable to a variety of purposes and used intensively by all members of the household; or the total space may be subdivided into a series of smaller regions each suitable for a particular range of activities.

The converted barn illustrated in Plate 7 (p. 42) obviously chooses the former point of view. Spacious, airy, and open, this group space functions as sitting room, entertainment center, music room, and game room; it flows easily up onto the balcony studio and into the library. Nevertheless, the space has been shaped imaginatively to partially segregate various activities. Exposed wood beams serve visually to break up the space and demarcate certain areas; the placement and orientation of furniture cause it to fall into several natural groupings; and positioning the studio on a balcony isolates it from the rest of the space both physically and psychologically to allow for a great measure of privacy.

For many homes a second discrete group space is the only way to meet the needs of differing age or activity groups and maintain a degree of civilization. Originally considered as a device to keep the living room neat and clean, such

52. A semisecluded nook offers the opportunity for one or two people to get away from more energetic group activities. With the alcove bed, this space doubles as a guest room. (*Courtesy U.S. Plywood, Champion International*)

areas—which may be called family rooms, playrooms, recreation rooms, or multi-purpose rooms—have increasingly become alternative spaces for group living. As a rule they are more informal, durable, and easily maintained (Pl. 8, p. 42). They can be partially visible extensions of the main group space but work best when they have the potential for total segregation. Typically, such rooms provide for children's or adults' play and possibly for hobbies. They are ideal locations for television, radios, and both live and recorded music. Family rooms often adjoin the kitchen for ease in serving informal meals or snacks, or they may be near children's bedrooms to provide overflow space for their play. Easy access to the outdoors is almost an imperative.

Taking the degree of separation one step further, many homes provide "seclusion spaces" where one or more members of the household can retire for quiet reading, work, or just thinking. Unlike the truly private space (see Chap. 3), seclusion rooms belong to no one person but are available to whoever needs a time of quiet and privacy. The seclusion space in Figure 52 is really just a corner of a larger area, but it acquires both serenity and isolation by means of the architectural details, particularly the raised seating platform that forms its perimeter. This space would lend itself equally well to reading, working on hobbies or crafts, listening to music, eating simple meals, and it can even double as a guest bedroom because of the daybed in a protected alcove. Natural materials—wood, hand-loomed fabrics, fur, and straw—create a warm setting for the peaceful withdrawal that recharges the spirit.

Group Spaces Outside the Home

When spirits need venting rather than recharging, a larger space is in order. The trend toward complexes of homes of fairly restricted size—such as townhouses, condominiums, garden and high-rise apartments—has brought into being new kinds of secondary group spaces. Community leisure and play facilities may consist only of children's playgrounds and some open green space (Fig. 53). As space and money permit, they might also include a kind of expanded family room, a clubhouse for communal gatherings and parties (Fig. 54), usually with kitchen facilities, plus swimming pools (Fig. 55) and saunas, tennis courts, and even golf courses and marinas. Such arrangements greatly enlarge group living space and bring people together in much the same way that the New England common, the swimming hole, the barn dance, and the social hall did for earlier generations. Moreover, they can add greatly to the livability of small homes if they provide what the individual tenants want and can use.

53. In a housing complex geared toward families with young children, rugged outdoor play areas and equipment are a necessity. A play sculpture of heavy wooden beams at various heights and set in a sand base allows young imaginations free rein and is virtually indestructible. Fisher-Friedman Associates, architects. (*Photograph: Joshua Freiwald*)

The many details discussed in this chapter are important, but they should not obscure major goals, which focus on basic human values. The social quarters of any home should give each person who lives in it a sense of belonging in the household group and encourage each to play a supportive but unconstrained role in the family pattern. Each individual deserves the opportunity to express personal aptitudes, feelings, and desires. In short, a successful group space should promote the security, self-realization, and socialization of each member of the family.

below: 54. When apartments and houses are small and clustered together, a community group space answers the need for large areas suited to musical entertainment, cards, games, and the like. Callister, Payne, and Bischoff, architects and community planners. See also Fig. 708. (*Photograph: Dean Jones; Courtesy Snapfinger Woods, Atlanta*)

right: 55. A community ''playspace'' for adults complements that intended for children (Fig. 53). Here the swimming pool is allied to a clubhouse. (Fisher-Friedman Associates, architects. (*Photograph: Joshua Freiwald*)

Private Spaces

3

Privacy can be many different things. It may be provided by a cabin deep in the woods; a secluded bedroom for one person or a couple within the larger household; a cocoon of sound created by enveloping oneself in music; a "symbolic" line of demarcation, such as a curtain or screen, that isolates someone's own territory; or simply the ability to concentrate so intensely, on work or reading matter, that the rest of the world is shut out. In a people-glutted environment privacy may be, in the words of Professor Alexander Kira, "one of the last luxuries left."

Yet privacy is also a necessity. Individuals require different degrees of privacy for sleeping, dressing, bathing, and the like. Other kinds of private spaces must be established when overnight guests visit the home or when a member of the household pursues tasks that demand seclusion. Most importantly, though, human beings need and deserve spaces in which to collect their thoughts or pursue their dreams, to get to know themselves as people.

Several factors challenge the quest for privacy, foremost among them, of course, the very existence of increasing numbers of people concentrated in increasingly smaller areas. Even vacationers seeking respite from the cities in the vast national parks often find themselves cheek by jowl with other families. Most households today probably cannot afford to provide individual rooms or suites for each member. The huge, rambling houses of a few generations ago—built when materials and labor were cheap and fuel simply a matter of chopping wood—have ceased to be practical. Nevertheless, with intelligent planning we can design homes that offer each inhabitant a private space in which to retreat.

Sleeping and Dressing

Primitive peoples slept on the ground, on rock ledges, or in trees, seeking only protection from the elements and from their enemies. With increasing civilization came the technique of building shelters, and while such dwellings reserved a place for sleeping, they rarely separated it from other areas. In fact, the notion of isolating the sleeping place from other parts of the house evolved quite late. In many parts of the Western world until the Renaissance, for example, people commonly slept on pallets on the floor, in rooms used for different activities by day. Medieval great halls often served in this way, with only a privileged few enjoying spacious private quarters. Today, most bedrooms are planned to accommodate only one or two persons, and considerable attention has been devoted to making the time spent in those rooms as pleasant and salubrious as possible.

The ultimate in privacy derives from encasing oneself in a windowless cubicle in which air, light, and sound are precisely and automatically controlled. Some research has indicated that effective sleeping time can be reduced by about two hours under such ideal conditions. A similar concept motivates the Closingbed (Fig. 56) designed by Joe Colombo, which incorporates in its headboard a radio, alarm clock, telephone, reading lights, cigarette lighter, and air conditioning controls. With the canopy down, the bed's occupant can regulate the interior temperature precisely. However, the Closingbed does have small plastic porthole windows to provide a glimpse of the immediate environment and perhaps reassure the anxious claustrophobe.

Most people probably would not be so single-minded about their sleeping spaces; furthermore, the scientifically optimum conditions for efficient sleep may not be the most psychologically gratifying. It is pleasant to retire early and read or watch television, occasionally glancing up at objects in the room or stars in the night sky. And the return to consciousness in a cubicle devoid of stimulus cannot possibly compete with the experience of awakening in a comfortable room filled with one's own personal things, penetrated by the morning songs of birds or the stirring rhythms of the city (Pl. 9, p. 59).

A well-designed bedroom affords a quiet retreat at any time of the day. It can be relaxing to curl up or stretch out on a bed during the afternoon. Often, bedrooms provide the best conditions in the home for concentrated reading, study, or meditation. For these reasons, a bedroom ideally should be a moderately sized, multipurpose, segregated space. The requisites for sleeping are:

- □ A **bed** or **beds** long enough and wide enough for one or two persons.
- □ A **bedside table** or built-in storage unit to hold the paraphernalia that may accompany one to bed—reading materials, clock and radio, tissues, cups and dishes, eyeglasses, a telephone, and so on.
- □ A **light source** next to or over the bed for reading and for emergencies.
- □ **Control of natural light** by draperies or blinds.
- □ **Ventilation** from windows or other air sources. The best solution calls for ventilating devices on opposite walls, next best on adjacent walls, minimum

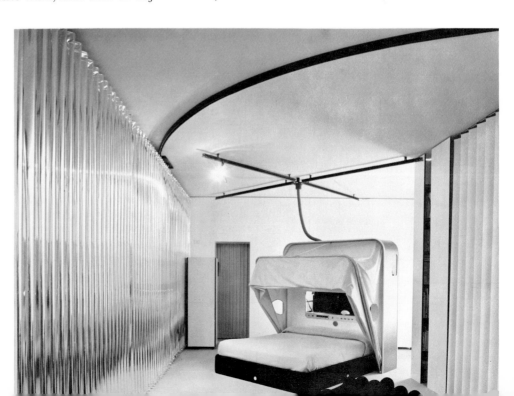

56. The "Closingbed" designed by Joe Colombo provides a micro-environment for sleep. When the canopy is lowered, light, air, temperature, and sound can be controlled precisely. (*Photograph: Aldo Ballo*)

57. A large freestanding unit gives ample closet, cupboard, and drawer storage for two people's wardrobes. On one side the storage unit serves as a headboard, on the other it creates a dressing area. Robert Stern and John Hagmann, architects. (*Photograph: Maris/Semel*)

on only one wall. Being able to let hot air escape through windows or ventilators at ceiling height greatly reduces summer heat. Air conditioning vents should be placed in such a way that the bed is protected from drafts.

□ **Quietness,** achieved by locating bedrooms away from—or insulating them against—noisier parts of the house, and by using sound-absorbing materials.

Dressing and undressing involve a variety of movements, many of them requiring conditions quite different from those best for sleeping:

□ **Space** sufficient to stand, stretch, turn around, and bend over
□ **Seating** to facilitate dealing with hosiery and shoes
□ **Storage** for all types of clothing; a minimum of 5 feet of hanging space per person, plus shelf and drawer space (Fig. 57)
□ **Counter space** with a well-lighted mirror, combined with a storage area for cosmetics and shaving equipment
□ A **full-length mirror** for the overall view, if possible
□ **Lighting,** either artificial or natural, that enables us to find things and evaluate the effect

Ideally, all of this takes place in a separate dressing area between the sleeping space and the bath, but too often it is sandwiched into whatever free space the bed and other furniture leave in the bedroom. Such conditions will be less frustrating if a "dressing center" is planned for each occupant of the room. Certainly, each person deserves a whole closet, including or near a chest of drawers. Adding a mirror, good lighting, and a chair completes the dressing unit.

In designing a bedroom, one must take several factors into consideration: the number of people who will occupy the room and their ages (children, teenagers, and adults may have quite different priorities); the various roles the room will have to play—that is, whether it is simply to be a place for sleeping or must serve as study, play area, den, or workroom as well; and the amount of space that can be utilized. Particularly when space is very limited, the amount of room available may be a major determining factor in planning a sleeping area.

Size of Sleeping Area

Sleeping spaces can range in size from the berths found in inexpensive accommodations on trains and ships—barely large enough to contain a human body—through extravagant quarters that include areas for reading or relaxing, for working at a desk or sewing table, and so on. In between we will find an entire spectrum of variations. No matter what the size, however, a sleeping space can be designed in such a way that it provides maximum comfort and efficiency for whoever occupies it.

Figures 58 and 59 suggest two novel ways of creating a sleeping space when there is no bedroom. By day the room in Figure 58 masquerades as an ordinary sitting room. Most people, upon entering, would not notice the bed held flush against the ceiling by metal cables. When night comes, the bed is simply lowered on pulleys to make an instant bedroom. Less eccentric, perhaps, and increasingly common in studio apartments, the sleeping loft (Fig. 59) takes advantage of a high ceiling

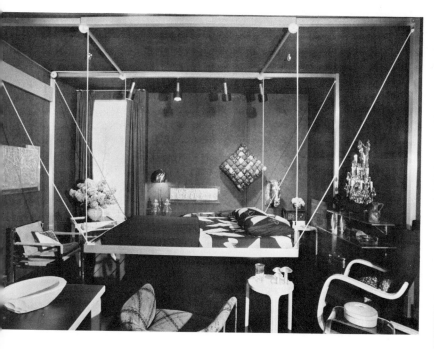

above: 58. Ceiling space is one resource few homes utilize. Here a bed raised and lowered on pulleys transforms a sitting room into sleeping accommodations at night. (*Photograph: The New York Times/Gene Maggio*)

right: 59. A sleeping loft greatly expands usable space in small but high-ceilinged apartments. (*Photograph: Michael Boys*)

60. The loft of an old barn becomes an expansive, gracious, and supremely comfortable bedroom. (*Photograph: Robert Perron*)

to double part of the space, making a workroom underneath. By contrast, the entire upper story of a barn, transformed into a bedroom (Fig. 60), provides spacious and luxurious accommodations for many different activities.

Number, Location, and Layout of Bedrooms

The number of sleeping areas in a home is conditioned by the size of the household, its economic status and lifestyle, and often by the stage of family life that prevails. One corner of a studio apartment may seem adequate to a young single person or an elderly retiree, both of whom are apt to have limited funds. Young children usually enjoy the companionship of siblings near their own ages, but teenagers will probably prefer a separate room to make their own territory and to ensure privacy. Dormitory-style sleeping may prove acceptable in vacation houses or for some types of households. In general, however, the number of bedrooms rises with the number of people to be accommodated and the amount of money available.

The location of bedrooms depends upon the emphasis a family places on opposing needs of supervision and seclusion. Young children must be near their parents at night, unless an intercommunication system exists to pick up distress signals. Placing children's bedrooms near the kitchen makes daytime control easier; convenient access to outdoor play areas saves housekeeping effort. With older children, the amount of surveillance they require must be balanced against a desire for the quiet and independence that separated private spaces will give to different age levels.

Placement of doors and windows contributes greatly to a bedroom's effectiveness. The doors, if more than one, should be as close together as is compatible with other requirements. Because the most frequently used traffic path connects the entrance door with the closet or chest of drawers, good sense suggests keeping this path short and direct. If the door is not directly in line with the bed or dressing area, there will be some measure of privacy even when the door is open. Grouping the windows on one wall can make the room seem larger and result in more usable wall space, although the need for ventilation may indicate placement of windows in two or more walls.

The demand for convenient storage in bedrooms is exceeded only by the same need in kitchens. Basic principles suggest designing storage space for whatever it is to hold, keeping all space for each person's clothing together, and having that space near the door. The bed illustrated in Figure 61 is an efficient and beautiful solution to the problem of many small objects that often clutter bedrooms. Not only the headboard but the entire underside of the bed incorporates drawers and open shelves. Thus, a normally wasted and dirt-catching area has been transformed into a practical storage unit.

Special Needs

Bedrooms are perhaps the most appropriate places in the home for members of the household to indulge their individuality. Bright, vivid colors may not be conducive to sleep, but if one person delights in them and the rest of the family does not, the bedroom would be a good place to satisfy this urge. Photographs with sentimental appeal or cherished collections differentiate one's own bedroom from those belonging to others. Even small rooms generally contain enough cubic footage for such memorabilia if bookcases, shelves, and cupboards are integrated with walls that will not be harmed by hooks and thumbtacks.

Children and young people especially enjoy rooms that have much free floor space and surfaces on which things can be displayed. Plenty of drawers and

61. A rustic handmade bed offers well-organized storage space beneath it with both sliding drawers and open shelves. Additional shelving forms a headboard. (*Photograph: Robert Perron*)

62. Intelligent planning created this sleeping-play-work space for two children. All materials are sturdy and easy to clean, so they will weather the onslaughts of very young children, yet the room is sufficiently adaptable to "grow" with its occupants. Sheltered bunks give a measure of privacy for sleeping. Douglas White, designer. (*Photograph: Robert Perron*)

cupboards help to store some of the clutter. Colors can be either bold or subdued, but durability is a prime consideration (Fig. 62). Movable partitions in or between children's bedrooms permit changing at will from large open areas to nooks for quiet seclusion.

When two people share a bedroom, a different situation arises, for the room should suit and express both. A hypothetical couple, for example, might want a room that could double as a study for either or both occupants, or even a bedroom that abuts—and could be absorbed into—the group space when large parties are in progress. The character of these two kinds of bedrooms obviously would be quite different, the furnishings in the latter more like those of a living room, with dressing and bath facilities concentrated in a separate area.

Hygiene

For several decades bathrooms were the home's most standardized utility, and until recently we took for granted the three unrelated white fixtures jutting conspicuously out into the smallest room of the house. Walls were invariably of plaster or tiles, timidly pastel in color. Small, hard-to-reach windows offered the only access to the outside world—if indeed they existed at all. Such bathrooms promised little beyond a dispiriting efficiency and often failed to live up to even that minimum essential. Fortunately, this tedium no longer characterizes bathrooms being designed today. In fact, some households have freed their thinking to the extent they can abolish the official bathroom altogether. One California family has developed a taste for outdoor bathing (Pl. 10, p. 59), a self-indulgence made possible by the predominantly gentle climate. A bath in this tub—surrounded as it is with trees and shrubs—would fall somewhere between the daily routine of hygiene and a dip in an icy mountain brook.

Nowadays people want more, larger, and brighter bathrooms with plenty of space—storage, counter, and elbow—to take care of grooming rituals. Bathrooms are being combined with dressing areas, often with a washbasin located outside the bathroom proper. Quick heat, lots of light, rapid and effective ventilation ensure comfort and convenience.

Research into the design of bathrooms has led to the reshaping of many standard fixtures for ease and safety. Most tubs now have nonskid bottoms and often grab rails for safety. They may include wide ledges and storage compartments with drop-down doors that become tables. Deeper tubs are designed for leisurely soaking (Fig. 63). Some showers offer two separate heads or a flexible shower spray to accommodate people of different heights; integral seats facilitate leg and foot washing and are safer for the ill or elderly (Fig. 64). Newer washbasins are more efficient and easier to clean. Above all, designers have finally recognized that bathing and grooming can be pleasurable as well as hygienic activities.

Related to the new interest in bathing as a therapeutic pastime is the popularity of the sauna, the relaxing (and invigorating) hot-air bath. The traditional Scandinavian sauna is a self-contained building, usually of cedar. A hot, dry atmosphere

right: 63. The new deeper soaking tubs acknowledge that bathing can be a pleasant, relaxing respite from the day's activities, as well as a necessary ritual of cleanliness. (*Courtesy American-Standard*)

below: 64. Tubs and showers fitted with seats are a boon to older people. They also facilitate leg and foot washing. (*Courtesy American-Standard*)

right: 65. Saunas range from small hinged units that wrap around the body to entire outside rooms. This comfortable space off a bathroom invites thought-suspending relaxation. (*Photograph: John T. Hill; courtesy McCall's Magazine*)

66–68. Careful placement of bedrooms and bathrooms within the home contributes to their effectiveness as private spaces.

right: 66. Bedrooms and bathrooms normally are grouped together in the quietest part of the house. Moreover, both parents and children may find greater peace if their bedrooms and baths are separated. Dreyfuss and Blackford, architects.

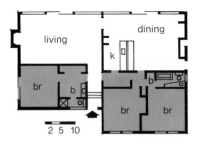

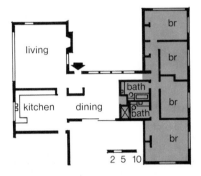

right: 67. In more complex plan shapes, bedrooms and baths can be in a segregated wing remote from household noises. Richard Pollman, architect.

above: 68. In two-story or split-level houses, the bedrooms and baths are usually upstairs, as in this house designed by James G. Durham.

is produced by pouring water on heated bricks, and true devotees will follow their basking with a dip in the snow. As interpreted for American homes, the sauna is often a cubicle adjacent to the bathroom (Fig. 65).

Location of bathrooms is primarily a matter of convenience, privacy, and cost (Figs. 66–68). In a one-bathroom house, this important room should be accessible from all bedrooms without the necessity of one's crossing, or being visible from, the group spaces. On the other hand, it is desirable that the bathroom be as near the kitchen and major group space as feasible. The plan shown in Figure 66 handles this tough assignment well.

Only cost checks the desire to multiply bathrooms. Ideally, a home for three or more persons should have at least two bathrooms, as should one with sleeping quarters on two floors. As the household expands, so should the plumbing. The optimum number of bathrooms can be lessened, however, if the tub or shower and the toilet are in separate compartments or if dressing areas incorporate washbasins.

Size, location of doors and windows, arrangement of fixtures, provision for storage, and finishes for walls, floors, and ceilings are important considerations in planning bathrooms:

- **Minimum size** is about 5½ by 6 feet, but these dimensions preclude use by more than one person at a time (often a necessary inconvenience), seriously limit storage space, and may give the occupant claustrophobia. A few more square feet usually justify their cost.
- The **door** should be located so that, when opened, it will not hit a person using any of the fixtures, will shield the toilet, and can be left partially open for ventilation without giving full view of the room.
- Critical factors in **window design** include light, ventilation, easy operation, and privacy. Ordinarily, this suggests high windows not directly over any fixtures, but new devices facilitate opening and closing windows even when they are high above washbasins or tubs. Skylights (Fig. 69) and vented fans can illumi-

nate and ventilate inside bathrooms. Even window walls are feasible if they open out onto a protected garden or balcony.

☐ Typical **arrangements of fixtures** are illustrated in Figures 66 to 68. Divided bathrooms (Fig. 70) increase utility considerably for relatively small expense.

☐ **Storage** at point of first use is a cardinal principle in housing the miscellany of things associated with hygiene and grooming. This indicates not only medicine cabinets (with locks for safety) but spacious cupboards and drawers.

☐ **Finishes for walls** permit great freedom. In addition to tile and painted plaster, the repertory includes brick and properly finished wood; laminated plastics (such as Formica) and molded fiberglass; waterproof wallpaper, textiles, or wallboard.

☐ **Flooring materials** range from practically impervious tile, through the somewhat more resilient plastics (such as vinyl), to the warmth of carpeting.

☐ **Color** is important for both its visual impact and its reflectance values, which can change skin tones. Oranges and pinks make a person look healthy; blues and greens may cast a sallow tinge.

☐ **Lighting,** both natural and artificial, is critical to provide good illumination for shaving and makeup.

☐ **Shape and size of fixtures** become critical factors in planning. Typical dimensions are listed in Table 3.1, but luxury fixtures can be much larger and of irregular shapes (Pl. 11, p. 60).

left: 69. A skylight may be the solution to bringing natural light into the bathroom while at the same time maintaining privacy. James Caldwell, architect. (*Photograph: Philip L. Molten*)

right: 70. A divided bathroom, here with sliding panels, permits use of the space by more than one person at a time. (*Courtesy Kohler Co.*)

Table 3.1   Standard Bathroom Fixture Sizes and Clearances*

Fixture	Small Depth		Width	Large Depth		Width
bathtub	30″	x	48″	42″	x	66″
soaking tub	40″	x	40″			
washbasin	15″	x	18″	24″	x	30″
toilet	24″	x	22″	30″	x	24″
bidet	25″	x	14″	28″	x	16″
shower	30″	x	30″	42″	x	60″
bathinette	21″	x	35″	24″	x	36″
vanity cabinet	30″	x	24″	32″	x	26″
Clearances						
space between front of tub and opposite wall	30″	–	42″			
space in front of toilet	18″	–	24″			
space at sides of toilet	12″	–	18″			
space between fronts of fixtures	24″	–	36″			

*Luxury fixtures are available in larger sizes.

71. A collection of primitive masks, arranged under a skylight, provides enrichment for an otherwise streamlined bathroom. Charles Warren Callister and Henry Herold, architects. (*Photograph: Philip L. Molten*)

No longer is laboratory starkness the most important determinant for bathroom design. Since fixtures, finishes, and accessories come in a wide range of colors and designs, their functionalism can be turned into visual delight. Paintings, graphics, sculpture, and plants all serve to humanize and individualize what was once a commonplace little cubicle. The bathroom illustrated in Figure 71 derives much of its luxurious quality from the collection of masks illuminated by a hidden skylight. And even a perfectly ordinary room can be transformed by the addition of dramatic color (Pl. 12, p. 60).

above: **Plate 9.** A cheerful, comfortable bedroom follows an Early American theme with its exposed cedar beams, antique furniture, and collection of handmade patchwork quilts. See page 49. (*Courtesy American Home Magazine*)

left: **Plate 10.** An outdoor bathtub would not suit every household, but in temperate climates it could be a delightful and refreshing innovation. Kipp Stewart, designer. See page 54; see also Figs. 456, 657; Plate 37, p. 265. (*Photograph: Morley Baer*)

left: **Plate 11.** Unusual custom-designed fixtures, including a contoured platform for "sunbathing," help give this bathroom its look of luxury. Charles Gwathmey, architect. See page 57. (*Photograph: Ezra Stoller ⓒ ESTO*)

below: **Plate 12.** A simple, old-fashioned bathroom can be transformed with the introduction of bold, primary colors. Robert A. M. Stern, architect. See page 58; see also Figs. 109, 247, 408, 440. (*Photograph: John T. Hill*)

left: 72. Vacation homes should be expandable to accommodate overnight guests. In this minimally divided bunkroom, recycled lumber makes the sturdy double-decker beds, while coat hooks take the place of closets for short-term use. Donald MacDonald, architect. (*Courtesy American Home Magazine*)

right: 73. A one-room guest cottage becomes a separate apartment for four, enabling hosts and guests to maintain their own rhythms of living. It has been fitted with kitchen equipment for an early breakfast or late snack, plus a library for browsing. Easy access to the outdoors permits guests to move about without disturbing the household. Richard and Sue Rogers with Norman and Wendy Foster, architects. (*Photograph: Ezra Stoller © ESTO*)

House Guests

Until only a few decades ago, entertainment of overnight guests represented a major form of recreation, a welcome change of pace from everyday living. The combination of great distances separating friends and relatives with typically large, commodious houses often staffed by servants made hospitality a simple pleasure. Guests could be entertained for long periods of time without seriously disrupting the household, and the visitor who arrived for dinner and stayed for a month need not be cause for dismay.

Today, houses are smaller and live-in servants almost unknown; even one unoccupied bedroom seems like a luxury. Nevertheless, with careful planning most houses can accommodate overnight guests in a civilized manner, particularly if their lifestyles correspond to those of their hosts.

For those who travel lightly with their own sleeping bags, comfortable surfaces on which to place them may be all that is necessary. Many vacation houses provide this minimum in bunk rooms (Fig. 72). Going one step beyond this, we should consider that house guests deserve the same elements of private space as do members of the family: a secluded area in which to sleep and dress, storage space for clothing, bathroom facilities, and the possibility of getting outside the social circle occasionally. The ultimate would be a separated **guest house** (Fig. 73), with its own kitchenette and eating counter. Other possibilities include:

□ A **bedroom-sitting room** with private bath, separated from family areas and always in readiness because it serves no other purpose

□ A **secluded room** or study that doubles as a guestroom—a sensible solution because a room well planned for seclusion has most of the qualities of a good guestroom

□ A **guiet alcove** or small room off the group space that can readily be made private by folding or sliding doors, curtains, or screens (Fig. 74)

□ An **extra bed** in one or more of the bedrooms—perhaps a bunk or a studio couch

□ A living room **sofabed** (Fig. 75)

Individual Work and Hobbies

Chapter 2 described group spaces that make provision for work, home crafts, and other hobbies. But some people desire greater privacy or total seclusion to pursue such activities, which may present a problem in an era when spare rooms, basements, attics, and backyard sheds have become scarce.

left: 74. By enclosing the tiny sunporch, architect Hobart Betts created a combined guest room and weekend workroom in his own vacation house. (*Photograph: Maris/Semel*)

above: 75. In many small homes overnight guests must be accommodated in the living room. This low-budget group space assures sleeping comfort by making a pair of sofas out of foam rubber mattresses placed on inexpensive plastic laminate bases. (*Courtesy American Home Magazine*)

Writing, paying bills, and keeping records all necessitate a desk, in and around which the needed paraphernalia can be stored conveniently. A desk in the group space, especially in a secluded corner of it, meets the needs of some families (Fig. 76). Others may find it more satisfactory to locate a desk in the kitchen or in one or more bedrooms. When desk work in the home is a normal day-to-day occupation, then a truly private retreat, such as a study isolatable from the rest of the house, becomes a necessity (Fig. 77).

Knitting and crocheting can be done wherever one can read, but mending, sewing, and needlework—either as profession or hobby—are not so easily taken care of. The collection of needles, scissors, and "findings" seems to invite disorder and the fingers of small children, to which they are a definite hazard. Adding a sewing machine and space for a cutting table brings further complications. In descending order of desirability would be: a special sewing room (nowadays a luxury); space in one of the bedrooms; or a spot in the already crowded kitchen or laundry. Chapter 4 shows an example of a well-planned sewing area with adequate work space and storage (Fig. 106).

above right: 76. Architect Douglas White's own home office provides ample work space and storage in a secluded corner of one room.

right: 77. A completely separated study gives the ultimate private space in households where one or more members normally work at home or often do concentrated reading. John Howard Gamble, architect. (*Photograph: Julius Shulman*)

right: 78. A bedroom large enough to serve as a studio allows the resident artist privacy and the freedom to leave work-in-progress exposed. A heap of handwoven pillows, macramé wall hangings, and natural wood furnishings establish the character of the room. (*Courtesy American Home Magazine*)

below: 79. The serenity of a meditation room away from the center of household living calms the spirit just by its simplicity. (*Photograph: Hans Namuth, Photo Researchers, Inc.*)

Such pursuits as weaving, woodworking, or painting deserve appropriate space and equipment. Important as these may be to individuals, such enterprises can quickly endanger the composure of other household members, unless they are isolated in a separate room or household studio (Fig. 78).

Solitude

For people who live in groups, for parents raising children—as well as the children being raised—occasional solitude is a rare and precious gift. Too often the bathroom provides the only haven in the home, the only area in which one feels reasonably secure from being disturbed—and this leads to certain difficulties. Much stress is laid upon the two-week vacation to "get away from it all," but travel cannot substitute for the half-hour vacations most individuals need every day. This returns us to the question of privacy. In the quest for solitude many families and individuals have planned tranquil "meditation rooms," in the home or in a partly or wholly separate building (Fig. 79). The opportunity to find total seclusion, free from interruption, can not only sustain the emotional well-being of individuals but enrich their contacts with other people when the private space is left behind.

Support Spaces

Those areas of a home responsible for the maintenance of daily living—for the stocking and preparation of food, the care and perhaps fabrication of clothing, the storage of equipment—may be termed "support spaces," in the sense that they nurture a lifestyle. Group spaces and private spaces would exist in a vacuum if they were not supported by the work areas of the home. The kitchen—the major support space—provides bodily sustenance and often emotional sustenance as well, when it serves as the principal gathering point for family members. Depending upon the requirements of the household, support spaces may also include facilities for laundry, sewing, different types of shop work, flower arranging and potting of plants, as well as various storage needs. Taken together, these areas constitute the foundation on which life in the home rests.

The relative effectiveness of a lifespace is partially rooted in the most mundane details—how easy it is to carry out all the tasks associated with day-to-day existence. For many people this will dictate making everything as maintenance-free as possible, with labor-saving appliances and step-saving design—perhaps to liberate them for activities outside the home. Others may wish to streamline *some* of the chores associated with maintenance in order to devote more time to specific activities generally thought of as "work," such as baking bread, preparing for a dinner party, raising children, making clothes, or building furniture. Space for these pursuits will then become paramount, but such space must also be maintained. The four concepts of **utility, economy, beauty,** and **character** assume sharper focus in support spaces than in any other part of the home. Under the general heading of **utility** would come:

☐ Planning rooms and outdoor areas that are appropriate in size, shape, and location to their intended functions
☐ Keeping related areas together, such as dining space, kitchen, garage, and service yard
☐ Finding equipment and furnishings that are genuinely practical
☐ Storing objects conveniently where they are needed

Economy suggests:
☐ Selecting durable and easily maintained materials and forms
☐ Limiting furniture and accessories to those that are really used or enjoyed

☐ Choosing appliances that minimize labor and save time (rather than those that actually increase labor by "simplifying" something it had not previously occurred to one to do)

Beauty lifts people's spirits and makes housework seem easier. Now more than ever it is possible to make the support spaces of the house, such as the kitchen, colorful and attractive (Pl. 13, p. 77).

Character, of course, implies that each support space has a special quality because it is tailored to the maintenance of a particular lifestyle.

Kitchens

Few areas of the home have received such intensive study as the kitchen. Manufacturers continually redesign the standard appliances and equipment to make them more efficient, more attractive, and thus more desirable to potential buyers. Now and then major companies will formulate experimental kitchens of the future that—while in the realm of fantasy—give us fresh insights into kitchen planning for today. Figures 80 and 81 illustrate such a dream kitchen.

Planned around changing social patterns, the tasks they generate, and the appliances and construction details that are or could be available by the late 1970s, this work center operates within the major group space. It takes as a basic premise the fact that cooking and cleanup are no longer isolated events solely in the province of the "housewife," but rather for many households an ongoing activity that can occur at any time of day and involve any number of people, separately or simultaneously. Therefore, the larger appliances have been redesigned and decentralized so as to be accessible to more than one person at a time. They have also been completely integrated with counters and storage cabinets, for both sanitary reasons and ease of maintenance. The many smaller pieces of equipment are stored at the point of primary use and reachable from both sides of a counter, with plenty of electrical outlets provided.

The Westinghouse dream kitchen is a prototype, designed to meet the requirements of a "typical" American family. By contrast, the kitchen illustrated in Figures 82 and 83 emerged from the very personal needs of a couple who not only cook a great deal but also teach and write about the art. Its special features include professional-quality appliances, optimum storage for every conceivable foodstuff and utensil (Fig. 87), an integrated office space and sewing area. The laboratory efficiency is humanized by wood counters, the gleam of tile, stainless steel, and

left: 80. A Westinghouse-designed kitchen of the future divides the "food center" into three integrated units—a Quick Meal unit, a Dinner unit, and a Storage Wall unit. It was planned to accommodate the needs of typical family lifestyles today. (*Courtesy Westinghouse Electric Corporation*)

right: 81. The plan of the Westinghouse kitchen shows relationships to the living area, formal and informal dining spaces, and the out-of-doors.

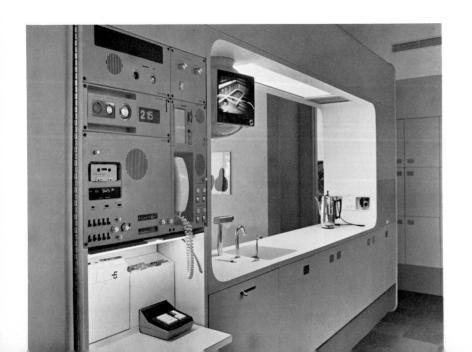

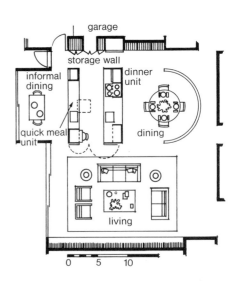

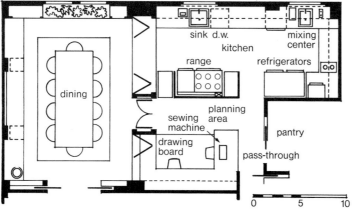

sink d.w. mixing
kitchen center
range refrigerators

dining

planning
area
sewing
machine pantry
drawing
board
pass-through

0   5   10

above: 82. An extravagant kitchen designed to the last detail according to the specifications of two master cooks provides the most efficient working spaces possible for preparation of all manner of foods. It also incorporates a sewing area and office, and serves as the major entertainment center for the household. Donald Mallow, architect. See also Fig. 87. (*Photograph: Norman McGrath*)

left: 83. The plan shows how various work centers have been arranged to allow for a smooth progression of activities.

brass, as well as by the arched glass cupboard doors. Ample light, some natural and some artificial, illumines all the various work centers. Truly a working lifespace, this kitchen doubles as entertainment center, study, even classroom for cooking classes. In very modern terms it fulfills the old concept of the kitchen as the "heart of the house."

Although quite dissimilar in appearance, both of these kitchens take into account research that has been done on functional kitchen planning over the last quarter century. Studies made by Cornell University, the University of Illinois, and the U.S. Department of Agriculture, among others, have provided designers with many facts, figures, and formulas that offer great help in organizing the physical layout of work areas.[1] Three concepts have emerged:

Table 4.1 Standard Kitchen Appliance and Cabinet Sizes*

	Small			Large		
	Height	Depth	Width	Height	Depth	Width
cooktop (built-in)		21″ x	26″ to		21″ x	36″
range (cooktop at 36″)	43″ x	24″ x	20″ to	66″ x	25″ x	40″
oven (built-in)**	27″ x	21″ x	22½″ to	42″ x	21″ x	24″
microwave oven	15″ x	12½″ x	18½″ to	15½″ x	21″ x	24″
refrigerator	52″ x	24″ x	20″ to	66″ x	29″ x	30″
refrigerator-freezer	65″ x	29″ x	31″ to	66″ x	29″ x	60″
freezer	33″ x	25″ x	42″ to	66″ x	29″ x	33″
dishwasher (built-in)				35″ x	24″ x	24″
dishwasher (portable)				38″ x	28″ x	24″
clothes washer	42″ x	25″ x	25″ to	45″ x	28″ x	29″
clothes dryer	42″ x	25″ x	27″ to	45″ x	28″ x	31″
ironing board	30″ x	44″ x	11″ to	36″ x	54″ x	14″
trash compactor				36″ x	24″ x	15″
sink	(single)	20″ x	24″ to	(double)	22″ x	33″
cabinets, base	30″ x	25″ x	15″ to	36″ x	25″ x	30″
cabinets, wall	12″ x	6″ x	15″ to	30″ x	13″ x	30″

*Larger sizes are available for special installations. Dimensions do not include
an allowance of 3 to 5 inches clearance behind large motored appliances and ranges.
**Cut-out space needed for single and double units.

□ The **physical limitations** of the principal cook or cooks should be a major determinant in achieving an energy-saving, comfortable working environment.
□ The kitchen is best organized around **work centers** that incorporate appropriate appliances with sufficient storage and work surfaces, and which are arranged in logical sequences.
□ The principle of **first use**—of storing items where they are needed rather than by category—fosters efficiency.

These findings say little about how a kitchen should look, but deal only in efficiency and comfort. Coupled with the chart of standard appliance sizes (Table 4.1), they can serve as a foundation for planning the work areas of the room. We must bear in mind, however, that functionalism and aesthetics need not be incompatible. The most efficient kitchen can also be beautiful (Pl. 14, p. 77).

Physical Limitations

In general, physical limitations vary with a person's height; to conserve human energy, we should consider normal work curves (Fig. 84) when planning the dimensions of counters and cupboards. Of critical importance in work comfort

84. Kitchen dimensions should be based on the height and reach of the person who will use the room most. The dimensions given here are for the average woman.

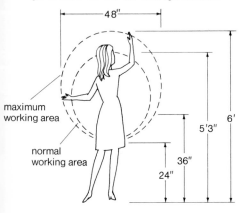

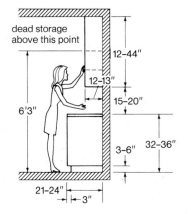

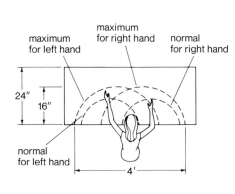

is the distance between one's elbow and the work surface. Most tasks can be performed easily on a counter that is 3 inches below the level of the elbow (with the upper arm vertical and the forearm horizontal to the floor). But when a particular chore—such as beating or chopping—requires force, a work surface 6 or 7 inches below elbow height serves better. This suggests that not all counters in the kitchen should be at the same level (Fig. 82).

The Work Centers

The design of work centers and the sequence in which they are arranged determines how smoothly a kitchen functions and how much energy will be expended in everyday tasks. Each work center should have adjacent counter and cabinet space of at least the sizes indicated.

The **refrigerator center** (Fig. 85) is placed either first or last in the work sequence—near the outside entrance and the sink for easy storage of food, or near the serving center and dining area for convenience of serving refrigerated items. In addition to the **refrigerator,** it should have:

- □ A **counter** at least 18 inches wide and about 36 inches high on the latch side of the refrigerator door for holding supplies. This often can be integrated with the counter space of adjacent centers.
- □ **Wall cabinets** to hold serving dishes for cold food and storage containers for foods going into the refrigerator. File space for trays often fits well here.
- □ A **base cabinet** with drawers for bottle openers, refrigerator and freezer supplies, and bottle storage.

The refrigerator center often incorporates a **freezer;** but a larger freezer could also be placed in a storage or utility room, basement, or garage outside the kitchen.

The **mixing center** (Fig. 86) handles all kinds of mixing—breads and pastries, salads and casseroles. It might be located between the sink and the refrigerator which holds many mix-first items, or next to the cooking center. It should include:

- □ A **counter** at least 3 feet wide and not more than 30 to 32 inches high (in contrast to the standard 36-inch height) to lessen fatigue. When considerable time is spent in mixing, knee space and a stool should be provided.
- □ Sufficient **electrical outlets** for small appliances—mixers, blenders, and so forth.
- □ **Wall cabinets** to store condiments, packaged foods, and cookbooks.
- □ **Base cabinets** with drawers for small tools and either drawers or sliding shelves for bowls, pans, and heavy items used in mixing.

Specially designed storage spaces for flour, sugar, and bread—as well as for small appliances such as mixers and blenders—will often be included in the wall or base cabinets of this center (Fig. 87).

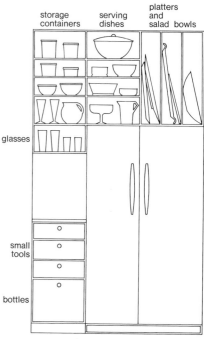

85. The refrigerator center.

86. The mixing center.

87. The mixing center of the kitchen shown in Figures 82 and 83 has special bins for dry ingredients, a marble top for rolling pastry, and a built-in two-unit cook-top. (*Photograph: Norman McGrath*)

88. The sink center.

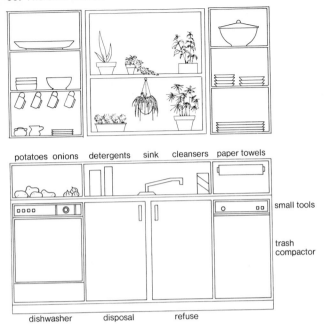

89. The cooking center.

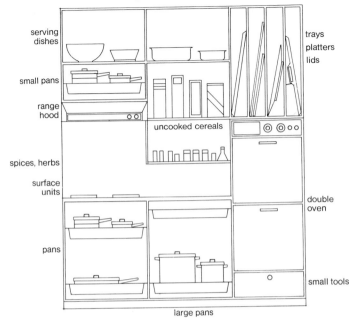

The **sink center** (Fig. 88) is indeed multipurpose, serving to wash fruits and vegetables, dishes, and children's hands, and providing water for mixing, cooking, freezing, and drinking. It can also be used for storage of tableware, although many households find the serving center more efficient for this purpose. The sink center is often located between the cooking and the mixing centers, since its proximity to both is desirable. This center needs:

□ **Counters** on both sides—at least 18 inches wide on the left, 36 inches wide on the right, and usually 36 inches high—with at least one of them a waterproof drainboard.
□ **A sink** or **sinks,** the design depending upon individual preferences. Double sinks facilitate hand dishwashing, but they may be too small for large cooking pans. With a dishwasher, a single large sink often suffices. Two separated sinks are especially convenient when more than one person uses the kitchen. For comfort, the sink should be about 3 inches below elbow height and not more than 3 inches in from the front edge of the counter.
□ **A dishwasher,** which will be easier to use if it is placed to the left of the sink. However, the location of dish storage must also be considered. The 24-inch counter width above a front-opening dishwasher is adequate for stacking dishes.
□ **Cabinet space** for those items generally used at the sink—utensils for cleaning, cutting, and straining food; dish cloths and towels, soaps and detergents. Many people find it convenient to store near this center the foods that need peeling or washing, a miscellany ranging from potatoes and onions to coffee and dried fruits.
□ **Provision for trash and garbage,** possibly including a **trash compactor.**
□ **A stool** and **knee space,** which ease the labor of cleaning vegetables and dishes, especially when conservation of human energy is a factor.

The **cooking center** (Fig. 89) becomes the busiest area of the kitchen during the half hour or so before meals. A location near the sink and mixing centers and convenient to the eating space will be most desirable. The cooking center should include:

□ Gas or electric **surface units** incorporated into a range or installed in a heat-resistant counter. Range tops are almost uniformly 36 inches high, but surface components can be installed on counters of whatever height the cook prefers. Usually, this would mean 3 inches below elbow height, but if the typical cuisine demands much stirring of sauces or use of a portable mixer, 6 or 7 inches below elbow height will be more comfortable.

□ A **heat-resistant counter** 24 inches wide and usually 36 inches high on at least one side of the surface units *and* built-in wall ovens.

□ An **oven** or **ovens,** either as part of the range or separate from the cooking surface. **Single ovens** below the surface units offer a compact cooking center, but the oven requires stooping to get things in and out. Many ranges incorporate a **built-in second oven** above the surface units, and this can be a desirable feature provided it presents no hazard to head and eyes. This arrangement, however, does not leave sufficient space for such oversize vessels as canning kettles and large soup pots. **Built-in wall ovens** should not interrupt the flow of counter space, although they need an adjacent counter area; they are best positioned so that the opened door is between 1 and 7 inches below elbow height for safety and convenience. **A microwave oven** for quick cooking of certain foods may be located in the cooking center or elsewhere, perhaps in the mixing center, serving center, or quick-cooking center.

□ **Wall cabinets** nearby for small cooking utensils and seasonings.

□ **Ventilation** provided by a quiet exhaust fan over the cooking surface.

In many homes, the availability of new equipment has caused the cooking center to explode into two or more smaller components. A kitchen might have, for example, a **quick-cooking center** (Fig. 90) in addition to the major cooking area. Quick-cooking apparatus could include a microwave oven, an electric broiler-oven, electric skillet, gas or electric barbecue, and a whole array of other small plug-in appliances. With the addition of a small sink and two or more surface units, even an undercounter refrigerator, this unit becomes totally self-contained. If it is properly arranged, a person working in this center would not interfere in the least with the activities of another cook in the major cooking area.

The **serving center** (Fig. 91) holds those items that go directly from storage to table—dishes and flatware, linens and accessories, toasters and waffle irons, and such condiments as sugar and catsup. Often integrated with either the cooking or the refrigerator center, it should be near the eating table and should have:

□ A **durable counter** at least 24 inches wide and from 30 to 36 inches high, with or without a pass-through to facilitate serving.

□ Ample **cabinet space** designed for the items to be stored. If the serving center is located between the kitchen and the dining area, then cabinet space should be accessible from either side. Usually, this space must be supplemented by cupboard space in the dining area or by a pantry.

Besides these centers, a **storage wall** or **pantry** serves to accommodate extra supplies and is especially necessary if wall-cabinet space over counters is lost to windows and ovens. Cleaning equipment and supplies need a well-planned closet either in the kitchen or in the laundry.

Storage Space in the Work Centers

The principle of first-use assumes primary importance in organizing storage space for the work centers. The cook will conserve time and energy if items are stored where they will be needed, rather than putting all similar things—pots and pans or sharp knives, for example—in one place.

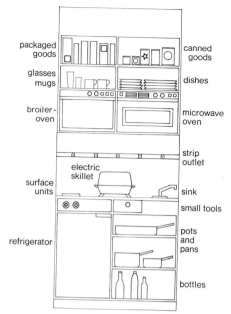

90. The quick-cooking center.

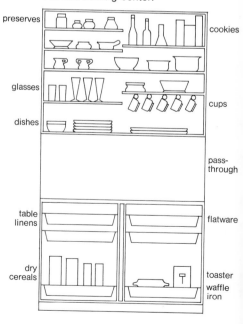

91. The serving center.

The *amount* of storage space in the work centers is a critical factor in their design. Research in this field indicates that the sizes given for counter space in each of the five work centers will ensure enough storage space for the average kitchen if wall and base cabinets are placed above and below the counters. When windows, range, or corners cut into these figures, compensating space should be provided elsewhere. If the work centers are placed alongside one another, all counters between appliances can be eliminated *except the largest counter, which then should be made 1 foot wider than usual.* According to these formulas, the counter space provided by the work centers totals at least 10 lineal feet, which is ample for kitchen supplies but leaves space for dinnerware to serve only four persons. Each set of dinnerware for twelve demands an extra 5 feet of wall-cabinet space. Families with many sets of dishes—or portions of sets—might consider an arrangement like that in Figure 92, which transforms mundane storage into a still-life of shapes and patterns.

Equally important, the *quality* of the storage space deserves careful consideration of when and how objects will be used and who will use them:

☐ **Visibility** suggests storing items (except for such identical articles as tumblers) only one row deep. Ideally, canned goods and condiments should be shelved in this manner to facilitate finding a particular item.

☐ **Accessibility** indicates putting the most frequently used items at the most convenient height, heavy objects below, and those seldom used above. Drawers in base cabinets are more convenient than fixed shelves, pull-out shelves intermediate. Space located above the maximum reach of a given person (Fig. 84) can be considered dead storage, since a stool or ladder would be required to reach articles kept there.

☐ **Flexibility** will be enhanced by adjustable shelves and drawers with removable dividers, which can adapt to changing family needs and design of kitchen tools.

☐ **Maintenance** generally recommends enclosed storage, but items that are used daily may to kept on open shelves.

Placement of the Work Centers

The cardinal principle of work-center organization is appropriateness to the desires and work habits of those using the kitchen most intensively. For most situations, however, the following generalizations hold:

- □ **Location** of the work centers usually starts with placing the sink, since it is used most, in the most desirable location—perhaps under a window—with the other centers located around it according to the busiest paths between them (often called the work triangle) and the dining areas.
- □ **Traffic** in and around the work centers should be limited to that connected with getting meals; miscellaneous traffic should be diverted elsewhere.
- □ **Distances** between counters and appliances that face each other should be 5 feet, and between counter and breakfast table at least 3½ feet. Distances between work centers are best kept short and the routes as direct as possible, while still allowing for the necessary counters and storage.
- □ **Standard arrangements** of work centers fall into four categories: one wall, L-shape, U-shape, and corridor (Figs. 93–96). At times, an island will be added to shield the work space from view or to supplement it. Although most kitchens relate basically to one of these four types, those designed to meet individual needs may differ markedly from standard practice.

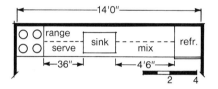

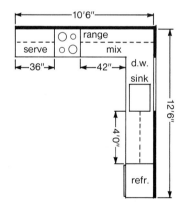

above left: 93. One-wall kitchens can be fitted into alcoves and concealed with folding doors when not in use. They are available in complete prefabricated units, and concentrate plumbing and wiring economically. However, if they contain standard-size appliances—rather than scaled-down "kitchenette" units—they require a great deal of walking.

below left: 94. L-shape plans have somewhat less distance between centers than one-wall kitchens. They leave room for eating and laundry and divert miscellaneous traffic a little.

above right: 95. U-shape kitchens generally are the most compact and efficient. They have the further grace of almost eliminating bothersome intrusion.

below right: 96. Corridor arrangements also decrease distances between work centers, but they invite unwelcome traffic when often-used doors are located at both ends.

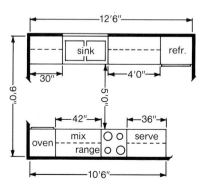

Designing the Kitchen

Plate 15 and Figure 98 show two kitchens designed with different criteria in mind, although both are for people to whom cooking is important. The narrow corridor kitchen in Plate 15 (p. 78) has two long walls given over to storage. Closed cupboards and drawers account for some of this space, but much of it is devoted to open shelving that displays the owner's large collection of dishes, pots, pitchers, containers, and other accouterments of cooking. Beyond the delightful visual effect, this solution opens up the narrow room to eliminate any feeling of constriction. The large windows at the end let in plenty of light, but plants and hanging utensils

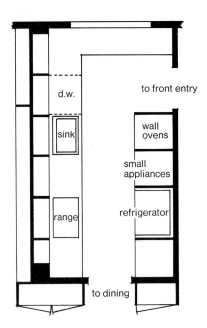

soften the glare. As the plan shows (Fig. 97), the kitchen is convenient to the group spaces but not exposed to them, so the cook can control the degree of privacy or interaction desired.

The other kitchen (Fig. 98) belongs to a furniture designer for whom cooking is a very social occasion. Actually, the "kitchen" has taken over one whole end of a high-ceilinged living area in this small remodeled house. Banks of closed storage cabinets and kitchen appliances fill a space that is only slightly demarcated by the heavy old butcher block table and the line of the bedroom balcony above. In a switch on the usual layout, a small enclosed dining ell is located off to the left behind the spiral stairs. This kitchen, although "supportive," could easily be considered part of the group space, since the cook would certainly participate in discussions and activities taking place in the living area, and guests would be encouraged to move freely into the kitchen.

above: 97. The plan of the corridor kitchen in Plate 15 (p. 78) shows how appliances have been grouped so the cook need take only a step or two between them.

right 98. A sleeping balcony demarcates the kitchen area of a multipurpose space in this delightful San Francisco house. Bob Steffy, designer. (*Photograph: Fred Lyons, Courtesy American Home Magazine*)

The kitchen illustrated in Figure 99 is noteworthy, since it incorporates many of the research findings reported earlier, plus those from a study of energy-saving kitchens for people with disabilities, to achieve a design that correlates efficiency with pleasantness. The latter study, developed by the Agricultural Research Service of the U.S. Department of Agriculture,[2] had as its goal the reduction of walking, stooping, lifting, and reaching in meal preparation and other kitchen activities.

The location of the kitchen in the total plan (Fig. 158) is one of the principal reasons for its success. Figuratively and literally the hub of the house, it serves as the connecting link between adults' and children's wings, is convenient to the formal dining room and outdoor eating area on the terrace. Proximity to both the carport and the front entry simplifies delivering supplies and greeting guests. This ample, almost square area is divided by an island into two zones—one for food preparation and the other for eating, planning, and storage. The working part of the kitchen is off to one side, out of the way of through traffic but easily accessible, while the circulation paths meet at the family dining table on the other side of the island. Although quite close, the utility room can be closed off.

The food-preparation zone adheres to a broken-U shape, with the three chief work centers in a step-saving triangle, and each center planned not only for storage at the point of first-use but also for conservation of energies. For example, the mix and dish-storage cabinets have accordian doors that open or close with minimum motion; knee space under the mix counter allows the worker to sit for time-consuming tasks. The dish-storage cabinet opens on both sides; high counters behind the sinks and the range serve as convenient pass-throughs to dining areas. The work sequence from the refrigerator to the dish cupboard has been planned for a smooth flow of motions. Maintenance is lessened by the choice of easily cleaned and dirt-resistant surfaces, such as laminated plastic countertops, well-sealed natural wood cabinets, and plastic tile floors. The plan is open enough to be pleasant and unconfining, closed enough so that the work areas need not be kept in strict order all the time.

99. None of the gracelessness characteristic of many kitchens that flaunt their utility in laboratory terms marks this pleasant cooking-eating space. The colors of natural wood serve as a foil for the floor and for counter tops, which can be any color the owner prefers. Loch Crane, architect. (*Photograph: Maynard L. Parker*)

right: **100.** A four-piece kitchen unit designed by Giancarlo Iliprandi combines range, oven, refrigerator, sink, and storage in a space less than 4 feet square. The individual segments can also be used separately. RB, Bergamo, Italy, manufacturer. (*Photograph: Aldo Ballo*)

below: **101.** A compact service core contains all the support elements for two units of a duplex townhouse—kitchens, bathrooms, stairs, closets, and air-conditioning equipment.

Some kitchens are planned for maximum efficiency, others with children foremost in mind; some for two-cook families (or more), others for households that do almost no cooking. At one end of the spectrum we would find the enormous, professionally equipped kitchen in which servants do most of the work; at the other, the modular unit that makes an instant kitchen wherever it is placed (Fig. 100). In every case the lifestyle of the particular family will determine the major factors in kitchen planning. However, some basic considerations apply to all types of kitchens:

Location of kitchens is a matter of critical importance, but there are many good solutions. A kitchen placed at the shortest feasible distance from indoor and outdoor eating areas, as well as from the garage and service areas, will save steps. Further, the kitchen should be convenient to the main entrance and to any service entrance, and if possible not far from a lavatory. (The last of these often follows naturally, since most homes centralize plumbing to save expense.) As long as these requirements are taken into account, there can be great freedom in placement, especially in a one-family home.

In a multifamily or high-rise construction, the economics of building often suggest an interior placement in a service core that concentrates utilities. Figure 101 shows a two-story factory-built service core, 12 by 40 feet, that contains kitchens, bathrooms, stairs, closets, and air-conditioning equipment for two units in a townhouse development.

Size is determined not only by the number of persons using the kitchen and the amount of food prepared for family or guests, but also by the kind and number of other activities that take place in the kitchen area. The space needed in small

above: Plate 13. A vividly colored, streamlined kitchen forms one wall of the major group space in this minimal-care beach house. The brilliant blue and red scheme contrasts strikingly with clean-lined Breuer and Miës van der Rohe furniture and a soft goat hair rug. John Fowler, architect. See page 66. (*Photograph: Norman McGrath*)

right: Plate 14. A large collection of baskets and Mexican tinware personalizes this warm, charming kitchen. Tozier and Abbott, architects. See page 68; see also Fig. 584; Plate 33, p. 231. (*Photograph: Julius Shulman*)

left: **Plate 15.** Every inch of space has been utilized in this long, narrow corridor kitchen. Much of its appeal derives from the owner's collection of pots and pitchers displayed on open shelves. Herbert Kosovitz, architect. See page 73; see also Fig. 97. (*Photograph: Fred Lyons, courtesy American Home Magazine*)

below: **Plate 16.** This delightful kitchen combines some modern appliances with bits of recycled nostalgia. Its focus is the old-fashioned Hoover cabinet painted in striking graphics. Richard Owen Abbott, architect. See page 81; see also Figs. 266, 267. (*Photograph: John T. Hill*)

homes for food preparation alone may vary from about 60 to 130 square feet, but larger homes may require even more. The addition of laundry or eating space, hobby or relaxation areas may raise the total to at least 300 square feet.

Shape has no readymade rules. Although typically rectangular, kitchens lend themselves to many other configurations. Experts generally agree, however, that a small food-preparation area requires fewer steps if its shape falls between that of a square and a rectangle with proportions of about 2:3.

Doors in kitchens are necessary evils—necessary as entrances and exits, evils because they take space, determine location of work centers, and invite miscellaneous traffic. The best solution is to keep doors to a minimum, set them as close together as possible, and locate no major work center between them. Of course, the overall design of a house may make this ideal impossible. In the Novak home (Pl. 15, opposite), the house plan necessitated a long, narrow kitchen with doors at each end, but the architect avoided permitting it to become a thoroughfare.

Windows make kitchens light and pleasant in addition to providing ventilation, but they do take space. Many people are more comfortable working in a kitchen that has some natural daylighting, perhaps a window over the sink that admits light and also gives an outlook. Architects have invented many ingenious ways of lighting kitchens. Sometimes small windows between counters and wall cabinets or high windows over the cabinets bring light in unexpected ways (Fig. 102). Skylights illumine many interior kitchens, and some rooms open over a counter

102. A dramatic two-story window topped by a stained-glass arch highlights this spacious kitchen. The plant shelf cutting across the window prevents the height from seeming overwhelming. Bill Shields, owner-designer. (*Courtesy American Home Magazine*)

above: 103. This small kitchen gets most of its natural light from sunshine streaming in through the large windows of the adjacent dining area. Allan Liddle, architect. (*Photograph: Julius Shulman*)

right: 104. When a kitchen opens directly onto a sheltered deck, it not only facilitates outdoor dining but makes the kitchen seem brighter and airier. John Reamer, designer. See also Fig. 421. (*Photograph: Harold Davis*)

105. Ideally, a laundry space should be pleasant to work in, as well as efficient. This cheerful room provides brightly colored bins for sorting, a sink for hand washing, and a folding table. (*Courtesy The Maytag Company*)

wall to a windowed dining area (Fig. 103). Among the most pleasant kitchens are those that lead directly to a garden or deck (Fig. 104). By concentrating windows at one end of the space, the architect of the Novak kitchen (Pl. 15) provided for ample light; the Steffy kitchen (Fig. 98) needs no windows because it is so open.

Kitchens require the most maintenance of any room in the house. They are noisy—and the center of all housework. These factors suggest choosing shapes and materials for floors, counters, cupboards, walls, and ceilings with an eye to *wear-resistance, ease in cleaning, sound control,* and *pleasantness* to sight and touch.

New life styles, new concepts of planning, and technological advances all play a role in transforming kitchens from necessary but dull and sterile work areas to cheerful, colorful centers of group living. Whether brand new and ultramodern or old and full of mellowed charm, a kitchen can happily reflect the tastes and character of its owners (Pl. 16, p. 78).

Utility Spaces

Undeniably, the kitchen is the most important support space in the home, and in some smaller houses and apartments it may serve as the *only* support space. But larger homes often delegate supplementary areas according to the particular needs of a given family. These may include provisions for laundry, sewing, shop work, flower arranging or potting, and storage.

Laundry Facilities

Every week millions of pounds of clothing and household linens are washed in American homes. But three factors have altered the nature of this chore: the development of automatic washers and dryers; the trend toward bringing laundry equipment up from dark, inconvenient basements; and the evolution of fabrics that require minimum care. Provisions for home laundering range from a sink or washbasin in which small things can be rinsed out to a fully equipped separate laundry (Fig. 105). Laundry planning will be affected by the size and age distribution of the household, the size of the home, and the attitude toward sending out laundry. If, for example, economy of time is more pressing than economy of money, a family may prefer to have the laundry dealt with by commercial services.

Laundry activities fall into four categories:

☐ **Receiving, sorting,** and **preparing,** steps that require a counter, a cart, sorting bins, or simply the top of the washer, plus a sink or tub for presoaking
☐ **Washing,** which necessitates laundry tubs and/or an automatic washer, as well as storage for supplies
☐ **Drying** in an automatic dryer or convenient drying yard, with some provision for drip-drying indoors
☐ **Finishing** and **ironing,** which require a folding counter, an iron and ironing board or ironer, plus space to put finished laundry and, ideally, space and equipment for mending

In small houses and apartments, laundry space may be reduced to a minimum and compacted into the kitchen or a closet. Utility rooms, however, segregate the clutter and noise of laundry processing. Rooms that have laundry tubs or deep sinks, even a shower, and are near the family entrance can serve as mud rooms—good places to clean up after work or play. In basementless houses, the utility room will also house heating and cooling equipment, a water heater, and perhaps a freezer.

Although space will be saved by incorporating a laundry in the kitchen, the inevitable noise of the machinery is bothersome. Basements and garages are practical alternatives, chiefly because they offer plenty of space and give sound insulation. Washers and dryers can be placed side by side or stacked on a frame in a closet in the bedroom area, usually in a space adjoining a bathroom. Since most laundry originates in and returns to bedrooms or bathrooms, and since laundering is seldom done at night when noise might disturb those trying to sleep, this location deserves consideration.

Nowadays many apartment houses provide laundry facilities on each floor for tenants, or there may be one large common laundry room somewhere in the building.

Sewing Areas

In recent years the popularity of home sewing has increased remarkably. Factors influencing this trend include: the rising cost of clothing and household textile goods; greater sophistication of home sewing equipment; an amazingly wide variety of yard goods available; and the development of quick, simplified construction techniques.

The household in which one or more members do considerable sewing almost mandates a permanent, isolatable sewing area, perhaps even a whole room. Extensive sewing not only requires a vast array of small tools and supplies but generates a fair amount of debris, in the form of fabric scraps and threads. A well-designed sewing center (Fig. 106) helps to organize all this paraphernalia and allows the work-in-progress to be left out. It should include:

☐ A **sewing machine,** either built into a cabinet or placed on a smooth surface, and so arranged that fabrics will not drape on the floor.
☐ An upright **chair** at a height that will permit the sewer to work comfortably without excessive bending.
☐ A **cutting surface** at least 3 feet wide and 6 feet long for laying out patterns.
☐ Adequate **storage** for fabrics and remnants, as well as for tools and supplies. Pegboards are useful for holding and keeping at hand the many small pieces of equipment needed.
☐ A **steam iron** and **ironing board,** possibly including a sleeve board.
☐ Good **lighting** directly over the machine and illumining the general area to facilitate hand work.

Optional equipment includes a dressmaker's dummy and skirt-hemming guide. There should also be provision for a library of sewing books and patterns.

As with kitchens and other support spaces, strict efficiency need not obviate charm and attractiveness. Bright colors, attractive furnishings, and perhaps a sunny window will help to make even the most utilitarian sewing more enjoyable.

Workshops and Garden Rooms

For many individuals woodworking and the many chores associated with home maintenance represent more than a hobby or a necessary evil. The serious cabinet-maker deserves a suitably equipped workshop, as does the person much involved in furniture refinishing and similar pursuits. Specific needs will vary widely according to the nature of the work, but most such activities require:

☐ A **location** reasonably isolated from the rest of the household so that the debris, odors, and noise created will not contaminate living spaces. Often this means a garage or basement, but a large-scale operation may suggest a separate shed or outbuilding. Some large housing projects provide special facilities.
☐ **Storage** for tools and supplies.
☐ Sufficient **electrical outlets** of the proper voltage for power equipment.
☐ If possible, a **sink** for cleaning hands and tools.

The dedicated gardener can, if space permits, indulge in a special potting or flower-arranging room either within or adjacent to the house (Fig. 107; see also Fig. 686). An ideal space would offer:

☐ Durable and easily cleaned **surfaces,** perhaps even a floor that could be hosed down
☐ **Storage** for vases, pots, soil, fertilizers, and tools
☐ **Plant lights** for starting seeds
☐ A **sink** for watering and for cleaning hands

General Storage

It is a lamentable fact that many small houses and apartments dash off the problem of storage, outside the kitchen, with a few small closets. This ignores the reality that *people,* by and large, have *things.* The kinds of storage that each household needs will depend, of course, on what kinds of things its members own, so we can give only general guidelines and show how some families have met their storage requirements.

A storage wall (Figs. 108, 109) with built-in shelves, drawers, and cupboards holds many diverse objects and can be decorative. Some units of this type are set at right angles to the wall and function as space dividers. More individual needs, however, require specific planning. For example, the family that enjoys games and puzzles might consider a bank of very shallow drawers or closely spaced shelves. At the other extreme, a large collection of bulky sports equipment warrants generous space and perhaps special hanging racks. One California family turned a partially finished garage over to the storage of their sizable array of backpacking gear (Fig. 110).

It is possible, but by no means necessary, to spend a great deal of money on storage facilities. The attractive headboard unit shown in Figure 111 consists of nothing more than old wooden milk crates—stained and fitted with hinged doors and knobs. Stacked behind the bed, the boxes provide storage for all manner of things and create a dramatic backdrop for the other furniture.

When either designing a house or renting an apartment, one must consider the availability of some empty, lockable, storage space for such limited-use items as suitcases and tents, summer furniture and winter sports equipment, out-of-season clothing and bedding, as well as furniture and other items not presently in use but not yet ready for discard.

108. In the Mexico City home of designer Luís Baragan, a storage wall built around the fireplace holds books and artifacts, with cupboard and drawer space below. The overall effect is warm and decorative. See also Plate 44, p. 317; Plate 58, p. 420. (*Photograph: Hans Namuth, Photo Researchers, Inc.*)

109. A clean-lined storage area designed by architect Robert Stern includes closet space, banks of drawers, and a ceiling-level cupboard for seldom-used items. See also Figs. 247, 408, 440; Plate 12, p. 60. (*Photograph: John T. Hill*)

above: 110. A partially finished garage area serves to store a sizable collection of backpacking gear. Wall racks both protect the equipment and allow for ready access. (*Photograph: Julius Shulman*)

left: 111. Except for the washstand at lower left, all the components of this attractive headboard unit were made from old wooden milk crates. Diane Cleaver, owner-designer. (*Photograph: The New York Times*)

The design of standard household fixtures and appliances has changed markedly over the past decade or so, as manufacturers have understood and demonstrated that function and beauty are not mutually exclusive. There is no reason, after all, why something that works hard at some mundane chore needs to advertise that fact by its drab appearance. With skillful planning, the support spaces in a home can be supportive not only of its daily maintenance but of its overall character.

Support Systems

Primitive peoples worshiped the elements they depended upon for survival—the sun, wind, rain, earth, and fire. Beyond propitiation of the gods inherent in these elements, they could do little to control their environments. Light and warmth derived from the sun and from fire, cooling and ventilation from the wind and rain. Today we have more dependable systems to provide for basic comforts, and we no longer need offer sacrifices to Ra or Demeter or Quetzalcoatl. Still, there is danger that, without referring to them as such, we have established other gods, called Electricity and Petroleum and Gas. Our present way of living relies so heavily upon these commodities that the threat of a shortage causes virtual panic.

Some evidence indicates that the pendulum has begun to swing in the opposite direction. Imaginative people are again thinking in terms of warmth from the sun, cooling from the wind. The 1970s have witnessed the revival of the bicycle, the wood-burning stove, even the windmill. All these symbols of a "return to the natural way" have charm and many have real value. But far more practical, for the long run and for the multitudes of people, will be an *intelligent* use of natural resources and modern technology. Our goal should be to maintain a reasonable level of comfort and convenience while simultaneously preserving environmental harmony.

Actually, the home itself is a kind of environment, one we create for ourselves and which we can control far more easily than we can our surroundings as a whole. James Marston Fitch[1] speaks of architecture as the "third environment" formed by building an interface between the *micro*-environment of the human body and the *macro*-environment of nature. This interface provides a selective filter capable of either excluding or admitting specific elemental forces. The *meso*-environment of architecture has as one of its primary functions the shielding of people from excessive energy in nature—severe cold, intense heat, driving wind and rain. But all too often such protection requires an excessive expenditure of energy. Certain office buildings and other public structures built during the late 1960s stand as the worst examples of this approach. Windowless, or fitted with windows incapable of being opened, they rely utterly upon artificial lighting, heating, cooling, and ventilation. Even noise control is dealt with artificially, when unpleasant sounds are masked by the hum of the air conditioner or by canned music. Given a power or fuel shortage, these buildings are useless.

If modern technology can devise artificial support systems, it can also teach us to refine natural systems of environmental control. Egyptians and Romans,

Eskimos and South Sea Islanders adapted their homes to their climates with an efficacy that should put many present-day architects to shame. Fortunately, not all contemporary builders ignore the most obvious devices for living in equilibrium with nature. The house pictured in Figure 112 rests on a knoll above the ocean in Hilo, Hawaii. Almost totally devoid of glass, it depends for privacy and protection from the elements upon a series of louvered shutters, which can be opened to let in fresh sea breezes and the appropriate amount of light, closed to keep out the rain. In a climate where cold and snow present no threat, this house acquires natural air cooling, ventilation, and regulation of light by its very design. Its contours hint at the inspiration behind these age-old solutions, for the architecture alludes to the round thatched huts common throughout the Pacific islands.

Another type of climate control motivated the house in Figure 113. Situated on the Gulf of California at the northern tip of Mexico, it endures the far less

left: 112. A house designed to exploit the natural elements of Hawaii also achieves distinctive cultural and structural expression. A series of louvered doors around the second floor can be completely rolled aside to catch sea breezes, partially closed to control the sun, or shut altogether to protect from the almost daily rain showers. Oda McCarty, architects. See also Fig. 270. (*Photograph: Julius Shulman*)

below: 113. On the hot, arid, windswept coast of the Gulf of California, insulation from the elements is of preeminent concern. Thick, projecting walls shelter both interior and exterior spaces of a house designed to moderate the climate. James Flynn, owner-architect. (*Photograph: Koppes*)

left: 114. Standard greenhouse blinds across the top and down the side of this solarium-dining room create fascinating patterns of light. Robert Stern and John Hagmann, architects. (*Photograph: Robert Perron*)

opposite: 115. The bedroom of a silo house brings an unconventional solution to a standard problem—that of bringing daylight into the home while maintaining privacy. The vertical slit windows are also an economy, since they avoid the necessity for curved glass. Mr. and Mrs. Louis Andette, owner-designers. See also Fig. 654. (*Photograph: Robert Perron*)

clement environment of the desert—intense heat, unremitting sun and wind. To overcome these factors, the architect planned thick curving and projecting walls, deeply inset windows, and covered patios, all of which insulate the interior from sun, wind, and blowing sand. A house designed to temper the impact of natural forces in its surroundings not only represents an economy for its owners and for the environment as a whole but simply makes good sense.

We in the United States have increasingly become a people who live the greater part of our lives indoors. We even travel about in a kind of meso-environment—the car—to a larger extent than any other nation. Nevertheless, we cling to our desire for union with nature, as evidenced by the widespread use of glass in houses, the popularity of a second home in the country. This apparent contradiction can be resolved only when we cease trying to bend nature to our will and learn the lesson that every other surviving species on earth has mastered: the technique of adapting ourselves to our environment. And one of the most pressing factors in that adaptation right now involves the rational use of energy.

The primary source of energy in this solar system is our star, Sun, but so far modern house design has used only one aspect of this resource in a positive and conscious manner—that of light.

Light

Light is a form of energy to which we react immediately, although often subconsciously. Much of our information about the world we live in comes to us through vision, but without light there can be no vision. Our responses to light rely upon a complex of physical and psychological phenomena as yet imperfectly understood. For purposes of home planning, however, it will be sufficient to mention certain qualities of light.

When light strikes an object, it may then be reflected, absorbed, or allowed to pass through, depending on the degree of transparency or opacity in the material and on its surface qualities. Light reflected from such smooth surfaces as metal is bright and sharp, that reflected from dull surfaces like brick more diffuse.

The appearance of objects is greatly affected by the kind of light that makes them visible. Strong contrasts of light and dark result when an object is illuminated by small, sharp light sources, less contrast when the light source is broad and diffuse, and almost no contrast when an object is evenly lighted from all sides. When small beams light an object, it will cast hard, sharp, dark shadows; a broad and diffuse

light source creates softer shadows; and light coming from more than one direction will cause an object's shadows to be multiple and overlapping. The shape of objects can be emphasized or subordinated according to the strength and direction of the light source.

Contrasts of brightness and darkness can create drama and emphasis; uniform lighting is good for many kinds of work but may be monotonous. Bright light is stimulating, low levels of illumination quieting. Warm-colored light tends to be cheerful, cooler light more restful.

Control of the luminous environment divides into two categories: natural daylight and artificial illumination.

Daylight

Sun worship did not die out with the disappearance of multitheistic religions. Many people today derive great physical and psychological pleasure from basking in the sun, although they rarely attach to it mystical connotations. Of course, as our principal source of vitamin D, sunlight is vital to the health of the human organism. But beyond this there remains the obvious fact that nearly everyone prefers a sunny day to a rainy one, refers to the former as a "beautiful" day.

The direct radiant energy of the sun, daylight, is a determining factor in the design of homes, especially when large wall areas have been devoted to glass. Plate 17 (p. 111) shows one way in which natural light can be brought into a house without overwhelming it. Located near the beach, where glare can be a problem one day, fog the next, the house has been sited among trees that temper but do not obstruct the ample light coming through large windows and skylights. Another kind of natural light, that from burning logs, flickers in the fireplace, which conserves heat by radiating it through a metal skin and flue.

Rather than simply allowing sunlight to pour into a room unchecked, many houses regulate the admission of light to create interesting visual effects. The dining room illustrated in Figure 114 has an all-glass wall and ceiling, but both are covered with slatted blinds. An intriguing striped pattern seems to continue all around the room because of the cast shadows.

Unique structural considerations led to the inclusion of many small slit windows in a home near Marlboro, Vermont (Fig. 115). Created from a standard grain silo, the house is, of course, completely round. Large areas of curved glass would have been prohibitively expensive, thus violating the owners' amazingly low

left: 116. Unique lighting fixtures demarcate the seating area, game table, and kitchen wall in a New York apartment. Christopher Owen, architect; Sylvia Owen, architect and designer. (*Photograph: Norman McGrath*)

below: 117. High opalescent fixtures provide even, general lighting for both a glass-walled living room and the terrace beyond. In contrast, lamplight and firelight bring intimacy and warmth to the conversation pit. Frederick Liebhardt and Eugene Weston, architects. (*Photograph: Julius Shulman*)

budget. Their solution not only provides for generous light but transforms the wall into a fascinating kaleidoscope of light and dark, a pattern that is echoed in the rug, bedspread, and hanging.

Artificial Light

Well-planned artificial illumination enables us to see without strain and helps to prevent accidents. But above all, it makes a vital contribution to the attractiveness of our homes. At night, much of a room's character is determined by its illumination. Even more than color, varying light can make rooms seem to shrink or swell, become intimate or formal. Important objects can be spotlighted, those of lesser interest deemphasized. And with the equipment available today, all this can be changed instantly by flicking switches or turning dimmers.

Artificial lighting built into a variety of ceiling fixtures served as the keynote for the total redesign of a typical high-rise apartment in New York (Fig. 116). A dropped ceiling with recessed fixtures defines the sitting area with its built-in sofa and table-cabinets, plus leather upholstered chairs. Another lowered ceiling highlights the curving wall around the kitchen. The lighting cylinder over the dining-game table dominates the design and gently repeats the arc of the window wall. All lights are controlled by dimmer switches, so that the intensity of illumination can be varied to suit the activities and moods of the occupants.

The living room and terrace shown in Figure 117 illustrate a different approach. One part of this high-ceilinged room is open and airy, extending through a two-story window wall onto a large outdoor terrace. Appropriate to the lighthearted spirit of this space, artificial illumination comes from two regularly spaced lines of floating shell bubbles that give multidirectional opalescent light indoors and outdoors. The other portion is an intimate, lowered conversation area facing the fireplace. Here light comes from table lamps for reading and from the glow of the fireplace. Furniture reinforces the mood of each area: low, compact, and built-in for the fireplace areas; generally space-making, lightweight, and movable in the other. When it is planned in relation to architecture, furnishings, and people, lighting can do far more than merely enable us to see. It is one of the most versatile aspects of home planning and powerfully affects our feelings.

In lighting our homes, we can learn much from theaters, aquariums, museums, stores, factories, and restaurants. Theaters have long exploited lighting as a vital part of dramatic production. Houselights lower, footlights come on as the curtains part, and from then on lights of all colors, brightnesses, degrees of sharpness and diffusion focus attention where it is wanted and underscore the mood of the play. Aquariums concentrate light on the fish, leaving spectators just enough light to let them see around, a practice sometimes followed in museums to rivet attention on a few things. At the opposite extreme are factories, laboratories, and offices flooded with bright illumination everywhere to step up production. Restaurants range from floodlighted and spotlighted lunchrooms to dark caverns with a candle on each table and gypsy music to reassure or unnerve you, according to your mood.

Types of Lighting

For untold ages people depended on the flames of fireplaces, candles, or lamps to illuminate their homes at night. Nowadays we seldom limit ourselves to flame light, except occasionally from candles and fireplaces indoors, barbecues and torches outdoors. Although inefficient, all give a warm, flickering, flattering light that seems hospitable, even festive. Electricity, though, is our major concern, and it produces light in two ways:

Incandescent light is produced by heating any material, but usually metal, to a temperature at which it glows. Typical incandescent bulbs have a tungsten filament in a sealed glass container. A visit to an electrical supply store will show that these bulbs come in many, many types. Incandescent lighting offers several advantages:

☐ Fixtures and bulbs cost less.
☐ There is no flicker or hum and less likelihood of radio or television interference.
☐ Textures and forms are emphasized because the light comes from a relatively small source.

Luminescence, or "cold" light, is not produced by heat. **Fluorescence** is the only luminescent light source commonly used in homes. A glass tube with an inside

118. Sections in the walls of this restored Connecticut farmhouse are illumined by cove lighting for an overall serene effect. Robert Stern and John Hagmann, architects. (*Photograph: John T. Hill*)

coating of fluorescent powder is filled with vaporized mercury and argon; then the ends are sealed with two cathodes. When electric current activates the gases, invisible ultraviolet rays cause the fluorescent coating to produce visible light. Although fluorescent tubes vary less in size and shape than incandescent, they have a considerable diversity. The desirable qualities of fluorescent lighting are:

☐ Tubes last about ten times as long as incandescent bulbs, produce three to four times as much light for the current used. Thus, they conserve energy.
☐ Almost no heat is produced.
☐ The light source is considerably larger, which spreads the light more and produces less glare.
☐ Tubes are available in a number of "white" colors, from the blue cast of "Daylight" to the pink of "Natural White."

In terms of purpose and effect, there are two major types of lighting.

General lighting illumines a room more or less uniformly, as the sun illumines the earth. It lets us see every corner of a room in a reassuring way and brings to equal attention the design and color of the whole space. At best, it minimizes the bulkiness of furniture, the darkness of shadows, and the often harsh contrasts of local lighting. General lighting very often emanates from ceiling fixtures or from lamps having reflector bowls and translucent shades. It is more truly general when lights concealed in coves evenly illuminate the ceiling or when lighting troughs "wash" large wall areas or curtained windows with light (Fig. 118). Finally, the entire ceiling or large sections of it can bring light through translucent plastics or glass.

General lighting can be either *direct* (with light shining full on objects to be illuminated) or *indirect* (when light is thrown against a surface, usually the ceiling, from which some of it is reflected). For general illumination, indirect light usually produces a softer effect than direct light, but it costs more to operate and may overemphasize the reflecting ceilings or walls. Overall uniform lighting is monotonous and seldom bright enough for reading or close work. For these reasons, most people combine it with local lighting.

Local lighting provides the kind and amount of illumination needed at specific places for specific activities, such as reading, cooking, or sewing. The light source can be high or low, but eye comfort suggests that it be shielded. Except in kitchens and bathrooms, local-lighting fixtures consist mainly of movable floor or table lamps, but fixtures attached to the wall, ceiling, or major pieces of furniture cause far less of a nuisance and are increasing in popularity. A major design factor, local lighting can create moods, emphasize important objects, and bring the visual delights of variety and rhythm.

The play of **brilliants,** seen in recent years only on Christmas trees or in fireworks now that crystal chandeliers and candelabra are uncommon, has experienced a revival and in a sense can be considered a third type of lighting. It is produced by fixtures that break light into many small, bright spots. Typical sources include candles, fixtures with many small bulbs, or those in which light passes through many small openings (Fig. 119). A similar effect will result when moder-

119. In a dining room designed to dramatize the play of light, hanging crystal pendants reflect and refract light from a ceiling fixture, spreading its sparkling brilliance over ceiling and mirrored walls. Rugs designed by Edward Fields serve as draperies and table covering. (*Photograph: Louis Reens*)

ately bright light is focused on accessories, wall surfaces, or lamp bases of reflecting materials, especially if they are intricately ornamented. The special contribution made by brilliants can be experienced immediately when one enters a room filled with sparkling light.

Specific Factors in Lighting

Planned lighting demands attention to brightness, location and size of light sources, direction of light, color of light together with its effect on colors, and the amount of light reflected by colors on ceilings, walls, and floors.

Brightness of Light   Our eyes are like fantastic miniature cameras that automatically adjust to different brightnesses. Perhaps their greatest defect is that they do not warn us quickly when they are being strained by ineffective light.

Light intensity is calculated in *footcandles,* an international unit of measure. For our purposes it would be overly complicated and superfluous to specify the particular quantity of light in one footcandle, but the term is useful for indicating *relative* intensities of light. Experiments have shown that people generally will select as most desirable the middle of almost any range of brightness they see. For example, if the range is from 10 to 30 footcandles, the typical subject will prefer 20. When, without the observer's knowledge, the range is stepped up from 30 to 100 footcandles, the middle will again be chosen. A great difference separates 20 and 65 footcandles, but over short periods of time our eyes do not tell us which is better. Many experts, however, agree that the quantities of brightness given in Table 5.1 represent the minimum needed for the activities listed and for the general illumination of rooms. The wattages necessary to obtain the desired footcandles of light will vary with the distance between light source and surface; the design of lighting equipment; the amount of reflection from ceiling, floors, and furnishings; and whether incandescent or fluorescent light is used, the latter giving three to four times as much light per watt as incandescent. Light meters that measure illumination are widely available.

Although the figures given are useful for planning the amount of lighting needed for any specific task, the following considerations should be kept in mind:

☐ Bright light is stimulating, calls forth energy, and makes us feel as though we should be up and about, but it may be ultimately boring and needlessly expensive in money and energy.
☐ Low levels of brightness may seem relaxing and restful, romantic, dingy and depressing, or even frightening—depending on the context.
☐ Moderately bright light brings no pronounced feeling other than general well-being.
☐ An appropriate distribution of light quantities results in an impression of balance and rhythm, of emphasis and moderation similar to those produced by nature.

Taking these variables into consideration, lighting engineers have made some general recommendations about the placement of light fixtures and the wattage that will provide an adequate amount of light for both general illumination and concentrated light for reading, sewing, and other close work. Table 5.2 lists these recommendations.

Glare results from exposed, bright sources of light; incorrectly designed fixtures; too much light, especially from one direction; and excessive contrasts. Worse yet, the contrasting glare and gloom frequently encountered in night driving and too often in homes creates an eye-fatiguing combination. For close work, the working area should not be more than five times as bright as the darkest part of the room, and a ratio greater than 1 : 10 is undesirable anyplace.

Table 5.1   Minimum Recommended Light for Certain Activities

	Footcandles
General Lighting	
most rooms	5–10
kitchen, laundry	10–20
Local Lighting for Activities	
card playing	10–20
casual reading, easy sewing, makeup, easy musical scores	20–30
kitchen, laundry	30–50
prolonged reading, study, average and machine sewing, difficult musical scores, shaving, benchwork	40–70
fine sewing, any small detail work	100–200

Table 5.2 Recommended Placement and Wattage of Light Fixtures

Type	Placement	Range of Wattage
wall fixtures (incandescent)	at least 66″ above floor	60–100w every 8′ for general lighting
wall fixtures (fluorescent)	faceboards at least 6″ out from wall, and as high in inches as they are in feet from floor, to shield fluorescent tubes	general lighting—approximately 1′ of channel (10w) for each 15 sq. ft. of floor area special lighting—approximate width of area to be lighted
cornice	at edge of ceiling, sheds light down	
valance	at least 10″ down from ceiling, sheds light up, down, or both	
wall bracket	50–65″ above floor, sheds light up, down, or both	
ceiling fixtures shallow	centered, symmetrically placed, or placed to illumine special areas	120–200w in multiple bulbs; 60–80w in multiple tubes
recessed	as above	30–150w bulbs
pendant	as above; see below when used for reading	120–180w in multiple bulbs
floor lamps (for reading)	stem of lamp 10″ behind shoulder, near rear corner of chair; bottom of shade 45–48″ above floor	as above
table lamps (for reading)	base in line with shoulder, 20″ to left or right of book center; bottom of shade at eye level when seated, about 40″ above floor	as above
wall lamps (for reading)	42–48″ above floor, 15″ to left or right of book center	as above

On the other hand, **blandness of light,** with every part of a room equally bright, is also fatiguing—to both the muscles of the eyes and the spirits of the occupants. If we remember that natural light modifies constantly—from dawn through midday to moonlight, filtered by trees and clouds, varying with the time of year—we will realize that change is normal and even beneficial. Our aim should be moderation, in both quantity and contrast of light.

Selective switches allow us to turn on or off different fixtures at will. With rheostatic dimmers, brightness of light from most fixtures can be smoothly adjusted to any point between candlelike glow and full brightness. The small cost of these dimmers could, in many instances, be more than compensated by reducing the number of separate fixtures that would otherwise be needed to achieve varied levels of brightness.

Location and Direction   Accustomed as we are to the sun being more or less overhead, lighting from above seems normal, that from other directions surprising. The following observations apply generally to location of potential light sources in the home:

□ Location of both the light source and any surface from which light is reflected will be important in the total effect.

120. Overhead artificial light diffused by louvers sustains the plants and gives the cheerful ambience of a light-filled space to this combination living room-conservatory. Douglas White, architect.

□ Light high in a room is at the same time serene and revealing. It can be efficient to the point of boredom or a striking revelation of an architectural highpoint (Fig. 120).

□ Light below eye level seems friendly and draws groups together. It is also useful while watching television.

□ Light coming from near the floor flatters people in the same manner as do theater footlights, and also contrasts pleasantly with more conventional lighting (Pl. 18, p. 112). Low light is a good safety device near steps and in halls.

□ Light from a number of sources, or well-diffused light, makes a room seem luminous rather than merely lighted, tends to spread interest throughout the area, and is comfortably undemanding.

□ Strongly directed light, for example that coming from one or two spotlights, may be dramatic, but it can seem harsh if not handled carefully. Our attention tends to follow its path—up, down, sideways, or at an angle—much as it does a solid form.

□ Light for working should illumine the task without forming distracting shadows and should not shine in the worker's eyes.

Size of Light Source   Much depends on the size of a light source. To understand this, we need only compare the luminous vault of the sky by day with its myriad play of brilliants at night.

□ Broad sources of light—the sky, a skylight, an illuminated ceiling, a window wall—give flat, glareless, uneventful light excellent for general vision, health, and safety, because they minimize contrasts and shadows. In decorative terms, however, they can be monotonous.

□ Smaller light sources that diffuse light broadly through lenses, translucent shades, or reflectors approximate this effect.

□ Very small light sources, especially bright ones, have high accent value, emphasize parts of rooms, and make silver and glass sparkle (Fig. 121). But such lights must be used with care, for they can be visually fatiguing and may cause a spotty effect.

Color of Light   Until recently, most people have been rather timid about using colored illumination in their homes. But the last few years have seen more experimentation with different colored bulbs or lenses, even with patterns of colored light, either stationary or moving, thrown on walls (Pl. 19, p. 112).

The color of light is determined by three factors: the light source, the diffusing or reflecting shade, and the room surfaces.

☐ White light shows colors as they are and has no pronounced emotional effect other than the important sense of normal well-being.
☐ Warm light flatters people, dispels the chill associated with darkness, and brightens warm colors but deadens blues and purples.
☐ Cool light makes rooms seem more spacious, separates objects one from another—and may make people look cadaverous.
☐ A combination of warm and cool light adds variety but needs to be planned with care.

Effect of Colors on Reflected Light   No surface in the home reflects or absorbs all the light that hits it; but high-value colors reflect a high percentage, and low-value colors reflect little. Table 5.3 lists the percentages of light reflected by some common colors. Clearly, white yields the most light for the money paid to the electric company, and black gives the least.

Lighting Fixtures

Ideal fixtures give the kind and amount of light suitable to a particular purpose, thus fulfilling the principle of **utility.** They represent sound **economy** in balancing their original cost with the electricity they use, in the ease with which they are cleaned and the bulbs are replaced, and in the space they take. They contribute

Table 5.3   Percentage of Light Reflected by Colors

Color	Percentage of Light Reflected
white	89
ivory	87
canary yellow	77
cream	77
orchid	67
cream gray	66
sky blue	65
buff	63
pale green	59
shell pink	55
olive tan	43
forest green	22
coconut brown	16
black	2

121. Tiny light sources in the ceiling, combined with candlelight, make china and crystal sparkle while they provide a restful atmosphere for dining. (*Courtesy C. I. Designs*)

left: 122. Spotlights focused upon the storage wall-bookcase lend an element of intimacy to this dramatic, high-ceilinged room. James Caldwell, owner-architect. See also Fig. 587. These photographs were taken at different times; note changes in furnishings. (*Photograph: Philip L. Molten*)

right: 123. A combination of high light sources gives excellent lighting and also emphasizes the interplay of ceiling planes in this striking kitchen. Fluorescent tubes are inset in the box beams, a plugmold strip of large clear bulbs follows the rise of the ceiling, and natural light pours in from a skylight set at the top level. Charles Moore and Rurik Ekstrom, architects. (*Photograph: John T. Hill*)

to the **beauty** of our homes. And they underline or create the distinctive **character** we seek. Almost inevitably lighting fixtures contrast with other furnishings, because they fill quite a different purpose. This suggests that *some* of them be deliberately chosen as accents. In general, though, sensible practice recommends having most fixtures appropriate in size, scale, and character to the rooms and other furnishings. Lighting devices can set up their own pattern of design running through the entire home, supplying a connective theme.

Fixtures are available in a bewildering diversity, but the light sources fall into three basic shapes. They can be **lines**—fluorescent tubes, long lighting tracks or plugmold strips, lighted valances and cornices—that lead the eyes in a strongly directional movement and that wash the ceiling, wall, or draperies with light. **Spots,** if large, resemble little suns, radiating light in many directions (Fig. 122); if small, as in candles, they are like sparks or stars. Whatever the size, spots tend to become more or less static centers of attention. The third category consists of broad **planes** that light large areas evenly.

Architectural and Built-In Lighting   As with built-in furniture, built-in lighting assures us that illumination was not an afterthought. It contributes to the total unity of a lifespace and can produce unique effects. The increasing use of large lighted ceiling panels illustrates a trend toward illumination of low intensity emanating from broad areas. The newer track lighting or plugmold strips (Fig. 123), which come in almost any length and have outlets every few inches, can accommodate bulbs of many sizes and shapes, even pendant fixtures. When used imaginatively, these strips can enhance the architectural outlines of a space—

whether left exposed or incorporated in a cornice, valance, or shelf—by spreading light over a wall, window, or ceiling. Closely allied to true architectural lighting are the many mass-produced fixtures ready for attachment to ceilings or walls.

Ceiling fixtures, once banished from consideration, have staged a healthy comeback through vastly improved design (Fig. 124). Some are inconspicuously recessed in the ceiling or flush with it, others soften light with louvers or diffuse it with lenses. Shallow glass or plastic bowls, dropped a few inches, reflect light from the ceiling and diffuse it through the bowl. They can also direct a pool of light downward, making them an inexpensive three-in-one way to light space for eating, hobbies, or homework (Fig. 125). Many fixtures are dropped well below the ceiling; those adjustable in height and position give welcome flexibility and facilitate maintenance. Adjustable spotlights and floodlights—now available with shades in many sizes, shapes, colors, and materials—can be turned on work areas or visual centers of interest for direct light, on ceilings for reflected light.

Wall fixtures, like ceiling fixtures, were once popular, fell from favor, and are now enjoying a renaissance, thanks to innovative new designs. Of course, such fixtures may interfere with hanging pictures or with changes in furniture arrangement (unless they are of the pinup kind), but they do remain out of the way and free the table and desk surfaces for other things.

below: 124. A beautifully designed permanent ceiling fixture stabilizes the dining area of an open group space. Wendell H. Lovett, architect. (*Photograph: Christian Staub*)

right: 125. Adjustable ceiling fixtures offer varying levels of light above a table for dining, reading, games, or work. This transparent modern fixture serves as elegant counterpoint to the carved antique table. O'Brien and Armstrong, architects. (*Photograph: Philip L. Molten*)

Portable Lamps   Floor and table lamps can be moved when and where they are needed. Moreover, they perform as lively decorative accessories. In some instances, lamps that are unornamented and inconspicuous seem best, but genuinely handsome, decorative lamps can greatly enrich a room at the same time that they provide light. A beautiful ceramic or glass piece, a richly modeled work of metal, profits from light above or in it. Some lamps could be described as light-as-object. The light is captured in a sculptural form that in turn spreads the ambience of its glow in the immediate vicinity (Fig. 126). Other types enclose the light source in an opaque base and emit light in one direction only. In still others, clear or frosted bulbs themselves become the lamp, while providing light. Chapter 17 discusses the design and selection of portable lamps as enrichment for the home.

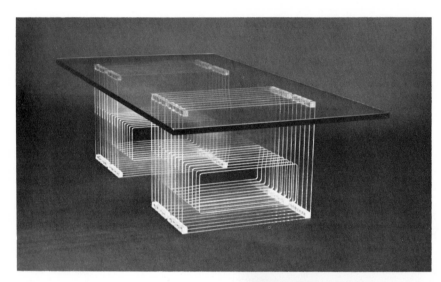

left: 126. The Plexiglas "Infinity" table designed by Steven Weiss achieves its floating, luminous effect from the juxtaposition of light-conducting edges with transparent planes.

below: 127. Good lighting at entrances and on stairs is important for safety as well as for providing a warm welcome. Callister and Payne, Henry Herold, architects. (*Photograph: Philip L. Molten*)

Lighting for Activities

In designing a home or revising the furnishings of a room, it pays to draw a plan with furniture arrangements. Once the furniture has been sketched in, lighting requirements can be assessed—where local illumination is needed, what kinds of general and accent lighting will best complement the character of the room, its colors, textures, and surfaces.

Entrance areas benefit from friendly, welcoming illumination as a transition from the dark outside to the brightness of the interior (Fig. 127). Guests and hosts see one another in a pleasant light, which provides a graceful introduction to the home. Diffused light from ceiling or wall fixtures, perhaps supplemented by more concentrated, sparkling light, creates a balanced effect.

Living rooms and **family rooms** need general illumination, preferably both direct and indirect, to bring walls and furniture, floors and ceilings into soft perspective. Flexibly controlled direct light is requisite where people read or sew, play games, or do homework. A touch of scintillating light adds interest.

Dining spaces deserve primary emphasis on what is most important—the table and the people around it. Light directed downward makes silver, glass and china sparkle, enhances the appetizing qualities of food and beverages. However, some indirectly diffused light lessens glare and diminishes unbecoming shadows on the diners' faces.

Kitchens absolutely demand good light, especially over the work centers. The eating table and the rest of the room should have a fairly high level of general illumination. Ceiling lights are almost indispensible, as are bands of light placed at strategic points along work counters, especially under wall cabinets. The kitchen will frequently be the most thoroughly illuminated room in the house. Much research has been devoted to kitchens, and we are likely to think in straightforward terms about this room.

Bathrooms require lights near the mirror to give shadowless illumination to the face. Bands of light on all sides of the mirror work best, lights on two sides or above and below almost as well. A bathroom also needs general illumination from a ceiling fixture or two.

Bedrooms should have light for dressing, reading in bed, and perhaps such activities as desk work, reading, or sewing. Direct-indirect lights over the beds, chairs, desks, and chests of drawers—as well as direct lights near mirrors—may be sufficient, but some general lighting is usually advisable.

Halls need some overall lighting; its source might be ceiling or wall fixtures that send glare-free light downward, but lighting near the floor, as in theaters, not only focuses on the area we need most to see in hallways, but offers a readymade opportunity for variety in lighting effects. Ornamental, colorful fixtures can dispel the dullness typical of most halls.

Stairways are hazardous. Light that clearly differentiates the treads from the risers—such as ceiling or wall fixtures that send even, glare-free light downward—can lessen accidents (Fig. 127). Spotty or distracting light is dangerous and best reserved for some other part of the house.

Exterior lighting seldom gets the attention it deserves. The minimum—seldom met—would call for illuminating the entrance of a house so that it can be recognized and the house number read from the street. Visitor and host should be able to see each other clearly in a good light at the doorway.

Terraces, patios, and **gardens** can be enjoyed at night, even from inside, if they are lighted. This effect has become especially important with the increasing popularity of window walls and with landscape design that is integrated with the house. Seen from inside, lighted outdoor areas greatly expand the apparent size of the interior and bring some illumination into the house. Also, light outdoors eliminates the rather menacing black windows that result in the absence of balanced illumination. Typical solutions are weatherproof fixtures mounted on exterior

128. Subdued outdoor lighting can create a magical effect, as in this pool area. (*From House & Garden Garden Guide*)

walls or overhanging roofs. More elaborate installations have spotlights and flood-lights concealed in the landscape. However, outdoor lighting must be handled with discretion, for high levels of illumination may seem unnatural and "stagy." A low glow will suffice to dispel the unwanted blankness (Fig. 128).

Switches and Outlets

Every room in the house needs a light switch beside any access door. Besides providing instant illumination of the room, this will encourage the household to turn off superfluous lights. Stairs should have switches at top and bottom, halls at both ends. Ideally, the switches will be selective, controlling the different fixtures appropriate for different occasions. Dimmers also serve for adapting the level of light to a particular task or mood. Each wall space 3 or more feet wide that is separated from other walls by doors or floor-length windows requires an outlet for lamps and appliances. On very long walls, two or more outlets diminish the hazards of extension cords.

☐ Switches controlling bed lamps should be within *easy* reach of a person lying on the bed.
☐ Switches for outdoor lighting are most convenient when they are inside the house.
☐ Outlets at table height present advantages in a number of situations: near ironing boards for electric irons; near dining tables for toasters, coffee pots, and so on; along the back of kitchen counter space for appliances used there; near sewing centers for sewing machines; and behind electric washers and dryers.
☐ Bathrooms require outlets for electric shavers, toothbrushes, and other small appliances.
☐ A workshop area should be equipped with heavy-duty outlets for power tools.
☐ Weatherproof outdoor outlets are desirable for electrically operated barbecues, portable lighting, or Christmas decorations.

It is relatively easy to focus sufficient light on work surfaces and to provide for some kind of general illumination. But a balanced combination of natural and artificial light throughout the home needs thoughtful planning (Figs. 129–131).

129–131. Varied levels of indoor lighting can change the mood of a room dramatically. Marlene Rothkin Vine and David Vine, owner-designers. (*Photographs: David Vine*)

right: 129. Natural daylight streams in through windows and a skylight for an overall cheerful effect.

below left: 130. General artificial illumination brightens every corner of the room to produce a mood suitable for group entertainment.

below right: 131. Subdued night lighting from lamps and the fireplace creates intimate "pockets" of light while leaving the corners in shadow.

Heating and Cooling

Our great-grandparents would be astonished at our assumption that central heating and cooling must be built into homes, for they typically depended on stoves and fireplaces for warmth, on open windows and porches for coolness. Our grandchildren may, in turn, wonder why we paid so little heed to the obvious fact that all-year comfort is a matter of house orientation and design, of materials and construction, as well as of mechanical equipment.

Natural Heating and Cooling

Designing for climate control varies from one section of the country to another; it can even pose different problems on sites only a few hundred feet apart because of changes in elevation, the presence of trees, or adjacent bodies of water. In some areas of the United States summer cooling is the overriding consideration, in others it is winter heating. Sometimes both factors must be dealt with, while a few areas experience neither extreme cold nor extreme heat. There are some fairly safe rules of thumb—such as keeping large areas of glass directed toward the south—but the wise architect studies the general and local climate carefully. Perhaps architects should give even more thought to environmental factors than to the family who will live in the house, because the house is less likely to move than the people.

The plan shown in Figure 132 represents a house in Stony Point, New York, which was designed with several environmental considerations in mind—sun, prevailing winds, slope of site, and view from the windows. Nearly all glass faces toward the south, the southeast, and the southwest, while the opposite side of the house is sheltered with opaque and insulated materials. Because the northwest portion of the building is partially submerged in a hillside, it acquires further protection from both cold winds and the hot summer sun of late afternoon.

After proper orientation of the house—the fundamental aspect of climate control—insulation is the next most important factor in keeping a building warm or cool, no matter what kind of artificial systems are used.

Insulation

The two basic elements in insulation are the materials in the house shell and the way they are put together. Generally speaking, dense and uniform materials, such as metal and glass, conduct heat and cold readily, while such porous substances as wood or lightweight-aggregate concrete blocks are poor conductors—that is, good insulators. Most houses, regardless of construction material, need further applied insulation.

Standard housing insulation comes in four basic forms:

- Porous substances—cellulose fibers, rock wool, fiberglass, and vermiculite granules—which imprison air in the small spaces between particles. Such materials are available either loose, for blowing into walls, or in batts to be nailed between studs and joists.
- Rigid panels that are installed above roof decking but under finished roofing.
- Thick panels of vinyl-faced fiberglass, which serve also as a finished interior surface.
- Sprayed polyurethane foam, another possible interior finish. However, polyurethane as insulation remains experimental, until questions of flammability and longevity have been fully explored.

The interior climate of the home can be affected in three other ways. Good *weatherstripping* around doors and windows reduces heat loss through leakage; in the absence of weatherstripping, there will often be perceptible drafts. Windows

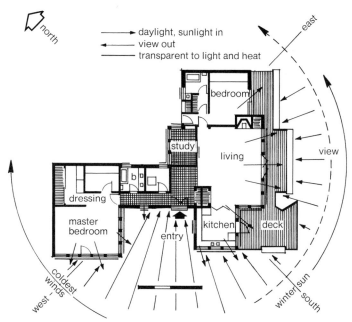

north

→ daylight, sunlight in
← view out
↔ transparent to light and heat

bedroom

study

living

view

dressing

b

master
bedroom

entry

kitchen

deck

coldest
winds

west

east

winter sun south

132. James Marsten Fitch designed and oriented his own house to take full advantage of the site and to moderate the climate in as many natural ways as possible. (*From* American Building 2: The Environmental Forces That Shape It)

with single glass transmit up to 35 times as much of the sun's radiant heat in summer, and 10 times as much as in winter, as insulated walls. *Double-glazing* reportedly reduces heat gain and loss from 45 to 60 percent (Fig. 133). *Storm windows* also help to keep out the winter cold and may even protect against summer heat if the windows do not need to be opened for ventilation.

It has been estimated that a properly insulated house uses only 50 percent of the energy required to heat a noninsulated one, and appreciable savings will also be realized in air conditioning costs.

133. Double-glazed windows warrant their expense in cold climates. Mositure condensation on the window at right comes from warm air hitting cold glass. Twin panes on the left keep cold out, warmth in, and the window free from moisture. (*Courtesy Pittsburgh Plate Glass Company*)

Artificial Heating

Heating systems are mechanically complicated. It is difficult to know which system would be best for a given house, and only experts should be trusted with the planning. However, the householder will benefit from knowing a few basic facts and principles.

Artificial heat for homes is produced by:

- □ Heating air in a warm-air furnace
- □ Heating water in a boiler
- □ Sending electricity through a resistant conductor, as in toasters
- □ Extracting heat energy by means of a heat pump

Heat is brought to the living space through:

- □ Registers, which are small openings in floors or walls emitting warmed air
- □ Baseboard heaters—comparatively long, high-temperature units along baseboards or sometimes ceilings
- □ Radiant panels with large, low-temperature surfaces
- □ Infrared heat lamps that provide quick, concentrated heat

Heat, then, affects us and our homes by *conduction* through solid matter, either continuous or in close contact, as when our feet are warmed by a warm floor; by *convection*, or moving currents of air, as when the warm air blown from a register decreases the heat loss of our bodies; and by *radiation*, when heat jumps from one solid to another without making the air uncomfortably hot and stuffy, as in infrared heating lamps. The general characteristics of different systems can best be understood if they are grouped in terms of the way heat is brought into rooms.

Registers convect air warmed in a furnace, give quick heat, and are moderately low in initial cost. The moving air, which can be cleaned and humidified or dehumidified, dispels stuffiness and tempers moisture content. Since the same ducts and registers can serve also for cooling, the cost of air-conditioning is lowered. The registers, though, may interfere with furniture arrangement. Except in the best installations, temperatures may fluctuate noticeably, and the air may seem uncomfortably hot at times.

Baseboard heaters circulate hot water or steam, or the heat generated by electric resistance coils, to provide relatively uniform temperatures, although rooms cannot be heated or cooled so quickly as with registers. Usually more expensive to install, they give no control of the air other than temperature.

Radiant panels, most often installed in ceilings but occasionally in floors or walls, are transformed into large warmed surfaces by means of water or air heated in a furnace or by wires that convert electricity to heat. The heat radiates to the opposite surface without affecting the air. Thus, they keep us, our furnishings, and the architectural shell pleasantly and uniformly warm while the air stays relatively cool. No intrusive registers or radiators mar the design of the room. Radiant panels require good insulation, they are rather expensive to install, and operating costs can be very high because of the expense of converting primary fuel, such as oil or natural gas, into electricity.

Infrared heat lamps can give quick heat in bathrooms or in any place where instant but not continuous heat is needed. They are inexpensive to purchase but fairly expensive to operate.

The specialized needs of each home should be assessed in order to provide optimum heating. Small units, individually heated by gas or electricity and usually placed in walls, may be quite adequate in mild climates. On the other hand, a house located in the far North might benefit from a combination of two or more heating systems.

Artificial Cooling

In many parts of the United States, home air-conditioning has come to be regarded as essential. Excessively high temperatures and humidity enervate us, so that we cannot function at full capacity for either work or play.

Operating on the same principle as mechanical refrigerators, air-conditioners remove heat and moisture from the air, keep clean air in motion, and reduce housecleaning. Central cooling systems—often combined with heating apparatus—generally are much more efficient and cheaper to operate than individual room units, although the cost of installation is higher.

In years to come the demonstrable advantages of air conditioning will have to be weighed against the potential dangers of excessive fuel consumption and detriment to the environment. One example demonstrates how an overdependence on artificial climate regulation can spiral out of control. The weather in New York City has actually changed over the last quarter century, partly because of the great amount of moisture released into the atmosphere by air conditioners. Night breezes no longer cool the paved streets and heat-retaining surfaces of the buildings. Instead, heat builds on heat, so that yet more air conditioners must be called into service. Unless such chains are broken, the results could be disastrous.

Ventilation

Good ventilation removes hot, stale air from the tops of rooms, brings in fresh air, keeps the air in gentle motion, and accomplishes all this without uncomfortable drafts. The major devices involved are doors and windows that can be opened, ventilating grilles, exhaust fans, warm-air furnaces with blowers, air-conditioning units, and portable fans.

Hot air rises, so it is best removed with windows, grilles, or exhaust fans placed high in the room or house. Ventilating skylights also release stale air. Forced-draft warm-air furnaces, with the heat on or off, circulate air, as does most cooling equipment. Failing one or more of these, a layer of practically motionless air will stay near the ceiling or in the attic. When this dead air is taken out, fresh air must enter to replace it. Usually, it comes through windows or doors, but ventilators strategically placed in the walls sometimes work better. These generally have horizontal louvers on the outside to ward off rain or snow, fixed insect screens, and hinged or sliding panels on the inside to control the flow of air. Their good points are numerous: being unobtrusive, they can vary more in size, shape, and location than can windows; since they do not interfere with privacy, they can be placed where windows are unsuitable; and their permanently fixed and inconspicuous screens lessen the need for visually distracting insect barriers at windows.

Of all rooms, kitchens need the best ventilation; most kitchens have exhaust fans, which can be used only as necessary, to supplement windows and doors. Bathrooms come next but seldom fare as well. Windows or grilles high in the wall help to remove stale air; controllable ceiling ventilators combine privacy with fresh air. Living and dining spaces also merit good air circulation, but the fact that they are typically large and have windows on two or more sides often takes care of the problem automatically. In contemporary planning, air flows through group spaces and to the outside as easily as people do. A good solution includes doors and windows plus grilles, some high and others low, located on different walls. Bedrooms benefit from fresh air without drafts. Again, high windows or ventilators on two walls, supplemented by other windows and doors, allow flexible control.

Energy in the Home

Lighting, heating, and cooling systems help to make our homes physically comfortable, cushioning the stresses imposed by natural cycles of weather. But these

134. "Solar One" was designed to make use of the sun's energy for heating, lighting, cooling, and the operation of electrical appliances. The 45-degree angle of the roofline, planned for maximum exposure to the sun in winter, gives the house a distinctive profile. Harry Weese & Associates, architects.

devices are heavy users of energy. According to some estimates, private homes account for nearly one-fifth of the energy consumed in the United States. Currently, some imaginative architects and planners, engineers and environmentalists are beginning to reexamine building practices and explore alternate ways of producing energy. One of the most exciting involves putting the sun to work.

Solar Energy

Except for its oversize "skylight," the house in Figure 134 looks fairly conventional. In fact, "Solar One" is a bold experiment in extracting power directly from the sun, without relying on subsidiary fuels such as oil, gas, or coal. The broad inset area in the steep roof is actually a series of panels composed of cadmium sulfide solar cells. When light strikes the panels, these cells generate direct current (DC), which can then be converted to alternating current (AC). Wires convey the electrical power directly to household lights and appliances. Excess energy can be stored in batteries. Methods of heating and cooling the house by means of the solar collectors are equally straightforward.

Pioneers in the study of solar energy estimate that, with presently available technology, 80 percent of the power requirements in a typical house could be met by utilizing these systems. The long-range advantages are obvious. While conventional fuel reserves are rapidly being depleted, solar energy is theoretically unlimited. It does not pollute the environment in any way. For the individual householder, the cost of building a solar house would be rather high today, but with mass-production techniques we can assume that the expense would lessen. The *operating* costs should become competitive with those we are accustomed to paying now for conventional fuels.

The house shown in Figures 135 to 137 takes a different approach in tapping the sun's energy. Here the owner-designer utilized an utterly simple, direct—and original—method for controlling the interior environment with two of our most basic elements—sun and water.

Unlike Solar One, this house is unique in shape. It consists of a cluster of "zomes"—a term devised by the architect to connote a dome with parallel zones. Banks of 55-gallon drums filled with water form the south-facing walls of the structure. In winter, the drums absorb heat from the sun all day, transmitting their warmth to the interior. At night massive insulated doors are raised to cover the drums so that the heat is retained. The process reverses in summer: only at night are the doors left open, so that cool air can lower the water temperature. An obvious

135–137. The "zome" house, a unique experiment in solar energy, uses huge drums filled with water to gather and store warmth from the sun. (*Courtesy Zomeworks Corporation*)

above: 135. The unusual design consists of a cluster of "zomes," or domes with parallel zones, for maximum architectural flexibility.

right 136. In winter, large insulated doors on the south side are left open by day to absorb the sun's heat, closed at night to preserve it.

137. The drum arrangement of the house in Figure 135 creates a fascinating interior design.

side benefit of this scheme is the interesting visual pattern created by the drums inside the house (Fig. 137). Although quite large, the zome house derives 85 percent of its heat from the sun. Moreover, its "natural" approach to supplying daily needs does not stop with solar heating. Water is pumped from a well by a windmill and run into the house by gravity; wind-driven fans in rooftop projections help to ventilate the house. Eventually, the owner hopes to generate all his own power.

Alternative Energy Sources

Many other ways of producing energy are now being investigated: windmills on land and ocean, geothermal energy from the heat of the earth's interior, hydro-electric power from tides that in some places form huge waves, nuclear fission and fusion, even biological methods that utilize bacteria to change organic materials such as algae and sewage into gas and oil.

Supplies of oil, gas, and coal are finite; we cannot continue tapping them at an ever-increasing rate. In order to cope with the problem of energy for the present and for future generations, we must undertake a two-faceted program: curtailment of waste in currently available energy resources and development of new methods to produce energy for the years to come.

Lighting, heating, cooling, and ventilation make our homes physically comfortable. Except for light, they have little to do with beauty or character, but they do seriously affect human happiness. The most attractively designed lifespace cannot be considered successful if it is too dark, too hot, too cold, or airless. Planning for support systems should begin at the very outset and continue through every aspect of home design.

opposite: Plate 17. Skylights extending a wall of glass bring the warmth and joy of sunlight deep into the living room of a house built on a wooded slope. Although the room faces south, the surrounding trees protect it from too much sun. Smith and Larsen, architects. See page 89. (*Photograph: Morley Baer*)

right: Plate 18. Recessed light, set high in the room behind a mirrored wall and low into indentations in the seating platform, provides unexpected but dramatic light sources. Jerome Ducrot, designer. See page 96; see also Fig. 505. (*Photograph: Dudley Gray*)

below: Plate 19. The daring use of red and pink lights brings a warm and exciting glow to this delightful room. Seymour Avigdor, designer; lighting by Ralph Bisdale. See page 96.

Organizing Space: The Plan

The plan seems like an innocuous and sometimes hard-to-read two-dimensional drawing, but its importance in determining the kind of life possible in any given space can scarcely be overestimated. It not only establishes the basic character of a particular structure but seriously influences the lifestyle that can be followed in the structure. For example, an open type of space with minimum floor-to-ceiling partitions could be occupied only by a family or group of people who enjoy the easy contact and group interaction such a plan engenders, or else the household would be quite miserable. Conversely, noncontact people who desire a certain amount of privacy—and prefer their interaction with others be confined to certain life rituals, such as dining together or social entertaining at prescribed times—will be happiest in a lifespace that provides designated, separated areas for various functions of living, areas that can be closed off both visually and acoustically.

The plan indicates the positions of walls and openings; the location, size, and shape of space for living; and sometimes the ways in which furnishings can be arranged. Many different aspects of planning the home have been considered in previous chapters; but creating an overall floor plan integrates the varied components discussed earlier into a single unified design. Space needs are translated into rooms of specific sizes and shapes; the living pattern hardens into an architectural pattern; walls, windows, and doors begin to define the nebulous allotment of space.

Space Modulation

Over the centuries the concept of space within the home has fluctuated between two basic arrangements: a single large, undifferentiated area in which most of the homelife took place, and a series of tightly segregated rooms with minimum intercommunication. In the late 19th and early 20th centuries, specialized rooms meant for designated activities appeared on the house plan. The terms card room, drawing room, music room, and even smoking room suggest the compartmentalization of a lifestyle now past. This century has witnessed changing lifestyles that in turn are reflected by more open space planning, with slightly demarcated but expansive spaces flowing into one another. As modern life has become less marked by formality, elaborate social rituals, and rigid distinctions, so our homes have changed in response to these demands. The active, mobile, informal lifestyles of today are inevitably recorded in new designs.

Open and Closed Plans

The **closed** plan (Fig. 138) divides space into separate rooms for specific activities. It has several points in its favor and still appeals to many people, because it affords privacy for different age groups and pursuits. A closed plan allows modulated levels of upkeep: for instance, children's play space does not necessarily have to be neat at all times, but adults often prefer a situation at least moderately ordered. Conflicting activities can take place simultaneously without interference. Furthermore, it is possible to close off certain portions of the house so that only those spaces in constant use need be heated or cooled at a given time—an important energy-conserving step. The house shown in Figure 138 exhibits such a plan as it is conceived today. If desired, the bedroom wing—or any individual bedroom—can be totally or partially shut off from the rest of the house and left unheated; levels of heat throughout the house can also vary according to need.

Open plans (Fig. 139) provide a minimum of fixed, opaque, floor-to-ceiling partitions and a maximum of flexible group space. Instead of being tightly closed into boxlike rooms, space is organized as a continuous entity, flowing from one section to another and from indoors to outdoors, all of which greatly expands the potential of any one area. The advantages of open plans include a sense of spaciousness beyond actual dimensions, diversified use of space, and recognition that family or group activities are not isolated events.

But open plans also have certain disadvantages. For one thing, noisy activities may interfere with those requiring quiet, and the retiring soul finds little opportu-

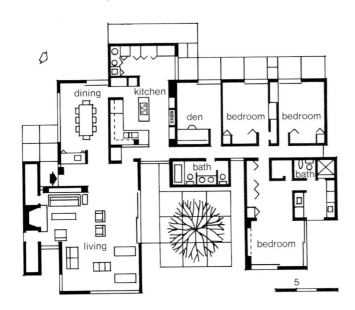

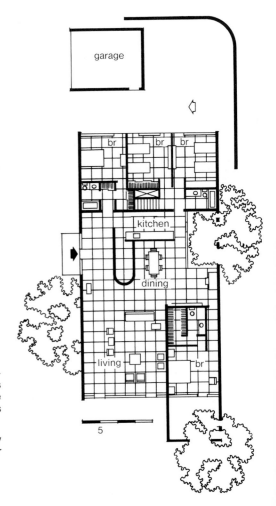

left: 138. A *closed* plan that permits separating each activity in a different room offers a great deal of privacy, which the U-shape arrangement accentuates. Donald Gibbs and Hugh Gibbs, architects.

right: 139. An *open* plan with a loosely demarcated group space offers greater flexibility.

nity for solitude. Also, if not sensitively planned, the large space may seem barnlike. These drawbacks can be overcome in several ways, as the barn reproduced in Plate 7 (p. 42) shows. First, by shaping the space with partial walls, different floor levels, and furniture arrangement, incompatible functions will be segregated. L-shape rooms, balconies, furniture set at right angles to the wall, and flexible screens or movable walls represent some of the major design possibilities. The second step consists of planning for noise control with surfaces that absorb sound waves. Third is the provision for some segregated areas—multipurpose or family rooms for active pursuits, seclusion rooms for quiet study, meditation, and relaxation.

The open plan owes much of its development to the inspiration of Frank Lloyd Wright with his prairie house designs (Figs. 824–826) and later to the innovations of Le Corbusier and Ludwig Miës van der Rohe (Figs. 831–834). It reached its full flowering in one-story houses that spread out over the land and into the landscape by means of terraces and decks, at a time when acreage was relatively inexpensive.

Vertical Space

A major interest in the design professions today involves the manipulation of vertical spaces, of volumes (Figs. 140, 141). The sense of excitement produced by soaring interior spaces has found a ready acceptance among large segments of the public; even speculative builders resort to high ceilings with mezzanine or balcony projections. This trend indicates a radical departure from the monotonous 8-foot

upper levels

lower levels

left: 140. Tantalizing glimpses of different levels and areas bring an exhilarating sense of the spaces beyond. In this house, each activity has its own separate but not isolated room. Charles Moore and Rurik Ekstrom, architects. (*Photograph: Maris/Semel*)

above: 141. The *multilevel* floor plan of the house in Figure 140 easily and naturally divides group and private spaces, a concept enhanced by the way rooms cluster around the space-saving circulation core.

Organizing Space: The Plan   **115**

ceiling that was standard for so long. Coincidental with the growing taste for verticality has been the pressing economic need to conserve square footage within the house. The hollowed-out effect of tall interiors with sloping ceilings tends to counteract our awareness of shrinking floor areas and to eliminate a feeling of constriction. Whatever the reasons, the results often have been dramatic.

The multilevel floor plan also has reestablished itself in popularity, after a period of disfavor caused by the aggressive onslaught of the one-floor ranch-type house. The split-level plan first reignited interest in multilevel living, since it offered the opportunity for three well-separated zones of activity over relatively small ground area. Even more square footage of living space results from the full two- or even three-story plan, without increasing the overall ground area occupied. At a time when acreage is scarce and expensive, we can no doubt anticipate a greater concentration on vertical building to exploit each plot of land more fully.

Organizing Space

The Program

When the designer first touches pencil to paper in beginning to draw a plan, a number of decisions should already have been made. In fact, there ought to be a carefully worked out program identifying the requirements of a home long before the graphic stage of planning is begun. The elements of this program include:

◻ Analysis of the site
◻ Space requirements
◻ Special functional goals
◻ Equipment needs
◻ A description of the desired character of the space
◻ Cost budget

The **site analysis** deals with topography, wind, sun directions, natural features, code and zoning limitations. Planning for **space requirements** generally takes the form of a list of space-consuming activities with a corresponding allotment of square footage. Of course, walls, closets, corridors, and support spaces also consume square footage, and these must be estimated. Special **functional goals** might include such activities as listening to or performing music, in which case special attention must be given to planning the acoustical qualities of the space, its reflective and absorptive characteristics. **Equipment needs** could be general (standard household appliances and the plumbing or electricity they require) or particular (a fully equipped power workshop, for example).

In describing the **character** of the proposed spaces, aesthetic goals can be established. This part of the program concerns itself with the emotional impact of the spaces and their design upon the occupants of the home. While vision plays an important part in our perception of this character, other senses contribute as well. The tactile sensation received in walking across a soft carpet produces quite a different response from that experienced in touching a polished marble floor. Also, the manner in which voices and other sounds are reflected or absorbed by an enclosed space gives us clear messages about the qualities of that space— messages that may elicit feelings of well-being, comfort, uneasiness, awe, safety, or fear. All these considerations should be taken into account during the earliest stages of planning.

The Schematic Diagram

Planning moves naturally from discussion of an overall program to the first graphic stage—the schematic diagram (Fig. 142). Here spaces are indicated by loosely

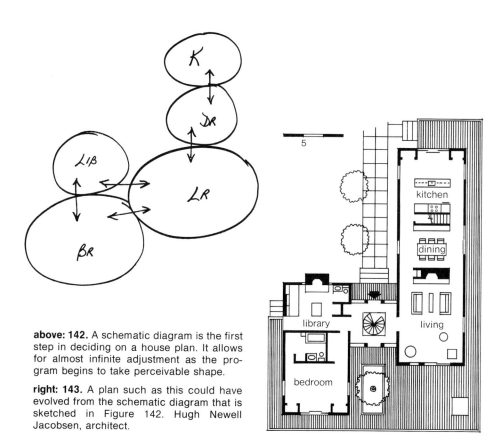

above: 142. A schematic diagram is the first step in deciding on a house plan. It allows for almost infinite adjustment as the program begins to take perceivable shape.

right: 143. A plan such as this could have evolved from the schematic diagram that is sketched in Figure 142. Hugh Newell Jacobsen, architect.

drawn circles or free-form shapes that roughly outline different space uses. In their proportion to each other the circles show the relative size and importance of each area. The schematic diagram also establishes relationships between various spaces—such as kitchen and dining area—by means of connecting lines. Arrows on the diagram signify ingress and egress, as well as circulation patterns.

The diagram may be reworked many times, with considerable adjustment of spaces, zones, and relationships. After these initial decisions have been made, the process of organizing space as a more precise two-dimensional drawing begins in earnest (Fig. 143).

Functional Planning

Winston Churchill once said, "First we build our buildings, then our buildings shape our lives." In fact, the converse of this statement should be a guiding principle in planning a lifespace. Ideally, our buildings—and particularly our homes—will reflect and fulfill the functions enclosed, rather than controlling them.

Functional planning begins with an analysis of activities to be carried out in the household, then moves toward an accommodation of space needs to those activities. Not only physical requirements but also psychological demands for space must be anticipated. From the smallest living module to the largest house, space divides itself into zones for different kinds of occupations: quiet and sedentary; noisy but sedentary; moderately noisy but active; very noisy and active (see pp. 44–47).

A helpful tool in gathering data to support functional planning is the "user survey," in which questionnaires are filled out to determine actual needs and desires of those who will occupy the space. This device was employed in planning Canter-

before

yard

living

utilities

k

porch

extra storage

after

yard

extra storage

den

k

utility

living

bury Gardens, a 34-unit apartment project in New Haven, Connecticut. Before construction began, the architect submitted a proposed floor plan to a selected group of future tenants. As a result of their comments, several important modifications were made (Fig. 144). Living rooms, which the tenant-advisors regarded as reception areas, were placed at the front of the building, while the large kitchen-dining-den space—considered the real "heart" of the house—moved toward the back. The long front hallway was eliminated for an improved utilization of space.

This example demonstrates the merits of a user survey for multiple-family dwellings, but it could as easily be applied to a single household. In planning space for a family, it would be wise to query in advance all members who are old enough to give informed opinions. The following sections offer general guidelines for the organization of various types of spaces.

Group Spaces

Chapter 2 treated in detail the design of group spaces; here we are concerned with the way in which these spaces relate to the overall home plan.

Group spaces that are subdivided architecturally—that is, by the shape of the room—can be most effective in isolating various kinds of activities without sacrificing the visual sense of spaciousness and freedom. The cruciform plan is excellent for this purpose, as is the modified cruciform, which creates three or four alcoves (Fig. 145). In fact, any plan, such as the L-shape, that affords different "compartments" gives a means of separating group activities. For even greater privacy, sliding or folding doors could be added (Fig. 146).

We can create the impression of separated zones in a square or rectangular group space by careful placement of furniture or screens (Fig. 147). Another possibility for establishing variety in the large undifferentiated space would be a

left and above: 144. The people who will actually use a home can give excellent advice on a proposed plan. In a low-income housing project, a plan (*above*) reworked in response to a user survey not only resulted in an apartment more in keeping with the probable lifestyle of the occupants (*below*) but also opened up the spaces to make the most of available square footage.

right: 145. In a plan designed in response to newly available modular service cores, group spaces flow around the module in a sequence of room shapes that allocate space without dividing it. Booth & Nagle, architects.

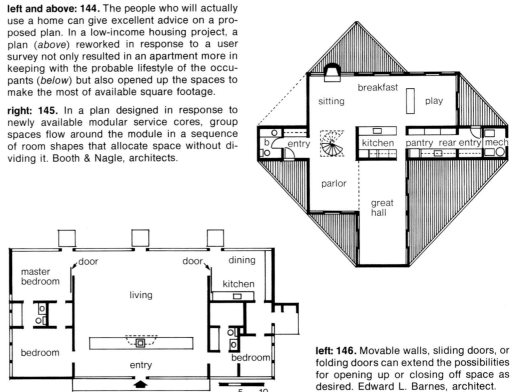

breakfast

sitting

play

b entry

kitchen

pantry   rear entry   mech

parlor

great hall

master bedroom

door

door

dining

living

kitchen

bedroom

bedroom

entry

5   10

left: 146. Movable walls, sliding doors, or folding doors can extend the possibilities for opening up or closing off space as desired. Edward L. Barnes, architect.

change of floor levels. For instance, altering the floor levels of dining, conversation, and music areas not only zones these activities but also adds a feeling of spaciousness and drama (Figs. 148, 149). Such a device must be planned carefully, however, for a change of only one step is too easily overlooked and can become a trip hazard. It is often better to have two gentle risers as a minimum for establishing a level change. Placement of furniture, plants, or a low railing will also call attention to the shift in horizontal plane. Obviously, a change in ceiling heights to demarcate certain areas can serve the same purpose (Fig. 19).

Generally speaking, group spaces are oriented toward outdoor living areas—toward a terrace, a garden, or even a balcony. For this reason, they must be shielded from the view of casual passersby, which can be accomplished by facing windows away from the street or by means of protective fencing and shrubbery.

above: 147. Furniture placement alone can establish zones for different activities without cutting up space into little boxes. Dining space, a library-study, and a conversation grouping all borrow from the surrounding areas without intruding on them. A low-walled bedroom-balcony further extends the feeling as well as the actuality of space. George C. Oistad, Jr., architect.

148–149. A group space is subdivided into areas of use by changing floor levels, counterpointed by varied ceiling heights. Barbara and Julian Neski, architects.

left: 148. Unexpected wall openings and the see-through fireplace enrich the visual experience of space. (Photograph: Maris/Semel)

below: 149. The plan illustrates how the sequence of spaces steps up around the central stairwell, achieving remarkable complexity within the geometric simplicity of a cube only 30 by 30 by 27 feet.

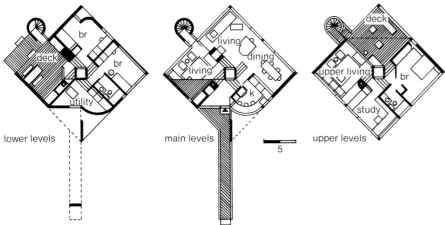

Group spaces relate closely in function to the support area of the kitchen and to access from the main entrance or parking facilities. The kitchen usually provides a link between automobile access and group space, since ideally it is contiguous to both (Fig. 150).

In many homes the provision of two or more completely separated group spaces helps to maintain harmony in the household or simply gives a choice of the kind of room in which to gather for various activities. A playroom opening off either the kitchen or children's bedrooms (Fig. 151) is a good solution in a one-story house. The latter arrangement also gives older children a degree of privacy and room to expand. When children are small and need fairly constant supervision, the kitchen-family room connection may be ideal. This solution also creates a relaxed entertainment center for adults and teenagers. A private study gives the seclusion needed for two or three people to get outside the group for quiet conversation. In houses with more than one story, a secondary multipurpose space on an upper or lower floor automatically produces some isolation.

Private Spaces

The primary consideration in locating private spaces is to ensure that they truly *are* private. A common error in house planning is placement of the bathroom—surely the most private of sanctums—in a position that offers a vista from hallways or even the principal group space.

Various possibilities exist for isolating private spaces, the most obvious being their segregation in a separate wing of the home (Fig. 138). In the so-called *bi-nuclear*

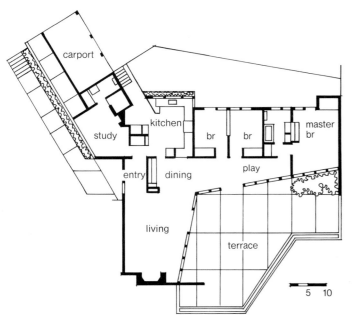

below: 150. A study in one wing of a house serves as a welcome retreat for individuals or small groups. The openness of the living, dining, and play space—expanding onto the terrace—functions well for family living and social events. Spencer & Ambrose, architects.

above: 151. A house plan divided by a glass-walled entry separates the quiet adult portion from the more active children's quarters, with the dining room approachable from either side. A useful indoor play area, within easy view for supervision from the kitchen, has been achieved by simply widening the bedroom hallway. Earl R. Flansburgh & Associates, Inc., architects.

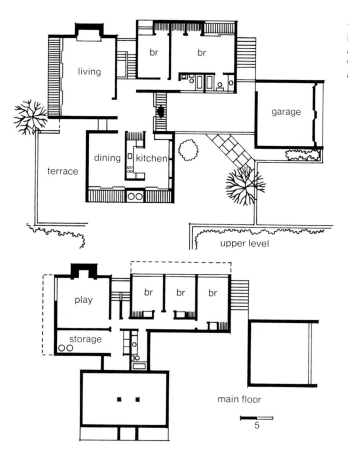

upper level

main floor

5

plan, the house divides into two wings, one for group living and support spaces, the other for private space. An entry area that serves both wings connects them. An extension of this system, the *tri-nuclear plan,* has an additional level for private spaces to supplement a private wing on the main level (Fig. 152).

Under the best of circumstances, private spaces are easily accessible from the cooking and eating areas. The heart of the home continues to be the food center, and all members of the household will tend to converge there (Fig. 153).

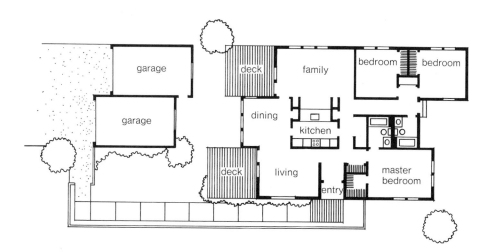

153. In modular house plans, the manufactured utility core suggests the placement of rooms in relation to it. Donald MacDonald, architect.

154. An open stairway provides circulation between two stories of a row of townhouses and indicates division of areas on the lower level without shutting them off from each other. The inset bands of closets, bathrooms, and kitchens between units result in an unusual degree of privacy for this type of housing. Ralph A. Anderson, architect.

When bedrooms and baths are placed on a second floor, the desired seclusion results automatically. Sometimes—perhaps with a hillside topography—an upside-down solution will be better, with the private spaces underneath the group living area (Fig. 152).

Support Spaces and Systems

The facilities we have labeled "support" include those for cooking, laundry, heating, cooling, and storage. Over the last several decades, the amount of space devoted to these functions in the home has been shrinking steadily—partly because of inflated construction costs and partly because of streamlined equipment. To reduce the size of homes, square footage is first eliminated from support areas, because these can sustain a cut without apparently reducing the living standard. Much of the equipment itself is smaller, cleaner, and less noisy: nowadays, a closet often suffices to house heating and air-conditioning equipment, a second closet holds laundry appliances.

For maximum efficiency, support areas should be centrally located in the house plan. This reduces the length of all sorts of umbilical cords that thread through the house to distribute energy in various forms. The shorter the run of the hot water supply, the sooner hot water appears at the faucet; the closer the kitchen to the various dining areas, the greater will be the likelihood of food being hot and appetizing when it is placed on the table.

Plumbing represents one of the most expensive elements of housing construction. For economy's sake, all plumbing fixtures—for kitchens, baths, and laundries—should be placed back-to-back whenever possible. In multistory homes stacking these facilities above one another accomplishes the same purpose (Fig. 154).

The utility core is a refinement of this idea. A predesigned industrial module, it contains all the equipment necessary for basic support functions: cooking, laundry, bathing, heating, air-conditioning, and water heating. Utility cores can be produced in standard sizes, shipped to the site in one piece, and installed with unskilled labor.

Sometimes it is possible to merge one of the support areas with the group space. As cooking becomes more of a family operation and less the exclusive province of one of its members, so this function can be more completely integrated with other family activities; thus, we find the lines that separate kitchens from major group spaces becoming increasingly blurred. Occasionally, the kitchen moves straight into the living room (Fig. 98).

Circulation

When economy is a factor, the barest minimum of square footage in the home must be allotted to circulation—entry halls, corridors, and stairways. Paths of circulation should be short and direct, should radiate from the home's principal entrance. Besides general circulation through the house, each room will have its own traffic paths. Various furnishing arrangements should be tried on the plan in order to analyze circulation paths to doors, bathrooms, windows, and major pieces of furniture.

The increased interest in two- and three-story house plans has brought with it research into different stairway designs. Spiral staircases occupy the least space, but this economy may be offset by the difficulty of moving furniture up and down, as well as the increased danger of accidents on the narrow treads near the center support. A flight of stairs broken at some point by a landing provides the easiest and most graceful way of bridging the approximately 9 feet of space typical between two floors (Fig. 155).

155. Staircases generally are more graceful and practical if broken at some point by a landing. Eliot Noyes, architect. (*Photograph: Hans Namuth, Photo Researchers, Inc.*)

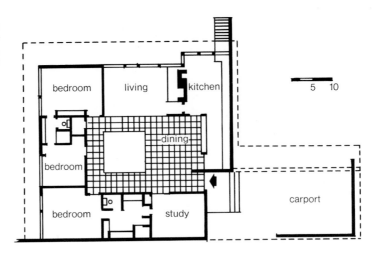

156. A skylighted atrium opens up the center of a small house in Dallas and becomes at once indoor garden, dining area, extended living room, and circulation space. Enslie O. Oglesby, Jr., architect.

The cooking area is subjected to the heaviest load of circulation. To this space all members of the household gravitate with dogged regularity. Thus, the successful plan will consider this intensive circulation demand and provide for it.

Some group spaces lend themselves more readily than others to the added function of general circulation. The dining area, since it is used at limited and stated intervals during the day, can easily double as circulation space without its effectiveness being destroyed. For homes built in mild climates, the atrium plan invented twenty centuries ago by the Romans solves the problem of circulation by providing that all rooms open directly into the atrium space. In a modern version (Fig. 156), the atrium is covered with a skylight outfitted with aluminum blinds to control the sun's heat and light.

Types of Living Plans

There are two basic determinants in shaping a plan—the intended occupants and the space available—and these can be interrelated in countless ways. Family size, resources, age of members, and way of life indicate the amount of square footage desirable and economically feasible, as well as the disposition of space for satisfactory living on one level or two, compacted or spread out. The size, shape, contour, and environment of the space, in turn, suggest whether a given amount of square footage can be contained in one story or will need more than one, whether the plan should be a square or rectangle or can be expanded into an L or T-shape or a cruciform, and perhaps whether an inward-turning court plan would be better than one that opens outward to a nonexistent view, to a street, or to nearby neighbors.

One-story plans are well suited to small houses and to larger ones for which the cost of greater land area and of an extended perimeter will not be an excluding factor. They avoid stairways, permit easy supervision of children, give ready access to the out-of-doors, and generally result in a horizontal silhouette that fits comfortably on level land. Until recently, individual apartments have also been predominantly one-story.

Multiple-story plans also offer several advantages. Given two homes of equal square footage, the double-story version would be cheaper to build than the single, because of its smaller foundation and roof. Heating and cooling are also less expensive. Moreover, vertically separated rooms simplify the problem of zoning spaces for different activities. As the cost of land rises, multiple-story houses seem more practical. They can fit onto awkward hillsides, tight city lots, or modest suburban sites, thus freeing more land for outdoor enterprises. Sometimes they rise

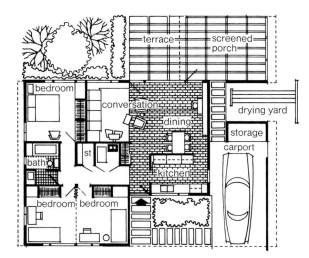

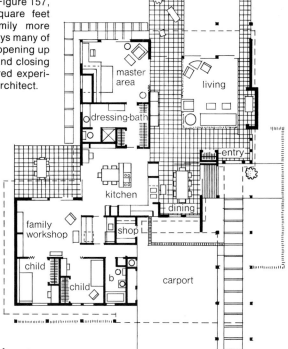

right: 158. More than twice as large as the house in Figure 157, this plan of 2030 square feet gives a growing family more elbow room but employs many of the same devices for opening up space when needed and closing it off for more sheltered experiences. Loch Crane, architect.

above: 157. Within an enclosed area of only 1000 square feet, this plan compacts most of the amenities that result in comfortable family living, while still allowing both physical and psychic expansion of space. Bruce Walker, architect.

to catch desirable breezes or an otherwise hidden view. The only real disadvantage of the two- or three-story house is the necessity of always climbing stairs.

Multifamily plans have been with us for many centuries. The Romans built thousands of apartment houses, some of them seven and eight stories high, during the 2nd century. Their presumed reasons were the same as those that motivate multifamily housing today: commerce and industry concentrated in specific large cities require a parallel concentration of people; also, land in such focal areas tends to be scarce and expensive, so it is more efficient to expand vertically than horizontally. The major disadvantages of such plans are the relative lack of privacy and the absence of outdoor living areas. Many newer multifamily dwellings overcome the latter problem with terraces or even outdoor decks (Fig. 41).

A Small One-Story Home

In the early 1950s Bruce Walker, an architect in Spokane, designed a small house to be built on a lot 60 by 100 feet (Fig. 157). That its excellent plan has stood the test of time is evidenced by the fact that even today many inquiries are still received for information about the house. The design features four distinct but integrated areas for group living: an all-purpose space and conversation alcove indoors, a terrace and screened porch outdoors. The arrangement allows for an easy flow of movement but also for stabilized furniture groupings.

Bedrooms and bath are well segregated in a unit away from the group spaces, with a sound barrier of coat closet, heater room, linen storage, and bedroom closets. The children's bedrooms occupy a small separate wing. Study of the plan will reveal many more details of thoughtful design.

A Larger One-Story Home

A design developed by architect Loch Crane for a larger lot (Fig. 158) organizes space ingeniously for livability, economy of time and energy, visual pleasure, and individualization. In purely graphic terms, the plan is a dynamically ordered

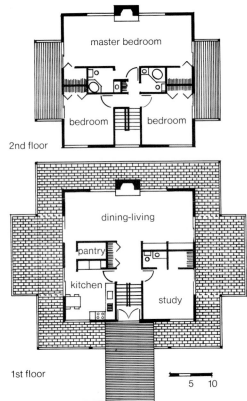

master bedroom

bedroom   bedroom

2nd floor

dining-living

pantry

kitchen   study

1st floor

5   10

complex of interlocking rectangles. Large windows and broad openings between rooms permit spacious views. Each room can be closed off completely by swinging, sliding, or folding doors. In order to minimize family conflicts, the group spaces have been divided into two separate areas: the more formal living-dining space, which merges with the master bedroom, for comparatively quiet entertainment and relaxation; and a child-centered space that links the kitchen, family workshop, children's bedrooms, and bath. Circulation is handled efficiently with a minimum of hall space.

A Small Two-Story Home

A two-story house in New Canaan, Connecticut (Figs. 159, 160), has excellent zoning and circulation. The first-floor study could double as a bedroom when someone in the house is ill, thus minimizing trips up and down the stairs. The balconies off the bedrooms give the second story access to the out-of-doors, while the split-level entry is convenient to both floors. What might have been boxiness in the exterior design (Fig. 159) is alleviated by extending the roof to provide shade for the windows and some protection of outdoor terraces, as well as by the bridge from driveway to entrance. Vertical posts standing tall and straight like trees counteract the flatness of the roof plane, as does the dark trim around the banks of windows.

A Row House

Row houses, townhouses, garden apartments, or attached dwellings have once again become a major solution to the problem of accommodating a large number

161. A remodeled row house makes the most of its 16-by-80-foot space through the virtual elimination of interior walls except where they are necessary for privacy. Peter Samton, owner-architect. See also Figs. 17, 30, 31.

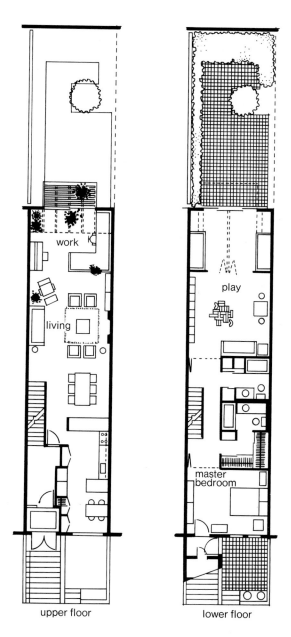

upper floor   lower floor

of families in a small area of land. Rising two to four or five stories in height, row houses by definition have their side walls abutting those of adjacent houses. Thus, they combine the psychological privacy of a completely integral structure with the economy of limited ground area to shelter a household of people.

A major disadvantage of the row house plan is the necessity of placing all windows on the two short walls at front and back. In older buildings, space tended to be broken up into many small rooms, with the result that internal spaces were completely deprived of daylight and fresh air. However, the current wave of interest in renovating townhouses has fostered new ideas for opening up the long, narrow space. The Samton house (Fig. 161; see also Figs. 17, 30, and 31) answers the problems of light, ventilation, and articulation of space admirably. Two main structural changes called for removing as many internal walls as possible to create a free-flowing space and the addition of window walls at back on both floors to flood the interior with natural light.

162–163. Basically rectangular plans are almost as economical as square, but they can be varied more flexibly. George Hampton, architect.

below left: 162. This plan adds a third story to markedly increase the square footage, allowing the house to be built on a steep hillside lot with minimum disruption of the site. (*Courtesy American Home Magazine*)

below right: 163. A view of the interior illustrates the way in which the three-story interior well opens up what could have been a rigidly divided space.

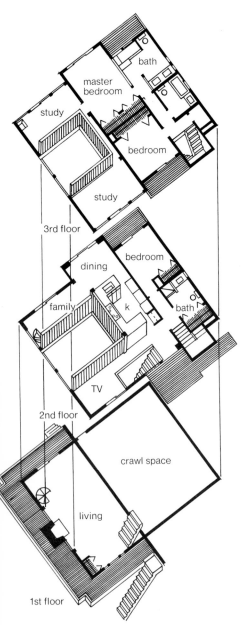

A Three Story Home

A steep hillside lot and sweeping view helped to shape a tall house designed by owner-architect George Hampton (Figs. 162, 163). The main entrance is on the second floor, where a bridge connects the house to the driveway. A 27-foot-high open well forms the core of the house, around which the living spaces cluster—spaces whose labels can change as family needs change. The family room now doubles as a conservatory, but it was once a workshop. The two hideaway study areas for the parents, accessible only through their bedroom, could be walled off to provide more bedrooms, with a new hallway cut through the other large bedroom. Because of the steep site, outdoor living is confined to decks, but their placement on various sides of the house allows for sun or shade. The kitchen occupies a key location in the group space. Adjacent to dining, family, and television rooms, it overlooks the living room and borrows daylight from glass window walls that ring these areas. It also abuts a bedroom on the same level, a great convenience when there is a young child or illness in the family.

A Cluster Plan Complex

An unusual floor plan consisting of four small separate pavilions loosely grouped around a court was conceived by an architectural firm for use by its members

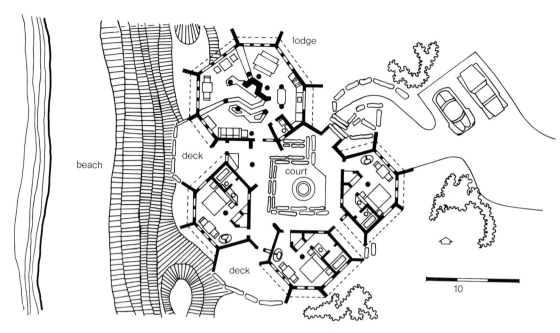

as a vacation retreat (Fig. 164). The courtyard serves as an outdoor gathering place and as circulation from the group space to the three private modules. This concept of isolated private spaces would function equally well for a family with teenage children or with three generations in the same house. Each unit could have windows facing in four directions, and each can be heated or cooled separately, even closed off when not in use.

An Expandable Floor Plan

Many young home planners are interested in a house that can grow along with their family needs and increasing financial resources. Such a long-range plan offers the householder the satisfaction of being on a pay-as-you-go program, plus the reassurance that the final structure will be an integrated design. The plan shown in Figure 165 expands with a minimum of disruption to the basic unit and would work quite well at each stage.

above: 164. A cluster plan complex, while expensive to build, can easily pay its way in privacy and flexibility of use, as well as in energy conservation when parts are closed off. Travers/Johnston, architects.

below: 165. An interesting aspect of some industrialized houses is their ability to expand, with minimum disruption, as family needs change. This version begins as a compact 507-square foot unit; grows to 845 square feet with the addition of a bedroom wing; and fills out to 1521 square feet as a master bedroom, family room, new living room, and deck are attached. Several other arrangements are possible. Mark Hildebrand, designer, for Rudkins-Wiley Corporation.

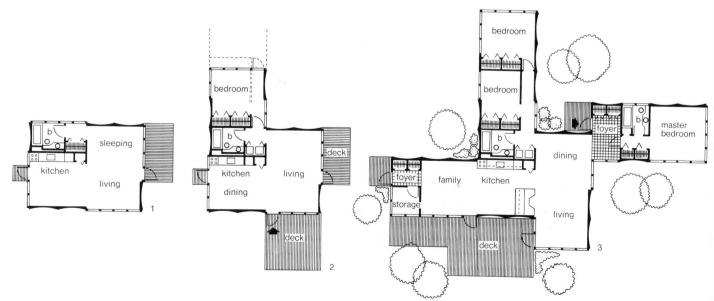

Industrialized Housing Plans

We tend to think that industrialized housing will look mass-produced and the plans be unimaginative and constricting. But this is not necessarily true, as Figures 166 to 170 show.

Panelized Housing   The first plan (Figs. 166, 167) represents a panelized house for which all the wall, floor, and ceiling panels and even some of the built-in furniture are factory finished but assembled at the site. The plan is a masterpiece of compact design that fits five bedrooms, two baths, two group-living areas—but privacy for the bedrooms when desired—into a total area of 1200 square feet. Built-in seating around the fireplace, plus built-in bunks, desks, shelving, and closets in the small bedrooms, make the most of that limited square footage. The simplicity of the rectangular plan suggests that a similar design would lend itself to a modular building scheme. Two long and easily moved mobile-modules could be transported to the building site and joined down the middle spine.

Modular Housing   The plans for a student housing project at the University of Massachusetts (Fig. 168) show the variety that is possible with modular components. Here the industrially produced modules—which are mostly 12 feet wide, 56 feet long, and 11 feet high—are completely finished at the factory, down to air-conditioning, furnace, and plumbing fixtures. But some variations in height,

166–167. Factory-built wall panels provide the modular basis for an extremely simple but comfortable house. Ronald L. Molen, architect.

above: 166. The exterior of the house is dignified and attractive, giving no hint of its industrialized construction. (*Courtesy Research Homes, Inc.*)

right: 167. As the plan shows, the house contains five bedrooms, one and one-half baths, and fairly ample group spaces—all within less than 1200 square feet. Built-in bunks, desks, and L-shape seating near the fireplace make the most of the available space.

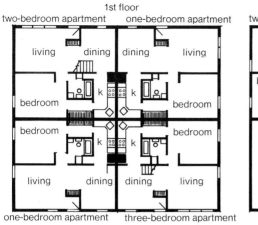

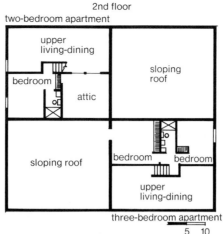

1st floor
two-bedroom apartment   one-bedroom apartment

living   dining   dining   living

bedroom   k   k   bedroom

bedroom   k   k   bedroom

living   dining   dining   living

one-bedroom apartment   three-bedroom apartment

2nd floor
two-bedroom apartment

upper living-dining

bedroom   attic

sloping roof

sloping roof

bedroom   bedroom

upper living-dining

three-bedroom apartment

5   10

168. The floor plans for a student housing project have been sensitively designed to allow alternative routes and to segregate acoustically the private and group spaces. Armstrong and Salomonsky, architects.

fold-up roofs, and field-applied panels give the exterior a lively silhouette and create diversity in the interiors. Although the layout of each apartment is essentially the same, the imaginative use of vertical space endows each unit with its own special distinction.

Analysis of the plans as adapted for one-, two-, and three-bedroom units demonstrate many niceties of detail. Starting at the entrance, which in each case is partially protected by a coat closet, circulation is efficiently routed to every room on the ground floor and to the stairs in the two-story units, leaving ample space for furniture groupings out of the traffic paths. Kitchens and baths are compacted into a plumbing core. The group space is open and expansive, yet the dining area can be partially secluded.

Mobile Homes The name mobile home clings to a certain type of industrialized housing, even though today the mobility is generally limited to the delivery of the home from a factory to a sales outlet and thence to a mobile home park. This form of housing now dominates the entire field of low-cost home construction in the United States. The list of amenities offered by a typical manufacturer is indeed impressive: complete kitchen equipment (including a built-in oven), laundry appliances, garbage disposer, gas-fired forced-air heaters, even draperies, fireplaces, and wall-to-wall carpeting. Many sales outlets also feature specially designed furniture. Clearly, all the comforts we once connected with "home" are present in this factory-produced replacement.

The 12-foot-wide limitation for transportation on highways governs the basic module of the mobile home. Luxury units, such as the one shown in Figure 169, consist of two 12-foot units placed side by side to form a 24-foot-wide structure. Lengths extend to 70 feet, depending upon the number of bedrooms contained, but in general, the design is limited in the disposition of spaces by the basic rectangular shape.

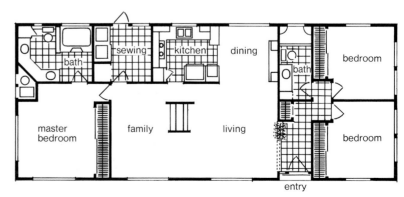

bath   sewing   kitchen   dining   bath   bedroom

master bedroom   family   living   bedroom

entry

169. The plan of a mobile home, although restricted to its basic 24-by-64-foot size, achieves separation of parents' and children's private spaces. It also cuts to a minimum the cross circulation through the group living area. (*Balboa Mobile Homes*)

Organizing Space: The Plan   **131**

The Home Without Space   The quintessential industrialized housing certainly must be the "suitcase home" illustrated in Figure 170. Three oversize and portable suitcases contain everything one could possibly need for daily living, down to television set, telephone, and tape recorder. To "build" this home it is simply necessary to move the three fiberglass suitcases—one each for living area, kitchen/dining, and bedroom—into any large space and open them up. To add a bedroom, you simply buy another suitcase! When it comes time to move to a new location, the suitcases are closed, rolled away on their own wheels, and opened in the new space. Obviously, this system allows for an infinitely flexible floor plan. At the same time, it is an essentially personal one, because the inner area becomes living room, dining room, or bedroom as the owner wishes, allowing for the multiple use of space according to individual time sequences.

Selecting a Plan

It is all very well to talk about the various planning possibilities and requirements, but sooner or later everyone must select a place to live. In order to effect the transition from abstract to concrete, the following section presents a series of questions designed to bring out the pertinent factors to consider in choosing a lifespace.

   Is the total amount of enclosed space, plus the usable outdoor space, suited to your needs? Many of us think we want as much space as possible until we see a large old house for sale or rent. Then we begin to wonder about cleaning, maintaining, and heating it, and how we and our furnishings would fit into rooms planned for another way of life. This suggests that the largest affordable space may not be ideal, even though there is no substitute for adequate square footage. It is probably worse to live in a space too small for the number of occupants than to cope with a rambling, inconvenient, hard-to-maintain old house. Too, many people are beginning to realize that the ample space provided by some old houses and apartments can be recycled to fit the kind of lifestyle we practice today.

Overall, the home should provide each occupant with a minimum of 200 square feet, although 250 square feet per person would be better and 300 would allow for truly comfortable living. These figures represent gross area, including walls, partitions, and all support spaces. To arrive at a per-person quota, it is simply necessary to take the entire gross area of the house plan and divide it by the number of occupants. The house plan illustrated in Figure 157 provides each of four persons with 250 square feet.

While these figures suggest a convenient rule of thumb, many factors—including, of course, finances—will influence the actual amount of space available to each member of the household. For one thing, as the size of the group increases, the amount of space required by each individual generally diminishes. Households composed of people who are heterogeneous in ages and interests, as well as those who are gregarious and extroverted, generally need more space per person than those whose members are homogeneous and relatively quiet. The home with flexible and multiuse space—enhanced by good zoning, convenient relationships among rooms, minimum traffic through rooms, thoughtful furniture arrangements, and livable outdoor areas—may be satisfactory with considerably less space per person.

Is the space appropriately allocated for your needs? The proportion of space devoted to **group, private,** and **support** spaces can vary markedly even in homes of the same size. The most significant relationship probably will be that between group and private spaces. One plan may offer a condensed group space in order that bedrooms and baths can be larger for individuals who like privacy; another could limit the bedrooms to mere cubicles, thus allowing for large or multiple group spaces. Support areas normally occupy proportionately larger sections of the overall plan in bigger homes, because, as noted earlier, when space is limited the support functions are the first to be compressed. However, families to whom the kitchen is very important may want to devote a greater proportion of the space to that room even in a small home. Divisions in private spaces vary mainly in the number of bedrooms and bathrooms allowed, but also in the seclusion given these rooms by a bedroom hall, movable partitions, and the potential of a separate space for individual pursuits.

Is the enclosed space well zoned and adjacent to related outdoor areas? The basic consideration involves segregating quiet areas from noisy areas. Plans can be checked quickly for this factor by coloring noisy spaces red, quiet ones green, then studying the resultant pattern. One of the most common zoning errors in one-story houses appears in the indoor-outdoor relationship: separating the kitchen from the garage (thereby precluding a convenient service entrance and yard) or facing the living room toward the street (which makes it difficult to unite the major group space with a protected terrace or lawn).

Is the pattern of circulation satisfactory? Short routes from point to point simplify housekeeping and make home life more pleasant, but they can be hard to achieve. Basic good planning suggests that:

□ Routes from the garage to the main and service doors should be short and offer protection in bad weather. Locating these doors near each other helps.
□ Ideally, it should be possible to get from the outdoors to any room in the house, and from any room to any other, without going through the middle of another room, except perhaps a multipurpose space.
□ Keeping doors close together and near the corners of rooms shortens traffic paths and promotes good furniture arrangement. This principle applies to entrance and closet doors, as well as room-access doors.
□ Living rooms should not invite traffic through the main seating area.

Are the rooms of suitable size? Beyond the *actual* square footage of a room, we must consider its *usable* and *apparent* size. These factors are affected by shape, location, and size of openings; relation to other rooms and to the landscape;

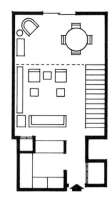

171-174. The same floor plan, with different furniture arrangements, can serve varying needs and lifestyles. This studio apartment with bedroom balcony lends itself to at least two plans.

left: 171. The tenant who is rarely at home during the day has little need of a view; hence, the seating area has been brought inside and assumes the quality of a library. (*Courtesy Apartment Ideas, Summer 1972.* © *Meredith Corporation, 1972. All rights reserved.*)

right: 172. As the plan shows, dining space has been deemphasized and removed somewhat from the kitchen, since the owner seldom has occasion to eat at home.

Table 6.1   Typical Square Footages for Certain Portions of the House

Room	Small	Medium	Large
entrance	25–30	35–40	45+
living space	150–200	220–280	300+
dining area	100–130	150–180	200+
dining space in kitchen	25–40	50–70	80+
kitchen	75–90	100–140	160+
bedroom	80–130	140–190	200+
bathroom	33–35	40–45	50+
utility room	12–15	18–25	30+

treatment of walls, floors, and ceiling; kind, amount, and arrangement of furniture. Some families prefer many small rooms, others a few large spaces. Table 6.1 lists typical square footages.

Will the rooms take the required furniture gracefully and efficiently? Naturally, the primary consideration here is adequate floor space for both furniture and traffic. But in planning a home we must also consider the question of suitable wall space—especially for such large items as beds and sofas—and the problem of arranging the furniture into satisfactory groupings. (Figs. 171-174).

Is there adequate storage space? A phenomenon almost everyone faces sooner or later is that storable items expand to fill and overflow the space allocated to

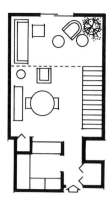

them, regardless of how commodious that space might be. Ample built-in storage reduces the amount of furniture needed and thus provides more living space. Specific storage requirements are discussed in Chapter 4.

Does the home lend itself to desirable or necessary change? It is impossible to predict just what the future will bring, but knowing that life and change go together suggests planning for flexibility. Family patterns change as children are born, develop, and leave home. The typically limited funds of young people may necessitate beginning with minimum quarters, but as financial stability increases, the question of upgrading or enlarging the lifespace—or moving to a new one— arises. Business opportunities, health, or simply the desire for something new can necessitate selling or renting a home.

Is the plan effectively oriented on the site? Orientation is best defined as relationship to the environment. This includes the sun, wind, and outlook; the size, shape, and slope of the site, as well as its relation to the street; existing trees, rocks, water, and so forth. Orientation affects the directions in which different rooms face, the location of windows and ventilators, and the placement of the building on its land (Fig. 175).

Skillful orientation for climate control is treated in Chapter 5. But other factors also deserve consideration: the presence or absence of a view, the degree of privacy needed in each room, and the amount of light—particularly sunlight—desirable in various parts of the house at different times of the day. All these are very personal decisions and must be dealt with on an individual basis. Still, we might list several typical situations:

left: 173. Cooking and entertaining at home are more important to this occupant, so the dining table is adjacent to the kitchen.

right: 174. In this arrangement the window—bringing light, air, and view—has been left unobstructed for the tenant who spends more time at home. (*Courtesy Apartment Ideas, Summer 1972.* © *Meredith Corporation, 1972. All rights reserved.*)

175. A house built on a rugged cliff in California seems almost to be a part of the wind-swept terrain. Although glass walls take full advantage of the dramatic view, the deep overhang of the roof protects the house. John H. Gamble, architect. (*Photograph: Julius Shulman*)

☐ Major group spaces deserve the best view, the privacy needed for living behind large windows, and the winter sun. South to southeast is preferred.

☐ Kitchens also merit a pleasant vista outdoors and ample daylight, preferably with morning sun. This suggests a northeast orientation.

☐ Bedrooms demand privacy; if the occupants enjoy the morning sun, the room should be focused generally toward the east.

☐ Bathrooms have no great need for outlook or sunlight, although both will be pleasant.

☐ Utility rooms can be anywhere, since they need few if any windows.

☐ Garages and carports must only be convenient to the street and house entrances.

All of these factors obviously represent ideals. Most people, in choosing a preexisting plan, find they have to compromise on a few essential qualities. Perhaps the overriding factors in site orientation will be knowing the house is not so dark that electric lights must burn all day, or so much subject to relentless summer sun that it can never be comfortable.

There is no ideal home plan. As with every other aspect of housing design discussed in this book, the plan best suited for a particular household will emerge from the needs, desires, personalities, and lifestyles of its members. When all these elements have been analyzed and understood, then the plan that begins as a graphic outline on paper can begin to take shape as a truly personal lifespace.

Design
and Color

7 The Nature of Design

Design is the selection and organization of materials and forms to fulfill a particular function. It has been with us since the first primitive hunter shaped a stone or twig to make a more effective weapon. In its simplest form this process of tool-making embodies all the basic concepts that still apply to the design of very complicated objects today: the hunter saw a need, sought the material that would best answer that need, considered how to shape and adapt the material, and worked out the process of forming to achieve a particular goal. Carrying this idea one step further, we should point out that the *second* hunter who saw the first's design, admired and imitated it, was not in fact designing but merely copying—unless the second weapon incorporated an improvement over the first.

No more can the beaver's dam, the spider's web, or the bird's nest be considered the products of design, for these creatures are following inborn instincts and learned patterns of behavior. Design as we understand it today is an intrinsically *conscious* process, the deliberate act of forming materials to fit a certain function, whether utilitarian or aesthetic. Still, the marvelous structures built by animals do refer to one of our most fundamental ideas of design—the so-called "grand design" of nature. From the tiniest unique snowflake to the mightiest mountain range, we find our world beautiful, satisfying, appropriate, in short well-designed. But beyond these isolated elements, it is the interrelationship of all the various earth's components that we call nature's design. Every living thing has its place in the food chain because of what it eats if it is an animal, what it absorbs if it is a plant; what it is eaten by or what it gives off to enable others to live. A rock is a rock, but at the same time it may be part of a mountain that catches rain clouds and helps dump the water out of them onto the thirsty land. A rock eventually breaks down into sand to form a totally different landscape with a different function—a place to which animals come when they emerge from the sea. One of the most serious concerns of our time revolves around the ways in which human beings, in the name of progress, have interfered with this natural design, perhaps paving the way for a total breakdown in its harmony.

In recent years we have become increasingly aware that manufactured things, as well as natural ones, have a part in this overall design. A chair is a chair, but it is also a former tree or hide or chunk of metal or collection of chemicals. When it has ceased to function as a chair, it must go somewhere—up in smoke, into some other product, or simply to the top of an ever-more-immense pile at the dump.

opposite: 176. Photographed from above, the main living area of a contemporary Michigan house, based on squares, rectangles, and occasional curving forms, takes on the quality of an abstract painting or an exercise in pure design with shapes and tones. Richard Meier, architect. See also Figs. 639, 640; Plate 48, p. 335. (*Photograph: Ezra Stoller © ESTO*)

left: 177. While exotic in its details, this reconstruction of an Egyptian bed is immediately recognizable as an object meant for reclining. The original was found at Kerma and dates from the Middle Kingdom (c. 2133–1786 B.C.). (*Museum of Fine Arts, Boston* [*Directors Contingent Fund*])

below: 178. A heavily ornamented bedroom set, exhibited at the Philadelphia Centennial of 1876 by Berkey and Gay Company, represents a type that was mass-produced during the late Victorian period. (*Public Museum, Grand Rapids, Mich.* [*Pictorial Materials Collection*]; *photograph: George W. Davis*)

Design becomes a very serious business indeed when we realize that its application to any object—from the largest building to the tiniest electronic component—is bound to affect other objects and structures, the people who use them, and possibly the environment as a whole. A chair made of wood demands that a tree be cut down; one upholstered in leather or fur exacts the life of an animal. Whether the tree will be replaced by planned reforestation, whether the animal's species will remain stable are factors the designer should keep in mind, even though they are largely beyond the individual's control. On the other hand, a chair with plastic components may be ultimately responsible for causing liver disease in workers at the plastics factory.

As far as disposal is concerned, it may be difficult for the designer involved in creating something beautiful to anticipate its eventual destruction. But most objects wear out sooner or later, and the combined refuse of more than two hundred million people in the United States alone makes for a staggering problem. Intelligent design takes into account the entire spectrum—the source of materials, the shaping of materials, and the return of materials to the environment.

179. An ultramodern version of the sofabed, this piece, called "Anfibio," can be buckled together in several different ways, thus making it unusually adaptable to today's changing lifestyles. When completely opened out, it makes a comfortable bed for two people. (*Courtesy International Contract Furnishings, Inc.*)

In this chapter we shall discuss design from a theoretical point of view—its nature and the influences upon it, the way it has changed over the last two centuries, and the directions it may take in years to come. Chapter 8 deals with the specific elements and principles of design, especially as they apply to the home.

Influences on Design

We might consider the "purest" form of design to be the creation of something that has never existed before, so that we have no preconceived ideas about how it should look. A bed designed for an Egyptian pharoah, a Victorian matron, or a 20th-century American couple will be readily identifiable as a bed (Figs. 177, 178, 179), and we can expect that the bed designed for an orbiting space station, although streamlined and ultramodern, will still look pretty much like a bed. But a machine invented for walking on the moon looks like nothing else in this world

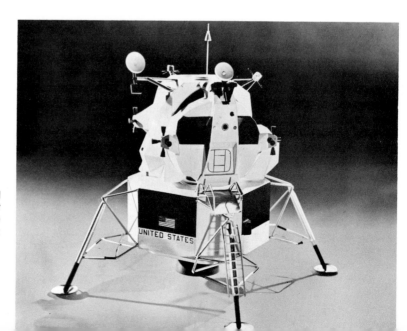

180. A function never before performed challenged designers to invent a totally new form. This is a scale model of the Lunar Module, devised for locomotion on the Moon. (*Photograph: NASA*)

181. Instead of hiding behind an incompatible cabinet, this Italian-designed television set flaunts its technological identity by revealing the working parts through a transparent casing. Marco Zanuso and Richard Sapper, designers, for Brionvega. (*Photograph: Aldo Ballo*)

(Fig. 180). Nevertheless, several factors inevitably influence the design of beds and lunar modules, as well as anything else we could think of. Among these factors are the *function* an object is to serve, the *material* or materials from which it will be made, changing ideas of *style* and appropriateness, and the *method of production* to be employed.

Design and Function

Without referring to it as such, we have already touched upon one of the ways function influences design. We recognize a bed when we see one because it incorporates a flat horizontal surface for sleeping. The design of most musical instruments had become conventionalized by the 17th century, partly because of the mechanics of sound production and resonance. Today's violin looks essentially the same as one made three hundred years ago, and one made three hundred years hence probably will not be very different. But what of a television set—a machine that did not become commercially viable until the late 1940s? Electronic designers of that era faced an enviable challenge in deciding what the new contraption should look like. For the most part, they failed completely. Early television cabinets were either sterile black boxes or elaborate pieces of furniture masquerading as something else. Only recently have designers begun to treat the television receiver as something unique, requiring its own design criteria. The response to this idea can be seen in built-in integral units (Fig. 37), and in new designs that celebrate the technology involved by permitting the circuitry, chassis, and operating parts to stand as their own design statements (Fig. 181).

Relatively few designers ever have the opportunity to create something totally new. Most design is actually *re*design, or improvement over designs that already exist. If a manufacturer presents a new line of tables and advertises them as a radically new design, this is true only up to a point, because tables have been with us for many thousands of years and serve the same basic purposes they did centuries ago. Furthermore, it is hoped that a new design means improved function, for we place very high value on things that work efficiently. The company that makes kitchen appliances may change their appearance every year, altering them physically if not functionally, to conform with prevailing tastes. But in advertising a new product, they will take pains to point out its improved features—additional jobs it can perform, ease of cleaning, quietness, speed, or whatever.

It is only since the Industrial Revolution that designers have systematically investigated the role of function in planning objects and whole systems. We will discuss the implications of mass versus unit design more fully later in the chapter, but for purposes of relating design to function we can point out that production of thousands or even millions of identical objects gives both the opportunity and the incentive to evaluate their effectiveness. Deliberate, scientific investigations of function have played a major role in shaping the contemporary home, and, as mentioned in Chapter 4 (p. 66), no part of the home has been more thoroughly researched than the kitchen. Time-motion studies, studies of work patterns and the flow of activities all relate function to design. Today's researchers utilize highly sophisticated methods, which result in such superefficient systems as the Westing-house kitchen (Figs. 80, 81). But the concept of utilitarian planning for the home is by no means new.

In the mid-19th century the thoroughgoing inefficiency of most American homes spurred Catherine Beecher, with her sister Harriet Beecher Stowe, to undertake a personal study of the ways in which function could be related to design. Although certainly not an advocate of women's liberation as we know it today, Catherine Beecher was greatly concerned with the idea of liberating women within the home in terms of economy of labor, money, health, and comfort. Her designs stressed function—in the kitchen, for example, cabinets and surfaces built for specific purposes and storage near the point of use (Fig. 182). Beecher designed a movable storage screen that could be placed in a large room to subdivide it for different activities at different times—a true multipurpose space. Surprisingly for that era, she gave serious attention to the quality of air inside the home. The Franklin stove, which was efficient in providing heat, had come into popular use, replacing the much less effective open fireplaces that gulped large quantities of air to keep the fires going. But the Franklin stove creates less turnover of air in the room, keeping

182. Deliberate, methodical planning went into the design of this kitchen work area published by Catherine Beecher and Harriet Beecher Stowe in *The American Woman's Home* (1869). It provides space for all the staple foodstuffs and working surfaces a cook of that era would need, while keeping an array of tools and cooking implements close at hand.

183. Revolutionary in its provision for closets, bathrooms, and ventilation, this house plan, also from the Beechers' *The American Woman's Home,* has the multi-room comfort and graciousness we associate with the 19th century.

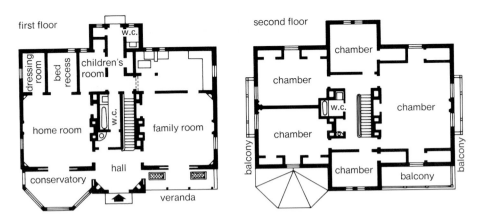

first floor

w.c.

dressing room | bed recess | children's room

home room | w.c. | family room

hall

conservatory | veranda

second floor

chamber

chamber | w.c. | chamber

chamber

balcony | chamber | balcony | balcony

it warmer but also keeping stale air inside. To counteract this, Beecher designed house plans that provided good circulation (Fig. 183). She advocated the inclusion of more bathrooms in the home and compartmentalized them for flexible use. All in all, Beecher's designs were predicated on function rather than style and emphasized a trend toward specific applications.

If we compare Catherine Beecher's ideal kitchen work area (Fig. 182) with the contemporary mixing center shown in Figure 87, we find many similarities. That the two kitchens, separated by more than a century, have so many points in common should not surprise us, for basic food-preparation techniques have changed little. What should surprise us is that so few kitchens incorporate planning of this nature. The task of the designer is to formulate ideas that answer the needs of function; the task of the consumer is to demand them.

Much has been made of the credo first announced in alliterative fashion by the architect Louis Henry Sullivan: *form follows function.* Yet function can never be an absolute determinant of form, since any given end-use might be satisfied perfectly well by two or four or a dozen different forms. Leafing through the pages of this book alone we might easily find twenty or thirty different chairs that fulfill the function of offering comfortable seating, but their forms seem to have little in common. The watering can shown in Figure 184 makes a good example. As a device for watering plants, it is highly functional: the curving handle would be easy to grasp; the spout set low on the container would drain water from the very bottom with minimum tilting; and the filling hole placed to one side opposite the spout would prevent water from coming out the top when the can is tipped.

184. This graceful watering can, plated in silver, exhibits the sleek polished surface as well as the slender curving forms that metal is capable of assuming. (*Courtesy Georg Jensen*)

opposite: 185. The ultimate in seating or lounging flexibility is represented by this modular unit consisting of an array of square cushions. The lower sections are all on casters for easy portability. Eleanore Peduzzi Reva, designer. (*Courtesy International Contract Furnishings, Inc.*)

However, none of these functional considerations account for the specific form of the can—the graceful proportions and slight taper of the container, the high arc of the handle, the slender tube of the pouring spout. To explain these we must turn to other design influences, in this case perhaps style and above all material.

Design and Material

With the possible exception of some plastics, the watering can in Figure 184 could not have been made from any material but metal. Certainly neither wood nor ceramic could easily assume the shape of a hollow tube as thin as this spout, and glass would be too fragile for the broad curve of its delicate handle. Metal, though, has the precise qualities needed to create a form such as this: strength when very thin, plus ability to sustain complex shapes such as curves.

During the 1970s possibly the single most important influence on interiors and their furnishings has been that of Italian designers. Their contributions have been twofold: the bold, imaginative use of new synthetics, both hard and soft; and the investigation of totally innovative forms that are flexible in use, made possible by these plastics. Chairs and sofas exist not as discrete objects but as parts of modular seating arrangements capable of being assembled, combined, rearranged, repositioned, even reshaped as needs and whims dictate (Fig. 185). The familiar seat, back, and four legs of a chair may disappear entirely into an amorphous or geometric shape that assumes contours only when someone sits in it.

Italian designers have exploited the universe of plastics in two directions. Rigid plastic chairs and tables may be light in scale and weight, assuming shapes not possible with the more conventional wood, but they are remarkably strong. On the other hand, soft plastics, such as polyurethane foam, have brought back the bulky look in furniture, because it is now possible to have solidity without weight. The success of Italian designs rests on the fact that their creators had the insight to go beyond traditional forms, techniques, and conventions to explore the possibilities for design that had never before existed.

right: **186.** Verner Panton's side chair, designed in 1968, is molded in one piece of plastic. Its contours are specifically engineered to accept the seated human form. (*Museum of Modern Art, New York* [*gift of the manufacturer, Herman Miller A.G.*])

far right: **187.** This replica of a side chair designed by Gerrit Rietveld in 1934 shows the natural grain and the joinings typical of wood. (*Museum of Modern Art, New York* [*gift of Mrs. Phyliss B. Lambert*])

Materials can both limit and inspire the designer—limit because no material should be forced into shapes contrary to its nature, inspire because an understanding of the particular qualities inherent in a material can free the designer to innovate. The two chairs shown in Figures 186 and 187 will illustrate this point. Both are simple, armless units essentially Z-shape in outline; both depend upon cantilever construction, and both are surprisingly comfortable. However, the first, a 1968 design by Verner Panton (Fig. 186), is a smooth, sinuous expression of the

188. The laminated wood furniture of Wendell Castle, with its sinuous, organic forms, refers back to the natural growths in which the material originated. See also Fig. 626. (*Photograph: John Griebsch*)

flowing qualities of plastic. It has no joints, nor does it require them, for the molded plastic, shaped imaginatively for balance, is sufficiently strong to hold the sitter's weight. Gerrit Rietveld's side chair (Fig. 187), designed in 1934, is an angular assembly of flat wood boards, joined in three places and reinforced at the joints. With appropriate construction, wood possesses adequate tensile strength to resist breaking, yet this chair actually is somewhat resilient.

While Rietveld's chair would seem to be an unusually honest and straightforward use of wood, designers of the 20th century have not restricted themselves to the board and plank forms we often associate with the material. By laminating together many small pieces of cherrywood, Wendell Castle created a chopping block that suggests—without directly imitating—the form of a live tree (Fig. 188). Its celebration of grain patterns and whorls highlights the most attractive quality of wood.

The classic example of curvilinear design in wood is the bentwood chair, developed in response to new methods of steaming wood that were introduced in the late 19th century (see Chap. 25 and Fig. 817). In its rocker form, the bentwood chair with caned back and seat has enjoyed enormous popularity during the 1970s (Fig. 189). This in turn has inspired contemporary designers to reinterpret the form in metal—a material also capable of assuming thin, curving lines (Fig. 190). Along with plastic, metal is very much a material of the seventies; although many people still prefer furniture made of wood or other organic substances, metal and plastics seem particularly in touch with the industrial age and could be considered a prevailing trend or—for lack of a better word—style. This leads us directly to consideration of another design influence.

Design and Style

It is extremely difficult to separate materials and technology from style, because they are interdependent. If the technological processes necessary for working with metals and plastics did not exist, there could be no style for metal and plastic

left: 189. A process for steaming and bending wood, developed by Michael Thonet in the 19th century, made possible the creation of the bentwood rocker, whose function seems appropriately mirrored in the medley of swirling curves. See also Fig. 817. (*Courtesy Thonet Industries, Inc.*)

right: 190. A modern adaptation of the bentwood rocker replaces the wood frame with metal, the cane seat and back with vinyl upholstery. (*Photograph: Bruce C. Jones; courtesy The Door Store*)

objects. With this in mind, we can say generally that styles and tastes and preferences do fluctuate periodically. For example, the fashion in Europe and the United States during the 19th century was for opulence, profusion of ornament, and a kind of heavy solidity in design. In the 20th century most people have come to prefer cleaner lines, less applied decoration, and an overall impression of lightness. To see these principles operating, we need only compare the bedroom from the 1870s (Fig. 178) with a bedroom from the 1970s (Pl. 20, p. 161).

The Victorian bedroom was the product of a society that held in high esteem the possession of material goods. The home existed as an expression of self-

left: 191. Despite today's emphasis on clean lines and the banishment of clutter, many people still harbor a nesting instinct that makes them treasure the old-fashioned rolltop desk, with its seemingly endless drawers, shelves, and cubbyholes. (*Photograph: David Vine*)

below: 192. This modern version of the rolltop desk, handcrafted of walnut by Espenet, has a more slender profile and no lower drawers. We would expect its contents to be considerably fewer and kept in better order than those of the desk in Figure 191.

importance and self-worth. Therefore, the reasoning went, the more objects it contained, and the more heavily decorated those objects were, the higher would be the owners' apparent position in the social scale. A contributing factor to this value system was the new availability of low-cost consumer goods made possible by the advancing machine age. For the first time, middle-class families could afford luxury items that had formerly been accessible only to the rich. Upward mobility and possession of objects became synonymous. Thus, the Grand Rapids bedroom contains heavy, ponderous furniture with pseudo-classical decorations and other enrichment over virtually every square inch. Precious objects—some useful, some not—occupy every flat surface. Color and pattern, however, are restricted to rich rugs on the floor and a decorative wallpaper.

To a certain extent, many of us still use our homes as the visible yardstick of material wealth and social status, but if this is true, then our criteria have changed. The bedroom in Plate 20 is all light and air and space, as compared to the rather dark and cramped Victorian version. Cleanlined, built-in furniture blends imperceptibly into the architecture. Most striking, of course, is the fact that bright color and pattern dominate the room. The brilliant red-yellow-and-black bedspread (and one live plant) provide the only notes of color against an overall neutral background, thus ensuring that the bed, even without any framework, remains the focus of attention. This bedroom incorporates an ample amount of concealed storage, whose unobtrusive character would have been out of place in a Victorian home, as well as an ease of maintenance that would have seemed quite superfluous to a world replete with servants.

An excellent example of the way in which the same kind of object can respond to different fashions appears in Figures 191 and 192. The first illustration is an old-fashioned rolltop desk made in the 19th century, filled with drawers and cubbyholes and, one hopes, secret compartments and sliding doors. A bastion of organized clutter, this heavy piece provides a refuge for endless papers and things to be stashed away, lost, and sometimes found again. The roll-down top covers and conceals everything—the clutter as well as the secrets. By contrast, the hand-crafted rolltop desk in Figure 192 is sleek and modern in design. Its compartments would hold many different kinds of things, but in a fairly regimented manner. We can imagine arranging pencils, stamps, paper clips, and writing paper in all the various sections, but their arrangement would be orderly and patterned to enhance the design of the desk itself. The 20th century does not place a high premium on clutter, so a different lifestyle demands different expression in design.

We could give numerous other examples to show how tastes and styles have changed over the centuries and how design in architecture, furnishings, and all kinds of objects have followed those trends. It is important to remember, however, that style is a cumulative process. It would not be impossible to find a room generally in the character of the Victorian bedchamber today, but the bedroom shown in Plate 20 could not have existed in the 1870s. This fact depends partly on the absence of built-in furniture, plastics, and metal structures in the 19th century, but it also relates to questions of taste, for the contemporary room would have seemed eccentric or even shocking a hundred years ago. As fashions change, many people change with them, but there will always be those who cling to the beauties of yesterday.

Design and Production

When a weaver sits down at the loom to create a tapestry, there is almost no limit to the design possibilities. A contemporary art fabric might be two-dimensional or three, have many colors and textures, and involve an array of yarns (Fig. 373). But if the same weaver were to design an upholstery textile for commercial production, very different rules would apply. No doubt there would be a restriction on the number of yarns and colors involved, and the complexity of pattern would

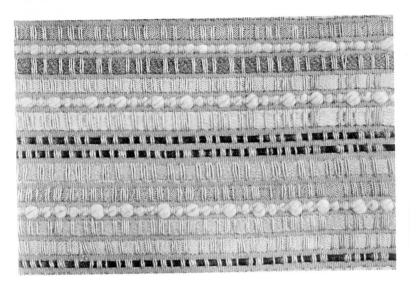

above: 193. "Jubilee" is a complex fabric made from many different kinds of yarns. It represents a triumph over the tedium long associated with machine production of textiles. (*Courtesy Jack Lenor Larsen, Inc.*)

right and below: 194. A complicated mold system had to be devised to permit the mass production of Warren Platner's steel-wire furniture. The one-piece frame construction results in an unusually graceful curving shape. See also Fig. 428. (*Courtesy Knoll International*)

depend on the sophistication of the looms involved. Whether a designer is limited or challenged by such restrictions will depend on his or her imagination.

Taking the example given above, the field of textiles, a number of contemporary designers have met the challenge brilliantly. Jack Lenor Larsen was among the first to refuse inhibition, demanding that the designs come first and the machines be adapted to cope with those designs. The result was a series of unique, sumptuous textiles that destroy the image of boring mass design (Fig. 193).

Often the best of modern design results from a combination of machine and hand processes, as is true for the steel-wire furniture created by Warren Platner (Fig. 194). A specially tailored mold system that involves some hand work in shaping the wires allows the Platner furniture to be made as one piece, with frame and supports an integral unit. The smooth flow of these weblike forms contrasts with older furniture styles in which separate parts had to be joined with nails, pegs, bolts, and glue. Thus, the design and the method of construction are practically inseparable.

The designer who creates a single object need not be too concerned about its method of production, for if one system doesn't work, there is always time to find another. But the vast majority of objects designed today are intended for mass production, and this raises all sorts of new questions. It was only in the mid-18th century, when it became feasible to manufacture many identical objects, that people began to analyze the nature, goals, and principles of design. From that point design, so to speak, became Design.

Mass Design

The Industrial Revolution had an enormous impact on the methods by which things were produced, but it also profoundly affected the design of objects. Machinery made it possible for the first time to turn out large quantities of goods at relatively low cost. In so doing, however, it dramatically changed the relationship of the designer to the object, the consumer to the object, and eventually the whole precarious balance among producer, consumer, object, and environment.

Before machines took over the business of manufacture, most articles—from spoons to houses—were designed and made either by the people who wanted them or by craftsmen in the community who were thoroughly familiar with the available raw materials and how they could be fashioned, how the objects would be used, and often how successful they proved to be in meeting the original needs. If a particular item did not serve in the way it was intended, it could be taken straight back to the maker, who might then be inspired to alter the design. Industrialization changed this situation drastically.

The immediate result of mechanized production was a standardization of form. Whereas previously each object had been personally designed and crafted by an individual or shop and evidenced the unique touch of the maker, the machines functioned best when they could spew out thousands of identical items. Following shortly upon this change was a sharp increase in design complexity—complexity for its own sake. Manufacturers with ever more sophisticated equipment could not resist the temptation to experiment with intricate decorative effects, piled layer upon layer in every conceivable type of product. By the mid-19th century this situation had snowballed to the point we might call decadence.

Another new phenomenon of the Industrial Revolution was the sizable inventory. The lone craftsman might keep a few samples of work produced in the shop, filling orders as they came in but never piling up a backlog of finished products, because this would have represented too much investment in materials. The entrepreneur, on the other hand, had to gamble on making thousands of a single object, hoping that the public would accept it. Designers therefore were forced to appeal to the lowest common denominator of taste, which did not exactly foster innovation. If the public rejected a design, the manufacturer would lose his entire investment. Thus was born the modern advertising industry, to create a favorable climate of acceptance for each new product.

If in preindustrial society design responded to felt needs—the lack of something inspiring its creation—then the reverse situation prevails today. Large manufacturers competing with one another produce vast quantities of items for which they must then generate a desire among consumers, and preferably a "need." The typical household did not "need" an electric can opener until it became aware that electric can openers existed. Particularly active in this field are makers of large appliances, which usually have a working life of from ten to twenty years. To encourage the consumer to discard an appliance before it ceases to operate, manufacturers annually introduce "improvements"—some of them truly useful, some at best whimsical. More often than not, design asks "What will the public buy?" rather than "What does the public need?"

Fortunately for the course of mass design, there always have been those who sought to maintain high standards within the framework of machine technology. The most organized and deliberate movement of this type occurred in the Bauhaus, a school of design active in Germany during the 1920s and early 1930s (see Chap. 25). The Bauhaus had as its guiding principle the establishment of standards of excellence in design and workmanship that would be compatible with mass production. Many of the designs formulated under its auspices, such as the side chair created by Marcel Breuer (Fig. 195), have remained modern classics and are still in production today.

One of the most unfortunate aspects of early mass production—and one the Bauhaus sought to overcome—was the fact that design often fell into the realm of individuals who understood far more about the operation of the machinery than they did about the products to be manufactured. Even now, many large companies entrust their advertising or public relations staffs with the weight of design decisions; it was considered revolutionary when, in the 1940s, a major textile mill hired master weaver Dorothy Liebes as design consultant. But this situation has by no means been universal, and some of the most successful mass products have resulted when design remained firmly in the hands of the designers.

The Industrial Revolution reached the Scandinavian countries considerably later than it did England and the United States, and the parallel disappearance of the traditional handcrafts that afflicted the latter two countries never occurred in Scandinavia. Thus, when mechanization arrived, there was a pool of trained designers available to guide its fortunes. Skilled artisans were acknowledged as the

195. A side chair designed by Marcel Breuer in 1928 demonstrates the strength of steel even in very thin tubes. (*Museum of Modern Art, New York* [*purchase*])

experts in design and encouraged to adapt their techniques to mass production. Among the results have been sturdy, clean-lined furniture; simple, elegant designs for dinnerware and other household objects; and honestly crafted textiles for a variety of purposes (Fig. 196). The pieces are well made and display to good advantage the natural qualities of their materials—wood, cane, leather, wool, clay, or steel. Today, many firms around the world copy both the underlying principles and the actual designs of Scandinavian industry.

The example of Scandinavian design raises again the question of design for single, one-of-a-kind objects, which was the kind of experience brought to mass production in that part of the world and, for that matter, in the Bauhaus as well. Although the Industrial Revolution effectively eclipsed unit design in the United States and parts of Europe for nearly two hundred years, the tradition of hand-craftsmanship has remained alive, even in industrial societies, and is now healthier than ever. In order to design many items, one must know how to design one item, so we turn now to a consideration of the unique object as a design challenge.

Unit Design

Many explanations have been given for the tremendous upsurge in all the crafts that occurred during the mid-20th century. Perhaps the most compelling sees a rebellion in the general public to consumer goods that are, on the one hand, exactly like the goods everybody else owns, and, on the other, cheaply—and often shoddily—made. A one-of-a-kind preindustrial product was not only unique but often lovingly and meticulously crafted. If it fell apart or had some flaw, the owner could go directly back to the maker and complain, which tended to minimize the occurrence of defective, insubstantial products. But it is difficult, at times impossible, for the lone consumer to establish communication with a giant industrial firm, and even when such contact bears fruit it is more likely to result in individual compensation than a change of procedures.

There is one more (seemingly contradictory) feature of industrial products that may have played a part in reviving interest in the handcrafts. In spite of a some-

above: 197. An upholstered armchair, side table, and desk set form a suite of *Craftsman* furniture, designed between 1898 and 1905 by Gustav Stickley. The lamps, made by San Francisco coppersmith Dirk van Erp, reveal the influence of Art Nouveau. (*Collection Mr. and Mrs. Terence Leichti, Hopewell, N.J.; photograph: Metropolitan Museum of Art*)

left: 198. The weavers of Appalachia have long been noted for their fine, meticulous work and love of pattern. This wool coverlet was handwoven in about 1920, but similar work is still being done today. (*Photograph: Alan W. Ashe; courtesy Southern Highland Handicraft Guild, Asheville, N.C. [Frances Goodrich Collection]*)

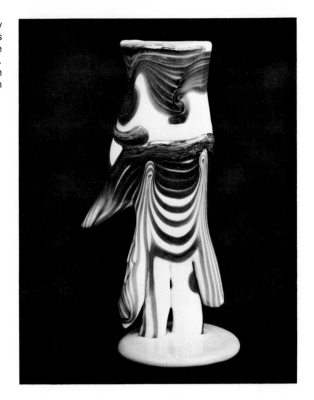

199. A hand-blown glass form by Joel Phillip Myers demonstrates how the traditional crafts have broken free of stereotyped forms. This piece is of white glass with silver and blue-green applied in a feathered technique.

times faulty construction, there is a kind of machined perfection about mass-produced objects that denies any touch of the human hand. Many precious handmade objects are treasured precisely because, in looking closely, we can see the tiny imperfections—the run of glaze on a ceramic pot, the mark of a tool on a piece of wooden furniture—that give evidence to the intervention of warm-blooded creatures. It might be said that, as a people, we seek perfection but we do not necessarily want to find it.

Most authorities trace the current craft revival to the writings of William Morris and to the ensuing Arts and Crafts Movement in England (see Chap. 25). In the United States a parallel movement, known as the Craftsman Style, resulted in such sturdy, well-made items as the suite in Figure 197. Contemporary furniture craftsmen like Wendell Castle (Figs. 188, 626) are in direct descendence from this tradition; while the styles have changed, the handcraft quality has not.

Further indices of the craft movement today can be seen in the textiles and other objects handmade by the mountain people of Appalachia (Fig. 198); in the serious attention given to all the conventional handcrafts, including ceramics, glassblowing, weaving, jewelry making, printmaking, and needlework (Fig. 199); in the design and fabrication of unique architectural members (Fig. 200); and ultimately in the creation of entire handmade houses (Figs. 5, 655).

The design process for any of these things will obviously be quite different from that involved in mass production. The individual craftsman has the time to test, develop, and evolve designs, because the span from initial conception through execution to use and evaluation is flexible. Relatively small amounts of money need be invested in a single object, so the designer is free to experiment and innovate. If a particular design fails, no real harm is done. By contrast, the large producer must invest many thousands or even millions of dollars in a new design and therefore cannot be too daring, because an unsuccessful product could spell disaster. Furthermore, the mass producer is always working months or years in advance, trying to guess what the consumer will want sometime far in the future.

200. Rough-hewn planks bolted to a tree trunk form a marvelous curving staircase that might be leading to a treehouse. (*Photograph: Barry Shapiro, from* Handmade Houses)

The individual craftsman normally works in direct contact with the consumer, and in response to mutually understood objectives.

If this whole discussion seems to suggest an innate superiority of handmade goods over those produced by machines, that impression is incorrect. We live in an industrial world, and there is no way this situation can be reversed. Machines can do many things that individual workers could not, and moreover they have brought within the reach of the majority of people a degree of comfort that could never be achieved by relying on painstakingly handmade goods. Perhaps the ultimate answer to the two-centuries-old love-hate relationship with industrialization is a dual one: to allow the machine to do what it does best and refrain from compelling it to do things it cannot, at the same time maintaining a climate for handcraftsmanship in areas where it cannot be excelled. This seems to be the direction in which design is now moving, but there are a number of other considerations that will help to shape design in the decades to come, and we might briefly try to anticipate what its general course will be.

Design for the Future

The Industrial Revolution focused attention on objects because, almost overnight it seemed, they could be made so easily. Emphasis was placed on objects as objects, as ends in themselves: what their functions were, what their forms should be, how these should be related to the materials used, eventually how they should relate to the people using them. But as objects multiplied, it became clear that their proliferation would not raise the general living standard, as had been hoped. In fact, increasing numbers of "things" seem actually to be lessening environmental standards for everyone. Objects of all sorts threaten to govern our behavior rather than enhance the overall quality of our lives.

Now designers in every field, from household equipment to huge urban developments, are beginning to ask, "Do we really need this?" Even if a new object is really an improvement over previous ones, we must consider how much energy it will consume, what servicing it will require, and how it will affect the environment as a whole. These concerns are particularly pressing in relation to the interior environment, because it touches upon every one of us.

According to some theorists, the interiors of the future will be more and more cleared of furniture. The French word for a piece of furniture, *meuble,* expresses the original definition of furniture as something movable. As we have seen however, the furnishings of the house have slowly been moving toward incorporation with its structure (Pl. 21, p. 161). Particularly in the bathroom and kitchen, almost everything is built in. Closets these days often encompass chests of drawers, and firepits may have built-in seating. Carpeted platform seating is essentially immobile, although it can be broken up into movable but permanent-looking pieces.

Italian designer Ettore Sottsass, Jr., envisions an interior environment composed of a series of movable boxes equipped to satisfy all our present needs: one would house a stove, another a refrigerator, still another a shower (Fig. 201). Beds, chairs, tables, and electronic equipment would all be in separate boxes that could be hooked up, moved around, added to, or discarded as desired. In the designer's words, "the idea of this environment of furniture on wheels is that through its neutrality and mobility, through being so amorphous and chameleonlike, through its ability to clothe any emotion without becoming involved in it, it may provoke a greater awareness of what is happening, and, above all, a greater awareness of our own creativity and freedom."[1]

Some designers conceive the whole habitat as a system of modular units to be combined with infinite variety. Component units housing equipment for all functions of living could also serve to separate the interior from the exterior

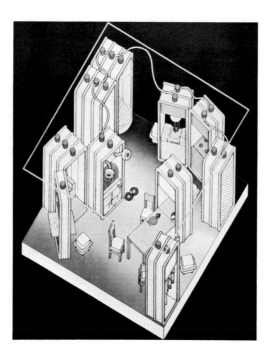

201. The huge plastic furniture boxes envisioned by Ettore Sottsass contain all the items that one needs for everyday living and move about easily on casters. The designer considers them more as a new way of thinking about furnishings than as actual prototypes to be built. (*Courtesy Centrokappa*)

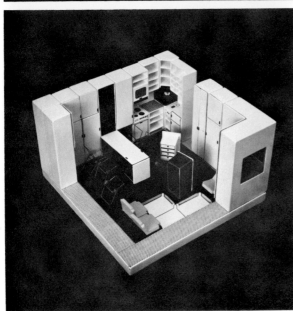

202. Modular design encompasses not only all the furnishings but even the enclosing walls of a lifespace in the vision of Italian designer Gianantonio Mari. All furniture and appliances can be folded up into the wall and floors to create a completely empty space, or various units can be opened up whenever they are needed for work, dining, sleeping, or relaxation.

environment (Fig. 202). The particular pieces of equipment needed for the various rituals of living could be opened up when needed and then folded up again into a section of floor, wall, or ceiling.

We have come a long way from the shaping of a primitive tool to the design of whole environments or even, what is not far in the future, of extraterrestrial structures (Fig. 729). In traveling this distance, we have begun to understand the implications of design. The hunter making a new tool seemed to affect only himself. Today we know that the creation of any object may have repercussions throughout the design continuum. The responsibility is enormous, and it remains to be seen how designers of the future will meet that challenge.

The Language of Design

8

Writers use words, mathematicians numbers, and musicians sounds to express their verbal, mathematical, and musical ideas. Literature is, of course, a refined coalescence of language preserved in durable form; but mathematics and music each have their own "languages," composed of symbols, words, and concepts that are as readily comprehensible to initiates as the letters of the alphabet would be to the layman.

In design, expression is achieved through organizing the elements of *space* and its counterpart *form*, of *line*, of *texture* and *ornament*, and of *color*. (The last of these, being highly specialized, forms the subject of an entire chapter.) Over the centuries designers, in putting these elements together, have evolved certain principles that help to explain why some designs are more successful—more functional and pleasing—than others. These principles include *balance, rhythm, emphasis, harmony, variety* and *unity, proportion* and *scale*. Taken all together, the elements and principles of design constitute its language.

The Elements of Design

Space

Space is the most vital element in home design. Simply by erecting walls we have enclosed a space, defined it, and articulated it. Painters often experience a kind of "block" when confronted with a pristine white canvas, writers when facing a pure white sheet of paper in the typewriter. The first mark on canvas, the first letter struck represents an enormous commitment and the establishment of all sorts of relationships. So it is with space, but to an infinitely greater degree. We deal with the mechanism of articulating space thousands of times during the day without realizing it. In placing an object on a surface, we are not filling a void but carving out sections of space around the object. Before a structure is built, the space it will occupy exists as a continuous, diffuse entity; the construction of walls and a roof isolates two segments of space—that inside the structure and that outside.

Space suggests the possibility of change, of freedom to move bodily, visually, or psychologically until we collide with or are diverted by a barrier. The element of *time* also plays an important role in our perception of architecture, for unless

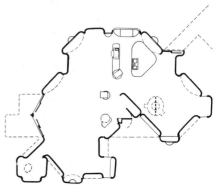

204. The plan shows how group spaces, clustered in the center of the house, lead outward toward increasingly private areas, culminating in small seclusion nooks.

203–204. Under the direction of Professor Felix Drury, a group of students at Yale University designed this house as an exercise in space planning.

above: 203. As a view of the kitchen-dining area shows, various spaces are demarcated by supports and configurations in the architecture, as well as by placement of built-in furniture. There are no "rooms" as such. The building material throughout was urethane foam, covered on floors, walls, and furniture with Acrilan Plus carpeting. (*Courtesy Monsanto Textiles Company*)

the space is very small, we cannot perceive it all at once, but must move through bit by bit, gradually accumulating impressions, until a sense of the whole has been assembled. In walking through a sensitively designed space like that in Figure 203, we participate in its expansion and contraction as naturally as we breathe. Space becomes a space-time continuum, because it changes constantly as we move.

This house, designed by several students at Yale University under the direction of Professor Felix Drury, was intended as an investigation into the question of organizing space. As an underlying concept the group resolved that there should be no rooms as such but merely spaces, very open and expansive at the center, then reaching out in many directions to the out-of-doors and to more sheltered and private areas, ending ultimately in very sequestered "nest" spaces (Fig. 204). Such a plan seems a logical extension of Frank Lloyd Wright's vision of organic architecture, as expressed in the Robie house (Fig. 825).

As we move through an organic space such as this, our eyes, our bodies, and our spirits explore its constantly changing contours—that which is open and that which is closed. Everyone recognizes the sense of exhilaration felt upon emerging from a forest into a meadow or walking across an open plaza in a city. Architects and city planners always have understood the drama implicit in passing from a constricted space to an expansive one. Entrance to the great urban plazas—the Piazza San Marco in Venice, the Zócalo in Mexico City, St. Peter's Square in Rome—typically is gained through narrow, congested streets, thus magnifying the element of surprise and delight upon reaching the square.

Splendid as these open spaces are, most people feel a need to return periodically to sheltered spaces that enclose and protect. We respond to the spaces that envelop and include us, and we adapt to them. In doing so, we share their triumphs or failures. The merging of open and closed spaces represents one of the hallmarks of modern architecture. Instead of sequences of boxed rooms, cut off from view of one another, we find spaces that flow together, expanding and contracting as the need arises.

The house designed at Yale is obviously a one-of-a-kind endeavor, but many of the same concerns can be seen in conventional, much less expensive housing. The "Unbox" (Fig. 205) is a modular house consisting of preassembled units that can be trucked along the highway, then lifted into position at the home site. As the name implies, however, this house overcomes the stereotype of tedious cube

right: Plate 20. A pristine white room with much built-in furniture has as its striking focal point a bed covered in a gaily printed spread of red, yellow, and black. The almost shocking color seems to float in a light, airy sea of white. Richard Meier, architect. See page 148; see also Plate 26, p. 180. (*Photograph: Ezra Stoller* © *ESTO*)

below: Plate 21. Nearly all major furniture in this modern home is built in. The long sofa unit incorporates table-storage sections at either end, a built-in fireplace has display recesses to one side, and even the dining table at right seems a part of the architecture. Colorful accessories, however—scatter pillows, flowers and plants—prevent the effect from seeming cold. Charles Gwathmey, architect. See page 157; see also Fig. 522. (*Photograph: Ezra Stoller* © *ESTO*)

left: Plate 22. This elegant three-story living space is conceived almost entirely in rectangles, with virtually no curves or diagonals. Even within the neutral color scheme, however, the result is not boring because of changes in size, shape, and progression. Paul Rudolph, architect. See page 167; see also Fig. 27; Plate 28, p. 197; Plate 61, p. 454. (*Photograph: Ezra Stoller* © *ESTO*)

below: Plate 23. A strong pattern of triangles in black and white echoes the colors that predominate in this room but provides a refreshing change of shape. Robert Fitzpatrick, owner-architect. See page 169; see also Fig. 480. (*Photograph: Ezra Stoller* © *ESTO*)

upon cube we tend to associate with such structures. Spaces flow into one another, opening both vertically and horizontally to meet specific needs throughout the home. The large living room, part of which is two-story, merges with the dining area (Fig. 205), but the two spaces attain a suggestion of separateness because of the second-floor walkway connecting the bedrooms. The multipurpose den (Fig. 206) is contiguous with both the large entry hall and the kitchen. As the plan shows (Fig. 207), there are no real "rooms" on the main floor (except, of course, for the bathroom), but instead a progression of spaces partially demarcated by half-walls, cut-ins in the external structure, and the second-floor bridge. Each area, then—living, dining, kitchen, hall, and den—gains additional space by borrowing from its neighbors. That all this could be accomplished within the limits of modular construction is a triumph of design.

The two most obvious and common space problems in homes are a lack of space and a surfeit thereof. Both conditions, however, tend to indicate an unwise *use* of the available space, rather than an unmanageable number of cubic feet. Row houses typically have been among the worst offenders in terms of cramped, awkward space. Long and narrow, several stories high, such houses as originally built had a series of rooms arranged railroad-car fashion from front to back on each floor. Since the house was usually one room wide, the internal space would resemble a single line of building blocks. We have already seen one example of

205–207. A prefabricated modular house dispels many of the typical impressions we associate with mass-produced housing, thus earning its name of "Unbox." John Sampieri, architect.

above left: 205. Diagonal sight lines have been used to counteract the essentially square format of the house, allowing the inhabitants to both see and move freely beyond the confines of any group space. (*Photograph: Maris/Semel, and House Beautiful*)

top right: 206. Just as in the living-dining area (Fig. 205), diagonal lines open up the relatively small all-purpose den plus entry. (*Photograph: Maris/Semel, and House Beautiful*)

above right: 207. The plan illustrates the way in which just a few irregularities in outline contribute to the flexible space within.

how contemporary renovators have dealt with this situation (Figs. 30, 31). The row house shown in Figure 208 confronts the problem of space both inside and outside. On the lower two floors the brick façade has been almost totally removed to create window walls; sliding glass doors on the first floor merge the inside spaces with the garden. The third floor has a semicircular balcony that both extends the internal space and breaks up the outside space, so that the long, flat rectangle of the façade takes on sculptural presence. Within the house, spaces are articulated by partial walls, and the whole is brightly lighted and painted in light colors to give the illusion of greater space.

At the opposite extreme, the barn shown in Figure 209 could be considered cavernous. As originally purchased, it was one huge undifferentiated space, of a quality that could make humans feel insignificant and threatened. We all appreciate the soaring, ennobling spaces of cathedrals and similar public buildings, but few of us would want to live in them. Here the need is for a delineation of space, to make it seem more personal and intimate. Several devices have been employed

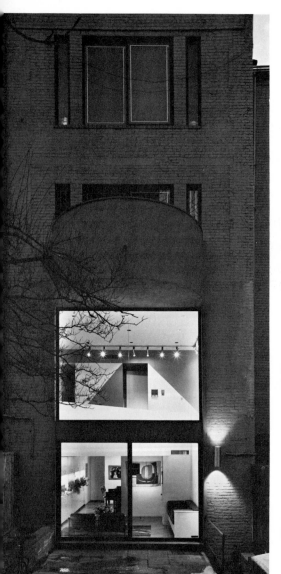

left: 208. In remodeling a typical city house, architects Stephen Lepp & Associates gained both actual space, by opening the interior through glass doors to a ground floor terrace and upper balcony; and the visual illusion of space through a large window wall in the second floor. See also Fig. 644. (*Photograph: David Hirsch*)

below: 209. Owners Roger and Constance Kenna introduced human scale into the overscaled space of a barn by treating the walls in horizontal strips that relate to normal head heights. The large, mirrored wardrobe, which also gives a ''sense of scale,'' is another step in the sequence down to the people who will inhabit the space. See also Fig. 615. (*Photograph: John T. Hill*)

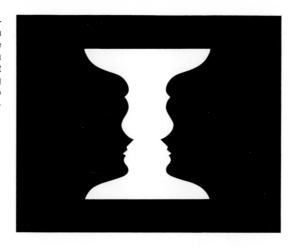

210. This classic visual device reverses constantly, depending upon how we focus our eyes. At one glance it is a white column on a black background; at another it shows two female profiles facing each other. Such tools help us to broaden our concepts of the relationship between space and form.

to achieve that goal. By leaving the structural posts and beams exposed, by painting some of the resultant panels light and some dark, by cutting windows into the massive walls, the owners created a patchwork pattern that breaks up the space. A bedroom balcony along one wall utilizes the extreme height of the room without diminishing its grandeur. A row of plants on the balcony and others scattered through the room also help to humanize its scale.

Space is among the most important elements of home design. Unless it is thoughtfully planned, nothing else will ever seem quite right. Yet almost any space, if sensitively handled, can be made effective, livable, even dramatic.

Form and Shape

Form is the counterpart of space, its three-dimensional structure, a limiting of infinity into human scale. Except for purposes of analysis, the two are inseparable, because form gives space whatever dimension it has, and space reveals, even determines form. The largest space—such as we would experience in the middle of the ocean or the desert—has form, for the horizon seems a circular line where sky and earth meet. The sky then becomes for us a dome, confining the limitless expanse of space into manageable proportions. Usually, form seems more constant and permanent than space, which implies the possibility of change and the infinity of space-time.

Form and *shape* are two terms often used interchangeably, both as nouns and as verbs: indeed, we have so used them in this book. But in the purest descriptive sense, subtle differences do distinguish them. *Shape,* the simpler of the two, refers to the measurable, identifiable contours of an object, generally expressed in relation to its outlines. We speak of a square shape, a round shape, a cubic shape, and so on. A much more inclusive term, *form* takes account of shape but may also encompass substance (solid or liquid form), internal structure, and even the idea implicit in shape. Two other terms associated with form and shape deserve definition. *Area* refers to the two-dimensional extent of a shape, such as the floor area of a house or the wall area of a room. *Plane* is a two-dimensional shape, which in today's usage has come to imply a spatial form that is an active force, such as the wall planes of the Unbox (Fig. 205).

In our discussion of interior design, we might do well to consider form and shape on two different levels. Form is best understood in relation to space, as the classic column-profiles silhouette (Fig. 210) illustrates. Looking at the drawing one way, we see the form of a Greek-style column with space on either side of it; when we allow the drawing to reverse, we see the forms of two female profiles with space between them. If we permit our perceptions to expand, we can apply the same

right: 211. Architect Wendell H. Lovett calls attention to the composition of geometric shapes in this house by outlining them in decisive colors. The window in the far wall illustrates the excitement generated by poising such a simple shape as a square on one corner, and then further emphasizing it by supergraphics. See also Figs. 483, 547. (*Photograph: Christian Staub*)

below: 212. In contrast to the house shown in Figure 211, this living room makes a serene counterpoint of rectangular shapes emphasized principally by their own light and color. Donald E. Olsen, architect. See also Figs. 394, 395. (*Photograph: Ronald Partridge*)

kinds of interrelationships to the home. The act of putting a chair into an empty room affects both the form and the space. When a second chair is added to the room, *both* forms and the space will be affected. The objects with which we fill our homes are not isolated, self-contained things but forms that relate to each other and to the spaces they articulate.

The more tangible element, shape is easier to understand and define. Despite the infinite diversity of shapes in our world, all can basically be categorized as *rectilinear, angled,* or *curved.* In their purest expression, these shapes become the geometric figures of rectangle, triangle, and circle; or in solid form cube, pyramid, and sphere. The circle often occurs in nature, the triangle occasionally, the square or rectangle rarely. Yet so perfect are these shapes, so satisfying in their completeness, that they serve as the basis for every kind of design, from massive buildings and the layout of whole cities down through the smallest implement. Geometric shapes are most obvious in the overall contours of things: buildings tend to be square or rectangular, sometimes with round components; bowls, dishes, and other household effects typically are round; streets are laid out in squared grid patterns, sometimes with triangular "islands" at points of convergence. This list could go on indefinitely. Today, however, designers are applying geometric forms to domestic architecture in new ways. Dramatic angles, unexpected planes, sculptured space, and architectural cutouts characterize some of the most innovative designs for interiors (Fig. 211). Where previously the circle, the triangle, and the square represented stability and repose, today's geometry provides an exciting freedom and a whole new concept for shaping internal space.

Not every shape, of course, is identifiable as a pure circle, square, or triangle; but every shape contains one or more of these elements, so we can discuss objects in terms of the predominant shapes and investigate the ways in which these shapes can be combined.

Rectilinear Shapes   The living room shown in Plate 22 (p. 162) is composed almost entirely of rectangles; its overall shape, the balconies ringing its perimeters, the steps leading up, the seating platforms, and individual pieces of furniture—all are pure rectangles. Yet although we have an overall impression of repose and order, there is no monotony. Variations of size and placement bring sufficient complexity to prevent us from being bored, even within the neutral color scheme. The solid plane of one towering white wall contrasts with the other three, which are cut with balconies, and a staggered pattern of steps offsets the side-by-side regularity of the seating platforms. Taken all together, this room is a virtuoso performance in design with shape.

Also based on a theme of rectangles, the room in Figure 212 seems more complex, somewhat less tranquil. Much diversity comes from variations of size and placement in the rectangles, but in this case contrasts of color have also been added. The dark squares of furniture, fireplace, stereo components, and storage recesses stand out against the flat white walls and neutral floor; the latter in turn are highlighted by illuminated cutouts and recesses. Three distinct gradations of color animate the rectangular format to bring the room to life.

As we have seen, when the rectangle or square is placed on end, it ceases to be restful and becomes a dynamic element (Fig. 211). In sum, then, rectilinear shapes can create very different effects and call forth a variety of emotional responses from the people who see them depending upon size, placement, color and orientation.

That rectangularity is typical of the larger spaces and forms in today's homes is evident in all but a few of the illustrations in this book. It prevails not only in entire houses and rooms but in such furniture as beds, tables, storage units, and television sets, plus many sofas, chairs, and benches, even putting in an appearance in smaller artifacts and textiles (Fig. 213). Among the reasons for this widespread acceptance, we might note that rectangles:

213. In "Quadrangle," designer Jack Lenor Larsen has expanded the elementary shape of the square to create a subtle but intriguing pattern by recessing the squares in deeper pile and using eight variations of weave and color.

□ Are easily handled on designers' drafting boards, by carpenters and masons on the site, and by machines in factories

□ Fit snugly together—an important factor when multitudinous elements coming from many sources are assembled on the job and when space is becoming increasingly expensive

□ Have a sturdy, secure relationship of exactly 90 degrees, which gives a sense of definiteness and certainty

□ Establish an incipient unity and rhythm when repeated

The qualities of clarity, stability, and certainty that combine to make rectilinear forms popular can also bring a harsh, boxlike monotony that many people deplore.

above: 214. In a home set into a natural woodland, a theme of triangularity echoes some of the shapes apparent in the branching tree trunks, but it brings an unmistakable human order. The sizing of triangular shapes—from the sheltering roof through the unusual fireplace configuration down to the pattern in the Oriental rug—makes a satisfying design progression. Thompson and Peterson, architects. See also Figs. 263, 646. (*Photograph: Morley Baer*)

left: 215. A massive triangular ceiling highlights this house, which was originally a cow shed, causing unusual angles to be produced in the fireplace and other internal elements. John Rawlings and James McNair, designers. See also Fig. 624. (*Photograph: John T. Hill*)

When handled imaginatively, however, the right angle has a pure, strong, absolute character—its own quality of beauty.

Angular Shapes   Triangles and pyramids differ from rectangles in their pointed, dynamic character. Among the most common angular elements in contemporary homes are the sloping rooflines that introduce a note of variety and surprise to the basic room cube. The living room in Figure 214 has a sharply angled ceiling, its shape echoed in the triangular fireplace and hearth jutting into the space. While remaining stable and welcoming, this room takes on life and spirit with the inclusion of dramatic angles.

From a structural point of view, triangles are among the most stable forms known, since their shape cannot be altered without breaking or bending one or more sides. Still, they express greater flexibility than rectangles, because the angles can be varied to suit the need. For example, the triangles formed by the legs of standard folding chairs (Fig. 206) can, with a flick of the wrist, be transformed from stable support to space-saving linearity. Used with discretion and in large size, as in the ceiling or gable end of a pitched-roof house, triangles are secure yet dynamic. Small repeated triangles or diamond shapes in textiles, tiles or wallpaper add briskness to interiors (Pl. 23, p. 162), while a three-sided table between two chairs sets up a congenial relationship. Diagonals generally increase apparent size; because angular shapes imply motion and are relatively uncommon, they usually attract and hold attention beyond what their actual dimensions would otherwise suggest (Fig. 215).

Curved Shapes   Curves bring together the lively combination of continuity and constant change. They remind us sympathetically of flowers, trees, clouds, and our own bodies. Until recently, large curvilinear elements, such as circular rooms, domed or vaulted ceilings, and curved stairways, have been rare in contemporary houses, but there is increasing interest in their possibilities (Figs. 115, 654).

The house illustrated in Figure 216 (see also Fig. 382) owes its great rounded spaces and sinuous curves to the owner's fascination with seashells. This is design

216. A fascinating mixture of straight and curved, geometric and amorphous shapes makes this house in Mexico a constant but ever-changing sequence of delights. G. E. Arenas, architect. See also Fig. 382. (*Photograph: Julius Shulman*)

inspired by nature, but abstracted to a high degree so that forms are compatible with architectural integrity. The roofline and walls are steeply angled, but we would be hard-pressed to find a simple rectangle anywhere in the house, so plastic and sculptural is its quality. Nevertheless, we sense a stability, because in spirit as well as in shape this delightful home recalls its source: Just as the tiny sea animal is protected by its shell, so would the inhabitants of this embracing home feel secure.

Circles and spheres have a unique complex of qualities:

☐ They are nature's most conservative and economical forms, since they not only enclose the greatest area or volume with the least amount of surface but strongly resist breakage and other damage.
☐ Although as rigidly defined geometrically as squares or cubes, they do not seem so static, probably because we cannot forget that balls and wheels roll easily.
☐ They have an unequaled unity, for every point on the edge or surface is equidistant from the center—a natural focal point, especially when accented.

Inside our homes, circles and spheres are most noticeable in plates (Fig. 217), bowls and vases, lampshades and pillows, and in a few tables, chairs, and stools. They also form the basic motif in many textiles, wallpapers, and floor coverings. Curvilinear forms seem particularly appropriate for fabrics, especially those meant to be hung, for the sinuous curves only enhance the quality of draping (Fig. 218).

Cones and cylinders, too, are curvilinear shapes, but they entail a definite, directional movement not found in circles or spheres. While cones and cylinders resemble each other, there is an important difference: Cones, like pyramids, reach toward a climactic terminal peak, whereas cylinders, like rectangles, could continue forever. This makes cones more emphatic and directs attention to a focal point. Both forms please us, because they relate to our own arms and legs. They frequently serve as the vertical supports of furniture, as lamp bases and shades, candleholders, and vases. Furniture legs of wood or metal often take the form of truncated cones, tapering toward the top or bottom for visual lightness and grace.

left: 217. Partial circles arching across this plate emphasize its roundness, thus creating the illusion of a sphere. Otto Piene, designer. (*Courtesy Rosenthal Studio-Haus*)

right: 218. A series of gossamer strips with curvilinear designs, hung in two parallel lines, change in response to the slightest air movement. This art fabric, by Gerhardt Knodel, could act as a room divider or window treatment, yet it remains a creative work in its own right.

Combining Shapes   Rarely do we find a home composed entirely of rectangles, triangles, or circles. The living room in Plate 22 is a notable exception. Instead, most interiors reveal a combination of shapes chosen to balance and counterpoint one another. Figure 219 illustrates a beautiful example of this. In outline an arrangement of boxes within boxes, the room carries out the rectangular theme in floor tiles, rug, storage wall, and some of the furniture. The ceiling, however, is angled up toward the center, with the narrow boards that form its surface emphasizing this angularity where they converge. The walls of the balcony slope upward to meet this pitch. Contained within an interior box, a spiral staircase curves upward to the balcony, and round wicker furniture echoes its contour. Were we to enter such a room, we probably would not consider it in terms of geometric shapes, but simply be aware of a pleasing juxtaposition of forms that achieve unity together. The essence of combining shapes lies not in seeing how many one can include but in making them work together. And in doing so, we can never forget that *shapes* inevitably draw *lines,* which introduces another element of design.

219. A few curved shapes usually bring some welcome relief to our predominently rectangular homes. In this living room they soften the many straight lines, promising adaptation to our own rounded contours. Francis Mah, architect. See also Plate 30, p. 198. (*Photograph: Alexandre Georges*)

left: 220. In this living room, especially as viewed from a high angle, lines become a dominant theme. Thin broken lines in the tile floor progress to definite lines in the area rug and then to the more substantial linear shapes of the posts and beams. Even the African wood sculpture on the fireplace is mainly a composition of lines rather than of mass. Julian Neski and Barbara Neski, architects. (Courtesy Hastings Tile Co., Inc.)

below: 221. Lines serve as a dominant theme in this wooden terrace. The spacing of floor boards to allow drainage creates lines that carry up through the more closely spaced fence boards to the solid roof. The whole is accented by the more open, trellislike effect of the structural supports and the safety railing. (Photograph: Harold Davis)

Line

Theoretically, line has only one dimension, since by definition it is the extension of a point; but in practice, lines can be thick or thin. In interior design, the word line is frequently used to describe the outlines of a form or space, or the dominant direction, as when the "lines" of furniture or of houses are said to be pleasing. But line has a more concrete meaning when it serves to ornament or accentuate

a form. In Figure 220 the rough wood beams draw lines within the overall space of a huge living room. Without question, though, the most striking element in the room is an area rug placed squarely in the center. Strong, dominant lines in contrasting colors are its only motif, and these naturally lead the eye from the fireplace to the sofa and back again. We can find other, more subtle lines in the pattern of floor tiles, the upward thrust of the chimney pipe, and the outlines of doors and windows.

Lines can act either to emphasize or to deemphasize shapes. In Figure 221 a long, narrow terrace has been made to seem even longer because of the lines formed by floor and ceiling boards laid parallel to its length. Had it been desirable to stress the outward thrust of the terrace, rather than its extent, the boards might have been laid crosswise, thus directing the eye out into space.

Textiles make a natural exponent of line, since the warp and weft yarns are themselves lines. When closely woven, textiles absorb the lines, but an openwork fabric such as the one illustrated in Figure 222 gives ample evidence of its linear structure.

Among the most expressive qualities of line is its direction. In studying the ways in which direction affects our feelings and our movements, psychologists and artists have come to such generalizations as the following:

□ **Vertical lines** imply a stabilized resistance to gravity. If high enough, they evoke feelings of aspiration and ascendancy.
□ **Horizontals** tend to be restful and relaxing, especially when long. Short and interrupted horizontals become a series of dashes.
□ **Diagonals** are comparatively more active in that they suggest movement and dynamism.
□ **Big upward curves** are uplifting and inspiring.
□ **Horizontal curves** connote gentleness and relaxed movement.
□ **Large downward curves,** seldom seen in homes, express a range of feelings, including seriousness and sadness. They may, however, bring a welcome sense of solidity and attachment to the earth.
□ **Small curves** suggest playfulness and humor (Fig. 223).

As interpreted for home design, these generalizations recommend that verticals be emphasized—high ceilings, tall doors and windows, upright furniture—for a feeling of loftiness and cool assurance; horizontals—low ceilings, broad openings, stretched-out furniture—for an impression of informal comfort; diagonals—sloping ceilings, oblique walls or furniture—for an environment that speaks of activity. Usually, several or all of these lines are brought together at varying levels of dominance and subordination so that the total effect seems varied and complete.

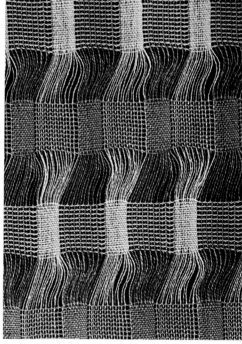

above: **222.** In "Gossamer," a leno weave fabric of long silky wool fibers, the lines produced by the yarns between the woven areas form a major design element. (*Courtesy Jack Lenor Larsen, Inc.*)

left: **223.** This silver-plated wire basket is composed entirely of lines in a sweeping double curve. Lino Sabattini, designer. (*Photograph: Ciceri*)

The Language of Design **173**

far left: 224. Designer Patricia Jorgenson used a variety of tactile textures as theme and variation in the design of an all-wool rug produced by a hand-tufting process. (*Courtesy V'Soske, Inc.*)

left: 225. The simulated textures in "Hudson Quilt" can be very lively in visual terms, because we know from experience that such fabrics are usually smooth to the touch. (*Courtesy Schumacher*)

226. The play of textures against each other—smooth against rough, tactile against visual—sets the dominant character of a large group space. Myron Goldfinger, architect. (*Photograph: Norman McGrath, courtesy Hastings Tile Co., Inc.*)

Texture and Ornament

Referring to the surface qualities of materials, texture describes how they feel when we touch them. Ornament, a somewhat broader term, relates to the decorative qualities visible on the surface of things. The two elements are closely related, because texture can serve as a kind of ornament, and ornament usually provides some texture. Every surface has a texture that affects us physically and aesthetically, but only when texture is consciously manipulated to beautify an object do we call it ornament.

Texture A distinction is often made between *actual* or *tactile* textures, in which the three-dimensional surface qualities can be felt, as in bricks and woolen tweeds or hammered metal; and *visual* textures (sometimes called illusionary or simulated), in which a material reveals a textural pattern under a smooth surface. The two fabrics shown in Figures 224 and 225 illustrate this difference. Several different levels of texture appear in the hand-tufted rug (Fig. 224), ranging from almost smooth through pebbled and fuzzy to very shaggy. Even without touching the rug, we know how soft it would feel and can perceive the gradations of texture. Moreover, the differences in pattern and direction within the rug create a texture of their own, which we would experience if we were to run a hand over its surface. By contrast, the screen-printed quilt fabric in Figure 225, although it seems to have a very complex texture, is perfectly smooth to the touch. Texture results from a translation of one sensory experience—touch—into another—vision.

The effectiveness of a texture is a matter of relationships between forms, colors, and the textures themselves. A decided tactile texture will be more obvious against a uniform surface than it will against a rough one. In home design texture plays an extremely important role in creating interest and variety, as the house illustrated in Figure 226 demonstrates. We can distinguish at least four different levels of texture here: the absolutely smooth surface of walls, ceiling, fireplace, and built-in furniture; the rougher textures of old wood and natural bricks; the soft plushness of upholstery fabrics and handwoven pillows; and the very delicate, almost frothy texture of plants and flowers. All these are judiciously distributed to provide pleasing contrasts as the eye moves back and forth through the space. One unusual application of texture contrasts can be seen on the balcony, where the antique hoist—a complex assemblage of gears, wheels, and pulleys—stands out against the plain white ceiling.

Texture affects us in a number of ways, all of which are reflected in the house just described. *First,* it brings a physical impression of everything we touch. Upholstery fabrics, for example, if coarse and harsh, can be actually irritating. If too sleek, they look and feel slippery and cold. The most popular fabrics tend to be neither excessively rough nor smooth. *Second,* texture influences light reflection and thus the appearance of any form. Very smooth materials—polished metal, glass, or satin—reflect light brilliantly, attracting attention and making their colors look clear and strong. Moderately rough surfaces, such as the brick floor in Figure 226, absorb light unevenly; hence their colors look less bright. Very rough surfaces set up vigorous patterns of light and dark, as can be seen especially in the plants. *Third,* texture is a factor in household maintenance. The shiny surfaces of brightly polished metal or glass are easy to clean but show everything foreign; rougher surfaces, such as bricks or rugs with high pile, call less attention to foreign matter but are harder to clean; and smooth surfaces with visual textures combine most of the good qualities of both. *Finally,* texture is a source of both beauty and character.

Ornament Many people distinguish two major types of ornament: structural and applied. *Structural* ornament comes from the intrinsic character of the materials, the way in which they are fabricated, or the sensitivity with which the object and each of its parts is shaped. It encompasses such sources as the natural beauty of wood grain or the qualities of silk or linen; textures and patterns originating in the weaving process or in the laying of a brick floor; the deliberate design and shaping of objects beyond utilitarian or structural demands so that they provide visual and tactile pleasure. Structural ornament inheres in the object it enriches; it seems natural and fundamental. Usually, it is less subject to physical deterioration, such as breakage or fading, and is less likely to go out of fashion than is applied ornament.

Applied ornament refers to that added to an object after it is structurally complete, such as patterns printed on cloth or wallpaper, carved moldings on walls, or designs etched on glass. Only two factors limit its range: the nature of the materials and the imagination and taste of the designer. Applied ornament can be admirably suited to an object's use, form, and materials—or it can be distressingly inappropriate. The most satisfying ornament fits the functions, form, size, and material of which it is a part, being, moreover, worthwhile in itself. Specifically, ornament should be:

□ Pleasant to feel, especially if it is touched frequently. Resting one's arms or back against sharp carving on a chair or handling angular silverware can be physically uncomfortable.
□ Supportive of the form it enriches. Ornament generally is at its best when it accentuates the particular quality of the object of which it is a part.
□ Related to the size, scale, and character of the form.
□ Appropriate to the material. Fine, linear decoration can be effective on smooth, light-reflecting metal or glass, whereas on wood it might look merely scratchy.
□ Vital in itself. Spirit and character are as crucial in ornament as in the design of form and space.

The stemware in Figure 227 embodies all these criteria. Taking the form of a delicate, perfect flower poised on a striated stem, these glasses contrast the pure, unadorned transparency of crystal against the overlapping pattern that is possible with molten glass. Beyond its decorative capacities, the textured pattern in the stem actually enhances function, since it provides a better grip. The ornament, while rich, has a light, linear quality in keeping with the size and fragility of the glasses, and it leads the eye upward to the expanding volume of the bowl.

Attitudes toward ornament, especially toward applied ornament, vary from one period to another; a glance at Chapters 21 through 25 will demonstrate this. In contemporary design two seemingly contradictory viewpoints are evident: on the one hand a distaste for any kind of applied ornament, with emphasis on keeping design clean and "minimal" (Fig. 21); on the other a great delight in ornament, especially as provided by old furnishings and handcrafted objects (Fig. 20). The quality that will be stressed in each home depends upon the tastes, personalities, and lifestyle of the occupants.

Our discussion of space, form, shape, line, texture, and ornament has necessarily been rather abstract, isolating one quality at a time for analysis. In practice, however, these elements are so closely interwoven that each reacts upon the others. To understand how these elements are combined, we must turn to the principles underlying successful design.

227. Ornament growing naturally out of the material, form, and function enhances these crystal goblets in a unique pattern. Pavel Hlava, designer. (*Courtesy Rosenthal Studio-Haus*)

Principles of Design

In the search for ways to create functional and pleasing objects, certain principles have become almost self-evident. They are observable in nature and in art. Balance, rhythm, and emphasis—a simple but inclusive trio of principles—explain why some combinations of space and form, of line and texture seem to work better and to look better than others. To these we might add such concepts as harmony, proportion, scale, variety, and unity. No one can set absolute rules for the creation of effective design. Indeed, some of the most striking designs seem deliberately to violate theoretical principles. But the qualities discussed below do serve as guidelines.

Balance

Defined as equilibrium, balance is a major principle in all phases of living, from furniture arrangements to bank accounts. Through balance we get a sense of equipoise, but this may range from static permanence through repose and from suspended animation to actual motion. Balance results when interplaying forces, attractions, or weights tend toward resolution.

Nature provides many examples of divergent kinds of balance. The Rock of Gibraltar typifies static permanence, with changes too slight to be noticed. Sand dunes are continuously shifting, but without loss of equilibrium. Trees, too, are always changing equilibrium, because their shapes vary as they grow and because winds and the seasons affect them. Thus, balance can be an ever-changing resolution of forces as well as an equalization of deadweights. It is also evident from nature that balance exists in four dimensions—time as well as length, breadth, and width.

In balancing an interior, we deal with the "visual weights" of architecture and furnishings. The visual weight of anything is determined by the psychological impact it makes on us. Objects of large size or of such physically heavy material as stone command respect. Bright colors or strong contrasts of all sorts are quickly noticed and vividly remembered. Elaborate detail arouses interest, while anything unusual or unexpected has an importance beyond its size. At the other pole, the small, the somber, the harmonious, or the typical usually settles into the background. For example, a small spot of bright color can balance a large grayed area; visually, a significant painting may be as "heavy" as many square feet of plain wall. Well-balanced interiors hold this interplay of forces in poise.

Balance in a home is as ever-changing as is nature's equilibrium, but in different ways. People are the first factor, for a room is never complete except when being used (Figs. 509, 510). As people walk about, they not only see a home from different angles but actually change the equilibrium by their movement and by the clothes they wear. The second factor is light. Natural illumination is altering every minute of the day and changes markedly with sky conditions and the seasons. Only within small limits can its effects be controlled, yet it affects our homes drastically. For example, subtle nuances of color and very fine detail can be readily appreciated in moderately bright light, but they are all but obscured in very strong sunlight or at dusk. Artificial light can be precisely controlled but has to be flexible to meet a number of needs, and flexibility brings variance. The third factor is the composite of all the little things that happen in the course of a day (the reading material and other portable paraphernalia brought in and left) as well as the modifications that come with the months and years (the scarcely noticed fading of textiles and mellowing of wood, to say nothing of the replacement of outworn or unwanted objects). What does all this mean? Simply that in view of these inevitable changes, many of them beyond our strict control, the fundamental pattern of equilibrium should be strong enough to take these onslaughts in stride, to gain from, rather than be destroyed by them.

It is customary to differentiate three types of balance: *symmetrical, asymmetrical,* and *radial.*

228. An almost perfectly symmetrical balance gives serenity to this very elegant sitting room, with furniture, paintings, and lamps reversing around an imaginary axis at the center. The occasional chair and stool to one side, plus the T'ang horse on the coffee table, prevent the composition from being totally static. (*Photograph: John T. Hill*)

Symmetrical Balance   Also known as formal or passive balance, symmetrical balance (Fig. 228) is achieved when one side of something is the exact reverse (or mirror image) of the other half. Our clothes, furniture, and household equipment are nearly all symmetrical to fit our symmetrical bodies. Such balance is easy to appreciate, because we can see quickly that, since one side is the reversed replica of the other, the two must be in equilibrium. The effect is typically quiet and reposed, perhaps because it demands little effort from the observer. Its overtones of stateliness and dignity are not easy to explain, but certainly people stand or sit as symmetrically as they comfortably can when they wish to appear dignified and in control. Symmetrical balance tends to stress the center, creating a logical focal point for something one wishes to emphasize. But the resultant division into two equal parts usually reduces apparent size.

Although the above observations are generally true of symmetrical balance as used in homes, we should note that totally different effects are possible. Violent rhythms or swirling curves, regardless of symmetrical arrangement, will not seem quiet or reposed. Shapes or colors that lead the eyes away from the middle weaken the focal point at the center.

Basically, symmetrical balance is as simple as *aba,* the pattern from which it is derived, and this simplicity contributes to its popularity. While very easy to handle at an elementary level, it can be imaginative, subtle, and complex. Few entire homes or even single rooms are completely symmetrical—utility and the need for variety rule this out—but many have such symmetrical parts as centered fireplaces or identical sofas or chairs facing each other. Often, however, symmetry is imposed arbitrarily or comes out of habit or laziness when it is not appropriate. Then it can lead to inconvenience or dullness. For example, doors in centers of walls are seldom logical because they leave two equal areas that may be difficult to furnish unless the room is very large.

above: Plate 24. This living room was planned in such a way that the view through large window walls to the rocky hillside outdoors became the dominant element. Works of art and the fireplace attract our attention next, while the furnishings, flooring, and ceiling are subdued. Keith Kroeger and Leonard Perfido, architects. See page 185. (*Photograph: Maris/Semel*)

left: Plate 25. An imaginatively painted arched panel, done in colors and shapes that suggest a brilliant sunrise, enlivens an otherwise dark, wood-paneled room. Painting by Bill Tapley. See page 185. (*Photograph: Robert Perron*)

above: Plate 26. The pure primary colors of red, yellow, and blue are seldom combined in homes, but here their bold use—together with bright green, a secondary color—brings to life a very streamlined kitchen and entry. Richard Meier, architect. See page 192; see also Plate 20, p. 161. (*Photograph: Ezra Stoller* © *ESTO*)

left: Plate 27. In a stucco pool house, one huge wall panel painted in swirls of red and yellow conceals the shower area. The warm colors and bold design set against an off-white background make the panel seem even larger than it is. Charles Moore, architect. See page 193. (*Photograph: Ezra Stoller* © *ESTO*)

Symmetry is indicated *but not dictated* when:

□ Formal or reposed effects are desirable
□ The designer wishes to focus attention on something important
□ Use suggests symmetry
□ Contrast with natural surroundings is a factor

Asymmetrical Balance   Also referred to as informal, active, or occult balance, asymmetry results when the visual weights are equivalent but not identical (Fig. 229). This is the principle of the lever or seesaw—weight multiplied by distance from center. Both physical and visual weights follow similar laws in that heavy weights near the center counterbalance lighter ones farther away. Asymmetrical balance is often found in buildings or gardens designed to harmonize with their natural surroundings and to use space most efficiently, as well as in furniture arrangements planned for convenience.

The effects of asymmetrical balance differ markedly from those of symmetry. Asymmetry stirs us more quickly and vigorously, and it suggests movement, spontaneity, and informality. Being less obvious than formal balance, it arouses our curiosity to see how equilibrium was found. Subject to no formula, asymmetry allows freedom and flexibility in arrangements for utility as well as for beauty and individuality.

Asymmetrical balance is indicated when:

□ Informality and flexibility are desirable
□ The designer seeks an effect of spaciousness
□ Use suggests asymmetry
□ Harmony with nature is a goal

229. Although the fireplace is symmetrically placed in the center of the far wall in this living room, most of the other elements are asymmetrically disposed. The heavy sofa balances a light, open chair before the window wall; the square-cut window at top left plays against a much smaller but round lamp at head level, the latter bouncing the eye down toward the fireplace tools to the left of the hearth. George Nemeny, architect. See also Fig. 233. (*Photograph: John T. Hill*)

230. Architect Reece Clark employed an unusual but effective radial balance in a vacation house designed to raise the living quarters for a panoramic view of the surrounding country. (*Photograph: Karl H. Riek, courtesy Red Cedar Shingle & Handsplit Shake Bureau*)

Radial Balance When all parts of a composition are balanced and repeated around the center—as in the petals of a daisy or the widening ripples from a pebble thrown in a pond—the result is called radial balance (Fig. 230). Its chief characteristic is a circular movement out from, toward, or around a focal point. In homes it is found chiefly in such circular objects as plates and bowls, lighting fixtures, flower arrangements, and textile patterns. Although of lesser importance than the two preceding types, radial balance makes its own distinctive contribution in many small objects.

Rhythm

Defined as continuity, recurrence, or organized movement, rhythm is a second major design principle and one through which an underlying unity and evolving variety can be gained. It is exemplified in time by the repetition of our heartbeats, the alternation of day and night, and the progression of one season into another. In form and space it appears in the more or less repetitive character of the leaves on a tree, the alternating light and dark stripes of a zebra, and the sequences and transitions of curves in a river.

Rhythm contributes to the beauty of homes in several ways. Unity and harmony are consequences of rhythmic repetition and progression. Character and individuality are in part determined by the fundamental rhythms—gay and light, dynamic and rugged, precise and serene. Lastly, homes gain a quality of "aliveness" through the implied movement and direction that rhythm induces. This, however, is fully achieved only when a congruent pattern of rhythms prevails—a pattern of which we may be consciously or only subliminally aware. *Repetition* and *progression* are the two primary ways of developing rhythm.

Repetition Repetition is as simple as repeated rectangles or curves, colors or textures; but it can be given more intriguing complexity by *alternating* shapes, colors, or textures (Fig. 231). Even the most commonplace home is full of repetition—evidence of its universal appeal and also of the fact that simply repeating anything anywhere is not very stimulating. Some useful guides are:

□ Repeat consistently the forms or colors that underline the basic character.
□ Avoid repeating that which is ordinary or commonplace.
□ Too much repetition, unrelieved by contrast of some sort, leads to monotony.
□ Too little repetition leads to confusion.

Progression A sequence or transition produced by increasing or decreasing one or more qualities, progression is ordered, systematic change (Fig. 232). Because it suggests onward motion by successive changes toward a goal, progression can be more dynamic than simple reiteration.

Progression is easiest to see in small things—in patterns on china and in textiles, for example. The chevron motif fabric in Figure 232 develops a rhythm of narrow-medium-wide-very wide stripes in different colors. But while it will necessarily be more subtle, progression is just as valid in design for the whole home, even in exterior design. The façade of a wood-sheathed house (Fig. 233) is broken by rectangles of different shapes and sizes, beginning with a small square at upper right, progressing through stacked vertical rectangles in the entry and at far right, and culminating in large horizontal rectangles in the center and at far left. This exterior also illustrates the principle of asymmetrical balance, for the visual weights of the windows on either side of an imaginary central axis (supplied here by the single leafless tree) offset each other to create equilibrium.

top left: 231. Repetition can become a lively design device when it is used in alternating sequences of color, as in "Matrix," a Jacquard-woven wool fabric. (*Courtesy Jack Lenor Larsen, Inc.*)

above left: 232. "Taslan," a cotton and nylon textile with a chevron pattern of stripes progressing from beige to dark brown, creates changing optical illusions of three-dimensional form. (*Courtesy E. I. DuPont de Nemours & Company*)

above: 233. The basic rectangular forms of this house are enlivened by a series of progressions in forms, placement, weights, and materials. George Nemeny, architect. See also Fig. 229. (*Photograph: John T. Hill*)

Emphasis

A third design principle, emphasis, is often considered in terms of dominance and subordination. Emphasis suggests giving proper significance to each part and to the whole, calling more attention to the important parts than to those of lesser consequence, and introducing variety that will not become either frittery or chaotic. It has to do with focal points, "rest areas," and progressive degrees of interest in between. Without emphasis, homes would be as monotonous as the ticking of a clock, and without subordination as clamorous and competitive as a traffic jam.

Many homes suffer from a lack of appropriate dominance and subordination. Such homes may have rooms in which almost everything has about the same dead level of nonimportance or, at the opposite extreme, rooms in which too many assertive elements compete for simultaneous attention. Those rooms in which attention is directed toward a few important elements are usually more livable—a substantial fireplace or a distinguished piece of furniture, a painting, or a window with an outlook—shown to advantage by quieter areas. Rooms of this kind result in neither boredom nor overstimulation. Attention is held and relaxed at many levels.

Two steps are involved in creating a pattern of emphasis: deciding how important each unit is or should be and then giving it the appropriate degree of visual importance. This is not so simple as the superficial concept of "centers of interest

234. A striking drum-shape staircase landing becomes the dominant element in this lofty group space, offsetting by its mass the angular shapes of the owner's collection of primitive art. George Nemeny, architect: Debora Reiser, associate. (*Photograph: Maria/Semel, and House Beautiful*)

and backgrounds," because here we are dealing with a scale of degrees of significance, not with two categories. A start can be made by thinking in terms of four levels of emphasis, such as emphatic, dominant, subdominant, and subordinate (although this, too, is an oversimplification because there can be innumerable levels). For example, the room shown in Plate 24 (p. 179) might break down in the following way:

- □ *Emphatic*—view of the outdoors through a window wall
- □ *Dominant*—fireplace, one important painting
- □ *Subdominant*—major furniture group, ceiling treatment, other paintings and sculptures
- □ *Subordinate*—floor, walls, accessories

If we analyze this room, it becomes clear that certain elements have been consciously manipulated to assume levels of importance they might not otherwise possess. Because the house sits on a rocky bluff overlooking a quarry, full access to the dramatic view was important to the owners. Three large window walls in the living room thus make the outdoor panorama the most emphatic feature in the composition. At the next level, the fireplace—dark and isolated in a plain white wall—stands out and assumes major significance, a not surprising treatment in the harsh climate of upper New York State. And, since the painting by Nicholas Krushenick on the wall at left has virtually the only color in a room full of neutrals (its hue echoed in a few sofa cushions), it too becomes dominant. Ordinarily, a large multisection seating unit would be a dominant element in any room, but here the sofa components have been upholstered in dark chocolate brown to blend with the carpet, so they take a secondary or subdominant role to the fireplace and painting. Conversely, a ceiling, if flat and painted white, recedes into a subordinate role, but here the exposed wood beams and dark color against white walls bring it up one level to subdominant status. The Louise Nevelson sculpture over the fireplace blends with the white wall it occupies; it takes on full significance only under close scrutiny, so in the overall view of the room it acts as a subdominant. The floor and walls, as neutral, two-dimensional planes, retain their accustomed roles as subordinate elements.

Other conditions and desires would lead to different solutions. In Figure 234, a remodeled townhouse, a huge cylindrical staircase landing and a collection of primitive art must be considered the most emphatic elements—the former because it is a striking curved feature in a landscape of rectangles and planes, the latter because the exotic contours of the primitive sculptures stand out dramatically against stark white walls. Even the two glorious Oriental rugs, which by their rich patterns and colors would normally demand our first attention, drop back one level before the staircase drum and the art.

Many people, however, do not have an impressive fireplace, an extensive view, a distinctive collection of paintings and sculpture, or a unique sculptural stairway. Fortunately, there are many ways of creating interest in a dull room. One approach is to concentrate spending on a single important piece of furniture, to locate it prominently, and to key it up with accessories, a painting, or a mirror. Funds permitting, one or two other distinctive pieces, less emphatic than the major unit, might be secured and made the centers of secondary groups. A strongly patterned wallpaper or a large map on one wall would also be effective. Very low in cost is an out-of-the-ordinary color scheme achieved by painting walls, ceiling, furniture, and perhaps even floor so that the color harmonies and contrasts become noteworthy (Fig. 406). A major focal point in the room shown in Plate 25 (p. 179) is the painted wall between two arched windows. The contours within the panel echo the curved shapes of the windows, but the colors—bright yellows and reds— are in sharp contrast to the dark wood all around them. At virtually no expense, what might otherwise have been a gloomy wall has been given exciting emphasis.

Harmony, Variety, and Unity

Even within the schema of different levels of emphasis, it is important to maintain an overall harmony, so that various elements do not seem to be thrown together arbitrarily or to be competing with one another. The painted panel in Plate 25, while emphatically contrasting in color, exists in harmony with the adjacent wall because of its similar shapes. Defined as consonance, concord, or agreement among parts, harmony suggests carrying through a single motivating idea and making good use of repetition and similarity.

In essence, harmony results when the other two principles—variety and unity—are combined. Variety without some unifying factor, such as color, shape, pattern, or theme, would be unsettling and discordant; unity unrelieved by variety would be nothing but dull. Several examples will illustrate how this works. A rug designed by Edward Fields (Fig. 235) has inherent unity, since it contains only two figures—the square and the diamond (the latter being a square tipped on end). Variety results from alternation of squares and diamonds, alternation of high and low pile, and contrasting colors.

The window treatment shown in Figure 236 makes splendid use of variety and unity to create a fascinating assemblage from mundane objects. Composed entirely of functional items found in the kitchen—spoons, rolling pin, wire whisk, meat pounders, and so on—the composition has overall unity in the similar shapes and materials involved. Variety comes from the ways in which different objects are hung, their orientation toward each other, and discrepancies in size.

A suggestion of how these principles can be expanded to apply to whole rooms is seen in Figure 237. A small room that could have been boring takes on vivid life from a patterned fabric used on walls, in draperies, and for upholstery. Thus, diverse shapes are tied together by thematic pattern, a system that tends to blur outlines. The carpeting, while composed of a different motif, is similar in character. In a reverse of the usual treatment, solid-color cushions—with the plain lampshades—relieve the profusion of pattern.

As should be clear from the foregoing discussion, variety and unity achieve a happy merger when one or more of the design elements—space, form, line, texture, ornament, and color—are held constant and one or more are changed.

Proportion and Scale

Two closely associated terms, proportion and scale both relate to the size of things. They deal with questions of magnitude, quantity, or degree. In architecture or interior design, *proportion* can be defined as the relation of one part to another part or to the whole, as well as of one object to another. *Scale* deals with the relative size or character of a thing in relation to other things. The fine shade of meaning between these two may seem elusive until we offer some examples.

In the most simplistic terms, proportions usually are said to be satisfactory or unsatisfactory, scale to be large or small. For instance, the design on a plate (Fig. 238) should have a satisfactory relationship to the size and heaviness of the object. If this floral design were much larger, it would overwhelm the form; if much smaller, it would get lost and seem like an afterthought. Similarly, the furniture

left: **237.** A room in which pattern becomes the interior design is unified by the lavish use of one motif, accented by just a few plain surfaces. (*Courtesy Schumacher*)

above: **238.** This dinner plate has an informal floral design pleasingly proportioned to the size and weight of the ceramic form and in scale with the visual weight of the slender bands of color around the rim. (*Courtesy Dansk Designs, Ltd.*)

in Figure 239 is large, massive, and bulky—almost monumental. In a small, low-ceilinged room, it would appear ludicrous, almost like standard-size furniture filling a doll's house. But here, in this towering, light-filled space, it is in perfect proportion.

No foolproof system of proportioning that holds good in all cases has been devised. The so-called golden section, which often gives safe, pleasing results, comes nearest. This consists of dividing a line or form so that the smaller portion has the same ratio to the larger as the larger has to the whole. The progression 1, 2, 3, 5, 8, 13, 21 . . . , in which each term is the sum of the two preceding ones, approximates this relationship. For those in need of formulas, this is as good as any, but its applications are limited. In practice, proportioning is more a trial-and-error problem, a system of varying the proportions of things until one arrangement seems "right."

above: 240. Heavy peeled pine log sofas are upholstered in positive and negative versions of the same bold, simple pattern to achieve a harmony of scale and proportion. (*Courtesy Jack Lenor Larsen, Inc.*)

right: 241. The massive scale of a vacation house on Long Island is carried out in every detail, but the informal and bulky but soft seating helps to humanize the effect. Norman Jaffe, architect. (*Photograph: Maris/Semel*)

Scale, as we said, is generally described as large or small, but by this we mean large or small in relation to something else. The sofas shown in Figure 240 have large, heavy frames compared to the furniture we normally see, and the upholstery fabric is an unusually large check. Both elements, then, could be spoken of as *large-scale* (and therefore in satisfactory proportion to one another).

A phrase one often hears is *grand scale,* and this certainly describes the house in Figure 241. Everything here is oversized, from the massive masonry wall, through the thick boards that form the uprights and immense wood beams, to the generous-size furnishings. A house as expansive and monumental as this needs very careful proportioning, for otherwise people would feel lost and intimidated.

A vital consideration in the home is "human scale." Physically, typical persons are between 5 and 6 feet tall and weigh between 100 and 200 pounds. These figures act as a yardstick for sizes of rooms, furniture, and equipment. Suitably scaled homes make us look and feel like normal human beings, not like midgets or giants. Yet within this framework, there is ample room for variation. The room in Figure 242, obviously the home of a child or children, has been deliberately *scaled down* to "small-human" size. Furnishings are low and shallow, spaces between things are relatively narrow, and in general the whole room would make a child feel comfortable and at home—not like Alice after taking the magic potion. Still, adults could be equally at ease in this room, for there is ample seating and walk space for full-size humans.

The elements and principles of design can seldom be applied self-consciously. Indeed, it is folly to imagine that by injecting suitable doses of balance, rhythm, emphasis, variety, unity, and proportion into a home we will inevitably arrive at the perfect design. More often, such principles come to our attention only when we have violated them, perhaps when two chairs placed together are obviously in horrible proportion to each other. However, once we have come to understand the factors involved, we can more easily grasp what is wrong and how we can correct it. The purpose of studying this language of design is not to memorize rules but, first, to recognize the basic elements we are working with and, second, to discover what principles have proved successful in other designs. By studying home designs that have worked for different situations, we will gradually develop a sense of how elements can be combined. And this is one of the most important ingredients of a personal lifespace.

242. A space furnished in child-scale would make youngsters feel it is uniquely their own and a welcome relief from the (to them) overscaled objects they have to contend with the rest of the time. Caswell Cooke, architect. (*Photograph: John T. Hill*)

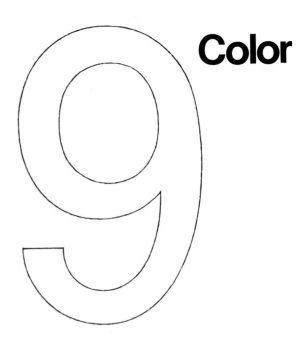

Color

Although color has long been considered a fundamental of home design, only recently have we become fully aware of its potentialities beyond mere pleasantness or unpleasantness. That it can be influential, for better or for worse, has been proved countless times. Such phrases as "functional color" and "color conditioning" describe its use in business for increased efficiency. And psychologists have reported studies that seem to show that young children tested in brightly painted rooms the children themselves thought of as "beautiful" made higher I.Q. scores than those tested in rooms of "ugly" (black, brown, and white) colors. In the theater the emotional effects of color have long been exploited. Color can work similar magic in homes, by cheering us or relaxing us. With receding colors or appropriate contrasts, the apparent size of a room can be markedly increased. Ceilings can be made to seem higher or lower with a coat of paint. Where there is no sunlight, its effects can be simulated with yellow walls, and excessive brightness or glare can be reduced with cool, darkish surfaces. Some or all furnishings can be brought into prominence or allied with their background by the use of color. In short, color can markedly alter the appearance of form and space, change our moods, and perhaps even affect our abilities.

The color of an object that we see results from two factors: the way in which the object absorbs and reflects light and the kind of light that makes the object visible. When light strikes an opaque object, some of its hues are absorbed and others reflected. Those that are reflected give the object its color quality. Lemons and yellow paint, for instance, absorb almost all hues except yellow. White objects reflect almost all the hues in light, while black objects absorb most of them. We say almost because pure colors are very seldom found. The true color quality of anything is revealed when it is seen in white light. Usually, however, light is not completely colorless.

The color of light depends on its source and whatever it passes through before coming to our eyes. White or apparently colorless light, such as that from the noon sun, contains all the spectrum's hues—violet, blue, green, yellow, orange, and red—balanced and blended so that the effect is colorless. Light from the moon is bluish, while that from open fires, candles, and the typical incandescent light bulb is yellowish. Incandescent and fluorescent lighting, however, come in many colors, and we can choose those that are most effective, even changing them for special occasions or blending colors by means of colored spot or floodlights. We can also alter the color of artificial light with translucent shades that are not white. Daylight can be changed by thin, colored curtains or by tinted glass. In general, warm light intensifies red, yellow, and orange and neutralizes blue and violet. Light that is cool and bluish does the opposite.

Color Theory

Organizing facts and observations on color into a systematic theory is the first step in understanding color relationships and effects. Three different kinds of theories have been developed: physicists base theirs on light, psychologists on sensation, and artists on pigments and dyes. Our interest is chiefly with the last, because anyone who works with paint or fibers—from the interior designer to the home do-it-yourself painter, from a fabric manufacturer to a handweaver— necessarily works with pigments and dyes. There are a number of accepted color theories, but basically all are predicated on the fact that to describe a color with reasonable precision at least three terms are needed that correspond to the three dimensions or attributes of color: *hue,* the name of a color; *value,* the lightness or darkness of a color; and *intensity* or chroma, its degree of purity or strength.

Hue

The simplest and most familiar theory is based on the concept that there are three primary colors—red, blue, and yellow—that cannot be produced by mixing other colors; however, mixtures of them will result in nearly every other color. When

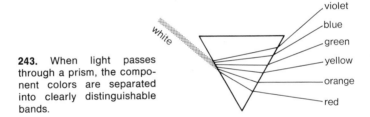

243. When light passes through a prism, the component colors are separated into clearly distinguishable bands.

natural light is passed through a prism, it separates into bands of violet, blue, green, yellow, orange, and red (Fig. 243). If these are bent into a circle and intermediate hues placed between them, they can be diagrammatically visualized in a color wheel (Fig. 244). The twelve hues divide into three categories:

□ **Primary hues,** labeled *1* in the color wheel, are red, blue, and yellow. Plate 26 (p. 180) shows a room painted in pure primary colors plus green, a secondary color.
□ **Secondary or binary hues,** labeled *2,* are green, violet, and orange. Each stands midway between two primary hues of which it is the product, as green is equidistant from blue and yellow.
□ **Tertiary or intermediary hues,** labeled *3,* are yellow-green, blue-green, blue-violet, red-violet, red-orange, and yellow-orange. These stand midway between a primary and a secondary hue of which they are the product. For instance, yellow-green is between the primary hue yellow and the secondary hue green.

Hues are *actually* changed, or new ones produced, by combining neighboring hues as indicated above. Red, for example, becomes red-violet when combined with violet. If more violet were added, the hue would be changed again. The twelve hues on the color wheel are only a beginning, because there can be an almost infinite number of hues. The effects of light and background also lead to *apparent*

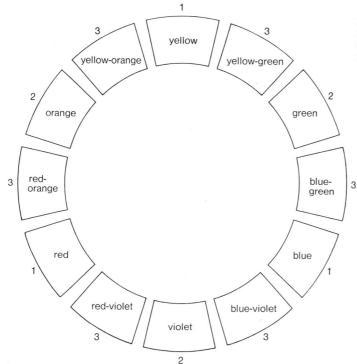

changes. Cool light will make any hue seem bluer, while warm light does the opposite. Backgrounds are equally important: red placed against cool blue or green seems warmer than when seen against orange or red-violet.

Effect of Hues on One Another   When placed next to each other, hues produce effects ranging from harmony to decisive contrast. Some combinations, such as blue, blue-green, and green, give a harmonious, restful sequence. But if blue is put next to orange, there is excitement and contrast. Two adjectives describe these relationships:

□ **Analogous hues** are adjacent to each other on the color wheel, as are yellow, yellow-green, and green.
□ **Complementary hues** lie directly opposite each other, as do yellow and violet, red and green, and blue and orange.

Hues can be combined to produce any degree of harmony or contrast. If only one hue is used in a room, a marked unity results. When *analogous* hues are placed next to each other, the effect is one of harmonious sequence. By actually mixing hues together, or by intermingling small spots of each, one creates another hue. *Complementary* hues, when placed next to each other, contrast vividly; each color seems to gain intensity if the area of each hue is large enough to be perceived as a separate color. But if the areas of two complementary hues are very small, as in a textile woven of fine red and green yarns, the effect at normal distances is lively but more neutralized. And if opposites are mixed together, a brownish gray is likely to be the result. Thus, many effects can be created with hues, ranging from strong contrasts to soft harmonies.

Warmth and Coolness of Hues   Each hue has its own "temperature" that affects us and our homes in several ways. Red, orange, and yellow seem warm and active (Pl. 27, p. 180); they tend to bring together whatever is seen against them. They are called *advancing* hues because they seem nearer to us than they actually are, which leads to two seemingly paradoxical results. Upholstering furniture in intense red increases its apparent size, but painting the walls of a room red decreases its apparent spaciousness because the walls seem closer. Blue, green, and violet tend to seem cool and restful. Because they appear to be farther away than they actually are, they are referred to as *receding* hues. They reduce the apparent size of objects, but when used on walls they seem to increase a room's dimensions.

Value

Value is defined as relative lightness or darkness. It is perhaps easier to understand in neutrals, where it indicates degrees of lightness or darkness between pure white (full light) and pure black (the absence of any light). But value gradations apply equally to colors.

There can be any number of value steps between white and black, but the seven shown in the gray scale (Fig. 245) make a convenient number. Even without considering color, for the moment, we can see how value levels affect the character of a home. The four kitchen and dining areas shown in Figures 246 to 249 have four different value schemes. The first (Fig. 246), a room composed of nearly all light values, seems bright, airy, and cheerful. Its effect is distinctly "uplift," but if not handled with care a system of all light values can seem cold and labora-

white

high light

light

low light

middle

high dark

dark

low dark

black

above: 245. A gray value scale shows seven gradations between black and white. The central dots are all of identical (middle) value, but, like objects in a room, they appear lighter against a dark background and darker against a light one.

right: 246. A light value scheme brightens an interior by reflecting all the light available—a quality especially useful in rooms without much natural daylight. (*Courtesy James Seeman Studios, Inc.*)

194   Design and Color

torylike. The second room (Fig. 247) also has predominantly light values, but with medium values in the table and floor to soften the effect. Concealed lights in the niche on the rear wall also create value contrasts in highlights and shadows. The third room (Fig. 248) consists of nearly all dark values—dark paneling, dark ceiling beams, dark-colored appliances, and so forth. Only the table, a medium value,

above: 247. A dining room with a mix of light and medium values is enlivened by concealed lighting over the built-in buffet. Robert A. M. Stern, owner-architect. See also Figs. 109, 408, 440; Plate 12, p. 60. (*Photograph: John T. Hill*)

right: 248. The kitchen-dining room of a basement apartment features predominantly dark values enriched by lighter areas and accents. Don Konz, owner-designer. See also Figs. 8, 466. (*Photograph: Hedrich-Blessing*)

and a few white accents provide relief. Because this design has been handled skillfully, we have a sense of security and solidity from this room, but without such care a scheme of all dark values can be very gloomy. Sharp contrasts of light and dark characterize the fourth room (Fig. 249), in which flat white walls are enlivened by dark ceiling beams, woodwork, and furniture. A few middle values, as in the rug, provide a transition and avoid harshness.

Value gradations become very important in a monochromatic color scheme (see p. 204) or in a design based primarily on neutrals. Plate 28 (p. 197) illustrates a masterfully subtle treatment of the latter. A bedroom of unusual tranquility and dignity, this room has been planned almost entirely around grays and beiges, with four slight transitions of value. The walls, an off-white, mark the lightest value, followed by the light beige macramé window curtain, the darker gray on the beds and stools, and the yet darker carpet. Even the last of these, however, could only be placed at middle value on the gray scale. A bowl of fresh flowers and the books (or whatever artifacts might be brought into the room over the course of the day) offer the only accents.

The seven intervals in the gray scale (Fig. 245) also correspond to the *normal values* of the hues in the color wheel (Fig. 244). We know from subjective experience that yellow is a light color and violet a dark color. But if we were to place the hues of the color wheel side by side with the gray scale, they would appear to have equal value in the following order:

Hue	*Value Step*	*Hue*
yellow	high light	yellow
yellow-orange	light	yellow-green
orange	low light	green
red-orange	middle	blue-green
red	high dark	blue
red-violet	dark	blue-violet
violet	low dark	violet

249. Dark and light values are balanced in a family room-kitchen furnished with beautiful Colonial antiques. The value scheme recalls that of Early American interiors (see Fig. 775). (*Photograph: John T. Hill*)

above: Plate 28. The neutral color scheme that dominates this bedroom takes on interest because of changes in value. A large macramé hanging behind the bed hides an unattractive outdoor view. Paul Rudolph, architect. See page 196; see also Fig. 27; Plate 22, p. 162; Plate 61, p. 454. (*Photograph: Ezra Stoller* © *ESTO*)

right: Plate 29. An analogous color scheme based on reds, yellows, and oranges provides a cheerful setting for this sunny dining corner. Ben Thompson, owner-designer. See page 205; see also Fig. 471; Plate 56, p. 419. (*Photograph: Ezra Stoller* © *ESTO*)

left: **Plate 30.** A modern painting and intricately patterned Oriental rug serve as the color keynotes in this room. The soft blue sofa picks up the blue of the painting, while color accents and accessories—even the warm yellow-brown of the wood furniture—also refer back to the painting's hues. Dark blue-black slate on the floor acts as a harmonizing base. When reassembled, the clear Lucite sculpture next to the painting becomes a dining table. Francis Mah, architect. See page 207; see also Fig. 219. (*Photograph: John T. Hill*)

below: **Plate 31.** Except for the mellow brown of the wood floor, pure saturated red is the only real hue used in this room, the color set off stunningly against the neutrals of black and white. Red's complementary, green, appears in one large plant. Robert Whitton, architect. See page 208; see also Plate 49, p. 335. (*Photograph: Ezra Stoller ⓒ ESTO*)

Every hue can range in value from high light to low dark, but we tend to think of hues at their normal values. Yellow, for example, comes to mind as the color of a lemon or dandelion rather than of a beige carpet. *Tints* are values lighter than normal; *shades* are values darker than normal. Pink is a tint of red, maroon is a shade of the same hue. Sky blue is a tint, navy blue a shade.

Values are changed by making them reflect more or less light. With paints, *actual* changes are made by adding black, gray, or white, by adding a color lighter or darker than the original, or hues that are complements of the basic color. Apparent changes can be made by reducing or raising the amount of natural or artificial light reaching a surface, or by placing it against backgrounds of differing degrees of light or dark.

Values affect one another much as hues do—contrasts accentuate differences. The same gray looks much darker when seen against a light surface than when seen against black. The same holds true for values of any hue.

Intensity

Any hue can vary in its purity or strength—in other words, in the degree to which it differs from gray. Pink, for example, is always red in hue and light in value, but it can be *vivid,* almost *pure* pink (Pl. 44, p. 317) or it can be *neutralized,* grayed pink. This is called intensity.

Scales of intensity can have many or few steps. Full intensities, which are possible only at the normal value of each hue, are often described as *high* or *strong,* the more neturalized as *low* or *weak.*

Intensities can be *actually heightened* by adding more of the dominant hue. They can also be *apparently raised* by illuminating the object with light of that hue or by throwing it into contrast with its complementary hue, a grayed tone of the hue, or a completely neutral color. A wall of grayed yellow can be intensified by repainting it with a purer yellow, by casting yellowish light on it, or by placing chairs in front of it that are upholstered in violet, a less intense yellow, or gray.

Actual and *apparent* intensities can be *decreased* in several ways. First, the designer can lessen the amount of the dominant hue by adding varying amounts of its complementary hue; yellow is grayed by adding violet, violet by adding yellow, blue by adding orange, and so on. A similar effect is produced by mixing a color with black, gray, or white. A second way calls for illuminating an object with light of the complementary hue. A blue wall, for example, would be grayed during the day by sheer, orange-tinted glass curtains and at night by translucent lampshades of the same hue. A third device is introducing something—a painting, a wall hanging, a chair, or a sofa—that is noticeably more intense in color than is the wall. This apparent change is most pronounced if the object and the wall are of the same or similar hues.

A great deal can be learned about the qualities of hue, value, and intensity by analyzing the color organizations that you see in rooms, furniture and textiles, and gardens. Trying a few simple experiments will give you firsthand information. Mixing different hues will show you how they change, and you can experiment by neutralizing them with complementary hues or with black, white, or gray. They can also be diluted with a suitable colorless thinner. Construction paper or textile samples can show what happens to the apparent hue, value, and intensity of any color when it is placed against varied backgrounds.

Changing any one dimension of a color almost inevitably changes the other two, at least slightly. Available pigments are almost never absolutely pure: grays, blacks, and whites tend to be either warm or cool and thus alter the hue with which they are mixed. It is possible to change intensity without altering value *if* you use a gray or complementary hue that absolutely matches the color's value, but this is seldom achieved. One of the dimensions can be modified much more than the other two, but it is difficult to change one and hold the others constant.

Table 9.1 Summary of Effects of Hue, Value, and Intensity

	Hue	Value	Intensity
feelings	warm hues are stimulating, cool hues quieting	light values are cheering; dark values range from restful to depressing; contrasts are alerting	high intensities are heartening; strong, low intensities are peaceful
attention	warm hues attract more attention than cool hues	extreme values tend to attract the eye; but contrasts or surprises are even more effective	high intensities attract attention
size	warm hues increase apparent size of objects; used on walls, they decrease apparent size of room	light values increase apparent size of objects; but strong contrast with background is equally effective	high intensities increase apparent size of objects; used on walls, they decrease apparent size of room
distance	warm hues bring objects forward; cool hues make them recede	light values recede, dark values advance; sharp contrasts in values also bring objects forward	high intensities decrease apparent distances
outline, or contour	warm hues soften outlines slightly more than cool hues; contrasting hues make outlines clearer than related hues	value contrasts are a potent way of emphasizing contours	intensity contrasts emphasize outlines

Effects of Hue, Value, and Intensity

Generalizations about color relationships and their effects are well worth knowing, although we should be aware that none of them always holds true.

How do colors affect our feelings and activity? Warm hues, values lighter than the middle range, and high intensities tend to raise our spirits and stimulate us to be active. Pronounced contrasts of any sort, such as blue-green and red-orange or deep brown and white have similar effects. Intermediate hues, values around the middle range, and moderate intensities are relaxing and undemanding. Cool hues, values below the middle range, and low intensities usually seem quiet and subdued. There are, of course, innumerable other ways of selecting and organizing varied hues, values, and intensities to achieve the effect that is desired.

What colors and combinations attract our attention? Any degree of dominance or subordination can be produced by skillful handling of color. We are immediately attracted by colors that are striking and bold, and these may be indicated where dominance is wanted. Extreme values and strong intensities also tend to attract attention, but no more so than emphatic contrasts or unexpected, out-of-the-ordinary color relationships. Colors that are grayed and moderate in value as well as any familiar color combinations are unemphatic and seldom noticed, which makes them passive backgrounds unless they are interestingly textured or otherwise patterned. Thus, with color alone attention can be directed toward that which is important and away from that which is less consequential.

How do colors affect apparent size and distance? The degree to which color can seem to alter the size of any object and its distance from the observer is often dramatic, but this too is a matter of complex relationships. In general, warm hues, values above the middle range, and strong intensities make an object look large.

Cool hues, darker values, and lower intensities reduce its apparent size. Decisive contrasts, textures, and ornamentation may or may not increase apparent size, depending on exactly how they are handled.

Apparent distance, or spaciousness, is increased by cool hues, the lighter values, and the lower intensities. Although some contrast is needed as a yardstick, strong contrasts usually make objects seem nearer than they actually are, while low contrast can increase the sense of spaciousness.

Putting all of this to work is fascinating but complex. Rooms with white or very light, cool walls seem more spacious than those with darker, warmer surfaces. Houses painted white seem bigger than those of red brick or natural wood. *But* the value relation between any object and its background is important because strong value contrasts make objects stand out, which tends to increase their apparent size. Thus against a white background a sofa with light upholstery might look much less conspicuous than it would set in a room of predominantly dark and middle values (Figs. 250, 251).

How can colors be used to accentuate or deemphasize the outlines or contours of objects? Differences in hues, intensities, and especially values make us conscious of an object's shape. White against black makes the strongest contrast, and as the values become closer to each other, forms tend to merge with their surroundings. The shape of a white lamp is much more emphatic when seen against dark gray or black than when seen against a light value of any hue. Diametrically opposite hues attract attention to outlines, but if the values of the two hues are similar, the edges seem fuzzy rather than distinct. Related hues also soften contours, and warm hues make the edges of anything seem less sharp than do those that are cool. We could summarize the effects of hue, value, and intensity, as in Table 9.1, bearing in mind that all generalizations about any one of these three factors assume

below: 250. The light value of a large sofa helps it to blend with the light values and apparent spaciousness of the room as a whole. (*Courtesy Selig*)

right: 251. A light sofa stands out in marked contrast to its setting of predominantly dark values—a scheme that increases the apparent size of the sofa. (*Courtesy Ege Rya, Inc.*)

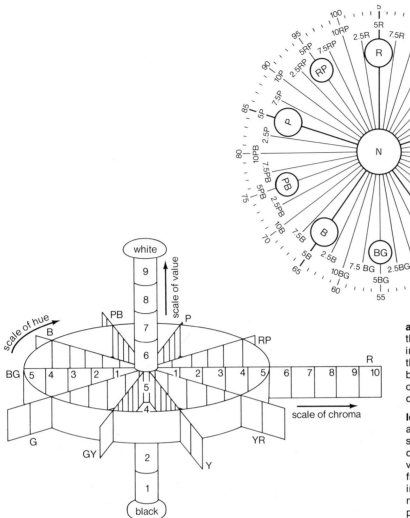

above: 252. The Munsell system divides the spectrum into five principal and five intermediate hues, indicated by letters on the color wheel. Each of the ten hues can be subdivided into ten more, creating the one hundred hues indicated by the outer circle of numbers.

left: 253. The relationship of hue, value, and chroma appears in a three-dimensional diagram. The circular band indicates the hues, as in Fig. 252. The central vertical axis shows nine value gradations from near black to almost white. Chroma, indicated on the radial spokes, goes from neutral in the center to full chroma at the periphery. (*Munsell Color Company*)

that the other two dimensions of color, the background, and so on, are held constant. For example, artillery red is normally more stimulating than peppermint green—both are of middle value and full intensity. *But* peppermint green is likely to attract more attention than cocoa brown, a color that is red in hue but low dark in value and tending toward neutral in intensity.

Color Theory: The Munsell and Ostwald Systems

Although similar to the color system discussed above—in that the hues are arranged in a circle, which becomes a three-dimensional form when fully developed—the systems formulated by Albert Munsell and Wilhelm Ostwald deviate from it in two basic ways. First, the primary hues are not the same, and second, both have intricate, standardized methods of notation with which innumerable colors can be precisely labeled and identified by referring to the appropriate color charts. These are of inestimable value in science, commerce, and industry where universal specifications of colors are necessary; they are also useful to professional designers and decorators for precise communication.

The Munsell system[1] of color notation has *five principal hues*—red, yellow, green, blue, and purple; and five intermediate hues—yellow-red, green-yellow, blue-green, purple-blue, and red-purple (Fig. 252). Each of these hue families has been sub-divided into four parts, indicated by the numerals 2.5, 5, 7.5, and 10, which when combined with the initial of a hue designates the exact hue. The number 5R, for example, refers to "pure" red, 7.5R is toward yellow-red, and 2.5R toward red-purple. Further refinement divides each hue into ten steps, as indicated on the outermost circle of Figure 252.

Figure 253 shows the nine *value* steps going from 1/, the darkest, to 9/ as the lightest, with 0/ and 10/ as theoretically pure black and pure white.

The term *chroma* is used instead of intensity. The chroma scale begins with /0 for complete neutrality at the central axis and extends out to /10, or further for very vivid colors (Fig. 253). The number of chroma steps is determined by the varying saturation strengths of each hue. Notice in the diagram that red, a very strong hue, extends to /10, but the weaker blue-green goes only to /5.

The complete Munsell notation for any color is written as hue value/chroma. Hue is indicated by the letter and numeral that defines that particular hue on the color wheel (Fig. 252). This is followed by a fraction in which the numerator designates value and the denominator specifies chroma. Thus 5R 5/10 indicates "pure" red at middle value and maximum chroma. Blue that is light in value and low in chroma is written 5B 9/1.

The **Ostwald system**[2] is developed from three pairs of complementary color sensations—red and green, blue and yellow, and black and white. The color wheel begins by placing yellow, red, blue, and green equidistant from one another. Placing five intermediates between each pair of hues makes a circle of 24 hues (plus six additional hues that are needed to complete the color range). These are indicated by the numbers around the equator of the color solid (Fig. 254).

No sharp distinction is made between value and intensity: the hues are lightened or darkened or neutralized by adding appropriate amounts of white and black. This expands the color wheel into a color solid composed of a number of triangular wedges packed together as in Figure 254. In each wedge there are eight steps from top to bottom and eight from center to periphery.

Colors are designated by a formula, which consists of a number and two letters (8 pa for example). The number indicates the hue. The first letter indicates the proportions of white in any color, and the second letter designates the proportion of black. The scale goes from a, which is almost pure white, through c, e, g, i, l, n, to p, which is almost pure black. Thus, these two letters tell how light or dark

254. The Ostwald color system is illustrated by a solid double cone, partially cut away to show relationships inside. Colors are most saturated at the equator and become increasingly neutralized as they approach the central axis of gray values. Colors become lighter toward the top, darker toward the bottom. At the right, a triangle illustrates 28 variations of one hue with lightest at the top and darkest at the bottom, proceeding from neutral at the black-white axis to saturation at the periphery.

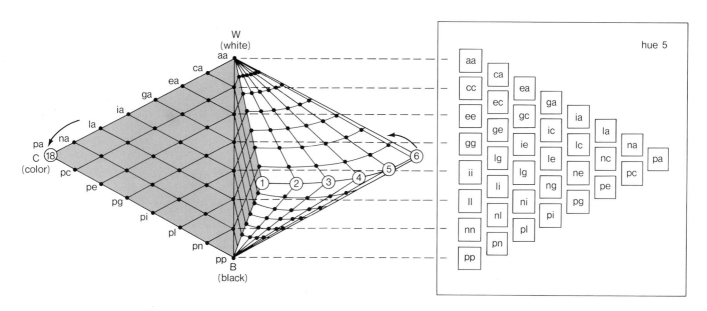

a color is, as well as the degree of saturation. In each triangle there are 28 colors, which multiplied by the 24 hues gives 672 chromatic colors. Adding the 8 neutral steps brings the total to 680, which is about as many as most people need. Study of the diagram and a few examples may possibly make this clear. Pure red has the symbol of 8 pa: the number indicates "pure" red, and the letters indicate that no black or white has been added. Intense orange-red has the symbol 5 pa, grayed orange-red has the symbol 5 lg, and dark orange-red has the symbol 5 pn.

A number of ways of developing color schemes that have an easily perceivable order are suggested in the literature on this system.

Types of Color Schemes

Planning a color scheme ranks high among the exhilarating aspects of home planning. You can assert your individuality and enjoy the freedom that comes from knowing that satisfying color costs no more than color that lacks character.

In theory, countless color schemes are suited to homes. Practically speaking, however, only a few can be classified, probably because these types just about exhaust the possibilities of orderly selection from the color wheel. In color, as in design, an underlying sense of order is satisfying; but stereotyped, commonplace organization is tedious. The standard color schemes are nothing more than time-tested basic recipes; rarely do actual color schemes fit perfectly into any of the categories. They can be varied and individualized, be simply points of departure, or be disregarded, as one wishes.

Typical color schemes fall into two major categories, *related* and *contrasting*. Related color schemes, which are composed of one or several closely neighboring hues, lead toward an unmistakable harmony and unity. Contrasting schemes, based on hues that are far apart on the color wheel, offer greater variety as well as a balance of warm and cool hues. The two types are basically different, but neither is inherently better than the other. Depending on the hues chosen and the dominant pattern of intensities, any of them can be vividly brilliant or comparatively quiet. Beyond this, we can subdivide color schemes into seven categories, of which the first two are considered related, the other five contrasting.

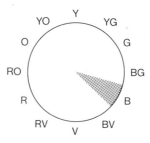

255. Monochromatic scheme.

Monochromatic Color Schemes

Monochromatic (literally, "one hue") color schemes (Fig. 255) evolve from a single hue, which can be varied from high light to low dark and from full saturation to almost neutral. White, grays, black, and small amounts of other hues add variety, as do applied and natural textures and decorative patterns. Thus, even with only one basic hue, the possibilities are legion.

The room shown in Plate 28 (p. 197) is monochromatic in the extreme, since it contains only the neutral grays and beiges; while it seems reserved, it could scarcely be described as dull. We might imagine this same room done in another hue—blue or green or red—with the same value gradations from light to middle.

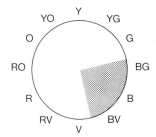

256. Analogous scheme.

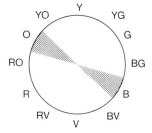

257. Complementary scheme.

The advantages of monochromatic color schemes are that some degree of success is almost assured, because unity and harmony are firmly established. Usually, spaciousness and continuity are emphasized, and the effect is quiet and peaceful except in those rare cases in which saturated colors predominate. A major danger—monotony—can be avoided by diversified values and intensities, and by differences in form, texture, and spatial relationships.

Analogous Color Schemes

Strictly speaking, analogous color schemes are based on three or more hues each of which contains some degree of one hue (Fig. 256). In other words, the hues fall within any segment of the color wheel that is less than halfway around it. Thus, if the common hue is blue, the colors could be as closely related as blue-green, blue, and blue-violet, or as separated as blue-green, blue-violet, and red-violet. Often, however, the range of hues is extended. Analogous color schemes, although basically harmonious, have more variety and interest than do monochromatic color schemes (Pl. 29, p. 197).

Complementary Color Schemes

Built on any two hues directly opposite each other on the color wheel, complementary schemes (Fig. 257) are exemplified by orange and blue, or yellow-orange and blue-violet (Pl. 30, p. 198). They offer a great range of possibilities. Yellow and violet, for example, can be as startling as gold and fuchsia, as moderate as ivory and amethyst, or as somber as olive drab and gunmetal.

Double-Complementary Color Schemes

A development of the complementary scheme, double complementaries (Fig. 258) are simply two sets of complements. Orange and red-orange with their respective complements, blue and blue-green, are an example. Worth noticing in this example is the fact that orange and red-orange, as well as their complements are near each other on the color wheel. This is usually the case, because if the hues are widely separated, it is difficult to see the order on which this scheme is based.

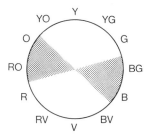

258. Double-complementary scheme.

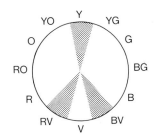 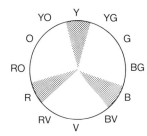 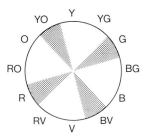

259. Split-complementary scheme.   **260.** Triad scheme.   **261.** Tetrad scheme.

Split-Complementary Color Schemes

Another variation on the complementary theme, the split complementary (Fig. 259) is composed of any hue and the two hues *at each side of* its complement, as in yellow with blue-violet and red-violet. Violet, the complement of yellow, is split into red-violet and blue-violet. This makes the contrast less violent than in the simple complementary type and adds interest and variety.

Triad Color Schemes

Red, blue, and yellow; green, orange, and violet; blue-green, red-violet, and yellow-orange—any three hues equidistant from one another on the color wheel—are known as triad color schemes (Fig. 260). In case such combinations sound shocking, remember that full-intensity hues are seldom used in homes. Red, blue, and yellow might be translated as mahogany, French gray, and beige. Green, orange, and violet could be sage green, cocoa brown, and dove gray. Thus, although triad schemes can be vigorous, they can also be subdued. In any case, the effect is one of well-rounded balance with variety held in check by a readily apparent, systematic unity.

Tetrad Color Schemes

Any four hues that are equidistant from one another on the color wheel produce a tetrad color scheme (Fig. 261), which is a special type of split complementary color organization. Yellow-orange, green, blue-violet, and red are an example. Such combinations lead to rich, varied yet unified, fully balanced compositions.

Deciding on a Color Scheme

Of the many ways of starting to develop a sense or feeling for color combination, the following have been found useful:

☐ Start a scrapbook or clipping file of color combinations that you like. Include advertisements, magazine covers, reproductions of paintings, and so on, as well as illustrations of domestic architecture and interiors.
☐ Collect swatches of cloth, wallpaper samples, paint color cards, and a package of assorted colored paper with which to try out ideas.
☐ Visit furniture stores, art museums, and model homes and make notes of what you especially like or dislike.
☐ Study original paintings or reproductions, because painters working freely with pigments to express their ideas are one source of stimulation.
☐ Study the colors in the nearby landscape and those more distant.
☐ Look carefully at the colors used in your home and those of your friends, paying attention to first impressions, as well as to the more important lasting effect.

□ Make a list of your favorite colors.
□ Look at color photographs that have been composed for aesthetic effect rather than as a simple record. Many of the color illustrations in this book are examples.

When you are reasonably certain you know what you want, borrow large samples—a full length of drapery material, a piece of upholstery large enough to cover a good portion of a chair or sofa. It may save money in the long run to get a large piece of wallboard and paint it the color you think is best for your walls. Study these at different times of day or night because their effect will change with the kind of light. Large samples are important because:

□ Increasing an area of color often changes its apparent hue, value, and intensity.
□ Color combinations at small scale only hint at the full-scale effect.

Factors to Consider in Selecting Colors

Color combinations generally are best when thoughtfully related to you and the other members of your household. Your possessions, specific rooms and their orientation, as well as the whole house and the surrounding environment, will influence possible choices.

People   The people using a home every day always come first. While it is risky to make generalizations, the following principles tend to hold true:

□ Active, vigorous people often prefer strong, contrasting colors.
□ Quieter persons sometimes favor rather cool, neutralized, harmonious schemes.

Possessions   The furniture and accessories now owned, as well as planned purchases, both limit and suggest possible color schemes.

□ A collection of antique furniture, good paintings, or individualized accessories might determine colors.
□ Miscellaneous furnishings can often be pulled together by a related scheme.
□ When starting from nothing, a favorite color or combination of colors might be the guide in selecting furnishings.

The living room in Plate 30 (p. 198) can be analyzed in terms of the colors in one dramatic painting and a beautiful Oriental rug. Dark slate floors with a bluish cast form a harmonious background for both; the sofa has been upholstered in a blue similar to one rectangle in the painting and in the rug's motif; accents of orange and red throughout the room pick up other colors from the painting. Even the warm tones of wood furniture and paneled ceiling seem to blend with the orange-and-blue color scheme for a totally unified effect.

Rooms   The walls of a room—including the windows and their treatment, the doors and fireplaces—are the largest color areas. Floors and ceilings come next in size, then furniture and accessories. In the past, typical color relationships broke down as follows:

□ Floors moderately dark in value and low in intensity to give a firm, unobtrusive base and to simplify upkeep
□ Walls usually lighter in value than floors in order to provide a transition between them and the ceilings, and typically quite neutral in intensity to keep them as backgrounds
□ Ceilings very light in value and very low in intensity for a sense of spaciousness and for efficient reflection of light

Although this standard approach can give a satisfying up-and-down equilibrium, there are many reasons for deviating from it. Light floors, for example, make a room seem luminous and spacious, and maintenance is no longer a problem with the new materials and textures. Dark walls give comforting enclosure, and they unify miscellaneous dark objects (Fig. 262). Intense colors for floors, walls, or furniture are a welcome relief from all-too-prevalent drabness. A survey of the color illustrations will disclose many of the devices that can be used successfully to personalize and individualize color schemes.

Room size, shape, and character seem to change with different color treatments, a factor often underestimated. In planning a new house, color should be considered along with the other aspects of design. Older houses are most easily remodeled by an "architectural" use of color. A few generalizations are:

☐ Cool hues, light values, and low intensities make small rooms seem larger.
☐ Rooms too long and narrow can be visually shortened and widened by having one end wall warmer, darker, and more intense than the side walls.
☐ Rooms that are too square and boxlike seem less awkward if one or two walls are treated differently from the others or if one wall and the ceiling or the floor are similar in color.

Plate 31 (p. 198) shows a room that is essentially a tall box, with a plain wood floor and white walls. That it becomes dramatic and exciting depends partly on the fact that furnishings have been kept very spare and simple, but also on the

opposite: 262. Walls painted chocolate brown create a sense of warm enclosure and make a coherent mass out of books and miscellaneous objects arranged on shelves across an end wall of the room. (*Courtesy Karastan*)

right: 263. Large windows shaded by overhangs illuminate a kitchen built with wooden floor, cabinets, and ceiling. Light-colored, highly reflective countertops brighten the otherwise dark interior. Thompson & Peterson, architects. See also Figs. 214, 646. (*Photograph: Morley Baer*)

introduction of striking color—a pure, saturated red—that stands out against the stark black and white. In other words, rather than trying to fight the boxiness of the room, the owners actually enhanced it and brought it to life.

Windows and their orientation affect the character of rooms and have a bearing on color schemes:

□ In rooms well lighted by large windows or good artificial illumination, colors will not be distorted. In rooms with less light, colors seem darker and duller (Fig. 263).

□ Rooms facing south and west get more heat and more light (of a yellowish hue) than those facing east or north. These differences can be minimized by using cool colors in south and west rooms, warm colors in east and north rooms.

The Whole House   Regarding the rooms of a home, especially those of the group living spaces, separately has dangers, because a home is a unit, not a collection of rooms. Unified color schemes recognize this and bring harmony and continuity; they increase visual spaciousness and make it possible to shift furnishings from one room to another without disturbing color schemes. This makes sense. But what about monotony? That is a matter of personal opinion—and of the colors used.

Architectural character of a sort positive enough to be a factor in color selection is regrettably uncommon. If, though, your home or even one room in a home has such a quality, regard it as an asset and emphasize it with an appropriate color organization (Fig. 264).

264. Color contrasts distinguish wall planes and emphasize the architecture of a house remodeled by owner-architect Tim Prentice. The partial wall at right and the staircase wall are painted vivid orange, with the stairs providing an accent; the fireplace wall is black. The remaining wall and ceiling surfaces are creamy white. (*Photograph: Norman McGrath*)

The geographical environment, regional and local, is a factor, but how much attention should be given to it is a personal decision. Connecticut, Louisiana, Arizona, and Oregon differ from one another in climate, geography, vegetation, and the architecture that such conditions indicate. Specific location is also of consequence. An apartment in San Francisco's fog belt might or might not suggest colors that would be appropriate to a ranch house on the sunny, rolling hills a few miles away (Pl. 1, p. 7). Sympathetic study of our surroundings helps us find colors that relate to their larger setting.

Economies with Color

Color can more than earn its cost; it can actually save money if wisely used:

- □ A coat of paint on one or more walls of a room will change the atmosphere more cheaply than any other single device.
- □ Old, battered, nondescript furniture takes on renewed vitality with new paint.
- □ Bands of color painted around windows are inexpensive substitutes for draperies: floors painted in suitable colors, possibly textured or patterned, lessen the need for rugs; painted graphics on walls cost less than wallpaper.
- □ A preponderance of light-value colors can cut electric bills and probably improve vision.
- □ Warm colors in the home make people comfortable at lower, probably more healthful temperatures.
- □ Cheering colors lessen the apparent need for vitamins and tonics.
- □ Colors that do not fade, or that fade gracefully, minimize replacement.
- □ Nature colors, especially if patterned, not only reduce daily and weekly maintenance but remain passably good-looking longer than do most clear, sharp colors.
- □ A unified color scheme throughout the house makes for economical interchangeability of furniture, draperies, and rugs.

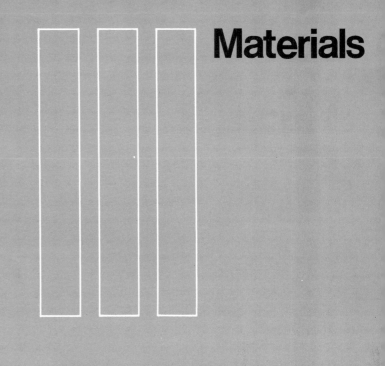

Materials

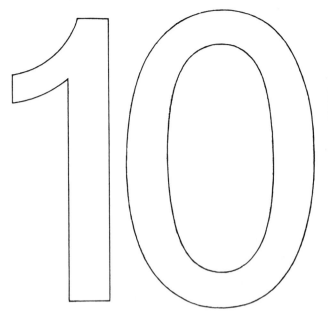

10

Wood and Masonry

Wood and masonry have served human beings as building materials ever since the earliest civilizations were inspired to improve upon animal skins and existing caves for their shelters. Both abundant in nature, wood and masonry offer the advantages of strength and relative permanence; yet both can be shaped with a measure of ease. In addition to its role in structural building, wood has functioned as a basic material for furniture and other artifacts in the home at least since the days of ancient Egypt. Today, despite the incursion of plastics, many people still think automatically of wood in terms of furnishings, particularly such items as tables, chairs, and chests.

Both wood and masonry possess special warm qualities that cause them to retain their popularity even though other newer materials may prove superior for practical considerations. In the case of wood, there is perhaps a subtle awareness of its once having been part of a living tree, and thus being more responsive to us as living creatures. Masonry, on the other hand, has as its major component the substance of the earth itself; a timeless, enduring quality inheres in masonry structures, which makes us feel safe and protected.

Wood

Wood was a natural selection as the chief material for a weekend house set on a narrow lot in a Connecticut village (Figs. 266–268), surrounded as it is by older houses built in the New England wood vernacular. Most immediately noticeable are the fences and wood curtain walls that afford privacy but still allow a feeling of movement around and through the house. Dark, 20-foot-high wooden poles support the walls and roof; combined with areas of glass and the wood panels, they create a handsome structural pattern of light and dark. Although the architect has maintained a strict geometry with rectangles predominant, the use of natural wood for the poles and walls, together with the exposed wall studs, results in an effect neither hard nor formal. A strong sense of precise order contrasts happily with the free-growing tree in the foreground. In winter, the tree casts lively shadows over the façade; in summer its foliage would give welcome shade.

There were many reasons for selecting wood as the principal building material of this house, quite aside from fitting it in with its neighbors. One is the remarkable strength of wood in relation to its size and shape. Notable in this respect is its

opposite: 265. Four different natural materials—metal, wood, ceramic, and concrete—arranged in simple forms combine to make an elegant, almost abstract still life. (*Photograph: Philip L. Molten*)

266–268. The nature of wood, its warmth and color, humanize the strict geometry of this vacation house in New England. Richard Owen Abbott, architect.

left: 266. Although the house is amply lighted by large glass window walls, the "privacy screens" of wood dominate the design and give the necessary seclusion to life within. (*Photograph: John T. Hill*)

below left: 267. A simply constructed sunken conversation pit, covered in blue carpeting, draws people in to the warmth of the open-faced metal fireplace. (*Photograph: John T. Hill*)

below right: 268. Much of the interior space consists of one large hall, partially subdivided for diverse uses. Only the bedroom and bath on the first floor have complete privacy; the studio and bedroom on the mezzanine are protected by their placement, but not walled in.

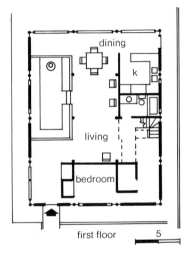

first floor   5

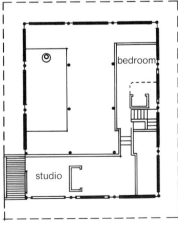

mezzanine floor

269. A great soaring arc that reaches up to encircle the bedroom-balcony of this house exploits the tensile strength of wood. Mark Mills, architect. (*Photograph: Morley Baer*)

tensile strength: it resists breakage when subjected to bending or pulling forces (Fig. 269), as anyone who has handled a bamboo fishpole knows. In the Connecticut house (Fig. 266) tensile strength permitted wood to be used for spanning gaps, such as those above the windows and in the wide stretch of ceiling. Tensile strength also suits wood to *cantilever* construction—a horizontal member projecting beyond a support. Both the roof, which extends freely beyond the house walls, and the suspended balcony that protects the entrance at one end and the kitchen area at the other are cantilevered.

Wood, further, has considerable strength in compression; that is, it retains its shape under pressure. This feature makes it practical for such upright forms as the poles supporting the structural framework. In addition, wood is slightly resilient, so it is appropriate for floors and furniture; a good insulator, it does not get so hot or cold as masonry and metal, nor does it readily transmit heat or cold.

Wood is comparatively inexpensive in original cost, and it can be maintained economically. Such woods as cedar, cypress, and redwood survive exposure to weather with little upkeep. The original cost of wood walls for interiors exceeds that for plaster walls, but wood requires less maintenance. At the end of ten years the total cost of wood and plaster is about the same; from then on wood costs less in time, energy, and money. Hardwood furniture requires relatively little care.

We would enjoy wood for its beauty and character even were it not for its utility and economy. Wood grain and color show a perfect union of variety and unity: no two pieces are identical—even the two ends or sides of one piece are not exactly alike—and yet a powerful, organic unity marks each piece and relates many pieces. The rhythms are as subtle and inevitable as those in waves or clouds, ranging from almost parallel linearity to an intricate complexity of curves. Some wood grains are emphatic, others quietly subordinate. Finally, wood is as pleasant to touch as it is to look at.

Wood has several major limitations: it burns, rots, and decays; insects attack it; and it may swell, shrink, or warp with changes in humidity. Also, as a natural resource it is finite in quantity. These factors, however, can be minimized to a great extent. Research has disclosed many processes for eliminating the less desirable qualities of wood, and with careful reforestation the supply can be renewed indefinitely. Basic measures include:

☐ Judicious **farming** and management of our forests to ensure a continuing stock, coupled with the consideration of other materials, such as masonry, metal, and plastics, where their qualities can serve to advantage.

☐ **Selection** of the best wood for specific conditions. Redwood and cedar, for example, resist rot and decay; walnut and mahogany have beautiful color and texture and can be carved intricately.

☐ Proper **drying,** which minimizes rotting, shrinking, and warping. In certain cases impregnation with plastics, such as polyester, will harden and stabilize the wood.

☐ **Designing** wood objects with respect for the nature of the material.

☐ Application of appropriate **finishes** or preservatives.

☐ Sympathetic **care** and maintenance.

Wood derives from plants ranging in size from pencil-thin bamboos through Australian eucalyptuses nearly 400 feet high to California redwoods as large as 100 feet in circumference. Differences in strength, hardness, durability, and beauty are almost as great as is the diversity of appearance among trees. Table 10.1 lists the significant characteristics of woods often used in homes.

Wood is usually classified as *hard* if it comes from broad-leaved trees that in colder climates drop their leaves in winter, such as maple, oak, and walnut; as *soft* if it comes from those trees with needlelike leaves retained throughout the year, such as pine, cedar, and redwood. In general, the hardwoods are in fact harder, as well as finer in grain, more attractively figured, and more expensive. The less costly softwoods shape more easily with typical tools, but they do not take fine finishes and intricate shapes as well. Considerable overlapping, however, occurs between the two types. For example, southern yellow pine is harder than chestnut, gum, basswood, or poplar, although the latter four are classified as hard because they derive from broad-leaved deciduous trees.

In selecting wood, you should keep in mind that every piece does not have to be top quality in all respects. Of course, wood must be strong enough to do its job, but for some purposes relatively weak wood suffices. Hardness offers an advantage when the wood is subject to wear but may be superfluous otherwise. Capacity to take a high finish, desirable in furniture wood, is unnecessary for exterior siding and shingles. Beautiful grain and figure provide a rewarding type of indoor ornament, but they would be essentially wasted outdoors. Plate 32 (p. 231) illustrates many potential uses for different woods inside the home: the walls and ceiling structure are warm-toned Western cedar, the floor hard oak, the sofa carved mahogany, the window chair bent cypress, the coffee table ordinary structural pine, the frames of the leather chairs sturdy maple. Each type of wood has been applied to the job it does best, yet despite the great variety an overall harmony prevails in the room.

Form in Wood

Many people today believe that the shapes given to wood—or to any other material—should develop out of its special qualities. Wood normally grows in tapering, pole-shape trunks and branches. Stripped of bark and cut into usable lengths, these poles have served in most parts of the world as the framework for tents covered with bark or skins, or for huts sheathed in bark or bunches of grass. Refined in shape, such poles are found in homes as posts and pillars (Fig. 270), as legs of tables, chairs, or cabinets, and as lamp bases. Tree trunks have been used, vertically or horizontally, as house walls in typical log-cabin fashion. Clearly, the pole is a basic wood shape, but further refinement is necessary to make the material truly versatile.

Trunks and branches can be squared to make heavy or light beams, or they can be sawed into planks or boards for furniture (Fig. 271), floors, ceilings, outdoor

left: 270. Partially squared wooden poles form the major supports for this house near Hilo, Hawaii. Further shaping of the pole into planks and boards serves as a theme that pervades the entire design. Oda/McCarty, architects. See also Fig. 112. (*Photograph: Julius Shulman*)

below: 271. Beautifully grained oak and rosewood, crafted to perfection, make a coffee table that is at once modern and classically elegant. (*Courtesy Dunbar*)

Table 10.1 Qualities of Selected Woods

Name	Source	Color and Grain	Character	Uses
alder (red)	one of few native hardwoods in Pacific Northwest	pleasant light colors from white to pale pinks, browns; close, uniform grain	lightweight, not very strong; resists denting, abrasion; shrinks little; stains well	chairs, other furniture
ash (white)	central and eastern United States; Europe	creamy white to light brown; prominent grain resembling oak; emphatic elliptical figures in plain-sawed or rotary cut	hard, strong; wears well; intermediate to difficult to work; intermediate in warping	furniture frames requiring strength; exposed parts of moderate-priced furniture; cheaper than most durable hardwoods
beech	central and eastern North America; Europe	white or slightly reddish; inconspicuous figure and uniform texture, similar to maple	strong, dense, hard; bends well; warps, shrinks, subject to dry rot; relatively hard to work, but good for turning; polishes well	middle-quality, country-style furniture; good for curved parts, rocker runners, interior parts requiring strength; also floors, utensil handles, woodenware food containers
birch	temperate zones; many species; yellow birch most important	sapwood, white; heartwood, light to dark reddish brown; irregular grain, not obtrusive; uniform surface texture; undulating grain	usually hard, heavy, strong; little shrinking, warping; moderately easy to work; beautiful natural finish; stains, enamels well	plywoods; structural, exposed parts of furniture, usually naturally finished (esp. Scandinavian); can be stained to imitate mahogany, walnut
cedar	north Pacific coast and mountains of North America	reddish brown to white; close-grained.	rather soft, weak, lightweight; easily worked; little shrinkage; resists decay; holds paint; red cedar repels moths	shingles, siding, porch and trellis columns, vertical grain plywood, cabinetwork, interior paneling
cherry	United States, Europe, Asia	light to dark reddish brown; close-grained	strong, durable, moderately hard; carves and polishes well	associated with Early American and Colonial furniture; now often used as a veneer
cypress (southern)	southeastern coast of United States; southern Mississippi Valley	slightly reddish, yellowish brown, or almost black; weathers silvery gray if exposed	moderately strong, light; resists decay; holds paint well	doors, sash, siding, shingles, porch materials; occasionally outdoor furniture
elm	Europe and United States	light grayish brown tinged with red to dark chocolate brown; white sapwood; porous, open, oak-like grain; delicate wavy figure	hard, heavy; difficult to work; shrinks; swells; bends well	somewhat sparingly in furniture; curved parts of provincial types; extensively used now for decorative veneers
fir (Douglas)	Pacific coast of United States	yellow to red to brownish; coarse-grained; irregular wavy patterns, especially in rotary-cut plywood; "busy"	rather soft, quite strong, heavy; tends to check, split; does not sand or paint well	plywood for exterior, interior walls, doors; cabinetwork; interior, exterior trim, large timbers, flooring; low-cost furniture, especially interior parts
gum (red or sweet)	eastern United States to Guatemala	reddish brown; often irregular pigment streaks make striking matched patterns; figure much like Circassian walnut	moderately hard, heavy, strong; tends to shrink, swell, warp; susceptible to decay; easy to work; finishes well	most-used wood for structural parts, with or imitating mahogany, walnut; also exposed as gumwood
mahogany	Central and South America, Africa	heartwood pale to deep reddish brown; darkens with exposure to light; adjacent parts of surface reflect light differently, giving many effects; small-scale, interlocked, or woven grain; distinctive figures	medium hard, strong; easy to work, carves; shrinks little; beautiful texture; takes high polish; always expensive	most favored wood for fine furniture in 18th century; much used in 19th century; used today in expensive furniture finished naturally, bleached, or stained dark
maple (sugar, and black, both called hard)	central and eastern United States	almost white to light brown; small, fine, dense pores; straight-grained or figures (bird's-eye, curly, wavy)	hard, heavy, strong; little shrinking, swelling if well seasoned; hard to work; has luster; takes good polish	Early American furniture; now used as solid wood for sturdy, durable, unpretentious, moderate-priced furniture; good for hardwood floors

Table 10.1   Qualities of Selected Woods (*continued*)

Name	Source	Color and Grain	Character	Uses
oak (many varieties; two groups: white and red)	all temperate zones	white oaks: pale grayish brown, sometimes tinged red; red oaks: more reddish; both have quite large conspicuous open grains; fancy figures rare	hard, strong; workable, carves well; adaptable to many kinds of finishes	standard wood in Gothic period, Early Renaissance in northern Europe, continuously used in United States; suitable for floors, wall panels, plywood; furniture, solid and veneer
Philippine mahogany (actually red, white Lauan, and Tanguile)	Philippines	straw to deep reddish brown according to species; pales when exposed to light; pronounced interlocking grain gives conspicuous ribbon figure	about as strong as mahogany, less easy to work; greater shrinking, swelling, warping; less durable, harder to polish	extensively used for furniture in past few decades; also plywood wall panels, which should be fireproofed
pine (many varieties similar in character)	all temperate zones	almost white to yellow, red, brown; close-grained	usually soft, light, relatively weak; easy to work; shrinks, swells, warps little; decays in contact with earth; takes oil finish especially well, also paint; knotty pine originally covered with paint	used throughout world for provincial, rustic furniture; in Early Georgian furniture for ease of carving, also paneled walls; often is painted or has decorative patterns; now used for inexpensive cabinetwork, doors, windowsash frames, structural members, furniture
poplar	eastern United States	white to yellowish brown; close-grained, relatively uniform texture	moderately soft, weak, lightweight; easy to work; finishes smoothly; stains and paints well	siding; interior, exterior trim; inexpensive furniture, cabinetwork, especially when painted or enameled
redwood	Pacific coast of United States	reddish brown; lightens in strong sun; becomes gray or blackish if allowed to weather; parallel grain in better cuts, contorted in others; decorative burls	moderately strong in large timbers, but soft and splinters easily; resists rot and decay	exterior siding, garden walls, outdoor furniture; some use for interior walls, cabinetwork
rosewood (several species, grouped because of fragrance)	India, Brazil	great variation from light to deep reddish brown; irregular black, brown streaks in fanciful curves	hard, durable; takes high polish	extensively used in fine 18th-century furniture, chiefly veneers, inlays; 19th-century solid wood; increasing use in furniture today
teak	Asia (India, Burma, Siam, and so on)	straw yellow to tobacco brown; striped or mottled in pattern	heavy, durable, oily; works and carves well; takes oil finish beautifully	widely used in Far East, both plain and for ornately carved furniture; now often used by Scandinavians for sculptural qualities
Tupelo gum	southeastern United States	pale brownish-gray heartwood merges gradually with white sapwood; lack of luster makes interlocking grain inconspicuous	hard, heavy, strong; good stability; moderately easy to work; tendency to warp	same purposes as red gum, although it is somewhat weaker, softer
walnut (American or black)	central and eastern United States	light to dark chocolate brown, sometimes dark irregular streaks; distinctive, unobtrusive figures of stripes, irregular curves; or also intricate, beautiful figures	hard, heavy, strong; warps little; moderately easy to work, carve; natural luster; takes good finish	in America from earliest times for good furniture, but especially in 19th century; now in high-grade furniture, paneling
walnut (Circassian,) (also called English, Italian, European, Russian, and so on)	Balkans to Asia Minor, Burma, China, Japan; planted in Europe for wood and nuts	fawn-colored; many conspicuous irregular dark streaks give elaborate figures; butts, burls, crotches add to variety	strong, hard, durable; works, carves well; shrinks, warps little; takes fine polish	a leading furniture wood since ancient times; used in Italian, French, Spanish Renaissance; in England, during Queen Anne period, 1660–1720, called age of walnut; imported for American furniture

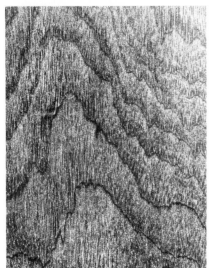

above: 272. The warmth of knotty pine wood paneling creates a background for a collection of gay, brightly printed fabrics and quilts. Edmund Stevens, architect. (*Photograph: Peter Reed*)

above left: 273. Quarter-sliced lumber is cut at approximately right angles to the growth rings, producing a series of longitudinal stripes—straight in some woods, varied in others. It shrinks less in width and also twists less than does plain-sliced lumber.

center left: 274. Plain-sliced lumber, cut parallel to a line through the center of the log, is usually cheaper than quarter-sliced lumber. The grain pattern generally is variegated parabolas.

below left: 275. Rotary-cut wood is peeled off the log into thin, continuous sheets by holding a cutter against the log while it is turning on a lathe—something like taking paper towels off a roll. It often produces complex wavy or ripple patterns. Rotary-cut veneers can be exceptionally wide. (*Courtesy Fine Hardwoods Association*)

siding, or indoor paneling (Fig. 272). Rectangularity facilitates fastening the pieces together. Timber can also be sawed into round blocks, suitable for such purposes as garden paving.

Wood structure is a complex organization of fibers and pores. Concentric *annual rings* increase the tree's girth; *vertical fibers* and *pores* run parallel to the trunk; and *medullary rays* radiate from the center at right angles to the vertical fibers and pores. When wood is cut, this structure becomes apparent and is called *grain* and *figure*. Therefore, the method of cutting will produce notably different results, as Figures 273 to 275 illustrate.

Beyond cutting and sawing, several other possibilities exist for handling wood. Small pieces can be glued or *laminated* together to create forms that would be impossible in straight-sawed lumber. The fanciful shapes typical of some hand-crafted furniture derive from lamination (Fig. 276). Another method consists of literally "unwrapping" the log by peeling it into very thin continuous sheets for veneers and plywood. Wood can also be subjected to heat and bent into curved shapes often seen in chairs (Fig. 189). Finally, one can grind or split wood into small pieces, then press the fragments together for wallboard and similar applications; grinding, softening, and bleaching are the first steps in making cardboard or paper; and many synthetic fibers depend upon dissolved wood as one component of the mixture.

These possibilities demonstrate the great virtuosity of wood, the manifold shapes it will take. Each has advantages that help determine its ultimate use.

Solid Wood   Solid wood needs no explanation. Its advantages are that:

☐ Satisfaction comes from knowing all the wood is the same as the surface.
☐ The edges of tabletops, chair seats, and so on do not expose the layer-cake construction of plywood (although these are usually concealed by another strip of plywood).
☐ The wood can be turned or carved.
☐ The surface can be planed in case of damage, or thoroughly sanded for refinishing, without fear of going through to another wood.
☐ The surface cannot loosen or peel off (as it may in improperly constructed veneers).

Major disadvantages are high cost and a tendency to warp, shrink, or swell.

276. New techniques of lamination have adapted wood to an even larger repertoire of form and ornament than was previously the case, as evidenced by this singular piece that serves as a seat-sculpture. Ralph Anderson, architect. (*Photograph: Julius Shulman*)

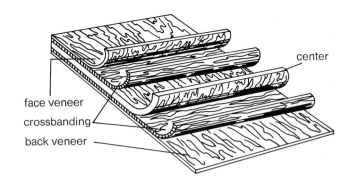

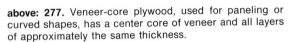

face veneer
crossbanding
back veneer
center

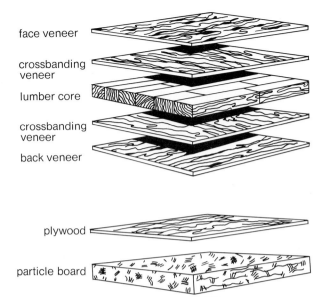

face veneer

crossbanding veneer

lumber core

crossbanding veneer

back veneer

plywood

particle board

plywood

above: 277. Veneer-core plywood, used for paneling or curved shapes, has a center core of veneer and all layers of approximately the same thickness.

above right: 278. Lumber-core plywood, suitable for table-tops and cabinet doors, has a thick center core of solid wood.

right: 279. Particle-board plywood, common in table or desk tops, has a thick center core of particle board (hard-board), a composite of small pieces of wood held together with resin binders.

Layered Wood   Veneers, plywood, and laminated wood are layered constructions consisting of one or more sheets of thin wood, thicker boards, or paper.

Veneers are thin sheets of wood produced by slicing with a knife, by sawing, or by rotary cutting. They can be glued to the top of thicker lumber to make what is referred to as "veneered wood," glued to paper for wall coverings, or glued to other veneers, as in plywood and laminates. Often, though, the term is used to refer specifically to the exterior surfaces that are usually of wood more expensive than that underneath.

Plywood is composed of an odd number of veneers glued together with the grain of adjacent sheets at right angles to each other (Fig. 277). Some plywoods have a center core of lumber or of pressed-wood board (Figs. 278, 279).

Laminated wood (as distinguished from an object made by lamination) is a type of plywood in which the grain of successive layers goes in the same direction. It is frequently used for those parts of furniture—such as the back and seat of Charles Eames' chair (Fig. 281)—that are bent and in which the major stresses and strains are in one direction.

The popular notion that veneers and plywoods are cheap substitutes for the real thing is a misconception. To be sure, they are usually less expensive than solid wood, especially in the better grades of hardwood, because the expensive wood goes much further when used as a veneer. But they also have other advantages:

☐ They are available in much larger pieces (up to 5 feet wide and 16 feet long) than solid wood.
☐ They are typically stronger than solid wood of the same thickness and weight.
☐ They are less likely than solid wood to shrink, check, or warp excessively.
☐ They are less liable to splitting by nails or puncturing by sharp objects.
☐ They give almost identical grain on several pieces that can then be matched to produce symmetrical figures.
☐ They permit use of fragile, highly figured woods that, if solid, might split apart or shrink irregularly.
☐ They lend themselves readily to curved and irregular forms.

□ They make possible flush surfaces of large size that are dimensionally stable.
□ They make possible a more extensive use of rare, costly woods.

These characteristics open many new design possibilities, some of which are shown in Figure 280. Factory-built wall panels of plywood have been used both as structure and as surface, interior and exterior, of a house designed to demonstrate the possibilities of plywood as an architectural system. The wall, roof, and floor panels, plus a prefabricated joint system, were trucked to the site and quickly attached. Plywood is available with many surface textures, from smooth to rough or with embossed patterns. Here the patterned, rough-textured surface in natural-color plywood creates a lively interplay with the sleek, smooth-surface fireplace and furniture.

Veneers and plywood are widely used today both as wall paneling and for furniture because of their superior performance and because they enable designers to match grain and figure effects. But perhaps no plywood constructions have approached the superb economy of form and material in Charles Eames' chair, which has become a contemporary classic (Fig. 281). The compound curves of the molded plywood seat and back have great strength, both literally and aesthetically, and show off the handsome pattern of the surface veneer. Attached to the tubular steel supports by an ingenious electronic rubber weld at one spot only, both seat and back are slightly resilient but nevertheless solidly supportive. The elegance of the design has resulted from an optimal correlation of material and process.

left: 280. Plywood paneling, arranged in sections at different angles, creates dramatic linear patterns in this prefabricated house. See also Fig. 461. (*Courtesy American Plywood Association*)

above: 281. Many of the characteristics of wood—such as tensile strength, slight resilience, and ability to be shaped and molded—are superbly demonstrated in this chair, originally designed by Charles Eames in 1946. (*Museum of Modern Art, New York [gift of the Herman Miller Furniture Company, U.S.A.]*)

Wood and Masonry   223

Ornament in Wood

Wood possesses a great diversity of inherent or structural ornament in its grain, figure, texture, and color. Not only does each species of wood have its own general type of pattern, but different aspects of these patterns can be brought to light by the way in which the woods are cut. In addition to the beauty of typical grains, some woods show amazingly intricate deviations of figures, which have long been cherished by furniture designers (Fig. 282). *Stripes* and *broken stripes; mottles* and *blisters* of irregular, wavy shapes; and *fiddleback, raindrop, curly,* and *bird's-eye* figures are but a few, to which must be added all the figures found in stump or butt wood: *crotches, burls,* and *knots.*

Texture   Actual surface texture makes a kind of ornament and largely determines the effectiveness of a grain. *Roughly sawn* wood, which has an uneven, light-diffusing texture that minimizes grain, is not pleasant to touch; wood designers normally reserve it for exterior work or for pieces that exhibit a rustic character (Fig. 283). *Resawn* wood is considerably smoother, with a soft texture not unlike that of a short-pile fabric; it reveals but does not emphasize the grain. *Smoothly finished* wood reflects light, emphasizes the figure, and is pleasant to touch.

above left: 282. Bob Stocksdale's shaped platter of black walnut shows off the beauty to be found within a block of wood.

above right: 283. The texture of rough-sawn wood has been enhanced by a heavy metal gate pull that confirms its character. (*Photograph: Morley Baer*)

left: 284. The pure beauty of superbly crafted wood joints has been emphasized in this chair to make an important design element. (*Courtesy C. I. Designs*)

Color   Different woods naturally display an enormous variety of colors, from whitest birch to darkest ebony. A room entirely paneled in redwood or knotty pine, for example, has a warm mellow quality (Pl. 33, p. 231). Vividly colored or plush fabrics seem a natural foil for broad areas of rich wood. Designers often exploit the contrast of different wood colors in such techniques as inlay and parquetry (Fig. 288).

Joints   The way in which different pieces of wood are brought together creates structural patterns of considerable importance. Overlapping shingles and siding have long been appreciated, not only for utilitarian reasons but because of their enlivening patterns of light and dark. A similar effect occurs when boards have beveled edges. Some modern designers emphasize and exploit wood joints for the sheer beauty of their pure forms (Fig. 284).

Moldings   Applied, narrow strips of wood that project from the surface of ceilings or walls are called moldings (Fig. 285). Today they have declined in popularity, because of our desire for simplicity and clean lines. In practical terms, however, wall moldings can help to maintain the home, since they prevent furniture from rubbing against the walls. They can also emphasize direction or set up a rhythmic pattern of their own; *board-and-batten* construction, in which narrow moldings cover the joints between boards, establishes a vertical or horizontal movement. Often, they frame such elements as paintings to separate them from their background; they also form transitions between planes, as in elaborate moldings that relate wall to ceiling.

Carving and Turning   The nature of wood has suggested **carving** from earliest days in all parts of the world, and the great periods of furniture are known as much for their carving as for their more basic qualities of design. Gothic carving in oak, Renaissance carving in walnut, and 18th-century carving in mahogany

285. Wooden moldings help to give this room a quality reminiscent of Shaker designs (see Fig. 816). The lower chair-rail molding prevents furniture from marking the wall; the upper one has pegs all around for hanging things, such as the candle fixture. (*Courtesy Better Homes and Gardens.* © *Meredith Corporation, 1972. All rights reserved.*)

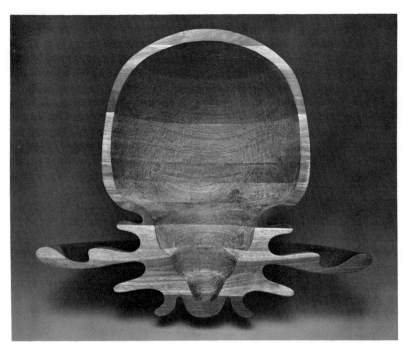

left: **286.** The age-old art of turning wood on a lathe inspired designer Stephen Hogbin to apply the process to laminated wood. The result is a fresh and spirited form. (*Photograph: Christl/Sliva*)

below: **287.** A heavily carved wood door provides a handsome introduction to a house constructed mainly of wood and glass. The rectangular pattern of the carving has been picked up in the chair coverings and in a wall hanging in the background. Tozier & Abbott, architects. (*Photograph: Julius Shulman*)

opposite: **288.** A dining table hand-inlaid with a pattern of beautifully grained and colored wood rests on a base of solid oak. (*Courtesy J & D Brauner*)

effectively enhanced form. **Turning** is also an old art, and ever since the lathe was invented we have enjoyed the many diverse ways in which a rapidly rotating piece of wood can be shaped for furniture parts, balusters, columns, and utensils (Fig. 286). Designers of almost every period produced turnings with distinctive profiles, such as the 16th-century melon bulbs, the 17th-century balls or sausages, and the spool, the bead and ball, the knob, the vase, and composite types that were popular in many countries at various times.

Elaborate turning and carving of high quality are rare but not unknown in contemporary design. They require much time and skill to produce and can increase household maintenance noticeably. But a beautifully carved element, such as a door, offers a wonderful decorative accent for an otherwise clean-lined design (Fig. 287).

Pieced Design in Wood   Inlay, intarsia, marquetry, and parquetry are techniques that combine different woods—or sometimes metals, ivory, shell, and other materials—in such a way that the contrasting colors and textures make patterns in a plane surface (Fig. 288). **Inlay** is a general term that has come to encompass all the various methods; **intarsia** refers to that type in which the pieces are inlaid in solid wood; **marquetry** applies to designs inlaid in veneers and then glued to a solid backing; and **parquetry** indicates geometric patterns, especially in floors and tables.

Contemporary taste has moved away from the harsh austerity often associated with "modern" design, but there is still very little complex applied wood ornamentation of good quality. Design in wood today covers a wide range, from the simple contrast of putting old, ornate furniture in a contemporary setting (Pl. 2, p. 7) to the exploration of concentrated enrichment suited to our own age (Fig. 287). Many designers are working with sculptural form in furniture that is pleasing when seen from any angle and that combines comfort and convenience with sensuous delight and lyricism (Fig. 276).

Wood Finishes

Anything done to a freshly sanded piece of wood takes away some of its pristine satiny beauty—but that beauty will soon disappear if no finish whatever is put on it. All but a few woods used in certain ways need some protective finish to keep the surface from absorbing dirt and stains; to give an easy-to-clean smoothness; to minimize excessive or sudden changes in moisture content; to protect the wood from rot, decay, and insects; and to prevent wood from drying out by

Table 10.2 Wood Finishes

Name	Composition	Application	Result	Use
bleach	various acids, chlorine compounds	brushed on (if bleaching agent is strong enough to affect wood, it will also affect skin)	lightens wood, neutralizes color, usually makes grain less conspicuous; not dependably permanent; wood loses some luster	to make furniture and inferior wood paneling pale, blond; also used on outdoor furniture and siding to give a weathered look
enamel	varnish mixed with pigments to give color, opaqueness	brushed or sprayed over undercoat since it has less body and covering power than most paints	generally hard, durable coat, like varnish; usually glossy, may be dull; wide range of colors	chiefly on furniture, cabinets, walls getting hard use and washing; also on floors
lacquer	cellulose derivatives, consisting of resins, one or more gums, volatile solvents, a softener, and a pigment (if colored)	regular lacquer best applied with spray since it dries rapidly (15 min.); brushing lacquers dry slowly, make brush application feasible	hard, tough, durable; resistant to heat, acids; not suitable for outdoor wood because of expansion, contraction; glossy, satiny, or dull	transparent lacquers much used on furniture, walls; opaque on furniture
oil	boiled linseed oil or various other oils; usually thinned with turpentine	brushed or wiped on, excess wiped off, allowed to dry, sanded or rubbed; between five and thirty coats—more the better; hot oil sinks into wood, brings out grain	penetrating, very durable finish with soft luster; darkens and yellows wood somewhat at first, considerably in time; protective, not conspicuous; must be renewed	oil, often mixed with beeswax, used in Europe from early times to 17th century; now used on indoor and outdoor furniture and on siding
paint	pigments suspended in linseed oil or, more commonly now, in various synthetics; usually contain a drier to hasten hardening	brushed, rolled, or sprayed on	opaque coating, varies from hard, durable gloss to softer dull finishes; hides character of wood; new types dry quickly with little odor, are easy to apply and have good covering power	protects and embellishes; painted furniture popular in ancient Egypt, the Orient, Europe since Middle Ages; much Colonial furniture was painted; widely used now on exterior and interior walls and furniture

289. A table finished with "Sideroclear"—a new process that is achieved by spraying several substances that meet, catalyze, and then cover the surface—is practically indestructible, being scratchproof, dentproof, even resistant to direct flame. (*Courtesy Intrex, Inc.*)

replacing lost oils. An appropriate finish might enhance the grain with oil; change the color with stain; or hide an unattractive color and grain with opaque paint. Table 10.2 lists the typical wood finishes and their characteristics.

Finishes can penetrate or stay on the surface; be transparent and colorless, transparent but colored, semiopaque, or opaque; and they can vary from a dull mat to a high gloss. To say that any one of these finishes is better than the others, except for a specific purpose, would be pointless. Today, however, many people like to see wood changed as little as is compatible with its use and therefore prefer transparent, colorless, satin finishes. On the other hand, extremely durable opaque finishes are becoming popular for certain applications. The following general principles may serve as guidelines in choosing the best finish for a particular wood and purpose:

☐ Opaque finishes hide the wood character, give a smooth uniformity, and offer great possibilities for color.
☐ Transparent finishes reveal the character of the wood and absorb minor damage that comes with use.
☐ Penetrating finishes, such as linseed oil, produce a soft surface which may absorb stains but will not chip or crack.
☐ Plastic-impregnated finishes harden wood, give it greater density and strength, and can make it almost totally impervious to damage. A new technique of applying a surface coating is said to resist even a lighted cigarette (Fig. 289).

Table 10.2 Wood Finishes (*continued*)

Name	Composition	Application	Result	Use
shellac	resinous secretion of an insect of southern Asia, dissolved in alcohol	brushed, rubbed, or sprayed on; dries rapidly; many thin coats, each rubbed, gives best finish	changes character and color of wood very little; soft satiny to high gloss finish; fragile; wears poorly; affected by heat, moisture; water spots	primarily as an easily applied, quick-drying undercoat
stain	dye or pigment dissolved or suspended in oil or water	brushed, sprayed, or rubbed on	changes color of wood without covering grain (often emphasizes grain or changes surface noticeably); usually darkens wood to make look richer	frequently used to alter color of furniture woods thought unattractive, or in imitation of expensive woods; outdoors compensates for weathering
synthetics	wide range of polyester, polyurethane, polyamide, vinyl; liquid or film; newest type finish; continuing new developments	usually factory-applied; *liquid* impregnates wood; *sprays* form a coating; *film,* typically colored, is bonded to wood with laminating adhesive	durable, long-lasting finish; resistant to abrasion, mars, chemicals, water, or burns; clear or colored, mat to glossy surface; film type difficult to repair	exterior siding; interior walls, floors, furniture; very good wherever abrasion, moisture, or weathering is a problem
varnish	various gums, resins dissolved in drying oils (linseed, tung, or synthetic), usually combined with other driers; dye or pigment makes varnish-stain	brushed or sprayed on; many thin coats best; dries slowly or quickly, depending on kind, amount of thinner used	thin, durable, brownish skin coating, little penetration; darkens wood, emphasizes grain; dull mat to high gloss; best when not thick, gummy	known by ancients; not used again until mid-18th century; widely used today on furniture, floors, walls, chiefly interior
wax	fatty acids from animal, vegetable, mineral sources combined with alcohols; usually paste or liquid; varies greatly in hardness, durability	brushed, sprayed, or rubbed on, usually several coats; often used over oil, shellac, varnish, but may be used alone	penetrates raw wood; darkens, enriches, emphasizes grain; soft to high luster; must be renewed often; may show water spots and make floor slippery; other finishes cannot be used	very old way of finishing wood; generally used today as easily renewed surface over more durable undercoats; some liquid waxes used alone on walls, floors, furniture

☐ Glossy finishes reflect more light than dull ones, are more durable because of their hard, dense surface, and facilitate cleaning, but they also show blemishes more readily. Gloss can be reduced by adding thinner to the paint or by rubbing with sandpaper, steel wool, or pumice. The shine also dulls with age and use.
☐ Many coats of any finish, sanded or rubbed between coats, give a more durable, attractive result than one or two coats applied thickly.

More than any other material, wood ties the house together structurally and visually. It remains one of our most useful, beautiful resources and has more than held its own in spite of the great advances in plastics, glass, and metal. In fact, the newer materials, having relieved wood of some applications to which it was never completely suited, have allowed us to see more clearly how wonderful wood really is. Much as we admire other materials, few of them arouse the deep responses that wood generates.

Masonry

Strictly speaking, masonry is defined as anything constructed of such materials as stone, brick, or tiles that are put together, usually with mortar, by a mason. Nowadays, however, the term also includes plastering and concrete construction. The materials of masonry derive from inorganic mineral compounds in the earth's surface. They are of crystalline structure and typically hard, dense, and heavy.

290. Large rocks, slightly shaped, give a rugged, enduring quality to the fireplace wall of a house in Beverly Hills. Further shaping produces the smooth slabs necessary for a level floor. John Lautner, architect. (*Photograph: Julius Shulman*)

Masonry materials offer numerous advantages. They do not support combustion, rot, or decay, nor do they invite insects or rodents. Most of them are long-lasting, require little maintenance, and retain their shape under great pressure. Their colors and textures range from the smooth whiteness of plaster to the abrasiveness of black lava rock. They can be shaped with rectangular solidity or curved buoyancy; some are left plain and simple, others laid up in complex patterns or carved. Above all, a timeless quality—their seeming imperviousness to destruction—makes us feel secure (Pl. 34, p. 232).

These properties explain why most historic architecture still in existence is of masonry. Best known are the large religious or public buildings, but throughout the world thousands of unpretentious houses of stone and brick still stand. The essence of historic masonry construction (with the exception of Roman work in concrete) was the piling of blocks on top of one another and usually joining them with mortar. Because such walls must be very thick and rest on solid foundations, they are expensive. They do not allow large unobstructed openings (unless these are arches), and they offer no space for the pipes and wires now so essential. Thus, solid masonry construction is seldom used today for an entire structure but often serves for one or more walls of a home (Fig. 290). Varied kinds of masonry also perform well in foundations, fireplaces, and chimneys, and in outdoor paving or interior floors that rest on the ground. In the 19th and 20th centuries, many new methods and materials have been developed. These include masonry reinforced with metal to decrease weight and bulk without lessening strength, hollow blocks of brick or concrete, and thin-shelled concrete structures (Fig. 303).

Masonry, though, has limitations other than high original cost. Although comparatively permanent, plaster and stucco crack, concrete blocks chip, and the softer stones disintegrate more rapidly than might be expected. All are difficult to repair. In comparison with wood or metal, masonry is not very strong in tension. Further, most masonry offers fairly poor insulation against cold and dampness, and most types reflect rather than absorb noise.

right: Plate 32. Many different woods are combined to create a warm, personal living space. The flowing curves of a Victorian sofa and bentwood chairs serve as a counterpoint to flat areas of wood in the paneling and curved inner wall, as well as to the angles of the ceiling beams. Alfredo De Vido, architect. See page 218. (*Photograph: Norman McGrath*)

below: Plate 33. Warm knotty pine paneling combines with wicker furniture, masses of baskets, and colorful fabrics to produce an unusually inviting interior. Tozier & Abbott, architects. See page 225; see also Fig. 584; Plate 14, p. 77. (*Photograph: Julius Shulman*)

above: Plate 34. An old mill in Bucks County, Pennsylvania, has a rubble masonry wall and rough-hewn beams, which contrast with a rather formal tile floor and traditional furnishings. The whole achieves a gracious ''country'' look. See page 230; see also Figs. 503, 585. (*Photograph: John T. Hill*)

right: Plate 35. The exposed brick wall, rustic cupboard, and colorful woven bedspread make a cozy and secure bedroom for this New York City apartment. L. Serota, designer. See page 235. (*Photograph: Wesley Balz, courtesy of House Beautiful. Copyright 1971, The Hearst Corporation.*)

right: 291. The rubble masonry walls of a house by the sea have rocks piled up in almost random fashion, the chinks filled in with smaller stones, giving a decidedly rough-hewn character in keeping with the site. John H. Gamble, architect. See also Fig. 295. (*Photograph: Julius Shulman*)

below: 292. Random ashlar masonry makes a striking, massive fireplace wall in this Minnesota house. John H. Howe, architect.

Masonry can be divided into two major categories. **Block materials**—stone, bricks and tiles, concrete or glass blocks—are delivered to a building site in their finished form and assembled on the job with mortar. Block masonry further subdivides into three basic types. *Rubble masonry,* rugged and informal, has untrimmed or only slightly trimmed stones laid irregularly. It is generally the least costly and least formal kind of stonework (Fig. 291). *Random ashlar masonry* is more disciplined but still rustic. The stones will be more or less rectangular in shape but will vary in size. Usually, it gives a decided feeling of horizontality, even though the joints are not continuous (Fig. 292). *Ashlar masonry* calls for precisely cut

right: 293. An old foundry, lovingly restored to become a dramatic contemporary house, has brick walls all around—a form of ashlar masonry. The hearth was originally an iron-monger's fireplace. Jerome Brown, architect; Cherry Brown, designer. (*Photograph: Hedrich-Blessing*)

below left: 294. A fireplace built of large stones embedded in concrete rests on one huge boulder that acts as a raised hearth. See also Fig. 637. (*Photograph: Morley Baer*)

below right: 295. In a California beach house, large smooth pebbles and stones embedded in concrete seem to make an unbroken path from the ocean right into the house and up the stairs. Such a floor is very easy to maintain. John H. Gamble, architect. See also Fig. 291. (*Photograph: Julius Shulman*)

rectangular stones (or bricks) laid with continuous horizontal joints. It tends to have a more formal quality and is the most expensive type of stonework (Fig. 293).

Moldable materials—including concrete and plaster—are shaped at the building site from a semiliquid state according to a variety of methods.

Stone

A concreted earthy mineral, stone has so many desirable qualities that it would undoubtedly be used more widely if it were not so expensive. Because of its resistance to fire, stone seems naturally associated with walls and fireplaces (Fig. 294). Belonging to the earth, it has a natural application in floors that are subject to hard use and in outdoor paving (Fig. 295). Its permanence gives garden or house walls a uniquely reassuring character. Wherever stone is used, its crystalline structure, varied colors and textures, and differing degrees of opaqueness and translucency provide a very special visual and tactile appeal.

Although innumerable kinds of stone could be adapted to homes, four are commonly seen today:

☐ **Granite,** an igneous rock composed of feldspar, quartz, and various minerals, is dense, hard, and fine to coarse grained. Available in light to dark grays, pinks, greens, and yellows, it can take a high polish and be precision cut, but in house design granite is most often used in its natural state for walls and fireplaces.
☐ **Limestone,** which includes various sedimentary rocks, is relatively soft and easy to cut. Colors range from almost white to dark grays and tans. Its most common use is in exterior walls and, as travertine, in table tops.
☐ **Marble,** a compact crystalline limestone, takes a beautiful polish, is often variegated, and comes in white, grays, pinks and reds, greens, and black. Contemporary designers, searching for structurally ornamented materials, have found it a handsome substance for fireplaces, tabletops, and counter tops.
☐ **Slate,** a sedimentary rock that splits easily into thin sheets with smooth surfaces, makes good interior flooring or outdoor paving. In addition to the typical bluish gray, slate is available in green, red, or black.

Brick

Among the oldest of artificial building materials, brick is still much in favor because, in addition to having the assets of masonry, it can be made by hand or machine from clays found almost everywhere. Brick weighs less than stone, an important factor in shipping and laying. Because of their relatively small size, bricks can be laid up around a hollow core or simply as a facing on one side of a wall, which leaves room for pipes and wiring and still forms a reasonably thin wall (Pl. 35, p. 232). Cavity-wall construction has the additional advantage that the trapped air acts as a nonconductor of heat, cold, and moisture. Bricks come in many sizes, shapes, colors, and textures; they can be laid in a number of patterns. Being fireproof, weather-resistant, and easy to maintain, they have long been a popular material for fireplaces and chimneys, as well as for exterior and interior wall surfaces. They make excellent garden paving, because their color and texture render them glareless and unslippery. No matter where they appear, bricks introduce an orderly rhythmic pattern of a scale appropriate for homes. They are particularly effective in large, comparatively simple masses. The only drawback is cost.

Typical **clay bricks** are blocks of clay hardened by heat in a kiln. A standard size is $2\frac{1}{4}$ by 4 by $8\frac{1}{4}$ inches, but the dimensions can vary considerably. Although *brick red* is a common designation, colors range from almost white, pale yellow, and pink through oranges and reds to browns and purples. On the basis of texture as well as resistance to breakage, moisture, and fire, clay bricks are conventionally divided into several types:

296. Handmade adobe bricks—a building material with a long history—take on new meaning when contrasted with walls of glass. Cliff May, architect. (*Photograph: Maynard L. Parker*)

☐ **Common** or **sand-struck** bricks, made in a mold coated with dry sand, have slightly rounded edges and are used for exposed side walls or as a base for better-quality bricks.

☐ **Face bricks,** generally formed by forcing clay through a rectangular die and cutting it with wire, have sharp edges and corners; they are more uniform in color and texture, as well as more resistant to weather than common bricks.

☐ **Paving** or **flooring bricks** are still harder, because they have been fired at higher temperatures to withstand abrasion and to lessen absorption of moisture.

☐ **Firebricks** are most often yellow; they make an ideal material for places subject to great heat, such as the backs of fireplaces.

Adobe brick differs from clay brick in that the clay is generally combined with a cement or asphalt stabilizer and dried in the sun (Fig. 296). Builders in the warm, dry parts of the world have employed adobe brick for centuries, and the material has recently come back in favor in the southwestern United States.

Like clay and adobe bricks, *clay tiles* consist of heat-hardened clay, but they are thinner than bricks and often glazed. Clay tiles are discussed in Chapter 11.

Concrete Blocks

Once an ugly duckling hidden apologetically in foundations, concrete blocks have now come out into the open and lend themselves to many applications. They share certain characteristics with clay bricks, but they are composed of cement and are not fired (although drying may be hastened with low heat). Concrete blocks tend do be much larger than bricks, so a single thickness of blocks forms a sturdy wall (Fig. 297). Nearly always they are hollow.

Most popular today are the lightweight-aggregate blocks made with such porous materials as cinders, pumice, or volcanic ash instead of sand and gravel. Their lighter weight—about half that of older concrete blocks—makes them less expensive to transport. Concrete blocks are larger than bricks, typical sizes being 8 by 8 by 16 inches and 4 by 8 by 16 inches. Consequently, they can be laid quite rapidly. Their porosity and hollow cores provide some insulation against heat and cold and also absorb noise. Moreover, the cores offer a natural space through which utilities can be threaded. Finally, the colors of lightweight-aggregate blocks are much pleasanter than the old, chilling gray. In mild climates, walls of these blocks need no treatment other than waterproofing, although they can be painted, plastered, or stuccoed.

Glass Blocks

Hollow blocks of glass capable of being set together in mortar come in many sizes and shapes. Different types vary in the amount of light and heat they transmit. Some, for example, reflect the high summer sunlight but allow the winter sun's low rays to warm a home's interior. Glass blocks are one of the few materials that admit light but give a degree of privacy, provide reasonable insulation against heat and cold, and make a supporting wall of any strength. Further, the manner in which they diffuse light and create changing abstract patterns from objects seen through them can be highly decorative. In the living room shown in Figure 298, glass blocks break up a solid wall of stuccoed concrete block, spreading the light and balancing that coming through a large window on the opposite wall.

above: 297. In a desert house, concrete blocks coil up from the rocky terrain to create a structure visually compatible with the environment. The blocks also insulate the house against heat and cold. Frank Lloyd Wright, architect. (*Photograph: Maynard L. Parker*)

right: 298. An informal, irregular pattern of glass blocks set in a stuccoed concrete-block wall actually lets in small amounts of light while figuratively lightening the large expanse of wall. Joseph Amisano, architect. (*Photograph: Gordon H. Schenck, Jr.*)

Concrete

Concrete is a mixture of cement with sand and gravel or other aggregates. One volume of cement to two of sand and four of gravel makes the usual mix. Concrete begins its existence as a thick slush, takes the form of any mold into which it is poured, and hardens to a heavy, durable mass often called "artificial stone." The Romans used concrete extensively; it is by no means new. But in the past century the variety of ways in which it has been employed, especially in large structures, makes concrete seem like a revolutionary material. Its great virtues are plasticity when wet and durability after it hardens. No other material combines these two qualities in the same degree.

Two factors have tended to limit poured concrete to such basic but unemphasized parts of the home as foundations, basement floors, walls, terraces, walks, and driveways. First, the cost of forms used only once on the site is very high for anything more elaborate than simple outlines. Second, ordinary concrete has a bland, rather institutional color and texture. Fortunately, there are many ways of getting around these disadvantages:

☐ Concrete can be prefabricated in blocks or slabs under efficient mass-production methods, using the same forms over and over. These slabs or blocks can then be assembled in different configurations on the building site to provide individualized homes.
☐ The inclusion of aggregates other than sand and gravel improves the color and texture of concrete, as well as its insulating properties.
☐ The surface can be varied by adding colored pigments, troweling it smoothly, or giving it any number of textures.
☐ The gravel used in concrete can be exposed in either of two ways: *terrazzo* refers to a concrete made with stone chips and polished to reveal an irregular mosaic-like pattern; *broom-finished* describes a pebbly-surfaced concrete made with round pebbles from which the surface coating of concrete has been brushed off.
☐ One can apply paints and dyes (of special types to withstand the strong alkaline reaction of concrete) to the surface. Paints generally are thick enough to smooth the surface, while dyes are transparent and penetrating.
☐ Plaster or stucco can also be applied as a surface coating.
☐ Concrete lends itself to carving in the same manner as stone (Fig. 299).
☐ Materials other than gravel can be embedded in the concrete to enrich the surface.
☐ New methods of spraying concrete often result in highly original homes (Fig. 300).

During the last few years concrete has come into its own particularly in the area of mass-produced, multifamily housing. The development of *reinforced concrete,* in which steel rods are embedded in the material before it hardens, unites the tensile strength of metal with the compressive strength of concrete to make possible relatively lightweight, fireproof units that are capable of almost infinite variation. Precast slabs, such as those described above, can be attached to a steel skeleton of virtually any height. Boxes can also be prefabricated at a factory to the point where electricity, plumbing, kitchens, and bathrooms have been installed and the walls finished. Such mass-production methods offer promise of lowering housing costs, but their potentialities and limitations are still being evaluated. The apartments shown in Figure 301 were constructed by an ingenious system of stacking prewired, preplumbed, reinforced concrete boxes in a checkerboard pattern, with the open cells then closed off by various prefabricated panels to become more rooms. The checkerboard pattern, by avoiding duplication of walls, floors, and ceilings, results in cost savings during construction and allows considerable flexibility in design.

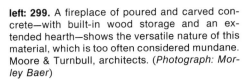

left: 299. A fireplace of poured and carved concrete—with built-in wood storage and an extended hearth—shows the versatile nature of this material, which is too often considered mundane. Moore & Turnbull, architects. (*Photograph: Morley Baer*)

below left: 300. "Earth House," designed by Paolo Soleri in 1956, is an experimental project in which concrete is cast over a mound formed from earth, with steel reinforcement added as necessary. The structure forms part of a studio complex near Scottsdale, Arizona. (*Photograph: Ivan Pintar*)

301. Precast concrete modules are lowered into place to form an apartment building. The spaces between modules will be partitioned off for additional rooms. (*Courtesy Shelley Systems, Inc.*)

302. A beautifully intricate plaster molding highlights this formal turn-of-the-century Brooklyn living room. The sliding doors—here unusually rich with stained glass—were a standard feature in townhouses of this era. (*Photograph: John T. Hill*)

Plaster and Stucco

Plaster and stucco have been popular building materials for centuries in many parts of the world because of their special qualities. **Plaster** is a thick, pasty mixture of treated gypsum and water, combined with such materials as sand and lime. **Stucco** refers to weather-resistant plaster most often used on exteriors. Both plaster and stucco generally are applied on a *lath,* a term now used for a lattice of thin strips of wood, metal sheets with grillelike perforations, or special types of hardboards. They can also be applied to any masonry surface that is rough enough to hold them, such as concrete blocks.

Like concrete, plaster and stucco will hold any shape given them before they harden. They can smoothly cover simple or complex surfaces with no visible joints. Both accept texturing, coloring, or painting, and interior plaster walls can be covered with paper or fabrics for embellishment and protection. Many older homes show how well suited these materials are to varied kinds of sculptural enrichment (Fig. 302). A further advantage is their moderate original cost.

Under some conditions both plaster and stucco create maintenance problems. Cracks or chips are common unless precautions are taken. On smooth, light colored walls these may be conspicuous, as are fingerprints, soot, and scratches. Although not expensive, the original cost of plaster is higher than for many of the hardboards, which provide better insulation against heat, cold, and noise.

Form in Masonry

With a few exceptions, the design of block masonry in contemporary American homes is limited to selecting stones or blocks available in the area and then organizing them into simple, usually rectangular masses. The shapes in which boulders and stratified rock appear can without much effort be adapted to rubble or random-ashlar masonry, which often seems more in the nature of the material than would a precise organization. Concrete blocks and bricks, having been molded to uniform rectangularity, typically are laid in the regularly repeated, clear-cut patterns of ashlar masonry. These treatments are, of course, traditional. What is particularly of this century is the way in which the weight and density of stone, brick, or concrete blocks are contrasted with the comparative lightness of wood and with the transparency of large areas of glass.

Another major category of masonry design is that possible with plaster and with sprayed or poured concrete. Holding any shape given by molds or mason's tools, these plastic substances are suitable for myriad shapes that are curved or angular, simple or complex. We see in architect John Covert Watson's own home (Figs. 303–305) an example of the fresh and imaginative forms that emerge when stereotyped notions of how a house should look are abandoned in favor of exploring new materials or new methods of dealing with old materials. In this case the spraying of concrete over a mesh made from steel rods of varying thicknesses produced a self-supporting shell that is at once walls, roof, interior, and exterior.

That masonry can be treated in many other ways is evidenced by the subtle forms created in marble by the ancient Greeks, by the soaring spires and lacelike tracery of the Gothic cathedral, by the majestic, formal structures of the Renaissance, or by the thinness of contemporary concrete shells that seem to float above their sites. And over the centuries, much masonry has been recycled. For example, archaeologists often find only foundations when they search for evidences of earlier civilizations; the stones or bricks from the old walls provided the raw material to build new structures. In our own time, many people prefer "used brick" to new for its more mellow look, and stone barns are recycled into homes or give up their stonework for new fireplaces. It is evident that masonry has its own very special appeal of enduring and substantial security.

303–305. The amorphous nature of sprayed concrete invites shaping, as this Texas house shows. John Covert Watson, owner-architect.

above right: 303. To form the shell, concrete has been sprayed over a basketwork of steel bars in domed forms that seem to grow from the land. (*Courtesy House Beautiful. Copyright 1973, The Hearst Corporation*)

above left: 304. The various textures and surfaces possible with masonry have been used to advantage in the living room, but concrete's essential unyielding quality has been softened with a deep pile rug, repeated curves in the furnishings, and plenty of greenery. (*Courtesy House Beautiful. Copyright 1973, The Hearst Corporation*)

right: 305. The plan shows how the concrete shell seems to protect and enclose the life within.

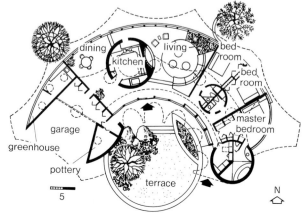

Ceramics, Glass, Metal, and Plastics

As materials, ceramics, glass, metal, and plastics share important characteristics. Since all are shaped while in a plastic, liquid, or malleable state, they lend themselves to a tremendous diversity of shapes. All are subjected to heat and/or pressure in processing. Except for some plastics, all are inert; that is, they will not burn, rot, decay, or appeal to insects and vermin. Each of these materials, nonetheless, has its own special potentialities and limitations that challenge designers and bring liveliness to our homes. As we go through the chapter, we will see how the specific qualities of each material have led to forms characteristic of its unique nature.

The materials that give a dining room in England its austere, uncluttered grace have been imaginatively fashioned and combined (Fig. 306). Although each—ceramics, glass, metal, and plastics—has been shaped to exploit special qualities, the result is not quite what we would expect from our usual contacts with the materials. The wall panels on the back and on one side are of aluminum, the lightness of which permits them to swing open on pivots. We have not been conditioned to seeing metal used for house walls, but nevertheless in this instance it works. The red brick floor is certainly common enough, but it brings an element of surprise in such a modern setting. Although the glass in the window wall on the left is familiar, its appearance in an unframed round dining table top, through which the simple metal X-supports and the brick floor can be appreciated, shows more innovation, as does the irregularly shaped mirrored construction over the serving unit. This unit is of brilliant white plastic, a material we might expect to see in a kitchen; here its pristine elegance of design suits it to a more formal setting. By treating these materials to expose their nature and then sensitively combining them, the designer has revealed their beauty.

Ceramics

Long before early civilizations began to write, they fashioned useful and symbolic objects from clay. Since then, this material has been of continuing and conspicuous importance in homes. All of us are aware of the dishes used for eating, of ashtrays, vases, and lamp bases. But this field also includes many sculptural pieces, bricks and tiles, chimney flues, and drain pipes. All these are *ceramics,* which is a short way of saying objects made of clay hardened by heat. Essential steps in the forming process are:

□ Combining clays to make a suitable *body*
□ Moistening the clay sufficiently to make it workable
□ Shaping the clay by hand, on the potter's wheel, or in a mold
□ Allowing the pieces to dry
□ Firing the pieces to harden them permanently

The process may also involve decorating the object with carving, painting, or other techniques; and perhaps *glazing*—that is, applying a glasslike coating to the outside and/or inside, and then firing the piece once again.

Clay Bodies

The clays used for a ceramic body naturally affect the characteristics of the finished product, and clays differ in many properties. Colors range from white through the most common reds, tans, grays, and browns to black. Textures vary from coarse, irregular, and open to fine, even, and dense. Clays also have different *maturation points,* or firing temperatures at which they will attain their maximum hardness but not yet begin to melt and deform. Generally, those clays that hold their shapes at high temperatures make the stronger objects, because the separate clay particles fuse together, or *vitrify,* into a homogeneous and waterproof mass. Almost never does a single clay offer all the qualities desirable for working and design; consequently, the ceramist will mix two or more clays in varying proportions to produce the desired combination. The result is a clay *body.* For convenience, ceramic bodies can be grouped into four major types, although each has a wide range of characteristics that may overlap those of the other types.

306. The special qualities of ceramics, glass, metal, and plastics have been used in distinctive ways to confer harmony and unity on this dining room in Yorkshire, England. Walker, Wright & Schofield, architects. (*Photograph: Michael Boys*)

Earthenware Coarse clays fired at comparatively low temperatures produce earthenware, a typically thick, porous, fragile, and opaque ware. Most often red or brown, earthenware is the material of bricks, tiles, and most folk pottery. Unglazed, it lends itself particularly well to flowerpots and planters, since the clay body "sweats" and allows the soil to breathe. Another common application is in special baking dishes for meat and fowl (Fig. 307), which permit food to cook in its natural juices. The glazes suitable for earthenware tend to be soft and may have very bright, glossy colors. In recent years many artists have begun to explore the possibilities of earthenware for sculptural form.

Stoneware Finer clays—generally gray or light brown—fired at medium temperatures result in stoneware, a relatively strong, waterproof, and durable ware. Most common in medium-price dinnerware (Fig. 308), to which such imprecise designations as *ironstone* may be attached, stoneware is also the predominant material of sculptural ceramics. Typical glazes have a mat finish, more subtle colors, and a much wider range of effects than are possible with earthenware.

China A somewhat general term, china describes a white, vitrified ware that is translucent if thin (Fig. 309). In common usage, china differs from porcelain only in its slightly lower firing temperature, but some manufacturers produce a ware called *fine china* that is indistinguishable from porcelain. *English china* or *bone china* has a white, translucent body and a soft but brilliant glaze; it actually contains a certain percentage of animal bone. *American vitreous china* offers unusual resistance to breakage and chipping of the body, to scratching in the glazes and decorations.

Porcelain High-grade, expensive dishes and ornamental ware represent the major products of fine porcelain (Fig. 310). A white ware fired at extremely high temperatures, porcelain is completely vitrified and often translucent. The body resists breakage, and the glazes are very hard.

top: 307. Earthenware casseroles, excellent for preserving nutrients, are decorated with traditional designs. (*Romertopf, courtesy Bloomingdale's*)

left: 308. A pattern reminiscent of kaleidoscopic designs fits neatly within the borders of plates and around the bottoms of cups in "Marbella" stoneware. (*Courtesy Royal Doulton*)

above: 309. The intricate detail in Wedgwood's Columbia Enamelled pattern seems in keeping with the scale and formality of the bone china forms.

left: 310. A tea service designed by Luigi Colani exploits the delicacy and grace of pure white porcelain. (*Courtesy Rosenthal Studio-Haus*)

The purist would say, with some justification, that earthenware suggests simple, vigorous shapes and ornamentation and that increasing precision and refinement should be expected as one goes from stoneware to china and porcelain. Not always, however, does this formula apply, for other factors affect ceramic design.

Form in Ceramics

The possibilities and limitations of form in any material are determined by its physical properties, the methods by which it is formed, the intended use of the end product—and the skill and sensitivity of the designer.

The physical properties of clay differ markedly before and after firing. In its unfired state clay consists of small powderlike or granular particles. When a small amount of water is added to the dry clay, the result is a malleable, plastic mass; the addition of more water produces a creamy liquid called *slip*. After firing, clay is hard and brittle, with little tensile strength. Ceramic objects, therefore, break quite easily when struck or dropped, and thin edges or protrusions are vulnerable.

The forming methods for clay divide into two general categories: hand techniques and mass-production techniques. In hand construction, the clay can be *thrown* on the potter's wheel, rolled into sheets or *slabs* (which may then be assembled in different ways), or carved and molded sculpturally. Mass-produced ceramic ware is shaped by pouring slip into molds, by pressing plastic clay in molds, or by *jiggering,* a process in which plastic clay on a revolving mold is formed by a template. Almost any shape is possible in clay, as the history of ceramics proves, but most dishes, vases, and similar household objects are round and relatively compact, because round forms come naturally from the wheel and the jigger. Rounded shapes are easy to hold, and they provide a pleasant relief from the basic rectangularity of our homes (Fig. 311). Important, too, is the fact that they have a minimum of edges to chip. In sum, rounded forms with compact outlines seem especially appropriate to ceramic dishes and ornamental objects.

311. A full-bodied round earthenware pot is hung against massive flat wooden timbers in such a way that each form complements and accentuates the other. See also Figs. 294, 637. (*Photograph: Morley Baer*)

below: 312. The spontaneous flowering of a sky-blue crystalline glaze on a cream background enhances the almost casual perfection of form in a covered jar by Jack H. Feltman. (*M. H. de Young Memorial Museum, San Francisco; photograph: R. W. Campbell*)

right: 313. A simply shaped stoneware bowl by Gertrud and Otto Natzler takes on great authority because of the boldness and texture of its "crater" glaze.

The practical aspect of round forms for certain purposes does not rule out other possibilities. Angular shapes are basic in bricks and tiles (Fig. 315); in household ceramics they can occasionally be useful as well as welcome surprises. Some extending forms, such as spouts on teapots or handles on cups, are worth the hazard of breakage. Then, fortunately, there is the creative urge to explore and experiment, to find forms that will reawaken our senses.

Ceramic Glazes

Glazes are coatings compounded from glasslike materials fused at high temperatures to the body of ceramic ware. In purely utilitarian terms, they increase efficiency by making the ware waterproof and easy to clean. More important, though, as an example of structural ornament, the textures and colors of glazes are primary sources of beauty.

Two examples will help to illustrate the limitless variety in glazes and the ways in which a glaze can be sensitively adapted to form. A delicate porcelain bottle by Jack H. Feltman (Fig. 312), simple in outline, has as its principal ornament a high-fire crystalline glaze. The intricate tracery of the glaze is perfectly at one with this slender, graceful form. By contrast, a rugged stoneware bowl by Gertrud and Otto Natzler (Fig. 313) seems part of the earth itself, with its pitted "crater" glaze and mat texture.

Glazes differ in the degree to which they join with and "fit" the clay body. A broken piece of glazed earthenware will show that the glaze forms a distinct layer on the porous body; but on most porcelains the glazes are so completely wedded with the clay that no sharp division can be perceived. Both clay and glazes shrink in firing. If the glaze and the body do not have the same rate of shrinkage, the glaze may develop a network of cracks. Some potters plan such effects deliberately for their ornamental value, but on dishes meant to hold food the cracks are more likely to be the result of poor workmanship.

Ornament in Ceramics

Often the basic form of a clay piece, with the addition of a glaze or glazes, is sufficient unto itself, making applied ornamentation unnecessary. However, because

of the ever-present urge to enrich a plain surface, ceramic objects have received their share of decoration. The medium seems to invite modeling, carving, and painting.

Modeling and **carving,** which give a three-dimensional play of light and shade, range from scarcely noticeable incised designs to vigorous shaping and cutting. Figure 314 shows both subtle incised designs and ornament that protrudes from the basic form. Sometimes stamps are used to impress designs on the clay while it is still plastic; in the case of Figure 307 the stamps were applied from both sides. *Sgraffito* (literally, "scratched") decoration results from coating a piece with slip—a thin liquid solution of clay—different in color from that of the base—and then scratching through to reveal the color underneath.

Colored pigments can be applied with a brush or through a stencil, transferred from decalcomanias, or printed mechanically. This decoration might be either under or over the glaze, and it offers endless design possibilities. *Underglaze* designs are applied before the final glazing (which is transparent), so they are protected from scratches and wear. *Overglaze* patterns are applied to the surface of glazed ware and fused with it at a low firing temperature. An overglaze design represents the cheapest and most common type of ceramic enrichment and when well done can be moderately durable.

With such possibilities, it is easy to see why ceramic design has always fascinated artists and industrial producers alike. Clay is, first and foremost, a sensuous material. A lump of it in the hands invites manipulation. Fascinated perhaps by this direct urge transmitted by the material and by the variety of modeled forms it would take and hold, ceramists have made clay one of the most versatile media known.

Ceramics in the Home

Bricks and tiles, glazed or unglazed and cemented together with mortar, play a very important design role in many homes. That tiles can be a significant component of domestic architecture is shown by the wide variety of patterns available in floor and decorative wall tiles (Fig. 315). Plates 36 and 37 (p. 265) show how two very different effects can be achieved with ceramic tiles. In Plate 36 the floor of an elegant sitting room has been surfaced in octagonal brick-red tiles with a

left: 314. In a covered jar by Donald Frith a fine, incised decoration is used in the sections that would normally be touched by hands, thus throwing into contrast the heavy modeling of the basic clay form.

right: 315. These glazed ceramic tiles from Spain, with an emphatic relief design, would make a colorful, easily maintained wall surface. (*Courtesy Country Floors, Inc.*)

left: 316. Humble earthenware drain tiles imaginatively shelter a passageway from extreme natural elements while still allowing in some light and breeze. Anshen and Allen, architects. (*Photograph: Maynard L. Parker*)

above: 317. Clay pots seem at home in almost any setting and take naturally to an informal arrangement of dried weeds. Charles Warren Callister and Henry Herold, architects. (*Photograph: Philip L. Molten*)

below left: 318. The heavy glaze on a classically shaped hand-thrown ceramic lamp base picks up a glow from the light above. (*Courtesy Design-Technics Ceramics, Inc.*)

clear glaze that allows the color to show through. The floor provides the major color element in the room. Plate 37 shows a renovated country cabin in which blue and white tiles, laid in a checkerboard pattern, circle the fireplace to provide a rustic quality in keeping with the setting.

An interesting and unique application of ceramics in the home marks a contemporary Mexican house (Fig. 316), in which ordinary clay drain pipes, banked in even rows, have been used to make a whole wall, filling the gaps between stone piers. They not only create an ever-changing pattern of light and shade but give protection against rain, sun, and wind.

Finally, of course, there remains the potential for "spot" enrichment in the home with individual ceramic pieces. Their design importance and character can range from the large, dramatic weed pot that is a major focus of attention (Fig. 317) to the simple, classic lamp base (Fig. 318). Either one represents a modern interpretation of a tradition for rounded clay objects in the home that is almost as old as civilization.

Glass

The evolution of glass from a semiprecious substance available only in small quantities—for making such things as beads and amulets—to a commonplace material that can be bought anywhere and installed in large sheets has altered our homes as much as any single factor. Its history is fascinating. Glassmaking appears to have developed from ceramic glazes, some of which were made at least six thousand years ago; but the oldest known glass objects are about four thousand years old. The Romans fabricated glass objects of such beauty that the best were valued higher than vessels of gold. Sheets of glass for windows were also known in the Roman Empire, but window glass was not common in small homes until the end of the 18th century. Today glass is an everyday, extraordinarily versatile material found in everything from cooking utensils to house walls (Fig. 319).

Glass is made by melting and fusing at very high temperatures the basic ingredients—silicates, alkalis, and lime—plus various other materials that give certain qualities. Crystal, the finest glass, contains lead. Color comes from minerals: red from gold and copper, blue from copper and cobalt, yellow from cadmium and uranium. Special effects—such as opacity, bubbles, or crystallization—and special forms, including glass fibers and insulation, result from chemicals or from the way in which glass is treated.

The general characteristics of glass are:

☐ Transparency unrivaled until recently by any other common material
☐ Capacity to refract light in a gemlike way
☐ Wide range of colors, degrees of transparency, and textures
☐ Plasticity, malleability, and ductility that permit a great variety of shapes, from threadlike fibers to large thin sheets
☐ Imperviousness to water and most alkalies and acids
☐ Resistance to burning (but will melt at very high temperatures)
☐ Moderately high resistance to scratching
☐ Low resistance to breakage through impact, twisting or bending, and sudden temperature changes (except with special types)

Glass is the standard material for tumblers and goblets meant for drinking liquids. Nonabsorbent, tasteless, and odorless, it feels pleasantly cool to hands and lips, is not harmed by anything that we can safely drink, and is inexpensive. Clear, colorless glass allows us to see what we are drinking and to enjoy the crystal clarity of water and the color of lemonade or wine. Colored glassware adds its own special

319. Only the introduction of glass with glareproof, reflective, and insulating properties made possible a house set in the woods of upstate New York in which walls almost entirely of glass wrap around the living core. Robert E. Fitzpatrick, owner-architect. (*Photograph: Joseph W. Molitor*)

qualities to table setting. The fragility of glass presents a major drawback, a small price to pay for its good qualities unless you have small children, eat outdoors, or snack casually in various parts of the house. Then, tumblers of anodized aluminum, stainless steel, or durable plastics are worth considering.

Glass is also used for other food receptacles with varying degrees of success. Glass salad bowls and plates are attractive when filled but become less appealing than opaque wares as the meal nears completion. Glass cups can hold hot tea or coffee but seem less appropriate than ceramics for ordinary use. Cooking utensils of glass have their special advantages, but they are harder to clean and less durable than metal.

Along with metal, glass seems particularly suitable for candleholders because of the way in which it sparkles. It makes attractive flower containers if you have good-looking flower holders, arrange the stems under water attractively, and keep the water very clear.

In sheet form, glass serves as the standard material for mirrors and windows, and sometimes for sliding doors and tabletops. For her Lunario tables, Italian designer Cini Boeri cantilevers severely plain round or oval glass shapes from bases of polished steel in a daring display of the transparency and relative tensile strength of glass (Fig. 320).

Unless it is kept polished, glass—especially colorless and transparent glass—loses most of its beauty. Finger and water marks or specks of dust are more conspicuous on clear, shiny glass than on most other materials. Under some circumstances the transparency of glass can make it a hazard to the unwary, especially in poorly designed window walls or sliding doors.

320. In the "Lunario" table, the transparency of glass reveals and accentuates the off-center poise of the table top on an ellipsoid base. Cini Boeri, designer. (*Courtesy Knoll International, Inc.*)

left: 321. A free-blown clear glass vase—an assemblage of three bubbles topping a hollow tube—strongly evokes the act of blowing glass. Willem Heesen, designer. (*Courtesy Glasvormcentrum Leerdam*)

above: 322. In these molded goblets, elongated globules of heavy glass provide a harmonious contrast of weight and structure to clear stems in the same material. Sigurd Persson, designer, for Ab Kosta Glasbruk, Sweden. (*Courtesy Sundahl*)

Form in Glass

What was said about form in ceramics might almost be repeated for glass, because, in both, an amorphous substance takes form while it is plastic or liquid; the final product is hard and usually brittle, and breakable; and process, material, and use lead naturally—although not exclusively—to rounded forms, Glass, however, adds a second major form category in flat sheets for house furnishings and architectural elements.

Two other distinctive qualities of glass should be mentioned. The first is that glass, technically speaking, always remains a liquid. Therefore, even when rigid, as it is at ordinary temperatures, it is actually a "supercooled liquid." Second, an almost perfect union of form and space can be achieved with glass. We look less *at* a transparent glass bowl or tumbler than *through* it to the space enclosed and the space beyond. Large windows give a similar effect. Contemporary designers and architects interested in the relation of form to space have a special feeling toward this material so closely uniting the two.

Hand-blown Glass   Just as the bowl is a natural shape for ceramics formed on the potter's wheel, the bubble is the natural form for hand-blown glass. In blowing glass by hand, the craftsman dips a hollow metal rod into molten material, blows it into a bubble, and then forms the hot, soft mass into the desired configuration by rolling, twisting, or shaping with tools while it is still hot and plastic. The bubble form of the vase in Figure 321 seems very much in the nature of the material and sympathetically appropriate. But because hand blowing is a time-consuming, expensive procedure, most household glass derives from procedures more suited to quantity production.

Molded and Pressed Glass   In a mass-production situation, molten glass is blown or pressed by machinery into cast-iron or wooden molds. The molds can be simple or intricate in shape and leave a plain or patterned surface on the glass (Fig. 322).

Drawn or Rolled Glass   Two processes apply to the manufacture of sheet glass. *Drawing*—the method by which inexpensive window glass is made, calls for molten glass to be drawn from furnaces in never-ending sheets, flattened between rollers, and cut into usable sizes. Although satisfactory for most purposes, drawn glass tends to be weaker, thinner, and more subject to flaws than plate glass. In *rolling,* the method for making plate glass, molten glass is poured onto an iron casting table, distributed and smoothed by rollers, then ground and polished. Today, sheets of plate glass more than 50 feet long are possible, and manufacturers can incorporate special qualities to make the glass shatterproof or to give sound, heat, cold, and glare control, as well as reflective properties.

Ornament in Glass

It is not easy to draw a sharp line between form and ornament in glass. Structural ornament can be added before glass is shaped by incorporating in the material substances that give color, make the glass translucent or cloudy, or produce such visual textures as bubbles or opaque streaks. Sometimes form becomes so complex that it serves as its own decoration, as do the globular shapes on the vase in Figure 321. An entire glass piece can be fluted, ribbed, or ringed with swirling patterns (Fig. 323). The glassblower can also "drop on" globs of molten glass to produce almost liquid ornament on the one hand or practical appendages such as handles on the other. Molded or pressed glass takes its texture, as well as its form, from the mold in which it is processed. Beyond this, several other types of applied enrichment are possible.

Cut Glass   Although glass was beautifully cut by the Romans, the technique experienced a renaissance about A.D. 1600, when a court jeweler in Prague applied gem-cutting techniques to glass. Rich effects come when the design is cut through an outer coating of colored glass to reveal colorless glass underneath. In colorless crystal, cutting gives many surfaces to catch and break up light (Fig. 324).

Engraved Glass   As with cut glass, engraving is done with wheels and abrasives; but engraving produces a shallow intaglio that by optical illusion often seems to be in relief. Firmness of form, sharpness of edge, and easy-flowing curves distinguish engraved glass from that which is pressed, cut, or etched.

Etched Glass   Either hydrofluoric acid or sandblasting will etch glass. The frosty etched surface can be left in that state or polished to smooth transparency (Fig. 325). Etching is often used to imitate engraving, but the designs are not so sharp nor so subtly modeled. Usually shallow and delicate, etching can be 2 inches deep, as it is in some heavy French pieces.

Enameled and Gilded Glass   After looking at some of the cheap enameled or gilded glass frequently seen today, we are tempted to call these processes inventions of the devil. But in the past some very beautiful glass was made by burning colored enamels or gold and silver into the surface.

Leaded and Stained Glass   Composed of small pieces of glass set in a pattern and held in place by strips of lead or copper foil, leaded and stained glass have recently undergone a revival because of their capabilities as enrichment (Fig. 326). Leaded glass usually refers to transparent glass, colorless or clear, often used as a window. Stained glass—enameled, painted, or colored by pigments baked onto its surface or by metallic oxides fused into it—can serve in windows, lampshades, or wherever its translucency can be highlighted by a strong light source. Some modern techniques laminate or bond colored glass to a sheet of glass or plastic, instead of piecing it together by means of lead or foil. The owners of the house

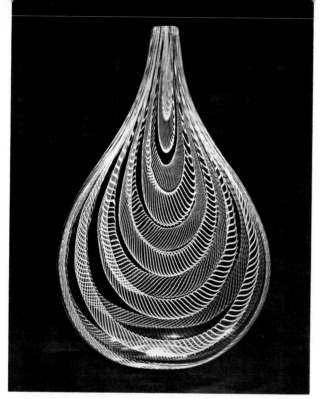

above left: 323. A *latticinio* pattern of white and amethyst threads of glass embedded in clear glass accentuates the teardrop shape of a bottle designed by Archimede Seguso of Italy. (*Corning Museum of Glass, Corning, N.Y.*)

above right: 324. Handcut lead crystal goblets, a sparkling accent on the table, reveal and intensify the gleam of any liquid they contain. (*Courtesy Waterford Glass, Ltd.*)

above: 325. A fresh approach to the design of etched glass resulted in these graceful goblets with the pattern confined to the lower part of the cup, where they would naturally be held. Björn Wiinblad, designer. (*Courtesy Rosenthal Studio-Haus*)

right: 326. A handsome old doorway with a clear leaded glass fanlight and stained glass side panels awaits recycling by an imaginative builder. (*Photograph: Thomas B. Hollyman, Photo Researchers, Inc.*)

shown in Plate 38 (p. 266) had their architect design the home around a collection of salvaged old glass windows. Sunlight coming through the surrounding trees and the glass creates a tranquil aura for their recycled furniture.

Architectural Glass

Although glass for buildings is generally thought of as transparent, colorless, smooth, and flat, it can be frosted or pebbly, ribbed or corrugated, and colored to control light, heat, even vision. Glass can also be curved to fit specific installations. Some architectural glass is tempered for safety; other types have a core of metal mesh that reduces the hazard of breakage in addition to being decorative. In the past, homeowners had to choose between opaque walls and transparent windows and then frequently cover the windows with curtains or blinds for visual protection. Now there is a glass that allows people to see out but blocks the inward view. And insulating glass, which has double panes welded together with a special dry gas between, makes possible large areas of glass even in cold climates. Architects have made use of these new capabilities to produce houses with walls almost totally of glass but still private and secure inside, such as that illustrated in Figure 319.

Glass Mirrors

Recently mirrors have served almost exclusively for utilitarian purposes in bedrooms and bathrooms, but they, too, are again coming into their own as sources of visual pleasure. Many metals can be given reflecting finishes, but mirrors as we usually think of them consist of glass with a metallic backing that provides distortion-free reflections of whatever is in front of them. They can be invaluable in visually expanding the size of a small room, as the dining room in Figure 327 shows. Mirrors also spread light throughout a room and bring sparkle into dark corners. Although most often given a plain silvery backing, they can be of other colors or of smoked glass; their usual flat surface can be curved to give interesting distortions or broken up by facets to create dazzling interplays of light and color.

Fiberglass

The great versatility of glass is indicated by the fact that its ingredients can also be spun into fibers for insulation, fabrics, or rigid forms. Spun glass was used for centuries in a purely decorative way, but not until about 1893 were its utilitarian values appreciated. Then neckties and dresses of spun glass and silk were exhibited as curiosities: they were heavy, scratchy, and too stiff to fold. As discussed in Chapter 12, glass textiles have come a long way since 1893. Today glass fibers provide insulation against extreme temperatures and sound. Another development is foam glass, made by introducing a gas-producing agent into molten glass. Filled with so many tiny air bubbles that it will float on water, it has excellent insulating properties. And we are all familiar with the many types of fiberglass panels that can make lightweight, translucent fencing or roofing materials. Fiberglass also appears in molded furniture that is so durable it can be used for public seating as well as less demanding home furnishings (Fig. 328).

Metals

Although metal was first reduced from ore about 5000 B.C., its application to domestic architecture was unimportant until recently. Today the typical "wood house" uses more than four tons of metal, but only a small portion is visible. Such is not the case with the house illustrated in Figure 329. Here the unique structural

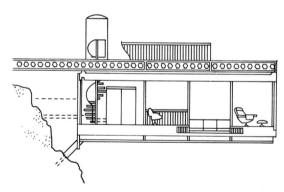

right: 329. The nature of self-weathering steel—its maintenance-free character and tremendous resistance to stress—is given dramatic evidence in a vacation aerie. The pattern of cutouts in the upper beams lightens their weight without diminishing their strength. Harry Weese, architect. (*Photograph copyright © O. R. Cabanban*)

above: 330. A section of the house pictured in Figure 329 illustrates its almost total independence of the site, except for the anchorage of steel beams.

qualities of metal, visibly exploited, permitted construction on a seemingly un-buildable site. The 1000-square-foot house, enclosed by walls of glass and of a self-weathering steel that never needs painting, is supported by a double canti-levered grid of steel beams that thrust it out from a steep cliffside in an audacious display of the tremendous tensile strength of steel (Fig. 330). For the stout of heart, this house makes a thrilling vantage point from which to view the changing displays of nature. It also expresses the owners' confidence in the engineering ability of their architect and the inherent nature of the material.

Metal—like masonry, ceramics, and glass—is inorganic and therefore does not burn, rot, or decay. But metal differs from these other inorganic substances in some important respects: most metals rust or corrode when exposed to moisture and air and have great tensile strength. Metal's capacity to transmit heat, cold, and electricity stands unequaled. The surface is usually shiny and nonabsorbent.

With the possible exception of plastics, no other material can be shaped in so many ways. Metal can be melted and cast in simple or intricate molds; in the solid state it can be rolled, pressed, or turned on a lathe, as well as hammered, bent, drilled, or cut with saws and torches; separate pieces can be welded together or joined with bolts and rivets.

This unique complex of qualities—tensile strength, meltability, ductility, malle-ability, conductivity, resistance to fire and decay, and potential beauty of color and surface—makes a house built today without metals hard to imagine. A partial list would include such inconspicuous but essential elements as structural members and reinforcing in masonry; conductors of water, heat, and electricity; weather-proofing and foil insulation; and nails and screws. Metals are thinly concealed by protective coatings of enamel in stoves, refrigerators, and other appliances. They become noticeable in hinges, handles, and doorknobs; in faucets, radiators, or warm-air vents; and in windows and door frames. Finally, metals are treasured for their visual attractiveness in tableware, furniture, cooking utensils, and lighting fixtures. The following metals have proved most important in the home.

Aluminum   Not until 1885 was it feasible to extract aluminum economically, even though it occurs in most common clays. A whitish metal, light in weight and easily worked, aluminum oxidizes to a soft gray but does not deteriorate indoors or out. Thus, it is valuable for cooking utensils, tumblers, pitchers, and trays. It makes a carefree material for screens, siding and roofing, gutters and drainpipes. The development of aluminum as a lightweight framing material for windows and doors probably accounts for the widespread use of sliding doors in contemporary architecture. Its imperviousness to water renders it particularly appropriate for versatile furniture that can be used either indoors or out and that requires minimum maintenance (Fig. 331). The surface can be highly polished or brushed to a silvery softness. Anodizing gives a satiny surface in a range of bright metallic hues.

Chromium   A blue-white metal, chromium takes and keeps a high polish and is widely used as a thin plating where durability, easy maintenance, and brilliant shine are desirable. It frequently appears on faucets, toasters, kitchen forks and spoons, lighting fixtures, and metal furniture. Because it is hard and resists corro-sion, it takes little care, but finger or water marks will be conspicuous. Typically, chromium is cold, hard, and glittery, assertive rather than harmonious. It can be domesticated, though, with a brushed finish.

Copper   Polished copper has a lustrous surface and a beautiful orange color that quickly oxidizes to a dull greenish brown or sometimes to a lively blue-green. Fortunately, oxidation causes no serious deterioration. Copper is soft and easily shaped but durable, which makes it excellent for pipes carrying water. Next to silver, it is the best conductor of electricity. It is long-lived and beautiful but expensive in first cost for eave troughs and roofs. Copper has a disagreeable taste

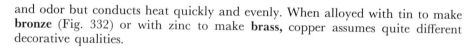

above: 331. Aluminum makes an ideal material for outdoor furniture; it is rainproof and quick to dry, sunproof and cool to touch, light in weight for easy portability, and available in many colors. (*Courtesy Tropitone Furniture Co., Inc.*)

right: 332. A cast-bronze door pull designed by Toza Radakovich expresses the contemporary craftsman's free interpretation of form in metal. (*Photograph: Richard Gross*)

below: 333. A relatively new material, stainless steel lends itself to innovative designs in flatware, unencumbered by the traditions that surround silver. It is also nearly maintenance-free. Wolf Karnagel, designer. (*Courtesy Rosenthal Studio-Haus*)

and odor but conducts heat quickly and evenly. When alloyed with tin to make **bronze** (Fig. 332) or with zinc to make **brass,** copper assumes quite different decorative qualities.

Iron and Steel   A grayish metal known for thousands of years, iron is widely available, strong, and relatively easy to work when cast in liquid form or wrought with tools. Contemporary decorative ironwork gives ample evidence of some of the inherent qualities of the material and the ways in which it can be worked. The great disadvantage of iron is the speed with which it rusts. However, it can be *galvanized* with a zinc coating or painted to discourage rust.

Steel is iron that has been made hard with chemically dissolved carbon. Its development has made possible an enormous quantity of things that today we take for granted—a spectrum ranging from high-rise buildings and suspension bridges to practical cookware and knife blades. Steel provides the structural material for much kitchen equipment, as well as for furnaces, many metal window frames, and the like. Most so-called iron furniture is made of steel. Because steel rusts like iron, it is almost invariably painted or enameled.

Stainless steels are another matter, for they have been made resistant to rust and staining by the addition of chromium. Hard, durable, and a pleasant blue-gray, stainless steels make the most durable and (in the long run) inexpensive of all cooking utensils, as well as thoroughly satisfactory, attractive, nontarnishable flatware (Fig. 333).

Self-weathering steel oxidizes to a rich russet color that is then impervious to further deterioration and so never needs painting. Until now its use in homes has been limited to the more imaginative designs, such as the cantilevered house in Figure 329.

Silver   It is no whim or happenstance that silver has long been cherished as the most desirable of metals for flat and hollow metal tableware. This whitest of metals reflects almost twice as much light as stainless steel and noticeably more than chromium. Moreover, it takes a genuinely beautiful polish (Fig. 334). Silver is a workable metal, so soft when pure that it must be hardened, usually with copper; sterling silver contains 7.5 percent copper. The one great drawback of silver is that it tarnishes rapidly and soon becomes blackish if the coating of silver sulfide is not removed; but unlike iron rust, this causes no serious damage. Manufacturers frequently plate silver over an alloy base, and if the plating is heavy enough, it will last a long time. But of course solid silver will remain in good condition indefinitely, and special finishes can retard tarnishing.

Form in Metal

Were it not for the fact that metal is heavy and expensive, we might say that almost any form imaginable lends itself to metal design. Metal will take and hold any shape that can be given to wood, masonry, ceramics, or glass. Its most distinctive quality, though, is its great tensile strength, which makes possible, as well as durable, quite slender shapes. Examples of this characteristic are the structural members of the house in Figure 329, and the slender legs of the bed in Figure 335. Sharp edges, as on knives, are more durable in metal than in any other material. When used expressively, metal contributes a precise thinness that distinguishes it from the comparatively heavy solidity of wood, masonry, and ceramics.

Ornament in Metal

The surface treatment of metal, which can give varied light-and-dark patterns and reflections, acts as a basic kind of ornament. The highly polished metal of the vases in Figure 334 gives mirrorlike reflections, interestingly distorted on their rounded forms. By contrast, the softly polished pewter of the bowl and cup in Figure 336 produces more mellow and diffuse patterns. Three-dimensional textures, such as those on stamped sheet metals (Fig. 337) can lead to myriad juxtapositions of highlights and shadows.

below: 334. The brilliance of highly polished silver has been emphasized by areas of satin finish in these "flower vases" designed by Lino Sabattini for Argenteria Sabattini, Italy. (*Photograph: Foto Ciceri*)

right: 335. The resistance of metal—in this case aluminum—to lengthwise stress makes possible the slenderness of this bedframe. Andrew Ivar Morrison and Bruce R. Hannah, designers. (*Courtesy Knoll International, Inc.*)

As with form, there are almost no physical limitations for ornament. If we wish to exploit each material's individuality, we will emphasize its most distinctive qualities. This leads to several suggestions. First, the strength of metal permits boldly projecting ornamental parts (Fig. 338); second, the very fine grain and smoothness make delicate embellishment effective; third, the hardness of metal reconciles linear or angular decoration with the material; fourth, the long life and cost of most metals may suggest relatively formal, controlled, and precise enrichment but does not preclude other approaches.

Plastics

The phenomenal development of plastics in the past few decades has affected our homes markedly and will continue to do so. Today's scientists transform wood, coal, milk, petroleum, natural gas, and many other substances into new compounds tailor-made for specific purposes, while designers and engineers invent efficient methods of shaping these materials. Thus, we can now produce on an enormous scale materials that in many instances are better suited to contemporary needs than the substances nature provides.

At first, plastics were considered cheap substitutes for more costly materials; a rash of plastic-pseudo-wood, plastic-pseudo-marble, and plastic-pseudo-metal objects flooded the market. Today we have learned to appreciate the material for

above left: 339. The development of foamed plastics has had a decided influence on furniture design. The ''Domino'' seating system is bulky but lightweight, extremely resilient but form-retaining. (*Courtesy Stendig, Inc.*)

right: 340. The ''Quattroquarti'' table of ABS plastic represents a new generation of furniture designs in which the pieces can be moved around to suit changing needs and desires. Rodolfo Bonetto, designer. (*Courtesy G. B. Bernini S.p.A.*)

above right: 341. Lucite is particularly adaptable for household objects because of its clarity and light weight combined with strength and durability. (*Courtesy Georg Jensen, Inc.*)

what it is, to exploit plastic-as-plastic. Not only can plastics assume shapes and perform tasks that no other material could, but the pure beauty of well-designed plastic form delights the eye and need not apologize for itself. Plastic dishes are lightweight and resist chipping. Chairs and other furniture can be molded from transparent, translucent, or opaque plastics (Pl. 39, p. 266); or shaped from foamed plastics whose density can be controlled to vary from rigid framework to soft cushioning (Fig. 339). Wall, floor, and ceiling panels and coverings come in great variety of plastic forms. Even houses in which plastics act as the major construction material, although still largely experimental, are slowly becoming available.

Plastic resins come to forming machines as powders, granules, compressed tablets, or liquids, which under heat and/or pressure can be shaped as designers wish. Many techniques exist for forming plastics; the materials can be compressed in molds; extruded through dies to form continuous sheets, rods, filaments, or tubes; injected into cavities of complex outline; drawn into molds by the vacuum method; blown full of gas or air to make rigid, semirigid, or flexible foams; or sprayed over forms.

Film and sheeting for shower curtains, upholstery, or laminates are made by spreading plastic solutions on wheels up to 25 feet in diameter, by extruding the compound through a wide die, or by calendering—that is, by passing the compound between several rollers to get the desired thickness and surface texture. Rollers also aid in giving other materials a plastic coating. In laminating such materials as Formica and Micarta, layers of cloth, paper, wood, or glass fibers are impregnated with uncured resin or alternated with uncured plastic film, then pressed into a single sheet.

Families of Plastics

Although innumerable plastics exist, some of those most used in homes derive from the types of resins discussed in the following paragraphs. Each name refers to a family of plastics with basic shared characteristics but with considerable diversity in form and application. And more and more resins are being cross-bred to produce plastics that demonstrate specific traits. Often, the terms *plastic* and *synthetic* can be applied to the same basic material; for example, molded nylon is called a plastic, but nylon threads are referred to as synthetic. In this chapter we shall consider only the plastics; Chapter 12 deals with synthetic fibers.

ABS and ASA   ABS (acrylonitrile, butadiene, stryene) and ASA (acrylonitrile, styrene, acrylic elastomer) are examples of the new cross-bred plastics that combine monomers to form polymer building block foundations. Such polymers then can be altered in many ways for specific applications, such as plating or alloying with other plastics. ABS and ASA compounds are tough and hard, with great tensile strength; exceptionally moldable; resistant to scratching, chemicals, and weather. They have good integral color and can be very lightweight. Their "fitting" ability predisposes them to everything from plumbing systems to modular furniture that can be assembled in various configurations (Fig. 340).

Acrylics   The most glamorous and glasslike of the plastics, acrylics include such well-known trade names as Plexiglas, Lucite, and Perspex. They are strong and rigid, show exceptional clarity, and have the ability to "pipe" light—qualities that have opened up new possibilities in furniture design (Fig. 126). Since acrylics can withstand outdoor weathering and sudden temperature extremes—and moreover are light in weight—they have contributed to architectural innovations in the form of self-supporting flat or domed skylights. They can be colorless or tinted, patterned or plain (Fig. 341). Although unaffected by most food and household chemicals, acrylics may scratch when brought in contact with gritty substances. However, the scratches can be buffed clean with jeweler's rouge or a buffing compound.

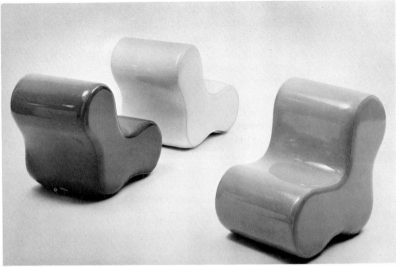

FRP   When reinforced, usually with glass fibers, plastics can be formed into strong but thin translucent sheets. *Fiberglass reinforced plastics* appear often in patio roofs, luminous ceilings, and light-transmitting walls and partitions. They can also be molded into lampshades, skylights, and exciting new furniture forms. The types range from stiff to flexible, from hard to soft; the color selection is good; and they show high resistance to chemicals and weather.

Melamines   The widespread use of melamines for countertops and tabletops, as well as for dinnerware, is based on their exceptional durability (Fig. 342). Hard and not easily scratched or chipped, they resist damage from water, food stains, and heat. When thin, as in the surfaces of high-pressure laminates like Formica and Micarta, melamines transparently reveal whatever pattern or material is underneath. If thicker, as in such dinnerware as Melmac, they become translucent or opaque. Colors, extensive in range, do not fade or lose their brilliance. The surfaces can be high-gloss, satiny, or mat.

Nylon   Nylon is the generic term applied to a group of plastics, but it is also a trade name. Transparent in very thin sections but usually opaque, nylon comes in many colors. Although resistant to abrasion, the hard, glossy surface can be scratched. Nylon has high tensile strength and is relatively rigid. Most common chemicals do it no harm, but coffee, tea, and colored foods leave stains. Neither freezing nor boiling temperatures affect it adversely. It is not, however, recommended for continuous outdoor exposure. These qualities make nylon useful for some tumblers and dinnerware, long-wearing gears and bearings, quiet rollers for drawers, and furniture.

Polyethylenes   Polyethylenes are easily recognizable in their flexible or semirigid form by a waxy surface. They have gained wide acceptance in squeeze bottles, nesting bowls, refrigerator dishes, and dishpans. Semitransparent to opaque depending on thickness, they are light in weight, come in many colors, and are very resistant to breakage and chemicals. Polyethylene objects perform well at subzero temperatures; boiling water can be poured into them, but they should not be boiled. In its rigid form, polyethylene is often used for molded nonupholstered chair shells.

Polystyrenes   The lustrous surface of polystyrenes, ranging from extreme smoothness to satin with many special finishes, is warm and pleasant to touch.

Crystal-clear types "pipe" light, as do the acrylics, and there is a limitless range of translucent and opaque colors. Polystyrenes are relatively inexpensive; they are tasteless, odorless, and resistant to household chemicals and foods (except cleaning fluids and citrus fruits). Hard and rigid, they stand up well under normal household use but not under bending or severe impact. The list of applications is long and varied—from kitchenware to modular furniture systems.

Urethanes Polyurethanes are interesting examples of a rapidly growing group of "cellular" plastics, so called because of their structure and ability to foam. They can be given almost any density and degree of hardness, from resilient to rigid. Those of densities resembling wood can be worked, finished, and repaired like wood. The insulating properties and very light weight of urethanes have made them valuable as architectural insulation and for curtain wall panels in house construction. Because they can be foamed in place and will bond to almost any surface, they serve as a surface coating. In the house shown in Figure 345 they become the structure itself. As resilient foams, urethanes have gained great acceptance for cushioning material, because the degree of softness can be controlled by the foam's density or even by a combination of densities. In Figure 343 such a cushion has been formed into a seating-play shape for a child and then covered with glossy vinyl. The resultant object is durable, easy to maintain, and comfortable.

Vinyls The versatile family of vinyls includes rigid, nonrigid, and foam or cellular types in any transparent, translucent or opaque color. Varied surface effects are produced by embedding, embossing, or printing. Vinyls are tough, strong, lightweight, and low in cost. Although they withstand foods, chemicals, and normal household use very well, they cut readily, and most types stiffen in cold. Among the diverse applications are curtains, tablecloths, upholstery, wall coverings, lamp shades, luminous ceilings, and counter surfacing. In its cellular form, vinyl often performs as a wood substitute. Vinyl floor coverings provide for the first time in a single material, durability, easy maintenance, resiliency, insulation, acoustical control, and a wide choice of color and design (Fig. 344).

In sum, certain qualities taken together differentiate plastics—despite their variability—from other materials. The range of color and texture, actual or simulated, seems limitless, and plastics exhibit all degrees of transparency and opacity.

344. Vinyl floor coverings can be designed to complement almost any kind of furnishings. Here a traditional Spanish tile pattern sets off the straight lines of the modern steel and plastic furniture. (*Courtesy Armstrong Cork Company*)

They feel warm and pleasant. Truly "plastic," they can be formed into almost any rigid or flexible seamless shape. Typically, plastics are tough and durable in relation to weight and thickness. Absorbing little or no moisture, they neither rot nor mildew. Their resistance to chemicals varies but is generally good. However, their strength and dimensions are with a few exceptions noticeably affected by extreme temperatures. Plastics cover a broad range of prices.

Two environmental problems have become apparent within the last decade in connection with the tremendous proliferation of plastics. In each case, research is being conducted to find answers, but the consumer should be aware of these concerns and press for solutions.

Flammability   While many plastics are rated as slow burning or self-extinguishing, a few types—including some acrylics, polyurethane foams, and polystyrenes—have been found not only to burn and/or melt or break down molecularly under certain conditions but to give off lethal and possibly explosive gases in the process. The plastics industry is attempting to overcome these hazards with new flame retardants, new chemical formulas, and the issuance of consumer information about the properties and appropriate uses of the materials. But the buyer of a mattress, for example, should seek guarantees that it is indeed fireproof.

Biodegradability   The possibility of a plastic being reabsorbed into the environment is also a matter of public awareness and demand for accountability. Plastics that can be melted down presumably could be reformed. In one experiment, plastics have been ground into chips and then combined with sand to make concrete. Other such uses could be found. Presently, chemists are working on new formulas for plastics that would eventually break down into harmless particles and decompose in the dump.

Form and Ornament in Plastics

Plastics differ from natural materials in that their basic qualities are chemically and physically determined by humans. Thus, instead of designing to suit a material, manufacturers can actually create a material to meet a specific need, real or imagined. This brings new challenges and problems. For one thing, such absolute flexibility indicates the need for close, steady cooperation among chemist, manufacturer, and designer. The designer is not only confronted with a characterless substance to mold, but has no age-old craft tradition in which to seek accumulated knowledge or inspiration. On the other hand, this absence of guidelines frees the designer from the stereotypes of past forms.

Design in plastics can be a completely liberated merger of designer, material, and machine. No longer hampered by preconceived notions of what is proper for any particular material, the imagination can soar in many directions, starting with the composition of the plastic itself and ending with new shapes and even new functions. This does not mean that shapes *must* be invented simply because the potential exists. The contours of plastic dishes and tumblers closely resemble those of clay or glass because these have been found serviceable and pleasant. But in some fields, major breakthroughs have been achieved. Furniture designers have been investigating whole new vocabularies of shape and function allowed by the properties of the new materials, while architects continue to explore the possibilities of free-form structures in strange and intriguing shapes (Fig. 345). And some of the simplest forms assume a completely new quality when translated into pristine plastic (Figs. 346, 347).

Successful ornament in plastics remains largely structural, where the inherent possibilities for varied colors, different degrees of transparency, translucency, or opacity, embedded materials, and molded form and surface texture seem to be in the nature of the materials and in the processes used to form them. Because

above: Plate 36. Glazed ceramic tiles in octagonal and diamond shapes make an elegant floor for this formal sitting room-conservatory. The furnishings have been pulled back to allow the floor to assume a dominant role. See page 247. (*Photograph: John T. Hill*)

right: Plate 37. Tiles have long been used around fireplaces because of their fireproof quality. Here the blue-and-white checkerboard pattern gives both color and Old-World charm to this rustic living room. Kipp Stewart, designer. See page 248; see also Figs. 456, 657; Plate 10, p. 59. (*Photograph: Morley Baer*)

above: Plate 38. Antique leaded and stained-glass windows, combined with newly crafted windows of colored and clear glass, comprise the walls of a romantic house in Mill Valley, California. Carved wooden railings protect the lower windows and children from each other. William W. Kirsch, architect. See page 254. (*Photograph: John Dominis, Time-LIFE Picture Agency*)

right: Plate 39. Purity of materials characterizes this pristine, formal dining room. The clear Lucite table and chairs, set with transparent dinnerware, seem to hover above the dark slate floor in a round space circumscribed by solid masonry walls. Neon tube lighting above heightens the effect of brilliance. See page 261. (*Photograph: John T. Hill*)

left: 345. The propensity for a new material to generate new forms is evident in this house of urethane foam sprayed over a scalloped shell fabric form. Much of the furniture is built in of the same material, and the basalt stone floor has been coated with polyester for easy care. Stan Nord Connolly, architect; Ron Kessinger, owner-designer. See also Fig. 652. (*Courtesy American Home Magazine*)

below: 346. A transparent plastic planter box is a new experience, bringing the soil and drainage pebbles into the total picture. (*Courtesy Architectural Supplements, Inc.*)

the conventional types of applied ornament are so closely allied with the natural materials they were originally designed to enhance, they are likely to appear weak, imitative, and inappropriate when used on plastics. Perhaps this is so because, as yet, little applied ornament has been developed for plastic that intensifies its unique quality, as, for example, etching or cutting heightens the sparkle of glass or intricate ornament throws into relief the luster of polished silver.

The history of plastics is very short, and the development of any new vocabulary takes a long time. Many consumers and manufacturers conservatively prefer that which is at least partially familiar to something wholly new. At the other extreme, the lack of restrictions imposed by the material has resulted in much poor design or in some cases an overexuberance of design.

Even though plastics are only beginning to receive distinctive qualities, they have had enormous impact on homes. Plastic cases for radio and television sets are cheaper than wood or metal. Plastic surfaces for furniture lighten housekeeping. Floors and countertops surfaced with plastic reduce noise and breakage and are easy to keep. Humble objects such as dishpans and mop pails come in bright cheerful colors. Plastic furniture is usually light in weight, easy to move around the house and from house to house; plastic houses of the future may change many of our concepts of home planning and furnishing. Finally, there is the whole realm—as yet hardly explored—of plastics as unexpected sources of visual delight.

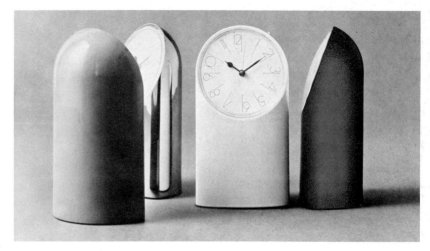

347. Clockworks enclosed in a case of plastic become form-objects as well as useful timepieces. (*Courtesy Stendig, Inc.*)

Fabrics

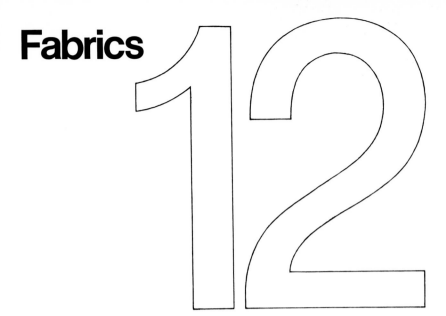

More than anything in a house except the people, fabrics humanize our homes because of their pliant responsiveness to our needs. Fabrics make us more comfortable, control light coming through windows and give privacy without solid walls, insulate against extreme heat and cold, and absorb noise. They provide easily removable and cleanable coverings for tables and beds, as well as pleasant-to-touch upholstery for chairs and sofas. Beyond these service functions, fabrics bring beauty and individuality unlike that of any other material. Several distinctive characteristics of fabrics are worth noting:

- □ No other materials come in such width and breadth and can be readily used in those dimensions.
- □ Uniquely pliable and manipulatable, fabrics can be folded, draped, pleated, or stretched; and they can be cut, sewn, or glued together.
- □ Of all the materials in the home, fabrics are most frequently and easily replaced.
- □ They are noticed because they appear in quantity throughout the home, look and feel softer than other materials, and are often brightly colored or patterned.
- □ Fabrics link together people, furniture, and architecture in a way unequaled by anything else. Carpets and other fabrics attached to floors and walls adhere strictly to the "architecture" of the home. Upholstery and table linens adapt themselves to the seating or to the tables on which they are used and at the same time relate those pieces to our clothing. Curtains and draperies can partake of the architectural quality of windows as well as relate openings to the enclosing structure and to the furniture in the room. Fabrics can even become the total interior environment, as in the sculpture-for-living planned by Aleksandra Kasuba (Fig. 348).

Beyond their everyday usefulness, then, fabrics have two important functions: First, they make their own visual and tactile contributions to the home; second, they can be strong unifying elements within a room and between rooms. This chapter focuses attention on fibers, the processes by which fibers are transformed into fabrics, and fabric design. In succeeding chapters we shall consider the potential integration of fabrics with walls, windows, floors, and furniture. Although it is important to understand the distinctive qualities of the various fabrics, we can never isolate them totally from other components of the home.

348. Weaver Aleksandra Kasuba, with the aid of designer Vytautas Kasuba, constructed an architectural fabric interior that would be a totally new experience for most of us—a world of enveloping softness, muted sounds, expanding and contracting vistas. (*Courtesy Allied Chemical Corporation*)

Fabric is a general term referring to anything manufactured by hand or machine, but it has come to be applied especially to *cloth*. *Textile* originally referred only to *woven fabrics*. Today, in the era of the art fabric, it is more freely interpreted. In addition to weaving, fabrics can be made by knitting, felting, knotting, or lacing together natural or synthetic fibers and also by fabricating plastics into films, sheets, or molded forms. Performance and appearance of a fabric depend on several factors: the qualities of the basic material, the process by which it is fabricated, the finish, and the applied ornamentation.

Fibers

The term *fiber* refers to a threadlike object or filament, but it has also come to mean that which gives substance or texture. Both meanings apply to textile fibers. Nature provides an abundance of such fibrous materials as reeds and grasses, flax and jute, the wool and hair of animals, the fibers enclosing the seeds of plants, and the filaments some caterpillars spin for cocoons. To these, scientists have added many of their own inventions. Table 12.1 gives basic facts about the qualities of the more important fibers. Fibers differ from one another in many ways: strength and elasticity; resistance to abrasion, stains, sun, moisture, mildew, and fire; and tactile and visual qualities. Each fiber has its strong and weak points. Although

Table 12.1 Textile Fibers

Fiber and Fiber Substance	Appearance	Uses	Maintenance	Special Characteristics and Processes	Resistances Poor	Resistances Good	Resistances Excellent
acetates (cellulose diacetate) Acele Avisco Celanese, and so on	drapes well; good color range	bedspreads, curtains, draperies, rugs, upholstery	fair soil resistance; dry-clean or wash; dries quickly; iron with cool iron	newer processes have color as integral part of fiber, increasing resistances to sunlight, cleaning	abrasion, aging, heat, sunlight, wrinkling	felting, fire, insects, pilling, shrinking, static electricity, stretching	
Arnel (cellulose triacetate)	pleasant luster; drapes well; excellent color range	draperies	slow to soil; dry-clean or wash; dries quickly; little ironing, higher setting than diacetates	excellent retention of heat-set pleats and creases; ability to withstand washing, ironing		abrasion, insects, pilling, static electricity, stretching	aging, felting, fire, mildew, shrinking, wrinkling, sunlight
acrylics (acrylonitrile and other monomers) Acrilan Creslan Orlon Zefran, and so on	warm, bulky, woollike touch; good color range in some types	blankets, curtains, rugs, upholstery	slow to soil; easy to spot-clean; dry-clean or wash; dries quickly; little ironing, under 325°	warmth without weight; retains heat-set pleats and creases	pilling, static electricity unless treated	abrasion, felting, fire, shrinking, stretching, sunlight, wrinkling	aging, insects, mildew, sunlight
modacrylics (modified acrylics) Dynel Verel, and so on	warm, bulky, heavy, dense	blankets, draperies, rugs, upholstery	similar to acrylics, but highly resistant to chemical stains; iron setting varies	self-extinguishing; special processes result in dense, furlike pile, textured, three-dimensional effects	heat, shrinking unless stabilized by heat-setting, sunlight (Dynel)	abrasion, pilling, static electricity, wrinkling	aging, felting, fire, insects, mildew, sunlight (Verel)
cotton (cellulose)	pleasant, soft, dull surface; fair drape; excellent color range	bed and table linen, bedspreads, draperies, rugs, towels, upholstery	soils, stains, wrinkles easily unless treated; dry-clean or wash; irons easily	mercerizing increases luster, softness, strength, dye absorption; wash-and-wear, spot- and wrinkle-resistant finishes	felting, fire, mildew, shrinking, wrinkling	abrasion, aging, fading, insects, stretching, sunlight	pilling, static electricity; all resistances greatly improved by special treatments and blends
glass (silica sand, limestone, aluminum, and borax) Beta Fiberglas Uniglass Pittsburgh PPG	lustrous, silky; good drape; fair color range in dyes, printed many hues	bedspreads, curtains, draperies, wallpaper	slow to soil; easy spot removal; hand-wash, hang with no ironing; dries quickly	*Beta* yarn one-half size of any other fiber; can be woven into very sheer fabric; fireproof, impervious to moisture and salt air; shed fibers can cause skin rash	abrasion, flexing (nonelastic) but new processes increase flexibility		aging, chemicals, felting, fire, insects, mildew, shrinking, stretching, sunlight
linen (cellulose, from flax)	clean, fresh, lintless; fair drape; good color range	curtains, draperies, household linens, rugs, upholstery	soils and wrinkles easily; washes and irons well	stronger when wet; *sanforized* to reduce shrinking; can be made wrinkle-resistant	fire, shrinking, wrinkling unless treated or blended	abrasion, mildew, pilling, stretching, sunlight	aging, insects, static electricity
nylon (polyamide) 6, 6/6; 501 Antron Caprolan Cumuloft, and so on	natural luster; good drape; good color range	bedspreads, rugs, upholstery	slow to soil; easy spot removal; dry-clean or wash, dries quickly; little ironing at low heat	outstanding elasticity, strength, and lightness; can be heat-set to keep permanent shape; sometimes damaged by acids; may pick up color and soil during washing	pilling, static electricity unless treated, sunlight	fire	abrasion, aging, felting, insects, mildew, shrinking, stretching, wrinkling

Table 12.1 Textile Fibers (continued)

Fiber and Fiber Substance	Appearance	Uses	Maintenance	Special Characteristics and Processes	Resistances Poor	Resistances Good	Resistances Excellent
olefins (ethylene, propylene, or other olefin units) *Herculon Vectra*	woollike hand; fair color range	blankets, rugs, upholstery, webbing	slow to soil; spot-clean or wash; little ironing, at very low heat	lightest fiber made; excellent insulator; transmits humidity well; is very cohesive (can be made into nonwoven carpets); low cost	heat, shrinking, static electricity	abrasion, felting, fire, stretching, sunlight, wrinkling	insects, mildew, pilling, aging
polyesters (dihydric alcohol and terephthalic acid) *Dacron Fortrel Kodel*, and so on	crisp or soft, pleasant touch; good drape; fair color range	bedding, curtains, draperies, upholstery	soils easily; dry-clean or wash, dries quickly; very little ironing, moderate heat	lightweight; ranges from sheer, silklike to bulky, woollike; as strong wet as dry; retains heat-set pleats and creases; picks up colors in washing	dust, soil, pilling because very electrostatic	abrasion, fire, sunlight	felting, insects, mildew, shrinking, stretching, wrinkling
rayon (regenerated cellulose) *Avril Cupioni Enka Fortisan*, and so on	bright or dull luster; drapes well; excellent color range	blankets, curtains, draperies, rugs, table "linens," upholstery	fair soil resistance; dry-clean or wash; iron like cotton or silk, depending on type, finish	most versatile fiber—can resemble cotton, silk, wool; absorbs moisture and swells when wet unless specially processed; reduces static electricity in blends; low cost; wash-and-wear and spot- and wrinkle-resistant finishes	felting, fire, mildew, shrinking, wrinkling	abrasion, aging, insects, stretching (poor when wet), sunlight	pilling, static electricity; all resistances greatly improved by blending, finishes
silk (protein from silkworm cocoon)	lustrous, smooth, unique crunchy softness; drapes well; excellent color range	draperies, rugs, upholstery	good soil resistance; dry-clean or hand-wash; irons easily, moderate heat	most desirable combination of properties of any fiber: smoothness, luster, resiliency, toughness, adaptability to temperature changes	fire (but self-extinguishing), static electricity, sunlight	abrasion, aging, felting, insects, mildew, shrinking, stretching, wrinkling	
wool (protein from sheep or goat and camel families)	soft or hard finish; dry, warm touch; drapes well; good color range	blankets, draperies, rugs, upholstery	good soil resistance; spot-clean, dry-clean, or wash in cold water; press over damp cloth at low heat	notable for warmth, absorbency (without feeling wet), resiliency, durability; wool-synthetic blends reduce shrinkage but have tendency to pill	insects, felting, shrinking unless treated	abrasion, aging, fire, mildew, pilling, stretching, static electricity, sunlight	wrinkling; new processes make it even more resistant to soil, stains, water, wrinkling

271

top: 349. A textile woven of only one fiber can have decided structural interest because of the yarn composition. In "Ticino" the yarn consists of a number of strands, almost casually laid and loosely twisted. (*Courtesy Stow/Davis Furniture Company*)

above: 350. Marianne Strengell's hand-woven off-white casement fabric of linen, fiberglass, rayon, and goat hair contrasts thick and thin, tightly and loosely spun yarns in a seemingly spontaneous construction. (*Photograph: Ferdinand Boesch*)

some are more versatile than others, none is ideally suited to every purpose. Moreover, important developments occur all the time—new synthetic fibers are created, familiar ones are modified, and processing and finishing techniques are improved.

All synthetic fibers share some desirable qualities: they are of unlimited length in contrast to the comparative shortness of wool and cotton; many of them repel, rather than absorb, moisture and soil; and they offer little foothold to insects and fungus. Some synthetics lend themselves better to specific uses than do any natural ones. As yet, however, few if any artificial fibers can serve with full competence *for as many purposes* as wool or cotton—in part, at least, because the natural fibers have been familiar for centuries. Natural fibers, to be sure, have their limitations, but these are being minimized by new ways of processing them. For example, manufacturers can make them resistant to soil and stains, shrinkage and moths, or crushing and wrinkling.

A textile may consist of only one fiber (Fig. 349) or may combine two or more to increase beauty, utility, or both (Fig. 350). Different fibers can be spun together into one yarn, or yarns spun from different fibers can be combined in a single fabric. These combinations of fibers have yielded some of the most successful changes in fabric characteristics. We are all familiar with the advantages of adding polyester fibers to cotton, in varying proportions, to produce textiles that are almost wrinkle-free and remarkably dirt-resistant. Nylon increases the strength of wool, and stretch nylon combined with cotton makes slipcovers that are form-fitting and pleasant to touch. The permutations are almost endless; they permit the manufacture of fabrics that can embody the best attributes of various fibers. But the fiber blends also present problems, for consumers must try to keep up with the advantages and disadvantages of all the new fibers and fabrics that keep appearing. Considerable progress has been made in consumer protection by requiring that fabrics be labeled with their fiber content and method of care. However, consumers will need to keep educating themselves on the characteristics of fibers so that their probable performance *in use* can be to some extent predetermined.

Yarns

Yarn results when fibers are twisted together to make a strand long enough and sufficiently strong for weaving or other fabric-construction processes. With natural fibers, yarn making includes cleaning the fibers, drawing them out so they are more or less even and parallel, then spinning or twisting them into yarn. Synthetic fibers are clean, continuous, and parallel as soon as they have been extruded as filaments, so the process is simply one of twisting them together. Yarns vary in the kinds of fibers used either alone or in combination, in the type and tightness of twist, in the ply (the number of strands in the yarn), and in the size of the finished product.

Long fibers laid parallel to one another and tightly twisted produce smoother and stronger yarns than do short fibers somewhat randomly arranged and loosely twisted. Nature provides only one long continuous fiber—silk—while all synthetics have that characteristic. Any of them, however, can be cut into short pieces for different effects. Length of fiber and tightness of twist lead to the following types of yarns:

- □ **Cotton** yarns differ in the degree of treatment to which the fibers were subjected. *Carded* yarns contain all but the shortest fibers, with the remaining ones somewhat straightened. *Combed* yarns are composed entirely of long fibers laid parallel before spinning, which makes the resultant yarn stronger, smoother, and usually more expensive.
- □ **Silk** of high quality derives from long, unbroken filaments, but *spun silk* is made from the short fibers that cannot be unreeled from cocoons.

□ **Wool** yarns include two types. *Woolen* yarns are soft, fuzzy, loosely spun yarns made from fibers only partially straightened; *worsted* yarns are tightly twisted from long, combed fibers, so they are smooth and strong.

□ **Synthetic** yarns come from fibers originating as continuous, parallel, more or less smooth strands called *filaments,* which are usually twisted into ply yarns. The fibers can, though, be cut into short lengths and blown apart, then brought together as a mass something like cleaned but uncombed cotton or wool; these *staples* then are twisted into soft yarns known as *spun* rayon, nylon, and so on.

Twisting fibers tightly or loosely is only one possible variation in yarn construction. Yarns can be given a right- or a left-hand twist, and the individual strands can be combined to make two-, three-, four-, or many-ply yarns. Special effects—such as crepe and bouclé yarns—result from different handling during the twisting process. Elastic cores can be covered with fibers to produce elastic yarns, and even metallic wires can be wrapped in with the fibers.

Yarn sizes range from spider-web single filaments to silk yarns of two hundred strands or ropelike cords. Many textiles contain only one size of yarn, but others combine several or many sizes (Fig. 351), depending upon the desired effect.

Fabric Construction

Although there are endless ways of making fabrics, all of them fall generally into one of five basic categories. Each of these methods has its own special advantages, and each lends itself to certain effects and end uses.

Felting   Probably the earliest method of constructing fabrics, and one of the latest to be updated by new methods, felting is simply the matting together of fibers to form a web. **Tapa cloth** (Fig. 352) results from pounding together the fibers of the bark of the paper mulberry tree, often with leaves or other decorative materials

top: 351. "Swazilace," designed by Jack Lenor Larsen and handspun and handwoven by Coral Stephens in Swaziland, is composed of only two fibers—mohair and linen. By varying size, twist, and regularity of yarns, and by the way they are put together, Larsen has created a textile of infinite interest.

right: 352. A handmade tapa cloth hanging serves as a headboard and makes a focal point in this bedroom. The rug evokes but does not duplicate the design of the bark cloth. (*Courtesy House Beautiful. Copyright 1972, The Hearst Corporation*)

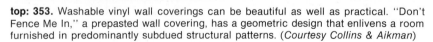

top: **353.** Washable vinyl wall coverings can be beautiful as well as practical. "Don't Fence Me In," a prepasted wall covering, has a geometric design that enlivens a room furnished in predominantly subdued structural patterns. (*Courtesy Collins & Aikman*)

above: **354.** Washable PVC vinyl suede upholsters a sofa whose softness belies its practicality. Byron Botker, designer. (*Courtesy Landes Manufacturing Company*)

right: **355.** Poured-on upholstery allows furniture shapes undreamed of or impossible with traditional upholstery fabrics. Liquid vinyl adheres to any polyurethane shape, never creases, and is easily washed clean. (*Courtesy Herman Miller*)

added. Traditional **felts** are of wool, hair, or fur fibers matted by a combination of moisture, pressure, and heat, a process that induces shrinkage and increases density. The result is a continuous dense cloth—firm, slightly fuzzy, and with comparatively low tensile strength. **Needle** or **needle-punched** felts, constructed by a newer technique, depend upon machines pushing barbed needles through a mat of fibers to entangle them without the intervention of heat or pressure. According to the characteristics and arrangements of the fibers and needles, products with low or high strength can be produced. Other nonwoven fabrics consist of layers of fibers **bonded** together by a binding agent that is set by wet or dry heat or by chemical action. In another technique, called **melding,** thermoplastic or "heat-softening" fibers are either introduced into the fiber mix or used as a sheath on a fiber with a higher melting point; when subjected to heat, the fibers fuse together.

Films   Films result from forming processes that—by means of extrusion, casting, or calendering—produce sheets instead of filaments. Some of the techniques for transforming synthetic liquids into fabrics were discussed in Chapter 11 in the section dealing with plastics. Originally appearing as thin plastic sheeting or film, the new plastic fabrics come in varied thicknesses, from the thin films suitable for shower curtains to heavier weights for wall coverings (Fig. 353). Upholstery grades are usually fused onto a knit or woven backing. Wall coverings may or may not be supported by a backing; they can also be laminated onto a layer of foam, which adds to the insulating and sound absorbing properties of the fabric. Textures range from leatherlike smoothness through suedelike softness (Fig. 354) to deeply molded, three-dimensional patterns. Vinyl fabrics can also be printed, embossed, or flocked with a soft fuzz. Not surprisingly, many of the designs imitate leather or textiles, but a few exploit the unique possibilities of these products.

The newest techniques in fabric construction eliminate the costly cut-and-sew operations necessary to make a fabric fit a particular form. Vacuum-formable fabrics can be shaped into a single piece of upholstery to cover a chair in as little as two minutes. Liquid vinyl flows onto polyurethane foam and becomes bonded to it, resulting in a no-seams, perfect-fit, and durable surface (Fig. 355). Another method utilizes short-cut fibers that are electromagnetically flocked to the surface of a chair or sofa to become the upholstery.

Knitting   Knitting is a process by which blunt rods or needles are used to interlock a single continuous yarn into a series of interlocking loops. Patterns result from a combination of plain, rib, and purl stitches, plus many variations (Fig. 356). Because machine knitting can be two to five times as fast as machine weaving,

356. "Brookville," a soft knit drapery material, derives its interest from the complexity of the fabric structure. The reverse, visible from outside the window, has a plain unfigured surface. (*Courtesy Robert Tait Fabrics*)

its possibilities have been reassessed in recent years. New fibers and techniques have produced dimensionally stable knit fabrics that have gained wide acceptance because of their stretch recovery, wrinkle resistance, and form-fitting characteristics.

Twisting The processes by which nets, macramé, and laces are made, twisting calls for the intertwining and sometimes knotting of yarns that run in two or more directions. Although lace has long been out of favor for household use, fresh and imaginative designs are opening the way to its reintroduction. The current revival of macramé as a handcraft attests to an interest in intricacy for design potential (Fig. 357), as well as to a desire for more personal involvement with our own spaces.

Weaving Weaving is the interlacing of warp and filling yarns, usually at right angles, to make textiles. *Warp* yarns run lengthwise on the loom and in the fabric. *Filling* yarns—also called *weft* or *woof*—run crosswise to fill and hold together the warp. The apparently enormous complexity of weaves can be reduced to three general categories: plain, twill, and satin.

Plain weave is simply one filling yarn carried over one warp yarn (Fig. 358). The variations include *broadcloth*, in which warp and filling are identical in size to give a smooth surface: *rep,* which has a definite ribbed texture produced by interweaving relatively heavy yarns with thinner ones; and *basket weaves,* a construction of two or more filling yarns crossing two or more warp yarns to produce a noticeable pattern, as in monk's cloth.

Twill weaves show a definite diagonal line or wale on the surface of the fabric (Fig. 359), caused by having the filling yarns "float" across a number of warp yarns in a regular pattern. Typical fabrics include serge, gabardine, and denim. Twill weaves resist soil and wrinkle less severely than do plain weaves of similar quality. They also tend to be softer and have a better drape.

Satin weaves differ from twill weaves in that the filling yarns make longer floats over the warp yarns, or the warp may float over the filling less regularly (Fig. 360). These floats minimize the over-and-under texture. If the yarns are fine and lustrous, the fabric surface will be smooth and will shine with reflected light. Satin, sateen, damask, and chino are examples of this weave category.

Within the three basic classes of weaves, there are special variations particularly relevant to home furnishings that should be mentioned. **Lace weaves** result when the warp yarns (or occasionally the filling yarns) are crossed or twisted at certain

357. A macramé hanging frames the fireplace in this high-ceilinged room, contrasting its delicate tracery with the flat, solid walls and fireplace. (*Courtesy American Home Magazine*)

right: 358. The regular over-and-under pattern of a plain weave textile becomes pronounced with the introduction of decided color variations. (*Courtesy Boris Kroll Fabrics, Inc.*)

far right: 359. The diagonal line characteristic of a twill weave can be emphasized to produce a visually exciting, kinetic effect by varying the angle and color of the pattern. (*Courtesy Stow/Davis Furniture Company*)

below: 360. A satin weave, with its long floating yarns on the surface, produces a shimmering, glossy fabric.

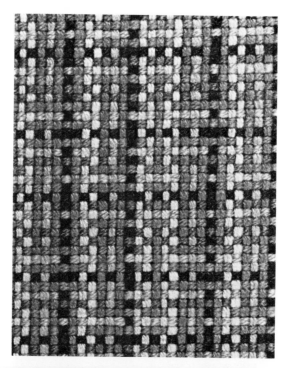

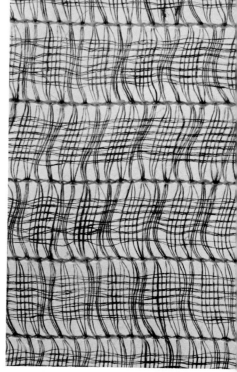

361. "Leno Sheer," designed by Hugo Dreyfuss, has a linen warp with hemp and rayon filling crossed and locked in the typical figure-8 leno weave. Its fragile appearance masks its actual strength. (*Courtesy Kagan-Dreyfuss*)

points to create an open, lacy effect. The most common lace weave is *leno*, exemplified by marquisette and similar porous textiles. Usually, the open weave has such a small scale that the design is hardly noticed, but coarser versions produce handsome patterns (Fig. 361). Leno weaves appear frequently in curtain fabrics.

Pile weaves add a third element to the basic warp and filling—a set of yarns that protrude from the background to make a three-dimensional fabric. In commercial production, the pile generally is added with a single continuous yarn that leaves loops on one side of the fabric. When the loops are left uncut, such textiles as terry cloth and frieze result. Cutting the loops produces velvet, plush, and the like. Patterns can be formed by cutting some loops and leaving the remainder uncut; by having some portions of the pile higher than others; or by employing different colored yarns (Fig. 362). Certain fine carpets—including rya and Oriental

rugs—are created by hand-tying individual strands of yarn onto the warp between rows of filler (Pl. 40, p. 283). This gives maximum flexibility in design. A variation on pile fabrics, *tufting* involves inserting pile yarns through a previously constructed backing, which may or may not be woven. The hand version of this technique is more often called *hooking.*

Jacquard weaves are pattern weaves produced on a highly complex machine—the Jacquard loom—that operates like a computer. They include flat *damasks,* raised *brocades,* complex *tapestries,* and some kinds of carpets. A Jacquard pattern can be almost anything, from a simple geometric motif to a complex, irregular design (Fig. 363).

Finishing the Fabric

Most fabrics, when they come from machine looms, are far from ready to be passed on to the consumer. Various kinds of finishing give them their ultimate appearance and qualities. We can divide these finishes into three types according to how they affect the function, the color, or the decorative qualities of the fabric.

Functional Finishes

Finishes that affect the basic appearance or performance of a fabric include the following:

☐ **Beetling,** or pounding with steel and wooden hammers, gives luster to linens and linenlike fabrics.

- **Calendering** is a process by which fabrics are pressed between rollers to give smooth finishes and to tighten the weaves. It can also polish fabrics to a highly glazed sheen or emboss them with moiré, crepe, or other patterns.
- **Crabbing** tightens and sets the weave in wool.
- **Fulling** shrinks, compacts, and softens a wool weave.
- **Gigging** and **napping** produce such textures as are found in flannel and fleece.
- **Heat setting** produces dimensional stability and aids in pleat retention.
- **Mercerization,** as applied to cellulosic fibers such as cotton, involves treatment with a solution of sodium hydroxide. If mercerized under tension, the fabric will be stronger, more lustrous, and more receptive to dyes; without tension (slack), mercerization causes the fibers and yarns to swell and contract, increasing the crimp of the yarn as well as its stretchability.
- **Shearing** and **singeing** remove surface fibers, fuzz, and lint, and prevent pilling.
- **Shrinking** lessens the tendency of most fibers to contract when exposed to moisture.
- **Weighting** compensates for gum lost by silk in the cleaning process.

By such means, lifeless, sleazy textiles are transformed into usable, attractive materials. In addition, there are some new, special treatments that notably change the behavior of fibers and fabrics. Textiles can be made:

- **Antistatic** to prevent the buildup of static charges and reduce soiling.
- **Bacteria-, mildew-,** and **moth-resistant** in varying degrees of permanence.
- **Crease-resistant** ("wash and wear," "easy care," "permanent press," and so on) by impregnating the fibers with resins or with agents that either cross-link cellulose molecules or build a "memory" into the fiber, causing it to return to its original shape. Crease-resistance gives textiles more firmness and sometimes better draping qualities; but it may also weaken fibers, reduce abrasion resistance, and wash out. Dyes become more permanent, and shrinkage of spun rayons, light cottons and linens, and velvets diminishes. Bonding to a foam or tricot backing also enhances wrinkle resistance.
- **Fire-** and **flame-resistant** through chemical treatments. A worthwhile safety precaution, these processes can be durable but sometimes need to be renewed. They may make textiles heavier and stiffer but may also increase resistance to weathering and sometimes to insects and mildew.
- **Elastic** by including spandex fiber in the blend or by inserting stretch properties through special construction techniques, such as the twisting or crimping of yarns, slack mercerization of fabrics, or heat setting.
- **Glossy** with resins that provide a more or less permanent smooth, lustrous surface. Glazed fabrics resist soil and have improved draping qualities. Glazing is usually limited to textiles meant for curtains, draperies, and slipcovers.
- **Insulating** through the application of a thin or foamed coating on the back, which keeps out the heat rays of the sun and keeps in winter warmth.
- **Soil-resistant** or **soil-releasing** by coating or impregnating fibers or fabrics with chemicals to make them less absorbent.
- **Stable,** chiefly through carefully controlled shrinking tendencies. In some processes, chemicals supplement moisture, heat, pressure, and tension.
- **Water-repellent** by coating or impregnating the fibers with wax, metals, or resins. Such treatment makes fabrics hold their shape better, as well as helping to keep dirt on the surface.

Coloring the Fabric

Dyes can be introduced at several stages of the fabric-construction process. As the need demands, manufacturers dye unspun fibers, spun yarns, or woven textiles. In some synthetics and plastics, the dye is mixed with the liquid from which the

364. A continuous design with a fairly small-scale repeat is well adapted to the technique of roller printing, with its un-interrupted, automatic processing. (*Courtesy Boussac of France, Inc.*)

fiber or film is made. Although generalizations about dyes cannot be absolute, the synthetic substances in which dye forms part of the fiber or film seem to be the most thoroughly colorfast. Next come the fibers and yarns dyed before fabric construction, and last the piece-dyed textiles. Today, however, less difference separates the latter two than was true in the past, thanks to new processes.

The kind of dye and its hue affect colorfastness, but almost all colors will fade in varying degrees when exposed to sun or polluted air, washed, or drycleaned. Unless we want to protect fabrics from sun and use at the possible cost of relaxed living, we should think about getting the most nearly fade-proof textiles available. Since all textiles change with time, it would seem sensible to select those that will mellow gracefully rather than those that will look tired and worn out when they fade. The following characteristics mitigate the results of fading:

- **Colors** most common in nature—grays, greens, browns, soft yellows and oranges—retain their appearance longer than do colors of higher intensity. Mixtures, such as in tweeds, do not become as listless as faded solid colors. Dark colors may lose richness and depth with even a little fading.
- **Textures,** with their play of light and shade, compensate for loss of color.
- **Patterns** that are intricate or diffused lose less of their character than those whose interest lies chiefly in brilliant contrasts, precision, or clarity.

It is worthwhile to consider whether a little fading or wear need be so deplorable. Fabrics that have mellowed and that show evidence of having been lived with give some people a comfortable feeling of continuity and cozyness. The softening of colors, textures, and patterns can result in a harmonious richness. We have only to compare, even mentally, an antique Persian rug with a modern equivalent to realize that this is so.

Nevertheless, it should again be emphasized that one of the simplest ways to introduce color into the home is through the fabrics. Textiles contribute the brilliance and stridence of primary hues, the richness and depth of purples or chocolate browns, the subtlety of pastels (Pl. 41, p. 283). Large or small areas of solid colors or of decisive patterns can be achieved easily and inexpensively, and just as easily and inexpensively changed (Pl. 42, p. 284).

Decorative Finishes and Enrichment

Printing The easiest, least expensive way to add design to fabric is by printing, a process known for at least four thousand years. Pigments mixed to the consistency of thick paste are applied to the finished fabric (or occasionally to the yarns before weaving) by one of the following methods:

- **Roller printing** (Fig. 364), by far the most common technique, involves the application of pigments from copper rollers engraved with the design. One roller is made for each color, but an effect of more colors than rollers can be achieved by engraving different parts of a roller to different depths or by printing one color over another. Sometimes the warp yarns are printed before weaving, which gives a soft, diffuse quality.
- **Block printing** is most often done by hand, although semimechanized methods now exist. Wood blocks that may be surfaced with metal or linoleum transfer color to the fabric. Block-printed textiles have the slight irregularities charac-teristic of handcraft designs (Fig. 365) and are expensive.
- **Screen printing** (Fig. 366; see also Pl. 42), often called *silk screen,* is a type of stencil printing especially suitable for patterns produced in relatively small quantities. The initial cost is less than that of roller printing, but stencils do not last as long as do the copper rollers. Screen printing involves forcing a thick dye through a mesh that has been coated with moisture repellant in some

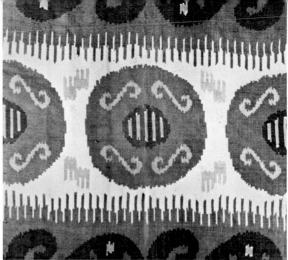

portions. Color passes through only the untreated areas. A number of screens may be used to add to or vary the colors. Automatic screen printing methods have greatly speeded up the process and lessened the number of workers needed, while still retaining many of the advantages of the medium.

□ **Batik** is a method of resist printing in which parts of the fabric are protected from the dye during each application. A dye-resisting wax or paste, applied to sections of the cloth, prevents dye from being absorbed in those areas. After each dye bath the wax is removed and perhaps reapplied to other parts of the fabric; the process can be repeated to form a design of more than one color. Still a much-admired handcraft (Pl. 43, p. 284), the technique is also being adapted to machine processes.

□ **Tie-dyeing,** another resist method, requires an arrangement of pleats, knots, and ties, causing portions of the fabric to resist the dye bath into which it is immersed. The resulting pattern is usually diffuse, since the dye advances and recedes around the bound areas.

□ **Discharge printing,** the reverse of resist dyeing, results when parts of the fabric are treated with a chemical to remove color.

Stitchery   The general trend toward increased enrichment in design has brought renewed interest in embroidery, appliqué, quilting, and other types of needlework. These may be done by machine in the factory, by hand in small workshops, or individually at home (Fig. 367). Many people enjoy adding some sketchy crewel embroidery to a pillow cover, or they may actually reconstruct the face of a fabric by needlepoint for a seat cover. Patchwork—old and new, real and simulated—exemplifies the tendency for rich, complex designs (Fig. 368; see also Pl. 9, p. 59).

left: 365. Block prints typically have small-scale repeats, because of the limitations on the size of the block, but the difficulty of lining up the design precisely causes the repeat to be more evident than in roller printing. Here the wood block is above, the printed cloth below.

right: 366. Screen printing adapts well to large designs, because the size of the screen—which can be quite large—determines the size of the repeat. "Pomegranate," a design by Jack Lenor Larsen, was handwoven and handprinted in Thailand.

367. Crewel embroidery is a relatively fast method of applying surface ornament to fabrics by stitchery. It lends itself to informal, meandering designs. Here the wing chair, hand-embroidered in six weeks, seems quite at home in a comfortable wood-paneled room. (*Photograph: The New York Times/Bill Aller*)

Fabrics   **281**

right: 368. A beautiful old patchwork quilt covers a bed set under an unusual window. The handwoven rug and extra quilt add enrichment. David Sellers, architect. (*Photograph: Robert Perron*)

below: 369. Alternating squares of plain weave and basket weave result in a distinctive structural design in Jack Lenor Larsen's wool fabric, "Spellbound."

bottom: 370. A large screen-printed design on Marimekko's "Kumiseva" takes advantage of the uninterrupted flat expanse of fabric. Here it is used as a murallike screen divider that leads the eye around it and beyond. (*Courtesy D/R International, Inc.*)

The explosion of interest in handcrafts as personally rewarding experiences has led many people to the creation of fabrics through weaving, knitting, or macramé. Others make rugs by braiding fabrics, hooking yarns, or even tying yarns on a loom or frame, as in the rya technique. The satisfactions that come from designing and making things by hand can be very real, and handwork of this type adds a dimension to the home that is sometimes amateurish but personalizing, and often surprisingly professional and spirited.

Fabric Design

Nothing in contemporary homes except wallpaper offers the freedom of design that comes naturally in fabrics. This is of special significance today, when other materials are likely to be handled with restricted simplicity. The increasing urge for intricate ornamentation and emotional impact can be most readily and inexpensively satisfied with textiles.

From the illustrations in this chapter, it should be apparent that fabrics are available to suit almost every taste and situation. The regular geometry of pattern loom-woven into a fabric and brought to life by varied color (Fig. 363) contrasts with the bold and exciting free-form designs of a batik hanging (Pl. 43). Small-scale, intricate motifs (Fig. 364) play against large, vigorous, discrete ones (Pl. 42). These and other fabrics throughout the book demonstrate the diversity of feelings and moods that textiles can bring into the home.

All that was said in Chapters 7, 8, and 9 about design concepts is generally applicable to fabric design. Design in textiles can be structurally integrated, applied to the finished cloth, or a combination of the two. In any case, fabrics have unique characteristics that should be taken into account. Some of the more important qualities—*structure, continuousness, flatness,* and *pliability*—are discussed and illustrated on the following pages.

The **structure** of fabrics is a basic factor in their design. Most woven textiles reveal the pattern of warp and filling to the eye and hand, and the way yarns are held together in knits and laces is equally apparent. The pattern may be of sufficient interest so that nothing more is needed (Fig. 369). If applied ornament is desired, the structure and the fibers merit respect. Delicate patterns lose their effectiveness on coarse fabrics; bold motifs may seem incongruous on fine materials.

The **continuous,** sheetlike nature of fabrics provides one of the few opportunities in homes for uninterrupted, endless patterns without a definite beginning or conclusion. Designs that lead the eyes easily in all directions seem especially appropriate (Fig. 370).

right: Plate 40. A brilliantly colored Danish rya rug brightens the rather dark study of a mineral collector, while its thick pile softens the effect of predominantly "hard" materials in the room. This design by Ege Rya, Inc., is called "Vesuvius." See page 278. (*Courtesy Harold J. Siesel Co., Inc.*)

below: Plate 41. Furniture upholstered in rich, pastel-colored fabrics makes for a bright and cheerful yet serene environment. Flat yellow walls and ceiling heighten the sunny effect. See page 280. Robert Perkins, designer. (*Photograph: John T. Hill*)

left: **Plate 42.** A brilliant swath of printed Mari-mekko fabric enlivens the off-white walls of this dining room, at the same time emphasizing the two-story height. Charles Moore, architect. See page 280. (*Photograph: John T. Hill*)

below: **Plate 43.** Marian Clayden's *Ceremonial Enclosure,* a huge silk panel with hand-printed designs, was made by a combination of resist-dyeing methods. See page 281. (*Courtesy the artist*)

Pliability recommends patterns that are supple and flexuous (Fig. 371), unless the fabric is intended only to be stretched flat on walls or floors. This does not rule out angularity, but it makes extreme rigidity or hardness questionable.

The two-dimensional **flatness** of most fabrics suggests two-dimensional compositions (Fig. 372). There are numerous exceptions to this statement, but in general an illusion of great depth or of strongly modeled forms will succeed only when the designer chooses deliberately to stress this ambiguity.

The Art Fabric

Beyond fabrics-used-as-fabrics there are the fabric constructions that can be considered in the same category with the other art media. The fabric environment shown in Figure 348 stands as an example of this concept carried to the point where the home itself becomes a sensuous fabric space-sculpture in which people live and move. In recent years fiber has begun to be accepted as a viable material for "fine art" just as stone and metal and oil paints always have been. Fiber artists are among the most innovative designers of the seventies; Magdalena Abakanowicz, whose tapestry is shown in Figure 373, occupies the forefront of this movement. An extremely vigorous creative statement, the tapestry uses yarns to provide at

373. Magdalena Abakanowicz' *Abakan 27* (1967) has an intensity of personal expression that characterizes the best recent work in the fiber arts. The tapestry, woven of rich brown and black sisal, is enlivened by brighter lips, spikes, and hanging threads that introduce a third dimension. (*Courtesy Jack Lenor Larsen, Inc.*)

once base, background, foreground, shape, color, and great textural diversity. If we try to imagine such a work done in any other medium, we realize that the artist's choice of yarn has opened up totally new dimensions in aesthetic expression.

List of Fabrics

The following pages list some of the fabrics most frequently used in the home. They have been divided into five categories, based primarily on thickness, which is an important factor in determining their applications. However, there is quite a range within each category and some overlapping between categories. Most of the fabrics can be woven from a number of different fibers, but a few are made from only one. Fabric names constitute a strange miscellany, being based on the fiber, such as *linen*, which has come to mean a special kind of linen textile; the weave, such as *satin*; the early use, such as *monk's cloth*; or a trade name, such as *Indian Head*.

Very Thin   Almost transparent fabrics are suitable for glass curtains and sometimes for summer bedspreads, table skirts, and table coverings. Most can be made from cotton, silk, synthetics, or even wool.

Bobbinet   A fine and sheer to coarse open plain lace with hexagonal meshes. Soft yet with character; most effective when very full; coarser types best for straight folds; sheer types well suited to tiebacks and ruffles. White, cream, ecru, pale colors.

Cheesecloth   Cotton in loose, plain weaves, very low thread count. Very inexpensive; short-lived; informal. Usually off-white.

Dimity   Fine, tightly twisted, usually combed cotton; plain weave with thin cord making vertical stripe or plaid. Often mercerized. Fine, sheer, crisp; suited to straight folds or tiebacks. White, tints, or printed patterns.

Filet   Square-mesh lace knotted at intersecting corners. Fine to coarse but usually giving a bold, heavy effect. White, cream, ecru, and plain colors.

Marquisette   Leno weave in many fibers. Sheer and open; soft or crisp; fine to coarse. Serviceable; launders well. White, cream, or pale colors; sometimes printed or woven patterns.

Net   Any lace with a uniform mesh, such as bobbinet or filet; fine to coarse, sheer to open; made of almost any fiber.

Ninon   Plain voilelike or novelty weaves. Very thin; smooth, silky, pleasant sheen. Best in straight folds. Plain colors; self-colored stripes or shadowy figures; sometimes embroidered.

Organdy   Cotton in plain weave; like sheer, crisp muslin, but crispness washes out unless specially treated. Folds keep their place. Often used without draperies; frequently tied back. Many plain colors; also printed or embroidered designs.

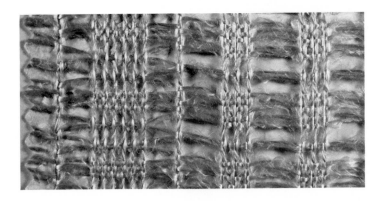

374. An openwork fiberglass fabric is ideal for window curtains, since it is not only attractive and translucent, but easy to care for. (*Courtesy Owens/Corning Fiberglas*)

Point d'esprit   Variation of bobbinet with dots that give it more body. White, cream, and pale colors.

Swiss muslin (dotted swiss)   Cotton in plain weaves; usually embroidered or patterned in dots or figures. Fine, sheer, slightly crisp. Can be used alone, usually draped; effect generally informal. White and plain colors, usually light; figures may be colored.

Theatrical gauze   Linen or cotton in a loose, open, crisp weave with a shimmering texture. Often used without draperies for colorful, informal effect. Wide range of plain colors, often two-toned.

Voile   Open, plain weave, sheer and smooth. Drapes softly; gives more privacy than marquisette. Various textures; many colors, usually pale; sometimes woven patterns.

Thin   Translucent fabrics are suitable for glass curtains or for draperies. They have sufficient body to be used alone and give a measure of privacy, although not at night. Thin fabrics can also be used for table skirts, table coverings, and summer bedspreads.

Batiste   Delicate and fine, plain weave, usually cotton or Dacron, often with printed or embroidered designs. Needs fullness to be effective; when embroidered, has considerable body. Light and dainty. White or pastel colors.

Casement cloth   Almost every known fiber in plain or figured weaves. Flat and lustrous. Often ecru, but can be other colors. Frequently used alone as draw curtains.

Fiberglass   Glass fibers in varied weaves and weights, from sheer marquisette to heavy drapery fabrics. Translucent to opaque; can be washed and hung immediately without shrinking or stretching. Good range of colors; plain or printed (Fig. 374).

Films (plastic)   Smooth or textured, plain or printed, thin or thick. Used for shower curtains, table coverings, upholstery, or wall coverings. Waterproof; wipes clean.

Muslin   Cotton in a soft, plain weave; light to heavy qualities. Bleached or unbleached; also dyed and printed. Inexpensive, durable, informal; often used alone at windows.

Osnaburg   Cotton yarns, coarse and uneven, in an open, plain weave; similar to crash. Usually medium weight, natural color, but can be light or heavy weight, any color, printed patterns. Strong and long-lasting; rough-textured; informal.

Pongee   Wild silk in plain weave with broken crossbar texture caused by irregular yarns; also imitated in cotten and synthetics. Fairly heavy; often used without draperies. Shrinks unless treated. Usually pale or dark ecru, but can be dyed. Also called tussah, antique taffeta, and doupioné (douppioni).

Sheeting (cotton)   Smooth, plain weave, medium to heavy weights. Inexpensive and informal. White, colors, or printed.

Silk gauze   Plain weave with a slight irregularity in threads, making an interesting texture. Hangs well; is never slick. Wide range of colors.

Lightweight   Light fabrics are suitable for draperies, bedspreads, table skirts, pillows, screens, wall coverings, table coverings, and slipcovers. They sometimes serve for upholstery in the heavier grades. Many can be made of cotton, silk, wool, or synthetics. They come in a wide color range and can be washed.

Antique satin   Variation of smooth satin, with a dull, uneven texture. Variety of weights but usually heavier than satin. Widely used for upholstery and drapery materials.

Broadcloth   Cotton, synthetic, or silk in plain or twill weaves; spun rayon or wool in twill weaves. Varies greatly in terms of fiber and weave. Cotton and synthetic types used for draperies, bedspreads, tablecloths.

Calico   Cotton in a plain weave, printed with small-figured pattern. Inexpensive and informal.

Challis   Wool, synthetic, or cotton in a soft, plain, firm weave. Usually printed with small floral designs but sometimes a plain color.

Chambray   Cotton or linen in a smooth, close, plain weave. White-frosted appearance on wide range of colors.

Chintz   Cotton in a close, plain weave, usually with a printed design and often glazed. Washing removes glaze in many types (Fig. 375).

Drill   Cotton in diagonal twill weave. Firm, heavy, very durable textile. Typical color is gray, but other colors available.

Faille   Plain weave with decided flat, crosswise ribs. Difficult to launder, but wears well if handled carefully. Varies from soft yet firm to quite stiff.

Gingham   Cotton or synthetic in light to medium weight, plain weave; woven from colored yarns. Strong; launders well. Checked, striped, and plaid patterns.

Homespun   Irregular yarns woven in loose, plain weave. Texture somewhat rough and irregular; informal character. Plain colors, dyed, or woven of mixed yarns.

India print   Printed cotton cloth from India or Persia with characteristic intricate design in clear or dull colors. Inexpensive and durable. Fades, but pleasantly.

Indian Head   Plain weave, firm and smooth. Trade name for a permanent-finish cotton, vat-dyed, colorfast, shrink-resistant. Inexpensive and durable.

Insulating   Fabrics coated on one side with metallic flakes to reflect heat or with foam plastic to trap heat.

Jaspé cloth   Plain weave; varied yarns give unobtrusive, irregular, blended stripes. Generally firm, hard, and durable. Can be in any color, but usually fairly neutral, medium dark, and monochromatic.

Linen   Flax in a plain, firm weave. Cool to the touch, good body, launders well; wrinkles easily unless specially treated. Often has hand-blocked designs (Fig. 376).

Moiré   Ribbed, plain weave with a watermarked appearance. Most moiré finishes can be steamed or washed out—more permanent on synthetic fibers.

Oxford cloth   Plain basket or twill weave, light to rather heavy weights. Durable and launders well.

Piqué   Plain weave with narrow raised cords running in one direction or at right angles to each other (waffle piqué). Durable; interesting texture.

Poplin   Plain weave with fine crosswise ribs. Firm and durable.

Rep   Plain weave with prominent rounded ribs running crosswise or lengthwise.

Sateen   Cotton, usually mercerized, in a satin weave; flat and glossy, with a dull back. Durable, substantial, but with a tendency to roughen. Often used for lining curtains.

Satin   Satin weave, smooth, delicate fabric with very high sheen. Durable; somewhat slippery.

Seersucker   Plain weave with woven, crinkly stripes. Durable, needs no ironing.

Shantung   Plain weave with elongated irregularities. A heavy grade of pongee, but with wider color range.

Stretch   Knit or woven of cotton, rayon, or other synthetic with special stretch properties or of spandex. Smooth to rough textures. Valuable for slipcovers and contoured shapes.

Taffeta   Close, plain weave, slightly crossribbed. Crisp; sometimes weighted with chemical salts; cracks in strong sunlight. Antique taffeta has unevenly spun threads.

Medium Weight   Fabrics of medium weight are suitable for heavy draperies and upholstery, as well as for wall coverings and pillows. Some also adapt to slipcovers, bedspreads, screens, and table coverings. Made of heavier fibers of cotton, flax, hemp, jute, linen, silk, synthetics, or wool, they are available in a wide color range; some are washable.

Bark cloth Cotton in a firm, plain weave with irregular texture due to uneven yarns. Plain or printed. Durable.

Brocade Woven on a Jacquard loom; raised designs are produced by floating some of the filling yarns. Usually has a multicolored floral or conventional pattern (Fig. 377).

Brocatelle A Jacquard weave similar to brocade but with a heavier design. Used mostly as upholstery on large sofas and chairs.

Burlap Loose basket weave. Heavy and coarse; interesting texture. Often fades quickly.

Canvas Cotton in a plain, diagonal weave. Heavy, firm, and durable. Strong solid colors, as well as stripes or printed designs. Often used for awnings, outdoor curtains, and upholstery.

Crash Plain weave with a rough texture caused by uneven yarns. Often hand-blocked or printed.

Cretonne Cotton in a firm, plain, rep, or twill weave. Fairly heavy texture and bold design. Similar to chintz but heavier, never glazed. Patterns are usually more vigorous.

Damask Any combination of two of the three basic weaves; flat Jacquard patterns. Firm, lustrous, reversible. Similar to brocade but design is not in relief. May be referred to as figured satin. One or two colors used (Fig. 378).

Denim Cotton in a heavy, close twill weave. Warp and filler often in contrasting colors; can have a small woven pattern. Inexpensive; washable; Sanforizing prevents shrinking; reasonably sunfast.

Duck Cotton in a close, plain, or ribbed weave. Durable; often given protective finishes against fire, water, mildew. Similar to canvas.

Hopsacking Loose, plain weave. Coarse and heavy. Inexpensive and durable.

Laminated Any fabric bonded to a lightweight foam backing, or two fabrics bonded together. Wrinkle-resistant; good for upholstery, slipcovers, insulating draperies.

Mohair Hair of Angora goats (now often a mixture of cotton and wool) in a plain, twill, or pile weave or with a woven or printed design. Resilient and durable. Novelty weaves, sheer to very heavy.

Monk's cloth Jute, hemp, flax, usually mixed with cotton or all cotton in a loose plain or basket weave. Coarse and heavy; friar's cloth and druid's cloth similar but coarser. Not easy to sew, tendency to sag. Usually comes in natural color.

Sailcloth Plain weave. Heavy and strong. Similar to canvas or duck. Often used on summer furniture.

Serge Twill weave with a pronounced diagonal rib on both face and back. Has a clear, hard finish.

Terry cloth Cotton or linen in a loose uncut-pile weave; loops on one or both sides. Very absorbent; not always colorfast; may sag. Not suitable for upholstery, but useful for draperies and bedspreads.

Ticking Cotton or linen in a satin or twill weave. Strong, closely woven, durable. Best known in white with colored stripes, but may have simple designs. Not always colorfast but washable.

Heavy Heavy fabrics are perfect for upholstery because of their weight and durability; in lighter grades they make draperies, pillows, bedspreads, slipcovers, wall coverings, even table coverings. Most are available in a variety of fibers and a wide color range. Few are washable.

Bouclé Plain or twill weave. Flat, irregular surface, woven or knitted from specially twisted bouclé yarns; small spaced loops on surface.

Corduroy Cotton or a synthetic in a pile weave, raised in cords of various sizes giving pronounced lines. Durable, washable, inexpensive (Fig. 379).

Expanded vinyl Plastic upholstery fabric with an elastic knit fabric back. Stretches for contour fit.

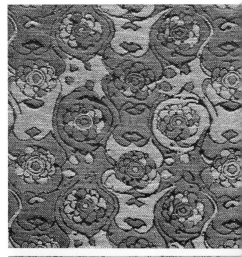

top: 377. A cotton brocade, "Harmony" has a conventionalized overall flower design formed by yarns floating over the plain-weave ground. (*Courtesy Boris Kroll Fabrics, Inc.*)

above: 378. An intricate design of wildflowers is woven into the fabric of "Santee Flowers," a damask. (*Courtesy Greeff Fabrics, Inc.*)

Felt   Nonwoven fabric of wool, rayon and wool, or synthetics. Nonraveling edges need no hemming. Available in intense colors; used for table coverings, pillows, even for draperies.

Frieze   Also called *frizé;* heavy-pile weave. Loops uncut or cut to form a pattern; sometimes yarns of different colors or with irregularities used. Usually has a heavy rib. Extremely durable.

Matelassé   Double-woven fabric with quilted or puckered surface effect, caused by interweaving to form the pattern. Needs care in cleaning, but otherwise durable (Fig. 380).

Needlepoint   Originally handmade in variety of patterns, colors, and degrees of fineness. Now imitated on Jacquard loom. At best, has pronounced character, from delicate (*petit point*) to robust (*gros point*); at worst, looks like weak imitation.

Plastic   Wide variety of textures from smooth to embossed; used for upholstering and wall-covering. Resists soil, wipes clean. Not for use over deep springs unless fabric-backed, which is more pliable, easier to fit, less likely to split.

Plush   Cut-pile weave. Similar to velvet but with a longer pile. Sometimes pressed and brushed to give surface variations; sculptured by having design clipped or burned out of pile, leaving motif in relief. Also made to imitate animal fur.

Tapestry   Weaves with two sets of warps and weft; woven on a Jacquard loom. Heavier and rougher than damask or brocade. Patterns usually pictorial and large.

Tweed   Soft, irregularly textured, plain weave. Yarns dyed before weaving; often several or many colors combined.

Velour   Short, heavy, stiff cut-pile weave. Slight luster and indistinct horizontal lines. Durable.

Velvet   Pile weave with loops cut or uncut. Luxurious but often shows wear quickly. Lustrous or dull; light to heavy grades; plain, striped, or patterned (Fig. 381).

Velveteen   Cotton or a synthetic woven with a short, close, sheared pile. Strong, durable, launders well.

Webbing   Cotton, jute, or plastic in narrow strips (1 to 4 inches) of very firm, plain weave. Plain, striped, or plaid design. Jute used to support springs; cotton or plastic interlaced for webbed seats and backs.

top: 379. Long used for clothing, corduroy also makes comfortable and attractive upholstery. (*Courtesy Directional Industries Incorporated*)

above: 380. "Coquille" skillfully utilizes the puffed effect possible with cotton-nylon matelassé to form a shell pattern raised above the surface. (*Courtesy Boris Kroll Fabrics, Inc.*)

right: 381. The soft, sensuous touch of velvet makes it one of the most luxurious upholstery fabrics available. (*Courtesy American Cyanamid Company*)

Major Elements

13 Walls, Stairs, and Fireplaces

Three elements of an eminently practical nature—walls, stairs, and fireplaces—have increasingly come to assume major design roles in the home. Walls are virtually essential for a dwelling; they give protection and privacy, affecting light, heat, and sound. At the same time, though, they demarcate areas and control our movements and vistas. If only because they constitute such a large area of square footage, walls and their treatment can largely determine the character of a home.

Stairs, of course, permit us to move easily from one level of an enclosure to another. By their very nature—as an efficient system for changing levels in minimum space—stairs usually cut a diagonal line or sometimes spiral upward. This feature introduces a diversion from the predominantly rectilinear quality of most homes. Unless they are completely buried behind walls, stairs attract—and deserve—much attention.

Fireplaces rarely function as the only source of heat in today's homes, except in the most gentle climates. Yet the very fact that we have not abandoned them (along with bootjacks, coal hods, and feather dusters) offers testimony to their psychological importance. A fireplace becomes the focus of any room; it is there people gather, even in summertime—partly, to be sure, because furniture is typically grouped around a hearth. Obviously, the focal point of a room, and of the principal group space, merits serious consideration in its design.

Walls

Walls govern the shape, size, and character of rooms or spaces; they become the enclosure against or with which we live. Increasingly, walls are being "used" as windows and doors, for built-in storage, and as supports for attached furnishings. That walls can be far more than innocuous backdrops can be demonstrated by the contemporary interest in geometrics, cutouts, overlapping, and interpenetration (Fig. 383). While cutout walls maintain their function of separating areas, they allow intriguing glimpses and half-views into the areas beyond to give the space a fascinating molded quality.

Well-proportioned walls are a continuing source of satisfaction. Appropriate colors, textures, and materials relate architecture to people and to furniture in a positive manner. Seen and used in relation to the windows, doors, stairs, and fireplaces that are parts of them; to floors and ceilings that complete the enclosure;

opposite: 382. The major interior elements in dancer Amalia Hernandez' own home in Mexico City create a fluid, constantly changing interplay of form and space. G. E. Arenas, architect. See also Fig. 216. (*Photograph: Julius Shulman*)

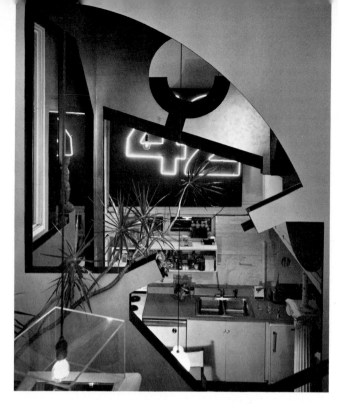

383. In the home of architect Charles Moore, walls lose their identities as passive, enclosing elements to become active, stimulating, and liberating components in the total design. (*Photograph: Norman McGrath*)

and to furniture, accessories, and people, walls should be considered as integral parts of a whole. Whether we are conscious of it or not, walls constitute a stage setting. The mood they establish is vital in its influence on everyday living.

The walls of the house shown in Figures 384 and 385 are architect Eliot Noyes' response to the challenge of building on a rocky site overlooking a valley. Two massive stone and concrete walls provide a structurally dominant vertical foundation from which lighter living areas are cantilevered, reducing the need for expensive and disruptive grading of the rugged terrain. The space between these two walls makes an indoor street (Fig. 386), lighted by large skylights and glass walls at each end, but essentially sheltered. It serves as a safe passageway to the various functional zones of the house. A half-flight of stairs up, the space becomes a semisecluded study; another short flight leads down to the dining room.

While the suggestion of a sheltered street works well in the central gallery, a street can be very impersonal. In the living room we find a substantially different

384–387. Massive masonry walls physically and visually support a country house designed by architect Eliot Noyes.

384. While the two masonry walls anchor the house solidly on a rocky outcrop, light, wood-sheathed rooms project freely from both sides. (*Photograph: Joseph W. Molitor*)

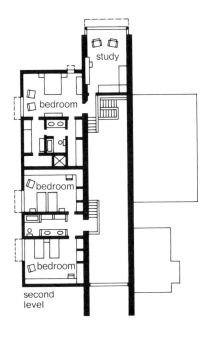

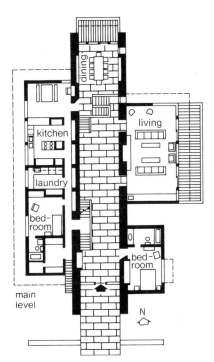

second level

main level

N

atmosphere (Fig. 387). A lower ceiling height immediately relates the room to human scale. But it is the walls that carry the theme of the architect's vision and establish the character. Three different types of walls appear in progression: the massive masonry bastion that provides anchorage for the cantilevered room; smooth plaster side walls, less bulky and more passive but still enclosing; and finally

above left: 385. The plan of the house also reveals the dominance of the stone and concrete walls but illustrates the way in which their weight has been moderated to some extent by a series of inset closets in the various rooms.

above right: 386. Glass walls at either end, large skylights, and stairs leading up and down eliminate any possible feeling of constriction in the interior gallery between the walls. (*Photograph: Joseph W. Molitor*)

right: 387. Stepping into the living room is a liberating experience, for the walls become progressively brighter and lighter in weight. The fireplace wall has been formalized with a broad, smooth hearth jutting into the room; the straight, clean edges of the fireplace opening play against the jumble of rock above. (*Photograph: Joseph W. Molitor*)

388–389. In a Vermont condominium, the walls themselves provide design interest while still fulfilling their function of shielding vistas and shaping space. Peter Gluck, architect.

left: 388. The interior walls make an endlessly fascinating pattern of solids and cutouts and slits, squares and rectangles and arcs, verticals and horizontals and diagonals. (*Courtesy American Home Magazine*)

right: 389. Instead of a bland, cold-transmitting window wall, the architect has conceived a well-insulated exterior wall with a group of smaller openings to frame views of the countryside and sky. (*Courtesy American Home Magazine*)

glass walls, framed in wood, light and open, exposing the view over the countryside. During the day this progression leads outside to the balcony, protected only by a low railing, and to an almost unlimited expansion of space. At night, possibly with the curtains pulled, the progression is reversed, drawing attention back to the stone wall with its promise of protection and shelter.

The design of the living room furnishings integrates the differing elements of the room. Sturdy and comfortable, the sofas and chairs complement the immensity of the stone wall and yet also have the crisp, square lines of the ordered glass wall. Placed opposite each other, the sofas invite focus on whichever scene, view of fire or panorama of changing seasons, is most rewarding at the time. The rectangularity of the seating arrangement reinforces the shape of the room and creates a setting conducive to conversation. Overall, the character of the room is one of a natural, relaxed poise established by the materials.

How different are the walls in the vacation condominium shown in Figures 388 and 389. Neutral walls of smooth plaster are a lively mixture of flat planes, curves, angles, and cutouts. The walls of the staircase have been dramatized by its changing forms, the dark wood railing that emphasizes those forms, and the painted design on the underside of the upper stairs. Half-walls partially segregate the dining and kitchen areas but leave them open to the major group space. Walls serve as open shelving in the dining area; closed, dropped cupboards in the kitchen; and a snug backing for the sofas in the living room. They create an animated, useful environment for vacation living.

Design of Walls

Contemporary architects and designers enjoy a freedom to use a vocabulary far more extensive than in the past, when walls were almost always fixed, vertical, thick, opaque, and supportive of the roof. Although many walls today have these characteristics, the following types are becoming common:

- Nonstructural walls that hold up nothing other than themselves
- Thin, transparent, or translucent walls of glass or plastic
- Walls that are integrated with ceilings
- Movable walls of all kinds that slide into pockets, fold like accordions, or are storage units on casters
- Storage walls that unite the enclosing functions of walls with many kinds of storage space
- Walls less than ceiling height to give visual privacy without tight, boxlike enclosure
- Spur or freestanding walls (or fireplaces) that stop short of joining the adjacent walls at one or both ends
- Walls that become furniture, with built-in seating or counter space
- Walls with cutouts and open spaces giving views to adjacent rooms

Of the specific qualities that can be combined to invest walls with the desired quality, some pertain primarily to utility, others to economy, beauty, or character. Taken together, they determine the expressive and functional properties of walls.

Degree of Formality or Informality   The living room of the Noyes house (Fig. 387) is more formal than that of the condominium (Fig. 388). Formality results when a room gives the feeling of a strict, firmly established, unchanging order, which the condominium certainly does not attempt to do. Symmetrical balance and pronounced regularity are the fundamental means to achieve this, but formality usually increases when the forms seem stable and precise, when surfaces are smooth, and when proportions make one feel upright. The Noyes living room, like many today, is semiformal. The walls are not symmetrically balanced throughout the room but achieve equilibrium through our unconscious awareness that the weight of the fireplace wall counterbalances the cantilevered section of the room with its appropriately lighter walls.

Degree of Activity or Passivity   Walls become active when their design and materials arouse visual interest, especially if they suggest movement. Patterned wallpaper or tiles, wood grain, or the design formed by the way in which wood is used can attract attention with their lively rhythms. Activity can also derive from built-in furniture, fireplaces, displays of collections, or the use of a wall for storage space. Typical smoothly plastered, uniformly painted walls remain passive unless their color is vigorous. Figures 390 and 391 show how very noncommittal walls can be activated by the use of paint.

390–391. "Before" and "after" views of a small bedroom show how forcefully paint can shape a space, with minimum difficulty and expense.

left: 390. In its original state the bedroom had neutral walls that served only to isolate the disparate elements for a rather drab effect. (*Courtesy Better Homes and Gardens.* © *Meredith Corporation, 1973. All rights reserved.*)

right: 391. As remodeled, a painted band of bright red links the two windows and swings around to form a headboard accented with a vertical panel of blue. A simpler window treatment unifies the design. (*Courtesy Better Homes and Gardens.* © *Meredith Corporation, 1973. All rights reserved.*)

392. A variety of wall surfacings—smooth plaster, thin wood strips laid horizontally, wider wood planks climbing the sloping wall to the roof, and glimpses of wood shingles—enliven an upstairs hall bounded by walls of varying heights, angles, and distances. Neil Goodwin, owner-designer. (*Courtesy American Home Magazine*)

Degree of Smoothness or Roughness   Wall textures range from glassy smoothness to stony roughness, with countless intermediate steps provided by plaster and gypsum board, tile and brick, wood and plastics. Smoothness is often associated with formality, roughness with informality. A basic pattern of companionable surface textures gives a sense of coherence, but variety and contrast are needed to awaken it. The upstairs bridge-corridor in Figure 392 has become an interesting passageway because of the changing surface textures on the walls.

Largeness or Smallness of Scale   Of tremendous importance is the scale of the walls in relation to the size of the space, the character of furnishings, and the personalities of the people using the room. The stone and concrete wall in the Noyes living room (Fig. 387) is bold and impressive but not overpowering, because the room and its furnishings are large in scale. In the bedroom shown in Plate 46 (p. 318), the small scale of the walls—and of the pattern in the wallpaper—relates to the delicate furnishings and the intimate character of the room.

Degree of Permanence or Mobility   In a mobile society, walls that can be moved to create the spaces current occupants need make a lot of sense. Movable walls that are at the same time storage walls can be doubly efficient. The owner or tenant of a large open space, such as a loft or barn, may be reluctant to break it up into smaller cubbyholes. Figure 393 shows an immense Manhattan loft that has been kept free of permanent interior walls. In place of them, the owner devised three movable hexagonal dividers of not-quite-ceiling height. These dividers, which also serve to display the owner's paintings, create "rooms" within and between them, yet they do not interfere with the sense of vast, flowing space.

Of course, movable walls give less privacy—both actual and psychological—than permanent ones. Some people feel insecure in the absence of permanent, fixed, floor-to-ceiling walls. Whether the goal should be stability or fluidity will depend on many factors, including the composition of the household, the lifestyle of its inhabitants, and the particular dispositions of individuals.

Degree of Enclosure or Openness   Enclosure results from such things as opaque, substantial-looking walls, warm dark colors, and noticeable textures. Small, separated, framed doors and windows with small panes and heavy draperies also contribute to a feeling of protectedness.

Openness comes with a maximum of transparent, translucent, or apparently thin unobtrusive walls and with a minimum of partitions that block view or movement. Receding colors and inconspicuous textures also contribute to openness. Of great importance is a continuity of materials, forms, and colors—not only inside a room but with the space in adjacent rooms and with the out of doors. The house in Figures 394 and 395 has freestanding walls to delineate the various areas of the group space, but it visually retains an impression of flowing spaciousness that continues out into the landscape. The kitchen, located behind the wall at far left, has been given glass walls above head height for noise and odor control without interrupting the open feeling.

Degree of Light Absorption or Reflection   Color value is the most critical factor in light absorption and reflection. White reflects up to 89 percent of the light striking it, black as little as 2 percent. But surface texture must be considered, because the smoother the surface, the more light is reflected. In the past, when windows were small and artificial illumination poor, very light walls were frequently needed to make rooms bright. Today, with large windows and improved artificial lighting, many people find that darker, textured walls create a sympathetic enclosure for themselves and their furnishings. Nevertheless, light-colored walls are

393. Mobile walls that double as display boards enable painter Lowell Nesbitt to enclose or enlarge the living spaces in what had formerly been an undivided industrial loft. (*Photograph: Dudley Gray*)

394–395. A head-height working divider wall demarcates group and support spaces in a large glass-walled pavilion. Donald E. Olsen, architect. See also Fig. 212.

above: 394. Throughout the house white walls intensify the feeling of spaciousness; the divider walls seem less bulky because of the dark-painted cutouts for bookshelves, cupboards, stereo equipment, and fireplace. (*Photograph: Ronald Partridge*)

left: 395. The plan shows clearly the flow of space around the divider spine.

refreshing, increase apparent size, make rooms easier to illumine, and serve as an effective background for anything placed against them. The owners of the house in Figure 394 report it seems the very essence of light, because the white walls reflect ample daylight coming in through sliding doors and high-level windows.

Durability and Maintenance   The amount of time and money needed to maintain walls affects the satisfaction they give. Some materials—masonry, tile, wood, and vinyl plastics—are durable and easy to keep. Others, including fragile but colorfast wallpapers, will endure with little care on walls that do not get hard use. The basic questions in selection are: What kind of use will the wall get? How easily is the material damaged? How easily can it be cleaned or repaired?

Degree of Sound Absorption or Reflection   Smaller houses and those with open plans, greater freedom for children, music systems and television, labor-saving but noisy appliances, and the trend away from heavy upholstery and draperies—all these make many contemporary homes noisy. It is possible to control this effect to a large extent, however, by means of wall constructions or finishings. "Hard" surfaces bounce and reflect sound; if they predominate in a room, noise is bound to be magnified. Conversely, "soft" materials absorb sounds and can noticeably lower the decibel level in a room. In terms of wall constructions and surfaces, the hardest materials are metal, plastic, and glass; wood and plaster are somewhat less sound-reflective; and the most sound-absorbing materials include cork, fabric, and the various "acoustical" devices.

We can imagine two extremes of noise and silence contrived by manipulating the structure and furnishings of a room. The noisiest possible environment might consist of a precisely rectangular space with walls, floor, and ceiling of smooth metal or glass; furnished with a few rectangular, smooth metal or plastic pieces set parallel to the walls. The quietest room could have broken walls and a projecting or recessed fireplace and storage cabinets; a ceiling plane interrupted by beams; walls surfaced with cork or fabric, a carpeted floor (the shaggier the better), and plaster or acoustical-tile ceiling; heavy upholstered furniture, thick draperies, large plants, and many books on open shelves. As noted, these two examples are extremes. The former would probably be so nerve-shattering as to drive us out of the house, but the latter could be so eerily silent that it became equally unsettling. Depending on the purpose of the room and the needs of the household, the best solution lies somewhere in between.

Degree of Heat-Cold Insulation   In the interests of both comfort and conservation of energy, the construction of walls with a high degree of heat and cold insulation is of the utmost importance. Chapter 5 deals with these matters. Undoubtedly, more materials will be made available to remedy poorly insulated walls.

Wall Construction and Materials

Although we often take walls for granted, the building of efficient, protective enclosures was a notable achievement for early peoples. Recently, there have been tremendous technological advances, especially in factory-made wall units. The technology of wall construction is beyond the scope of this book, but some knowledge of what walls are and how materials affect their characteristics can help in deciding on the walls most appropriate for homes.

Walls that are fixed, opaque, and of one material are easiest to understand. Examples include houses built of heavy timbers—such as log cabins and Swiss chalets—and structures of solid stone or adobe brick. These are rare today, being expensive and comparatively poor insulators. Moreover, they leave no concealed space for pipes and ducts and are not amenable to the broad, unobstructed openings now in favor unless combined with heavy steel or wood beams. Walls entirely of masonry have great appeal, however, with their comforting sense of permanence as well as their color and texture. Steel reinforcing increases their stability, and space can be left for insulation and utilities. The possibilities of concrete as a distinctive material have received relatively little attention in residential architecture, but its use in multiple-family dwellings has risen enormously.

Today, most walls consist of more than one material, or of the same material used in different ways. Wood-frame walls are most common in single-family homes, since they are familiar to builders and not expensive. In addition to resilient stability, they allow space for insulation and utilities. Usually, but not necessarily, they support the roof. Surface treatment, inside and out, can be varied. Although wood-frame walls may have five or more layers, they can be thought of as three-layer sandwiches:

- □ **Structural frame** of wood studs (closely spaced two-by-fours or more widely spaced heavier posts) from floor to ceiling. Studs typically are set with 16 inches separating their centers—a useful thing to know when hanging things.
- □ **Exterior layers** of diagonal wood sheathing and insulation or sheets of strong insulating composition board, covered with weather-resistant surfaces of wood, asbestos, plastic, or metal siding, shingles or sheets; with lath and stucco; or with a veneer of brick or stone.
- □ **Interior layers** of lath and plaster, plywood, gypsum board, or wood paneling.

Table 13.1 Wall Materials

Material	Character	Use	Finishes	Advantages	Disadvantages
		Exterior and Interior			
absbestos (panels, shingles, siding) cost: moderately low	new textures and colors make it interesting; may resemble wood from a distance	occasionally in interiors where durability and easy upkeep are important; exterior walls	none needed, but can be painted	rare combination of low cost and upkeep; high resistance to fire, weather, and insects	potential health hazard for workers and consumers
brick (adobe) cost: varies greatly from one locality to another	earthy solidity combined with handcraft informality; large in scale; noticeable pattern of blocks and joints unless smoothly plastered	interior-exterior walls, chiefly in mild climates	stucco, special paints, or transparent waterproofing	unique character: resists fire and insects; newer types made with special binders and stabilizers are stronger and more weather-resistant	older types damaged by water; walls must be thick or reinforced; sturdy foundations required; comparatively poor insulation for weight and thickness
brick (fired clay) cost: high but less than stone	substantial and solid; small-scale regularity; many sizes, shapes, and colors; can be laid in varied patterns	interior-exterior walls, exterior surfacing or garden walls; around fireplaces	none unless waterproofing necessary; interior walls can be waxed	satisfying texture and pattern; durable, easily maintained; fireproof	none other than heat-cold conduction and noise reflection
concrete cost: moderately high	typically smooth and solid-looking, but can be highly decorative	interior-exterior walls in mild climates; exterior walls elsewhere	exterior painted or stuccoed if desired; interior painted, plastered, or surfaced with any material	permanent, durable, low maintenance; can be cast in varied shapes and surface patterned	comparatively poor insulator; requires sturdy foundations and costly forms
concrete blocks (lightweight aggregate) cost: moderate.	typically regular in shape, moderately textured, and bold in scale, many variations	interior-exterior walls in mild climates; exterior and garden walls anywhere	exterior waterproofing necessary; no interior finish needed but can be painted	durable, easily maintained; fireproof; fair insulator	none of any consequence, except perhaps lack of domestic character
glass (clear, tinted, and patterned) cost: moderately high	open and airy; patterned glass transmits diffused light	interior-exterior window walls; patterned glass for translucency; tinted for privacy, glare	none (except for curtaining for privacy and control of light, heat, and cold)	clear glass creates indoor-outdoor relationships; patterned and tinted glass combines light and varying degrees of privacy	breakable; very poor heat-cold insulation unless thermopane; needs frequent cleaning
metal (panels, siding, shingles, and tiles) cost: moderate	varies greatly depending on size, shape, and finish; often regarded as unhomelike	sometimes used in kitchens and bathrooms; exterior house and garden walls; mobile homes	aluminum and steel available with long-lasting factory finishes in many colors	lightweight in relation to strength; resistant to fire; enameled and aluminum panels need minimum upkeep	although very durable, metal surfaces are difficult to repair if damaged
plaster and **stucco** cost: moderately low	typically smooth and precise but can be varied in texture; only surfacing material that shows no joints, breaks; quiet background	plaster in any room; stucco usually for garden or exterior house walls	special weather-resistant paints; paint, paper, or fabric for interiors	moderately durable if properly finished; suited to many easy-to-change treatments; fireproof; special types absorb sound	often cracks or chips
plastic (panels, siding, glazing; often reinforced with glass fibers) cost: moderate	opaque or translucent, often textured and colorful; thin and flat or corrugated; thicker with cores of varied materials	interior walls where durability, upkeep are important; partitions; interior-exterior walls, exterior siding; translucent for garden walls	factory finished	similar to patterned glass except breaks less easily, lighter in weight; can be sawed and nailed; siding prefinished, durable; low upkeep	not thoroughly tested for longevity
stone cost: high	substantial, solid; impressive; natural colors and textures	around fireplace; exterior and garden walls	none unless waterproofing is necessary	beauty and individuality; durability, ease of maintenance; fireproof; ages gracefully	poor insulator; reflects sound; not amenable to change
wood (boards, plywood, shingles) cost: moderate	natural beauty and individuality of grain and color	interior and exterior walls; garden fences	needs protective finish to seal it against water, stains, dirt	fairly durable, easily maintained; good insulator; adaptable; ages well inside	few kinds are weather-resistant unless treated; burns; attacked by termites

Table 13.1 Wall Materials (*continued*)

| Material | Interior Only | | | | |
	Character	Use	Finishes	Advantages	Disadvantages
cork cost: moderately high	sympathetic natural color and texture	any room; only plastic-impregnated types suitable for baths and kitchens	none needed but can be waxed	durable, easily kept; sound-absorbent; good insulator	harmed by moisture, stains, and so on, unless specially treated
plastic (thin, rigid tiles) cost: relatively low	similar to clay tile except variety is sharply limited	kitchen and bathroom walls	no finish needed	easy to keep and apparently durable; simple to install; lightweight	similar to clay tile
plastic (resilient tiles or sheets) cost: moderately high	great variety of colors, patterns, textures	where durable, resilient walls are wanted, such as in play space or above kitchen counters	some need waxing; many now do not	very durable and resistant to cuts and stains; easy maintenance; can extend into counter tops	none of consequence
tile (clay) cost: moderately high	repeated regularity sets up pattern; great variety in size, shape, ornamentation	kitchens, bathrooms, and around fireplace; occasionally used for exterior ornament	no finish needed	can have great beauty and individuality; very durable, easily maintained; resistant to water, stains, fire	hard and cold to touch; reflects noise; can crack or break
wallboard (gypsum) cost: moderately low	noncommittal; joints show unless very well taped and painted	any room	paint, wallpaper, or fabric	not easily cracked; fire-resistant; can be finished in many ways	visually uninteresting in itself; needs protective surface
wallboard (plastic laminates) cost: high	shiny, mat, or textured surface; varied colors and patterns	kitchens, bathrooms, or any hard-use wall	none needed	very durable, unusually resistant to moisture, stains, dirt; cleaned with damp cloth	although wear-resistant, it can be irremediably scratched or chipped; reflects noise
wallboard (pressed wood) cost: moderate	smooth, mat surface with slight visual texture; also great variety of patterns	hard-wear rooms	needs no finish but can be stained, waxed, painted	tough surface is hard to damage	none of any importance
wall covering (plastic) cost: moderately high	many patterns; pleasing textures; mat or glossy surfaces	good for hard use walls	none needed	very durable; resists moisture, dirt, stains; cleans with damp cloth	none of importance
wallpaper and fabrics cost: moderately low	tremendous variety of color and pattern	any wall	usually none but can be protected with lacquer	inexpensive; can give decided character; some kinds very durable and easy to keep	must be chosen and used carefully

Increasingly, metal and plastic structural framing systems take the place of wood, because of their labor- and cost-saving potentials. And the need for efficient insulation becomes apparent to decrease our dependence on energy resources for heating and cooling.

Although walls of this type are still the most familiar for single-family homes, manufacturers have made great strides in the prefabrication of walls. Panels of wood, metal, or plastics—comprising in one component the layers of materials mentioned above—can be made in factories, which results in lowered construction costs without loss of individuality. There are hundreds of different designs available.

Wall Materials and Surfacings

Table 13.1, a comparative list of wall materials, enables us to evaluate the many differences in structures and surfacings. We should also be aware that:

□ All exterior materials can be used for inside walls, a possibility highly regarded by contemporary architects and designers because it accentuates indoor-outdoor relationships, and by householders because it often reduces maintenance on interior surfaces.
□ Some materials usually thought of as flooring—such as cork, vinyl, or carpeting—bring to walls the same serviceability they give floors.
□ Many new materials expand the range of possibilities.

None of this need concern those who are happy with plaster or gypsum board painted white or low-intensity colors, which become passive backgrounds. But the sampling of old and new products may provide inspiration for those who want more distinctive walls.

Wood   As boards, shingles, or panels, wood is available in an immense variety of grains, colors, and styles. The patterns produced by shingles or by boards laid horizontally or vertically—the joints beveled, shiplapped (overlapped), or covered by battens—make up part of the architectural vocabulary that can set the character of the wall (Figs. 272, 283, 287; Pl. 33, p. 231). A quite different effect results when plywood sheathes the wall, either as exterior siding or as interior paneling (Fig. 280). Another variable is the way in which the wood is finished, whether smooth

399. An interesting wall surface can be achieved simply by recycling small pieces of used lumber to create a lively pattern. Bernard Langlais, designer. (*Courtesy American Crafts Council*)

or rough-sawn, treated with vinyl or other substances to preserve attractiveness and reduce maintenance (Fig. 396).

Shingles, normally thought of as exterior sheathing, make a casual interior wall surface especially useful in rooms subject to much dampness—such as garden rooms, bathrooms, and saunas—because they absorb moisture (Fig. 397). Other unusual types of wood wall surfacings include bark (Fig. 398) and randomly sawed and nailed plank ends (Fig. 399). Cork, which is actually the thick, elastic outer bark of the cork oak, gives both sound and temperature insulation, in addition to serving—in children's spaces particularly—as surfaces for tacking things onto. In the living room shown in Figure 400, the single dark cork wall provides a warm and pleasant contrast to the otherwise stark white walls and ceiling.

400. A dark cork wall at one end helps to square off a long, narrow living room while at the same time providing a surface for posters and other objects on display. Barry David Berger, designer. (*Photograph: John T. Hill*)

Masonry Various types of masonry walls were discussed in Chapter 10. They include cement block (Fig. 73), exposed brick and stone (Figs. 290, 291, 293; Pl. 35, p. 232), ceramic tile (Figs. 87, 315; Pl. 11, p. 60) and stuccoed brick (Fig. 401). Ceramic-tiled bathrooms have come a long way since the days of stark white uniform tiles bordered in a row of black (Fig. 402). And custom ceramic walls come in a wide variety of patterns and colors, from the "natural," earthlike effect to sleekly modern designs (Fig. 403). What appears to be a rubble stone wall in Figure 404 is actually exterior plywood to which small stones have been attached with epoxy cement. Such a wall surfacing could be used either indoors or out.

above: 401. Stucco makes an excellent wall surfacing material when used over rough brick, and the method of finishing can enhance the casual, uneven effect. In this studio loft, stucco seems a perfect foil for the heavy shag carpet and deep comfort of a sofa piled with cushions. (*Courtesy E. I. DuPont de Nemours & Co.*)

right: 402. The possibilities for design with ceramic tile have a long history. In this bathroom, a stylized "weeping willow" pattern of small glazed and unglazed mosaic tiles of different colors brightens the stall shower while providing an almost impervious surface. (*Courtesy American Olean Tile Company*)

Glass, Metal and Plastics   Broad areas of glass represent a fairly new development in home design, but for the most part this innovation has been confined to window glass. In a sense we might see this as an expansion, rather than a change—with windows growing larger and larger until they take over whole walls. Another common use for glass in walls, more popular now than ever before, is in the form of mirrors (Fig. 327), which expand the apparent size of a room and create brilliant patterns of reflected light. One genuinely new effect, however, comes with glass blocks, either patterned (Fig. 405) or plain and usually set into concrete-block walls (Fig. 298).

Metal seldom appears on interior walls, being primarily confined to outside sheathing. But used with taste and imagination, metal can provide a striking wall surface, as the aluminum panels in Figure 306 illustrate. The extreme sound- and light-reflective qualities must be handled carefully.

Rigid plastics, of course, are used with increasing frequency as both exterior siding and interior paneling. They masquerade as other materials or stand on their own to make superior wall surfacings for special installations, such as bathrooms, or any place where their imperviousness to water and soil as well as their ease of maintenance can act as an advantage.

Paint   Paints today are made from a broad range of natural and synthetic materials selected for their special attributes, and new types and combinations appear often. Their properties are impressive. Some can be applied to wood, masonry, stucco, metal, asbestos, or gypsum board; many resist sun, fading, and blistering; and most dry in a short time. Others are fire-resistant or rust-inhibiting. The newer paints are easier to apply than older varieties; they usually go on with a roller and have little paint odor. When dry, they offer mat, semigloss, or high-gloss surfaces. Water-base paints are extremely easy to handle, because paint spots can be wiped up with a damp cloth and brushes cleaned with soap and water. After a short period of curing, they become impervious to water. Solvent-base paints may be more durable, but the application and clean-up are somewhat more tedious. The number of different colors available has been greatly increased by the automatic mixing machines most paint dealers have.

Being the easiest of all finishes to apply, paint leads many people into doing their own wall finishing. Nothing so quickly and inexpensively changes the character of a room. Paint finds its place in the smallest apartment and the most elaborate mansion, in good part because it is an excellent, unobtrusive background for furnishings, art objects, and people. In itself paint has little beauty or individuality, but these goals can be attained by choosing exactly the right color or a distinctive combination of colors that seem eminently suited to the walls they cover and to the people who live with them. Figure 406 and Plates 44 and 45 (p. 317) show three quite different effects that can be achieved with ordinary paint. The dining space in Plate 44 is a perfectly plain square box of a room; its stuccoed walls and ceiling have been painted all over in a single color. But that uniform color is vivid pink! Highlighted by a fire-engine-red door and natural wood furniture, the pink color creates a striking effect and also gives a certain flavor to this home, which is in Mexico.

Another essentially boxy room (Fig. 406) assumes trompe-l'oeil curves from the painted stripes on walls and ceiling. Taking his cue from the fireplace, which juts out slightly into the room at bottom, the owner carried the pattern of light against dark out across the ceiling in an expanding swath that makes the ceiling appear to slope upward. A dark stripe to the left of the fireplace curves out into the entry hall to unite the two spaces, thus also helping to enlarge the room visually. In a period when odd-shape rooms are popular—but most of us retain the basic cube—an ingenious use of paint can almost miraculously transform a static space into a dynamic one.

The owners of the apartment in Plate 45 made no attempt to dispel the boxlike character of the space, but rather enhanced it by creating patterns of boxes-within-boxes through a dramatic red-and-white color scheme. The contrast of brilliant red inserts and panels against flat white walls makes for an exciting, graphic design, but the whole is softened by live plants and a handwoven rug.

Next to color in importance is paint's ability to give a uniform surface to whatever it covers. Sometimes smooth paint will not cover all blemishes, and occasionally smoothness is not wanted. In such cases, paint can be *stippled* with a stiff brush to obliterate brush marks and to provide a soft, mat finish; or it can be *spattered* with one or more colors to give some vibrancy and minimize spots or scratches. More pronounced textures are produced with special paints, by applying the paint with special rollers, or by going over the wet paint with a sponge or a whiskbroom. These are easy and inexpensive ways to cover plaster cracks or gypsum board joints, and they create unique surfaces.

Wallpaper   Long known in the Orient, wallpaper has been used in Europe for about five centuries and in the United States since the Colonial period. "Poor man's tapestry" was a good name for it, because wallpaper came into use in humble homes as an imitation of the expensive textiles used by the wealthy. Wallpaper's advantages are many:

406. The transformation of a room by paint is one of the delights of interior design. Here the white boxiness of a living room has become an apparently sculptured flow of space through the judicious use of a supergraphic that carries through the group spaces. Donald MacDonald, architect-designer. (*Photograph: Morley Baer*)

□ It can be used in any room in the home.

□ It can be tested for its effect in advance by borrowing large samples.

□ It is available in many colors, patterns, and textures, and in varying degrees of durability.

□ It is a quick and easy way to remodel with prepasted or self-adhesive (peel-and-stick) types.

□ It has the most positive character of any wall surfacing in its price class.

□ It makes a room seem to shrink or swell, gain height or intimacy, become more active or subdued, more formal or less formal.

□ It minimizes architectural awkwardnesses by illusion or camouflage.

□ It hides disfigured walls.

□ It makes rooms with little furniture seem furnished.

□ It distracts attention from miscellaneous or commonplace furniture.

So virtually infinite are the patterns, colors, and designs available in wallpaper that we can barely suggest the range of effects possible. In Figure 407 the structural awkwardness of an under-the-eaves bedroom was turned to positive advantage by a brown-and-white graph-paper print on the wall surfaces. The bedspreads carry out the theme but are not identical in pattern; in one, the colors reverse to give a progression of emphasis to the dark bolster coverings.

Wallpaper seems natural for many traditional or restored rooms. The Early American bedroom in Plate 46 (p. 318) is a charming assemblage of authentic antiques and muted, subtle colors. The small-scaled pattern and light color of the wallpaper join with frilly white curtains to provide a background for the mellowed furnishings and magnificently soft, faded patchwork quilt.

Wallpaper has a few inherent disadvantages. Some people may not like its "papery" look, and many patterns are dull or ugly. But these are not faults of the material. It is possible to find papers appropriate to almost any way of living, any kind of furnishings, any exposure or special factor. Wallpapers range from solid colors through textured effects, small and large patterns, to mural or scenic designs. Most have a dull, mat finish that may or may not be washable, but some are glossy. Then there are the less usual types. Flock papers with their raised, fuzzy nap look like textiles. Marbleized papers hint at the gloss and depth of marble, and metallic papers bring luster and can help a little in insulating rooms against heat and cold.

Selecting a pattern and color is not easy. Wall-length samples of several patterns can be brought home, fastened up, and observed at different times of day and night. Wallpaper is a kind of applied ornament that may noticeably affect the apparent size, shape, and character of rooms. Consider it in the light of the criteria for ornament discussed in Chapter 8, making these more specific by keeping in mind that the wall and paper are flat and continuous, like fabrics, and that in most instances the pattern will cover very large areas. In addition:

☐ Plain colors look much like paint but come in varied textures.
☐ Textural patterns are more active, more pronounced in character, and more effective in concealing minor damage than are plain colors.
☐ Abstract patterns do not go out of fashion quickly and seem especially suitable to walls.

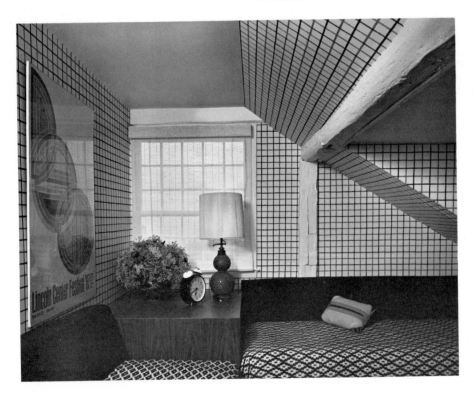

407. For a bedroom in a remodeled horse barn, the strong linear pattern established by exposed posts and beams is emphasized by the wallpaper design; the bedspreads repeat the diagonal of the sloping walls. George Washington Orton 3d, designer. (*Photograph: Hans Namuth, Photo Researchers, Inc.*)

above: 408. An overscale pattern by painter Roy Lichtenstein on silver Mylar dramatizes the stair wall in a house remodeled for his own use by architect Robert Stern. Its pattern repeats the rectangular wall paneling but shocks it into life with bold diagonals and circular motifs. See also Figs. 109, 247, 440; Plate 12, p. 60. (*Photograph: John T. Hill*)

right: 409. "Greenwich," a wall covering of Vymura, produces a strong architectural quality in both its subject matter and the overall pattern. (*Courtesy ICI America, Inc.*)

□ Scenic wallpapers are somewhat like murals, and may open up the space.
□ Repetitive, bold, conspicuous patterns may reduce the visual importance of the space, furniture, and people, but a supergraphic can provide a focal point.
□ Conspicuous, isolated motifs often make walls look spotty.

Plastic Wall Coverings   Nearly all the things that were said about wallpaper apply equally to plastic wall coverings. However, certain qualities are easier to achieve with the new and increasingly popular synthetic materials. For example, because plastics present fewer problems in application than does wallpaper—and are thus easier to match at the seams—they lend themselves well to supergraphics and large pattern repeats (Figs. 408, 409). Textured, three-dimensional effects and metallic shine are the particular strong points of plastic coverings (Figs. 410, 411).

below: 410. The nature of vinyl lends itself to heavily textured effects, as in this wall covering called "Glacier." Tough and heavyweight, it comes in sixteen colors ranging from bright hues to neutral shades. (*Courtesy Stauffer Chemical*)

right: 411. Metallic foil wall coverings add an unexpected brightness to otherwise dull walls. This pattern is known as "Illuminations." (*Courtesy General Tire & Rubber Company*)

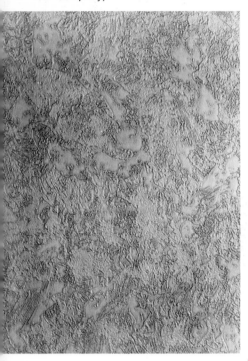

In terms of maintenance and long life, of course, they tend to be superior to wallpaper, but the initial cost may be higher. With proper application they can hide serious wall defects, even to holding cracked plaster in position. Some vinyls come with special backings for sound insulation, and a number of them perform well as upholstery, thus allowing for harmony between two elements of the interior.

Wall Fabrics   Just about every fabric known has at one time or another been draped over, stretched on, or pasted to walls. Today, such effects usually fall into two main categories: wall fabrics that surface a wall and cover at least one section completely; and those that are simply hung on walls as enrichment.

Almost any fabric can be made into a wall covering by tacking it to the wall (if that is allowed) or to a wooden frame, as well as by using double-faced carpet tape or vinyl adhesive. In Figure 412 a vibrantly colored stretch fabric has been stapled on a wooden frame to create a wall-size mural that acts as a headboard.

The various kinds of grass cloth, long-time favorites for adding texture to a wall, are also easy to apply, because they are glued to a tough paper backing and then handled much as wallpaper. They come in textures from comparatively smooth to bold and in many colors, although we tend to think of them as being most appropriate in their natural colors (Fig. 413).

Carpets have also begun to climb the walls, providing sound insulation, a soft, sensuous texture in an unexpected place, and continuity between floor covering and wall. This technique can be especially successful when it serves to tie built-in seating into the structure of the room (Pl. 18, p. 112).

Wall hangings of many types can add enrichment wherever desired. A single length of textile with a bold pattern makes a headboard, a second a footboard, a third an adjustable screen in Figure 414. Heavier woven or stitchery panels—even rugs—open up many new possibilities for walls, to replace the standard paintings

above: 412. By using one of his own stretch fabrics, designer Jack Lenor Larsen concealed a cracked plaster wall and established a dramatic focus for an apartment bedroom. (*Photograph: John T. Hill*)

right: 413. Grasscloth can mask wall defects while adding an undemanding and informal but pleasing texture and character to a room. (*Courtesy Hercules Incorporated*)

below: 414. In this studio apartment textiles assume the identity of walls, but they can be rolled up like window shades to eliminate spatial divisions, thus allowing for changing functions and moods. Romuald Witwicki, designer; Marimekko fabrics. (*Photograph: John T. Hill*)

or prints. In Figure 415 a casement fabric construction acts as a partial wall, separating but not shutting off one part of the room from another. All told, fabrics give variety and mobility, often with little time or effort.

Stairs and Staircases

If we think of stairs as physical entities, they are a series of steadily rising small pieces of flooring. Visually, however, stairs belong to walls: they become part of the wall if set against it or act as dividers—a wall function—if they are freestanding.

418. In an unusual combination of functions, a brick fireplace column provides the structural support for a spiral stair, doubling the use of the space. Ford, Carson, and Powell, architects. (*Photograph: Julius Shulman*)

The basic stair consists of a straight set of risers, attached to a wall on one side and supported by another wall opposite; the latter may go all the way to the ceiling or end in a simple balustrade for protection. But architects always have been fascinated by the inherent sculptural possibilities of stairs. The two houses at the beginning of this chapter illustrate two points of view. In the Noyes house (Fig. 386) the stairs are simply a way to get from one level to another. They do not draw attention from the drama of the masonry walls. But the condominium staircase acts as a focal point, its constantly changing forms enlivening what could have been a dark, uneventful inner corner (Fig. 388).

Some of the delight possible in a freestanding staircase is apparent in Figure 416. Here a wood stairway, reduced to its simplest elements—treads, supports, and protective railing—curves down from the upper floor and divides, without visually closing off, areas of the living room.

A particularly exciting stairway treatment is that which integrates the stair with a fireplace. The stair in Figure 417 moves diagonally up a stepped brick chimney, cutting sharply across its otherwise square façade. The bricks of the fireplace themselves become the stairs and risers, while the wooden handrail thrusts its bold diagonal upward to counterpoint the brick. In Figure 418 the metal staircase actually spirals *around* a freestanding fireplace; combined with the metal grillwork of the partially open second floor, the staircase creates an effect not unlike that of the grilled balconies in New Orleans. In addition to its aesthetic qualities, this stair eliminates the feelings of insecurity and vertigo that often accompany spiral staircases, since a solid brick wall—the fireplace—is always on one side.

419. Oak treads and a steel railing spiraling upward to a secluded studio loft bring a playful, delightful contrast to the basic rectangularity of this architectural setting. Fisher-Friedman Associates, architects. (*Photograph: Morley Baer*)

Design of Stairs

Stairs cannot be considered only from the point of view of visual impact. The physical dimensions and their comparative proportions are of the utmost importance for the comfort and safety of those negotiating the stairs. These points should be considered in appraising stairs for use. In general:

- A tread deep enough to take the entire sole of the shoe feels most secure.
- A rise (the vertical measurement between each tread) of about 5 inches seems easiest for most people. Some authorities recommend that the sum of the tread and rise be between 17 and $17\frac{1}{2}$ inches.
- Bare treads can be slippery; carpeting provides firmer footage.
- A landing offers a welcome breathing space on long stairs.
- Ample headroom at the top of the staircase is a self-evident safety precaution.
- Variation in the size or spacing of steps (except for well-defined landings) can be a trip hazard.
- Winding stairs may be perilous, especially if the inner edge of the tread is too narrow to accept a firm footstep.
- Some kind of handrail running the length of the stairs is essential for safety. When the household includes a person whose limited eyesight or other physical condition makes stair-climbing precarious, there should probably be a rail on *both* sides of the stairway.

This list of utilitarian considerations may seem confining, but it need not be considered binding for every flight of stairs. When planning a secondary staircase or one that leads to a hideaway area of the house—not to the essential rooms—you can give your imagination freer rein. In Figure 419 the spiral stair, rising up to

above: Plate 44. The home of designer Luís Baragan exploits the warm, tropical colors of Mexico in its brilliant pink stuccoed walls and ceiling. Storage is typically built into the almost-bare walls. Bright red touches and blonde furniture complete the effect. See page 308; also Fig. 108; Plate 58, p. 420. (*Photograph: Hans Namuth, Photo Researchers, Inc.*)

left: Plate 45. Chinese red against white highlights the effect of boxes within and upon boxes in this Washington, D.C. apartment. The ceiling-height cutouts at left contain guest bunks, reached by means of the ladder with its plants removed. A full wall of storage cubes holds magazines and books. George Hartman and Ann Hartman, owner-designers. See page 308. (*Photograph: John T. Hill*)

right: Plate 46. The bedroom of a remodeled New Hampshire house seems cast in the soft, earth colors of an old daguerreotype. A small-scaled pattern in the wallpaper makes an unobtrusive background for antique furnishings and gently faded fabrics. White frilly curtains and a lace canopy complete the charming ambience of yesterday. See page 310. (*Photograph: John T. Hill*)

below: Plate 47. A red-lacquered chest, hand-woven rug, and above all the magnificent metal stove dominate the living room of an upper New York State farmhouse. The elaborate stamped and wrought designs on the stove would qualify it as an object of delight, even if it were not a functioning heat source. See page 324. (*Photograph: John T. Hill*)

the owner's studio, brings a delightful, romantic accent, its curves echoed in the old stained glass window and the bentwood rocker.

In one-story dwellings stairs usually are not a consideration, except for an occasional one- or two-step drop or rise in floor level to define different areas of a larger space. Nevertheless, consideration should be given to making these steps both evident and safe for the unwary. Clear definition by furniture arrangement, a low wall or railing, or the placement of large plants and other accents can prevent a twisted ankle or even a broken leg.

Fireplaces

Fireplaces and fires are extravagant. A fireplace may cost as much as a bathroom, and in many places a good log fire is about as expensive as a home-cooked meal for two. Further, storing fuel takes dry space, getting it into the firebox requires labor, and the later cleanup is a chore. Most fireplaces are actually used for fires less than 1 percent of the time. When lit, they provide physical warmth, perhaps heat for cooking, and some light and ventilation—but all of a hard-to-control sort.

Still, open fires are beautiful, and fireplaces even without fires can be substantial centers of interest. A fire's warm, constantly changing, beautifully shaped and colored flames and embers produce a kind of lighting equaled only by sunrises and sunsets. Open fires are also associated with pleasurable outings and probably deeply buried feelings about the importance of fire to humankind. Nothing lifts the spirits on a cold, cheerless day or night like a fire, warming hands and hearts. Then, too, every fire has its own character; in fact every moment of a fire differs from every other, and fireplace design need follow no stereotypes (Fig. 420). Thus, even though the most perfectly designed fireplace is hopelessly out of date in terms of utility and economy, open fires are not outdated in terms of human satisfaction. And they do serve some useful purposes, which are discussed below.

Light is a major contribution of fireplaces today, because the illumination they provide is unique. It is restfully soft and warm enough in color to make even pallid complexions look suntanned. The concentrated, flickering light can be hypnotically relaxing and draw people together like a magnet.

Heat from a fireplace on a cold day seems well worth its cost, even though it creates drafts on the floor and may throw thermostatically controlled furnaces off balance. Heat output can be increased and controlled by designing the firebox

420. A small fireplace made from the same material as the wall it projects from creates a spot of warmth as well as sculptural interest. The main fireplace of this house is shown in Figure 423. Judith Chafee, architect. See also Figs. 47–49; Plate 57, p. 420. (*Photograph: Ezra Stoller ©ESTO*)

319

to throw heat into the room, by having a damper to control the draft and a projecting or suspended hood to radiate heat. Prefabricated fireboxes and vents, like small warm-air furnaces, circulate heated air effectively.

Cooking over an open fire is a pleasant way to make fun out of work. It is informal and divides the labor among family members and friends. The household that often cooks over fire needs certain equipment. Essentials include adjustable grilles, long-handled forks and pans, and a floor not harmed by sparks or grease. Work is lightened if a fireplace is in or near the kitchen, if there is a special cupboard for permanent storage of equipment, and if a wheeled cart is at hand. All this may sound complicated, but it can be worth it, especially for those potentially difficult occasions when adults and children share the same party.

Ventilation is hardly a major function of fireplaces, but they do air rooms—violently with a good fire, moderately when they are cold and the damper is open.

The *symbolism* of "hearth and home" continues to be important. The experience of gathering around a fire for stories, popcorn, or whatever unites people of all ages and interests can make a group feel relaxed and secure.

Finally, fireplaces provide busy householders with a place to burn trash and the hyperactive host or hostess with a harmless outlet for nervous energy.

Fireplace Design

Certainly the most important functional aspect of a fireplace is how well it draws, because one that does not draw well enough to start a fire or keep it going—or one that sends smoke into the room—negates its original purpose. This matter should be left to experts. Equally important is safety; the several hazards can be reduced by fireproof roofs and chimney tops that retard sparks; by screens to keep sparks out of the room; by andirons or baskets to keep fuel in place; and by hearths high enough to keep babies at a safe distance. Then comes fireplace maintenance, which can be lessened if both indoor and outdoor wood storage is nearby. The most efficient fireplace has a wood bin that can be refilled from the outside, an ash pit to permit outside ash removal, and a fire pit lowered a few inches below the hearth to restrain the ashes.

Location   When fireplaces were used for heating, nearly every room had one. Today, few houses have more than a single fireplace, and this generally is located in the living, dining, or family space. Sometimes the same chimney serves a social fireplace in the living room and a barbecue in the kitchen or family area. Occasionally, one or more additional fireplaces will be put in seclusion rooms or bedrooms. Because of its traditional association with food preparation, the fireplace located in a kitchen seems natural, even though it may be used seldom for cooking. The tiny fireplace shown in Figure 421 was created when renovation exposed a hidden chimney behind a kitchen wall. Finally, outdoor fireplaces tend to be in or near outside group spaces—such as terraces and patios—although they may be at some distance for short, inexpensive vacations away from the house.

No rules mandate where a fireplace should be placed in a room. However, several factors should be kept in mind. Fireplaces most often are large, more-or-less dominant elements. They demand considerable maintenance when a fire is burning and therefore should be accessible. Fireplaces make natural centers for furniture arrangement and usually attract as many people as space around them permits. When the fireplace abuts an outside wall, the chimney can be an exterior design factor. Energy conservationists, however, recommend indoor chimneys, to ensure that any heat will be given off to the interior, rather than lost to the outdoors.

A typical location is the center of a long wall. While such an arrangement allows maximum visibility for large groups, it also suggests a symmetrical furniture placement, which can lead toward static symmetry. This solution also tends to shorten the room visually. A fireplace in the center of one of the short walls is

also familiar but somewhat less common. Another stable situation, this location can make the room seem longer and may inspire one furniture grouping near the fireplace and another at the opposite end.

A fireplace can also be in the end of a spur wall that acts as a room divider; it might be a freestanding structure that delineates continuous space into areas for different activities (Fig. 422); or it could serve as the focus for a recess specifically designed as an intimate area away from the main group space (Fig. 423). Locating a fireplace in the corner of a room emphasizes that room's longest dimension and limits furniture grouping to a quarter circle.

above left: 421. A tiny kitchen fireplace offers actual and visual warmth, as well as providing a potential for open-fire cooking. Its rough brick makes a good transition between the paneled dining area and the stucco of the kitchen proper. See also Fig. 104. (*Photograph: Harold Davis*)

above right: 422. A fireplace in the center of a space is reminiscent of a campfire around which everyone can gather. Here the smooth suspended hood fulfills its purpose of drawing off smoke and brings an easy contrast to the white brick firepit. Burde, Shaw and Associates, architects. (*Photograph: Morley Baer*)

right: 423. A fireplace recessed in an inglenook promises warmth and companionship or a cozy place to read. The hearth raises the level of the fire so it can be seen more easily from the length of the room. Judith Chafee, architect. See also Figs. 47–49; Plate 57, p. 420. (*Photograph: Ezra Stoller © ESTO*)

Prefabricated fireplaces sometimes deliberately assert their independence of the surroundings. In a converted dairy barn (Fig. 424) the owner, a sculptor, placed a freestanding Heatilator—a prefabricated unit around which a fireplace is usually built—on a concrete base to become a sculptural statement in its own right. This makes an extremely efficient way of heating the large space, since two small grilles on either side return the heated air in the wall behind to the interior.

Appearance   Although consistency with the whole house is a major consideration, fireplaces can have their own special beauty and individuality. The questions to be answered are much like those about walls:

☐ What degree of formality is wanted?
☐ Should horizontal or vertical lines predominate?
☐ How active and dominant should the fireplace be?
☐ What degree of roughness or smoothness seems best?
☐ Which materials are most appropriate?
☐ Should the fireplace be large, small, or intermediate in actual size and in scale?

Size will be governed primarily by the size and scale of the room and its furnishings, the effect the fireplace is intended to produce, the materials from which it is made, and the kind of fires wanted. Of all elements in the home, fireplaces lend themselves best to overscaling without seeming unpleasantly obtrusive (Fig. 425). But very small fireplaces can have a certain refreshing charm (Fig. 420). It is easy to increase the importance and apparent size of fireplaces by enriching them with bands of contrasting materials, by integrating them with bookshelves or built-in furniture, or by making them an integral part of large areas of masonry. Also, fireplaces seem larger on small walls than on big ones.

Relationship to walls, floors, and ceilings profoundly affects the character of fireplaces. They can be simply holes, perhaps framed unobtrusively, in an unbroken wall—the least noticeable treatment. Some project from the wall a few inches or several feet, which increases their impact. The fireplace outlined by a mantle and possibly a molding remains classic, in modern as well as traditional homes (Fig. 426). When the fireplace leaves the wall entirely, as a freestanding block of masonry or an independent unit in metal, it becomes still more conspicuous. In Figure 427 a beautiful old iron stove and semicircular wood holder serve as focal points in

424. An unadorned prefabricated metal Heatilator unit is an efficient heating plant and a strong focal point in the sweep of open space in sculptor Sydney Butche's living-dining room. (*Courtesy House Beautiful. Copyright 1972, The Hearst Corporation*)

right: 425. A huge brick fireplace soaring to ceiling level does not seem out of scale with its surroundings, partly because of the unifying color and horizontal striations. Alfredo De Vido, architect. (*Photograph: Ezra Stoller © ESTO*)

below: 426. A fireplace projecting slightly from the wall and capped by a mantelpiece gains an unobtrusive prominence that sets the character of this quiet, comfortable room. Thomas A. Gray and William L. Gray, owner-designers. See also Fig. 660. (*Photograph: The New York Times / Bill Aller*)

a wide-open group space. Perched on a round island of asbestos paint, these two curving elements act as a counterpoint to the basically rectilinear quality of the space, thus further increasing their importance.

The fireplace unit may extend to the ceiling, which accentuates its verticality (Fig. 425). If it terminates a little or well below the room's top, it can create a horizontal or blocky effect. The bottom of the fire pit can be either at floor level or at seat height; in the latter case, the hearth usually is extended to give sitting space. Raised fires seem more a part of the room than do those at floor level. Another possibility is depressing the fire pit below the floor, sometimes with space

427. An ornate old iron stove and a plain modern log holder have been related to the wall behind by the imaginative use of asbestos paint called for by the local fire code. Don Metz, architect. (*Photograph: John T. Hill*)

large enough for furniture around it. This arrangement tends to draw people into a convivial huddle and subdivides a room without partitions.

Materials turn our thoughts at once to masonry and metal, since neither is damaged by fire. Brick and stone look substantial and permanent, tile can be plain or decorated, and metal not only lends itself to shaping in many ways but transmits heat, thus using all of the fire's energy potential. These materials come in many colors and textures: smooth tile and polished marble, shining copper and dull iron, brick and stone in all gradations of roughness.

The present concern with energy conservation and with fuel shortages has led many families to consider returning to wood as a partial or emergency source of warmth. Homes that do not have fireplaces have begun to sprout old-fashioned wood-burning stoves, which require only a heavy-duty pipe outlet through the ceiling or a wall, rather than a full chimney. The farmhouse living room in Plate 47 (p. 318) boasts such a piece—a splendid example of iron craft enriched with touches of brass. Given the superior efficiency of freestanding metal stoves, this unit could keep such a small room comfortable on all but the coldest nights. But even if it could not, it earns its place in the room by the charm of its design and embellishment. A feeling of safety and stability emanates from its squat, sturdy contours as surely as from the glowing embers within.

Of the three elements discussed in this chapter, only one could be considered essential—the walls that surround our enclosures. Yet just as walls give protection and privacy, stairs contribute mobility and fireplaces both actual and psychological warmth. When handled with taste and imagination, each of the three elements can bring its own design integrity into the home.

Windows, Window Treatments, and Doors

Windows and doors relate spaces to one another both visually and physically. The "wind's eye" of old was a narrow opening to let out some of the fire's smoke and let in a little fresh air, to help light the room, and to permit peephole glimpses of what was going on outside. Today we think less in terms of one self-contained "inside" standing firm against the forces of nature than of different kinds of spaces, carved by walls, penetrated by windows and doors. The types of window treatments we adopt—curtains, draperies, shutters, shades, blinds, plant screens, or nothing whatever—govern the amount of interrelationship two adjacent spaces will have.

Windows

Of the three functions performed by windows—*ventilation, light admission,* and *visual communication*—only the last is unique. Ventilation often can be handled better through louvered and shuttered openings, air-conditioning, exhaust fans, and other mechanical devices. Electric light is sometimes more convenient and is capable of more precise control than natural light. But only through transparent windows, doors, and walls can we enjoy a view of the outdoors from protected enclosures. When windows expand to fill large areas of a wall, interior and exterior spaces become closely united. In the house shown in Figure 428 a window wall at one end of the huge living room serves as a natural magnet for an intimate seating group. Overlooking a pond and gently rolling hills, the window affords a peaceful view to the outside, the pleasure of which is enhanced by soft textures and muted colors. At night, shutters close off the window and turn the focus inward.

Types of Windows

Despite immense variation in the appearance of windows, all can be classified in one of two general categories: *fixed* windows meant essentially for light and views, and *movable* windows that are additionally useful for ventilation. In this century movable windows have predominated; however, the increasing popularity of air conditioning and changing concepts in architecture have caused, in the last few years, a dramatic rise in the use of fixed glass, even for private dwellings. We might question this tendency in view of the need to conserve energy and of general ecological concerns. Both air conditioning and heating consume fuel; either can have a deleterious effect on the environment by its generation. It makes little sense, then, to imprison ourselves behind totally fixed glass when the simple act of opening or closing a window can solve the problem of controlling heat, light, and ventilation under certain circumstances. Modern heating and cooling devices represent a tremendous technological advance, but they should be regarded only as supplementary to the natural controls we have had all along.

Rather than a strict reliance on either form of window, a combination of movable and fixed glass windows—and of various types of glass—often provides the best solution to climate control in the home, from both an aesthetic and an environmental point of view. Fixed and movable windows come in standardized sizes and in systems of prefabricated units, which have lowered the cost of acquisition and installation. In the housing complex shown in Figure 429 the use of fixed and movable window components becomes a pleasant repetitive motif on the changing façade.

Wood and metal are the materials typically used to hold the panes of glass in windows and walls. Metal is stronger (which makes thinner strips possible), does not shrink or swell noticeably, and has a uniform texture harmonious with glass. With the exception of aluminum and stainless steel, metals in windows must be protected by paint; and because all metals conduct heat and cold readily, moisture may condense on the inside of metal sashes in cold weather. Wood shrinks, swells, and requires a protective finish, but it does not encourage condensation. The use of plastic as a material for framing windows is also rising because of the relative stability of many plastics, their indifference to heat and cold, and their integral finishes.

Movable Windows   Figure 430 shows some of the types of movable windows available. Each has certain advantages and disadvantages.

Double-hung windows generally have two sashes that slide up and down. A sash is the frame, usually movable, in which panes of glass are set. Weights, springs,

428. A bay window-wall in furniture designer Warren Platner's own house makes an elegant composition of wall and window elements. The projection of the bay into the landscape gives the visual pleasure of the outdoors, the bodily comforts of the protected interior. See also Fig. 614. (*Photograph: Ezra Stoller* © *ESTO*)

right: 429. Fixed and movable prefabricated window components of aluminum have been set in slightly projecting wood frames to further enliven the rhythmic progressions of the façade in a San Francisco redevelopment project. Jonathan Bulkley and Igor Sazevich, architects. (*Photograph: Joshua Freiwald*)

below: 430. Prefabricated movable window units allow great freedom of choice.

or friction holds them in place when open. Usually, they are higher than wide, and the sashes in each window are of the same size and shape. The advantages of double-hung windows are numerous. They are easy and inexpensive to install and seldom warp or sag. Hardware is simple, weatherproofing effective. They can be opened top or bottom, and they do not project to get in the way of people and curtains inside or people and plants outside. The major drawbacks are these: not more than half the area can be opened, and when open, the window affords no protection from rain. Double-hung windows are difficult to clean from inside unless the sash can be removed or pivoted and inconvenient to operate when furniture is under them. In addition, some people find the horizontal crossbar that cuts the window in half visually annoying.

Horizontal sliding windows are like double-hung windows placed on their sides, and they share the same advantages and disadvantages. Usually, though, they have

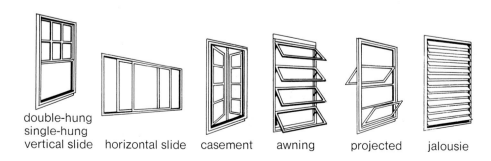

double-hung
single-hung
vertical slide   horizontal slide   casement   awning   projected   jalousie

431. This arched window of fixed glass permits the owner to overlook the constantly changing seashore as the tide moves in and out. Mark Mills, architect. See also Fig. 500. (*Photograph: Morley Baer*)

the horizontal proportions popular today and are often combined with fixed glass, which eliminates the distracting middle bar.

Casement windows, hinged at one side and swinging in or out, were in common use long before sliding types. Their major assets are that the whole area can be opened and that they can be adjusted to direct breezes into the room or to reduce cold drafts. Equipped with crank-operated hardware, casement windows are easy to manipulate even when over furniture. In the better types, both sides of the glass can be washed from inside. Casement windows also have drawbacks. In-swinging casements are seldom used because they interfere with furnishings, and those that swing out over terraces or walks make potentially serious hazards. They offer no protection from rain and are not easy to weatherproof tightly.

Awning and **projected windows** resemble casements but are hinged at the top or occasionally the bottom. Disadvantages are similar to those of casements: small panes of glass, sashes that take space when open, difficulty in sealing them tightly. In addition, they collect dust when open. But they have the notable advantage of giving precise, draft-free control of ventilation while blocking rain or snow.

Jalousie windows are of the awning type but with very narrow strips of glass or plastic—even wood if ventilation without view is the goal. They have all the advantages of awning windows and, moreover, take little space. Odd shapes are not costly. Jalousie windows, with their many small panes, are difficult to clean and to weatherproof; they may also interfere somewhat with views. But for precise control of ventilation, they excel all other types.

Fixed Glass   Fixed glass windows free the architect from the constraints of standardized shapes and sizes that apply to movable windows (Fig. 431). The bay window illustrated, angled downward and focusing on a tidepool at the edge of the Pacific, was designed purely for delight. Often, large sheets of glass need no frame other than the materials used in the construction of a wall, so they become one with the wall rather than a dissimilar component. Moreover, windows made

left: 432. A row of clerestory windows brings daylight into the house at the topmost levels, thus balancing illumination from other sources below. Alex Riley, architect. (*Photograph: Philip L. Molten*)

right: 433. A huge skylight angling across the raftered ceiling creates a dramatic architectural statement as well as a light source in the living room of architect Ivan Poutiatine's own home. The redwood paneling was salvaged from a seventy-year-old aqueduct. (*Photograph: Joshua Freiwald*)

from large sheets of glass or plastic are economical compared to movable windows, because they cost less to install and require no hardware or screens. The extensive use of fixed glass calls for caution, however, because it can be difficult to control transmitted light and heat and to clean large, inaccessible areas of glass.

Skylights and Clerestories   Windows in the ceiling or high in a wall between two roof levels—skylights and clerestories—were originally invented to illuminate and ventilate interiors without loss of privacy or interference with furniture arrangements. Traditionally, skylights provided the constant north light desired by artists. A compact plan can have kitchen, laundry, and bathrooms grouped far from conventional windows, yet allow these rooms to be well lighted and ventilated from above. Skylights and clerestories bring daylight (and also moonlight) into the center of the house and make it unnecessary to stretch out the plan for light in all rooms. They also balance the light coming in through other windows (Fig. 432). If the glass is movable, a high window makes a very efficient ventilator, since it lets out the hot, stale air trapped at ceiling level. Beyond such practical considerations, light coming from overhead also reveals hitherto unnoticed qualities in furniture, sculpture, and plants, giving new dimension to form and space. The skylight in Figure 433 brings light deep into a large living room to create constantly changing patterns across the walls, furnishings, and floor.

Design and Location of Windows

Views and privacy, light and ventilation, heat and cold, and furniture arrangement are among the major factors determining window design and placement. Accessibility for cleaning follows closely. Interwoven with these is the larger concern of architectural composition—the relationship of windows to the mass and space of the whole structure and its site.

Views and Privacy   Normally, large windows face the best outlook: a view out over a city, into a private garden, or toward a body of water (Pl. 48, p. 335). When such a vista does not occur naturally, it is possible to create one. The architects of the house shown in Figures 434 and 435 built a two-story courtyard in the center of the space to bring in light and air, at the same time ensuring absolute privacy from the street. The four major rooms—living room, dining room, library, and

434–435. In remodeling a 19th-century Boston stable, the owners were restricted by local ordinances that prohibited altering the façade. Childs Bertman Tseckares Associates, Inc., architects. See also Fig. 481.

left: 434. The solution came from opening up the interior with sliding glass windows around a private interior courtyard.

above: 435. The section shows placement of the court adjacent to four of the main rooms; skylights and clerestories provide light for other parts of the house.

436. A plant-filled bay window gives privacy to those on the inside, a pleasant aspect to those on the outside. (*Photograph: Alex M. Noman*)

master bedroom—all overlook the courtyard, and all have glass window walls to take full advantage of the outlook.

Windows facing the street or nearby neighbors most often are smaller, higher in the wall, or of more opaque materials than those with sheltered views. Otherwise, privacy can be achieved by building fences or planting hedges, and as a last resort by closing off the window with view-blocking curtains. Quite a different solution was chosen by the owner of the house in Figure 436. Here the bay window directly overlooks a busy country road and adjacent bridle path. With its collection of plants, pottery, and baskets (plus the ever-present cats), it has become a pleasant tableau for passersby—motorist, pedestrian, and equestrian alike. Except at night, when the interior is lighted, the screen of plants offers sufficient privacy.

Light　　Natural light is cheerful; for eyes and spirit, no room can have too much daylight. But it is unfortunately easy to design rooms that seem unpleasantly bright because strong contrasts of light and dark lead to glare. Oddly enough, glare generally comes not from too much light but from *too little light* in the *wrong places*. More light means less glare if the windows are well planned. Until recently, most windows were holes cut out of the wall, and the first thoughts were of getting curtains to "soften" the light. In the best contemporary design, however, large areas of glass seldom cause excessive brightness. Major factors in planning include:

□ Light coming from more than one direction minimizes heavy shadows and makes one feel enveloped by light, rather than being caught in a spotlight.
□ Light entering near the top of a room illumines the ceiling and spreads through the room more than does light penetrating the lower levels.
□ Overhangs projecting beyond windows reduce the glare of the sky and mellow light entering a room (Fig. 437).

- Windows to the floor will admit less glare if the surfacing material outside does not reflect light unduly. Light-absorbing materials or the shade from trees or trellises help solve this problem.
- In extreme situations it may be necessary to use nonglare glass, which can be clear, smoke, or gold-colored. Some types are also sound- and heatproof, even reflecting.

The lightest elements of a room by day, windows are very dark—almost ominous—at night unless they are lighted or curtained, or unless the immediate view outside is illumined.

Ventilation   The most comfortable ventilation unnoticeably lets stale air out from near the room's top and draftless fresh air in from the floor level. High windows, skylights, exhaust fans, or louvered openings above windows accomplish the first, while low windows or ventilators do the second. There are times, though, when we want to feel a breeze sweeping through the house from wide-open doors and windows. Rooms are most quickly aired if the openings are on opposite sides, one of which faces the prevailing winds.

Heat and Cold   To date, most colorless, transparent materials are poor insulators. Hence, extreme temperatures will be important factors in window design and placement. By reducing costs for heating and air-conditioning, special types of glass, such as double insulating glass and glass that reflects excess solar heat, usually pay for themselves in a few years. Orientation of windows, however, is more important in achieving equable temperatures indoors at the least cost. Chapter 5 gives more information about this factor.

- Glass facing south brings welcome winter sun, but with a properly designed overhang it excludes summer sun because then the sun is high in the sky (Fig. 437).
- Glass facing east admits the morning sun, cheering in winter and seldom too hot in summer.
- Glass on the west side lets hot afternoon heat deep into the house.
- Glass on the north brings in winter cold.

Undesirably oriented windows necessitate relying on insulating curtains or on something outside, such as nearby shade trees, vine-covered arbors, very wide overhanging roofs, or awnings. Generally speaking, in terms of heat and cold—and in most parts of the United States—glass on the south is best, followed by that on the east.

Furniture Arrangement   The location and design of windows and doors largely determines how furniture can be arranged. The more openings the walls have, the harder it is to place furniture. This situation is aggravated if the openings are separated from one another or if windows come below the ordinary table height of 27 to 30 inches. Windows grouped in bands high enough to allow the placement of tables, desks, or sofas beneath them facilitate furniture arrangement. Of course, skylights and clerestories present no problems. And in larger rooms or open spaces, the tendency is to group furnishings away from the walls, thus minimizing the influence of windows except when they provide a view. Windows that extend to the floor make indoor and outdoor space seem continuous, but they lose most of their value if heavy furniture must be put beside them. In other words, window walls increase *visual* space but may reduce *usable* space. The house shown in Figure 438 illustrates these points. In the living room, with its window wall, furniture is grouped near the interior walls; the study above has higher windows to allow placement of a desk beneath.

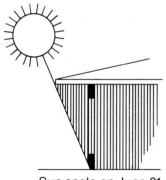

Sun angle on June 21

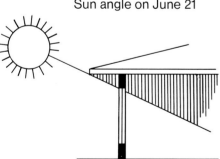

Sun angle on December 21

437. Properly designed roof overhangs let in desirable winter sun through south windows but keep hot summer sun off the glass; they also reduce glare and soften the light.

left: 438. In living room with a large window wall, heavy furniture has been placed to take advantage of the view, with only a movable easy chair and transparent table near the window to shield it from traffic. The vertical window-door-wall exposes the focus of the architectural design—the stairs rising in easy stages to the spiraling levels of the house around a heavy pole support. William Morgan, architect; Edward Heist, Jr., interior designer. See also Fig. 643. (*Photograph: G. Wade Swicord*)

below: 439. The freestanding three-story window wall of a house in Connecticut creates an architectural composition that dominates the design. Opening the house to a lakeside view, it is protected by the almost solid wall that wraps around the private spaces. Richard Meier, architect. (*Photograph: Ezra Stoller © ESTO*)

Cleaning All glass needs cleaning occasionally, especially in dusty or sooty locations or where it can be reached by small children. It is easiest to clean when the panes are large, when they can be reached without excessive stooping or climbing, and when they are accessible from outside as well as inside. Clerestories and skylights bring special cleaning problems, often lessened with translucent glass.

Architectural Composition

So far we have discussed windows in terms of what they can do to make home life more comfortable; however, the architect cannot stop here. Openings today, as in the past, are a vital factor in architectural design, but no single aspect of home planning shows greater change. The general aims and principles of window design still prevail, but the specific patterns are notably different from anything known heretofore. Contemporary trends can be summarized as follows:

□ Windows and doors are considered as integral parts of the architectural shell, rather than as isolated, evenly spaced, cutout holes.
□ Windows typically are grouped in bands, usually horizontal but with a recent tendency toward vertical strips (Fig. 439). When feasible, windows and doors are combined in harmonious units.

left: **440.** In adding a modern sun porch to his own gray-shingled house, architect Robert Stern retained something of the character of the original, while introducing a bold structural counterpoint. The projecting sun porch has windows wrapping around three sides in the lower half, clerestory windows in the upper section of the flat side, so that any available sun will be captured. See also Figs. 109, 247, 408; Plate 12, p. 60. (*Photograph: Hans Namuth, Photo Researchers, Inc.*)

right: **441.** A window-walled bay ensures privacy for the diners by setting them up among the treetops for an ever-changing panorama of the seasons. Edward A. Killingsworth, architect; John Hallock, interior designer. (*Photograph: Chuck Crandall*)

□ Architects place large areas of glass where they serve best; small windows are strategically located for balanced lighting and ventilation, with privacy.

□ Unity and simplicity of effect result from using as few shapes, sizes, and types as possible, with the tops of windows and doors aligned.

□ A less formalized attitude toward the design and placement of windows is becoming evident, with odd-shape windows sometimes being set in unusual locations for a forceful design impact (Fig. 440).

From an architectural point of view, the design of openings is at least as important as the design of opaque portions of the home. Windows are conspicuous day and night, inside and outside. Their thin, smooth, light-transmitting material contrasts strikingly with what is around it. Beyond these physical characteristics, the fact that enclosed and unenclosed spaces interpenetrate one another through windows and doors endows them with a unique psychological importance.

Window Walls

The act of audaciously opening the home to its surroundings is, in some respects, as significant as the age-old struggle to secure dwellings against the environment. Box-tight enclosure has never been completely satisfying, and the urge to combine the paradoxical goals of security and openness has a long, varied history. Walled gardens allowed the early Egyptians, Greeks, and Romans to open part of their homes to the outdoors. In the medieval period, areas of glass large enough to be called "window walls" were introduced. Many houses built fifty or more years ago had sizable "picture windows." Though seemingly *revo*lutionary, window walls represent an *evo*lutionary step toward broader expanses of glass.

Window walls are now standard features even in some tract houses, but many designers and builders fail to understand them completely. A window wall should be thought of not as merely a bigger window but as a different way of planning the house and garden. Two superb examples of this concept will illustrate the point. The dining space in Figure 441 gives the illusion of being in a treehouse, because

Plate 48. A house overlooking Lake Michigan has walls almost entirely of glass to take advantage of the stunning view. The pristine white color, prevalence of railings and pipes, and the basically layered horizontal design all create the impression of a huge luxury liner ready to be launched on the lake. Richard Meier, architect. See page 330; see also Figs. 639, 640. (*Photograph: Ezra Stoller © ESTO*)

Table 14.1   Special Considerations for Window Walls

Problem	Solution
loss of privacy	Face window wall toward private part of property or above sight lines. Build fences or plant hedges. Use curtains and draperies.
glare of light	Balance light with windows in other walls or with skylights. Have overhanging roof or trellis. Plant suitable shade trees nearby.
excessive heat or cold	Orient toward south or southeast. Use insulating glass. Provide overhead protection or trees. Have insulating draperies that can be drawn when necessary.
more glass to clean	No easy solution; use professional window-washer's techniques.
greater quantity of curtaining	Place window wall so that curtains are not essential.
furniture arrangement	Plan room so that major furniture group is related both to window wall and other dominant units, such as fireplaces.
color schemes	Take account of relationship between colors inside and those seen through the glass.
danger of being mistaken for an open door	Use proper design—a raised sill, obvious supports, or colorful stick-on designs—to indicate physical presence of a window wall. Arrange furniture and/or floor materials indoors and out to steer traffic to a door, not a window.
fading of colors	Choose colors that do not fade or that fade pleasantly. Exclude sun with projecting roof, planting, or curtains.
black and cold at night	Illumine window with lighting trough above it. Light terrace or garden outside. Use draperies or reflective glass.
design and maintenance of landscape	Plan at least the immediate landscape architecturally to harmonize with interior; use paving, fixed outdoor furniture, sculpture, and plants that will remain attractive all year with little care.

the projected room it occupies is completely walled in glass. Indoors and outdoors are thoroughly integrated, yet the diners remain protected from heat, cold, and insects. An even bolder plan unites the living room in Plate 49 (opposite) with a swimming pool by means of a sliding-glass window wall. In this Florida house use of the pool is possible through most of the year; insects present the only problem, and this has been solved by screening in the pool area completely. The glass wall, then, exploits the possibilities of indoor-outdoor living to the fullest.

At best, window walls flood rooms with light; at worst they admit glare, heat, or cold. By visually uniting house and landscape, they affect furniture arrangements and color schemes, as well as the design of the exterior. It should be remembered that curtains generally make unsatisfactory solutions to the problems offered by window walls, since they defeat the primary purpose by limiting the feeling of openness. Table 14.1 lists several of the difficulties created by window walls and ways of dealing with them.

There are innumerable ways of designing window walls. When they fill an entire wall from floor to ceiling, a minimum break remains between indoors and outdoors. If they begin above the floor, they leave room for furniture. Window walls may have few divisions or a strong pattern of verticals or horizontals. They can join a room with an extensive view or focus attention on a small enclosed court. Although typically associated with living or dining areas, glass walls can make kitchens or halls expansive. If well planned they are quite feasible in bedrooms—

even bathrooms—in almost any part of the United States. Figure 442 shows the ultimate window wall, which dispenses with glass altogether. Sliding wood doors protect the interior at night and in inclement weather.

Large windows magnify the cost of a home. Glass is expensive to buy and replace, difficult to make weathertight around the edges. It must be cleaned often and is likely to increase heating and cooling bills. Movable glass needs screens and window hardware. Almost all windows bring the added expense of curtains, draperies, or blinds. But sensibly large, well-placed windows are worth their cost in aesthetic delight.

Window Treatment

It is tempting to say that perfectly planned windows need no "treatment," but we would then ignore the great changes in outdoor light and heat and the varying needs of the people inside. Thus, for the sake of *utility,* we often need curtains, draperies, blinds, or shades inside to control the privacy of the home, the amount and kind of light that enters it, and heat and cold. From the point of view of *economy,* the fewer accessories used at windows, the more money will be available for other purposes, although efficient window treatment can reduce heating and cooling bills. Furthermore, whatever is put in the window should be durable; resistant to the ravages of sun, moisture, and moths; and easily maintained. *Beauty*

left: **442.** The most daring window wall imaginable is the one that shuns even transparent glass between a home's interior and the countryside. This living area can be totally opened to the grounds in clement weather, protected by sliding walls at night. Charles Moore, owner-architect. (*Photograph: Morley Baer*)

right: **443.** Adjustable wooden louvers shield the three-story window walls of a Florida house to permit flexible control of the semitropical climatic conditions of bright sun tempered by daily breezes, sometimes heavy rainfall and high winds. Dwight E. Holmes, architect.

comes from the inherent attractiveness of the materials chosen and from the way in which they relate the windows to the whole room. *Character,* here as elsewhere, is less a matter of being "different" than of solving problems well.

Exterior Window Treatments

Too often overlooked, exterior window treatments have one overriding advantage: They provide climate control without interfering with furniture or taking wall space within the room.

Awnings   Awnings made of weather-resistant fabrics can be adjusted as the weather varies to protect windows from sun, rain, and dirt, while casting a soft, pleasant light inside and outside. They come in many designs and colors. Unfortunately, fabric awnings have a relatively short life, since they are subject to fading, soiling, and wind damage. Metal awnings, usually aluminum, can either be stationary or roll up. They are higher in initial cost than fabric types but pay for themselves over the years. The major design problem with awnings is making them look like integral parts of the structure, rather than afterthoughts.

Shutters   Seldom used today, true shutters can temper light, heat, and cold. Occasionally they serve to secure vacation houses against marauders or windows against violent storms. More common are the dummy shutters employed to make small windows look larger on pseudo-Colonial houses.

Cutouts and Projecting Elements   Overhanging roofs and trellises are popular exterior shading devices. In addition, they can shelter outdoor living areas and visually relate a house to its site. Walls that extend beyond the perimeter of the structure to create semiprotected outdoor spaces appear increasingly in cluster developments where privacy from nextdoor neighbors is sought. But they can also control the quantity and quality of light entering the windows. Cutouts are semiopen spaces, missing a wall or two or perhaps a roof, that nevertheless seem an integral part of the structure.

Grilles and Fences   Masonry, wood, plastic, or metal grilles and fences—placed close to windows or some feet away—control privacy, sun, and wind in any degree desired depending on their design and location.

Louvers   Ventilating panels of wood, metal, or plastic can be especially effective as sunshades and for weather protection (Fig. 443). Normally used over windows, they can take the place of glass completely in very temperate climates (Fig. 112).

Interior Window Treatments

Besides the traditional curtains and draperies, interior window treatments include shades, blinds, panels, and shutters. These elements can move sideways or up and down, the latter having the definite advantage of being completely out of the way when not wanted.

Shades   Fabric roller shades are inexpensive; they may cover part, all, or none of the glass. Shades reduce light and give privacy in relationship to their thickness and opaqueness. The newer ones are easy to clean and come in many colors, textures, and patterns. A fabric used elsewhere in the room can be laminated onto a plain shade or more softly draped onto one to give unity and individuality (Fig. 444). Gather shades (Fig. 445), while performing in the same manner as roller shades, have a different mechanism for raising and lowering them. The drawbacks of shades include the fact that, when pulled down, they cut out the light from

top: 444. In this bedroom, patterned fabric on the window shades matches that used for the bedspread to create a unified, tailored effect. The octagonal pattern in the rug provides more visual interest, but this is balanced by clean-lined built-in furnishings. David Hicks, interior designer. (*Photograph: John T. Hill*)

above: 445. A gather shade, sometimes called Roman or Austrian, of striped bouclé fabric used lengthwise, counters the diagonals of the unfinished pine walls and ceiling with a decided horizontal line. The shade softens but does not block light entering the room. (*Courtesy Monsanto Textiles Company*)

right: 446. Thin strips of bamboo, usually thought of as a casual material, form a subdued, elegant shade for this very large window. See also Fig. 475. (*Photograph: John T. Hill*)

447. Vertical Venetian blinds can control the exact degree of light and privacy desired; also, they require less maintenance than the horizontal variety. Peter Samton, owner-architect. See also Figs. 17, 30, 31, 161. (*Photograph: Robert Perron*)

the top of the window first—and that is the best light. Some shades roll from the bottom up, but these interfere with the operation of the window. Shades also block the breeze and may whip around noisily. They have neither the architectural quality of blinds nor the softness of draperies.

Bamboo and split-wood shades function much like those made of fabric. They differ in that they usually let more light through, give a better view of the outside, and have pleasantly natural textures and colors (Fig. 446).

Venetian Blinds Colonial homes used Venetian blinds made of wood, but they are available now in metal and plastic as well. Their special advantages include almost complete light and air control—straight into the room, down toward the floor, or up toward the ceiling—as well as complete disappearance behind a valance or other fixture, if desired. Venetian blinds are durable and not expensive. They create pleasing horizontal lines, and some of the newer versions are constructed with very thin slats, causing minimal interference with the view. They do, however, collect dust and dirt and are difficult to clean.

Vertical blinds of metal, plastic, or fabrics can be shaped easily to fit and unify odd-size openings. They control light from side to side, rather than from up or down, and emphasize the height instead of the breadth of windows and walls (Fig. 447). Of importance for household maintenance is the fact that they collect less dust than horizontal blinds.

Grilles and Screens Under certain circumstances—when windows are not well designed, when there is no view, or when privacy becomes necessary—grilles or screens of wood or other materials deserve consideration. The grille shown in Plate 50 (p. 336) covers the window of a city apartment to mask the unfortunate view while at the same time admitting plenty of light.

Shutters The old-fashioned indoor type of shutters has recently become popular again. Shutters can serve as a unified part of a wall and, because they are usually in sections, can open and close off the windows as desired. This feature is shown to advantage in a house in Sweden, where the natural wood texture and slat design is repeated in the ceiling and bookcase (Fig. 448). Although their initial cost is rather high, they last almost indefinitely, and for many people they have pleasant associations with the past.

448. Movable wooden shutters become a variable design composition in a Swedish home; their lines and textures relate to the bookcases and ceiling and complement the tactile qualities seen throughout the room. (*Courtesy House Beautiful. Copyright 1973, The Hearst Corporation*)

449–450. The same room takes on quite different aspects when its shutters are open and when they are closed. John Saladino, designer.

below left: 449. The shutters fold out of sight into piers between the windows. A grouping of plants, by their placement and feathery foliage, softens the incoming light. (*Photograph: John T. Hill*)

below right: 450. When the shutters are closed, they join the panels beneath to become an interesting wall composition, as well as affording privacy and banishing the blackness of night. (*Photograph: John T. Hill*)

Figures 449 and 450 show how dramatically "hard" treatments like shutters can transform a room. The first photo shows the shutters open by day; light streams into the room, making it seem expansive, airy, and cheerful. In the second picture the shutters have been closed; as if by magic the room has become smaller and more intimate. There is an overall sense of security and coziness. Some people find that the ritual of "closing in" for the night retains the aura of tranquility associated with lighting the oil lamps a century ago.

Plants Plants can serve as effective window treatments, filtering but not shutting out light and giving any degree of privacy needed (Fig. 451). The ultimate would be a jungle of live plants that completely block visual communication in and out.

Bare Windows When window design is truly striking, any added "treatment" becomes superfluous and could even detract from the effect. Such is the case in Figures 452 and 453. The living room of a house in Greece (Fig. 452) has small windows inset in its thick walls. The steep angle of the inset admits sufficient light while keeping out the heat as well as the inquiring looks of passersby. The house shown in Figure 453, in direct contrast, stands as a daring experiment in living with glass. Curved windows dominate a walkway connecting two levels of the house, letting in light and sunshine and giving an unobstructed view, in this case to the

top: 451. The garden area of this city apartment was created by closing off an outside terrace. Built-in seating units occupy the spaces where the original windows were. William Machado, designer. (*Photograph: John T. Hill*)

above: 452. The sunlight of Greece, as of some portions of the United States, can be almost overpowering. The architect of this house tempered its brilliance by admitting some light only through randomly arranged small panes of glass inset deeply in the thick concrete walls. Nico Zographos, architect. (*Photograph: Michael Boys*)

right: 453. A huge curving window wall, uncurtained in any way, permits unobstructed views to the surrounding terrain and makes the outdoors seem to be part of the house. Richard Meier, architect. See also Plate 20, p. 161; Plate 26, p. 180. (*Photograph: Ezra Stoller © ESTO*)

Windows, Window Treatments, and Doors **343**

sea. Here the owners and architect have made a conscious choice between privacy and openness—and opted for the latter. Any curtaining would destroy the drama.

Curtains and Draperies

In addition to controlling privacy, light, and heat, curtains and draperies soak up noise in proportion to the area they cover, the thickness of the fabric, and the depth of the folds. They make rooms homelike and effectively cover up the bareness of those not completely furnished—a point worth remembering if you do not get all your furniture at once. With curtains and draperies you can change the apparent size, shape, and character of a room or conceal architectural awkwardnesses. Small rooms look larger if curtains and draperies blend with the walls; low rooms look higher if draperies go from ceiling to floor. Gloomy rooms seem brighter when gay colors or invigorating patterns are used near windows. Walls chopped up with windows or jogs can be unified by generous glass curtains and draperies, and some eyesores can be completely concealed.

You can direct almost any degree of attention toward windows by the fabrics you select and the way you hang them. Unpatterned materials similar to the wall color, acting as inconspicuous transitions between opaque walls and clear glass, encourage us to look *through windows.* Moderate color contrasts and patterns direct attention *toward windows.* Bold or unusual colors and designs usually cause us to *look at the draperies* rather than the windows. A few definitions will help to clarify the terminology of "soft" treatment for windows.

- **Glass curtains** are of thin materials and hang next to the glass.
- **Sash curtains** are a type of glass curtain hung on the window sash. They can be stretched taut between rods on the top and bottom of window sashes or hung in loose folds.
- **Draw curtains,** usually of translucent or opaque fabrics, are mounted on traverse rods. In the past, they came between glass curtains and draperies; nowadays they are more often used alone.
- **Draperies** are any loosely hung (not stretched) fabric. Thus, the term really includes all curtains. Generally, though, draperies are thought of as heavy fabrics that can be drawn or that stand idly at the sides of windows purely for decoration.
- **Cornices** are horizontal bands several inches wide placed at the window top (or the ceiling) to conceal curtain tops and the rods from which they hang. They can also function more positively in relating the whole window treatment to walls and ceiling.
- **Valences** are simply wide cornices. They vary in shape and can be of hard materials or of fabrics.

Glass Curtains   Softening and diffusing light, glass curtains temper the glitter of window panes and relate them to the rest of the room, as well as giving partial privacy (Fig. 454). As a bonus, they also decrease the necessity of keeping windows spotless. Thin curtains come into play when the outlook is unattractive or when the household desires some privacy at all times. Along with lampshades and translucent plastic or glass panels, glass curtains make one unique visual contribution: they bring light into the room *through* color and pattern, somewhat in the manner of stained glass.

A great variety of simple *materials* have taken the place of our great-grandmother's beautifully rich curtains. Some of these are listed under "very thin" fabrics in Chapter 12. Any fabric that hangs well and withstands sun, washing, or cleaning is suitable.

Color is especially important, because the light filtering through glass curtains will take on their color, thus tinting the whole room. Also, glass curtains are

above: 454. Loosely woven net, hung from the ceiling, completely covers windows and walls in a city apartment, unifying these elements and tempering the light. Edward Wormley, designer. (*Photograph: J. Alex Langley; courtesy Dunbar Furniture Company*)

right: 455. When desired, the folds of draw curtains can clothe the windows of this living room with a light-diffusing film, but the curtains can also be pulled back to expose the view outside. Ellis G. Reuness, architect. (*Photograph: Harold Davis*)

conspicuous from the outside. Therefore, they are usually a neutral light color and, for exterior harmony, identical or very similar in all rooms. They can, however, be pink or yellow to warm a cool room or pale green, blue, or lavender to cool a hot one. Although customarily plain, suitable fabrics are available with woven or printed patterns, which are useful in rooms that need interest at the windows without adding draw curtains or draperies.

If combined with draperies, glass curtains usually hang inside the window frame, close to it and the glass; they are long enough to clear the sill without leaving a noticeable gap. Used alone, they can be hung outside the frame and cover two or more grouped windows with a unifying film. Sometimes two or more sets of glass curtains are hung in the *café* or *tier* manner to emphasize horizontality or give privacy without always reducing light from the window tops.

Draw Curtains and Draperies   Flexible control of light, heat and cold, and privacy are the primary functional purposes of curtains and draperies that slide on rods. Often they are used alone, and then they take over all the aesthetic functions of window treatment as well (Fig. 455).

Fabrics used for draw curtains need sufficient strength, durability, and flexibility to withstand being pulled back and forth and to hang gracefully when stretched or pulled together. Thus, many thin glass-curtain materials and some heavy

left: 456. The living room of a renovated California house takes visual accent from brightly colored handwoven curtains in the arched window. The curtains also enhance the quality of natural beauty in materials evident throughout the room. Kipp Stewart, owner-designer. See also Fig. 657; Plate 10, p. 59; Plate 37, p. 265. (*Photograph: Morley Baer*)

below left: 457. A glazed cotton fabric with a sprightly naturalistic design has been used as wall covering, chair upholstery, bedspread, and bed and window draperies, turning the bedroom into a delightful bower. (*Courtesy Schumacher*)

below right: 458. In a small bed-sitting room, the architectural treatment of the recessed bed acquires further coziness because of tied-back drapes in crisp chintz, the whole pulled together by the matching spread and wall covering. An upholstered pouf and table skirt carry the theme out into the room. (*Courtesy E. I. DuPont de Nemours & Co.*)

upholstery fabrics are suitable. Between these two extremes there remains a challenging array in the drapery, bedding, dress, and suiting sections of almost any store. Coarse or fine nets soften without obscuring windows. Organdy, pongee, and silk gauze are relatively smooth and rich looking. Such textiles as monk's cloth, Osnaburg, and tweed are thicker, rougher, and more casual. Denim is sturdy and durable, Indian Head clean and crisp; chambray has a smooth, slightly silky texture; gingham is informal. Glazed chintz offers a crisp, shiny surface that intensifies its colors and patterns. Satin hangs in soft folds, is dressy when woven of smooth yarn, informal when made of heavier, loosely twisted threads. Damasks, brocades, and brocatelles have woven, often formal, patterns. To this list can be added bamboo and wood textiles, substantial and informal, plus many plastic and synthetic fabrics.

Appropriateness to the home and its occupants is the only defensible criterion for *color* and *pattern*. Draw curtains are least noticeable when related to the walls. They become more conspicuous if they repeat or echo the color and character of such large units as furniture or floor, make emphatic statements when they contrast strongly with the rest of the room (Fig. 456).

Color, chiefly color value, is typically the most noticeable quality of curtains; very dark curtains against a light wall, or the opposite, stand out sharply. Scale and character come next: large-scale patterns with vivid contrasts or those that differ from other large areas in the room become dominant. It is a matter of deciding what degree of dominance or subordination, harmony or contrast, will be most appropriate. A sampling of the myriad possibilities can be seen in Chapter 12.

Draw curtains are almost invariably most effective and serviceable when they hang in straight folds that at least cover all the window frame and begin and stop at sensible points. They fit their setting best when they begin either slightly above the top of the frame or at the ceiling and when they end slightly below the bottom of the frame or near the floor. Usually, the longer draw curtains are, the better they work in the room, unless there is a good reason for stopping them short. Also, fuller curtains (from $1\frac{1}{2}$ to $2\frac{1}{2}$ times the width of the space they cover) hang more gracefully. When pulled back, curtains should cover the frame and wall, rather than the window itself. French, box, or pinch pleats take care of fullness at the top, and a generous bottom hem, often weighted for a proper hang, helps them drape well.

Draperies began their life in the heavy textiles that physically and visually warmed the cold walls of early homes and then migrated from the walls to beds and windows (Fig. 457). Today they are still found at windows, and sometimes on four-poster beds or secluding a bed alcove. Occasionally they serve as wall hangings. Draperies differ from draw curtains only in that they tend to be heavier and do not necessarily pull across the opening they guard. They often have a valence, either tailored or draped, and sometimes are tied back, evoking an earlier, more romantic era (Fig. 458).

A major element of the architectural shell, windows have gone through many developmental phases, from a slit in the wall to becoming the wall itself. Each stage has brought with it the need for window "treatment," modifications that will make this hole in the wall comfortable as well as appealing. Many such modifications—shutters, curtains, and the like—can be dispensed with if the building has been well-designed or if the location, size, shape, and type of windows make them unnecessary. The design factor may well become even more important as we enter an era where we can no longer depend entirely on artificial means of lighting, heating, and cooling our homes. Here we have another example of the great need to think about *all* factors in advance of construction and to solve as many problems as possible architecturally. An ecological approach may well change the aesthetics of architecture.

Doors

Doorways allow us and our vision—as well as light, sounds, smells, breezes, warmth, and cold—to travel in and out of the home and from one room to another. Doors control this travel in varying degrees depending on their location, design, and material. Contemporary doors run the gamut from stout, opaque barriers of wood or metal that shut everything in or out, through sheets of translucent glass or plastics, to transparent glass. Folding doors of wood, bamboo, or fabrics offer additional possibilities. Further, doors can be designed so that only part of them opens, such as Dutch or barn doors, in which the top can be open but the bottom closed (Fig. 459). The sliding *shoji* panels—which are at once walls and doors—of traditional Japanese houses (Fig. 460) allow a flexibility in design that has had a marked influence on contemporary American architecture.

In rented quarters or in a home already built, you can do less about the doors than about the windows, but the following are possibilities:

□ Remove unneeded doors to create greater openness.
□ Seal up or cover with a wall hanging doors that are unnecessary for traffic.
□ Refinish doors and their frames so that they blend with the walls.
□ Paint some or all doors in contrasting colors or decorate them so that they become dominant features.

If you plan to buy a house or rent an apartment, it pays to look carefully at the location and design of doors. And, of course, when building your own home, you should consider very carefully how doors and openings can serve best.

Types of Doors

As with windows, doors can swing or slide and they can also fold.

Swinging Doors   By far the most common type, swinging doors are hinged at one side, like casement windows. They are widely used because they are easy to operate, have simple hardware, can be made to close automatically with closing devices, and lend themselves to effective weatherproofing and soundproofing. Their major disadvantage is that the arc through which they swing must be left free of furniture.

Sliding Doors   Sliding doors need not take otherwise usable room or wall space when opened and can disappear completely to give a great sense of openness. They do, of course, have to go someplace, often into a wall. Or they can slide in front of a wall, which is often done when door and wall are of glass. Although sliding doors can be suspended entirely from overhead tracks, they usually perform better if they also slide along tracks or grooves in the floor (which are hard-to-clean dirt-catchers). On the debit side, the movements required to open and close them are not so easy to make as for swinging doors, and there is no inexpensive way to make a sliding door, especially a screen door, close itself. Many sliding doors do not glide so quietly and smoothly as one would wish, and the backs cannot have narrow shelves or hooks, which are especially convenient on closet doors. The fact that they can be very much wider than swinging doors emphasizes horizontality and spaciousness.

Folding Doors   Sliding along tracks, usually at the top, folding doors open and close like an accordian. They take little space when collapsed and come in diverse colors and textures. In general, they are not so soundproof as other types and sometimes tend to stick, but they are excellent for those situations in which one wants to be able to open or close a large opening inexpensively. In a prefabricated

above left: 459. A Dutch door, its top half lined up with the horizontal bank of windows, allows a quick airing of the kitchen while still guaranteeing safe enclosure for a small child or perhaps a little dog. William Parkins, designer. (*Photograph: Harold Davis*)

left: 460. The classic Japanese house is simply made of wood, with a pole and beam construction. Sliding walls known as *shoji* divide the different areas and can be opened and closed easily to change the character of the space. (*Courtesy Consulate General of Japan*)

above: 461. Hinged plywood panels become a wall when unfolded, but when doubled back on themselves they reveal an ever-widening doorway into the room beyond. Donald McDonald, architect. See also Fig. 280. (*Courtesy American Plywood Association*)

vacation house, simple panels of plywood slide along an overhead track to open up a possible sleeping area to the general group space (Fig. 461).

Location of Doors

Because doors and windows have so many points in common, almost everything said about locating windows applies to doors, but there are two important differences. Doors govern traffic paths, and they are often opaque.

Traffic paths, like highways, are usually best when short and direct and when they disturb areas for work or quiet relaxation as little as possible.

Furniture arrangement is in part determined by the location of doors, because a traffic path should be left between each pair of doors, and space must be allowed for those that swing. From this point of view a room should have as few doors as is feasible, with necessary ones kept close together if other factors permit.

462. French doors of glass covered by adjustable louvers give an almost infinitely adjustable scale of light, ventilation, privacy, and outlook. Walter Dunivant, owner-designer. (*Photograph: Harold Davis*)

Views and privacy are controlled by door location and material. In a bedroom, for example, a well-placed door, even when open, should not bring the bed or dressing area into full view. Doors between cooking and dining areas function best when they do not direct attention toward the major kitchen work areas. Opaque materials are typically used where view is nonexistent and privacy always needed. Translucent materials serve well where there is neither view nor the need for absolute privacy. Transparent materials allow two-way vision.

Light can come through doors as well as windows, and transparent doors are frequently combined with windows as a means to architectural unity. Glass doors give a special pleasure in that they permit one both to *look* out and to *go* out. The dining room shown in Figure 462 has a wall of louvered doors to provide maximum control of light admission. Light entering the room can vary from none at all, with the louvers totally closed; through partial translucence with the louvers adjusted; to full communication with the garden when some doors are open.

Ventilation can be accomplished quickly by opening doors, especially in opposite walls. There is nothing like opening doors to "air out the house"; but ordinary doors are not suited to gentle, controlled venting.

Heat or cold coming through light-transmitting doors has the same characteristics as that coming through windows, and thus the same comments apply. Opaque doors stand somewhere between windows and walls: They do an adequate job of climate control if well weatherproofed and concentrated on the side away from winter winds.

Cleaning a glass door is like cleaning a window, except that finger marks are more frequent, and it is easier to get at both sides. Opaque doors, too, get their full share of finger marks, particularly around the knobs. Metal or plastic plates help a little and offer a logical place for ornament.

Curtaining for glass doors is usually accomplished with draw curtains that can cover or expose the entire area of glass. The best solution locates glass doors where they need never be curtained, but this is not always easy. In older houses, "sash" curtains are sometimes used on glass doors.

left: 463. Doors with curved tops close off the shallow archway between dining room and kitchen and repeat the design of the archway in the foreground, thus adding architectural interest to a familiar boxlike shape. Kirsten Childs, architect. (*Photograph: Robert Perron*)

above: 464. A door designed to seem like part of the wall when closed makes an impressive accent when open, although it still retains its affinity with the vertical character of the wall paneling. Edward L. Barnes, architect. See also Figs. 509, 510. (*Photograph: John T. Hill*)

Design of Doors

The doors most characteristic of today's design concepts are those as visually simple as possible. This style includes the plain wood doors in which plywood sheathes a strong but light core, as well as doors of glass or plastic framed unobtrusively with metal, plastic, or wood. Many units that are little more than sheets of glass function as both windows and doors, calling attention not to themselves but to what they reveal. These are popular today, because they are inexpensive and easy to clean; moreover, they blend with the shell of a house to give a strong feeling of continuity. However, large transparent doors should be made from safety glass and must be so designed that a closed door is obvious from both sides. Folding doors of wood, bamboo slats, or fabric-covered frames can provide some visual interest with their textures and patterns.

Paralleling this taste for simplicity is the still-popular concept of doors as accents, now given special emphasis with the liberation from stereotyped shapes and proportions. Curved doors with an almost nautical flavor connect the kitchen and dining space of a house that is very graphically oriented (Fig. 463). And a supertall door with a slanted top—divided so the two sections can operate independently—joins a double-story study with the adjacent living room (Fig. 464). These two examples prove that doors can be as fully sympathetic with today's dramatic architecture as any other element.

left: 465. Handsome salvaged paneled doors with leaded glass insets at the tops create an impressive entrance for a remodeled home. Jerome Brown, architect; Cherry Brown, interior designer. See also Fig. 293. (*Photograph: Hedrich Blessing*)

below: 466. A beautiful leaded-glass door, preserved when the house it occupies was remodeled, maintains a continuity with the past yet seems quite comfortable in its new setting. Don Konz, owner-designer. See also Figs. 8, 248. (*Photograph: Hedrich Blessing*)

Even without unusual shape, size, or scale a door can serve as a point of emphasis and visual enrichment in the home. The classic wood-paneled door (Fig. 465) seems just as comfortable in many contemporary homes as it did in the 19th-century manor house, and salvage companies do a thriving business in selling old doors to be recycled for new applications. In remodeling the house shown in Figure 466 the architect used the original leaded glass as a border around opaque paneled doors, making the entrance area bright and visually interesting.

Location and design of windows and doors are fundamentals in home planning, and they deserve far more thought than they often get. In many historic houses these elements gave architects and craftsmen a unique opportunity to use their inventiveness in enriching interiors and exteriors. This principle still applies today.

Floors, Floor Coverings, and Ceilings

The current interest in vertical space has had a profound effect on the design of floors and ceilings. For many years these elements were considered relatively innocuous blank surfaces serving utilitarian purposes only; but some homes now treat them as strong architectural members with decisive influence on the character of the space. Instead of a flat, horizontal plane covered with the ubiquitous gray-beige tile or a neutral beige-gray wall-to-wall carpeting, floors now often bridge many levels: a few steps up or down to define different areas of the main group space; balconies overlooking other parts of the house; even two or three stories flowing into one another. At the same time, interest in floor coverings has revived. We see greater variety in hard-surface flooring, more conspicuous colors and textures in carpeting. Area rugs once again function as strong accents in the interior design vocabulary.

Both architects and homeowners have shown renewed interest in the positive effects of ceilings. All of us are aware of how we instinctively duck when we go through a lower-than-usual doorway, how we tend to look up when we come into a space with a soaring ceiling. These almost unconscious physical reactions have psychological overtones that can be usefully employed in the design of space for different moods and activities.

In a house built on a hillside bordering a lake (Figs. 467–469), the stepped-down configuration of the plan takes on vivid definition because of the treatment of floors and ceilings. Entering at the top of the hill, one is immediately aware of the ceiling that swoops down over the living room and then descends over a long central hall-stairway linking and separating the various zones of the house. A curved skylight that borders the dark wood ceiling throws it into relief, to provide illumination by day, a glimpse of the sky at night. The dark slate floor balances the visual weight of the ceiling and heightens the effect of protective white walls alongside the stairs. The floor also halts, at intervals, the downward plunge of the stairway.

The living room has an area rug with an abstract pattern reminiscent of the rectangular floor tiles. This defines the generous conversation group of sofas and chairs, which assumes warmth and intimacy because it is under the lowest part of the ceiling in the living room and because the hard floor has been softened by a deep pile rug. Beyond the living room windows, a terrace built on the roof of the next lower level counters any tendency to acrophobia. Floors and ceilings

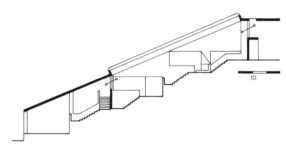

467–469. A steeply sloping site provided the incentive for distinctive architecture in this Vermont house. Peter L. Gluck, architect.

top: 467. The sharp angle of the ceiling over the group space and hall of the house brings a dramatic and constant reminder of the slope. (*Photograph: Norman McGrath*)

left: 468. A view back over the seating area shows one of the exposed steel beams that support the wide span of roof visually as well as structurally. Daylight coming in through the long skylight above the stairs illuminates the far wall to lighten and brighten the total effect. (*Photograph: Norman McGrath*)

above: 469. A section of the house illustrates the way in which the stairway ceiling ties together the various terraced levels. The placement of large pivoting windows at top and bottom creates a natural air-conditioning effect.

have been used contrapuntally, to state the theme of the steep site yet anchor the house firmly on its foundations in the hillside.

Floors and ceilings, together with walls and windows, are the big enclosing surfaces that keep us warm, dry, and safe. But depending on their design and materials, they can raise, depress, or ignore our spirits.

Floors

Floors are flat, horizontal surfaces meant to be walked on, less often to be run, jumped, or danced on, and sometimes to be sat on. They take a limited amount of wheel traffic such as vacuum cleaners, service carts, children's toys, and occasionally wheel chairs. They support us and our furniture and provide insulation against the earth's cold dampness. As we all know but sometimes forget, floors get the greatest wear and the most dirt of any part of the house. But floor design and materials are not so completely mundane as these factors imply. In fully developed architecture, they contribute to the expressive character of the whole house. They can define and separate areas without benefit of walls, can suggest traffic patterns, and can be as dominant or subordinate as one wishes.

In houses with basements, the floors are typically of two sorts. Basement floors are concrete slabs poured directly on the earthen subgrade or on a foundation of crushed rock. Those above grade (on the main story and second or third floor, if any) usually consist of supporting floor joists, a layer of inexpensive wood or plywood for strength, and perhaps an insulating membrane to retard the passage of air and moisture. All this will be topped by a finish flooring of hardwood, masonry, tiles, sheet vinyl, or carpeting.

The growing popularity of ground-hugging, basementless houses on the one hand, and precast concrete slab high-rise apartments on the other, has changed these procedures. In both types of construction, all floors may be concrete slabs basically like those in basements, but with important differences: They are reinforced with metal to minimize cracking; intermediate floors may have much thinner slabs, with the space between them and the ceilings underneath used for sound and temperature insulation; and the upper and lower surfaces can be integrally colored or patterned through the use of various materials in the concrete mix or with wood or metal screeds, which also allow for expansion. By heating concrete floors or covering them with resilient floor coverings, the householder can lessen one unfortunate side effect—cold, tired feet. It appears that combined coldness and hardness, rather than hardness alone, results in fatigue. In summer, however, with the heat turned off, the coolness of concrete floors is welcome.

Types of Flooring Materials

The rock ledges of caves and earth beaten down by use were probably the first hard-surface floors. Stones smoothed and set into place represented on improvement, constructed floors of brick, tile, and wood yet a further refinement. Until a century or so ago these were the only possibilities for permanent flooring. Today, many new materials supplement the standard ones. Table 15.1 briefly summarizes the characteristics of flooring materials commonly found in contemporary homes. Compared with carpeting, almost all are durable, cool, either hard or moderately resilient, more or less stain-resistant, and easy to clean with water. But these general similarities should not obscure the equally important differences in appearance and behavior among them.

Masonry Floors Stone, brick, and ceramic tile have a high original cost but last for generations, indoors or outdoors. Stone floors of slate, marble, or other composition can produce almost any effect, from the very rugged to the coolly formal, depending upon how the stones are set. Irregularly cut stones placed in random

Table 15.1 Flooring Materials

Material	Source or Composition	Use	Size and Shape	Patterns
		Hard		
concrete cost: least expensive flooring; can be both base and finish flooring	cement, sand, aggregates, and water; can be integrally colored	can be left uncovered indoors or outdoors; the standard base for clay tile, brick, and stone; can be covered with wood, resilient flooring, or carpets	usually poured in slabs but tiles are available; sometimes marked off in rectangles by wooden or metal screeds	can be given surface interest by exposing aggregates; terrazzo has mosaic-like patterns from marble chips
stone cost: very expensive	slate, flagstone, marble, and so on	chiefly entrances, outdoor paving, and near fireplaces, but can be used in any room	usually not more than 2' square; rectangular or irregular	natural veining, shapes of stones, and patterns in which they are laid
tile and brick (clay) cost: expensive	heat-hardened clay; tile is usually glazed	areas getting hard wear, moisture, and dirt: entrances, hallways, bathrooms, or any place where effect is wanted	tiles are $\frac{1}{2}''$ to 12'' square or rectangular, hexagonal, and so on; standard bricks are approximately $2'' \times 4'' \times 8''$	tile has varied designs; typical brick patterns come from the way in which the bricks are laid
wood (hard) cost: moderately expensive	oak, birch, beech, maple, pecan, teak, walnut; can be impregnated with liquid plastics, finished with synthetic finish	any room; often covered by carpets	strips $1\frac{1}{2}''$ to $3\frac{1}{2}''$ wide; planks 2'' to 8''; parquet blocks $9'' \times 9''$ and so on	color and grain of wood; usually laid in parallel strips; also blocks or varied parquetry patterns
		Resilient		
asphalt tiles cost: least expensive composition flooring	asbestos or cotton fibers, plasticizers, pigments, and resin binders	recommended for laying over concrete directly on ground; especially suitable in much-used areas	standard is $9'' \times 9''$ but others available	tiles are plain or marbleized; laying creates typical tile patterns
cork tiles cost: moderately expensive	cork shavings, granules compressed and baked to liquefy natural resins	floors not subject to hard wear, water, grease, stains, or tracked-in dirt	squares $9'' \times 9''$ or $12'' \times 12''$; also rectangles $6'' \times 12''$, $12'' \times 24''$, and so on	chunks of cork of different color give fine to coarse textural patterns
linoleum cost: inexpensive	wood flour, ground cork, gums, linseed oil, and pigments pressed onto burlap or felt	floor and counter tops for kitchens, bathrooms, children's rooms, activity spaces	standard tiles are $9'' \times 9''$; in rolls 6' to 15' wide	practically unlimited; ease of inlaying permits individual designs
rubber tiles cost: moderately expensive	pure or synthetic rubber and pigments vulcanized under pressure	similar to linoleum except that it can be laid directly over on-grade concrete floors	$9'' \times 9''$ to $18'' \times 36''$	usually plain or marbleized
vinyl-asbestos tiles cost: inexpensive	similar to asphalt but with vinyl plastic resins	any indoor floor including on-grade and below-grade concrete floors	$9'' \times 9''$ tiles are typical	wide range of patterns, printed or embossed
vinyl-cork tiles cost: moderately expensive	same as cork but with vinyl added as a protective sealer	any floor where heavy-duty durability is not important	same as cork	same as cork
vinyl sheets and tiles cost: moderately expensive	vinyl resins, plasticizers, pigments, sometimes fillers in cheaper grades, formed under pressure while hot; sheet vinyl usually laid on backing of alkali-resistant materials.	any indoor floor; special types available for basement floors; also counter tops, wall covering	usually $9'' \times 9''$ tiles; also by the roll, 6' to 15' wide; new types poured on floor for completely seamless installation	great variety, new designs frequent; marbled, flecked, mosaic, sculptured, embossed, veined, and striated

Table 15.1 Flooring Materials (*continued*)

Colors	Durability	Maintenance	Comments
Hard			
concrete limited range of low-intensity colors, but can be painted, waxed with colored wax, and so on	very high except that it often cracks and can be chipped; serious damage difficult to repair	markedly easy if sealed against stains and grease; waxing deepens color and gives lustrous surface but is not necessary	hard and noisy; cold (welcome in summer) unless radiantly heated
stone usually black, grays, and tans; variation in each piece and from one piece to another; marble in wide range of colors	very high but chipping and cracking difficult to repair	easy—minimum sweeping and mopping	solid, permanent, earthy in appearance; usually bold in scale; hard and noisy; cold if floor is not heated
tile and brick (clay) glazed tiles in all colors; bricks usually red	generally high but depends on hardness of body, glaze; may chip or crack, fairly easy to replace; appearance of brick, unglazed tile, improves with wear	easy—dusting and washing; unglazed types can be waxed; porous types absorb grease and stains	satisfyingly permanent and architectural in appearance; can relate indoor to outdoor areas; noisy and cold
wood (hard) light red, yellow, tan, or brown; can be painted any color	high but shows wear; irradiated types very durable	medium high—must be sealed, then usually waxed and polished; irradiated need minimum care	natural beauty, warmth; moderately permanent; easy to refinish; but fairly hard, noisy
Resilient			
asphalt tiles full range of hues, but colors are neutralized; becoming available in lighter, clearer colors	excellent but can be cracked by impact and dented by furniture; some types not greaseproof	moderately easy—mopping and waxing with water-emulsion wax	eight times as hard as rubber tile; noisy; slippery when waxed
cork tiles light to dark brown	moderately high; dented by furniture, and so on	not easy; porous surface absorbs dirt, which is hard to dislodge; sweep, wash, and wax	luxurious in appearance; resilient and quiet
linoleum practically unlimited; new types come in light, clear colors as well as dark and neutral	moderately high in better grades; resists denting better than asphalt, not so well as vinyl	moderately easy—wash and wax, do not use varnish or shellac	attractive, flexible, quiet; no real disadvantages, except need for frequent waxing
rubber tiles unlimited range; often brighter and clearer than in linoleum or asphalt	similar to linoleum but more resistant to denting; some types damaged by grease	average—washing, wax or rubber polish	very similar to linoleum, but twice as resilient
vinyl-asbestos tiles almost unlimited	high general durability, resistant to grease, alkali, and moisture; can be dented by furniture, and so on	among the easiest; resilient underlay retards imbedding of dirt	somewhat hard and noisy but more easily kept than asphalt
vinyl-cork tiles same as cork	same as cork, but more resistant to denting, dirt, grease	very easy—sweep, wash, and wax as needed	vinyl makes colors richer; less resilient and not so quiet as cork
vinyl sheets and tiles wide range including light, bright colors; in some, translucency gives depth of color similar to marble	excellent; cuts tend to be self-sealing; resists almost everything including household acids, alkalies, or grease; denting, chipping, and so on	very easy; built-in luster lasts long; imperviousness keeps foreign matter on surface; can be waxed but not always necessary, especially for some types	pleasant satiny surface; quiet and resilient, some types have cushioned inner core; patterns developed from material itself seem better than those imitating other materials

patterns (Fig. 470) tend to be more casual than identical stones set close together in an even configuration. Unglazed red bricks seem especially suited to kitchens and bathrooms (Fig. 471), because of their natural, domestic quality.

The popularity of ceramic tiles for flooring has persisted through many centuries and remains high today, despite the introduction of newer materials. In fact, many types of vinyl tile and sheet vinyl imitate clay-tile flooring. The classic terra-cotta red tiles nearly always create a warm earthy effect. In the dining room illustrated as Plate 51 (p. 369) they form a perfect backdrop to the sun-drenched colors of a Mexican house. Their durability permits the same tiles to surface the terrace, thus uniting indoor and outdoor group spaces. On the other hand, small glazed tiles can be as elegant as the most sumptuous marble floors (Pl. 36, p. 265). Ceramic tiles come in many sizes and shapes—square, oblong, hexagonal, octagonal, round, and fluted, for use alone or in combination (Figs. 472, 473).

Concrete floors, as mentioned previously, take on a completely different quality when colored or textured aggregates are added to the mix. In Figure 474 the blocks of concrete are bordered with wood strips that complement the architectural composition.

Wood   The most popular of the hard flooring materials, wood varies in cost with the type and method of placement. It requires a good deal of day-to-day maintenance but is fairly easy to repair and refinish. Some wood floors must be waxed, but if the wood has been irradiated or impregnated with polyurethane or simi-

left: 470. A studio added at one end of an old Bucks County, Pennsylvania, farmhouse has a slate floor that seems in harmony with the original stone wall, old furniture, and rustic artifacts. (*From* The Personal House *by Betty Alswang and Amber Hiken*)

right: 471. Unglazed ceramic tiles make up the floor, shower stall, and tub platform in a remodeled house. The shag rug adds a touch of softness. Ben Thompson, owner-architect. See also Plate 29, p. 197; Plate 56, p. 419. (*Photograph: Ezra Stoller* ©︎ *ESTO*)

above: 472. The varied shapes possible with clay tiles, the many patterns they can assume, help to explain their long and continued history. (*Courtesy Country Floors, Inc.*)

right: 473. Terra-cotta tiles in two simple shapes—the square and the hexagon—combine to make an elegant pattern in this dining room floor. Richard P. Donohoe, designer. (*Courtesy Don Primi, Hastings Tile*)

474. The wood screeds in this concrete floor allow for expansion and thus eliminate the danger of cracking, but they also take part in the rhythmic motif of rectangularity on which the design of the interior is based. The owner designed and built most of the inside fixtures and finishes himself over a period of several years. Bob Batchelder and Dick Whittaker, architects. (*Photograph: Philip L. Molten*)

above left: 475. Narrow, regularly spaced boards create a neutral, rather formal floor in this New York apartment. The pattern of stair and balcony rails echoes the parallel linear motif. See also Fig. 446. (*Photograph: John T. Hill*)

left: 476. In architect Alfredo De Vido's own vacation house, the flooring is rough knotty pine sawed in random lengths. Its rustic character blends with the wood paneling and exposed structural members. See also cover photos. (*Photograph: Ezra Stoller © ESTO*)

top right: 477. Parquet floors with their rich patternings are once again coming into favor, now that they are available in block form for easy installation. This design is called "Saxony." (*Courtesy Harris Manufacturing Company*)

above: 478. Vinyl flooring mimics a pattern traditional in ceramic tiles. Luran "Airtred" has a layer of vinyl over a core of vinyl foam and an asbestos backing for resilience, quietness, and insulation. (*Courtesy Sandura Company*)

lar plastic, it can be cleaned with a damp mop. Above all, wood has a homelike, enduring character that appeals to many people.

Wood floors generally take one of three forms: narrow, regularly spaced strips of similar-grained wood (Fig. 475); random-width, rough-finished boards typical of barns and country houses (Fig. 476); and inlaid squares of alternating grain known as parquet (Fig. 480). Most often highly polished, parquet floors follow many different designs and configurations (Fig. 477).

Resilient Tiles and Sheet Flooring   An endless variety of resilient flooring materials—most synthetic but some of natural composition—are now available. Cork and rubber are much more resilient than asphalt or concrete, and some of the newer types of vinyl flooring have an inner core of foam to increase springiness and warmth (Fig. 478). Sheet vinyl comes in rolls 6 to 15 feet wide and up to 100 feet long; it has fewer dirt-catching seams than do tiles of the same material, but tiles can be installed with less waste if the floor is irregular in outline. Tiles also permit replacement of an area that is subjected to unusual wear. The self-sticking versions enable any handy person to change the character of a floor with little effort. Superior-quality vinyl is moderately expensive, highly diversified in color and pattern, and probably the nearest approach to the ideal of an attractive, easily maintained, smooth-surface flooring material now available (Fig. 479).

Design of Floors

Depending upon the design effect to be achieved, floors can either unify or demarcate various sections of the home. Three examples will illustrate these devices. In Figure 480 a large expanse of wood parquet flooring pulls together an open group

left: 479. Vinyl floor tiles offer virtually endless possibilities for the creation of visual design. (*Courtesy Armstrong Cork Company*)

right: 480. A wood parquet floor unifies the very large group space in this house, while area rugs demarcate "islands" for the furniture groupings in the living area and dining space. See also Plate 23, p. 162. (*Photograph: Ezra Stoller © ESTO*)

481. Oriental rugs with their rich and subtle patterns make an excellent foil for the clean lines of much modern architecture. In this remodeled Boston stable they are also a step in the progression of textures and another link with the past. Childs Bertman Tseckares Associates, Inc., architects. See also Figs. 434, 435.

space of massive proportions. A spiral staircase curving up to the second story is made from the same type of wood, which further unifies the design. An area rug in tones that blend with the wood flooring outlines the principal seating group, thus marking but not barricading its perimeters. In the dining area beyond, a second area rug serves as an island for the table and chairs, providing an anchorage in what might otherwise be a too-nebulous space. Taken all together, the harmonious floor and floor coverings heighten the effect of a flat, extensive plane leading outward beyond the window wall to a lawn and the woods.

The house in Figure 481 suggests a floor that leads the eye inward rather than outward. Its focus is an atrium courtyard, brick-paved to denote its "outsideness" as opposed to the protected inside flooring of wood. The sharp break between indoor flooring and the courtyard is emphasized by a brick column in the window wall and a solid brick wall on one side of the atrium. Oriental scatter rugs make elegant stepping stones to connect one end of the house with the other.

Traffic patterns submit to an almost whimsical control in the house illustrated as Figure 295. A path made of stone and concrete leads up from the beach, into the house, and up the stairs, contrasting with the more regular flooring of the living spaces. The informality of this house permits creation of a "yellow-brick road" effect to make one feel one is still walking along a pebbled path outdoors.

Selection of Flooring Materials

The matter of choosing suitable floor materials deserves careful planning, especially in view of the possibilities hardly dreamed of a generation ago. Some of the important factors are these:

- **Durability** is of primary importance, because floors take severe punishment from the abrasion of feet and the weight and possible movement of furniture. Durable floors have a surface sufficiently tough to prevent wearing through to another material. They do not crack, splinter, or disintegrate, nor do they become permanently indented or otherwise make noticeable the hard use they get.
- **Economy of upkeep** allows us to enjoy the attractiveness of flooring materials. Upkeep is lessened when floor materials resist stains and bleaches, do not absorb liquids or dirt. Camouflage patterns and neutralized colors near middle in value reduce labor, regardless of the material or surface texture. Floor areas without jogs or crevices are easier to sweep, vacuum, or mop than those of complicated shape. And, somewhat surprisingly, tests indicate that carpeted floors take less labor to maintain than those with hard surfaces.
- **Resilience** cushions impact, thereby reducing foot fatigue, breakage, and the noise produced when we move around.
- **Warmth,** actual and apparent, is welcome in all but excessively hot climates. There are three ways to make floors *actually* warm: putting the heating elements in the floor, having the heat in the ceiling so that the floor will be warmed by radiation, and insulating the floor. There are also three characteristics that make floors *look* warm: warm hues, middle to dark values, and soft textures.
- **Light reflection** is generally associated with ceilings and walls, but much light hits floors day and night. The more light floors reflect, the brighter the home will be and the lower the utility bills. Part of the reason the house in Figure 480 seems so bright and open is the high degree of light reflectance from the pale parquet flooring.
- **Sound absorption,** as differentiated from the noise reduction that comes from resilience, relates to muffling of sounds at the point of origin. Especially in large apartment buildings, the use of sufficient sound-insulating material between the floor of one apartment and the ceiling of the next beneath is greatly to be desired. Within each home, flooring of soft, porous materials helps to absorb the sound of footsteps and of things being moved across the floor. Of course, carpeting, the thicker the better, makes the most efficient kind of sound insulator.
- **Appearance** depends on appropriateness to specific situations and on the individual tastes of the household. Many people overlook the strategic potential of floors as sources of personalized aesthetic expression and satisfaction. Floors can be keyed up (Figs. 467, 468) or subordinated; can alter drastically the apparent size, shape, and character of a room; can suggest division of space without walls.

Obviously, these are broad generalizations to which we could point out many exceptions. For example, durability and economy of upkeep are vastly more critical in a kitchen or a family room than in a study, where appearance might be more significant. These factors also set up conflicts, for there is as yet no one flooring material that is perfect in every respect. Thus, once again, it is only sensible to decide what is most important and to make such compromises as are necessary.

Getting suitable floors takes time, but the dividends from thoughtful planning are large. You can save money and increase the potential for long-term enjoyment if you give more than a passing glance to every floor you see, not only in homes, but in shops, restaurants, and public buildings. Mail-order catalogues and stores that sell floor coverings show what is generally available. Periodicals on interior design—especially those written for professional architects and decorators—report new developments. When this information is related to an analysis of a specific situation, such questions as the following can be answered:

How much and what kind of use will the floor get? A main entrance hallway clearly will take much more traffic than a bedroom; the former may be constantly exposed to mud, dirt, and tracked-in moisture, whereas the latter may never see anything but clean shoes and slippers. Another factor is the distribution of traffic—whether concentrated in particular spots or paths or evenly spread across the floor.

How much will the floor cost? In evaluating which type of flooring will be the better buy, one must take into account not only initial cost but the amount of money and time that upkeep will require.

What kind of beauty is indicated? The choices include informal or formal, delicate or rugged, active or passive, and several other alternatives. Flooring should be planned in relation to the walls and ceiling of the room it will occupy and perhaps to adjacent rooms or the out-of-doors, if this kind of harmony is desirable.

How individualized ought the floors to be? A floor can contribute greatly to the character of a home, either enhancing the personal qualities expressive of the household members or remaining a neutral background to other elements.

Whatever the answers to such questions, it is best to study large samples of materials in the rooms for which they are intended. Floors are too big, too expensive, too permanent, and too heavily used to be considered lightly.

Floor Coverings

Soft floor coverings add warmth, visual softness, texture, resilience, quietness, and a friendly intimacy to floors. As with wallpaper, floor coverings give rooms a "furnished" look, even with little furniture. In Figure 482 neutral-toned wall-to-wall carpeting covers the vast expanse of a loft and moves up to upholster a central seating platform. The solid sweep of carpet ties together isolated furniture groups, which are anchored on area rugs.

Floor coverings explicitly relate the floor to upholstered furniture, curtained windows, and clothed occupants. With their color, texture, and pattern, they contribute markedly to the character of homes, and, like hard materials, they can alter the apparent size and shape of rooms. Technical advances, together with changing tastes and concepts, have added new possibilities for individual expression.

Types of Floor Coverings

A few definitions will help to classify the broad range of floor coverings. *Rugs* are made in or cut to standard sizes and are seldom fastened to the floor. *Carpeting* comes by the yard in widths from 27 inches to 18 feet or more, must be cut (and pieced if necessasy) to cover all the floor, and is fastened down. *Broadloom* refers to floor textiles woven on looms more than 36 inches wide. The term does not describe the weave, fiber, color, pattern, or any quality other than width. For purposes of this discussion we will apply the word *carpet* to all soft-surface floor coverings, because this seems the more inclusive term.

Beyond these general definitions, we might distinguish carpets according to several different characteristics. These include *size, method of construction, pattern, texture,* and *materials.*

Size   At the risk of belaboring the obvious, we could point out that floor coverings can blanket the entire floor, none of it, or part of it. The last of these arrangements—rugs covering part of the floor—are often termed *area rugs.* Personal preferences, the way of living and character of the home, cost, and the appearance of the flooring itself are determining factors in the amount of soft floor covering a home will have. Rugs, carpeting, or a combination of both can be appropriate for different situations.

Wall-to-wall carpeting makes rooms look luxurious and comfortable. If the pattern is quiet and the color muted, it lends an aura of spaciousness. Carpeting is one of the best means of unifying a room or of relating several adjacent spaces (Fig. 482). Sometimes, an area rug will be placed on top of the carpeting to highlight a furniture grouping or other important point of focus (Fig. 483). Because

right: 482. In the huge living loft owned by painter Frank Stella, wall-to-wall carpeting unifies the space, moving up to cover a central seating platform. Oriental rugs create internal spaces to break up the expanse. See also Fig. 4. (*Photograph: John T. Hill*)

below: 483. Here wall-to-wall carpeting with a subdued diamond pattern gives a firm but undemanding foundation for the more dramatic treatment of walls and ceilings. The dark area rug, however, brings attention back to the seating group. Wendell H. Lovett, architect. See also Figs. 211, 547. (*Photograph: Christian Staub*)

it fits a room exactly and is fastened to the floor, carpeting gives a sense of security and permanence. Covering a larger area than a typical rug, it is more expensive, but it can serve as a finished floor covering, eliminating the need for expensive flooring underneath. Maintenance costs are less than those of resilient floorings that need constant washing and waxing; but wall-to-wall carpeting cannot easily be sent to the cleaners, moved to another room or house, or turned to equalize wear. Once thought appropriate only for the more formal areas of the home, carpeting now appears in all rooms, even the kitchen and bathroom, because of the variety of materials and qualities available.

Area rugs, the smaller versions of which may be called **scatter rugs,** are highly adaptable. They can be purchased in many sizes and shapes. If they cover the entire floor or most of it, the effect is similar to that of carpeting. Rugs can also be small accents calling attention to a special part of the home (Fig. 481) or, when larger, can hold together a grouping of furniture. In homes with open plans, they can define areas without enclosing walls. Area rugs are usually (though not neces-

below: 484. A large Oriental rug defines an open area at one end of the open living space in photographer Morley Baer's home. Thus, its handsome, decided design can be fully appreciated, much as if it were hanging on a wall. Wurster, Bernardi, and Emmons, architects. See also Figs. 591, 617, 645; Plate 60, p. 453. (*Photograph: Morley Baer*)

right: 485. Carpet tiles with self-adhesive backings lend themselves to personal decorating. These tiles are actually of sisal fiber woven with an inch-thick cut pile. They come in solids and stripes, in five colors. (*Courtesy Jack Lenor Larsen, Inc.*)

below right: 486. Carpets woven on a Wilton loom can have the subtle or decided patterns made possible with Jacquard attachments. Here a prismatic effect is achieved by a progressive change of tonality over 72 inches, with a one-half drop repeat. (*Courtesy Jack Lenor Larsen, Inc.*)

sarily) striking in color, pattern, or texture. Oriental, Scandinavian rya, and generally speaking any handwoven rugs fit into this category (Fig. 484).

A recent innovation in floor coverings takes the form of **carpet tiles,** which have a self-stick backing and can be laid just like their vinyl-surfaced counterparts. If desired, they can function as wall-to-wall carpeting, since the tiles are easy to cut and therefore follow the contours of a room without difficulty. Carpet tiles can be uniform in color and texture; if the pile is sufficiently long, the seams will

487. A 19th-century American rug of wool and cotton on a canvas backing has a delightful informality held within the conventionalized chain design of the border. (*Metropolitan Museum of Art, New York [The Sylmaris Collection; gift of George Coe Graves, 1930]*)

not show. On the other hand, the 9-inch-square or foot-square tiles readily lend themselves to combination for making patterns (Fig. 485).

Methods of Construction   The typical carpet-construction processes fall into several categories:

Tufting now accounts for the greatest percentage of soft floor coverings. In this process, pile yarns are attached to a preconstructed backing by multineedled machines.

Weaving and **knitting** interlock the surface yarns and backing simultaneously. Machine-woven rugs are sometimes subdivided into *Axminster, velvet,* and *Wilton* (Fig. 486), according to the types of looms on which they are made. Most Oriental rugs are woven, usually by hand, as are Navajo and similar tapestry (free-woven) designs (Fig. 490).

Needlepunched or **needlebonded** carpetings have a dense web of short fibers punched into a backing, resulting in a feltlike surface. Originally confined to kitchen and indoor-outdoor use—because the polypropylene fibers used resisted liquids and did not dye well—needlepunched carpets, with newer dye and printing techniques, have moved into every part of the house.

Flocked carpeting is made of short, chopped fibers electrostatically embedded in an upright position on a backing fabric to make a very dense plush surface.

Hooking, a hand process related to tufting and needlepunching, calls for pile yarns to be forced through a woven backing. Hooked rugs generally exploit their potential for free use of color and intricate, nonrepetitive designs (Fig. 487).

Braiding, too, originated as a hand process. In Colonial times it provided a second life for used garments, sewing remnants, and other fabric scraps, which were braided together in strips (like hair) and the strips sewn together. Today, commercial braided rugs are available; they give a particular warm, homey quality to traditional rooms (Pl. 52, p. 369).

Carpet backings, as distinguished from separate padding or cushions, are also important in the life of a carpet and can affect the way it lies on the floor. In many processes, the backing is coated with latex or a similar product to hold the surface yarns securely; other methods will add an extra layer of backing for greater strength. Both techniques help in keeping the carpet flat, prevent it from skidding, and aid in noise control.

Pattern   The pattern in a carpet can be anything from a tiny, almost imperceptible figure to a striking one-of-a-kind design. Commercially manufactured carpets most often have repetitive designs, because of the exigencies of industrial looming; but this very uniformity can serve as an asset in the room where floor

covering functions as a subdominant feature (Fig. 488). Almost invariably a vivid, handwoven rug calls attention to itself, becoming the focus of a room. In Figure 489 the tapestry rug echoes the spirit of fabric and graphics on the wall, even the dark sofa with white furry throws.

One special characteristic of rich patterned rugs deserves mention here—their tendency to migrate to the walls. Rya rugs, for example, which are universally marketed as floor coverings in the United States, would never have been used for this purpose in the Scandinavian countries of their origin. So ornate are the patterns—and so intricate the process of weaving them—that the rugs earned a place of honor on the wall. Such is also the case with the beautiful Navajo rug shown in Figure 490.

right: **Plate 51.** The dining room of painter Rufino Tamayo's Mexico City house has a traditional red terra-cotta floor extending through sliding glass doors onto the terrace. A brilliant red cotton rug, handwoven by local craftsmen, anchors the table and chairs. See page 358; see also Figs. 618, 620. (*Photograph: Julius Shulman*)

below: **Plate 52.** A huge braided rug with concentric bands of color provides the classic floor covering for this Colonial-style bedroom. The canopy bed and other antique furnishings, soft old wallpaper, exposed beams, and rough-hewn wood paneling are all in character. Mr. and Mrs. James Tyson, owner-designers. See page 367. (*Photograph: John T. Hill*)

above: **Plate 53.** A dropped ceiling with neon strip lighting demarcates the table area of this large dining-conference room, part of the home-office complex. Mayers & Schiff, architects. See page 377. (*Photograph: John T. Hill*)

right: **Plate 54.** The sumptuous culmination of this early 20th-century hunting lodge dining room is an ornate brick-tiled ceiling fashioned in recessed squares. Plain brick walls have been enriched with related patterns near the ceiling line. Hendrik Petrus Berlage, architect. See page 378. (*Photograph: John T. Hill*)

491. In this room, a heavy shag rug balances the weight of the sloping ceiling and invites one in to share the deep comforts of the upholstered furniture. John D. Bloodgood, architect. (*Photograph: Hedrich-Blessing*)

In the past few years great innovations have been made in dyeing and texturizing techniques, so that pattern has become easier to create in industrial carpets. Printing, similar to fabric printing or rotary news printing, is now possible over pile textures with deep penetration of colors. Programmed processes drip and jet dyes onto the face of carpeting to give a brindled effect or draw washes of color. Fibers themselves can be constructed with multiple sides to reflect a shimmering light. Combinations of colors, as many as twenty per carpet—in high or low pile, cut or uncut—result in distinctive patterns.

Texture   Carpets generally divide into two texture categories—*low-pile* and *high-pile*—although the classification is really one of degree rather than kind. Most carpets made today have some type of pile, from the very low plush of flocking, through uncut loops of varying heights, to the cut loops of velvets and shags. Long-pile carpets offer the potential for complete self-indulgence as few other materials in the home do (Fig. 491). Flat-surface carpets generally are confined to the needlepunched indoor-outdoor types or to braided and other handcrafted rugs (Fig. 489).

Materials   Many changes have taken place in the manufacture of carpets during the past decade. Above all, there has been a great increase in the use of synthetic fibers. Fibers affect the cost, cleaning time, and appearance of carpet; many of the synthetic-fiber carpets are durable, dirt-resistant, and easy to clean. Moreover, they are less expensive than natural fibers and come in almost any color or texture. The acrylic fibers, for example, have exceptional resilience, softness, and warmth; nylon is amazingly long-wearing; spots are easy to remove from both. Still, wool retains its popularity, despite the expense. It is wiry, long-lasting, and resistant

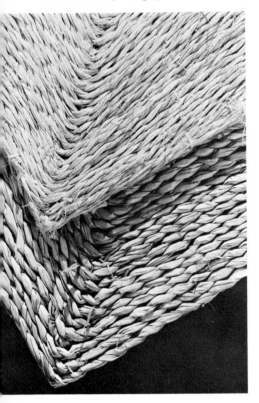

to burns (whereas many synthetics will melt if touched by a flame and retain a permanent scar). Not to be dispensed with quickly is the fact that wool appeals to our ingrained love for natural materials.

Cotton and linen frequently appear in flat-woven rugs. While not as durable as wool, these materials can contribute special qualities, such as intense color and a soft, hand-loomed effect (Pl. 51, p. 369). Cotton or linen carpets are also less expensive than wool and easier to clean. Other cellulosic fibers sometimes used as floor coverings include jute, sisal, hemp, and various grasses (Figs. 485, 492). In some parts of the world, particularly tropical regions, grassy materials are basic for floor coverings. *Tatami* or grass mats take the place of carpets in Japanese homes; and many contemporary Western homes have adopted them for casual, informal situations (Fig. 493).

New fibers and combinations of fibers, new techniques and finishes, are constantly appearing, so it is important to find out as much as possible about a carpet's specific fiber and processing before deciding on a purchase.

Selection of Floor Coverings

Most of the same factors listed for consideration in choosing a flooring material apply to floor coverings as well. They, too, represent a substantial investment of money, so the purchaser should be well informed. Three factors in particular that can affect the suitability of a carpet for the home are durability, color and finish, and noise control.

Durability   The durability of rugs and carpets depends on several elements:

☐ Fibers vary conspicuously in the wear they will take, as discussed on pages 270 and 271.
☐ In pile carpets, density of pile is of primary importance: the more tufts per square inch, the longer the life of the rug. Length of pile is also important, because carpets with high pile last longer than those with short pile. The backing should be strong and flexible, tightly woven, and capable of holding the tufts securely. In flat-woven rugs, the fibers and thickness plus tightness of yarn and weave prolong usefulness.
☐ Cushions can add years to a carpet's life, while making it more pleasant to walk on. Under scatter rugs, the cushions should be skid-proof.
☐ Rugs that can be turned to equalize wear or that can be reversed save money. A sound economy, especially with wall-to-wall carpeting, calls for covering heavily used portions with small, replaceable rugs.
☐ Good care is essential. Embedded dirt can harm carpets, as can many stains and spots. Moths and mildew destroy or weaken some fibers.

Color and Finish   Not a few rugs are replaced before they have completely worn out because they have faded, become permanently stained, or grown tiresome. With today's large windows it pays to seek permanent colors or those that fade pleasantly. Stain-resistant fibers or soil-retarding treatments are good investments, but no more so than floor coverings that will please as long as they last.

Noise Control   Carpets have one function that has become vital in today's world, and that is in the area of noise reduction. Together with the pads or cushions placed under most carpeting, floor coverings can alter noise levels substantially, provided there is an optimum combination of pile height, thickness, and pad composition. In general, the more permeable the construction of the rug—so that air pressure changes can penetrate and be trapped—the more sound will be absorbed. In some instances, this has led to the use of carpeting on walls, to further reduce the almost constant noises of the city or perhaps of neighbors and the household itself. A partial example appears in Plate 18 (p. 112).

The design of floors and floor coverings can be very complicated, since there are so many variations available. It is easy to see from the examples reproduced in this chapter and elsewhere in the book how important a role floor treatment plays in establishing the character of a home.

Ceilings

Although they are rarely *used* in the same sense that other major elements of the house can be, ceilings do have several important functions. They not only protect us but affect illumination, acoustics, heating, and cooling. Typical ceilings are the same size and shape as the floors they parallel, are surfaced with plaster or composition board, and are painted white or some very pale hue. There are several reasons for this stereotype. A flat, neutral ceiling literally designs itself and is inexpensive to build and maintain; it gives unobtrusive spaciousness; and it reflects light well. In most cases we barely notice ceilings and do little about them. Perhaps it is just as well in a busy world to retain one large undecorated surface in every room for visual respite. Nevertheless, ceilings need not be so plain, as we shall see in discussing their height, shape, direction, materials, and general design.

Ceilings are the outstanding motif in the house shown as Figures 494 and 495. They sweep up to a height of 28 feet above a dining-kitchen area, hover over a glass-enclosed passageway, then dip down to a more intimate level in the living room. As a structural unit the ceiling makes an exhilarating, character-defining

494–495. For clients who like warmth, simplicity, space, and high ceilings, architect Warren Callister created a personal house.

above left: 494. Rooflines are the dominant design element both inside and outside the house. (*Photograph: Stone and Sticcati*)

above right: 495. The soaring ceiling over the large kitchen-dining section is further articulated by the glassed-in gable end and the long skylight. (*Photograph: Stone and Sticcati*)

left: 496. A very high ceiling creates dramatic planes when furniture and wall elements are held close to the floorline. Hidden skylights under the roof admit fascinating shafts of light at different times during the day. Alfredo De Vido, architect. See also Figs. 425, 677. (*Photograph: Ezra Stoller © ESTO*)

below: 497. Many apartments, like this one in Minneapolis, have ceilings only 8 or 8½ feet high, but they can be made to seem higher by placing furniture low to the floor and painting the ceiling in light colors. (*Courtesy Apartment Ideas, Summer 1972. © Meredith Corporation, 1972. All rights reserved*)

498. In the very large, very open group space of this Montreal house, the floors and ceilings make up the dominant elements, taking over the function of walls in defining areas and determining their character. Victor Pros, architect. See also Fig. 32. (*Photograph: Julius Shulman*)

feature that produces changing moods as one walks through the spaces it shelters. The walls in the central part of the house seem to disappear, giving a sense of overhead protection above horizontally expanding space.

In the more enclosed kitchen-dining area (Fig. 495), the roof is even more dominant; sight lines are inevitably drawn up to the apex of the ceiling by the sweep of laminated wood beams and the design of the concrete posts that support them. The overall effect is one of soaring vertical space. A long skylight and the glass gable ends bring in daylight and allow views of the surrounding treetops, thus eliminating any feeling of constriction. Still, there is nothing frightening or disconcerting about this sweeping space, partly because the triangulated design of the Oriental rug pulls us firmly back to earth again.

Height

Ceiling heights are determined by reconciling our needs for head room, air, and economy with our desire for space pleasantly proportioned and in character with our living. Minimum human heights are 7 feet for basements, $8\frac{1}{2}$ feet for the main level, and 8 feet for upper stories. Heights beyond these may well be justified for aesthetic reasons, and lowered ceilings, especially in part of a room, may seem cosy and sheltering.

There are notable differences in the moods established by low and high ceilings, as Figures 496 and 497 demonstrate. In both of these rooms, the focus of interest is toward the bottom of the space, with furnishings, textures, and colors hugging the floor. The bedroom, moreover, has a distinct low horizontal established by the line of door, fireplace, and window. Yet the overall impression created by these two designs is quite different. The small apartment living room (Fig. 497) seems sheltered and intimate; the fact that all seating—and even lighting and art—is close to the floor gives a sense of burrowing in. By contrast the bedroom (Fig. 496), with its soaring vertical space, deliberately contradicts the normal ceiling line to achieve an open, airy expansiveness. Light cutting across the room from a skylight heightens the drama.

When different ceiling heights appear in the same space, the effect of transition is magnified. A huge group space divided into two areas gives a California house (Fig. 498) ample room for large social gatherings. The larger section, centered around a fireplace (Fig. 32) has a partially raised ceiling to open up its volume.

Farther back the ceiling drops to shelter a comfortable sofa that might be used for more quiet conversation. The ceiling remains low over a stepped courtyard area punctuated by unusual ceiling supports, then rises again over the second half of the group space.

Ceilings of different heights can energize space and differentiate one area from another. For example, dining rooms can be set apart by lowering the ceiling as well as the floor, and quiet conversation spaces can be demarcated by ceilings appropriately lower than those in the rest of the group space (Figs. 36, 37). Even a desk corner in the living room benefits from being anchored by a supplementary ceiling, low and horizontal, while a dropped ceiling over a hallway will emphasize the sudden, exhilarating elevation of ceiling over the larger living space.

In remodeling older buildings, which often have the high ceilings of a more extravagant age, the owner can make use of that verticality to provide more floor area and the contrast of varied ceiling heights with balconies and lofts (Fig. 59).

One other aspect of high and low ceilings should concern us now, at a time when the energy required to heat and cool our homes has become an important consideration. Low ceilings reduce winter heating costs but make rooms warmer in summer, because the rising hot air has nowhere to go. High ceilings bring in cooler air at floor level, so they are more comfortable in summer, but they require much more energy to keep them warm in winter.

left: 499. A domed ceiling seems a natural terminus for a round kitchen-dining space in this renovated barn. Its circularity is emphasized by the concentric pattern of the wood boards supported by radiating beams, by the pattern of the tile floor, and by the central placement of the round dining table. See also Figs. 560, 621. (*Photograph: John T. Hill*)

below: 500. A coved ceiling capped by a glass dome seems almost weightless in comparison to the wooden one in Figure 499. But the impression of concavity is heightened by other elements—the curve of the fireplace and the adjoining built-in bench, porthole windows, and rounded furniture shapes. Mark Mills, architect. See also Fig. 431. (*Photograph: Morley Baer*)

Shape and Direction

While it is often suitable to have ceilings that are nothing more than uninterrupted horizontal planes, some other possibilities offer more interest.

Dropped ceilings can enliven the overhead plane even on the first floor of a two-story house, where horizontal ceilings are almost mandatory. They can demarcate certain areas and provide a handy recess for indirect lighting that will softly illuminate a room. The lowered ceiling shown in Plate 53 (p. 370) actually flaunts its role as a light-carrier with bright-colored neon tubing that brings a theatrical quality to the dining area.

Coved ceilings, in which walls and ceiling are joined with curved surfaces rather than right angles, make space seem more plastic and flexible. If carried to their logical conclusion, such ceilings become domes or vaults. Contrasting materials, such as the heavily wood-beamed dome in Figure 499, add visual as well as actual weight to enhance the sense of enclosure in a room. In the living room shown in Figure 500, the walls flow gently into the ceiling until they meet a domed skylight, which in turn creates interesting washes of light and shadow.

Shed, lean-to, or **single-slope ceilings** (Figs. 467, 468) provide excellent acoustics and call attention to the highest part of the room, often in a quite dramatic manner.

Gabled or double-pitched ceilings (Fig. 292) encourage one to look up, and they activate and increase the apparent volume of a space. If the beams are exposed, the eye tends to follow their direction. For example, if the ceiling slopes gently and has beams running from one end of the room to the other, this will accentuate the room's length. When large beams follow the direction of steeply pitched ceilings, they emphasize the room's height dramatically. Ceiling planes can also slope in four directions. A-frame houses have double-pitched ceilings that come down almost to floor level for an unusually strong architectural statement.

Sculptured ceilings are those that defy classification because they are uniquely themselves. The ceiling shown in Figure 501 exposes structural members to create a striking radial pattern, which is interrupted by the curving fireplace and the plane of the adjacent space cutting across it. Clearly this ceiling is not a neutral backdrop but the focus of the whole room.

501. In this house of curves and planes, heavy wood beams and steel reinforcement flaunt their structural role and transform utility into a thing of beauty. The striking radial pattern of the ceiling, cut by a large triangular window, becomes the focal point of the room. (*Photograph: Ezra Stoller* © *ESTO*)

Materials

Plaster and wallboard are today the most common ceiling materials, since they are inexpensive and easy to apply. But these conventions by no means exhaust the possibilities for ceiling embellishment.

Plaster provides an uninterrupted surface that can meet plastered walls without joints, thereby passively unifying the sides and top of a room. It can be smooth or textured, plain, painted, or papered. In the days of more leisurely craftsmanship, plaster often was embellished with designs, a refinement preserved with care in many remodeled townhouses (Fig. 502).

Gypsum board resembles plaster, except that it leaves joints that must be concealed with tape or with wood battens. The latter provide lines of emphasis.

Ceiling tiles come in many sizes and patterns; they can contribute a readymade texture. Some are easy to apply by the householder to cover a less-than-attractive surface; many are acoustical and offer the very obvious advantage of reducing noise at its source. There are also tiles with foil backing that cut down on air-conditioning costs. The elegant room shown in Plate 54 (p. 370) has been patterned with a rich mosaic of glazed bricks—scarcely one's image of ordinary ceiling tiles—for a rich, sumptuous effect.

Wood—in the form of strips, planks, or plywood—is both handsome and homelike (Fig. 503). It can be left in its natural state (in which case it will need minimum care over the years) or painted, perhaps to brighten the room.

Fabrics are rarely used on ceilings, but they can add warmth and softness to a room in unexpected ways. The bedroom shown in Figure 504 has its ceiling draped with a brightly colored Indian marriage tent, which gives the effect of a canopy enclosing the whole room.

Transparent materials like plastics and glass admit natural daylight, or artificial light from fixtures concealed above them, to provide allover illumination to the room (Fig. 505).

Besides the surface materials that finish a ceiling, of the utmost importance are insulating materials placed between ceiling and roof or, in a multistory building, under the floor of the level above. Chapter 5 discusses these matters in relation to heating and cooling.

Design of Ceilings

Heaviness overhead is usually unpleasant, unless the weight is clearly supported from above and balanced from below, as it is in the domed ceiling (Fig. 499). This fact, together with the advantage of having ceilings that reflect light, explains the frequency of light colors and fine textures on overhead surfaces. Certainly this characterizes most apartments, in which ceilings tend to be low and daylight comes in through windows on one exterior wall. The tiny living room in Figure 497 has been expanded visually by lowering the seating onto a soft yellow carpet. Any available light reflects upward off the carpet onto the totally bland ceiling, which in turn spreads it throughout the room to give an airiness at head height and above.

It should be remembered that ceilings, especially at night if much light is directed toward them, bathe everything below with their reflected color. A yellow ceiling, for example, would enliven yellows, oranges, or yellow-greens beneath it but would dull any blues or violets. Special effects of considerable impact, however, can be achieved with ceilings painted in strong colors or made of a dark wood.

Among the most telling aspects of interior design are the treatments of floors, floor coverings, and ceilings. Together with walls, they give a room or an entire dwelling its basic character and, once established, begin to channel decisions about other steps in home planning. A sympathetic integration of these three elements constitutes a major step in creating a personal lifespace.

left: 502. In renovating this floor-through New York apartment, painter Robert Motherwell retained the 19th-century decorative plaster ceiling and wood moldings. The effect is a splendid mixture of old and new. James Baker, architect. (*Photograph: Hans Namuth, Photo Researchers, Inc.*)

below left: 503. Exposed wood beams form the ceiling of this restored 18th-century mill in Pennsylvania. French and Italian antiques seem perfectly at home in the rustic setting. Lilias Barger and Raymond Barger, designers. See also Fig. 585; Pl. 34, p. 232. (*Photograph: John T. Hill*)

below right: 504. A billowing fabric ceiling hung over a mobile suspended bed adds brilliant, bold color and pattern to an otherwise unadorned room. See also Plate 18, p. 112. (*Photograph: Dudley Gray*)

left: 505. Lights concealed behind translucent panels cover the entire ceiling and bring a soft glow of illumination to this inside kitchen. James Maul, architect. (*Photograph: Philip L. Molten*)

Furniture Selection and Arrangement

16

Furniture provides the major transition between architecture and people. In the most basic sense, it is a tool for relieving the stresses of gravity. It exists to provide comfort in the things we do: working, eating, sleeping, and relaxing. We expect each piece of furniture to fulfill the specific functions we require of it. An easy chair and a dining chair, for instance, while meant basically for sitting, differ in design because they serve us in different situations. Moreover, furniture also performs as an architectural element by organizing the space within a room: defining conversation areas and traffic paths, suggesting separation of areas, and so forth. Finally, furniture enables us to impress our personal tastes on our life-spaces, even when they are architecturally the same as those of our neighbors. Very much as an expression of our lifestyles, we choose furniture that allows us to use various rooms as we see fit. We manipulate the character of the furnishings, and their arrangement, to define the type of living we expect a room to foster.

The two living rooms in Figures 506 and 507 exemplify two different approaches to furniture—its selection and arrangement—that we find prevalent today. Basically, the two rooms are much alike—rectangular, with windows across one end, and having no distinctive architectural features. In each case, the major furniture units have been placed around the edges of the room to make the most of available space; but there the similarities end. In the first living room (Fig. 506), the furniture becomes almost part of the architectural shell. It is hard to tell where one ends and the other begins. Built-in seating units fitted with soft cushions function as a transitional element between walls and floor. Arranged in a broad L shape around a rug and coffee table, they fill the roles of sofa, lounging platform, and tables. Two metal-and-leather sling chairs plus built-in storage complete the equipment of this group space. The traffic path is well-defined, with free circulation space allowed inside the seating area. People could move around easily, sit or lie in different ways; many flat surfaces provide places to put a book or magazine, an ashtray or a glass, a sculpture or a plant. Overall, within a rigidly contoured area, there is ample freedom of movement and choice of ways to relax.

The apartment living room in Figure 507 shows a totally different concept of furnishing space. Here everything is movable, and if the owners feel like arranging the room differently, they can do so without difficulty. Except for one large sofa and the bentwood chairs, all furniture consists of modular units that could be regrouped in different configurations to suit changing needs. The chairs are light

enough to be drawn up for joining any conversation or to be placed elsewhere in the apartment as a means of opening up the space for a larger, more mobile party.

The two furniture arrangements could also be considered with other factors in mind. In terms of maintenance, the first room would probably be more efficient than the second; most of the large elements would stay in place because they are built in, there is plenty of storage at hand for the smaller items that accumulate in living rooms, and surfaces generally would show little soil and clean easily with

above: 506. An apartment living room gains serenity and space by having most of the furniture built in. Harmonious neutral tones provide a background for art and for people. Joseph Merz and Mary Merz, architects. (*Photograph: John T. Hill*)

right: 507. A living room similar in character depends for its effect on completely mobile furniture. The theme of the bay window has been picked up by placing the seating units in bays created by the large cube tables; a counterpoint of circles and squares carries over into the design of the cutout Styrofoam panels that camouflage the old windows. Sughash Paranjpe, architect. (*Photograph: Norman McGrath*)

508. An old Art Deco chair, discarded as trash by one owner, becomes—with the help of a little refurbishing—the focal point of a new owner's living room. See also Plate 50, p. 336. (*Photograph: Robert Perron*)

509–510. The influence of people on the design of a home becomes immediately apparent from these two views of the same room. Edward L. Barnes, architect. See also Fig. 464.

left: 509. The living room has a built-in seating platform along one side wall to accommodate many people; a shaggy rug seems comfortable to young people and a dog, while the rattan chairs and stool can be moved around wherever they are needed. (*Photograph: John T. Hill*)

above: 510. With only one occupant in the room we become aware of individual elements and especially of the role textures play in establishing the desired informality. (*Photograph: John T. Hill*)

either a vacuum cleaner or a duster. In the second room, things would get out of place more easily because of the very mobility of the furnishings, there is little storage space, and the tops of the cube tables, especially the glass tops, would show soil and scratches.

Should the occupants decide to move to new quarters, neither group of furnishings would present much of a problem. The first apartment has no really bulky items; the seating units would either be left behind or dismantled, and the cushions could be adapted to a new module. In the second apartment the sofa is the one piece large enough to be cumbersome for moving.

Considered in design terms, the first room seems quietly composed and unified, a background for people. Most of the forms are rectangular, their edges softened in varying degrees, with the round table, the pillows, and the circular painting as accents. The second room contrasts geometrically precise angles and circles throughout, with this juxtaposition culminating in the window panels and the pictures on the walls. It is a visually active space that achieves unity through the repetition of circles and squares but is softened by the curvilinear forms—the bentwood chairs, the plants, and the patterns on the rug and cushions—that serve as transitional elements between the two rigid forms.

In character, neither of the rooms is pretentious. Both promise a comfortable, relaxed kind of living. However, the carpeted, padded, and cushioned surfaces of the first room would encourage perching, sitting, lounging, and stretching out on the floor or sofa for quiet talk, listening to music, or even dozing. The second room suggests more upright postures on pieces of furniture designated for that purpose. Its floor does not invite sitting or lying upon, because it is too hard and there are no protective corners to back into. Generally, the space could foster lively and animated interaction among people, but the upholstered pieces are comfortable enough and well-lighted by lamps on flexible brackets for those who like to read.

Equally practical and pleasing in their different ways, these two rooms show how people with differing needs and attitudes can personalize their homes through the furnishings they choose.

Furniture has been discussed and illustrated on many of the preceding pages. In the first part of the book it was considered as a factor in group and private spaces; the next chapters focused on design quality, and then materials were considered for their impact on design and use. Keeping these previous discussions in mind, we can now approach the selection and arrangement of furniture with particular emphasis on personal values.

Selecting Furniture

The vast array of furnishings currently available testifies to a wide divergence in the ways people live. There is mass-produced furniture that reflects and enhances every pattern and style of living; furthermore, increasing numbers of people are finding satisfaction in constructing their own furnishings—either freely or from components—and in rehabilitating furniture others have discarded. The Art Deco chair shown in Figure 508 was picked up off the street, where it had been left for the garbage collectors; with new upholstery and minor repairs to the frame, it makes a delightful contribution to the new owner's living room.

In order to sort through the many types of furniture and find what pleases you most, you should build a personal scale of values that will allow you to evaluate furniture as it relates to your particular necessities and aesthetics. Deciding on physical requirements is the first step, although it seems like a rather prosaic one. Considerable thought should be given to how and in what situations you are going to use your furniture and who will use it. The single-person household will obviously have quite different needs than the family that includes, say, seven children and a dog (Figs. 509, 510). The living room pictured offers a long built-in seating platform, comfortable wicker chairs, and a large shaggy rug, all suitable for sitting, sprawling, or reclining. Excellent lighting illuminates these areas. It is interesting to note what a different effect the room presents when it is full of people, as opposed to having only one child curled up in the corner. The former situation makes the room seem animated and busy (even though all the occupants are engaged in sedentary activities); in the latter case there is an overall impression of intimacy and tranquility.

Before selecting furniture you should also consider how much space is available, what scale of furniture will relate well to the room, and possible arrangements. "Practice buying" with these aspects in mind is a profitable investment of time.

In stores, catalogues, magazines, books, and your friends' homes you can see many kinds of chairs, tables, cabinets, and furniture systems—both new and old. Compare and contrast them, noting the excellences and weaknesses of each. Very few are totally good or bad. When you have the opportunity, sit on, look at, and feel furniture. You are going to be the one using it, so find out what looks good and is comfortable to you.

As you continue to look, think, and compare, you will be consciously sharpening your aptitude for seeing and evaluating differences. At the same time, you will develop the ability to decide which aspects are most important for your own needs and for your personal scale of values. With some people, comfort or beauty may transcend all other considerations, although most of us seek a balance. Good as a general scale of values is, however, none can be rigidly applied to every specific situation.

Utility and Economy

Whether furniture is for sleeping, sitting, eating, working or playing, practical considerations should not be minimized. Important factors for utility and economy are the following:

Convenience applies to efficient storage and to the ease with which often-moved furniture—such as dining chairs or beds that must be pulled out from the wall for making up—can be handled. Almost all furniture is moved from time to time, so it should be no heavier than necessary for use, strength, and appearance. Large pieces, especially if they are heavy, should be on casters or gliders.

Mobility is a fact of life in our society, and many households must cope with packing, shipping, and resettling at frequent intervals. Furniture that is lightweight, collapsible, or capable of being disassembled may provide the answer (Fig. 511). Some people who move often find it easier to either rent furniture or to buy cheap or second-hand pieces that can be sold and left behind. While this expedient makes it more difficult to personalize a space, it does offer what for many individuals is the exciting challenge of designing a new environment every few years.

Comfort relates to pieces on which we sit or sleep, as well as to the height of tables and desks and to the leg room under them. The table-desk shown in Figure 511 has removable pegs in the supports so that it can be adjusted to almost any height. Sometimes comfort overrides every other factor in choosing a particular item of furniture. The classic example of this is the ugly, broken-down easy chair whose owner would never part with it. The age of household members becomes important here, for elderly and young people have definite but quite different requirements for comfort.

511. A drafting-work table that could be used for dining is remarkably adaptable. The file unit can be removed, the top can be tilted, raised, or lowered, and the whole table comes apart for ease in moving. (*Courtesy The Workbench*)

Flexibility pertains to furniture that can be used in more than one room or for more than one purpose. Until recently, most furniture was designed very specifically, such as the typical dining sets of a few decades ago. Only the chairs could be moved about freely, but no matter where they were placed they carried a "dining room" character. Now many pieces are multipurpose; the table-desk in Figure 511 tilts to make a drawing table and, without its drawer components, could serve as a small dining table. Endlessly flexible is the modular unit shown in Figure 512, which consists of interlocking hardwood posts, butcher-block surfaces, drawers, closets, and shelves. Rearranged into different combinations, this piece would be equally at home in a den, a home office, a student's bedroom, even a work corner of the group space.

Space required becomes increasingly important as homes grow smaller. Accordingly, many contemporary designers have eliminated protruding moldings and curved legs, so that pieces can be fitted together snugly; brought storage units to the floor or hung them on walls; designed cupboards and drawers to fit their contents flexibly; employed materials—metal, plywood, foam—that reduce size; developed folding, stacking, and nesting tables and chairs (Fig. 513); and in some cases reduced both size and scale to a minimum.

The concept of modular and built-in furnishings has had great impact on the space in homes, as we have mentioned before. By eliminating the separate piece of furniture that must stand alone, designers utilize the spaces-in-between, so that *more* furniture requires *less* floor area. Floor area is also freed when furniture is attached to walls.

Length of service depends on both physical and psychological durability. The physical life of furnishings, of course, is determined by materials, construction, and finish. Psychological longevity, while equally critical, can be harder to appraise. It makes no sense to buy a piece of furniture solid enough to last for generations if you are going to hate it within a year or two. "Fad" styles have particularly short staying power. There is no reason why you cannot buy an inexpensive bit of whimsey occasionally to brighten the home, but when investing in basic articles

left: 512. KD6 Modular Furniture can be added onto or separated and easily rearranged to suit the user's needs by an ingenious system of exposed bolts that add interest as well as sturdiness to the design. (*Courtesy John Adden Furniture*)

right: 513. Small tables of lightweight but sturdy and colorful plastic can be set side-by-side to form a larger unit, or stacked by fitting the ends of the legs into small depressions on the table tops. This design is called "Demetrio." (*Courtesy Owens/Corning Fiberglas*)

of furniture, you will do far better to choose well-made, well-proportioned items in which the materials have been honestly and suitably used. Some designs have an exceptional capacity for standing the test of time, as two of Philip Johnson's own houses demonstrate (Figs. 23, 25). The Barcelona chairs, stool, and lounge —modern classics dating from about 1930—appear in the Cambridge house (Fig. 23) and again in the Glass House (Fig. 25) as it is today, with only reupholstering needed to preserve their beauty and character.

For some families, durability may no longer be the imperative it once was. When furnishing temporary quarters or anticipating a period of mobility—such as a business training program or military service—you may find solid, expensive furnishings to be actually a handicap. Built-in furniture also has drawbacks in these situations, because it may be too large to move without tearing it apart, and the next tenants may find it objectionable. The length of service each article is capable of giving should depend on the length of service that will be required.

Cost of maintenance includes cleaning, repairing, refinishing, and reupholstering. The choice of appropriate materials can lighten cleaning burdens, while strong materials and firm construction lessen the need for repairs. Durability of finish and ease of refinishing are important: painted furniture, whether wood or metal, needs new paint every few years; transparent finishes on wood, supplemented by wax or polish, last a long time, and some of the new synthetic finishes reportedly are almost indestructible (Fig. 289). Such materials as aluminum and chromium can last indefinitely without being refinished. Upholstery fabrics may serve from two to twenty years or more depending on the material and the wear it is subjected to. Several factors govern the cost of reupholstering: the price of the fabric, the amount needed and the labor involved. The use of zippered covers wherever possible facilitates both cleaning and recovering.

Beauty and Character

Whether furnishings have beauty and character depends on an entirely subjective appraisal, because individuals vary so markedly in their tastes. It is in this realm that you must know yourself. We have already discussed the concept of different standards of beauty (see pp. 22–24). Insofar as furniture is concerned, some people consider to be beautiful only the most streamlined, sleek, ultramodern designs (Fig. 514), while others prefer the grace and charm of antiques (Pl. 46, p. 318). For those who cannot afford real antiques, there are many good contemporary reproductions of classic pieces—some available in kit form—that blend well with today's homes and lifestyles (Fig. 515). Beyond this, other alternatives exist: the beauty of natural materials and that of synthetic materials (Figs. 28, 345); the glow of primary colors and the subtlety of neutrals (Pl. 26, p. 180; Pl. 28, p. 197); the precision of geometric order and the opulence of flowing curves (Figs. 176, 382). We could list many other contrasting styles and tastes. In the end, each individual, and the household as a unit, will decide what types of furnishings are beautiful and have character. At a time when more and more people live in architecturally similar spaces, it is more than ever important to choose furnishings that are personal, that will individualize a space and make you feel you are coming home—not to a hostile or indifferent environment but to your own lifespace, which gives you the freedom to expand mentally, psychologically, and spiritually.

Furniture Types

The first furniture probably consisted of a natural rock ledge found in a protected spot and used for sitting or sleeping. Refinement of such existing surfaces led to recesses in the walls of the hut or cave occupied by primitive peoples. In effect, this was "built-in" furniture—the prototype of units integrated with the architectural shell that we are accustomed to today. Historians theorize that the earliest individual pieces of furniture were hammocks and mats for sleeping, which in colder climates would have been made of skins, in warmer climates of grasses and reeds. From these ancestors all the myriad furniture articles we know evolved.

Once established, the preference for isolated furniture prevailed well into the 19th century. Even clothes closets were unknown, and people stored their garments in bulky wardrobes or chests. Then in the late 1800s home designers began to use walls more intensively, and by the early 20th century built-in furniture had staged a revival that is still vigorous today. Combined with the interest in furniture that is at one with the architecture is the development of *unit* or *component* pieces, which in a sense offer a compromise between built-in and individual furnishings. Unit furniture organizes a variety of furniture elements into a cohesive structure.

Because it is at once ancient and up-to-the-minute, we might consider built-in furniture first.

Built-in and Unit Furniture

More often than not, built-in furniture promotes flexible living, although this may seem like a contradiction. Because the furnishings take less room than movable pieces, they leave a maximum amount of free space around and between them. Built-in furniture can also minimize dust-catching crevices, give a feeling of permanence and security, and break up the boxiness of typical rooms. At the same time, it reduces the visual clutter brought by many isolated pieces of furniture, which have an irritating tendency to get out of their best positions. Many people trace the current interest in built-in furniture to Frank Lloyd Wright, who early in his career began thinking of the house as a unified whole, with storage, seating, and tables forming an integral part of the architecture (Fig. 824).

The room in Figure 516 might be considered a descendant of prehistoric caves with rock ledges for furniture. Here varied floor levels terraced up to window walls of different heights provide surfaces for walking, sitting, and reclining. Covered with thin upholstered pads and a generous scattering of pillows, the platforms suggest an easy, comfortable, and casual lifestyle. The only actual pieces of furniture in the room are a low table and two stools in the center, which would be ideal for light meals and snacks.

left: 514. A collection of furniture pieces designed by Pierre Paulin makes a landscape of curves and circles and arcs. Although very sleek and streamlined, these units are extremely comfortable. Stretch fabrics make a crushproof, easy-care surface. (*Courtesy Turner, Ltd.*)

above: 515. A corner cupboard that can be assembled from a kit is modeled after an 18th-century piece. Its simplicity would make it equally at home in a modern setting. (*Courtesy Cohasset Colonials*)

Furniture Selection and Arrangement   **387**

left: 516. The no-furniture room seems particularly suited to a vacation home, with the seating pads doubling as mattresses for an overflow crowd. Windows of various sizes and proportions frame outdoor scenes. Moore-Turnbull, architects. (*Photograph: Morley Baer*)

left: 516. The no-furniture room seems particularly suited to a vacation home, with the seating pads doubling as mattresses for an overflow crowd. Windows of various sizes and proportions frame outdoor scenes. Moore-Turnbull, architects. (*Photograph: Morley Baer*)

517–518. An apartment planned entirely around built-ins causes architecture and furnishings to merge into one integral unit. A very relaxed lifestyle and absolutely minimum housekeeping would be two benefits of such a space. Gamal el Zoghby, owner-designer.

below left: 517. The major group space has two large seating platforms connected by partial walls and built-in lighting to the ample storage units at the other end of the space. (*Photograph: John T. Hill*)

below right: 518. A cozy alcove for informal meals emerges behind built-in partial walls. Both table and seating are integral with the framework. (*Photograph: John T. Hill*)

The apartment illustrated in Figures 517 and 518 has nearly all of its furnishings built in. The major group space (Fig. 517) is a landscape of strict geometric cubes—jutting out into the room as a sofa, open on one side for books, closed all around and rising to the ceiling for concealed storage. In the tiny dining alcove (Fig. 518) are padded benches and a table suspended on a single pedestal. Behind the alcove, a cozy recess has been integrated with the wall and softened with a fake-fur throw. Overall, it is impossible to tell where the furnishings begin and

519. Modular furniture that has the ability to create a "room" within its boundaries would make sense in any large space, such as a loft apartment. Here the mattress is foam on a simple, tiltable frame. (*Courtesy International Contract Furnishings*)

the architecture leaves off, so thoroughly are the two integrated. This concept of total, unified design appeals to our sense of harmony and order.

Like built-in furniture, unit or component furniture answers our desires for coherence and spaciousness. The module shown in Figure 512 offers a good example of this, being work surface, open storage, closed storage, and potentially bed all in one. A similar multiple role is played by the unit in Figure 51, where most of the major furniture elements have been assembled into an integral structure.

We will have occasion to refer to built-in and component furniture again in relation to specific types of pieces.

Beds

Reducing physical strain to a minimum is the major purpose of beds. Individuals vary in their specific ideas about sleeping comfort, so the only real way to find out whether a bed is right for you is to try it. We have been conditioned to believe that a bed should have a springy foundation and a resilient mattress. The typical foundation consists of either inexpensive, lightweight flat springs or more bulky, expensive coil springs, but a flat plywood foundation can also be comfortable if the mattress is thick enough, particularly for people who enjoy a very firm surface.

Mattresses have been filled with just about everything from straw to hair, even air and water. Today the least expensive are thin pads of polyurethane foam. The better grades have 4- to 6-inch cores of polyurethane or latex foam or innersprings covered with padding. Innerspring mattresses are still the most popular, probably because people are familiar with them. They vary in the number of coils, their design, whether or not they are individually pocketed, and in the type or thickness of the padding that protects the user. All of this affects their conformity—the way in which they respond to a person's distributed body weight—hence the individual's comfort, which can only be ascertained by trial. Foam mattresses are lightweight in proportion to their size and harbor no insects or allergy producers. They seldom need to be turned and come in various degrees of resilience (as, of course, do innerspring mattresses). Foam mattresses can also be handmade, which allows them to be cut to size in the thickness and density desired or even built up of layers of foam in different densities for greater comfort. In Figure 519 a foam

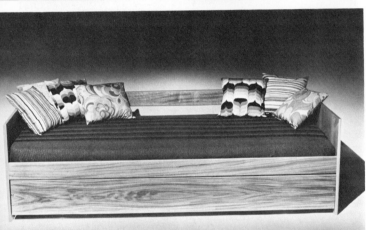

top left: 520. Sofabeds now come in a range of designs comparable to those offered in ordinary sofas. This comfortable, plush-upholstered piece conceals a full-size mattress. (*Courtesy Selig*)

above left: 521. A bed fitted with arms and a back to make it usable as a sofa hides another trundle bed beneath it. The trim design results from high-density foam mattresses. (*Courtesy The Workbench*)

above right: 522. A bed has been transformed into an alcove—a lifespace within a lifespace—by surrounding it with built-in units that bring many amenities close to hand—lights, television, telephone, books, and shelf-space for whatever else the owner desires. Gwathmey & Siegel, architects. See also Plate 21, p. 161. (*Photograph: Ezra Stoller © ESTO*)

mattress covers a built-in bed that forms the hub of a complete lifespace in miniature. Ample storage, both open and closed, allows one to keep at hand not only clothing and personal effects but books, magazines, perhaps working materials. The upper portion of the bed tilts up for reading or writing comfort, something that would be difficult to achieve with a heavy innerspring mattress.

Even if funds are low, good beds should be a priority in furnishing the home. For safety's sake, each mattress should carry a label stating that it conforms to the flammability standard established by the Consumer Product Safety Commission. They can be supported on simple wood legs or the more convenient metal frames on casters that permit the bed to be moved for bedmaking. Headboards, night tables, and footboards, while nice to have, are not essential and can be added later. In small quarters or for occasional guests, sofabeds make a sensible economy. Today, many of these are quite handsome (Fig. 520). Also, the various types of bunk beds, fold-down beds, and trundle beds can be excellent space-savers (Fig. 521).

Two new types of beds—waterbeds and built-in beds—have their adherents; their comforts may or may not outweigh certain disadvantages.

A waterbed consists of a heavy-duty plastic water bag, a solid frame that supports the bag, a watertight liner between the bed and frame to guard against floods, and a special heating pad that warms the water to a comfortable temperature. (The heating pad should bear the Underwriters' Laboratories label of safety testing.) Waterbeds are firm and strongly supportive, because they can shape themselves exactly to body contours, but some people find disconcerting their quick reaction to changes in position. They also weigh a tremendous amount when filled (about 1600 pounds for a standard-size model), must be emptied for moving —distinctly not an easy task—and present problems in adjusting sheets, blankets, and bedcovers. They can be used only in buildings with strong foundations, and some landlords will not allow them at all. But for those who can overcome or overlook these obstacles, waterbeds do provide a new experience in sleeping comfort.

Built-in beds offer a certain reassuring protectiveness and bring many conveniences close to hand—lighting, possibly a slanted end for reading in bed (Fig. 519), bookcases and stereo components or controls, surfaces on which to place things. The main difficulties lie in moving the bed and in making it, although in the latter case the necessary stretching might be considered good exercise. Sometimes storage facilities are combined with the bed as in Figure 522, which was designed by the architects as a smaller total environment within the larger bedroom.

Children, especially small ones, require different kinds of sleeping furniture. Bunk beds are popular, because children possess both the necessary agility to get into an upper bunk and the spirit of adventure that delights in climbing up and down (Fig. 523). In the bedroom occupied by only one child, a bunk bed supplies accommodation for overnight visits by friends. Infants, of course, must have well-protected sleeping spaces to prevent them from tumbling out. Figure 524 shows a unique kind of "built-in bed" for babies—a cradle suspended between the upright supports of a chest and cabinet structure. While such an arrangement would serve its occupant for only a very short time, it remains a beautifully crafted object.

Sofas

We have chosen the inclusive term *sofa* to refer to a seat for two or more people, but many other names are or have been applied to such pieces of furniture. Some are used interchangeably, but the various terms may convey shades of meaning:

- **Chesterfield** refers to an overstuffed sofa with upholstered ends.
- **Couch** originally meant a sofa with a low back and one raised end; nowadays the name is synonymous with sofa.

left: 523. Bunk beds can double as children's hideouts and play sculpture. In this case, storage recesses have also been built in. Douglas White, architect. (*Photograph: Robert Perron*)

above: 524. A lovingly handcrafted cradle-storage unit would be a treasured piece of furniture long after the baby had outgrown the cradle. Sam Maloof, designer-craftsman. (*Courtesy National Collection of Fine Arts, Renwick Gallery, Smithsonian Institution, Washington, D.C.*)

□ **Davenport** is used in the United States to describe an upholstered sofa often convertible into a bed, but originally the word designated a small writing desk named after its maker.

□ **Divan** is a Turkish term for large, low couches without arms or backs that developed from piles of rugs for reclining.

□ **Lounge** once referred to a type of couch with no back but with one high end for reclining. Today the term indicates either a flat padded surface on which to stretch out or any supercomfortable seating unit that invites relaxation.

□ **Loveseat** means a small sofa or "double chair" for two people.

□ **Settee** refers to a light double seat with a back and sometimes with arms, often upholstered.

□ **Settles** are all-wood settees, used in Colonial days before a fire to trap heat.

□ **Sofa** comes from an Arabic word; in the United States it describes any long upholstered seat for more than one person.

The variety of sofas is legion: straight, curved, or angled to fit a room; with or without arms; in one piece or sectional; long enough for a tall person to stretch out on or more modest in scale; heavy and massive, delicate and graceful, or light and simple. When shopping for a sofa, you should keep in mind the functions you will expect it to perform. In different situations individuals will need a sofa:

□ Long enough to stretch out on

□ Low and deep enough for relaxation but high and firm enough so that most people can get up under their own power

□ Fitted with arms for comfort

□ Convertible into a bed if extra sleeping space is required

□ Sectional if rearranging furniture is a hobby or moving a necessity

□ Upholstered in a material that combines beauty and durability

below: 525. Modular seating cushions that can be rearranged in an infinite variety of ways make up nearly all the furniture in this converted brownstone apartment. Steve Kiviat, owner-architect; Susan Kimber, interior designer. (*Photograph: Norman McGrath*)

right: 526. A large floor mattress gives lounging space and contributes to the informal, tropical character of this colorful living space. Unexpected contrasts are restrained by the simplicity of the architectural detailing. Taylor and Ng, architects. (*Photograph: Morley Baer*)

In some homes the sofa is losing its identity as a separate piece of furniture to merge with the floor or wall as part of the shell of the house (Figs. 506, 510, 517), or else has disintegrated into components that can be assembled in several configurations as moods and needs dictate (Fig. 525). And increasingly we encounter the "sofa" that is nothing more than a flat pad or mattress strewn with many loose pillows (Fig. 526).

Chairs

For most people in the United States today, the greater part of our waking hours are spent sitting down. We work, study, relax, eat, and travel in a seated position. Leading such sedentary lives, we should be expert sitters; but we are not, because until recently no serious studies of sitting had been made. Now, however, we know that maximum comfort results when weight and pressure are distributed and tension eased by having:

- The height of the seat somewhat less than the length of the sitter's lower legs, so that the feet rest on the floor and the legs be relaxed
- The depth of the seat a bit less than the length of the upper leg to avoid putting a pressure point under the knee
- The width of the seat ample enough to permit some movement
- The seat shaped or resilient, so that pressure is not concentrated on the small weight-bearing edge of the pelvis
- Both seat and back tilted backward slightly to buttress the weight
- The angle between seat and back 95 degrees or more
- The chair back in a position to support the small of the sitter's back
- The position of the seat and back adjustable for different persons (as in typists' chairs) or for different ways of relaxing (as in the old-fashioned Morris chairs and some of the new reclining chairs)
- A place to rest the head and relax the neck, plus supports for arms

The wing chair was one of the first types of seating devised for comfort. Over the years many variations have appeared. A contemporary design by Charles Eames (Fig. 527) resulted from a thorough exploration of new and old materials and techniques and a detailed study of sitting comfort, which showed that flexibility is essential. The Eames version has been so successful and has achieved such wide popularity that innumerable copies have appeared over the years.

527. Charles Eames' swivel lounge chair of molded rosewood with cushioned leather upholstery adjusts to many positions; with the ottoman, it promises complete semireclining luxury. (*Museum of Modern Art, New York, gift of the manufacturer, Herman Miller, Inc.*)

528–530. New experiments have caused some designers to reevaluate the ideal proportions for various furniture pieces. In these diagrams, the first number is that currently recommended, the number in parentheses the dimension considered standard up to now. (*Adapted from* Nomadic Furniture)

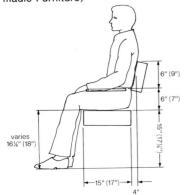

528. Armchair dimensions.

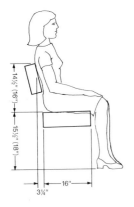

529. Side chair dimensions.

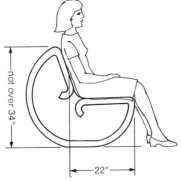

530. Easy chair dimensions.

531. An easy chair designed by Mario Bellini would provide maximum comfort for relaxed activities. (*Courtesy Atelier International, Ltd.*)

In their book *Nomadic Furniture,* James Hennessey and Victor Papanek offer a series of sketches (Figs. 528–530) as suggested measurements for making chairs and, by extension, for buying them. These figures differ from the ones typically recommended; on the drawings, the parenthetical number is the size of chairs generally available today, the first number the one the authors have determined from measurements made of themselves, their families, and friends. Beyond this, they advise measuring the actual users for the best fit. Chairs meant for people who fall outside the 5-foot-5inch to 6-foot range could well vary seat heights and depths for greatest comfort, rather than forcing them always to accommodate to an "average" world. Children need child-size furniture, while exceptionally tall or heavy people have quite different requirements.

Chairs serve a number of purposes, and their forms should mirror their functions. The typical household needs chairs suitable to at least three categories of activity.

Relaxed Activities   In the group space, in a study or seclusion room, and in bedrooms if possible, it is desirable to have seating that allows each person who regularly uses the room to relax completely for reading or simply for a brief "quiet time." The Eames chair (Fig. 527) and other types of reclining furniture meet this specification, as do sofas and most well-cushioned chairs, which adjust to varying individuals and are comfortable over long periods. Padded upholstered chairs and rocking chairs (Figs. 531, 532) have long remained favorites for relaxing, but new designs expand the range of flexibility for supercomfortable chairs (Fig. 533). Also, new types of springs and foams have greatly decreased weight and enable us to obtain pieces that are trim and neat, or even big and bulky but still movable.

Relaxed-Alert Activities   Talking, listening to music, watching television, and similar pursuits can be enjoyed in the kinds of seating described above, but smaller side chairs that are fairly easy to move and give good support make helpful adjuncts. Such chairs can have shaped seats of wood, metal, or plastic, or they might be lightly upholstered, webbed, canvas-covered, or caned (Figs. 534, 535). Whatever the material, these chairs should be easy to grasp, light to lift, and strong enough to withstand frequent moving.

above left: 532. An old refinished rocking chair adds a nostalgic note to this contemporary bedroom with redwood paneled walls, but it also gives good back support and a remarkable sense of ease to the sitter. (*Courtesy Simpson Timber Company*)

above right: 533. A convertible mattress-lounge chair of fabric-covered polyurethane foam depends on belts and buckles to hold it together when serving as a chair. Umberto Catalano and Gianfranco Masi, designers. (*Photograph: Aldo Ballo*)

left: 534. A spring base and frame of metal with overlapping leather upholstery straps makes a lightweight but comfortable chair. (*Courtesy Herman Miller, Inc.*)

below: 535. A continuous metal frame covered with rattan results in a chair that is very light to move about. The cantilever construction gives a comfortable springiness to the design. (*Courtesy Founders Furniture, Inc.*)

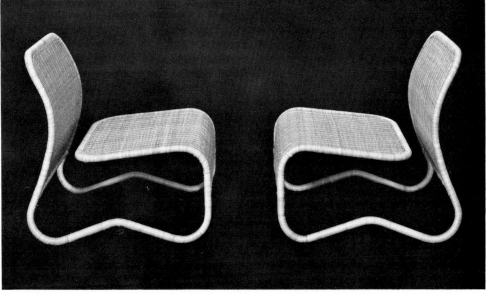

above: 536. A favorite since its conception in 1925 by designer Josef Hoffmann, the Prague bentwood armchair is a comfortable and handsome pull-up chair for many uses. (*Courtesy Stendig, Inc.*)

top right: 537. One of the newest designs in pull-up chairs is this adjustable swivel-and-tilt armchair that is essentially two comfortable foam cushions attached to a cast-aluminum frame. Andrew Ivar Morrison and Bruce R. Hannah, designers. (*Courtesy Knoll International*)

above right: 538. This chair—with its simple wood frame and sling seat and back—would be comfortable for dining, playing cards, or moving up to a conversation group. See also Fig. 553. (*Courtesy C. I. Designs*)

Alert Activities   Dining, working, and games require sturdy, easily moved chairs with relatively upright backs to keep the sitters alert; seats and backs that are shaped or lightly padded to lessen pressure; and upholstery that resists abrasion and dirt (Figs. 536–538). The most frequently used group dining space should have enough chairs or built-in seating always ready to accommodate the entire household, but it is helpful to have more of the same type of pull-up chairs (not necessarily identical) to bring out for larger gatherings.

Tables

The essence of table design calls for supporting a flat slab off the floor. This is reduced to its lowest common denominator when a home craftsman balances a piece of plywood or a flush door on prefabricated, easy-to-attach metal or wood legs or sometimes on a pair of sawhorses—which, incidentally, is an inexpensive way to get a striking table. There are problems, however, in all table design, and these include providing for:

☐ Necessary strength and stability
☐ Supports out of the way of feet and legs
☐ The right height, size, and shape for its use
☐ Durable materials

As with chairs, each home needs a variety of tables that differ in function and therefore in size, shape, height, and materials.

539. A dining table of oak and rosewood expands with two 18-inch leaves to seat six to eight people. (*Courtesy Dunbar*)

Dining Tables   Sit-down meals require a table that is sturdy enough not to be jarred by the unpredictable movements of children or the force of someone carving meat; that has a top large enough to give each person at least 2 feet of elbow room and high enough to allow leg room between the chair and the lower surface; that keeps supports out of the way of sitters' feet and knees; and that can be extended in size if necessary. Rather than extending a table, many people now use more than one for a larger crowd, if the space available permits this.

The surface of a dining table will be an important feature in its selection, because this—covered or uncovered—will form a background for china, crystal, silver, and linens. Plate 55 (p. 419) shows a unique solution to the question of table coverings. Here the entire surface of the plastic table has been illuminated with a hidden light source. The quality of light shining through the table depends upon the color and degree of opacity of the table covering, in this instance a thin yellow plastic sheet. Tablecloths have become increasingly rare for daily meals, often being replaced by mats, so it pays to look closely at the durability, ease of maintenance, and beauty of the top surface.

Shape is the other major consideration in choosing a dining table. Most are rectangular, because a basically squared shape harmonizes with rectangular rooms, can be pushed snugly against a wall or into a corner, and is slightly less costly to make (hence to buy). In the right place, however, a round or oval table will give an inimitable friendly feeling. Many kinds of rectangular, round, or oval tables can be extended with leaves (Fig. 539)—the round thus becoming an oval. A polygonal or odd-shape table makes a refreshing change and gives a handcrafted quality (Fig. 540). Drop-leaf tables, in use since Elizabethan days, expand or

540. Fitted together like a jigsaw puzzle, this hand-crafted table of random-shape boards has an outside octagonal contour. A beautiful, natural piece such as this should never be hidden by a cloth. (*Photograph: Barry Shapiro, from* Handmade Houses)

left: 541. This walnut drop-leaf table occupies minimum space when closed and pushed against the wall, but with the leaves opened it is sufficiently large for dining or games. Lawrence Hunter, designer. (*Photograph: Richard Gross*)

below: 542. A low, sturdy table in front of the fireplace anchors the seating group and provides extra storage space for magazines, matches, and miscellany. The table is part of a modular system that supplies continuity to the room's theme of informal comfort. (*Courtesy Armstrong Cork Company, Founders Furniture, Inc.*)

below left: 543. A sewing table with functionally planned drawers and drop leaves can double as an occasional table almost anywhere in the house. Hans J. Wegner, designer. (*Courtesy Pacific Overseas Inc.*)

below right: 544. The "Poker" table designed by Joe Colombo has removable legs for easy storage. Swivel-out panels hold glasses and other effects to prevent them from being knocked over. (*Photograph: Aldo Ballo*)

contract with ease (Fig. 541). Some contemporary folding tables can be compacted to 9 inches or stretched to 110 inches, which latter dimension provides space for fourteen people.

It is important to check dining chairs and tables together, because often their legs interfere with each other, the heights of the two are not coordinated, or the space between chair and table is insufficient for the sitters' comfort.

Coffee Tables   We have come to think that no sofa is complete unless faced with a long, low table on which ashtrays, books, magazines, newspapers, accessories, plants, flowers, and snacks abound. Most coffee tables, though, seem to have been designed only for the long, low, open look; they have no storage space for the little things needed in a conversation area, are too low to be reached comfortably from the sofa and to give foot room, and if in scale with the sofa usually block traffic. The most useful coffee tables are about 20 inches high and offer some storage space (Fig. 542). Their tops are durable and their supports strong, so they cannot be tipped easily.

Occasional Tables   It might be said that the old-fashioned living room table that once sat in the middle of the room disintegrated into many little tables; convenience now seems to demand a horizontal surface, however small, within reach of every seat. Thus we often find a table at each end of the sofa and one for each group of chairs. Unlike coffee tables, occasional tables seldom interfere with the legs of sitters and may provide shelves or drawers for supplementary storage (Fig. 543). They look better if they are of the same height as the arms of upholstered sofas and chairs, but a somewhat lower or higher level makes for greater convenience and diminishes spillage of beverages. Occasional tables often hold lamps, although strictly speaking a lamp table should be a little higher. Nests of tables, the top one acting as an end or coffee table, greatly simplify entertaining, as do stacking tables (Fig. 513). Clusters of cubes not only serve the same purpose but double as extra seating.

Card and Game Tables   Although rarely handsome, the folding or break-down card table is a wonderful invention (Fig. 544). Most people find it more comfortable to play cards and other games at tables several inches lower than those meant for eating. Collapsible card tables are ideal for occasional games, bridge luncheons, buffet suppers, and supplementary serving at festive dinners. Space permitting, a permanent card table with at least two chairs always handy could be a fixture in any household where games or casual eating occur frequently.

Kitchen Tables   Once banished in the drive for compact efficiency, tables in kitchens or adjacent alcoves have again found popularity. Since they often serve for eating and meal preparation, they differ from dining tables only in having greater strength and durability.

Desks   An efficient desk has two essential properties: a suitable writing surface and convenient and accessible storage for papers and supplies. It should be obvious that every household needs at least one good writing place, but the size, complexity, and location of the unit will depend on individual propensities. A desk can be a table with only one or two drawers (Fig. 511), a compartment in a modular unit (Fig. 512), or a piece of furniture designed for serious work (Fig. 77). Space-saving devices include writing surfaces that fold or slide out of the way. A vertical file drawer or two is the most sensible place to store compactly all the pieces of paper related to household operation. The file can be part of a desk or purchased separately in units of one to four drawers. A two-drawer unit makes a good pedestal for an instant desk, with a piece of plywood for the top and a support of some kind at the other end.

545. A relatively small number of components can be fitted together in almost endless configurations to suit exacting storage requirements in this furniture system. Doors can be attached to the various sections if desired. (*Courtesy International Contract Furnishings*)

Storage Units

Storage is a major problem today. Living quarters have steadily become smaller, while attics, spare rooms, basements, barns, and sheds have all but disappeared. More people have more things to put away and apparently less time in which to do it. Yet many favor the uncluttered, clean-lined look, and having the proverbial "place for everything" does simplify housekeeping. This suggests the following measures:

☐ Discard things that are neither used nor enjoyed.
☐ Cut down on purchases of unnecessary articles, especially bulky ones.
☐ Plan active storage in terms of the criteria listed on page 72.
☐ Provide as much dead-storage space as needed for seasonal objects of all sizes and shapes. Typical households can use space equivalent to that of a one-car garage (10 by 20 feet), but greater convenience results when this space is distributed where it is needed, rather than concentrated in one spot.

All of this means giving at least as much thought to storage in all parts of the home as is typically devoted to the kitchen. Convenience, visibility, accessibility, flexibility, and maintenance are just as important in group spaces and bedrooms. Examples of the ideal to be sought include tapes and records near the player, books convenient to reading chairs, toys where children play.

A total concept of household storage goes beyond what most of us call furniture, because efficient storage is part of overall home design. The minimum that one should expect is empty space for cupboards and chests, for suitcases, strollers, bicycles, outdoor furniture, and the like. These facilities can be built into the house or added as modular units.

We store things by standing them on floors or shelves, by hanging them on walls or the backs of doors, by suspending them from ceilings, or by putting them in drawers or chests. Which of these solutions is best depends upon the use, size, shape, fragility, and value of the object to be stored.

Bookshelves   The simplest pieces of storage furniture are bookshelves. Despite the fact that books come in many different sizes and shapes, easily adjustable shelves can store them efficiently. Books on open shelves do get dusty, but they make a handsome display and also absorb noise. Nowadays, bookcases generally double as display space for all sorts of objects that have aesthetic value or interest.

Nearly every room can profit by some book and magazine storage. In the kitchen a single shelf may store all the family's cookbooks, while a bookcase or a few shelves in the living area and in bedrooms suffices to hold current reading materials. The principal center for the household's collection of books could be the living room, dining area (Pl. 6, p. 41), study (Fig. 77), family room, or even a separate library or gallery (Pl. 45, p. 317). Low bookcases double as tables and—if sufficiently long and well planned—can unify a wall. A bookcase that reaches to the ceiling often becomes a forceful architectural element. Shelves can frame and relate doors and windows or serve as freestanding partial or complete dividers between two rooms or parts of a single room.

Drawers   Although we take sliding drawers for granted, they were not widely used until the 17th century. Chests of drawers work best when they have strongly joined, dustproof drawers that slide easily and handles that can be grasped without difficulty. Shallow drawers at the top are a great convenience, and flexible dividers for them well justify their cost. Relatively small units that fit together increase flexibility of placement. Drawers combined with shelves and/or cabinets of different sizes can store a multitude of variously shaped items (Fig. 545).

Cabinets   Although they appear infrequently outside kitchens, dining space, and bathrooms, cabinets with doors and adjustable shelves or vertical dividers are welcome in every room. The family room illustrated in Figure 546 has a combination unit incorporating cabinets, drawers, and open shelves, which not only serves for storage and display but acts as a partial room divider between sections of the space.

Doors on cabinets present the same problems as doors between rooms. Swinging doors work easily and accept narrow storage racks on the back, but they get in the way when open. Sliding doors open only part of the cabinet at a time and allow for no door-back shelves. When space in front of cabinets is at a premium—or

546. Modular cabinets and drawers assembled into a unit placed at right angles to the wall articulate one section of a long, narrow family room, while providing much useful storage space. (*Courtesy U.S. Plywood, Champion International*)

547. Architect Wendell H. Lovett planned stereo equipment as part of the design motifs of circular and rectangular forms in the living room of a music-oriented household. See also Figs. 211, 483. (*Photograph: Christian Staub*)

when doors are left open while people move about—sliding doors offer a good solution, but in other places swinging doors have distinct advantages.

Cabinets for radios, stereo components, and television sets have no historical precedents; hence, the early ones were overly conspicuous. Nowadays, audio-visual equipment is often integrated with cabinets and bookshelves (Fig. 37) or is built into the wall, where it may become a striking design element (Fig. 547). Perhaps because they are highly engineered pieces of technology that lend themselves to visual expression of function, stereo components emerged quite early from the dark ages of pseudo-style. Television sets, with their unfortunate bulk and blank faces when not operating, lingered longer either in cabinets that tried to disguise their identities or in the plainest of black boxes. Designers are now attempting to develop more imaginative solutions (Figs. 181, 582). Too, we are growing less aware of the unlighted screen, just as we accept the unlit fireplace.

Outdoor Furniture

Interest in outdoor living has led to many kinds of weather-resistant furniture in a surprisingly wide range of materials. Redwood, cedar, and cypress are long-lasting and attractive (Fig. 548). Aluminum never rusts, stays cool in the sun, and is light in weight (Fig. 331). Wicker and rattan bring the charm of natural materials to an outdoor living area (Fig. 549). Some of the newer plastics stand weathering quite well and are a good solution for use either indoors or out (Fig. 550).

Tables present no special problems, nor do the frames of chairs and chaises, but it is not easy to make upholstery both weatherproof and resilient. Few springs, cushions, and pads remain unharmed by a lot of water, although some plastic materials can take moderate amounts. The seating most nearly approaching carefree comfort has metal frames with synthetic-webbing seats and backs (Fig. 331). Then come the wood, plastic, or metal chairs and lounges with cushions, which should not be left out in the rain. For the latter, it is advisable to have a roofed outdoor living area or weathertight storage nearby.

Materials and Construction

There is no quick and easy way to size up furniture materials and construction. When buying new furniture we could all save much time and disappointment if the manufacturer's specifications were available for each line—a provision consumer groups have been advocating. Lacking these guidelines, you will do well to look at every piece of furniture literally from every angle; to get all possible information from the salesclerk; and to try to purchase only from stores that stand behind their merchandise. Furniture can be no better than the materials, the joinings, and the finishes that go into its makeup. Some preliminary test questions include the following:

left: 548. Chairs, benches, and a table of weather-resistant redwood require little maintenance. A fence, screen, and overhead protection define the outdoor living area, give it privacy and shade. Henry Hill, architect. (*Photograph: Morley Baer*)

below left: 549. Woven rattan furniture is remarkably weatherproof, although it would deteriorate if exposed to much rain or snow. The distinctive design of this chair, however, would render it equally useful indoors. Danny Ho Fong, designer. (*Photograph: Richard Gross*)

below right: 550. Fiberglass furniture withstands weathering and can be left outdoors even in severe climates. Its new forms add interest to the garden scene. This version is by Homecrest Designs. (*Courtesy Owens/Corning Fiberglass*)

□ Does the piece stand firmly on the floor and resist efforts to make it wobble? This is particularly important in tables (even more so in expandable ones), as well as in desks and chairs.

□ Do all movable parts, such as drawers and drop leaves, operate easily and steadily?

□ Are all joints tightly and smoothly fitted together with some type of interlocking construction?

□ Is the finish durable, smooth, and evenly applied? Is it composed of one or many coats properly applied or of one or two coats that look thick and gummy in any crevice or indentation?

Having answered these questions, you should next look at the points of greatest wear and stress.

Flat surfaces—tops of tables, desks, counters, bookcases, cabinets, and chests—should resist scratching, denting, breaking, staining, and wetting. Properly finished hardwoods generally prove satisfactory if kept reasonably free from liquids. Plastic finishes on wood are durable, some exceedingly so; however, the problems of refinishing such surfaces have not been solved completely. Vinyl tiles or sheets provide quiet and good resistance to stains and cuts, while plastic laminates are even more durable but noisier. We have not yet come to the point of considering wear on plastics as a plus factor, as we may on wood that shows its age but has been lovingly cared for or restored. Glass is light and airy but presents a breakage hazard; it also requires almost constant cleaning. Marble, although rich and heavy, makes a noisy surface that can break and stain.

Edges of tables, doors, and drawers are the points most easily nicked and marred. All but the most durable materials will show wear, but hardwood or replaceable metal or plastic strips help.

Runners of drawers should be made from hardwood, plastics, or noncorrosive metals. Large and heavy drawers are best suspended on rollers and tracks.

Handles, knobs, and hinges show ample evidence of the use they get in the soil that collects on and around them. Hardwoods and dull metals are still the most serviceable materials, but plastics now have taken over a portion of the field. Hinges should be of the best possible quality and securely fastened into a base material hard enough to hold screws under strain. Plastics have one important advantage in furniture manufacture in that functional devices can be part of the unit itself, rather than being applied, which makes them much more durable. Of course, if self-handles and hinges *should* be broken, repair might be difficult or impossible.

Legs and bases suffer assault from kicking feet, mops and brooms, vacuum cleaners, and children's toys. Damage can be reduced by minimizing the number of parts that touch the floor and then having these made of medium-dark wood, plastic, or metal, with finishes that do not scratch or chip readily. Indenting bases so they are not easily seen and covering them with carpet are two other possibilities.

The following sections list the virtues and drawbacks of various materials for furniture and the ways in which these materials are fabricated.

Wood

The standard furniture material, wood should be thoroughly dry and of a variety that is stable in size and shape to minimize shrinking, swelling, and warping. Each wood has its own qualities, and the knowing craftsman may combine several kinds in one piece. Structural parts need not take a good finish but are best when of strong wood, such as ash or birch. Exposed surfaces ought to wear well, be hard enough to resist scratching and denting, have a pleasant finish, and be beautiful in themselves; mahogany, walnut, oak, maple, and birch display these qualities. Redwood has a pleasant color and stands weather, but it is soft and splintery.

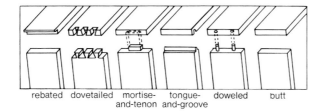

rebated   dovetailed   mortise-   tongue-   doweled   butt
and-tenon and-groove

The advantages of plywood have been discussed, and some hard-pressed composition boards prove their value for tabletops, backs of chests, and parts of drawers.

Wood in furniture can be joined in a number of ways (Fig. 551):

- □ **Rebated** or rabbeted joints have a groove cut from the edge of one piece to receive the other member.
- □ **Dovetailed** joints have flaring tenons (or tongues) on one piece and mortises (or grooves) on the other. They are used in most good drawers.
- □ **Mortise-and-tenon** joints have a mortise (a hole or cavity) in one piece of wood into which a tenon (projecting piece) cut in the end of the other fits securely. They are usually stronger than doweled joints.
- □ **Tongue-and-groove** joints resemble mortise-and-tenon joints, except that the tongue and groove extend the width of the boards.
- □ **Doweled** joints have wooden pegs (or dowels) inserted into holes in the two pieces of wood to be joined.
- □ **Butt** joints are the simplest and the weakest; they have no place in furniture unless reinforced with corner blocks.

Most joints need glue to reinforce them, and synthetic resins have joined the older vegetable and casein glues for this purpose. Frames of chairs, sofas, and case goods also require triangular wood or metal corner blocks tightly screwed and cemented in place for reinforcing. Screws strengthen joints much more than nails do.

Until a few decades ago wood joints were among the highlights of a fine piece of furniture—the sign of a master craftsman. After a period in which joinings declined in both interest and quality, we are now beginning to see again the emphasis on wood joints as things of beauty and structural design (Figs. 284, 552). Some of the newer knock-down furniture does away with rigid joints so that the pieces can be disassembled for moving (Figs. 13, 553).

top: 551. The ways in which wood is joined critically affect the durability and appearance of furniture. This illustration shows the most typical joints.

below left: 552. Simple board furniture, in which the method of joining is clearly exposed, has an ingenuous but ingratiating quality. Roger Fleck, designer. (*Courtesy Bluepeter, Inc.*)

below right: 553. In a meticulously crafted wood and leather chair, a simple dowel holds the sling back in place. See also Fig. 538. (*Courtesy C. I. Designs*)

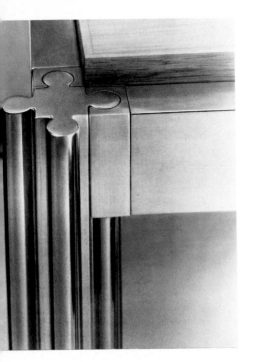

Metal

Mass-produced metal furniture is relatively inexpensive, which is a factor in its popularity. In recent years designers have begun to exploit metal for its inherent structural properties, finding it uniquely suitable for pieces that are strong and durable but not bulky. Steel with a baked enamel finish is familiar in kitchens and bathroom cabinets, as well as in indoor-outdoor chairs and tables. It comes in many colors, is easy to wash, and maintains its good appearance if not kicked or banged. Steel is also widely used for legs and frames of chairs, tables, and storage units. Rods and tubes of steel can be coated with any color, and some metallic enamels have a soft but rich glow. Chromium-plating gives lasting protection and surfaces that range, visually, from glittering hardness to pewterlike mellowness.

Notably different from the earlier "pipe and angle-iron" designs are those based on the sculptural potentialities of metal itself. In the hands of a sensitive designer steel wire becomes an inspirational, responsive medium for chairs that are both graceful and comfortable (Fig. 194). Lightweight and nonrusting aluminum has also led designers to explore forms that have no association with plumbing shops or forges. Some of the sculptured pieces are elegant far beyond their cost. Aluminum's natural color is pleasantly sympathetic, but it can be permanently treated with a wide range of hues.

Metal can be joined by welding, riveting, bolting, or just shaping. Welding gives smooth, strong joints, but bolts and rivets suffice if you do not mind seeing what holds the pieces together. In Figure 554 the legs are shaped from solid aluminum ingots to fit like pieces of a jigsaw puzzle into the receptive frame. Most metal furniture is so much stronger than normal household use demands that construction generally presents less of a problem to the consumer than does furniture made of wood. However, repairs are much more difficult.

Plastics

Synthetic materials have affected furniture design and maintenance in three markedly different ways. Most obvious are the durable surfaces—vinyl and laminated melamine sheets for tabletops and counter tops, vinyl upholstery for chairs and sofas—that have greatly extended the range of easily kept colors. More striking is the use of molded plastics for chairs and tables (Figs. 340, 513). Thin and lightweight, amazingly strong yet slightly resilient, polyester reinforced with fiberglass can be molded so that the seat, back, and arms of the chair are one continuous piece, thus eliminating the need for joining. The plastic shell, much warmer and more pleasant to touch than metal, can be left as is, coated with vinyl, or upholstered with foam rubber and fabric. Transparent or translucent plastics, such as Plexiglas and Lucite, offer designers opportunities for a totally new vocabulary in furniture design (Fig. 555).

Foamed plastics represent an even newer development—one that has radically changed the look of certain types of furniture over the last decade. Foams have also revived the bulky look in furniture, although in this instance it is bulk without weight. These cellular plastics are quite versatile, since the density can be controlled to produce either rigid structural parts or soft cushioning (Fig. 514). Integral-skin foams on some pieces of furniture eliminate the need for separate upholstery (Fig. 355).

Certain of the foamed plastic units need no joining; they are simply blocks of the material, perhaps enclosed within a rigid frame. Others have zippers or buckles to hold the coverings of variously shaped blocks together; a few types are built up of shaped slabs of foam in different densities held in place by contact cement.

Exciting as these developments are, they must be regarded with some caution. As has been mentioned, the possibility exists for eventual dulling or discoloration,

554. Furniture made from interlocking metal legs and rails is very strong, demountable, and capable of being combined in many ways. The four-sided leg joint brings a sculptural quality to the plain structure. George Ciancimino, designer. (*Courtesy Jens Risom, Design, Inc.*)

555. A chair molded from a single slab of Lucite gains resiliency from its cantilever shape. (*Courtesy John Harra Studio*)

left: 556. A maharajah's chair and two stools of rattan—plus the profusion of tropical plants—transform this American terrace into an exotic Eastern garden. (*Photograph: Ezra Stoller* ⓒ *ESTO*)

above: 557. Although usually thought of an inexpensive and casual, rattan furniture can be as formal and elegant as the designer makes it. Here the rigid rattan has been bound at the joints with rawhide for an extremely durable construction. (*Courtesy McGuire Company; photograph: Ezra Stoller* ⓒ *ESTO*)

pitting or scratching, even breakage or breakdown of the material. To date, repair or refinishing runs the short gamut from difficult to impossible. Problems of flammability and ultimate solid waste disposal have still to be worked out. Of course, these are common problems with wood and metal also, but the natural materials have been around longer, so their dangers, environmental insults, and recycling possibilities are fairly well known. With plastics, it becomes a matter of learning as we go along, of insisting on more thorough testing and disclosure.

Upholstered Furniture

The padding and covering put on chairs and sofas to make them conform to our contours can be of several degrees of comfort.

Fabric Stretched on a Frame   Until the Renaissance, upholstery consisted chiefly of textiles, rushes, or leather stretched over frames and often supplemented by loose cushions. Furniture with backs and seats of leather or fabric is still common today (Fig. 13) and provides lightweight, inexpensive resilience. The use of cane, rush, wicker, or rattan for furniture parts or whole pieces also prevails; in cost and extent it ranges from the cane seats familiar in bentwood and other occasional chairs (Fig. 189); through exotic imitations of Eastern furniture (Fig. 556); to the elegant rattan pieces that would be at home in the most formal setting (Fig. 557). The latter two types often have upholstered cushions for greater comfort. In any event, the frame on which fabric is stretched should be strong as well as attractive, the upholstery durable and securely fastened to the frame but easily removable (Fig. 553).

Simple Padding   The next step in comfortable seating would be a padding made from thin layers of resilient materials covered with fabric and secured to a frame. Since the 17th century this has been the standard way of making frequently moved chairs comfortable. Until recently, long curled hair was the best and most costly padding, with kapok, moss, and cotton relegated to less expensive pieces. But today, various types of foam padding are more common. As a rule this arrangement takes the form of a foam cushion on a plywood base, on webbing, or on a sling of resilient material (Fig. 558). Zippered covers make cleaning easy, and in some cases the foam may have a plastic fabric laminated to it, which means it can simply be wiped with a damp sponge.

Stuffing and Springs   Although furniture designers began to place springs under stuffing during the 18th century, it was not until about 1914 that massively overstuffed pieces came into fashion. The materials and steps of this complicated process, a version of which is shown in Figure 559, may include:

□ **Frame** of strong wood with secure joinings or of metal or plastic
□ **Webbing** woven in a simple basket weave and tacked to the frame
□ **Springs** usually coiled, tied to the webbing and frame and close enough to prevent sagging but not so close that they rub against one another
□ **Burlap** covering the springs to protect the padding
□ **Padding** or stuffing (similar to simple padding), which gives smooth, soft contours
□ **Muslin** to cover the padding (only on better furniture)
□ **Final fabric** hiding all of the above and presenting its finished appearance to the world

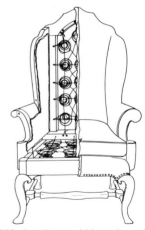

left: 558. Leather webbing slung from a wood frame and padded with leather-covered cushions makes these twin sofas both comfortable and practical. Robert L. Rotner, architect. See also Fig. 629. (*Photograph: James Brett*)

above: 559. This drawing shows in cross section the several components of stuffing-and-spring upholstery.

560. Wing chairs upholstered in a tapestry-weave fabric seem comfortably at home in this converted barn setting, with many old objects used as enrichment. See also Figs. 499, 621. (*Photograph: John T. Hill*)

As a rule, only the last of these—and perhaps some of the frame—will be visible, so it deserves special attention.

Upholstery Fabrics   Fabrics become almost an integral part—and the most conspicuous part—of the furniture to which they are fastened, and they are what we usually touch. In a sense, then, upholstery fabrics could be considered furniture. The least we might expect is that they look comfortable to sit on, feel good to hands and arms, and resist abrasion and soil. Visual relationship to the shape they cover and the setting in which they are placed lifts them above mere usefulness (Fig. 560). Beyond this are fabrics with their own distinctiveness or those treated with originality (Fig. 367).

Seeing identical pieces of furniture covered with varied fabrics alerts us to the forcefulness of color and design in altering the apparent shape, size, and character of any form (Figs. 561, 562). In rooms with several or many upholstered items, the whole effect can be changed with different furniture covers. All that we know about the psychological effects of hue and value, emphasis and scale, can be brought to bear in selecting upholstery. Also strategic is a knowledge of fibers, yarns, and weaves—of how, for example, wool compares with cotton or silk or nylon or vinyl. In upholstery fabrics, it pays to look for long fibers and tightly twisted yarns, for weaves that are firm, because loosely woven textiles snag easily. Pile weaves and flat weaves behave very differently, as do solid colors and patterns. Leather has long since earned its place because of durability and easy maintenance: its surface is pleasant to touch and to look at. Today, leather has been challenged by plastic fabrics that give excellent service in hard-wear situations and come in a vast array of colors and textures.

Planned Buying

Without a plan, the acquisition of furniture can become as frantic and disordered as holiday shopping often is. In fact, it can be even worse than holiday shopping, because much more money is involved, and one has to live with one's purchases. However, the plan should not be a static blueprint, but rather something that grows and develops. A sensible approach calls for buying the large essential pieces first, then filling in with the smaller and less costly items. Over the first two years of home planning, it might work out this way:

First Year	Second Year
living room	
sofa or mattress on a platform	one or two chairs
one easy chair and one side chair or two of either type	occasional tables
	desk
coffee table	draperies if needed
carpet or area rug	accessories
a lamp or two	
flexible window treatment	
dining space	
table	two more chairs
four chairs	additional storage units if needed
carpet or rug	draperies if needed
window treatment if needed	accessories
bedroom(s)	
springs and mattresses on legs or frames, or mattresses on platforms	bedside tables
	room-size rug, if desired
chest of drawers for each person	accessories
mirror	draperies if needed
one chair	
lamps	
area rugs	
window treatment	

Obviously, this conventional system will not work equally well for everyone. Many individuals and families are perfectly willing to spend a year or two living with orange crate furniture and bare windows in order to be able to afford an extraordinary Oriental rug they will have for a lifetime—to give only one possible example. Others might pour all of their savings into sophisticated stereo components or a magnificent piano, letting the rest of the household equipment manage as best it can. It is really a matter of what each family considers most important.

561–562. The same piece of furniture can take on very different characteristics depending on the upholstery fabric used.

above: 561. A wing chair upholstered in velvet.

right: 562. A wing chair upholstered in leather.

Instead of firm rules, then, you should follow general guidelines insofar as they apply to your own goals and ideals:

☐ Take your time and avoid impulse buying, especially when it involves a great deal of money. The piece of furniture you keep coming back to again and again in the shop or catalogue or whatever will be the one to give enduring pleasure.

☐ Buy only what you are sure you need or want.

☐ Keep in mind the total pattern of your furnishings, but also buy only those pieces that are good in their own right.

☐ Express yourself and your own personal lifestyle, rather than trying to imitate or impress your friends.

Arranging Furniture

Furniture arrangement is a matter of coordinating furnishings with both people and architecture. To do this well we need to consider the alternative ways in which furniture can be positioned and the amount of space needed for these placements.

Group Spaces

Even the tiniest homes benefit by having the spaces devoted to group activity demarcated—definitively or subtly—into different zones. We will consider three possibilities: a primary seating group, a secondary seating group, and a home entertainment area.

Primary Seating Group   The major conversation center is typically the dominant furniture group in any home. When a home has only one such relaxation area, this grouping may also serve for music and television, reading and buffet suppers, even games, although the noisier activities should be segregated if at all possible. Studies of small-group interaction have shown that people like to sit opposite each other at some slight angle unless there is too much space between, in which case they choose to sit side by side.[1] In large, impersonal spaces the limits of the opposite seating configuration seem to be about 5½ feet between heads, but evidence indicates that in the home conversational distance can be much longer because of the smaller scale and lower noise level.

Basically, we can say that the most satisfactory major conversation groups are more or less circular in shape and allow a maximum distance between people of 8 to 10 feet. The furniture is usually, although not always, stabilized in some way: in a corner, around a window wall or fireplace, or built up into a substantial arrangement (Figs. 563, 564). Possibilities for seating configurations include:

□ Seating units in a generally circular or rectangular arrangement around a table
□ Sofa with a chair or two at each side, all facing a coffee table (Fig. 565)
□ Two sofas opposite each other or one sofa facing two chairs, often at right angles to a fireplace or other center of interest in large rooms
□ Two sofas at right angles to each other or one sofa at right angles to two chairs, often in a corner although one unit may project into the room
□ Entirely mobile units that can be changed at will

Circulation paths cannot be ignored; enough space must be left so that those sitting in a corner feel free to get in and out at will.

Secondary Seating Group A secondary conversation or reading center often supplements the major group in larger rooms (Figs. 566, 567). This usually is planned for one to four people and occupies a subdominant position. The possibilities include:

□ Two chairs and the necessary table angled toward each other
□ Two, three, or four seating units facing each other over a table

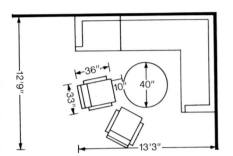

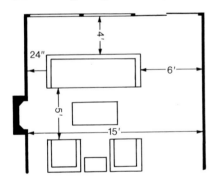

563–564. Two possibilities for arranging furniture in the major group space.

above: 563. A corner group with coffee table and occasional chairs.

below: 564. A sofa facing two easy chairs and set at right angles to a fireplace.

565. This pleasant family room has a comfortable sofa and two chairs for relaxing, a game table with upright chairs suitable for many activities. The window seat along the wall at right provides extra storage. George Nemeny, architect. (*Photograph: Ezra Stoller* © *ESTO*)

566–567. Two possibilities for a secondary furniture grouping in the main living space.

right: 566. Two easy chairs flanking a table with a reading lamp.

far right: 567. A game table with four chairs.

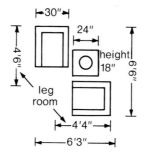

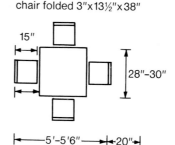

□ A built-in unit or window seat
□ Four chairs at the sides of a game or card table
□ A large lounge chair with a table and good lighting for relaxed reading

The room shown in Figure 565 has both a game table (partially visible at left) and a window seat in addition to the major conversation group.

Home Entertainment Area   The placement of home entertainment facilities —television sets, radios, stereo equipment, musical instruments—will be a serious consideration for any home, but particularly so when the household includes individuals with different interests or tastes.

   Television cabinets are conspicuous and often not very attractive, but they must be placed for comfortable viewing by a number of people. Several solutions are possible:

□ Relating a television set to a fireplace usually gives an unobstructed view from the major seating group, while minimizing the set's bulkiness (Fig. 582).
□ The set can be integrated with a storage wall or perhaps with a whole audio-visual center (Fig. 37).
□ A set on casters or a cart allows it to be moved into position for viewing, out of the way when not in use.
□ Sets on swivel mounts can be placed in walls or cabinets between two rooms where they will serve both.

   Radios and stereo components can be difficult to position satisfactorily; individual households vary greatly in the importance they place on such equipment.

□ Small radios and record players can be put almost anywhere but often are integrated with other cabinets.
□ Records and tapes require convenient storage space; if the collection is large, a corner of the room or part of one wall can be given over to them.
□ Combining equipment and record cabinets with other unit or built-in furniture keeps them accessible but not obtrusive.

   Pianos and similar instruments are large and impressive. They need free space around them to permit effective acoustics and the gathering of an audience.

□ Upright models can be flat against the wall or at right angles to partition a room.
□ Grand pianos are physically large and should not be crowded (Fig. 39). The curved side should face into the room for proper sound dispersion.
□ Pianos should be subjected to as little change in temperature as possible, suggesting placement away from windows or heating units.
□ An instrument that is also a beautifully crafted piece of furniture deserves a place of prominence (Pl. 56, p. 419).

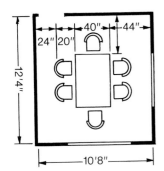

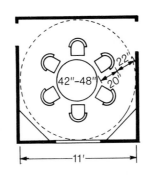

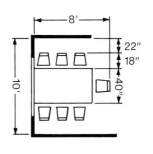

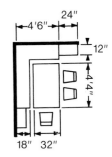

left: 570. A rectangular table with one short side placed against a wall.

right: 571. A table placed for built-in seating along two sides.

568–571. Four possibilities for the arrangement of dining furniture.

left: 568. A rectangular table in the center of the room.

right: 569. A round table in the center of the room.

Dining Space

Dining tables and seats, no matter what room they occupy, can be arranged in many ways, including the four shown in Figures 568 to 571.

□ A rectangular or round table in the center of a dining room or large kitchen, or at one end of the general group space, increases the importance of meals and simplifies serving. Figures 572 and 573 show standard sizes of rectangular and round tables, indicating the number of people they can accommodate.

□ A table with one end against the wall takes less floor space and fits into the room architecturally.

□ A table and seating in a corner, especially built-in, require minimum space and have the advantage of staying in position, but they somewhat complicate moving in and out as well as serving the meal.

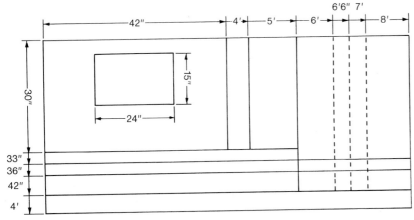

572. Standard sizes for rectangular dining tables. (*Adapted from* Nomadic Furniture)

573. Standard sizes for round dining tables. The figure in the center shows the number of people that can be accommodated comfortably by each. (*Adapted from* Nomadic Furniture)

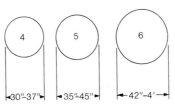
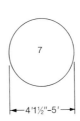
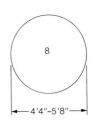
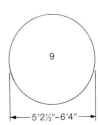

Bedrooms

The two major factors in arranging bedroom furniture are circulation paths and the placement of the bed or beds. The most-used traffic paths link the entrance door with the closets and drawer units, so these should be as short and direct as possible. Beds are large and inflexible; moreover, convenience usually enforces certain types of placements. Figures 574 to 576 show three possible bedroom arrangements, while Figure 577 gives the dimensions of standard-size mattresses. (Extra space must be allotted for head and footboards, Table 16.1.)

- Beds are typically, but not necessarily, placed with heads against a solid wall. Adequate space should be left on three sides for ease in making up the bed. Alternatively, the beds should have easily rolling casters.
- Single beds placed broadside against a wall or in a corner give more free space and can double as seating units, but they should be on easily rolling casters to facilitate making up.
- Double-decker beds conserve space very efficiently, but the upper bunk will be hard to make up.
- Drawer units are best next to or in closets, near windows if they have mirrors above, or both. Two chests side by side or one double chest will save space, as well as visually balancing the bulk of the bed.
- Drawers combined with cabinets and possibly a desk constitute a compact unit.
- A chair adjacent to the closet and drawer units completes the dressing center.
- An easy chair, a lamp, and a small table set near a window form a pleasant reading spot in a bedroom.

Furniture Sizes and Shapes

A working knowledge of the sizes and shapes of specific pieces of furniture helps immeasurably in arranging a room, as does familiarity with recommended clear-

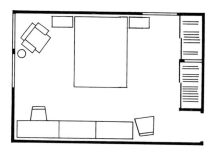

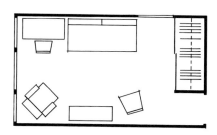

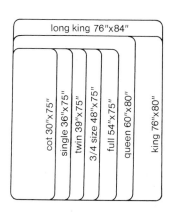

574–576. Three possibilities for the arrangement of bedroom furniture.

above left: 574. One large bed placed at right angles to the wall.

above right: 575. One single bed set parallel to the wall.

left: 576. Two single beds placed against adjacent walls and at right angles to each other.

right: 577. Standard mattress sizes. (*Adapted from* Nomadic Furniture)

ances between pieces, between furniture and walls, and so on. Figure 578 shows a selection of typical furniture items drawn to a scale of $\frac{1}{8}$ inch equaling 1 foot. Table 16.1 lists a range of sizes and shapes, but it must be borne in mind that custom, built-in, and free-form pieces can vary widely from these measurements.

Arranging Furniture on Paper

To save time and money, to avoid disappointments, you should know what you want and how it will fit into your space before buying or attempting to place furniture in rooms. Planning on paper is worth many times the small effort it takes.

- [ ] List all activities you want to provide for, the furnishings and equipment each requires.
- [ ] Make accurate drawings of the plan of each room so that $\frac{1}{2}$ or $\frac{1}{4}$ inch represents 1 foot. Cross-section paper helps greatly. First, measure total length and breadth of the rooms and draw the major outlines on paper. Then locate doors, windows, fireplaces, radiators or heating vents, jogs, and any built-in features.
- [ ] Make cardboard cutouts of your furniture, similar to those in Figure 578 but at the same scale as the drawings of your room. Label each one.
- [ ] Put the cutouts on the plan, placing large pieces first and working down in size to accessories. Move them until the arrangement seems best to you. Then check circulation paths by drawing them on the plan.
- [ ] Review the arrangement a day or so later and revise if necessary.

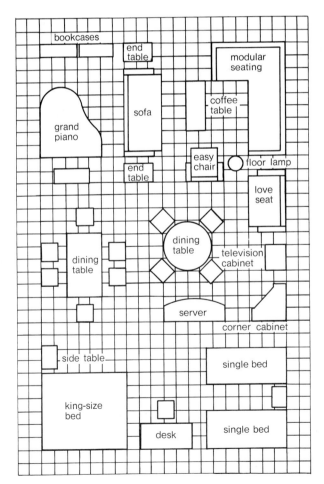

578. Becoming familiar with furniture sizes and shapes is an important early step in planning arrangements. Each square on this drawing represents 1 foot. (*Adapted from a drawing planned by Victor Thompson*)

Table 16.1 Furniture Sizes and Clearance Spaces

Living Room	Small		Large	
	Depth Width		Depth Width	
sofa	2'6" x 6'	to	3' x 9'	
love seat	2'6" x 4'	to	3' x 5'	
easy chair	2'6" x 2'4"	to	3'4" x 3'3"	
pull-up chair	1'6" x 1'6"	to	2' x 2'	
coffee table, oblong	1'6" x 3'	to	3' x 5'	
coffee table, round	2' diam.	to	4' diam.	
coffee table, square	2' x 2'	to	4' x 4'	
occasional table	1'6" x 10"	to	3' x 1'8"	
card table	2'6" x 2'6"	to	3' x 3'	
flattop desk	1'6" x 2'8"	to	3' x 6'	
secretary	1'6" x 2'8"	to	2' x 3'6"	
upright piano	2' x 4'9"	to	2'2" x 5'10"	
grand piano	5'10" x 4'10"	to	9' x 5'2"	
bookcase	9" x 2'6"	to	1' x —	

Clearances

traffic path, major	4' to 6'
traffic path, minor	1'4" to 4'
foot room between seating units and edge of top of coffee table	1'
floor space in front of chair or sofa for feet and legs	1'6" to 2'6"
chair or bench space in front of desk or piano	3'

Dining Area	Small		Large	
	Depth Width		Depth Width	
table, square, 4–8 people	2'6" x 2'6"	to	5' x 5'	
table, rectangle, 6–12 people	3' x 5'	to	4' x 8'	
table, round, 4–10 people	2'7" diam.	to	6'4" diam.	
straight chairs	1'4" x 1'4"	to	1'8" x 1'8"	
arm chairs	1'10" x 1'10"	to	2' x 2'	
buffet	1'8" x 4'	to	2' x 6'	
serving table	1'6" x 3'	to	2' x 4'	
china cabinet	1'6" x 3'	to	1'8" x 4'	

Clearances

space for occupied chairs	1'6" to 1'10"
space to get into chairs	1'10" to 3'
traffic path around table and occupied chairs for serving	1'6" to 2'

Bedroom	Small		Large	
	Depth Width		Depth Width	
twin bed, head and footboard	6'6" x 3'3"	to	7'6" x 3'8"	
full bed, head and footboard	6'6" x 4'6"	to	7'6" x 6'	
cot	5'9" x 3'			
crib	2' x 4'	to	2'6" x 4'6"	
night stand	1' x 1'3"	to	2' x 2'	
chest of drawers	1'6" x 2'6"	to	1'9" x 5'	
wardrobe or closet	1'7" x 3'1"	to	2' x —	
easy chair	2'4" x 2'4"	to	2'8" x 2'8"	
pull-up chair	1'3" x 1'6"	to	1'6" x 1'9"	

Clearances

space for making bed	1'6" to 2'
space between twin beds	1'6" to 2'4"
space fronting chest of drawers	3'
space for dressing	3' to 4' (in both directions)

Furniture Arrangement as Personal Expression

The foregoing discussions have dealt with the many possibilities for arranging furniture. Figures 579 through 582 show some of these in actual applications. The first two rooms are practically identical spaces in a remodeled townhouse only 9 feet wide. On the main floor (Fig. 579), the living room conversation group centers on a comfortable sofa and two fairly solid easy chairs placed in a long and narrow configuration around a glass coffee table. The two smaller chairs opposite are light and open, their curves encouraging easy movement around them to the secondary furniture group of a permanent card table and chairs in the bay window. A thick white area rug consolidates the major group. Mirrors on either side of the fireplace wall and the sweep of draperies around the end wall visually enlarge the constricted space. The space underneath this room has been treated in quite different fashion (Fig. 580). Called a den by the owners, it has two small sofas placed at right angles to the walls, forming a solid island on the Indian rug—a stopping place in the long sweep from kitchen through to the greenhouse. The fireplace on one side and a Lucite étagère on the other, plus lamp tables and lamps, build up this grouping, but the circulation path to the garden room beyond remains direct and open. Although all the furniture in both rooms is movable, each piece seems so perfect in its selection and right in its placement that we find it hard to envision any other arrangement.

579–580. Two different group spaces in a very narrow townhouse reveal varying design treatments. Audré Fiber, designer.

below: 579. The living room gains an easy formality through the choice of simple, timeless modern furniture and older refurbished pieces arranged in an open oval for social gatherings. The understated simplicity of architectural details and the gradual transitions of color from beiges to shades of red allow the low-keyed approach to dominate. (*Courtesy House Beautiful. Copyright 1973, The Hearst Corporation*)

580. The family room, taking its cue from the heavily beamed ceiling, has a much more assertive central grouping. Although the loveseats are again of unelaborated contemporary design, they are keyed up by the decisive pattern of the rug, the solidity of the tree-trunk table contrasted with the transparent Lucite shelf unit—the whole set again the old wood plank floor and brick walls. (*Courtesy House Beautiful. Copyright 1973, The Hearst Corporation*)

right: Plate 55. Much of the light and color in this dining room come from the dining table itself—a Plexiglas case lit from within by fluorescent tubes. The translucent plastic "cloth" spreads yellow light through the whole area, and the color could be changed easily by switching to another hue in plastic. Joan Sprague and Chester Sprague, owner-architects. See page 397. (*Photograph: John T. Hill*)

below: Plate 56. A beautifully crafted harpsichord occupies its own recess in this Cambridge, Massachusetts, home. While paying full respect to the piece as a musical instrument, the owner also focuses upon it as an elegant piece of furniture. Ben Thompson, owner-designer. See page 413; see also Fig. 471; Plate 29, p. 197. (*Photograph: Ezra Stoller © ESTO*)

left: **Plate 57.** The kitchen-dining space of this Connecticut home has been designed almost entirely in subdued earth tones—brick red floor, natural wood cupboards, trim, and furniture, plus muted upholstery fabric—all set against off-white walls. What vivid color there is comes from the food, cooking utensils, and other accessories. Judith Chafee, architect; Christina A. Bloom, interior decorator. See page 432; see also Figs. 47–49, 420, 423. (*Photograph: Ezra Stoller ©* ESTO)

below: **Plate 58.** A festive table setting takes its key from the warm pink color scheme that pervades much of this Mexico City home. Tall candles, pink table accessories, flowers, and fruit are the only additions necessary to make this already happy space seem gala. Luís Baragan, owner-designer. See page 432; see also Fig. 108; Plate 44, p. 317. (*Photograph: Hans Namuth, Photo Researchers, Inc.*)

The house in Figures 581 and 582 adheres to a totally different furnishing philosophy. Much of the furniture is built-in: the cabinets and the cantilevered dining table in the dining area, a bank of shelves and stereo units in the living area. Other furniture—foam seating units and dining chairs—is precisely but lightly placed. One can easily imagine the foam units regrouped, the dining chairs drawn up to the conversation circle or placed around a folding card table somewhere in the open areas. In an upstairs sitting room, all of the furniture is built in (Fig. 582). A desk spans an alcove under a skylight that encourages some potted plants to grow. The steps leading down to this area have two similar white boxes (facing built-in seating opposite) that contain the television set and the fireplace, frank statements of one of the main purposes of the space—a place for easy, relaxed television viewing by the warmth of the fire.

Study of these four rooms reveals some fundamentals. Each room achieves a singleness of effect, each is unified by the repetition of forms and general character. Variety is brought in to add life: the two French chairs in the townhouse living room and the étagère in the den contrast sharply with the solid character of the rest of the furnishings, although the contrast is of surprise rather than dissonance. The country house living area features a play of smooth, restrained curves against the strict rectangularity of the architecture.

Above all, each room is deeply personal. Just by looking at them, our imaginations conjure up the owners. Although the two rooms in the townhouse at first glance seem very dissimilar, both show an admixture of formality and informality that is gracious yet easy and comfortable, for owners who have some prized objects that they enjoy seeing and using. The other house promises a carefree mobile kind of lifestyle precisely because the sparse and mostly built-in furnishings eliminate the need to spend much time in housekeeping chores. The house works for its occupants, rather than the other way around. And in the broadest sense, this is the basic goal of all furniture selection and arrangement.

581–582. Furniture takes a secondary role in both major group spaces of a contemporary house. Robert Whitton, architect.

left: 581. In the living-dining space, much of the furniture seems part of the architecture. Cabinets and shelving are built in, the dining table is cantilevered, and the remainder consists of seating units reduced to their simplest elements, cane surfaces suspended on steel tubing, or thick foam seat and back units that comprise a chair. (*Photograph: Ezra Stoller © ESTO*)

right: 582. The furniture in the family room is even more architectural. Here the seating itself is built in, as is the desk. A television receiver and fireplace occupy harmoniously designed white boxes. (*Photograph: Ezra Stoller © ESTO*)

Enrichment

That human beings have an inherent desire for aesthetic enrichment can scarcely be refuted. Almost as soon as primitive peoples learned to build shelters, to fabricate tools and useful objects, they were impelled to add purely decorative touches. This of course is ornament, no different from the embellishments we are accustomed to seeing on a sofa or chair or even a wall. In a sense, enrichment does mean ornament—something that heightens the visual or textural interest of a piece, possibly a piece of furniture. But in the context of home design, enrichment usually is considered from another point of view. Our homes abound with objects that are either purely decorative and serve no functional purpose, or, if they are utilitarian, have been designed in such a way that they provide enrichment against a contrasting or simpler background. These are the elements with which we will concern ourselves primarily in this chapter: the designs, arrangements, embellishments, and objects that contribute a quality of richness to our daily lives and our personal lifespaces.

Depending upon one's interests and tastes, enrichment can be approached in at least two ways: objects may serve as enhancement of the total design in architecture and furnishings, or they may constitute the very focus of the design, with other elements subordinated to them. A country house owned by architect Charles Moore expresses the latter treatment (Fig. 583). Here enrichment dominates totally—a collection of antique musicians, a wall of ceramic and wooden sculpture and figurines, a fluorescent light sculpture, a fur throw. The architectural elements, including wall, floor, and ceiling design, are extremely simple and straightforward and are played down to cast the objects in a central role. Upon entering this room, the visitor's eye would be drawn immediately to the display wall for its overall impact. Next, one could spend a pleasant time absorbing details, studying each individual piece as it competes for attention. The richness of interest and visual design is so complex that each subsequent visit to this home would be a new adventure, as previously undiscovered subtleties became apparent. If all the objects of enrichment were removed from the space—or a completely new set substituted—the room would take on a dramatically different character.

Objects also provide the focus in the kitchen illustrated as Figure 584. The owner's collections of baskets, straw trivets, tinware, and copper utensils have taken over the walls and ceiling of the space to become a major design statement. Here the effect is one of overall pattern, for the individual pieces vary little in shape

above: 583. A room with low-keyed, meticulously detailed interior surfaces seems specifically designed as a show-case for some of architect Charles Moore's many interests—old furniture, "found" architectural details (here made into a coffee table), and native handcrafts. Colorful fabrics and a seg-mental flexible lamp in the foreground highlight the composition. (*Photograph: Robert Perron*)

right: 584. Collections are a prime source of individualized enrichment as in this kitchen, where assemblages of trivets, baskets, copper, and tin brighten the surfaces and at the same time remind the owners of their delight in searching out the objects. Tozier & Abbott, architects. See also Plate 14, p. 77; Plate 33, p. 231. (*Photograph: Julius Shulman*)

left: 585. Old artifacts, including an oval painting in an antique frame, seem the most appropriate enrichment for this renovated mill in Pennsylvania's Bucks County. Lilias Barger and Raymond Barger, owner-designers. See also Fig. 503; Plate 34, p. 232. (*Photograph: John T. Hill*)

below: 586. Heavy crystal, fine porcelain, and an antique mirror in a gold-leaf frame enrich this formal, traditionally paneled dining room and foyer. (*Photograph: John T. Hill*)

or decoration. Instead of being treasured as single precious objects, the pieces have been organized so that their shared quality creates an enrichment.

Basically the same approach might be followed by the household lucky enough to possess a treasured work of art. We have already seen one extreme example of this—an apartment owned by people so thoroughly absorbed in art that they wish to subordinate everything else to it (Fig. 21). Most of us would not be so single-minded; a subtler method of focusing attention on a painting is to repeat or recall its colors elsewhere in the room, so that the eye is inevitably drawn back to the source of the color (Pl. 30, p. 198).

A thoughtful application of enrichment can also enhance the design of a home to bring out certain architectural or stylistic features. Three very different examples will illustrate this point.

The house shown in Figure 585 takes its character from the rustic architecture—thick masonry walls, deeply recessed windows, exposed rough-hewn beams. To emphasize the quality of an old country farmhouse, the owners have added several integral touches: a soft-hued painting in an antique frame, folk pottery and wood carvings, a wooden light fixture hanging from the ceiling, touches of wrought iron, an old butcher's block, and so on. The overall impression is one of harmony, warmth, and coziness.

Figure 586 shows another traditional home—in this case a very formal one. The aura of 19th-century elegance is established by graceful paneled walls, an ornate carpet, and antique furnishings, but this effect would be incomplete without the enrichment provided by the crystal chandelier and candelabrum, the elaborate gold mirror frame, and porcelain ware on the table and sideboard. Period authenticity—or simply authenticity of feeling—is only one aspect of enrichment, but it can be a very important one in certain situations.

The points to be emphasized in a particular home may have no clear relation to any style or period or type of design, but rather be a distinctive aspect of the architecture. One of the most striking features of the house illustrated in Figure 587 is its soaring vertical height. To focus attention on the raised ceiling, the owners have added a unique form of enrichment—a row of plants suspended near the roofline and illuminated by skylights. Set off against white walls, the plants naturally draw the eye upward, but they also refer back to plants massed around the fireplace to bring us down to ground level again.

These several examples not only demonstrate how enrichment can either carry a design or support it, but also reveal a spectrum of tastes. We know much about

587. Areas of concentrated enrichment, such as a grouping of plants, have long been used to heighten the effect of architecture, but in this case the effect is achieved in a very modern way, with the plants calling attention to the high, sloping ceiling. James Caldwell, architect. See also Figs. 122, 675. (*Photograph: Philip L. Molten*)

588. Patterns of ceiling beams, supporting poles, window and door frames, and outlined wall panels provide the major enrichment in this house. Thus, the architecture itself becomes a kind of embellishment. Alex Riley, architect. (*Photograph: Philip L. Molten*)

the occupants of each of these homes without ever having met or seen them. Some of us might empathize with the collector of charming native handcrafts (Fig. 583), others with the person who cherishes classic accessories (Fig. 586). This points up an important aspect of home enrichment: a collection of objects without personal significance to those who live with them will never blend comfortably into a lifespace. Freedom of taste allows us to choose and combine what we like most, to express ourselves in completing the design of a home.

So far we have talked about enrichment as something deliberately added with the conscious desire to "enrich." In so doing we overlook a very basic form of enrichment—the kind that develops spontaneously or as a side effect from some other element. Because it is so fundamental, we should consider such incidental embellishment first.

Incidental Enrichment

The most obvious enrichment in any home is the one we are most likely to forget about—ourselves. No two people look alike or dress alike. Their varying personalities, changing moods, and different activities all affect the background against which they move. We can recall what a different quality the room shown in Chapter 16 has when it is populated and when it is not (Figs. 509, 510). Like actors bringing to life a stage setting, people enrich the lifespaces they inhabit.

Another basic form of enrichment may be provided by the architecture of the home itself. This is certainly the case in Figure 588, where the patterns of ceiling beams, door and window frames, supporting columns, and wall panels enrich the

otherwise planar surfaces. Small details are kept in harmony, as in the lighting fixtures near the ceiling and along the hall, which mimic the dark-framed panels. What little furniture there is in this space has been kept very simple, while art works and other incidental decoration have been held to a minimum.

Patterns in draperies and upholstery, in floor coverings and wall treatments, in furnishings and lighting fixtures all can provide a measure of enrichment. So too might the implements and materials of one's profession or hobby, especially when they involve the visual arts. No space could be visually richer than the inside of a weaving studio, with its profusion of multicolored yarns, the satisfying form of the loom, and works in progress scattered about; a painting, sculpture, or ceramic studio creates the same kind of delightful image (Figs. 28, 78).

We do not choose books and magazines for their physical appearance on a shelf, but it cannot be denied that a wall of books brings enrichment to any room (Fig. 589). In this instance our personal involvement with certain books may add an emotional enrichment to bolster the visual; but even without this attachment we take satisfaction from the rows of similarly shaped objects with their colorful bindings and dust jackets.

Windows and doors contribute two kinds of enrichment, in the patterns of light they admit (Fig. 114) and the vistas they allow of the outside environment. The bedroom in Figure 590 benefits from both of these; the enrichment of this rather

591. The shapes and placement of beautiful objects here enhance the natural beauty of the environment and the strong architectural design to create a concentrated focal spot of permanent yet ever-changing enchantment. Wurster, Bernardi, and Emmons, architects. See also Figs. 484, 617, 645; Plate 60, p. 469. (*Photograph: Morley Baer*)

austere space comes as much from the outside as the inside, with its outlook on dense woods and a huge spreading tree. Interior embellishments have been kept to a minimum, but the heavily fringed rugs and floral-patterned bedspread recall the lush natural foliage outside.

A special set of circumstances led to the very individual type of enrichment pictured in Figure 591—masonry walls that are 2 feet thick cut with a window offering an extraordinary view of mountains and coastline. The owner took advantage of the wide window ledge to create a still life of precious objects—a hot toddy maker, a tray and decanter, some elegant jars. The contrast between this precise, tranquil grouping and the turbulent vista beyond the window would cause endless fascination. We might say that this tableau represents a combination of two kinds of enrichment—the incidental from the window and the deliberate in a placement of objects chosen for their beauty.

We turn now to a second kind of enrichment—that contributed by small utilitarian items.

Enrichment in Functional Objects

With one or two possible exceptions, the objects to be considered in this section are relatively inexpensive. The typical household, over the years, will accumulate several—or several sets—of each, so that the possibility arises for altering the effect of enrichment from day to day. All have a very specific utilitarian purpose, but all come in a vast range of designs, so that one can exercise a great deal of personal taste in selection.

Lamps

Chapter 5 dealt with lighting in terms of architectural units and permanent fixtures. Here we are concerned with portable lamps, which often are chosen as much or more for their physical attractiveness as for the kind or amount of light they supply. There are basically two types: the classic base, bulb, and shade arrangement; and the integral all-in-one piece.

Some lamps today might be described as light-as-object. Light is captured in a sculptural form that in turn spreads the ambience of its glow in the immediate vicinity (Fig. 592). A variation on this is the fixture in which a shaped bulb, usually frosted, becomes the "lamp" to be supported by a compatible base.

Bases, bulbs, and shades, although different in function and usually in material, comprise a unit when organized into a lamp (Fig. 593). This suggests a basic agreement among them—some qualities in common but seldom exact repetition. The shape of a lamp ought to grow from its function: the base supports the bulb and shade; the bulb sends out light; the shade protects our eyes from glare, directs and diffuses light. But materials also play a determining role. The simplest base of a traditional table lamp is a cylinder with a foot large enough for stability (Fig. 318). The breadth-to-weight ratio is important in keeping a lamp upright; a support of metal, plastic, or wood can be more slender than a clay or glass one. Bulbs now come in a great variety of shapes, sizes, and colors. When they are meant to be used unshaded, they should not produce glare or become too insistent.

Shades generally take the form of drums, domes, or truncated cones to spread the light downward and sometimes upward as well. A tall, steep shade gives concentrated light, a low, wide one dispersed light. Of course, shades can be square, triangular, or any other shape, but rounded forms seem more congenial to light, and we welcome their curves in our predominantly rectilinear homes.

The optimum size of a lamp will be determined by illumination requirements and by the size of the room and its furnishings. High lamps with large spreading shades illumine broad areas and match large furniture in scale. Deliberately overscaled lamps can create dramatic focal points, but unless they are sensitively used, they may crowd small spaces. The more lamps a room has, the smaller each can be, but too many small lamps may give the appearance of clutter.

Color is important, especially in translucent shades but also in the whole ensemble, because lighted lamps are very conspicuous. A preference for warm, flattering artificial light would tend to rule out translucent shades of blue, green, or violet, but opaque shades in these colors could be effective for certain rooms.

Although many innovative lamp designs have been introduced, most of us would still think of the standard base-and-shade arrangement when "lamp" is mentioned. To our grandchildren the word may conjure up quite a different image, while our grandparents might have envisioned something like the hurricane lamp in Figure 594. While hurricane and kerosene lamps rarely provide the only source of light in today's homes, they can be an attractive kind of enrichment, at the same time giving off their special warm glow.

top: 592. Thin porcelain lamps rely on the light within to emphasize their perfection of form, while they cast a soft, diffuse glow. Stig Lindberg, designer.

center: 593. In this very streamlined lamp, a polished aluminum cylinder base supports an adjustable long polished aluminum shade that houses a fluorescent bulb. (*Courtesy Robert Sonneman*)

bottom: 594. Lamps are not necessarily lighted by electricity. This modern version of the hurricane lamp allies beauty of shape and sparkle of glass with the ever-captivating flickering light of a candle. Orrefors design. (*Courtesy Georg Jensen*)

Screens

With a venerable history as ornamental space dividers, screens are especially welcome in open-plan homes or in multipurpose rooms (Fig. 393). They can be moved or adjusted to divide areas into comfortable units without completely shutting out what is beyond (Fig. 595); or they can be folded inconspicuously against walls. There are no limits to the possible materials: sheer silk and rice paper, clear or translucent glass and plastics, tapestry, brocades, leather, shutters and bamboo poles, curved or flat plywood, wallpaper or fabrics (Fig. 596). Some screens are almost as heavy and substantial as walls, others light and freestanding. They can be plain or ornamented, identical or different on the two sides, harmonious or contrasting with their surroundings.

left: 595. In this New York apartment a screen-divider built of eight hollow-core doors hinged together and on casters creates areas for different activities and also serves for storage, display, and as inherent enrichment through its angled configuration. Judy Klein and Stephen Marc Klein, designers. (*Photograph: David Hirsch*)

below: 596. An elegant screen decorated with a painted landscape establishes the living-dining space in this traditional room. (*Photograph: John T. Hill*)

Table Settings

Many households have come a long way from the routine of three meals a day set forth on a table around which the family was expected to gather—if, indeed, this ever was the norm. However, many experiments, as well as our own personal experiences, indicate that the environment in which we eat can affect our health and happiness. Dining with companions, either family or friends, can be a pleasurable experience, and many elements go into enhancing that pleasure—the food served, the setting, and certainly the accouterments of eating. Meals are significant in any kind of group living, possibly being the only time the household congregates; they also play a significant role in entertaining guests, because the giving of food is a traditional emblem of hospitality. For these reasons, the atmosphere for dining deserves more than routine treatment.

Table settings represent a creative experience in enrichment, since they can be changed with relative ease. The same table set with different kinds of dishes, glassware, flatware, table coverings, and accessories will take on quite a different quality. Books on etiquette used to divide table settings into formal and informal categories; actually, this is a rather limited classification, and we could identify several other possibilities.

The table setting illustrated in Figure 597 really is about as "formal" as one sees nowadays. A clear glass table forms a shimmering background for fine china, crystal, and sterling silver, causing all these to gleam even more brilliantly with reflected light. Although orderly and reserved, the arrangement presents an overall curvilinear quality. The floral theme stated in the china is repeated in heavily decorated silver, subtly echoed in the embroidered linen napkins, and very gently restated in the fluted stemware. A long centerpiece of live plants completes the picture. We would expect this kind of setting to appear only for very elaborate dinner parties and similar occasions.

Less formal but still quite special and charming is the setting shown in Figure 598. A subdued, classic pattern in the china seems in keeping with the utterly plain, graceful silver and stemware. The coarse-weave linen tablecloth and bright napkins

left: 597. A sparkling formal table setting that promises gourmet dining is consistent in its use of delicate, curvilinear forms played against the rectangular framework of the table and the diamond-shape motif of the supports that show through the glass tabletop. (*Courtesy Tiffany & Co.*)

right: 598. Classic china, silver, and crystal seem less formal when arranged in a seemingly artless manner on a heavy linen cloth, the whole setting sparked by bright napkins. (*Courtesy Royal Copenhagen Porcelain*)

contribute to the more casual effect. Instead of a single set centerpiece, each place setting has its own miniature bouquet of tulips.

A light afternoon meal for family or for one or two friends could have inspired the delightful setting shown in Plate 57 (p. 420). This beautiful kitchen has an overall neutral color scheme, with its white walls, terra cotta floor, and natural wood trim, thus leaving the opportunity for food and cooking utensils to provide enrichment with touches of vivid color. An old wood table, left bare to show off its wonderful weathered surface, has been set with plastic dishes, stainless-steel flatware, and bright cotton napkins in four colors. The only centerpiece—and the only one needed here—is a basket of oranges and lemons, which pick up the colors of the cane-seat chairs. Unquestionably, this meal has been planned for its visual appeal as much for its flavor. In fact, everything in this room seems to have been thoughtfully designed to create the pleasantest atmosphere for casual dining.

Festive occasions—holidays, birthdays, anniversaries—deserve equally festive settings, and the table shown in Plate 58 (p. 420) meets this criterion perfectly. With its high beamed ceiling, natural wood furniture, and shocking pink cushions, this room would be cheerful under any circumstances, but the addition of brightly colored table linens, flowers and fruit, and especially the pink candles in tall candelabra makes it truly gala. We might almost imagine that the room is poised, waiting for a happy group of people to enter and bring it to life.

Selecting Tableware   The table settings just described obviously derive their success as much from the appropriateness of dishes, silver, glass, linens, and accessories as from their arrangement. This is especially evident in the traditional beauty of the first table, in the independence of taste in the latter two. But before tables can be set, the equipment must be in hand—chosen with an eye to its probable uses.

Selecting tableware differs from most other aspects of home planning and furnishing in several important respects because of the ways in which it is typically accumulated and used. The household acquires pieces not only through planned (and occasional impulse) buying but by unpredictable gifts and inheritances. Sets and individual objects can be variously combined and arranged with no cost other than imagination and a little time. The several kinds of tableware usually arrive in sets, and quick replacements may be indicated because of breakage, damage, or loss. Nothing else except cooking utensils will be handled, moved from place to place, and washed as frequently. Also, tableware requires easily accessible and specially planned storage to make the constant flow from cupboard to table to sink or dishwasher and back to cupboard as convenient as possible. Finally, many families have everyday and guest tableware and linens, a distinction seldom made elsewhere in the home. Putting these factors together raises unique problems and, more significantly, great possibilities for enriching—and personalizing—the home.

The household's preferences in kind of food and method of serving, the present or planned dining and storage space as well as furniture, and the lifestyle—all of these have direct bearing on the selection of tableware. Utility and economy are important, as always, but in this instance beauty and character may be more heavily weighted. Because tableware is seen only a few hours a day, there is much greater freedom to have patterns and colors that might be too demanding if always in view. Each piece can be used in different contexts, so it should have its own intrinsic beauty that is versatile yet affirmative. In few other phases of home life is change so easily and economically possible, and each change presents a new design challenge.

Selecting Dishes   Dinnerware is generally the most conspicuous part of the permanent table equipment and often delineates the character of table settings. The following points pertaining to utility and economy should be kept in mind in selecting dishware:

- Size and shape are significant (Fig. 599). Each dish should be large and deep enough to hold an adequate amount of food without spilling. Plates with rims permit easy grasping and provide a resting place for silverware but do not hold so much food as rimless ones. Cups should have finger-contoured handles, rims that fit the lips. Dishes that can be stored easily save time and space.
- Replacement, as well as original cost, merits consideration. "Open stock" patterns permit buying or adding to a set as needed, but they no longer guarantee permanent or long-time availability. The buyer should read warranties and suggestions for maintenance carefully. Vitreous ceramics and better plastics resist chipping and breakage. Hard glazes reduce unsightly and unsanitary scratches; underglaze decorations are more durable than overglaze. Low-fire folk pottery must never be used to contain acid foods (and preferably no foods at all), since the lead in the glaze can leach out and cause lead poisoning. Such wares, of course, are perfectly acceptable for decoration and nonfood applications. Compact shapes lessen breakage. Raised ornament increases cleaning time and is more subject to chipping and scratching.
- Dishes that double as cooking and serving containers save time and assure hot food.

The following points pertaining to beauty and character should also be kept in mind when choosing dishes:

- Dinnerware comes in great variety, opening the path to many colors and patterns that should have lasting appeal (Fig. 600). Relation to other table appointments, furniture, and lifestyle is at least as important as the beauty of pieces seen by themselves.
- Originality, in a mass-production age, derives less from finding one-of-a-kind pieces than from choosing those that seem compatible with individual preferences and are adaptable to varied settings. Personalization comes with the ways

left: 599. Dinnerware in an unusual octagonal shape is well designed from a utilitarian standpoint and would add interest to a table setting. This stoneware pattern is from the "Franciscan" line. (*Courtesy Interpace*)

right: 600. Royal Copenhagen's "Flora Danica" porcelain dinnerware would be harmonious with a traditional house or add a touch of concentrated enrichment to a modern setting. (*Courtesy Royal Copenhagen Porcelain*)

above: 601. Heavy stoneware with a free asymmetrical pattern teams well with the bare wood of an old table and the casual arrangement. (*Courtesy Tiffany & Co.*)

left: 602. An unusual combination of stoneware and porcelain in dinnerware could stimulate innovative and creative settings. Wolf Karnagel, designer. (*Courtesy Rosenthal Studio-Haus*)

in which they are combined and arranged (Fig. 601). Flexibility is to be prized, since it indicates the possibility of fitting the same dishes to various table settings, surroundings, and moods. The service pictured in Figure 602 consists partly of stoneware, partly of porcelain. Therefore, it could be "dressed up" with fine crystal, silver, and lace; "dressed down" with linen, stainless steel, and bare wood. Dishes that are compatible with many different table settings should give satisfaction for a long time.

Selecting Flatware   With proper care, flatware endures for several generations, since it is seldom broken or seriously damaged. Therefore, potential longevity of appeal is more important than in other kinds of tableware. The following points pertaining to utility and economy should be kept in mind when selecting flatware:

☐ Flatware, like dinnerware, is much handled and it ought to have a pleasant feel—be easy to pick up and hold firmly, balance well in the hand or on the plate, and have no irritatingly sharp edges.
☐ Use does not harm silver, pewter, or stainless steel but, with ordinary care, improves them by mellowing the surface.

- It is no longer considered necessary to have all of the flatware in a place setting or a table setting of the same pattern. Variety can add interest.
- Pieces that cannot be put in a dishwasher raise problems.
- Place settings, the units in which silverware is often but not necessarily acquired, may vary in the number and kind of pieces they include; customarily they consist of knife, fork, teaspoon, salad fork, and dessert or soup spoon, and sometimes butter spreader.

- **Sterling silver** flatware is originally expensive but does not wear out (Fig. 603). **Silverplated** flatware costs less, but the plating wears off rather quickly unless it is double- or triple-plated and reinforced at points of greatest wear. **Pewter** is somewhat less expensive than sterling silver and has a softer, mellower shine (Fig. 604). **Stainless steel** is durable, nontarnishable, and seldom discolors (Fig. 605). The price of flatware varies by weight, material, and design.
- The extra cleaning time that heavily ornamented patterns take may or may not be compensated by their rich beauty and the way in which they obscure scratches.

The following points pertaining to beauty and character should also be kept in mind:

- Flatware adds elongated forms and soft sparkle to table settings, but its real beauty is quite as much a matter of how it feels in the hands as of how it looks.
- Plain ware has a simple dignity and can be used in any context. But metal is an ideal material for intricate ornament.
- Flatware, because of its small size and distinctive qualities, offers unusual opportunities to bring modest contrast and variety into the home.
- Its cost and long life place flatware (and hollow ware too) at the bottom of the list of objects with which to indulge faddish, possibly transitory tastes.

Selecting Glassware   Since almost everything said about dinnerware applies to glassware, only a few specific points are worth emphasizing.

- "Glassware" for everyday meals can be of unbreakable aluminum, stainless steel, or durable plastic.

above: **603.** Silverware of a unique pattern that shows off the nature of the material would be comfortable to handle and treasured for years. (*Courtesy Georg Jensen*)

below left: **604.** Pewter flatware has experienced a new wave of popularity in the last few years, making an interesting addition to the repertoire. The simple shapes and restrained ornament on these pieces take their cue from Colonial designs. (*Courtesy Reed & Barton*)

below right: **605.** Stainless steel, a modern material, is often given a modern, fresh interpretation. Here the usual break between handle and bowl or blade has been moved up, changing the balance of each piece, and the customary four long tines become three shorter ones. (*Courtesy Dansk Designs, Ltd.*)

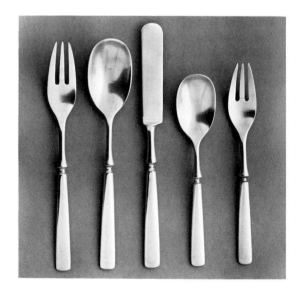

right: **606.** The choice of table covering will characterize a setting. A flowered tableskirt, topped by a thin organdy cloth, seems delightfully appropriate to a leisurely afternoon tea. (*Courtesy Schumacher*)

below left: **607.** A grouping of salt shakers and pepper mills, fashioned from natural teak in unusual designs, resembles a set of sturdy little chessmen. (*Courtesy Dansk Designs, Ltd.*)

below right: **608.** Plastic table accessories, either clear or in colors, could brighten many casual settings. They are almost indispensable for outdoor and casual meals. Gunnar Cyren, designer. (*Courtesy Dansk Designs, Ltd.*)

□ Colored glassware enlivens a table—but the color cannot be changed for different occasions and it alters, sometimes unattractively, the color of the liquid.
□ Stemware has a buoyant quality that gives an airiness to the table setting (Fig. 598); but it is hard to wash, breaks easily, and takes much storage space.

Selecting Table Coverings   Comparatively inexpensive and easily stored, table coverings enhance variety and change. New fibers and weaves, easily cleaned plastics, strong or subtle colors are a challenge to those with self-reliant discrimination. The following points pertaining to utility and economy should be kept in mind when selecting table coverings:

□ Protecting table surfaces and lessening noise are major functions.
□ Original cost is typically low to moderate, but maintenance time and energy add their own "costs."
□ Tablecloths are harder to wash, iron, and store than table mats unless they are permanent press. Designs in permanent-press cloths have improved vastly in the last few years.
□ Resistance to stains and wrinkles is a significant factor.

The following points pertaining to beauty and character should also be considered:

□ Typically regarded as backgrounds to dinnerware and food, table coverings often are plain or subtly patterned, but conspicuous colors and patterns can be refreshing.
□ Tablecloths can function as decisive unifying factors (Fig. 606).
□ The soft textures of most table coverings supplement the typically hard smoothness of dishes, silver, and glass.
□ A change of table covering can revitalize long-familiar dinnerware and alter its character from one meal to the next.

Selecting Table Accessories   The incidental pieces that bring further enrichment to the table include: serving pieces, centerpiece containers, salt and pepper shakers, candlesticks, ashtrays, napkin rings, and so on. All of these are available in the same materials as eating utensils—ceramic, metal, and glass—so the principles discussed above apply here also. For more casual table settings, however, wood and plastic accessories offer a pleasant contrast of color and texture (Figs. 607, 608). Often it is the accessories, the most variable element of the setting, that most strongly underscore the table's theme.

Planning Centerpieces   The word "centerpiece" can be a bit misleading, because of course no rule demands that a floral or other decorative arrangement occupy the center of the table. As we have seen, a centerpiece can even disintegrate into many individual pieces to brighten each person's place setting (Fig. 598). Except for this type of situation, however, the centerpiece is commonly the dominant enrichment on the table, so it could be considered to play a central role. We have come to expect that centerpieces be interesting but not conspicuously distracting. Flowers, leaves, and live plants, fruits and vegetables are the standard components (Figs. 597, 598; Pl. 57) and come in almost inexhaustible diversity. Most of these must be changed frequently to keep them looking fresh. Rocks and shells, a piece or two of sculpture, or a cluster of candles have the advantage of durability and can often be renewed by the addition of one or two transient items, such as flowers. Beyond this, a centerpiece can present the opportunity for a free play of creative imagination. The unlikely combination of eggs and dried weeds makes a striking ornament for the buffet table shown in Figure 609. While this would not be appropriate for every table, it does give some idea of the potential scope.

609. A buffet table lends itself to an over-scaled decorative arrangement—here of eggs and dried weeds—to balance the lay-out of many smaller objects. (*Courtesy Royal Copenhagen Porcelain*)

The relation of centerpieces to the rest of the setting, as well as to the size of the table and the room, is all important. If people sit or walk around the table, centerpieces should be attractive from all angles. Nearly always it is desirable that the centerpiece be low enough to permit those at the table to hold a conversation without interference.

In sum, the challenge and delight of planning a table setting—on a daily basis or for festive occasions—not only brings the potential for enrichment but serves as a responsive medium of personal expression. We can tell much about a person from the table setting she or he creates—more perhaps than from the overall design of the home. In microcosm, the dining table represents one's personal lifespace.

Bed Coverings

Like table settings, the linens, blankets, comforters, and spreads used on a bed bring the potential for very flexible enrichment, since they are relatively inexpensive and easy to change. It seems hard to believe that until roughly a quarter century ago colored and patterned sheets were almost unknown, pure white the absolute standard for bed linens. The extent of this revolution in design can be realized when we see world-famous fabric and clothing designers applying their talents to sheets and pillowcases.

Since the bed or beds will nearly always be the focus of any bedroom, the bed coverings that dominate the surface must strongly effect the room's overall design. Moreover, bedspreads and quilts allow an immediate kind of personal expression, for they are often the products of widely popular crafts and hobbies. We have seen a number of examples of patchwork quilts, both old and new (Fig. 368; Pl. 9, p. 59). In Figure 610 a handwoven spread with a long macramé fringe serves as a neutral but lush background for brightly colored scatter pillows—another form of enrichment. Cascading down off the bed and onto the floor, the fringe blends with a high-pile rug to give an overall sense of warmth and comfort to the room.

Bed coverings can also act to unify a room, as Figure 611 demonstrates. Here a graphic print by Victor Vasarely was the inspiration for a hand-crocheted bedspread that picks up the colors and overall motif of the print without duplicating it exactly. An even simpler method of unifying a room depends on patterned sheets (Fig. 612). Sheeting fabrics used on the bed can also cover a table or a scattering of pillows, can become window curtains, canopies, or drapes, can even run up the wall to make a self headboard.

Pillows covered in bright colors and patterns represent one of the most pervasive and versatile forms of enrichment (Fig. 613). They are easy to make, lending themselves to all kinds of fabric arts. We mention them here under bed coverings, but pillows can just as easily migrate to other parts of the house (Fig. 526).

While nominally useful in providing comfort, pillows of the sort we have been discussing often take on a primarily decorative role, especially when intricately worked or heavily ornamented. This leads us directly to consideration of objects that have no function whatsoever except just to be, for the sensuous delight they give us.

Enrichment in Decorative Objects

In saying that the objects discussed below—plants and flowers, paintings, prints, and sculpture, handcrafted items and accessories—serve no useful purpose, we are severely limiting our definition of "useful" to a rigid, almost Puritan standard. Works of art, whether fabricated by nature or by human beings, play a very important role in enrichment, for they enrich the very essence of our selves: our minds, our spirits, our sensibilities. A world—or a home—devoid of objects that exist purely for the joy of existing would be almost like a world without sounds.

left: 610. Bed coverings must be utilitarian as well as decorative. This handwoven spread serves as an important design element, but it is functional besides; it could be stretched out on, taken off and put on the bed on a daily basis, and still maintain its aplomb. Raymond E. Wark, interior designer. (*Photograph: Leland Y. Lee*)

below left: 611. A crocheted wool bedspread is versatile and integral with the room's design; furthermore, it contributes warmth. Oxley & Landau, architects. (*Photograph: Julius Shulman*)

below right: 612. The many handsome designs now available in patterned sheets have encouraged their migration to the tops of beds, as well as to other traditional fabric applications, such as wall coverings. Maija Isola, designer, for Marimekko. (*Courtesy D/R International, Inc.*)

left: 613. A scattering of custom-designed pillows adds both pattern and comfort to this family room, in which most of the furniture is built in. (*Courtesy Monsanto Textiles Company*)

Enrichment **439**

below: 614. A large, spreading plant forms almost an abstract design, adding curvilinear interest to this small, cubic kitchen. Warren Platner, owner-designer. See also Fig. 428. (*Photograph: Ezra Stoller ⓒ ESTO*)

right: 615. A superplant ties together two levels of a remodeled barn and balances the myriad small leaves that might otherwise have seemed spotty against the white balcony wall. Roger Kenna and Constance Kenna, owner-designers. See also Fig. 209. (*Photograph: John T. Hill*)

bottom: 616. A swirl of sparkling crystal shows off to perfection a seemingly artless but masterful arrangement of white roses and green leaves. (*Photograph: Erich Hartman, ⓒ 1968 Magnum Photos; courtesy Steuben Glass*)

Plants and Flowers

Live Plants   Live plants are so much a fixture in today's homes that it seems difficult to imagine doing without them. A glance through the pages of this book will show that few rooms banish plants altogether and many enlist them as important design elements. Several factors explain this penchant for bringing part of the outdoors inside. The first is, of course, the widespread desire to introduce a natural touch in a synthetic environment; this could be considered a psychological goal—to maintain touch with what has traditionally been an agrarian culture. In purely visual terms, plants contribute colors, textures, and ungoverned forms that contrast pleasantly with the human-controlled parts of an interior environment. Lastly, there remains the emotional satisfaction of watching something grow and change and develop. The degree to which individuals or families will want to get involved in horticultural process is a question of personal interests. However, we could point to the incontrovertible fact that, with reasonable care, plants *do* get larger and in some cases may bloom (thus altering their physical appearances), which distinguishes them from any other element of home design.

As visual design, plants can play many roles. A single, strategically placed plant may be a dramatic—almost abstract—outline (Fig. 614), whereas masses of plants— filling a bay window (Figs. 47, 436), softening a garden room (Fig. 556), or cascading from a balcony (Fig. 615)—might create an effect ranging from a soft screen to a jungle. Big, bold plants are good for major effects or to fill a space where furniture does not fit; small ones, whose interesting foliage merits close study, could occupy a place of prominence on a table or window ledge. Perhaps the best plan is to nurture the plants one loves and let them seek out their own lifespaces.

Acquiring plants for their purely visual appeal can be a perilous adventure. If no one in the household has the slightest interest in gardening, the carefully chosen specimen that precisely fits one's design needs will inevitably wither and die—thus destroying the effect as well as the plant. Some plants, including cactus, philodendron, and certain members of the *dracaena* family, seem to flourish in spite of being ignored, while others demand the most meticulous care merely to survive. Before purchasing a plant, you should weigh the amount of attention it needs against that you are willing to give.

Each type of plant has its own requirements of light, heat, soil, water, and humidity for best growth. Almost none like dark, hot, poorly ventilated rooms any more than humans do, but a few will survive under such unfavorable conditions.

- **Hot, sunny windows** suggest cactus and other succulents. Coleus and similar plants with colorful foliage also thrive with many hours of sunshine a day, as do geraniums and citrus trees.
- **Moderately cool** east or north windows will support a variety of plants: begonias, which range from a few inches to several feet tall; African violets; many kinds of ivy, plain or variegated, which can be trained around a window or up a wall; all the philodendrons; and even some varieties of orchids.
- **Low-light** areas not directly adjacent to a window call for such foliage plants as philodendrons, rubber trees, and ferns.
- **Bathrooms,** which typically are warm and moist, make ideal settings for lush ferns and many tropical plants.

The containers in which plants are kept have much to do with both their ornamental value and their physical health. However, once the requirements for proper drainage, root spread, and soil aeration have been met, almost no container can be ruled out, the materials ranging from the classic unglazed pottery through glazed ceramics, metals, glass, and plastics (Fig. 346). (Wood, unless lined, will split and rot from constant watering.)

Fresh Flowers   Raised to the level of an eloquent art by the nature-loving Japanese, and assiduously practiced by many in the United States, flower arrangement can mean anything from stuffing some blossoms into a vase to a fascinating art. The effects that can be produced are limitless. There are as many steps between symmetrical, strict formality and casual, spontaneous grouping as there are kinds of blossoms. For some, flower arranging begins with a walk down a country road to find the most colorful wildflowers and leaves; for others, it means a visit to the florist to select the most perfect specimens to enhance a crystal bowl (Fig. 616). Whether ingenuous or sophisticated, fresh flowers in the home bring a special kind of enrichment that cannot be duplicated with anything else.

The flowers, branches, and leaves obtainable play a decisive part in determining the kind of arrangement that is possible, because each plant has its own character and habit of growth. Some flowers, such as irises, grow tall and upright and lend themselves to vertical arrangements. Poppies and tulips have flexible stems and tend to curve into spreading designs that can be basically either horizontal or vertical. Short-stemmed blossoms and sinuous vines give naturally horizontal compositions, although many materials can be deliberately modified to give a low-spreading effect when this is indicated. Flowers will cooperate up to a point, but little is gained by pushing them beyond it. Arrangements that emphasize the distinctive personalities of the blossoms used are likely to be most successful.

617. Another window of the house shown in Figure 591 becomes a still life with an arrangement of dried weeds, delicate against the heavy masonry wall. Wurster, Bernardi, and Emmons, architects. See also Figs. 484, 645; Plate 60, p. 469. (*Photograph: Morley Baer*)

The relation of flowers to their containers is important also but not dictated by rules. In Figure 616, the brilliance of the crystal bowl is matched by the sparkling perfection of the roses. But any degree of similarity or dissimilarity between flowers and containers can be effective. Usually, the container is subordinate to its contents, and simple glass, ceramic, or metal bowls or vases will happily hold varied flowers. Sometimes, though, a distinctive urn, cornucopia, or vase is almost as important as what it holds. Those who enjoy arranging flowers appreciate having varied containers, because it is stimulating to be able to call upon a vase or bowl just right in size, shape, color, and texture.

Dry Arrangements   Dry arrangements can be divided into the "semidry" compositions of fruits and vegetables that last from a few days to several months and the "bone dry" compositions of everlasting flowers, weeds, and seedpods, leaves and bare branches, driftwood and rocks. They cost little or nothing and require no care other than the somewhat tedious job of removing dust. The principles are the same as those from which pleasing arrangements of fresh flowers develop.

Often, though not always, dried flowers and weeds are subservient to the containers they occupy, acting more as enhancements or complements rather than statements in their own right. Such is the case in Figure 317: we can be sure the clay pot takes precedence and that the weeds were chosen because their angular, spindly shapes complement the solid round form of the pot. In Figure 617 a bunch of feathery weeds contrasts with the heavy masonry walls of the house and strict rectangularity of the window frame to create a striking tableau in the window.

Paintings, Drawings, Prints, and Photographs

For many households, the very next step in home design after choosing major pieces of furniture will be deciding what "pictures" to put on the wall. Of course, there is really no reason why any pictures at all *must* be put on the wall. If the purpose in hanging a painting or print is simply to fill a void or carry out the color scheme, there is not much point in bothering. Works of art are as personal and emotionally charged as the books we read, the music we enjoy, the types of entertainment we pursue. Most of us, however, either have some objects of visual art that give us particular pleasure, or we are eager to seek them out. In terms of home enrichment, then, three factors must be considered: choosing works that evoke a special response; framing them appropriately; deciding where and how to display them to best advantage.

Choosing Works of Art   The several categories listed at the head of this section differ substantially in medium, effect, content, and, naturally, in cost to purchase.

Paintings are original, one-of-a-kind works done in oil, tempera, watercolor, acrylics, or other pigment bases on canvas or similar backing. Along with original sculptures, they are the most expensive works of art one can buy. Few of us are in a position to purchase masterworks of a caliber visible in museums, but it must be remembered that the vast majority of paintings that today command prices in the hundreds of thousands—or millions—of dollars initially were sold to discerning collectors for a tiny fraction of their current value. Local art shows and galleries, art schools, even auctions can be the source of treasures that awaken particular responses and may, incidentally, have intrinsic value.

Drawings—in pencil, crayon, charcoal, or ink on paper—tend to be much less expensive than paintings, even when done by recognized artists. Because they are often preliminary sketches for other works, drawings may be more relaxed than paintings, a more direct revelation of the artist's concept; but they can also be precise delineations or full-bodied statements, as developed as a painting.

Prints, often known as multiples, are impressions on paper resulting from such processes as *woodcut, etching, drypoint, lithography,* and *silk screen.* They are considered to be original works of art when struck directly from plates made or supervised by the artist; numbered according to which impression in sequence each is from the initial print; signed or authorized by the artist. Prints are much less expensive than paintings or drawings; even works by established artists are within the range of average collectors and could represent a sound investment.

Photographs are self-evident—a medium of expression uniquely of the 20th century (although its principles were developed somewhat earlier). The content of a photograph can vary from the "art" subject—indistinguishable from that of paintings, drawings, or prints—to the picture that has only personal significance—a snapshot of family and friends. Either is valid as an image for home enrichment, as long as it means something important to the individual.

Reproductions of art works have no direct connection with the artist. They are inexpensive impressions on paper made photographically or by a commercial printing process. Such reproductions do not give the total impact of original works, for they lack the full range and brilliance of color, the special interests of texture and materials. Still, if one has particular empathy with a certain painting or drawing, and reproductions are all that one can afford, they should not be scorned. High-quality reproductions, especially of drawings, are sometimes quite faithful to the originals.

Frames, Mats, and Glass   Frames visually enclose pictures and contribute to their importance and effectiveness. Also, they form a boundary or transition between the free, intense expressiveness of pictures and the architectural backgrounds. Lastly, they safeguard the edges, may hold protective glass, and facilitate moving and hanging. Their first duty is to enhance the pictures, their second to establish some kind of relationship with the setting. Generally this means that frames should either supplement the size, scale, character, and color of what they enclose or simply be unobtrusive bands. Occasionally, marked contrast can accentuate the qualities of a painting. Only exceptionally should the frame dominate the picture. The wide, heavily carved and gilded frames of the past or any that project at the outer edges "set off" pictures from their backgrounds. Those of moderate width and simple design, harmonious in color with the walls and either flat or stepped back, relate pictures to walls. Today, many paintings are meant to be hung without frames, the impact of the boundary of a painting against its background being part of the total concept.

Mats and glass are typical accompaniments of watercolors, photographs, and graphic prints. Mats enlarge small pictures and surround them with rest space as a foil, especially important if the picture is delicate or if the background is competitive. In color, mats are usually of white or pale-hued paper, because these tones concentrate attention on the picture. For special effects, mats can be of pronounced color and of textiles or patterned paper, cork, or metal.

In size, mats vary with the size and character of the picture as well as with the frame and the location. Heavy frames lessen the need for generous mats, while large or important locations increase it. To correct optical illusions and give satisfying up-and-down equilibrium, the width of the top, sides, and bottom of mats may be different. In matting a picture, as in creating one, the elusive interaction of form, line, and space—not a set formula—should determine the result. The discerning eye of the owner or framer will be the best judge of the correct mat for any particular picture in its intended location.

Glass is necessary for pictures that need to be protected from surface dirt, moisture, and abrasion. It also seems to intensify colors. But glass also produces annoying reflections, a problem partially alleviated with the new nonreflective glass, as well as with Lucite, Plexiglas, and other plastics. Nonreflective coverings should be approached with care, however, for they tend to gray and soften what is underneath. Mats and glass generally go together on watercolors, prints, pastels, and photographs. Paintings seldom have or need either.

left: 618. In painter Rufino Tamayo's living room in Mexico City, a large, dramatic painting becomes a focal point, irresistibly drawing the gaze back from the vista into the room beyond. See also Fig. 620; Plate 51, p. 369. (*Photograph: Julius Shulman*)

right: 619. A display of drawings and watercolors all but fills the walls of this comfortable sitting room, but the effect is prevented from being "busy" or overpowering because of the subdued color scheme and regular pattern in which the works are hung. (*Photograph: John T. Hill*)

Hanging Pictures   Both aesthetic and prosaically physical considerations come into play in hanging a picture. Once the latter are dealt with and mastered, the former can be given free rein:

☐ Nails and hooks can be driven securely into some types of walls. In frame houses with interior walls of plaster or wallboard, it is necessary to find the wooden stud (or upright post) to anchor the nail. (Studs most often are 16 inches apart.)
☐ Some wall surfaces—and some landlords—will not permit nails to be driven in. For this purpose there exist picture hooks on superheavy tape that can be affixed to the wall.
☐ Concrete and similar walls may demand special plugs that expand on the other side to create a permanent, immovable projectile for the picture.
☐ In general, pictures should be hung flat against the wall, with no wires or hooks showing, although sometimes the wires are decorative.

Locating paintings, drawings, photographs, and prints so that they interact happily with each other and their setting is an art. Since pictures help relate furniture to walls, they are often placed over something—a sofa or group of chairs, a desk, a table, a bookcase, a piano, or a fireplace. Keeping pictures at eye level lets them be viewed comfortably, relates them to furnishings, and emphasizes the room's horizontality. From time to time, though, it is refreshing to have a painting stand for what it is worth on an otherwise blank wall. Large, dominant paintings, by their forceful presence, almost demand this kind of treatment (Fig. 618). Smaller, more modest works can be grouped successfully, provided each is in a position to invite leisurely study (Fig. 619).

Sculpture

Bringing into three dimensions the intensity and expressiveness found in painting can have serious impact on the home. An important piece of sculpture, regardless of its size, commands a place of importance and becomes the focus of attention.

Large pieces that are freestanding can—from a purely organizational point of view—be treated as articles of furniture. That they will gather an aura of specialness about them depends as much upon their visual integrity as upon placement. Smaller pieces may occupy prominent positions on a shelf or table (Fig. 228), on the wall, in a niche, or possibly suspended from the ceiling. The collector who is fortunate or diligent enough to amass many pieces of related sculpture will certainly want to create a display area particularly for them (Fig. 620).

Crafts

Pottery, glassblowing, weaving, woodcraft, metalwork, basketry—all have experienced a tremendous surge of popularity in the last several years. As collectors have increasingly turned their attention away from the "fine" arts toward an appreciation of the so-called applied arts, crafts have begun to throw off their "homey" image and assume their rightful place as serious expressive works. A beautiful ceramic object may be no less significant than an official piece of sculpture, a handwoven tapestry no less important than an oil painting (Fig. 621). Happily, craft objects are still much less expensive and much more readily accessible to the public than paintings and sculpture. In many homes such precious articles have begun to replace the traditional picture-on-the-wall as prized objects of enrichment. For example, the suspended seclusion balcony shown in Figure 622 has as its major adornments the art fabrics on two walls and a beautiful handmade basket. Plants hanging from the three-story ceiling complete the tranquil picture.

left: 620. Rufino Tamayo, who designed his own house (Fig. 618), made one wall into a honeycomb of display spaces for his collection of pre-Columbian art. (*Photograph: Julius Shulman*)

right: 621. A magnificent tapestry becomes a wall in a remodeled barn, where its rich, strong detail equals the dominant setting. See also Figs. 499, 560. (*Photograph: John T. Hill*)

below: 622. A piece of ancient fabric mounted in a frame to protect it, a double-height sweep of an art fabric down one wall, a small piece of basketry used as the hypnotic center of a built-in seating circle—all attest to the current interest in crafts as important objects of enrichment. (*Photograph: Norman McGrath*)

right: 623. An intricately woven basket provides a spot of color and abstract pattern in this modern, clean-lined house. Charles Moore, architect. See also Fig. 123. (*Photograph: John T. Hill*)

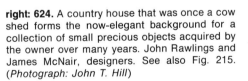

right: 624. A country house that was once a cow shed forms the now-elegant background for a collection of small precious objects acquired by the owner over many years. John Rawlings and James McNair, designers. See also Fig. 215. (*Photograph: John T. Hill*)

Throughout this book we have shown many examples of the potter's and glassblower's art enriching contemporary interiors. Baskets, when their design is sensitive and closely adapted to the materials, take the place of sculpture and make a pure aesthetic statement (Fig. 623). While often divorced from their original utilitarian functions, such objects retain the suggestion of sturdy serviceability that relates them to the basic activities of everyday living.

Accessories

We have not yet touched upon one major category: objects that are not quite works of art or craft (since they are mass-produced) and not quite utilitarian (although they may perform some marginal task), but are simply kept about because they delight the eye or hand or intellect. Figure 624 illustrates a collection of such articles—brass candlesticks, heavy glass forms, a whimsical ceramic goose, a globe. If we try to imagine this same room stripped of these little islands of enrichment, it seems very dull indeed. That is because they, together with books and plants scattered about, delineate the very character of the room. Without them, the space would be impersonal and bland. In a sense, this sums up the underlying nature of enrichment—that which personalizes a home, gives it its particular quality, and makes it peculiarly one's own.

Location and Background of Enrichment

There are two logical types of locations for enrichment: those places where people normally look and those places where we want them to look with interest and pleasure.

People tend to look more or less straight ahead; through doors, windows, or wherever distance invites exploration; and at anything that is large, different, or well illuminated. Thus, it is reasonable to think about putting some enrichment opposite the home's entrance door, somewhere in the first view of the major group space, more or less opposite seating for conversation and dining, on the wall opposite a bed, in the space above a desk, and at the end of a hall. Outdoors, the major views from inside the house or from the terrace, as well as the ends or turning points of garden paths are logical places on which to concentrate interest.

Entrance areas are introductions to the home. Usually they are small, which suggests something best seen at close range in a short period of time. A good table or chest with flowers, plants, or a small sculpture below a mirror is one possibility, if space permits. Or the enrichment can be on the wall—a distinctive lighting fixture or mirror, an uncomplicated painting or print, a colorful textile.

The first view into the living room is another matter, for the opposite wall or window may be some distance away. In many contemporary homes this first view carries attention through the room out into the garden, which then becomes the place for interesting planting or fences, decorative urns or sculpture. In other houses, the fireplace wall is the first thing seen, and it may or may not need more than the architect has given in its design and materials. If the fireplace is small and simple, the wall above may have a painting or textile large enough and strong enough to balance the opening below and to make itself understood from across the room—and also with sufficient interest to be worth looking at over long periods of time. In still other quarters the initial view may end in a blank wall that, typically, has a group of furniture and accessories. Whatever the situation, it is gratifying to have something of interest greet the eyes.

Then there are the spots in most homes where we have to entice attention, such as uninteresting corners or small wall spaces that must be used. A small, separate furniture group can be reinforced with congenial illumination; by having prints, paintings, or textiles on the wall; and by placing interesting objects on the table. Then, what was an unused corner becomes inhabited space, chiefly through appropriate furniture but to a surprising degree through distinctive enrichment.

The effectiveness of any enrichment can be increased or decreased markedly by its setting. Large, significant objects can proclaim their presence by being put in important positions, by being given backgrounds against which they can be readily seen and by being built up with smaller objects. At the other extreme, some enrichment can take its place unobtrusively, a little murmur in a harmonious setting. Thus varying degrees of emphasis and subordination are achieved.

Enrichment as Total Design

There remains for consideration the space in which the overall design is a form of enrichment, where architecture, furnishings, and embellishments are so thoroughly integral as to blend into one cohesive statement. We offer two quite different examples of this approach. The first, a California house (Fig. 625), is entirely wood-paneled inside, with exposed beams and posts; partial openings between rooms; sensitive wooden moldings around windows, doors, and other focal points; and much subdued detailing in wood. The house has many levels, and a large portion of the furnishings are built in. Suspended light fixtures framed in wood merge gracefully with the architecture. Even where isolated objects of enrichment have been added, in a patterned rug or throw pillows, they seem to settle into their surroundings, rather than contrasting with them. Few areas of this house could be seen as devoid of enrichment, yet it is of a subdued, harmonious nature.

Much more active is the enrichment shown in Figure 626, the upstate New York home of a prominent woodcrafter and potter. Here a fantastic potpourri of handmade objects compete for the viewer's attention, turning the eye first in one direction then in another. There is endless involvement with the beauty of materials and shapes and colors and textures, from the free-form wood furniture set against molded plastic chairs to the numerous handwoven, hand-thrown, and hand-blown objects. Lush Oriental rugs both anchor the composition and present their vivid colors and patterns for attention. It would be difficult to find a lifespace more personal than this, filled as it is with a total enrichment of objects fabricated by the owners and their friends.

The Extended Environment

18 Exterior Design

Despite the tremendous variety of their exteriors, today's homes are immediately distinguishable from those of the past. Unfortunately, attempts often are made to conceal this fundamental distinction. The 19th-century idea that every building should have the clothing of a recognizable historic style still persists, so that we find contemporary homes "packaged" in imitations of French Provincial, Spanish Colonial, and American Colonial styles. These styles, however, originated under technological, social, and economic conditions that no longer exist. Providing for one or more automobiles, for example, can throw the carefully organized façade of an American Colonial house completely off balance. Two large blank doors tacked onto one side may have become a familiar sight, but they cannot be termed authentic. Modern architects and designers, rejecting the artificiality of the historic style syndrome, have sought to find new forms as suitable to our own culture as the original Colonial architecture was to its time.

Why do today's houses look the way they do? The modern approach to architectural design begins with the most basic issues. For whom is the home intended and what purposes will it serve? Where will the house be situated in terms of general environment, climate, and specific site? Of what materials will it be constructed? How will those materials be put together to form a stable structure? Function, site, climate, materials and structure all act as "form determinants"—factors that inevitably affect the character and appearance of every building.

As their name implies, form determinants impose limitations on exterior design, but they also provide latitude for creativity. By definition, every house must meet certain functional requirements in providing a lifespace for its inhabitants, but the diversity of modern lifestyles allows for a wide range of exteriors expressive of individual tastes and preferences. Site and environmental factors require designs responsive to terrain, to natural features such as trees, rocks, and bodies of water, and to neighboring streets and houses. Climate can be an essential factor: the desert sun suggests small and strategically placed windows, heavy snow loads slide off a steeply pitched roof, and tropical climates need specific solutions to problems of humidity and rainfall. Masonry construction usually requires thick walls to support the roof, while a skeletal frame of steel leaves room for large windows and unobstructed open spaces. Yet a structural system can be exposed or concealed, dramatized or understated in the final exterior design. Similarly, a single material used throughout a house will underscore the continuity of shapes and contours,

opposite: **627.** Uniform shingle siding, staggered façades, and changing ground levels contribute to the intimate pedestrian space shared by residents of Solana II, a development at Solana Beach, California. Oxley and Landau, architects. See also Fig. 611. (*Photograph: Julius Shulman*)

while a skillful combination of different materials often produces a more exciting variety of colors and textures. The first half of this chapter examines the role of these form determinants and their expression on the exteriors of today's homes.

In addition, however, the external form of a house is affected by its means of production—whether custom-built or mass produced, remodeled or prefabricated, single-family or multiple-unit. The custom-designed home naturally offers the greatest opportunity for individual expression. But ours is a diversified society, and many forms of housing exist to meet our varied needs. One person may prefer the pace and excitement offered by an apartment in the city, another the peaceful solitude of a cabin in the country. Many individuals enjoy moving into an older house and gradually fixing it up over a period of years, while others require the convenience of maintenance-free housing or the total mobility of a house on wheels. Within a given type of housing, there remains a wide variety in the formal treatment of function, materials, structure, and environmental relationships. Thus the selection of a particular type of dwelling inevitably reflects the needs and personalities of individuals. Some of the choices available in one type—the single-family house—are outlined in the second half of this chapter. Multiple housing and the larger environment form the subject of Chapter 20.

Expression of Form Determinants

Function

The exterior of any structure should convey an impression of the functional purposes for which the building is intended. In other words, our houses should shape themselves around our living and working patterns and then take their outward form from the interior arrangement of space. This premise is indeed the beginning point in all modern design. A careful analysis of the functions involved and life patterns to be accommodated provides the architect with the underlying facts of the building program. A house with rooms of different sizes and shapes at varying levels can be given an exterior boldly revealing these features, as if the walls and roof have been simply wrapped around the various living functions (Fig. 628). Houses designed as simple volumes of continuous, freely adaptable space acquire exteriors of a different character (Fig. 319).

The diverse appearances of today's homes testify to the wide range of individual lifestyles and special interests that can be expressed in exterior design. For a homeowner who wanted to see over the trees of a heavily wooded site, architect

628. Architect Robert Whitton employed concrete blocks covered with sprayed white stucco in his Florida home. Interior spaces project outward as boldly sculptural forms on the exterior. (*Photograph: Maris/Semel*)

above: **Plate 59.** Architect Arthur Ericson composed a home in Vancouver, British Columbia, as a series of interlocking horizontal terraces. Natural materials and a reflecting pool relate the structure to the lake and rocky cliff on either side. Tall panes of glass and vertically ribbed cedar walls are surmounted by horizontal wooden slabs that project beyond corners as geometrical accents. See page 460; see also Fig. 42. (*Photograph: Ezra Stoller © ESTO*)

right: **Plate 60.** Irregular stone masonry creates a massive, rough-textured surface whose rich, natural colors come to life in sunlight. Plants, brick paving, straw, and weathered wood enhance the greens and browns of the stone wall, while a Dutch door, painted white, makes a crisp contrast. Wurster, Bernardi, and Emmons, architects. See page 463; see also Figs. 484, 591, 617, 645. (*Photograph: Morley Baer*)

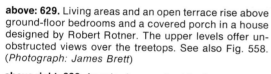

above: 629. Living areas and an open terrace rise above ground-floor bedrooms and a covered porch in a house designed by Robert Rotner. The upper levels offer unobstructed views over the treetops. See also Fig. 558. (*Photograph: James Brett*)

above right: 630. Angular forms reflect the irregular plan of this shingled house in Roseau, Minnesota. Windows and decks are oriented toward a nearby stream and golf course. Thomas N. Larson, architect. (*Photograph: Phokion Karas*)

right: 631. Cedar covers the circular walls and conical roof of a working studio for designer Jack Lenor Larsen. Other "huts" for living and sleeping complete the informal vacation compound. (*Photograph: Kal Weyner; courtesy U.S. Plywood, Champion International*)

Robert Rotner designed a house with living quarters and an outdoor dining terrace on an upper level (Fig. 629). A different consideration—the desire for internal and external privacy—led to the functional but unique exterior of a house in northern Minnesota (Fig. 630). Here separate rooms and a private sun deck face unobstructed views in one direction, while neighboring areas are blocked by solid walls and a tall windscreen.

Vacation homes are apt to be among the most exciting architectural productions to be found. The design of a vacation house reflects the easygoing informality of holidays in the mountains or at the seashore. Planned around play activities for all ages, the "home away from home" often features easy maintenance and free indoor-outdoor communication. The mood created is one of easy living, delight, and occasionally fantasy. Depending upon individual preferences, the program may call for togetherness or allow for the separation of different groups, and a special retreat or studio can provide space for meditation, hobbies, or homework outside the office (Fig. 631). Wood exterior finishes help the vacation house to blend with its natural environment, but glass areas tend to be large in order to bring the beauty of the site inside.

opposite: Plate 61. Paul Rudolph created an elegant exterior for this remodeled carriage house in New York City. Steel frame construction is frankly expressed but decoratively handled in a delicate composition of thin, straight lines and tinted glass. Lower sections are recessed to create a sense of volume. See page 471; see also Fig. 27; Plate 22, p. 162; Plate 28, p. 197. (*Photograph: Ezra Stoller © ESTO*)

above: **632.** A house designed by Robert B. Browne is stretched over, and elevated above, its flat Miami site in deference to tropical winds, rains, and temperatures. (*Photograph: Ezra Stoller © ESTO*)

right: **633.** Cooling breezes flow between and through the two enclosed areas of the Miami house.

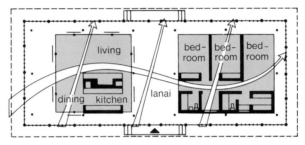

Climate

Climate forces act continuously and relentlessly on buildings, and their importance for exterior design is fundamental. While various materials may be equally suitable, no architect can afford to ignore the year-round weather conditions in which a house must stand. Often, the very survival of a building depends on the designer's recognition of this factor in the choice of materials, structure, and site. The decisive effect of climate on exterior design is most clearly expressed in houses built to withstand climatic extremes.

Tropical or Semitropical Climates   Humidity, hot sun, hurricane winds, high tides, and insects can make most semitropical areas less than paradisiacal unless dwellings take these facts of nature into account. Lifting houses off the ground is an old way of letting cooling breezes or surging water go underneath. When this is done with concrete, the material used for the house in Figures 632 and 633, the arrangement also discourages insects. Extending the house over its site allows moderate winds to go through the rooms, as in this example, where the center is a genuine breezeway. Sliding doors control storm winds, which go harmlessly over and under this low house, while overhanging roofs and insect screens provide protected outdoor areas on four sides. A roof cover of heat-reflecting coral chips is another device to make this an architecturally, rather than mechanically, air-conditioned house.

Similar conditions led to the equally satisfying but very different exterior of a wooden, shingle-roofed house in Hawaii (Fig. 112). The elevated main floor is surrounded by adjustable louvered panels, which can be opened for cooling breezes, partially shut against the sun's heat, and completely shut to keep out heavy rainfall.

634. Tall windows and an open deck bring views of the high Sierra to the upper level of this winter vacation home, while the downstairs playroom offers direct access to the snow-covered hillside. (*Photograph: Bruce Harlow; courtesy California Redwood Association*)

Snow Country   The relentless force of accumulated snow can cause roof collapse, seal off a house from access and egress, and even displace a structure from its foundations. Snow loads on the roof actually aid insulation, but heat escaping from the interior tends to melt the snow into water, which may then leak through the roof or freeze at run-off points. Serious problems can be prevented only if climate conditions are accommodated in the structural system and exterior design.

Aesthetic as well as practical considerations led to the design of a vacation home set on a wooded mountainside (Fig. 634). A steeply sloping roof with projecting eaves sheds snow away from the walls of the house, while the pointed silhouette has a strong visual affinity for the surrounding mountains and pine trees. Concentrated areas of glass are protected by the overhanging eaves and a raised deck, which also provides spectacular views over the countryside.

The Desert   Homes built in the desert, whether in Egypt or the southwestern United States, share many design features that stem directly from the hot, dry climate. Because it does not require protection from prolonged rainfall, the desert house often has a flat roof, which is easy to construct. Thick walls give as much insulation as possible in temperatures that may vary as much as 40 degrees between day and night extremes. During the daytime, the massive walls absorb the heat slowly, keeping the inside cool. At night, the heat retained in the walls gradually passes off to warm the interior. By morning the heavy walls are once again cool, providing a kind of natural air-conditioning.

Glass must be employed carefully in homes built for a desert climate. Windows tend to be small, often deeply inset, and heavily protected by shutters, grilles, and other devices. Where large areas of glass are used, they are sheltered by overhangs and trees, if possible, and the openings usually face away from the hot afternoon sun. Thick walls, flat roof, and a small number of shielded openings all appear in the house in Figure 113, whose inventively curving forms deflect constant seaside winds and harmonize with the surrounding sand dunes.

Climate considerations are increasingly important in exterior design today. We now realize that the world's supply of energy is limited, and its conservation requires a great deal of effort and long-range planning. The utilization of solar energy, now in the experimental stage, may eventually offer practical solutions of wide application (Figs. 134–136). In the meantime, exterior designs carefully integrated with climatic conditions can increase the efficiency and reduce the cost of conventional heating and air-conditioning systems.

Site

The location of a house, in terms of both the immediate site and the surrounding environment, obviously has a strong influence on exterior design. In many ways the relationship between house and site is the central issue of architectural design, since not only the choice of materials and structure but even the disposition of interior spaces may depend on site conditions. Eliel Saarinen, the great Finnish architect and teacher, often told his students, "In designing any object, always look to the next largest context to establish relationships." By this principle, the design of tableware should relate to its placement on a table, that of a rug to the room it occupies, and that of a house to its immediate environment.

Architects and designers are by training sensitized to this basic issue, and the custom-designed home almost invariably takes form only after the owner has chosen a site. Through study and careful analysis, the architect makes certain that the house will relate to its particular setting. Each location has a unique set of characteristics that must be considered in the design of the home. A sloping lot, for example, does not permit the same freedom of placement as does a flat site (Fig. 635). Existing trees, shrubs, and natural forms such as rocks and water impose further limitations. Problematic factors like these can be eliminated arbitrarily by simply leveling the site—an unimaginative and unsatisfactory solution. On the other hand, the architect can accept the challenge and exploit natural features to achieve particular advantages. Thus, the sloping lot provides a perfect opportunity for separating different living functions, ensuring privacy through vertical organization of space, and allowing for varied means of access, lighting, and outward views (Fig. 635).

The Natural Environment   "Falling Water," the home designed by Frank Lloyd Wright for the Kaufmann family in 1936, represents a vigorous architectural response to a natural site of great beauty (Fig. 636). In densely wooded, hilly terrain, a mountain stream runs over a ledge of rock to create a small waterfall. Wright avoided the obvious solution—placing the house to give it a view of the waterfall—

635. Barbara and Allan Anderson made the most of a steep, rocky site in the design of their own home in Rye, New York. Weathered shingle siding helps the house to blend with the natural setting, which the architects altered as little as possible. (*Photograph: Ezra Stoller © ESTO*)

left: 636. "Falling Water," the home built for Edgar J. Kaufmann in Mill Run, Pennsylvania, was designed by Frank Lloyd Wright in 1936. Cantilevered concrete balconies and thick, rough walls in local stone paraphrase the landscape below and around the house. (*Photograph: Hedrich-Blessing*)

below: 637. Low roof lines and natural materials tie this multilevel house to the hillside overlooking Big Sur, California. See also Figs. 294, 311. (*Photograph: Morley Baer*)

and instead built the home practically on top of the waterfall. The house, he said, was designed to become a part of the site rather than assuming a secondary role as observer of the waterfall. The cantilevered balconies of the house repeat the shape of a rock ledge below and mirror the direction of the waterfall, while the core of the building—a stone chimney—echoes the colors and textures of the surrounding area. Falling Water admirably fits Wright's definition of a good building as "one that makes the landscape more beautiful than it was before."

Each site presents unique problems requiring design decisions, but, as with other form determinants, there is often more than one valid solution. Open hilltops, for example, have been treated with marked contrast in a pair of houses, one resting high above the Pacific at Big Sur, California (Fig. 637), the other perched above

above left: 638. Sharp-edged sculptural forms dramatize the emphatic orientation of a Long Island home by architect Myron Goldfinger. (*Photograph: Maris/Semel*)

639–640. The white geometrical forms of a house designed by Richard Meier rise from a steep waterside slope at Harbor Springs, Michigan. See also Fig. 176; Plate 48, p. 335.

above: 639. Bedrooms, kitchen, and service areas lie behind the glass-enclosed dining room and two-story living room. (*Photograph: Ezra Stoller © ESTO*)

left: 640. Outdoor decks, joined by open stairs, extend the living areas. The elevated setting offers spectacular views across Lake Michigan. (*Photograph: Ezra Stoller © ESTO*)

641. A roof covered with sod and vegetation insulates and partially conceals a house in the hills of New Hampshire built by designer Don Metz. (*Photograph: Robert Perron*)

a rocky beach on the north shore of Long Island (Fig. 638). The Big Sur house, terraced down a hillside whose gentle slope is echoed in the low, canted rooflines, seems to nestle into the landscape and become a part of it. The wood is left natural, the structural system frankly exposed. In the Long Island house, a low but steep groundswell interacts with the large, dynamic forms and emphatic orientation of the structure, which seems to rise up in a dramatic gesture against the sky. Large circular shapes cast hard shadows, as if in response to the boulders below, while the continuous decks and windows provide the interior with broad vistas up and down the shore.

Waterside locations, among the most coveted sites for homes, encourage strongly oriented exteriors with ample exposure to outward views. A high, steep, and heavily timbered bluff overlooking Lake Michigan inspired the tall, prismatic shapes of a house designed by Richard Meier (Figs. 639, 640; see also Pl. 48, p. 335). Gleaming white above the shore line, the house acquires a nautical ambience from external stairs and handrails made of steel, staggered wooden decks, and a pair of prominent, tubular chimney stacks. Windows, set in an asymmetrical pattern of rectangles, surround the lakefront half of the house to permit maximal views and light. Smooth, white surfaces and hard edges assert the technological character of the house, which, like the previous example, stands out against its natural surroundings as a bold, dramatic statement.

A contrasting treatment of lakeshore conditions appears in a house by Arthur Erickson in Vancouver, British Columbia (Fig. 42; Pl. 59, p. 453). Set between a small lake and a low, rocky cliff with light foliage, the house is organized as a group of terraced, rectangular shapes topped by jutting, vertical slabs of wood that repeat the jagged contours of the landscape. Oil-finished cedar, bricks in various shades of brown, and dark stone tiles harmonize with the natural colors of the setting. Water becomes a part of the house by means of the reflecting pool, where large boulders, stone steps, and terrace walls of irregular masonry again recall the rocky backdrop.

The relationship of site and exterior form is capable of seemingly endless variations. Aiming at a literal integration of natural and constructed elements, Don Metz designed a low, one-story house with a concrete roof strong enough to support 18 inches of sod (Fig. 641). Wildflowers and grass took root in the soil, so that the house now seems to blend into the gently sloping mountainside. A southward orientation provides light and a vista over neighboring valleys and hills.

Exterior Design **461**

Even a relatively flat site receives imaginative treatment in a house near Cedar Rapids, Iowa (Fig. 642). The steel framework is sheathed in vertical planes of unfinished cedar, which repeat the colors and slender lines of the wooded setting. But projecting cantilevered balconies and roofs temper the dominant verticality and echo the horizontal terrain.

The Built Environment Existing structures and avenues of traffic are just as important as natural conditions for the relationship between house and site. Homes in medium-density suburban areas often allow open views in only one direction and close the other sides to ensure privacy. For example, windows fill one side of the house in Figure 643, while the remaining faces have only minimal exposure. Other examples achieve the same effect with different exterior forms (Fig. 630).

An urban site on a crowded street demands careful planning in order to provide privacy and noise protection as well as natural lighting and outward views. A townhouse in New York City displays a vigorous handling of these problems (Fig. 644). Varied fenestration distinguishes each floor and gives the house individual character, while the simplicity of the planar façade avoids any suggestion of visual arrogance toward neighboring buildings (see also Pl. 61, p. 454). High land values invite the efficient use of space throughout the city dwelling. At the rear of an urban site, walled-in privacy allows a more open arrangement of courtyards, decks, and windows (Fig. 30).

Structure and Materials

Among the most fundamental determinants of exterior form are the materials chosen and the structural system by which they are combined. The structural properties and expressive potentials of wood, masonry, metal, concrete, and other materials have already been discussed (see Chaps. 10 and 11). All the myriad structural systems available today can be divided into three major categories: *load-bearing wall* construction, *skeletal frame* construction, and *monolithic* construction. These divisions

left: 642. Unfinished rough cedar siding covers the steel structure of a three-story house near Cedar Rapids, Iowa. Crites & McConnell, architects. (*Photograph: Julius Shulman*)

right: 643. Solid walls ensure privacy from neighbors and street traffic in a Florida house by architect William Morgan, while large glass windows provide maximum exposure toward the nearby lake. See also Fig. 438. (*Photograph: G. Wade Swicord*)

are not exhaustive, however, for there are many variations that combine the qualities of more than one system. A single building can incorporate different structural principles as well as a range of building materials. Theoretically, any material can be combined with any type of construction, although at present only reinforced concrete has such complete versatility in practice.

The selection of a given material and structural system brings with it a particular set of limitations and opportunities. Each combination has its own technology, tools, and methods of construction, but there are many different ways of articulating the "skin" and "bones" of a house. The examples illustrated in this section demonstrate the variety of exterior effects that can result from the frank exposure and sensitive handling of structure and materials.

Load-bearing Wall Construction   In the load-bearing wall system, the weight of the roof is carried to the foundations by means of thick, continuous walls built of stone, brick, adobe, or concrete-block masonry, even poured concrete. Because of their structural importance, load-bearing walls usually have narrow windows and doors, though a lightweight roof permits large openings between masonry piers (Fig. 645; Pl. 60, p. 453). While generally expensive and lacking hidden spaces for pipes and wiring, stone and adobe walls offer excellent soundproofing, and their capacity to absorb heat is especially useful in hot climates. Concrete-block walls, with their hollowed-out interiors, have spaces for the support cords, and poured-concrete walls can easily have them embedded during fabrication. Masonry walls also resist fire and the effects of weathering, but the primary attraction comes from their natural colors, rich texture, and feeling of massive permanence.

left: 644. Brick and glass are elegantly combined in a townhouse built on a restricted site in New York City. A high wall in front of the façade preserves ground-floor privacy, while a window in the floor above offers ample light and a view to the street. Stephen Lepp & Associates, architects. See also Fig. 208.

right: 645. The thick, load-bearing walls of a clifftop house are built of large, irregular stones that respond to the natural colors and textures of the site. Wurster, Bernardi, and Emmons, architects. See also Figs. 484, 591, 617; Plate 60, p. 453. (*Photograph: Morley Baer*)

left: 646. Different-color woods clearly articulate the frame construction of a house in California. The overhanging roof is cut away at the right to bring direct sunlight to the deck. Thompson & Peterson, architects. See also Figs. 214, 263. (*Photograph: Morley Baer*)

below left: 647. Architect Jacques C. Brownson built his own home in Geneva, Illinois, during the 1950s. The slab-like steel roof is suspended from above and cantilevered over a paved terrace.

below right: 648. A house designed by Marcel Breuer derives its simple, arresting shape from monolithic concrete construction. Concrete is also employed in the rectangular slabs that fill the segmental façade and in the darker-colored privacy fence. (*Photograph: Ezra Stoller © ESTO*)

bottom: 649. Fiberglass wall-and-ceiling modules provide a lightweight, durable, and inexpensive material for this prototype house. A core of urethane foam provides insulation. (*Courtesy Rudkin-Wiley Corporation*)

Skeletal Frame Construction   The vast majority of modern buildings, ranging from simple country shacks to towering skyscrapers, depend on the principle of skeletal frame construction. A structure of this type consists of a supporting framework or "skeleton" of posts and beams, to which a "skin" of walls and windows is fastened. The juncture of vertical and horizontal members may be strengthened by diagonal cross-pieces to create a *braced frame*. When used for small wooden houses, this type of construction is usually called a *balloon frame*.

In the house in Figure 646, a darker wood clearly distinguishes the structural frame from the nonsupporting walls, windows, and roof. Vertical posts are square in section, while rectangular ceiling beams are positioned with short edges up to ensure maximum strength. The *cantilever* principle, by which a horizontal element projects beyond its support, appears in the overhanging eaves of the wood roof. Throughout the house, the straightforward revelation of structure and materials creates an atmosphere of openness, warmth, and invitation.

The greater compressive and tensile strength of steel permits thinner supports, and greater clear spans between them, than is possible in wood construction. The walls of steel frame houses can thus be filled entirely by sheets of glass, and the resulting exteriors have a light and spacious character (Figs. 319, 647). With steel, not only roofs and balconies but whole interior spaces can be cantilevered boldly into space (Fig. 329). In Figure 384, cantilevered rooms are anchored, both visually and statically, on a pair of rugged masonry walls—a scheme that emphasizes the special properties of two different materials.

Glass walls and cantilevers appear again in a house designed by architect Jacques Brownson (Fig. 647). Brownson's house also illustrates *suspension*, another variant of frame construction for which the tensile strength of steel is essential. The ceiling is actually hung, or suspended, from four horizontal steel beams, which are supported by vertical posts standing outside the house proper. Brownson's treatment of this feature clearly articulates the independence of the structure from the glass-walled spatial envelope.

Monolithic Construction   Monolithic construction, as its name implies, is a system in which the continuity of all forces acting on the building is assured by the unity of the structural material. Reinforced concrete, with its initial moldability and final combination of compressive and tensile strength, suits this type of structure especially well. Set in curving shapes calculated to balance the forces of load and support, concrete hardens as a single, continuous material with the strength and rigidity of a giant seashell. In a house designed by Marcel Breuer, the interior space is defined by a thick, broadly arching shell of concrete, which acts as both walls and roof, both "skeleton" and "skin" (Fig. 648). The vaulted form is completely self-supporting, but the architect adds visual interest by filling the open front of the house with a network of vertical and horizontal slices of concrete. When handled by a master, concrete monolithic construction can lead to exteriors of vigorous elegance.

Fiberglass and other plastics, though lacking the strength of concrete, also lend themselves to monolithic construction. Lightweight three-dimensional units can be prefabricated and then bolted together at the site to form complete one-story houses (Fig. 649).

Variant Structural Systems   The structural systems described above can be enlarged to include a number of variants, hybrids, and mutants. The great strength and versatility of concrete, for example, allows it to be employed in an endless variety of structural ways. Concrete offers great potential for modular prefabrication, in which a limited number of units are mass-produced in the same molds and then combined in different patterns. As discussed in Chapter 10, these units can be either two-dimensional panels or three-dimensional modules. Prefabricated concrete panels are stacked on top of each other as load-bearing walls, but the enormous strength of the material allows for ample window openings and thin dimensions, while the low cost of mass production eliminates a major drawback of both masonry and one-time-only concrete production (Fig. 650). Three-dimensional units may be placed on an independent framework, but more often they serve as hollow "building blocks" bearing the load of the units above (Fig. 301).

The distinction between structural skeleton and attached "skin," which has led to such dramatic results in the modern skyscraper, allows for many variations with different materials. The tepee, developed by native Americans, is a type of membrane structure now attracting widespread interest because of its structural, functional, and environmental efficiency (Fig. 651). A flexible membrane, originally of buffalo hide but today usually of canvas, envelopes a structural cone of radially placed wooden poles. As in monolithic structures, walls and roof are one. An inner lining provides insulation and air circulation, sending smoke from the fire, traditionally built inside for warmth and food preparation, up through the opening at the top. The conic shape of the structure ensures stability, while the simple construction process permits demounting with virtually no defacement of the land.

above: 650. An integrated system of prefabricated concrete panels includes bearing and nonbearing walls, with or without windows, and units for balconies, stairs, and the like. (*Courtesy Sepp Firnkas Engineering, Inc.*)

above right: 651. Portability, structural economy, and a built-in ventilation system are among the many virtues of the tepee. (*Courtesy Nomadic Tipi Makers*)

right: 652. Plastic foam, sprayed over balloons, created an igloolike house near Denver, Colorado. The material serves as an excellent insulator. Stan Nord Connolly, architect. See also Fig. 345. (*Photograph: Roberts Commercial Photography*)

Houses built of plastic foam begin with an inflated balloon or skeletal framework of wire mesh, wood, or fiberglass. The foam, sprayed in liquid form, assumes the shapes of the framework. When dry, however, the hardened plastic supports itself as a lightweight monolithic structure (Fig. 652). The material assumes almost any shape imaginable—with the possible exception of sharp, straight edges—so that the exteriors of foam houses usually reveal an abundance of free-flowing curves. Similarly fluid forms can result when concrete is sprayed over a mesh of steel bars (Fig. 303).

Perhaps the most innovative structural system devised since the introduction of reinforced concrete is the "geodesic" dome, developed by R. Buckminster Fuller and successfully adapted by others (Fig. 653). The geodesic dome is a self-supporting spherical network of steel or paper rods, joined in triangular patterns to ensure rigidity. Few other systems enclose so much space with so little material, and the process of construction is equally efficient. A membrane of glass, transparent plastic, or almost any other material can be attached to the skeleton to provide shelter, insulation, and light. The house illustrated here was designed as a transparent

653. An experimental house of aluminum rods and a plastic skin rests high in the hills above Hollywood, California. Bernard Judge based the design on the geodesic domes of R. Buckminster Fuller. (*Photograph: Julius Shulman*)

bubble affording unobstructed views of the area in all directions. Ventilation is provided by a screened opening around the base and another opening at the top of the dome, protected by a raised plastic cover. Inside, an independent steel frame supports high floors for optimum views, while screens provide areas of privacy. Because of its light weight and great strength, the geodesic dome has great potential for the "megastructures" of the future (see Chap. 20).

Stressed skin construction has attracted much interest in recent years, especially among do-it-yourselfers. Large triangular, hexagonal, or polyhedral panels can be fitted together in a rigid structure similar to that of a geodesic dome, but with panels acting as both skeleton and skin at the same time. Panel shapes must be calculated to ensure an equal distribution of forces and minimize strain on the joints. The structural system finds direct expression on the exterior, as in the "zomes" of Steve Baer (Fig. 135). Such houses have yet to prove themselves in terms of cost, livability, and longevity, but the concept remains intriguing.

Types of Single-Family Housing

In the last half century or so the single-family dwelling has become the predominant form of housing in Western societies. Although the changing fabric of modern society has weakened the validity of this type of land use—while urbanization, environmental concerns, and population pressures have increased interest in multiple-unit housing—the single-family detached home continues as a prevalent form of dwelling to which many aspire. It offers individuals, families, and other groups a plot of land and independent home they can call their own and change, within limits, to suit personal needs and fancies. Physical boundaries separate the residence from surrounding areas, permitting a high degree of privacy. And the homeowner's monthly outlay for housing accrues in the form of a capital investment.

All single-family houses are not alike, however. Choices range from the custom-designed to mass-produced, with many variations between the two extremes. A preexisting house can be left as it is, partially or completely remodeled, expanded, or restored to its historic state when first erected. Personalized new homes may be constructed of anything from prefabricated modular units to materials and objects found on the site. All these factors by which a house is brought into being have important effects on exterior design.

The Custom-Designed Home

We are all builders at heart, and the prospect of creating a personal form of shelter appeals to our most basic instincts. Custom design offers a family or individual the opportunity to build a unique home, tailor-made to suit personal needs and preferences.

Selecting a site, hiring an architect, and setting the budget are usually among the first steps of custom design. The future occupants discuss their space requirements and living patterns with the architect, and together both parties outline the house in terms of size, plan, siting, materials, and cost. Homeowners can stipulate specific design features and even supply sketch plans and elevations, or they can leave all details to the professional's expertise. When the owners have approved the final design, contractors are commissioned to supply the materials and skilled labor necessary to lay foundations and erect the structure, and to install plumbing and electrical equipment. Special arrangements may be required, depending on the site, for driveways, electricity, water supply, and sewage. Rising costs and changes of mind during the period of planning and construction inevitably compromise budget estimates. Yet the satisfaction of seeing the project to completion—plus the pleasure of moving into the final result—almost always outweighs the headaches encountered on the way.

The custom-designed house evolves directly from the lifestyle of a particular family or group. Exteriors are thus free to express individual patterns of living, as in the houses already discussed, which satisfy their owners' requests for views over the landscape (Fig. 629), privacy (Fig. 630), and vacation hideaways (Fig. 631). Even without special requirements, a home designed by a talented architect can transform the habits of daily routine into visual substance and aesthetic excitement (Figs. 628, 639, 640).

Mass production and custom design are by no means incompatible. One of the best ways of cutting costs is to take advantage of materials available in prefabricated form. Particular ingenuity in this respect led to the creation of a remarkable "silo house" intended for weekend living (Fig. 654; see Fig. 115). A standard grain silo, purchased from the manufacturer, was transformed into a home by the addition of windows, an upper floor, and a stairwell. Aided by friends, the owners erected the structure themselves in order to reduce the cost of labor, which often accounts for half the expenses of building a new house. The result is a uniquely personal mixture of custom design, mass production, and handcraft.

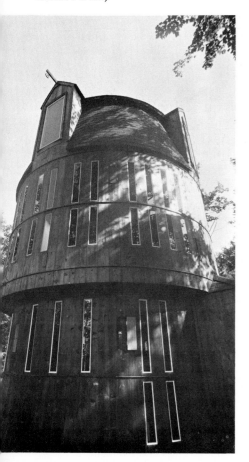

654. An ordinary grain silo became a distinctive home for the Audette family, who erected and adapted the structure themselves. See also Fig. 115. (*Photograph: Robert Perron*)

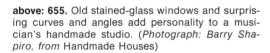
above: 655. Old stained-glass windows and surprising curves and angles add personality to a musician's handmade studio. (*Photograph: Barry Shapiro, from* Handmade Houses)

left: 656. The people of Alberobello in the south Italian province of Apulia build their own cone-roofed dwellings by hand, using irregular slabs of local stone without mortar. The form and technique of these structures, known as *trulli*, has remained essentially unchanged since the protohistoric period. (*Photograph: Alinari–Art Reference Bureau*)

Handmade Houses

The ultimate in personalized architecture is the handmade house. This type of home is a rare and often exotic interlude in modern housing. It exists in response to that urge to create by hand that lies deep within our nature. Handmade houses serve as ruggedly individualistic protests against the inevitability of industrialization (Fig. 655). They are usually found in an exurban location far from the reach of restrictive zoning and the building inspector. They range in form from the geodesic dome in variations undreamed of by Buckminster Fuller to rambling, ever-expanding "follies" composed of bottles, bricks, and other scraps. Some are based on the shelter-building techniques of early peoples (Fig. 656).

Remodeled Homes

One of the most viable alternatives to the custom-designed home is to remodel an existing older home into a new form. The remodeling process often calls for more imagination and ingenuity in planning than the custom-designed home that starts from scratch. Like a double exposure in a photograph, the present-day inhabitants are superimposed over the shadowy images of yesterday's family. The new owner must in fact build on the past and carefully relate old and new. Living patterns today demand a freer and more flowing arrangement of space than previously, both within the home and out into the surrounding spaces. Opening up walls into larger window areas and installing doors to terraces or decks often substantially change the exterior design. The sensitive architect, however, tries to integrate the new with the old by means of materials, recurring details, or general character (Fig. 657).

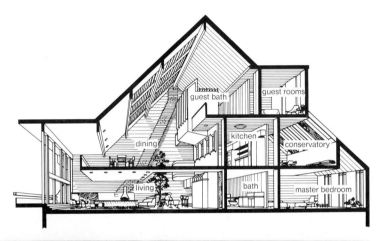

above: 657. Architect Kipp Stewart remodeled and expanded a small cottage, employing simple, natural materials like those of the original structure. The result is a charming retreat for informal living. See also Fig. 456; Plate 10, p. 59; Plate 37, p. 256. (*Photograph: Morley Baer*)

658–659. A Boston warehouse, built in 1888, was converted by architect Gerard Cugini to provide offices for rental and a triplex apartment for himself.

above right: 658. The upper levels of Cugini's apartment rise under a sloping roof invisible from the street (Fig. 659). Skylights provide ample daylight for three floors, linked by internal balconies.

right: 659. The cantilevered exterior balcony, built of concrete, offers a view across Lewis Wharf (Figs. 717, 718) toward the Boston harbor. (*Photograph: Louis Reens*)

The reconciliation of old and new is especially important in the case of remodeled homes in the heart of the city. Much ingenuity is required to meet the special needs of a new owner while not disrupting the visual rhythm of the existing urban fabric. In Boston, for example, an old warehouse has been converted into three floors of rentable office space and a triplex apartment with a glass wall and cantilevered balcony looking onto the harbor (Figs. 658, 659). Harmonious integration can be achieved even with a contrast of materials, as in a New York townhouse remodeled with a façade of steel and glass by Paul Rudolph (Pl. 61, p. 454; see also Fig. 27 and Pl. 22, p. 162). Thin, delicate lines and a fine sense of proportions relate the house to the Greek Revival structure next door.

The current awareness of the need to conserve resources and preserve our architectural heritage has led to the recycling of many older buildings. While many old homes and commercial structures are being turned into essentially contemporary dwellings, a few enthusiasts, sometimes with governmental support, are restoring historic homes to their original condition (Fig. 660; see also Fig. 426). Modern conveniences can be incorporated unobtrusively, while the spirit of the past becomes an everyday reality.

left: 660. This 1825 clapboard house stands in a historic restoration district in Winston-Salem, North Carolina. Two brothers, Thomas and William Gray, purchased the house, restored the exterior to its original, austere appearance, and adapted the interior to their own living needs. See also Fig. 426. (*Photograph: The New York Times / Bill Aller*)

right: 661. Colonial styles are revived in a row of attached houses built by developers in the new town of Columbia, Maryland. A mixture of designs based on different periods and geographical areas makes little historical sense but adds variety to the street. See also Figs. 712, 713. (*Courtesy: The Rouse Company*)

Developers' Homes

By far the greatest number of homes constructed for single-family living during the past fifty years have been those built by developers on large or small tracts of land. Often using only one plan, with or without variations in façade and orientation, developers have been able to build more cheaply and quickly than the individual homeowner. From the rows upon rows of identical boxes each centered on its own tiny plot of land, to the larger and more thoughtfully sited houses that may each have an identifying form, orientation, and variation in plan, these dwellings have been produced to meet the needs of the greatest number of potential home buyers. In essence they have been mass produced but individually built by workers going from one house to the next, employing their particular skills.

A new town such as Columbia, Maryland (discussed in more detail in Chapter 20) illustrates an unusually successful example of large-scale speculative building. Projected eventually to house about 110,000 people, Columbia contains a wide choice of housing types and styles built by a number of subdevelopers. Most of the dwellings have been specifically designed for certain groups of potential purchasers. Although often unimaginative, the exteriors are less homogeneous than in most developments (Fig. 661). The result illustrates the main characteristic of

left: 662. A modular system for prefabricated panels, designed by architect Alfredo De Vido, can be arranged to form a small, one-story house. (*Photograph © Louis Checkman*)

right: 663. A different arrangement of De Vido's panels produces a larger, two-story home with carport and covered decks. (*Photograph © Louis Checkman*)

this type of housing: It is built to appeal to general tastes shared by the greatest number of people.

The most apparent influence on exterior design in this type of housing is the continuing interest in historic styles, which apparently satisfy many people. However, an opening wedge of more functional exterior design is becoming more prevalent to meet the needs of new types of housing, which may feature such elements as staggered façades, cluster planning, and grouped structures of varying heights. The older styles just do not lend themselves as readily to the indoor-outdoor-but-still-private type of living that so many people desire today.

Mass-Produced Homes

The industrialization of housing seems inevitable, given the high cost of building, but the trend has certainly been slow in becoming a practical reality. For some thirty years the dream of low-cost housing made possible by prefabrication and mass-production techniques similar to those that gave us the low-cost automobile has tantalized the prospective home builder and buyer. Currently two types of mass-produced homes are available from an increasing number of manufacturers: modular homes and mobile homes.

Modular Housing   According to Professor Joseph Carreiro of Cornell University, who has made extensive studies of factory-produced homes,[1] modular housing is a kind of "systems approach" with great potential for the future. Components, both panels and three-dimensional modules, are almost totally prefinished at the factory, then placed on a prepared foundation at the site and fastened together. The concept is broad and encompasses a wide variety of designs and ways of putting the components together.

Mass production offers the possibility of greatly reduced labor costs in both fabrication and assembly. The success of modular construction, however, depends on the flexibility of each system, so that the modular units can be arranged in different combinations to suit the needs, budgets, and tastes of individual households (Figs. 662, 663, 166–168).

Most prefabricated single-family homes now available are panelized, arriving at the site as a collection of beams, girders, and wall, floor, and roof components, which can be erected on a prepared foundation in a short time by largely unskilled labor. A number of companies produce this type of house: exteriors usually display established styles but occasionally achieve distinctive results (Fig. 664). Vacation homes in particular lend themselves to this method, because they are often placed in locations far from a ready supply of skilled labor.

Panelized systems complete with do-it-yourself instructions provide less flexible but very inexpensive homes (Fig. 665). The cost of the example illustrated here has been greatly reduced by replacing the foundation with simple concrete piers like those employed for mobile homes.

Three-dimensional modules are as yet less widely applied in single-family than in mass housing. A demonstration house suggesting some of the possibilities is illustrated in Figure 666. Modular kitchen and bathroom units stacked one on top of another form a central spine around which panelized components are assembled to create group and private spaces. The potentials of such a system are immediately evident.

Based on the theory that maximum prefabrication involves minimum cost, some firms offer houses prefinished at the factory and basically ready for occupation as soon as they are lifted into place (Fig. 667). The only other work at the site is the laying of a foundation. Except for this feature, prefinished houses are essentially mobile homes, and the two types of dwellings share many similarities in exterior form.

Mobile Homes   The mobile home is the most rapidly growing form of single-family housing in the United States. Production of this type of housing is exploding in response to the demand for low-cost housing that will provide some of the amenities associated with single-family living. The mobile home offers a degree of privacy, independent ownership, easy financing, liquidity of investment, and reduced real-estate taxes. Ironically, the very mobility that gave a name to this type of housing has long ceased to be a major factor in its popularity. Today, mobility is apt to be limited to the initial move from the factory to the mobile home park. Once settled on its minuscule site, the mobile home often remains at one location through a succession of owners. Factory produced, the mobile home is limited by law to a maximum width of 12 feet in order to be transported on the highway. However, many designs today provide a double unit with two 12-foot sections joined side by side to provide a house 24 feet wide (Fig. 169). Mobile homes are produced in a number of different lengths up to a staggering 70 feet.

In exterior design, this type of housing suffers from ambivalent tendencies. Its appearance straddles a line between its origins as a trailer hauled about by a streamlined automobile and the small cottage it becomes when parked on its site (Fig. 668). Progressive designers, rejecting both extremes, have attempted to give the mobile home an exterior design expressive of both its function and its industrialized means of production (Fig. 669).

Motor Homes   Domestic mobility achieves its ultimate expression in the motor home (Fig. 670). Large windows provide light but can be sealed for privacy, while vents ensure the proper circulation of air. Heat, power, and plumbing mechanisms are exposed or easily accessible from the outside in order to maximize interior space and facilitate servicing. The motor home's compact, streamlined design reveals its dual function as both house and automobile.

The tremendous variety in exterior design shown in this one chapter amply demonstrates the diversity of cultural expression we take for granted today. In our complex society, many dissimilar lifestyles coexist in one community, while two families living on opposite sides of the continent may be more like each other than their respective neighbors. One of the chief opportunities for the expression of personal needs, tastes, and aspirations lies in the selection of a particular type of home with a particular handling of function, site, materials, and structure.

right: 669. Sleek, simple lines enhance the steel and plastic "capsule lodge" called "Yadokari" manufactured by the Nikko Kasei Company of Tokyo. Like most mobile homes, the small vacation house is transported by truck and quickly lifted into place by crane. (*Photograph: Yoshiyuki Sakai, courtesy GK Industrial Design Associates*)

below: 670. The motor home reconciles the demands of domestic comfort with the advantages of total mobility. (*Courtesy Owens/Corning Fiberglas*)

Landscape Design

19

Designing the landscape surrounding a home is an important and integral aspect of total design for living. The careful placement of a house in relation to its site can be supplemented by adjustments to the landscape in order to increase the integration of indoor and outdoor spaces. Individual living patterns often call for specific design features in the garden or yard, just as they do in the organization of the house interior. Households with young children need outdoor amenities different from those required by swimming enthusiasts or amateur gardeners. Similarly, problems of access and privacy are often best met by altering the terrain or planting new trees and shrubs. A homeowner may choose to plant a lawn around the house, install large concrete terraces, or leave the site as much as possible in its natural state; each choice offers distinct advantages in terms of the amount of maintenance required and the extent to which the garden can serve as an extension of the house. Everyone appreciates the beauty of nature, but the dissimilarity of human tastes ensures an endless variety even in gardens intended purely for visual enjoyment. In all of its aspects, landscape design allows the natural setting to become an integral component of personal lifespace. One individual prefers an expanse of open ground for active sports and games, another favors a shady retreat or a framed view from the house. Formal or informal, carefully planned or left in natural condition, requiring minimal or constant attention—the home landscape can be designed to fit personal needs and tastes.

Formal gardens, which reached the peak of their popularity in the 18th century, survive only under special circumstances today, as in a topiary fantasy maintained by the enthusiastic owner of a historic home (Fig. 671). Here, animals and geometrical shapes have been sculptured from privet hedge within a symmetrically planned garden of carefully tended flower beds. Although they demand the studious, full-time attention of a professional or amateur gardener, such creations offer an appealing display of whimsey and virtuosity.

Contemporary gardening tastes, indebted to English and Japanese influences, usually prefer more informal, varied, and "natural" effects—however carefully planned they may be. Irregularity, unpredictability, and a play of contrasting shapes and textures create an impression of composed informality in the example illustrated in Figure 672. An irregularly shaped pool, scattered rocks, different types of foliage, and a rough-textured, low, wooden bridge seem to harmonize with the existing trees, as if this were a "discovered" corner of an enchanted forest.

above: 671. Animals and geometric shapes fashioned from privet hedge and baling wire make up the topiary garden on the grounds of what was once a simple Colonial farmhouse in Portsmouth, Rhode Island. The garden has been carefully maintained since its original creation almost sixty years ago. (*Photograph: The New York Times*)

right: 672. Existing pine trees are carefully incorporated in the design of a relaxing sylvan retreat. (*Photograph: Morley Baer*)

Functions of Landscape Design

In an ideal situation, both outdoor and indoor spaces are planned at the same time as a single, unified concept. Usually, however, the garden environment must be designed around an existing home. Either way, the role of landscape design in relation to architecture is, first, to strengthen the relationship of the house to its site, and, second, to provide usable outdoor spaces for living and recreational purposes. Other considerations might include:

☐ A preferred level of maintenance requirements
☐ Privacy from and/or integration with surrounding areas
☐ Attractive "garden pictures" from windows or terraces
☐ Provision for active outdoor play for both children and adults
☐ Room for growing flowers, fruits, or vegetables, and perhaps a potting shed
☐ Storage space for gardening equipment, outdoor furniture, and games

Access

The functional aspect of the house-site relationship centers on the provisions for access and movement between the house and its grounds. The means by which we enter a house are important for obvious functional reasons and because of the basic emotions evoked by the experience of coming home or visiting others. Contemporary architects generally avoid the traditional imposing façade with a prominent central doorway directed toward the public street. Functionally conceived with an emphasis on privacy, today's exteriors often open to the public domain

opposite: 673. A short bridge carries automobiles and pedestrians to the upper living areas of a house in Mountain Park, a planned community outside Portland, Oregon. Windows are concentrated on the sides facing away from the street to provide privacy and views over the landscape. Campbell-Yost and Partners, architects. See also Fig. 1. (*Photograph: Julius Shulman*)

right: 674. Architectural space blends with dense vegetation around an open but protected pedestrian approach. Exposed aggregate in the concrete adds colors and textures in keeping with the natural setting and the unfinished wood surfaces of the house. Callister & Payne, Henry Herold, architects. See also Figs. 127, 625, 689. (*Photograph: Philip L. Molten*)

only through a driveway or walk leading to a relatively modest entrance. Approaches can be concealed or given twisting routes to preserve privacy, or opened conspicuously as a welcoming gesture.

Each site presents special problems, especially for motorized access. Hilly sites are often treated by leading the driveway to one level, the pedestrian path to another. The driveway in Figure 673 is carried on a bridge, which provides a direct, level approach while articulating the separation of the house from the public road.

Thanks to the greater maneuverability of human beings, pedestrian access offers the opportunity for more variety in turns and level changes than is possible in the placement of driveways. In one example, a wide pavement of wood-framed concrete slabs, placed alongside the house and protected by overhanging eaves, leads the visitor through lush foliage up a few steps to a landing at the rear (Fig. 674). The resulting impression combines invitation and security.

Indoor-Outdoor Communication

One of the chief advantages of low-density land settlement is the opportunity it affords for outdoor as well as indoor living. Given a suitable climate, contemporary homes offer free communication between the two areas. Doors opening off interior living spaces provide direct access to the outdoors and encourage fluid movement. Sliding glass doors are especially useful, since they maintain visual communication even when closed, but nonsupporting walls can be opened up in more inventive ways as well (Fig. 442).

One of the most popular and efficient means of linking house and landscape is through the use of decks and terraces—open to the sky, but convenient for most

left: 675. A uniform material—wooden shingles and boards—harmonizes the outdoor deck with the exterior of a home designed for himself by architect James Caldwell. The open, raised deck acts as an extension of indoor living areas and prevents dirt and mud from being tracked through the house. See also Figs. 122, 587. (*Photograph: Philip L. Molten*)

below left: 676. A wooden deck has been cut away around existing trees to preserve a natural source of shade, moisture, and beauty—as well as sturdy hammock supports. Liebhart, Weston, & Goldman, architects. (*Photograph: George Lyons, courtesy California Redwood Association*)

below right: 677. Covered porches and an open terrace seem contained by the geometric, sculptural exterior of a shingled house by Alfredo De Vido. Tall proportions express the striking vertical spaces of the interior. See also Figs. 425, 496. (*Photograph: Ezra Stoller © ESTO*)

of the activities that normally take place indoors (Figs. 675, 46). Such elements can be carefully arranged to make a gradual transition from house to landscape, combining maximum convenience with a sense of living in the middle of a natural setting (Fig. 676). Immediate access to outdoor recreational pursuits is another important consideration for some families (Pl. 49, p. 336).

Covered porches and verandas offer protection from sun and rain without excluding outdoor scents and breezes. Like decks and terraces, they serve as transitions and as living spaces in themselves. The house in Figure 677 features two porches placed close to the ground to allow easy communication with the lawn and, at the rear, a paved open terrace. Both porches support second-story rooms, so that the open spaces appear as integral parts of the building's prismatic exterior design. The ceiling of the front veranda also protects the sliding glass doors that give access to the interior.

Outdoor Living Areas

For the owners of a house on a restricted suburban plot, with neighbors on three sides, privacy is usually the first landscape requirement. Some form of fence or hedge generally serves to define boundaries and cut off the view toward and from the surrounding houses. The suburban back yards in Figures 678 and 679 are fairly typical in size and nearness to neighbors, and both are enclosed by fences. Each yard also has an intermediate zone that serves as an easily maintained transition between the house and garden. In Figure 678, a broad wooden deck allows rain to pass through the spaced boards—a pattern repeated in the enclosing wooden fence. In Figure 679, shallow stepping platforms or *engawas* lead from the house floor to the Japanese-style gravel garden with its carefully placed rocks and plants. The tightly joined boards of the engawas echo the solid design of the privacy fence.

left: 678. Paved areas and an open deck invite casual, active use in a rear yard designed by landscape architect Lawrence Halprin. (*Photograph: Morley Baer*)

right: 679. Low wooden engawas, raked pebbles, and carefully placed rocks and plants give this suburban garden a contemplative, Japanese flavor. Watanabe, landscape architect. (*Photograph: Morley Baer*)

The gardens themselves also reveal differences of treatment. In the first, circular areas of paving stones draw people out to sit or sun themselves, while the surrounding ground cover requires minimum care. A few shrubs and carefully placed trees are set against the fence but do not obscure it. The other garden contrasts the green grass of a carefully tended lawn with the gray gravel terrace, but the two surfaces share a peaceful, ordered quality. Here the fence is partially obscured by foundation planting and low rock walls. A few boulders and small trees create focal spots and complete the intimate mood. In comparison to the first example, this garden requires devoted attention, and it attracts quiet contemplation rather than carefree activity.

Larger pieces of property can be landscaped with less concern for privacy than is true in medium-density suburban areas. Owners and architects alike usually prefer to leave the grounds largely in their natural state, altering the terrain only for access and other functional considerations. More extensive landscaping, however, sometimes improves the overall home environment. The removal of a natural outcropping of rock may open a pleasant vista, for example, while replanting a deforested site will attract birds and other wildlife. Level ground not only offers the greatest convenience for many outdoor activities but can also enhance the visual effect of a particular house. In Figure 628, a trim, carefully tended lawn offsets the abstract forms of an architect's home.

In an urban environment, restricted space, dense population, and excessive air pollution demand special solutions in the design of outdoor living spaces. Hard surface materials, such as brick and stone, promise the easiest maintenance. In

left: 680. Brick provides the practical and attractive surface of a terrace in New York City. A cedar fence, bleached gray, ensures privacy, while low brick walls serve as planting boxes as well as low seats. Richard Dattner & Associates, architects.

right: 681. A J-shape bench provides informal seating and serves as a step between the two levels of a narrow city garden. Ivy and other plants surround activity areas covered in gravel. Thomas D. Church, landscape architect. (*Photograph: Morley Baer*)

682. Swimming becomes an integral part of outdoor living in a house equipped with dressing rooms and a pool-side terrace. Smith & Larson, architects. (*Photograph: Morley Baer*)

Figure 680, different levels of brick paving divide a terrace garden into separate spaces for dining and relaxation. The same material is used for low-maintenance planting beds, providing shrubs and small trees that soften the strongly architectural setting. Potted plants are especially handy to the city gardener, since they can be rotated with the seasons for continual blooms.

The long, narrow dimensions of many urban lots present a challenge to the landscape designer (Fig. 681). Such sites are best broken up into separate areas. A careful balance of greenery, pavement, seating, and level changes creates a relaxed, free atmosphere—equally pleasurable for active use and as "garden pictures" viewed from inside the townhouse. Enclosed by walls for privacy, the city garden tends toward introverted design, with the intimate scale of an outdoor room.

Play Areas

Provisions for outdoor play depend on the kinds of activities enjoyed and the ages of the participants. An open space of lawn often suffices for a variety of games from football to croquet. If swimming is a favorite sport, a pool and perhaps dressing rooms can be provided, even on small lots. In Figure 682, a concrete terrace beside the pool gives space for drying out, lounging, and eating snacks. Flowering shrubs around the pool cut the glare from concrete and water and make the pool seem a natural part of the garden. Dressing rooms under a low shed roof form a visual and functional transition to the house proper.

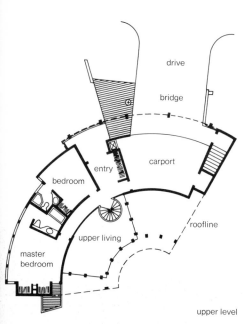

drive

bridge

carport

entry

bedroom

roofline

upper living

master bedroom

upper level

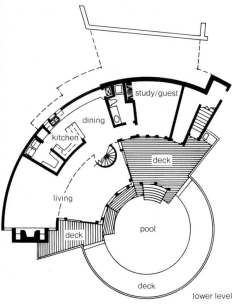

study/guest

dining

kitchen

deck

living

deck

pool

deck

lower level

above: 683. The segmental plan of Charles F. Pensinger's home outside Birmingham, Alabama, seems to radiate outward from a circular pool at the center. John M. Fuller, architect.

above right: 684. The hillside location of the Pensinger house allows an unobstructed view toward downtown Birmingham. (*Photograph: Don Henderson*)

Swimming served as the focus of exterior design in a house whose living areas radiate from a circular pool and shield it from the street (Figs. 683, 684). Suspended among the trees on a steep slope, the swimming area achieves a high degree of privacy in an open, natural setting.

When young children are part of a household, a swimming pool can be hazardous, and must be fenced off or covered for safety. A play yard will be more to the point, with plenty of room for the children's constantly changing games and activities. Play equipment can range from the usual slides, swings, and sandpile to elaborate tree houses or simple climbing sculpture (Fig. 685). The equipment need not be elaborate, however, for children often have more fun with a pile of sand and a collection of boards that they can use inventively in their play. Some hard ground surfacing is helpful for riding wheeled toys, jumping rope, and bouncing balls. If play space is visually screened from other areas, adult standards of neatness can be relaxed, but easy accessibility to the kitchen and children's rooms is an important asset.

Service Spaces

As food becomes more expensive while its quality suffers from industrialized processing, many households today grow their own fruits and vegetables, to be eaten fresh or preserved for later use. The placement of a working garden depends less on visual effect than on favorable soil, light, and drainage conditions. Plants must have ample sunlight and protection from wind; tools and supplies should be readily accessible.

Every home requires storage space for tools, recreational equipment, trash cans, and the inevitable accumulation of things with nowhere else to go. An outdoor shed for garden tools and supplies can also serve as a studio for home crafts (Fig. 686). Usually located near the kitchen and carport, a suitably designed storage facility relieves the house and yard of much unnecessary clutter.

left: 685. A climbing structure of thick, wooden blocks permits improvisational play while embellishing the yard as a sculptural accent. (*Photograph: Ron Green, courtesy Timberform*)

right: 686. Natural, rough-grained wood and a concrete floor create a convenient but attractive garden shed-studio. Skylights provide the necessary abundance of natural light. (*Photograph: Barbeau Engh, courtesy California Redwood Association*)

left: 687. Extended roofs, floor-level decks, and an inner porch promote free indoor-outdoor living in a small interior patio. Driftwood, rocks, plants, and rough-sawn wood siding contribute natural textures, while concrete paving with exposed aggregate offers maximum convenience. William Gillis, architect. (*Photograph: Morley Baer*)

below: 688. Windswept trees and a cantilevered balcony shade an open deck suspended above iceplant, a natural soft ground cover. Louis Alley, landscape architect. (*Photograph: Morley Baer*)

opposite: 689. Wood fences create privacy screens and decorative foils for a lush concentration of plants and flowers. Callister & Payne, Henry Herold, architects. See also Figs. 127, 625, 674. (*Photograph: Philip L. Molten*)

Materials of Landscape Design

A knowledge of materials is as necessary in landscape design as it is in house planning or interior design—perhaps even more so, for the materials are primarily natural ones with very specific temperaments and needs. Because living materials grow and die, the anticipation of natural changes is important. Designing in tune with nature produces the best results.

Ground Surfacings

Like floor coverings, ground surfacings are either hard, such as stone and brick, or soft, such as lawns and ground covers.

Hard ground surfacings, more than any other single factor, make gardens livable. Once installed, they require almost no maintenance and keep the design of the garden clearly defined. Hard pavements also help relate the house to the land. *Stone* can be tightly joined and mortared to provide a continuous surface or laid in flagstones to bring a rustic, informal look to garden paving. *Brick* ranges in texture from rough to smooth, and in color from rust to a dark chocolate brown. This versatile material can be set in many patterns and used for walls and steps as well as pavements (Fig. 680). *Concrete* offers great durability and moderate installation costs. *Exposed aggregate* in the concrete provides an attractive surface for gardens, because the exposed pebbles add color and texture to an otherwise cold material (Fig. 687). *Blacktop* or *asphalt* makes a good surface for games. Flexible and easily patched or resurfaced, it also lends itself to meandering garden pathways. *Gravel,* an inexpensive material, comes in a wide variety of colors and textures (Fig. 681). *Wood,* when raised as decking above the decay-producing moisture of the soil, also serves as an excellent ground cover (Fig. 688).

Soft ground surfacings serve a double purpose: to prevent erosion from wind and rain, and to unify the garden design. Some soft covers withstand considerable trampling, but others are too delicate for pedestrian traffic. A lawn of grass or dicondra is the most popular method of achieving a regular green surface. Other soft but durable coverings are *shredded bark,* often used for children's playgrounds, and *outdoor carpeting,* installed over a concrete base. Soft ground covers unsuitable for heavy traffic include wild strawberry, ivy, creeping juniper, pachysandra, and many carpetweeds, such as iceplant (Fig. 688).

Fences, Walls, and Hedges

Comparable to the walls of a room, outdoor fences, walls, and hedges give privacy, lessen wind penetration, and create a background for plants and embellishments (Fig. 689). Architecturally, they delineate the three-dimensional space of the landscape. Walls and fences require little maintenance and can be squeezed along a property line, leaving the ground free for other uses. Given sufficient space and a patient gardener, a hedge provides both privacy and a backdrop of natural beauty and fragrance.

Overhead Protection

The comfort of outdoor spaces often depends on tempering the impact of natural forces. Various types of overhead protection can reduce the impact of the sun's heat and glare, deflect the force of wind, and protect living and storage spaces from rain and snow. Eaves projecting beyond the walls of the house shelter outdoor areas and enhance the livability of a home (Fig. 687). Arbors, trellises, and sun-

above: 690. Wooden trellises cast flickering highlights and shadows over stone and concrete floors, walls of wood and rough masonry, and a variety of plants and shrubs in a house remodeled by architect Howard Backen. (*Photograph: Philip L. Molten*)

left: 691. Trellises arranged in an octagonal pattern shield a city garden from both neighbors and excessive sunlight. In the foreground, however, an upper-level deck offers direct exposure to the sky. Taylor & Ng, architects. See also Fig. 526. (*Photograph: Morley Baer*)

692. Serpentine curves, large boulders, and overhanging trees and plants give this swimming pool the appearance of a natural lagoon. The entire design reveals a love of nature and a minute attention to detail. See also Figs. 283, 694. (*Photograph: Morley Baer*)

shades utilizing vines, canvas, or wooden slats help to create comfortable outdoor spaces enlivened by changing patterns of light and shadow (Fig. 690). An inventive arrangement of trellises adds privacy as well as comfort to a city garden (Fig. 691). Horizontally branching trees, such as mulberry, evergreen, elm, and oak, provide the most natural means of overhead protection (Fig. 688).

Plants

The large vocabulary of plant forms available for garden design increases each season with new specimens introduced by growers. The selection of particular plants depends on factors such as size, nature and density of foliage, rate of growth, climatic adaptability, as well as intended placement and final effect. *Low-growing plants* that serve as ground covers have already been mentioned. *Shrubs,* low- to moderate-height woody plants with multiple stems, are used as backdrops, screens, and decisive accents. *Evergreens* offer year-round color, while *annuals* and *perennials* mark changing seasons. *Trees,* of course, are the biggest plant forms in the garden and must be chosen and planted with their ultimate size and shape in mind. Many a novice gardener has made the mistake of planting trees too close together, neglecting to consider their maturing bulk. Trees are nature's own device for tempering climate conditions. In addition to providing shade, color, and shelter, they cool the air by the moisture from their leaves. It is the lucky householder who has some mature trees for natural protection and delight. *Flowers,* both perennials and annuals, enliven a garden with brilliant colors and delightful fragrances. They are also a practical source of interior enrichment.

Water

For centuries, water has formed an important element of garden design. The gardens of ancient Persia, Italy, and other Mediterranean countries made extensive use of pools, cascades, and fountains. No single element brings more delight to the outdoor setting of a home. A pool of standing water extends the vista, reflects the changing moods of the sky overhead, and responds to the slightest ripple of breeze (Fig. 692). The gurgles and splashes of jets and fountains delight the ear

above: 693. A single stream of water harmonizes with the linear elegance of a Japanese-style garden. Geraldine Scott Knight, landscape architect. (*Photograph: Morley Baer*)

left: 694. Functional necessity turns to decorative enrichment in the concrete-filled drain tiles lining the curving edge of a pool. See also Fig. 692. (*Photograph: Morley Baer*)

as well as the eye (Fig. 693). While the use of water introduces special problems of pumping, drainage, and safety, this important element should not be neglected by the garden planner.

Enrichment

The final touch of garden design is the inclusion of special features purely for the pleasure they afford. Objects such as rocks, ceramics, and sculpture require little maintenance but can add decisive personality to the garden environment. Free-standing sculpture, exploited fully in the gardens of the Baroque period, appears occasionally in today's homes. More common is the sensitive detailing of functional features, as in the drain tiles filled with concrete that form the rhythmic, curving edge of a pool in Figure 694. Ceramic pots and urns, with or without plants, provide visual accents (Fig. 311). Given a site of sufficient size and appropriate character, a gazebo serves as the picturesque focus of a rambling landscape (Fig. 695).

695. A screened-in gazebo, with spreading roof topped by a large, decorative finial, provides a quiet retreat for outdoor relaxation while enhancing the landscape as viewed from a distance. The rustic whimsey of the garden structure contrasts with the dynamic masses of the house proper. (*Photograph: Ezra Stoller* ©️ *ESTO*)

Community
and
Environment

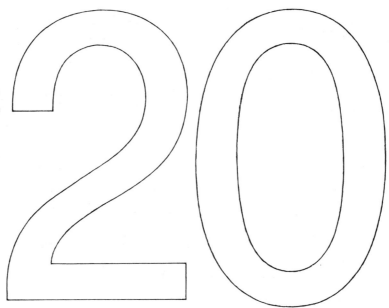

Population growth and urbanization throughout the world have strained traditional relations between humankind and nature. Today, more than one-half the population of the United States lives in urban areas that occupy only 1 percent of the total land area. Overcrowded cities have outgrown the systems of transportation, communication, and life-support that once seemed sufficient to their needs. Excessive congestion, noise, and pollution have contributed to the physical and spiritual deterioration of urban life (Fig. 696).

Since the end of World War II, the primary response to urban overcrowding has been the settlement of large tracts of land on the peripheries of major cities. Suburban living promised independent ownership of land—however small the plot—and motorized access to the employment and cultural attractions of the city. Hoping to prevent overcrowding and other urban ills, community governments passed zoning ordinances regulating lot size, set-back distance between house and street, house orientation, type of structure, even architectural design. Although well-intentioned, such laws often bring questionable side effects: where restrictive, they may bar the kinds of enlivening variety that would benefit the community; where permissive, they have tended to foster sprawls of identical houses lined up in straight-jacket patterns (Fig. 697). Large-scale developers often level sites and repeat the same design in house after house in order to build, at minimum cost, as many single-family dwellings on a given tract of land as permitted by local zoning regulations.

Zoning restrictions prohibiting the mixture of residential and commercial buildings led to the emergence of "bedroom suburbs," in which most activities beyond eating and sleeping—such as work, shopping, and recreation—required travel by automobile. This type of sprawl settlement is now seen by many as a stifling environment, without flexibility for individual expression or the social amenities necessary for a beneficial community life.

Massive emigration from the city to unplanned suburbs tends to diminish the quality of life in both areas. Suburban dwellers develop an excessive dependence on the automobile and spend much of their time in transit, while each family's standard of living becomes measured against the identical pattern shared by all. At the same time, heavy motorized traffic adds to the congestion and pollution of the city, whose residents find it increasingly difficult to enjoy the pleasures of the countryside. The gradual segregation of economic and social groups encourages

mutual distrust, and the decline in the number of people who work and live in the same place contributes to a breakdown of neighborhood cohesion.

Population growth and urbanization may decelerate in years to come, but the trend cannot be entirely reversed. Despite the continuing popularity of the single-family home, other types of living arrangements will play an ever-increasing role in the housing of the later 1970s and 1980s. Environmental considerations also loom larger than before, as planners seek to balance the natural and built environments for the benefit of our own and succeeding generations. This chapter presents a brief survey of the types of multiple-unit housing available, the role of landscape design in shaping community spaces, and the promises of planned communities. A concluding section offers a glimpse at living environments of the future.

Multiple-Unit Housing

World-wide population growth and urbanization confront the individual in the present-day scarcity and spiraling cost of land. This factor, together with the drawbacks of conventional urban and suburban housing, has led to an increase in denser types of living arrangements. Separate dwelling units of all sizes can be combined in larger structures ranging from high-rise towers to garden apartments, attached townhouses, and even clusters of independent houses sharing common grounds. The individual can either rent a living unit or own it jointly with an incorporated association of fellow occupants of a building or housing complex.

left: 696. Absentee landlords, inadequate services, overcrowding, and community apathy all contribute to the decline of urban areas abandoned by businesses and homeowners alike. (*Photograph: Dan W. Wheeler*)

right: 697. Three basic house types are arranged with slight variations to mask the rigid uniformity of a suburban sprawl development in Staten Island, New York. (*Photograph: The New York Times/Neal Boenzi*)

698. Clouds obscure the central floors of the 100-story John Hancock Center in Chicago. Upper floors move as much as 18 inches during high winds. Skidmore, Owings, & Merrill, architects. (*Photograph: The New York Times/Gary Settle*)

The residents of such *cooperative* buildings and *condominiums* own their own homes as an investment but share the cost of upkeep, services, and communal grounds and facilities. At its best, multiple-unit housing offers financial advantages, moderate maintenance requirements, the convenience of nearby shops and services, and a fruitful interaction with other people.

Complex problems face the designers of multiple-unit housing. High density must be reconciled with individual privacy, and efficient construction methods must be adjusted to allow variety in design. The relationship between built and open space requires careful study in terms of quantity and placement. Site, materials, cost, scale, and design must somehow satisfy investors, architects, builders, the surrounding community, and the prospective inhabitants. The complexity of these issues has elicited a variety of contemporary responses.

Urban Solutions

Inadequate housing continues to pose a central problem to all of our cities, where large numbers of people live on a small amount of land and both real-estate and construction costs are at their highest. Urban housing must supply its residents with adequate living spaces, a variety of services, and as much open air and sunlight as possible, while at the same time enhancing rather than disrupting the immediate neighborhood environment.

Mixed Land Use   The zoning laws of many cities still enforce the segregation of residential from business and commercial areas. While useful for protecting homes from the noise and pollution of heavy industries, this arrangement often means that individuals must travel to work or shopping centers, and that in the evening residential areas are crowded while commercial districts stand empty. Urban planners today favor the mixture of housing with office space, stores, and community facilities in order to reduce unnecessary traffic and increase land-use efficiency. The principle of mixed land use has been applied to large buildings, housing developments, and entire new towns.

High-Rise Living   In densely populated areas where land is expensive but foundations can be laid in firm bedrock, tall apartment buildings provide a logical answer to housing needs. High-rise buildings not only conserve land but save energy as well, for they consume 55 percent less gas and 45 percent less electricity than single-family homes to accommodate the same number of people.

The tallest residential building in the world is the John Hancock Center in Chicago (Fig. 698), one hundred stories high and serviced by half as many elevators—which have a unique ability to regenerate power on their downward trips. Here the concept of mixed land use has been applied to a single building. Apartments, originally rented but later converted to condominiums, occupy 48 floors in the upper half of the structure; offices (28 floors), parking (7 floors), stores, restaurants, and recreational facilities fill the remaining space. Commuting from home to office might consist of a three-minute ride on the elevator. Accentuated by a tapered exterior form, the extreme height of the building suspends some of its residents literally above the weather.

Although a plain "box" will house the most people on the least amount of land, many architects today break up the façades of their buildings by means of oblique angles, inset or cantilevered balconies, and variations in the shape and placement of windows (Fig. 699). Such devices add variety to internal spaces and give sculptural life to exterior forms. In the example illustrated here, 1650 apartments are housed in two towers edged between an expressway and the Harlem River in New York City. Facilities housed at lower levels provide parking, shopping, recreation, and education, while a waterside park serves residents and the public.

699. The handsomely designed Harlem River Park Houses in the Bronx, New York, provide multiple housing and community services in a distinctive, landscaped setting. Davis, Brody & Associates, architects; M. Paul Friedberg & Associates, landscape architects.

Medium- and Low-Rise Housing   Just as vertical space promotes individual privacy in the detached home, high-rise buildings discourage interaction between vertical neighbors and often give residents a sense of isolation from the natural world as well. The depersonalizing effects of the high-rise structure have led to a renewed interest in medium-rise buildings of five to ten stories, which allow the inhabitants a greater sense of "place," of belonging to a neighborhood, and, it is hoped, stronger feelings of responsibility toward the building and its inhabitants (Fig. 700). Moderate scale and horizontal proportions give such buildings a greater sense of stability and a more domestic quality.

Even in crowded cities, low-rise structures offer a practical type of housing, if zoning laws or monetary considerations do not require maximum density. An unusually attractive development for low-income families in Pittsburgh provides 114 units on a small city block (Fig. 701). Exterior façades are staggered and grouped around curving pedestrian walkways, which gives the complex the intimate scale of small village.

Suburban Solutions

Cluster Planning   The shortages and rising costs of land, construction, and fuel for heating and transportation all affect housing problems in the suburbs as much as in the city. One of the most significant trends in contemporary suburban housing is the cluster plan, which offers many advantages over the inefficiency, environmental drawbacks, and depersonalizing effects of conventional "tract" or "sprawl" developments (Fig. 702; compare Fig. 697). Instead of a rigid grid of streets with each house set on a tiny independent lot, clustered units "pool their resources" to allow for greater open space accessible to all residents—a scheme that encourages cooperation rather than competition. The shorter lengths required for roads, driveways, and underground wiring and plumbing help to reduce initial costs.

The advantages of cluster over conventional planning can be seen in a diagram comparing the two methods as applied under identical conditions (Fig. 703). The cluster plan offers 41 acres in home sites, 51 acres in usable open space, and a changing succession of pleasant views. Conventionally subdivided, the same area would have 80 acres filled by home sites, almost half as much land devoted to circulation, and none for playgrounds and parks.

Suburban Townhouses   Ideally suited for both cluster planning and the contemporary desire for maintenance-free living, the attached "townhouse" represents the strongest trend in suburban housing today. The townhouse presents a low profile of two or three stories, with front and back exposures often extended by patios

left: 702. Cluster planning at the Knolls development in San Rafael, California, allows an average density of 10 units per acre. A ring of attached townhouses shields the central, shared garden and pool from outside noises and traffic. Bushnell, Jessup, Murphy, & Van De Weghe, architects. (*Photograph: Robert Royston*)

right: 703. Cluster planning (*above*) offers greater open space, shorter roads and utility lines, and safer, more varied streets than is possible with conventional tract subdivision (*below*). (*From William Whyte, Cluster Development*)

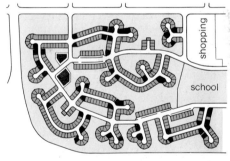

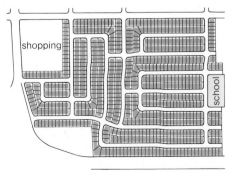

and decks (Fig. 704). Shared masonry or concrete walls of sufficient thickness ensure sound insulation on the interior, while on the exterior, walled balconies and gardens make attractive outdoor living areas with a degree of isolation from neighbors. Although exteriors imitating historic styles still persist in many such developments, others reveal a sensitive handling of the contemporary vocabulary of architectural design, with an emphasis on straightforward, functional expression.

It has been estimated that new housing built over the next few years will divide into three groups of approximately equal volume: townhouses, apartments, and detached homes. Outside the city, "garden" apartments usually resemble suburban townhouses and offer a similar combination of privacy and low maintenance in an area of medium-density population (Fig. 705). Cluster planning and careful landscape design can provide a pleasant natural environment for communal enjoyment.

Community Landscape

The importance of landscaping around housing developments of all sizes has become increasingly apparent, for aesthetic, social, environmental, and monetary reasons. Concern for environmental quality has led to an emphasis on designing in tune with nature in order to prevent the deterioration of local ecology, reduce energy consumption, and preserve natural beauty. Planners have also found that the better the development looks, the more pride the inhabitants will take in keeping it so. Adequate space for outdoor recreation for children and adults is imperative, and more units can be clustered on a given area if the spaces in between are landscaped for community use (Fig. 702).

The designers of the Martin Luther King, Jr. Community in Hartford, Connecticut, evolved a plan that clearly delineates community and private outdoor areas for both active play and quiet enjoyment (Figs. 706, 707). Paved and lightly planted courts between the low buildings provide protected areas for socializing and children's play. The recessed entrance to each unit is through these courtyards, which also have built-in storage cupboards for rubbish containers—an amenity

704. Walled-in gardens bring outdoor privacy to a row of townhouses in Carrollwood Village, a development planned around a golf course near Tampa, Florida. Eugene R. Smith & Associates, architects.

right: 705. Garden apartments and four-story structures line the shores of an artificial lake in "Sixty-01," a development in Redmond, Washington. Frank August, of Riley Bissell Associates, architect. (*Photograph: James K. M. Cheng*)

706–707. Diagonal shapes aid privacy and create community spaces in the Martin Luther King, Jr., Community in Hartford, Connecticut. Tai Soo Kim and Neil R. Taty, of Hartford Design Group, architects.

below left: 706. Low-rise structures are grouped in sawtooth patterns between open areas of lawn and trees.

below right: 707. Inner courts are paved for convenient access, active play, and socializing.

not always considered in planning. On the outer sides of the buildings, private yards open off the living rooms of each dwelling and outward onto communally shared, tree-shaded lawns.

In large developments and urban areas, children's play areas equipped with built-in seating for parents become social centers for families with small children. Play devices for climbing, sliding, and pretending may take imaginative sculptural forms fascinating to adults as well as children (Fig. 53). Suburban developments may take adult recreational pursuits such as swimming, boating, or golf as a point of departure, or the parklike quality of the natural landscape may be emphasized.

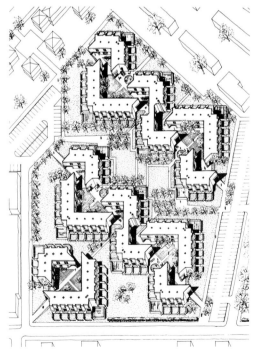

In Figure 708 attached structures housing three or four residences each have been carefully sited among existing trees. Exterior finishes of fir and cedar harmonize with the oak and pine trees of the natural environment. Unobtrusive roads provide motor access to each cluster of houses, while pedestrian and bicycle paths wind across the gentle contours of the site to preserve the atmosphere of a wooded glen.

The problems of large-scale landscape design have implications for the important issues confronting us today. Stressing our dependence on a balanced and self-renewing environment, landscape planner Ian McHarg argues strongly for designing *with* nature, rather than attempting to subdue it. In his words: "The farmer is the prototype. He prospers only insofar as he understands the land and by his management maintains its bounty."[1] McHarg and others have devised sophisticated techniques for analyzing the equilibrium of natural forces existing on a site before development, and for planning the distribution of land uses in a way that takes advantage of the ecological cycle without destroying it. Landscape planning is now an integral part of designing balanced new communities.

Planned Communities

Most communities have reached their present physical form through a series of different and often conflicting responses to natural conditions and earlier structures. The result of such unplanned growth can be a varied and interesting mixture of buildings and spaces, as seen in many older towns that have somehow escaped both deterioration and short-sighted "renewal," but inadequate planning all too often leads to chaotic jumble or suffocating drabness. Today we realize the pressing importance of comprehensive planning for all types of habitation. As we have seen, many communities have responded to this challenge by enacting zoning laws that allow for mixed land use, cluster planning, and higher-density housing. Even greater potential lies in the design of whole new communities that will eventually become largely self-sufficient. In projects of this nature, architects and landscape designers work together from the outset, along with developers, government agencies, civil engineers, sociologists, city planners, and financial experts. A planned

708. Clusters of multiunit dwellings blend unobtrusively with the carefully preserved trees and irregular terrain of Snapfinger Woods, a suburban development outside Atlanta. Callister, Payne, & Bischoff, planners; John M. Payne, architect. See also Fig. 54. (*Photograph: C. W. Callister, Jr.*)

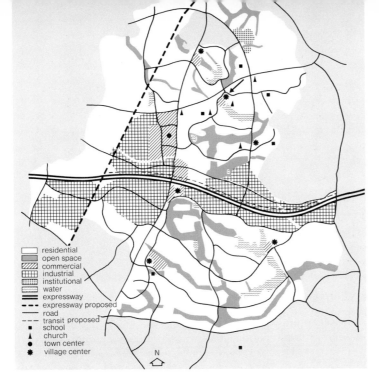

residential
open space
commercial
industrial
institutional
water
expressway
expressway proposed
road
transit proposed
■ school
▲ church
● town center
✳ village center

N

709–711. Reston, Virginia, a new town begun in 1962, will eventually comprise seven villages, each with a population of 10,000.

709. Reston's plan follows the gentle contours of the natural terrain. A town center, near the intersection of a major highway and a railroad, supplements the seven village centers. The land is divided into separate zones for light industries, park space, office and commercial areas, and housing of various densities.

community can range in scale from 20 to 20,000 acres, and in population from several hundred to 100,000 or more. The major forms are the "new town," the Planned Unit Development, and various types of special-interest communities. An unusual but related form is the megastructure.

New Towns

The new town is designed and planned as a self-contained unit with a limited population. Relatively few completely new towns have been built in the United States, whereas numerous examples already exist in Great Britain, France, and West Germany, where the pressure of population growth has been more acute. The Government of the United States has not actively engaged in the development of new communities, but the Housing and Urban Development Act of 1970 has encouraged their planning. This law authorizes grants and bond guarantees to private developers who meet stringent requirements set by the Department of Housing and Urban Development. These requirements include a detailed and complex planning process covering physical, environmental, social (including health, recreation, and cultural) goals, as well as financial, economic, governmental, and management programs. Most new towns now being developed, however, have been promoted with private capital, necessitating compliance only with state and local regulations. New York is the only state whose government has developed planned communities on its own initiative.

The complex planning of a new town usually begins—as is often now required by law—with an environmental impact study to indicate whether the site is feasible for development without having an adverse effect on the ecology of the region. Economic and financial analyses must be made at the same time, as well as programming for community service systems.

The goals of new towns include a balance of different housing types and densities to encourage a mix of social, ethnic, and economic groups among the inhabitants. Commercial, industrial, recreational, educational, and public areas are spaced in zones which prohibit the limitless expansion of one type of land use at the expense of the other community needs (Fig. 709).

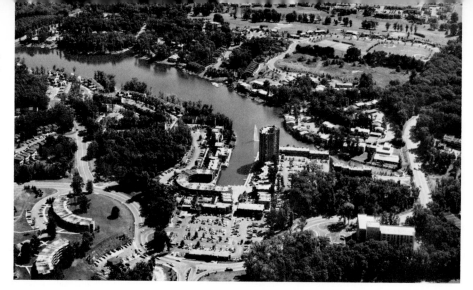

Residential areas usually consist of single-family homes interspersed with low-rise multiple-family housing and often some high-rise apartments as well—a mix intended to attract all age groups and households in a range of income brackets. Many new towns make extensive use of cluster planning, with detached homes closely spaced on small lots or with rows and groups of attached houses. Housing clusters are normally separated by open green areas, so that each home has direct access to a common park or recreation space (Fig. 710). Park areas often provide pedestrian and bicycle paths for easy off-street circulation through the residential areas and to schools, shopping, and recreational and cultural centers.

Carefully designed street, highway, and parking systems attempt to solve the problem of living with the automobile. The street patterns of most of our communities have been inherited from the horse-and-buggy era. New planning concepts increase the size of the city block, reduce the area occupied by streets, and distinguish between thoroughfares and residential streets, which are designed as cul-de-sac or loop systems discouraging fast automobile traffic. Roosevelt Island, a high-density development in New York City, will ban private automobile traffic entirely, relying on minibuses for transportation on the island (Fig. 714).

Public amenities and services are concentrated in a major center for the entire new town and in smaller neighborhood or village centers, which serve an important role as the focus of community identification. A thoughtfully designed example appears in the Lake Anne Village Center in the new town of Reston, Virginia (Fig. 711). A J-shape structure containing ground-floor commercial and civic facilities and topped by two stories of apartments encloses an intimate but open public plaza at the tip of a small, narrow lake. Outside parking enforces pedestrian-only traffic on the plaza, and the mixed-use zoning ensures lively evening as well as daytime activity.

The principle differences between the new town of today and the unplanned bedroom communities of the last thirty years is in the provision of a wide range of uses to ensure a complete lifespace. The enormous proliferation of light industries—relatively quiet and pollution-free enterprises that do not require large, unsightly plants—has made it possible to zone such employment sources adjacent to residential areas, allowing some individuals to work within walking distance of their homes. Commercial and shopping centers meet many of the needs of surrounding households, while recreational and cultural facilities provide the lively ambience traditionally a part of city living. All of this, established in parklike settings within a surrounding open space, offers a new way of life that in theory sounds utopian, but in practice has yet to stand the test of time.

One of the most successful new towns, at least from the developers' point of view, is Columbia, Maryland, located just off the major expressway between Washington and Baltimore and about 20 miles from the center of each city (Figs. 712, 713). A group of urban designers, behavioral scientists, architects, and developers began the initial planning in 1963. A number of villages of different sizes, each with a village center and subdivided into neighborhoods, are spaced in the open, rolling countryside around a more densely built "downtown" center with two department stores, more than a hundred retail shops, plus other types of commercial buildings. Large areas around the town's periphery have been set aside for employment centers, which, it is hoped, will provide 65,000 jobs when Columbia reaches it maximum population of 110,000. Expansive greenbelts, criss-crossed by pedestrian and bicycle paths, run through the development, and schools, meeting rooms, and athletic facilities are spaced throughout.

The housing is largely being built by subdevelopers, who naturally build what they hope the prospective tenants want—and in this they seem to have been quite

712–13. The new town of Columbia, Maryland, begun in 1963 on a 17,000-acre site, is scheduled to house a population of 110,000 at its completion in 1981.

left: 712. Like Reston, Columbia is planned with a town center and several village centers, as well as areas reserved for open space and for job-producing light industries.

above: 713. Repeated designs reduce the cost of attached townhouses designed by subdevelopers in Columbia's Wilde Lake Village. See also Fig. 661. (*Courtesy The Rouse Company*)

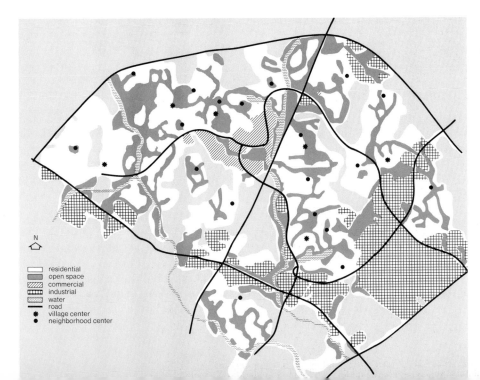

N

residential
open space
commercial
industrial
water
road
* village center
• neighborhood center

714. Roosevelt Island in New York City, shown under construction in the autumn of 1974, follows a master plan by Philip Johnson and John Burgee. Buildings are tallest along the central street, whose angular path adds spatial excitement to the downtown area. (*Courtesy Roosevelt Island Development Corporation*)

successful. One can find almost any housing type—single family, townhouse, garden apartments, and even medium-rise—in almost any style from the ubiquitous Colonial and Federal (Fig. 661), through a kind of French style with mansard roof, to the contemporary shed-roof barn style (Fig. 713). Villages are separated by hills and trees, so that only one section is usually visible at any one time, with perhaps glimpses of other developments across open green fields. Much of the landscaping is provided by the developers, who have in many cases sought to retain the natural advantages of a gentle rolling terrain. Each tenant pays a fixed charge to the Columbia Association, which provides maintenance and services. Residents who wish to use swimming pools and golf courses pay additional fees.

The success of Columbia, apart from its architecture, lies in the fact that it has attracted a wide variety of social and ethnic groups, that it is rapidly becoming largely self-supporting, and that it provides a viable alternative to both urban and exurban living, with many of the inducements of both. Moreover, it supplies vastly needed new housing in an attractive setting, uncrowded but near potential work, with the retail and service amenities of a small city.

Planned Unit Development

The advantages of the new town as a self-contained, socially beneficial environment can be applied on a smaller scale in the form of Planned Unit Developments, or PUDs. The Urban Land Institute defines a PUD as a "project, predominantly of housing, with the following elements: dwelling units grouped into clusters, allowing an appreciable amount of land for open space; much or all of its housing in townhouses or apartments or both; most economical and efficient use of land, making possible higher densities without overcrowding; where desired, part of the land is used for nonresidential purposes, such as shopping and employment centers."[2] These principles obviously lie behind the planning of new towns like Columbia and Reston. But they are also applicable to smaller urban and suburban complexes, and to urban developments large enough to be called *new-towns-in-town.*

Roosevelt Island is a new-town-in-town PUD to be built on a 147-acre island in the East River in New York City (Fig. 714). An eventual population of 17,000

residents will be housed in U-shape apartment buildings 4 to 22 stories high, stepped down and opening toward the river on both sides of the island. Automobiles will be allowed only as far as a parking garage at the entrance; from there, minibuses and a walkway system will link the various facilities. Refuse is to be collected from various buildings and channeled to a central point by an underground pneumatic system. Schools will be scattered throughout, but commercial and civic functions will be integrated with apartments along the central spine, creating a lively "main street." Large areas of the island are reserved for open park space to act as a buffer between the housing and the existing hospitals that occupy each end of the island and which, it is hoped, will provide jobs for many of the residents. This new-town-in-town is an innovative experiment in developing a population mix reflecting that of the city as a whole, and in establishing new forms for improving the quality of urban living.

A smaller project that follows many of the PUD concepts is the Buffalo Waterfront, designed by architect Paul Rudolph (Figs. 715, 716). A densely packed but low, winding chain of mostly two- and three-story buildings rises to an occa-

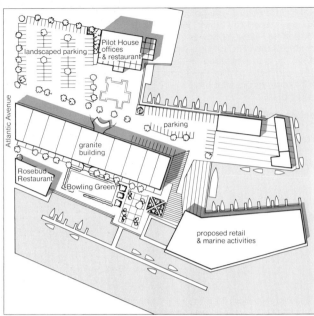

left: 717. A warehouse built in 1836 now houses retail shops, offices, and condominium apartments at Lewis Wharf in Boston. Carl Koch, architect and developer. (*Photograph: Wayne Soverns, Jr.*)

right: 718. The plan of Lewis Wharf shows how architect Koch converted the disused industrial district into an attractive, harborside residential area. The "granite building" is the converted warehouse shown in Figure 717.

sional six-story elevator apartment house. The broken rooflines, irregular balconies, and brown, rough-textured surfaces of the complex have been likened to those of a European hill town. Adjacent to the city center, with municipal buildings and a number of office towers, the project rejuvenates a run-down section with a residential density and a large amount of pedestrian space. Later phases of construction will add schools, a large new park, and commercial and recreational facilities, as well as additional residences. Those along the waterfront are envisioned as a mix of townhouses and apartment towers.

The principles of Planned Unit Development have even been applied to the rehabilitation of historic districts and buildings, as in the case of Lewis Wharf on the Boston harbor (Figs. 717, 718). Architect Carl Koch converted an 1836 warehouse and some neighboring structures into a downtown community with rental and condominium apartments, offices, three restaurants, and several retail shops. Lewis Wharf offers its new residents a historic atmosphere, open space, and interesting views—all on a waterside location not far from a subway stop and the central business district.

Specialized Communities

In direct contrast to new towns and PUDs, which aim at a balance in population and land use, specialized communities are designed to appeal to a particular age group or lifestyle. Retirement, mobile home, religious, and vacation communities fall into this category. Residential complexes restricted to single people, young married couples, or adults are among the alternatives.

The Retirement Community   The specialized community that limits its permanent population to adults of retirement age has found widespread acceptance. Land developers have been encouraged by the buyer acceptance of this lifestyle and by favorable government financing.

The retirement community provides a wealth of amenities, such as recreational facilities, art and craft studios, adult education classes, and cultural events. Housing ranges from detached homes to townhouses, garden apartments, and even high-rise buildings. The dwelling unit is sold as a condominium to the occupant, who pays

right: 719. Heritage Village is a retirement community designed to accommodate about 4500 persons on a 1000-acre site in Southbury, Connecticut. The hilly, wooded setting has been preserved as much as possible. (*Courtesy Heritage Development Group, Inc.*)

below: 720. Mobile home technology is inventively exploited in Paul Rudolph's experimental townhouse complex in New Haven, Connecticut. Dwelling units of different sizes are assembled from 12-foot-wide, prefabricated plywood modules and arranged to give each household a private courtyard. (*Photograph: Donald Luckenbill*)

a monthly charge for maintenance, insurance, taxes, and carrying charges. These charges sometimes include medical care and hospitalization.

Heritage Village in Connecticut, one of the best known of these communities, features townhouses grouped in cul-de-sac clusters, an extensive network of pedestrian paths, and a green, wooded setting enhanced by ponds and rolling hills (Fig. 719). With a full range of shops, professional and business offices, an 18-hole golf course, a library, and other recreational and communal facilities, Heritage Village achieves many of the goals set by full-scale new towns.

The Mobile Home Community Mobile home communities have been forced to develop in a specialized manner, because most zoning ordinances regard them as a substandard form of housing. Typically eight or nine mobile homes are crowded on an acre of land—in contrast to the older suburban developments, which allow four or five homes per acre. Normally barred from residential areas by zoning

above: 721. A jagged roofline and contrasting surfaces of white concrete and dark wood relate the exterior of a condominium ski resort to its setting in the wooded, snow-covered mountains of Aspen, Colorado. Bruce Bicknell, architect. (*Photograph: Bruce McAllister*)

right: 722. The irregular balconies of the vacation town of Port la Galère, in southern France, climb a steep cliff that rises up from the Mediterranean Sea. The 60-acre development accommodates some four hundred dwelling units. Jacques Couelle, architect. (*Courtesy Arthur Sworn Goldman & Associates, Inc.*)

restrictions, the mobile home community seeks refuge with a nonconforming use permit in industrial, commercial, or agricultural zones. Therefore, it usually offers few of the amenities provided in a balanced community—although there are exceptions (Fig. 720). Economy is the major attraction, and mobile homes supply the largest segment of low-cost housing in the United States today. The low initial cost of the dwelling unit can be financed easily, and the monthly rental of a parking space equipped with utilities and basic services is equally low. By not owning the land on which it is placed, the buyer can sometimes sell the home easily. But the resident of a mobile-home park is at the mercy of the management, whose rental agreements may give them unexpected degrees of control.

Vacation Communities   Vacation communities, whether for year-round or short-term use, are developed on sites of striking natural beauty or designed around a certain type of recreation, as in the case of ski resorts in the mountains. New towns in fact but not in spirit, many such developments are built without regard for the balanced land use essential to a self-sustaining community. In addition to housing units, ski resorts usually offer a large complex of amusement facilities accompanied by restaurants and shops (Fig. 721). But schools, general commercial enterprises, and any forms of employment beyond those required to run the resort seldom exist. What cannot be ignored, however, is the impact of the development on both the broader environment and the character of the area.

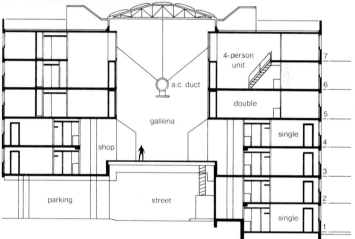

The aesthetic and environmental issues of relating design to both natural and built surroundings have been sensitively met in Port la Galère, a vacation new town built on the cliffs of the French Côte d'Azur (Fig. 722). Architect Jacques Couelle designed the community in clusters of attached dwellings overlooking the Mediterranean and joined by winding roads. Rising in a vertical mass that continues the rugged texture of the bluff, Port la Galère resembles the dozens of small hilltop villages that have grown up piecemeal throughout southern Europe. Yet the impression of spontaneous growth and irregular stuccoed-masonry construction was created from prefabricated components of reinforced concrete. The result is a community planned on an intimate, human scale with all the unexpected turns of an old village—a new structure perfectly in tune with the natural and cultural aspects of the Mediterranean environment.

The Megastructure   The megastructure attempts to combine all the functions of a single, large community into one building. Covering a greater area than any simple high-rise building, the megastructure is naturally characterized by bulk, but it can take a variety of architectural forms.

One such form appears in the 950-foot-long housing structure built around a glass-roofed interior street, or *galleria*, at the University of Alberta (Figs. 723, 724). A weatherproof pedestrian mall, lined with shops, restaurants, and recreational facilities, covers a service roadway and parking areas below. Opening to

725. A megastructure designed by Paul Rudolph would utilize existing methods of prefabrication to create a vertical city of complex silhouette. (*Photograph: Ezra Stoller © ESTO*)

the exterior on the outer sides of the structure, apartments of different sizes flank the concourse-level facilities and, as floor-through units, overlook the interior space through large glass walls. At this scale, the megastructure seems less like a building than a part of the landscape—a long, low, linear city contained within solid walls.

By contrast, Paul Rudolph's model for city development resembles an artificial mountain with all the irregularities of a natural landscape (Fig. 725). Constructed of modular concrete boxes, the dwelling units would be piled up in such a way that each would have ample sunlight, fresh air, and outward views. The project was designed to contain offices and workshops for the printing industry, leaving about 40 percent of the space for apartments. The dense, vertical configuration suggests that mass transportation by moving platforms and elevators would be more practical than the automobile. Staggered projecting and receding forms create a complex silhouette that disguises the bulk of the structure and minimizes its visual impact on the surrounding area.

Selecting a Community Lifespace

In the long run, the community is perhaps more important than the individual dwelling. A lifestyle embraces a host of activities outside the home, and every community offers a unique mixture of opportunities whose appeal will vary from one person to the next. Thus choosing a place to live is an essential part of planning a personal lifespace.

From the outset, the search should be directed toward finding a community that promises the kind of life you would like to live—that seems congenial and attractive. A particular geographical area may be desirable in terms of climate or proximity to relatives and friends. Individual preferences will also affect the choice of a specific location, whether city, suburb, or country. The intangible "feel" of a community should not be ignored, for the best choice is an environment that satisfies both practical and psychological needs.

Community assets and deficiencies deserve careful consideration. In general, assets include: a good school system; parks and recreational facilities; cultural amenities, including newspapers, radio, and television as well as libraries, concerts, plays, movies, and the like; convenient shopping areas and ways to get there by foot, bicycle, and public transportation, as well as by automobile; external transportation connections; centers of worship; and fire and police protection. Possible nuisances should be surveyed, such as nearby traffic thoroughfares, railroads, and airports, as well as noisy or smog-producing factories. Light industry—quiet, clean, and sometimes even attractive—can be advantageous because of employment opportunities.

Deciding on a community, as in all other aspects of planning a lifespace, is a matter of balancing all factors in order of their personal desirability. Like people, however, communities seldom stay the same, and their patterns of growth should be the concern of every resident.

In contrast to the design of our homes, most of us have only a little control over the nature and design of the community we select to live in. Helping to direct community growth, however, is a system of checks built into the development process by various governmental agencies for planning, environmental health, and building inspection. Land use and zoning regulations may be adopted by city, county, or state in an effort to channel growth in a predetermined pattern. These regulations are enforced by a planning commission composed of public-spirited citizens serving on a volunteer basis. In addition to the planning commission, many communities have access to a full- or part-time professional city planner, who can supply technical guidance to the lay group. In this way citizens *can* exert some influence on the nature, design, and growth patterns of their communities.

Future Lifespaces

That designs of the future will be very different from those of today seems inevitable as the pace of technological and environmental change continues to accelerate. As forms of the 20th century emerged in response to the functions, materials, and technology of the time, so will our future forms respond to new conditions. Future designs will undoubtedly reflect the following requirements:

The need to conserve and utilize new sources of energy, especially that of the sun, will certainly change the way our homes are built (Fig. 134). Improved methods of industrial fabrication may save time and energy and make more efficient use of materials. There will be greater emphasis on the orientation of buildings, proper window-wall-mass distribution to take advantage of the sun and shield from wind (see Chap. 5), natural air-conditioning by means of cross ventilation, and external shading devices. Exploiting new energy sources will bring new forms to both interiors and exteriors. In the words of a recent publication: "The great designers will be inspired by the engineering honesty of solar collectors and will find ways to express them as elements that help cause the architectural experience to happen. These new forms will be appreciated for their beauty as well as for their economic use of energy."[3]

The need to conserve land resources will result in their more efficient utilization through higher-density living arrangements combined with environmental plan-

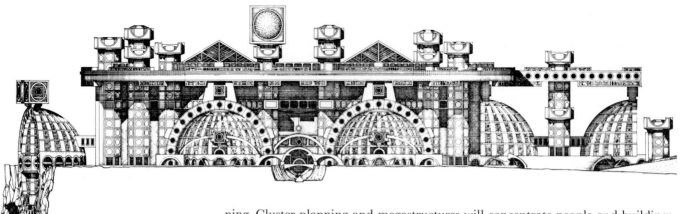

ning. Cluster planning and megastructures will concentrate people and buildings while preserving the natural surroundings.

The need to maintain the world's self-renewing environment will perhaps lead to megastructures that operate in themselves as complete life-cycle enclosures. The depletion of material resources through wasteful consumption may someday be eliminated by products designed with a built-in means of recycling at the end of their usefulness. Professor Arthur J. Pulos sees it this way: "The optimum object should be designed to serve its function as directly and as humanely as possible and then to disappear gracefully without fouling man's living spaces or imposing itself on following generations. . . ." In this way, "products will begin to behave in a manner not unlike living organisms whose existence is assured by their constant renewal in newly-born forms."[4]

Within a highly technological environment, the need for adaptability and flexibility—like that of organisms in the natural world—may lead to many changes in the homes of the future. Not only, for example, will mobile and motor homes receive more inspired designs, but totally new forms of structures and interiors will be developed.

The contemporary awareness of these many needs has already brought about some visionary designs for our future.

above: 726. Paolo Soleri's design for "Arcosanti," a community dedicated to the arts and handcrafts, reveals the architect's love of geometric forms, especially the semicircle. Parts of the structure have been constructed in the Arizona desert.

right: 727. A massive, hollow cone of terraced apartment units encloses an artificial lake in Giorgio Grati's visionary "Nucleo 1000," whose residents would be fed by agriculture developed on the surrounding open land.

Ecological Megastructures

As already discussed, the megastructure concentrates structure and people on a limited amount of land in order to leave an expanse of open space all around it. Unlike the suburban sprawl that consumes the landscape with small buildings, small plots, and ever-expanding freeways, the megastructure offers a method of preserving the land for agriculture and recreation, while at the same time housing a growing population.

Paolo Soleri's "arcologies"—combining architecture and ecology—are megastructures on a truly visionary scale. A single arcology might stand three hundred stories high, cover 14 square miles of land, and house perhaps a million people. It would provide all the living, working, educational, recreation, and service needs of its residents, for whom the surrounding miles of farmland and recreational space would be close at hand.

"Arcosanti," a miniature test-model arcology 150 feet high and designed to house three thousand residents, is currently under construction in Arizona (Fig. 726). When asked why he wants to house this many people in a concentrated structure when there is still so much open land in Arizona, Soleri replies: "Dispersal is antagonistic to life. Density is not an evil we have to accept for ecological reasons; it is the only morphology that can give us a lively existence."[5] He also points out that such concentration results in land and energy conservation as well as desegregation of different segments of the population.

Soleri believes in the rich and full life that comes when people live and work together, and to this end Arcosanti is being built by workshop members and full-time apprentices whose tuition helps pay for the materials of construction. Eventually, these payments will be redeemable as credits toward the rental of living units at Arcosanti.

Ecology and a concentrated population also figure in Milanese architect Giorgio Grati's "Nucleo 1000," a 21-story cone-shape structure enclosing an artificial lake in the center (Fig. 727). The project would house one thousand apartments, with outside terraces overlooking the countryside, as well as retail, service, and entertainment facilities. The inside lake and beach would be lit and heated by the sun and quartz arc-lamps as needed. Land surrounding the structure would be used as farmland, fertilized by a biologically degradable sewerage effluent. To further the cause of natural balance, food would be sold only in reusable refrigerated containers meant to go back and forth between shops and individual kitchens.

Plug-In Homes

Another vision of future forms has already been constructed in Noriaki Kurokawa's capsule tower in Tokyo (Fig. 728). Self-contained, one-person dwelling units, totally prefinished at the factory, are cantilevered from a central structural core that also provides utilities. With all living amenities built-in, the modules are ready for occupancy as soon as they have been lifted into place and connected with the utility terminals. Kurokawa's design offers intriguing possibilities for the future. Capsules could be "docked" in different places and in various assemblages to provide living quarters for an individual, group, or family. We would take our lifespace with us, instead of moving to another space.

Extraterrestrial Structures

M. C. Escher's 1954 woodcut *Tetrahedral Planetoid* reveals the artist's fascination with visual perception and surrealistic imagery (Fig. 729). Escher's prescience has been justified, however, by Princeton physics professor Gerard K. O'Neill, who has proposed a space construction for a small colony of perhaps two thousand people that would follow the orbital path of the moon. The asteroid belt has almost pure

728. Self-contained living capsules are "docked" on a steel-and-concrete shaft in Noriaki Kurokawa's Nakagin apartment house in Tokyo. (*Photograph: Orion Press*)

729. M. C. Escher's *Tetrahedral Planetoid,* a woodcut dated 1954, presents a visionary city suspended in space. The artist seems to have looked at Italian hill towns through a fish-eye camera lens. (*Haags Gemeentemuseum, The Hague* [*Escher Foundation*])

nickel-iron chunks that could be processed easily for structural uses; other building materials would be taken from the moon's abundant supply or transported from the earth. Solar energy would provide electric power and sustain crop raising in a controlled atmosphere. Shaped as a cylinder, the space station would rotate at a rate calculated to generate a centrifugal force similar to the earth's gravity. As time went on, larger space stations could be built as self-sufficient, nonpolluting environments—the ultimate in continuous life-cycling. Eventually, in Dr. O'Neill's words, the earth might become "a worldwide park, a beautiful place to visit for a vacation."

If these concepts seem cold or frightening in the impersonality and mechanization of their Utopian vision, we must remember that people have an infinite capacity for asserting their individuality and adapting space to suit their own needs, rather than following the program of an unseen planner. As circumstances change, people will find new ways to leave a personal imprint on their lifespaces, and there will always be eccentrics who insist on doing the opposite of prevailing trends. The appreciation of older customs, handmade objects, and other products of outmoded technologies will no doubt—and happily—provide pleasure for several generations to come.

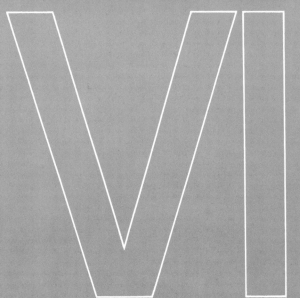

Our Historical Heritage

21 The Renaissance

Much of our present-day culture rests on a tradition that began in 15th-century Italy. The artists and thinkers of the Renaissance saw their age as the rebirth of a way of life that had ceased with the fall of the Roman Empire. Reacting against medieval emphasis on the soul and the afterlife, Renaissance humanism asserted the dignity of the individual and the importance of secular life. Rather than relying on scripture as the authority for all knowledge, Renaissance man studied nature directly and explored the world beyond the Mediterranean. Inspiration for these interests came from classical antiquity as it was preserved in literary manuscripts, the ruins of ancient buildings, and surviving works of art.

The spirit of the Renaissance found its clearest expression in the arts, especially architecture. A classical vocabulary of columns, entablatures, and arches was applied to buildings of simple geometrical shapes and compact proportions—all of which contrasted sharply with the soaring forests of pointed arches and pinnacles that had characterized the great Gothic cathedrals of the later Middle Ages. But the Renaissance adopted more than the outward forms of Greek and Roman architecture; it also embraced the classical principles of clarity, balance, and proportional relationships among the dimensions of a building or object.

Private palaces, filling whole blocks in Florence, Urbino, and other cities, were among the first successes of the new style. Small windows and few entrances made the Renaissance *palazzo* a defensible stronghold as well as a luxurious family home. The cubic shape of the exterior and the restrained treatment of walls gave the dwelling a sense of secure equilibrium.

Domestic interiors and furnishings followed the direction set by monumental architecture. Interiors consisted of simple rectangular rooms, often articulated by real or simulated architectural forms (Fig. 731). Furniture was designed to reveal its construction without appearing severe. The predominant rectilinearity of architecture and furnishings was moderated by a sparing use of curved forms and enriched by columns, arches, volutes, acanthus scrolls, and other classical details. Venetian trade provided many additional embellishments, from the silks and luxury goods of the East to the elaborate, colorful tapestries of northern Europe. Interior, exterior, and furnishings were often consciously harmonized in the ambitious houses of the wealthy, but each unit of a larger composition always retained its identity.

A brief summary can only hint at the character and variety of Renaissance interior design, but a broad view of the period reveals the following characteristics:

opposite: 730. Contrasting colors, vigorous curves, and boldly modeled forms enliven the Baroque staircase of Guarino Guarini's Palazzo Carignano in Turin, Italy. See also Fig. 753. (*Photograph: Aschieri*)

The Renaissance			
Italy	Spain	France	England

	Italy	Spain	France	England
1400	**Early Renaissance 1420–1500**	**Medieval** (Gothic with Islamic influence)	**Medieval** (Gothic)	**Medieval** (Gothic)
				Henry VII (1485–1509)
1500	**High Renaissance 1500–80**	**Early Renaissance, or Plateresque 1492–1556**	**French Renaissance 1500–1650**	**Tudor-Elizabethan 1509–1603**
			Louis XII (1498–1515)	Henry VIII (1509–47)
	Mannerism 1520–80	Charles V (1515–56)	Francis I (1515–47)	
		High Renaissance or Desornamentado 1556–1650 Philip II (1556–98)		Elizabeth I (1558–1603)
	Baroque 1580–1750			
1600				**Early Stuart 1603–49**
			Henry IV (1589–1610)	James I (1603–25)
		Baroque 1620–1750	Louis XIII (1610–43)	Charles I (1625–49)

- □ **Aims**—order, clarity, moderation
- □ **Character**—reposed, static; embellishments applied to a strong design frame-work
- □ **Design**—balanced, symmetrical; architectural rhythms predominate; clear separation of parts; equal emphasis given to plain and ornamented surfaces
- □ **Scale**—moderate
- □ **Shapes**—simple, geometrical, with clear outlines; horizontal emphasis
- □ **Ornament**—columns, entablatures, arches, and classical moldings; arranged to articulate the underlying structure
- □ **Colors**—strong hues; primaries preferred; related in complementary, harmonizing combinations

The Renaissance in Italy was an exceptionally unified phenomenon that had a profound effect on all aspects of culture. From the beginning of the 16th century, the movement spread to other parts of Europe, largely through the encouragement of a few imaginative and well-traveled kings and princes. The new style was adopted differently and in varying degrees from country to country; some features were taken over while others were rejected, and local traditions invariably affected the final result. Furthermore, the Renaissance style in Italy was supplanted in the 16th century by the Mannerist and Baroque styles (see pp. 522 and 532). Thus, later imitations of Italian work elsewhere in Europe incorporated elements of both the Renaissance and the reactions against it. Yet the later "Renaissances" of France, Spain, and England shared a fundamental sympathy with the original Italian movement. The similarity of purpose underlying these various movements demonstrates the compelling attraction of the style. For us, the Renaissance shows that the forms and ideas of the past can inspire new creations of great originality.

Italy

Italy was the home of the Renaissance. The remains of Roman civilization were readily at hand, and the Italians shared with their ancient ancestors a common geography, climate, and urban way of life. Fierce competition between cities, families, and individuals fostered great achievements by naturally gifted artists.

The Early Renaissance: c. 1420–1500

The early flowering of the Renaissance took place in Florence, where artists first experimented with classical orders in architecture, representational realism in sculpture, and linear perspective in painting. *Palazzi* and suburban villas of the wealthy rose on carefully formalized and often symmetrical plans. Thick walls and small windows provided insulation against extreme weather, while verandas, porticoes, and inner courts allowed maximum enjoyment of the summer climate.

Interiors   Moderately scaled to human needs, interior spaces conformed to the simple, rectangular shapes of the building. Tiled floors offered insulation and durability; raftered ceilings were either exposed or plastered over, but usually painted. Walls were whitewashed, painted with decorative designs and figural scenes, or sometimes covered in marquetry (inlaid pieces of wood), in which dazzling pictorial illusions could be created through perspective (Fig. 731).

An ideal interior of the period appears in *The Dream of St. Ursula*, a painting by Vittore Carpaccio (Fig. 732). St. Ursula's room is a trim, cubic space embellished by statuary, plants, and furnishings. Classical architectural moldings make the transition from walls to ceiling and divide the walls into horizontal registers, while entablatures, columns, and capitals frame the door and the round-arched windows. Although very popular, classical ornament did not always articulate the structure

left: 731. Perspective creates the illusion of three-dimensional cupboards and built-in benches in the corner of a room in the Ducal Palace at Gubbio, Italy. Books, musical instruments, and a Latin inscription reflect the learned interests of the Duke of Urbino, who commissioned the marquetry decoration in about 1480. (*Metropolitan Museum of Art, New York [Rogers Fund, 1939]*)

right: 732. *The Dream of St. Ursula*, painted about 1495 by Vittore Carpaccio, presents an artist's conception of an up-to-date Venetian Renaissance interior. The sparse, architectural quality of the room is relieved by statuary, plants, and furnishings, which include a canopied bed, simple stool and writing table, and a portable bookcase. (*Accademia, Venice; photograph: Alinari–Art Reference Bureau*)

left: 733. The principal bedroom of the Palazzo Davanzati, built in Florence in the second half of the 15th century, features tile floors, an exposed wood ceiling, and richly painted walls. The furniture dates from the 16th century. (*Photograph: Alinari–Art Reference Bureau*)

below: 734. The "Savonarola" or X-chair derives from the folding stools used by the ancient Egyptians, Greeks, and Romans. Reflecting the sturdier construction introduced in the late medieval period, this 15th-century Italian example is constructed of interlacing beechwood slats, with simply carved arms, back, and base. (*M. H. de Young Memorial Museum, San Francisco [gift of M. H. de Young Endowment Fund]*)

so coherently in real interiors. For example, in the principal bedroom of the Davanzati palace (Fig. 733), the walls are painted in three registers: a tapestrylike design with heraldic motifs; imitation marble paneling behind an illusionistic fence; and an arcade (arches on columns) framing scenes that illustrate a contemporary love poem. The arcade gives the upper part of the room a sense of added space, but painted and real architecture are not integrated: the ceiling rafters do not align with the painted columns, and in the corner a painted arch begins on one wall and ends on the other.

Furnishings   Rooms were furnished sparsely in the Early Renaissance, the furniture generally designed to harmonize with the architectural context. Most pieces were made of wood, especially walnut, with large areas of plain surface relieved by accents of carved ornament. Homes of this period offered a variety of seats: three-legged stools (Fig. 732); benches, which were sometimes built into the wall (Fig. 731); panel-back armchairs; and many variations on the "Savonarola" or X-shape chair of late medieval design (Fig. 734). Household goods were stored in long, low chests called *cassoni*. Beds rested on platforms that provided both insulation and additional storage space (Fig. 733). The board and trestle (a wide board resting on sawhorses, which could be dismantled and moved from room to room) gave way to the permanent table with decoratively carved legs.

The High Renaissance: c. 1500–80

Building on the experiments of the earlier period, the High Renaissance developed a mature concern for total planning, consistency of purpose and design, and the organic relationship between ornament and underlying form. The expansion of papal power made Rome the major center of art patronage, and here many artists from northern Italy had their first direct contact with the Roman ruins. A sustained study of these remains enabled artists to reach beyond the externals of ornament and grasp the basic principles of classical architecture. Thus inspired, the artists of the High Renaissance learned to combine a strong design framework with a careful adjustment of proportions and details.

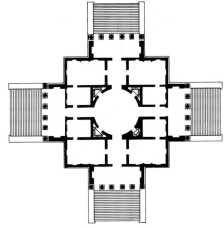

left: 735. The walls of this stately, marble-floored room in the Villa Farnesina in Rome were painted between 1508 and 1511 by the building's architect, Baldassare Peruzzi. The illusionistic wall paintings represent a screen of columns and piers, punctuated by views of the Roman landscape as it existed around the villa. (*Photograph: Gabinetto Fotografico Nazionale–Fototeca Unione*)

736–737. The Villa Rotonda, built at Vicenza in 1550–51 by Andrea Palladio, epitomized the Renaissance interest in bilateral symmetry, axial alignments, and the centralized plan.

below left: 736. A circular hall fills the center of the square structure, whose every exterior side has a gabled, columnar porch atop a long flight of stairs. (*Photograph: Alinari–Art Reference Bureau*)

below: 737. The plan reveals strict unity and precise proportional relationships.

A major concern of architects in this period was the integration of parts with the whole. One way of achieving this was through bilateral symmetry—the arrangement of matching parts on either side of an imaginary central line or axis. The use of bilateral symmetry and axial alignments gave a geometrical unity to individual rooms (Fig. 735), series of rooms linked by the alignment of doors, exterior façades (Fig. 736), and plans (Fig. 737). In his famous Villa Rotonda,

Andrea Palladio created symmetrical compositions on either side of two perpendicular axes; the result is a centralized building that presents an identical façade on all four sides. Gardens, too, were often linked with architecture in a grand composition based on axial relationships.

Interiors   Princely families hosted the elaborate social life of the High Renaissance in spacious, richly furnished homes. Interior designs struck a balance between two conflicting intentions: to articulate the structure of the room by means of real or painted architectural forms, and to deny the solidity of the walls through the painted illusion of receding space with open vistas to the outside world (Fig. 735). Ceilings often boasted gilded *coffers* (recessed wooden panels), while floors might be laid in patterns of multicolored marble. The whole interior became a unified, clear-cut design of stately regularity and balance.

Furnishings   Bold carving, a strong sense of tectonic design, and the full range of classical ornament made High Renaissance furniture an important component in the total ensemble. Benches and stools remained in common use, but the new padded chairs, with finely tooled leather seats and backs (Fig. 738), offered greater comfort. The *cassapanca* (a *cassone* set on a platform and given a back and armrests) combined the functions of seating and storage (Fig. 739). Elegant curves and figural embellishments gave some examples a sense of graceful poise. Cabinets often resembled little buildings through their mammoth scale and strict architectural treatment (Fig. 740). Textiles, imported from Brussels or woven in Italy by northern craftsmen, added warmth and color. Finally, the great homes were filled with precious objects including sculpture, paintings, ceramics, decorative bronzes, and delicate Venetian glass.

France

The centralization of France under monarchic rule was well under way when Louis XII (1498–1515) initiated military campaigns into Italy and other foreign territories. These expeditions brought the Italian Renaissance to the attention of the French ruling class, who responded by taking home ideas, objects, and even artists. The new style met strong resistance, however, in the Gothic tradition still thriving in residential architecture and in the artisan guilds.

Stimulated only by a few individual patrons, the Renaissance in France never became more than a curious, if often happy, mixture of imported and native elements. Thus, the many castles of the 16th century showed a new regularity of plan, greater simplicity in the treatment of wall surfaces, and more horizontal proportions than before. But the French were loath to surrender the picturesque silhouettes created by pointed roofs with projecting dormers, chimneys, and towers. Similarly, interiors combined Renaissance ornament with Gothic pointed arches, and it was only gradually that coffered ceilings replaced the lofty rafters of the earlier style—as was also true in England (Fig. 747).

The period of greatest receptivity came during the reign of Francis I (1515–47), who assembled a miniature colony of Italian artists at his new residence in Fontainbleau. A distinctive school emerged as French artists learned from Italian masters, who worked in the Mannerist style then at its peak in Italy. Reacting against the High Renaissance, *Mannerism* employed classical forms to create anticlassical effects, such as tension, ambiguity, and surprise. We might compare, for example, the cabinets illustrated in Figures 740 and 741. Despite its basically rectilinear composition, the Dijon buffet loses structural coherence through the suppression and decorative treatment of architectural forms and through a profusion of ornament over all surfaces. The late date of the piece shows that Mannerism continued to influence French design until the emergence of the Baroque style in the middle of the 17th century (see Chap. 22).

above left: 738. A 16th-century Italian chair exemplifies the clear-cut, balanced design favored during the High Renaissance. Tooled decorations on the leather back, decorative nailheads, fringes, and the bowknot and volutes of the pierced front stretcher embellish a strongly rectilinear framework. (*Courtesy French & Company*)

above right: 739. A sparing use of ornament offsets the graceful curves and natural grain of this walnut *cassapanca*. A pair of female figures recline on volutes beside the heraldic arms of the Orsini family, for whom the piece was made about 1550–75. See also Fig. 733. (*Metropolitan Museum of Art, New York [funds from various donors, 1958]*)

above: 740. Pilasters and a full entablature frame this monumental walnut cabinet, made in Italy in the 16th century. Projecting lion heads recall those found on the doors of ancient Roman buildings, as well as the gargoyles of medieval cathedrals. (*Fondazione Giorgio Cini*)

right: 741. A complex silhouette harmonizes with the elaborate decorations of a French Mannerist walnut buffet carved in Dijon about 1600. (*Brooklyn Museum [gift of Mrs. J. Fuller Feder]*)

French chateaux of the 16th century were especially rich in tapestries woven in Brussels, Arras, and other Flemish towns. Intricately woven cloth served not only for wall hangings but for upholstery, bed covers, and other furnishings.

Spain

The Spanish peninsula had been settled since the 11th century B.C. by a succession of Iberians, Celts, Romans, and Visigoths, but the Moors—Arab Moslems who came from North Africa in the 8th century A.D.—had the most pervasive impact. The political coexistence of Moslem and Christian populations ended with the expulsion of the Moors in 1492—the same year in which Columbus claimed vast New World territories for the Spanish crown. The gold and silver of the Americas helped Spain to become the leading power of Europe in the 16th century.

As was true for France, the products of the Italian Renaissance, especially portable luxury objects, reached Spain as the result of military and political acquisitions in Italy. At the same time, however, the rich tradition of Moorish decoration exerted a strong influence on Spanish art long after 1492. Indeed, Moors comprised the majority of the artisan class in southern Spain until the "Moriscos," or converted Moslems, were driven out in the early 17th century. Spain's mountainous terrain divided the country and contributed to the survival of local artistic customs. These factors gave Spanish art a character all its own.

The Renaissance in Spain can be divided into periods that vary in the degree of Italian influence and the extent to which that influence affected interiors and

below: 742. The library in the Casa de Lope de Vega, a 17th-century house in Madrid, reveals the austere simplicity of most Spanish interiors and furnishings. (*Photograph: MAS*)

right: 743. Brilliantly colored, richly patterned ceramic tiles cover a nook in the Casa Cabanyes, a 17th-century house in Argentona, near Barcelona. (*Photograph: MAS*)

furnishings. Receptivity was strongest in the early period, from 1492 through the reign of Charles V (1516–56). Acanthus scrolls, classical moldings, profile busts set in roundels, and other Italian-derived motifs appeared on both architecture and furniture (Fig. 744). The precious delicacy of the craftsmanship, recalling the work of silversmiths (*plateros*), has given the name *Plateresque* to the first Renaissance style in Spain.

Under Philip II (1556–98), Spanish architecture adhered closely to Italian models in a style known as *Desornamentado,* or "disornamented," after its austere simplicity, or *Herreran* after Juan de Herrera, architect of Philip's Escorial palace. The style had little effect on domestic design. Similarly, the Baroque style of the 17th century sometimes penetrated interiors and furniture (Fig. 746), but its most extravagant expressions were better suited to churches than to houses.

Interiors   Houses in Spain generally followed the Mediterranean practice of arranging rooms around an open court that served as both a living space and a means of getting from room to room. Thick walls, small windows, and flat roofs responded to a climate of hot, bright sunlight and scant rainfall. Stone floors and heavy, whitewashed walls sometimes made for austere interiors relieved only by furnishings and decoratively carved woodwork (Fig. 742). Often, however, brightly colored tiles produced stunning effects, covering surfaces in a dense optical pattern (Fig. 743). This emphasis on abstract surface pattern, as opposed to the articulation of structure, lay at the heart of the Moorish tradition.

Islamic custom also introduced carpets to Spain well before they appeared in other European countries. Spanish products imitated the designs of Oriental imports as well as contemporary northern textiles. The thick, colorful textures enlivened interiors while providing insulation for chilly stone floors.

Furnishings   Although they often followed Italian designs, Spanish artisans created a distinctive type of furniture in the *vargueño,* a chest of drawers with a drop front, which was supported by an open stand or a high cabinet (Fig. 744). Wood remained the basic material for furnishings (Fig. 745), but Spain's wealthy

left: 744. A walnut *vargueño* exemplifies the *Plateresque* style of 16th-century Spain. Italian influence appears in the roundels with profile heads and the delicate, naturalistic carving of foliage and fanciful animals. (*Victoria & Albert Museum, London* [*Crown Copyright*])

right: 745. Islamic traditions persist in the geometric star patterns carved on the apron of a long walnut table made in Spain about 1600. (*Courtesy French & Company*)

patrons could afford silver, ivory, ebony, and other luxury embellishments. Leather formed the seats and backs of chairs and served as a covering for chests. Iron ore mined in the northern mountains gave craftsmen wrought iron for decorative work (Fig. 746), supports, and even whole pieces of furniture. Despite Renaissance influences, the Moorish tradition persisted, as in the surface pattern of abstract shapes on a 17th-century *vargueño* (Fig. 746), and in the geometrical flower designs on a sturdy walnut table (Fig. 745).

England

Under Henry VII (1485–1509), England emerged from civil war and entered a period of economic prosperity and political stability. Marriages with European families and a growing maritime trade brought England into contact with the Renaissance.

The damp English climate precluded the acceptance of many features of Italian architecture, while strong medieval traditions and conservative tastes inhibited the

adoption of the new style. Yet an English Renaissance did take place over a period of a century and a half, which can be divided into two phases: the Tudor-Elizabethan and the Early Stuart. Like his French contemporary Francis I, Henry VIII (1509–47) imported Italian artists, but the new movement did not really take hold until the reign of Elizabeth (1558–1603). Renaissance ideas gained wider consensus under the Stuart dynasty of James I (1603–25) and especially Charles I (1625–49), whose chief architect, Inigo Jones, introduced a thorough understanding of the principles of Italian design.

The Tudor-Elizabethan Period (1509–1603)

Designers of the 16th century hoped to reconcile the new fashion for symmetry and regularity with the old love of flexible planning and picturesque silhouettes. The standard feature of older English houses had been the great *hall:* a large, high-ceilinged room in which food was cooked on a central open fire. The hall was the center of family life in every home, where exposed wooden ceilings created a sense of warmth as well as spaciousness (Fig. 747).

Halls took on a more ceremonial function in Elizabethan homes, which were designed as stately settings for the Queen's royal progress. Living functions were transferred to long galleries and smaller, more private rooms (Fig. 748). Gothic pointed arches and general verticality yielded to rectangular and round-arched openings with a horizontal emphasis. Large, closely spaced windows admitted as much sunlight as the English climate offered. Wood wainscoting, divided by classical pilasters and simple moldings, typically covered the lower walls.

Furniture was large in scale and heavy in proportions. Oak provided the most common material, but the occasional use of walnut permitted finer detail. Seating included benches; panel-back chairs with sloping arms; and triangular "turned" chairs, whose legs, turned on a lathe, were carved as cylinders with thick, ring-shape embellishments. Canopied beds and massive tables were conceived with a ponderous solidity, their vertical members often carved with bulging "melon" shapes distinctive to the Elizabethan period (Figs. 748, 749).

left: 748. Pilasters frame the wood paneling in a room of 1580–1610 from Hingham Manor in Suffolk, England. The ceiling and a wall frieze above the paneling are covered in decoratively molded plaster. (*Minneapolis Institute of Arts [John Washburn Memorial Room, William Hood Dunwoody Fund]*)

right: 749. A monumental Elizabethan bed from the late 16th century is made of oak inlaid with walnut, ebony, and ash. An awkward assortment of pedestals, urns, and colonnettes support the canopy. At night the hangings would be closed for warmth and privacy. (*Metropolitan Museum of Art, New York [gift of Irwin Untermyer, 1953]*)

right: **750.** Geometric patterns and stylized floral motifs, inlaid with holly, cherry, and stained woods, enhance the charming design of an oak armchair from the first quarter of the 17th century. Volutes, scrolls, and stubby columns indicate the growing influence of the Italian Renaissance during the Early Stuart period. (*Victoria & Albert Museum, London* [*Crown Copyright*])

below: **751.** A substantial, comfortable armchair of the early 17th century displays a low, rectangular outline. The turned arms, legs, and stretchers, as well as the colorful upholstery, are typical of this phase in English furniture. (*Nelson Gallery–Atkins Museum, Kansas City* [*Nelson Fund*])

The Early Stuart Period (1603–49)

In the early 17th century, architects continued to assimilate ideas as well as motifs from the Italian Renaissance. Plans were regularized; interiors and furnishings acquired a greater consistency of scale and ornament. Ceilings displayed lavish plaster decorations, while the fireplace often served as a major focus of interest in generously proportioned rooms (Fig. 752).

Furniture became smaller and lighter with shallower carving than before. Panel-back chairs were sometimes decorated with beautiful designs in marquetry, as the chair in Figure 750 illustrates. The squat, bulging columns that form the legs, and the volutes in the back of this piece are not "correctly" proportioned by classical standards, but they have a charming character of their own. Gateleg and drop-leaf tables were introduced at this time, as were chairs and sofas with colorful upholstery nailed to the frame (Fig. 751).

Inigo Jones   England produced an architect of international stature in Inigo Jones (1573–1652). Twice traveling to Italy to study ancient and "modern" buildings, Jones was profoundly influenced by the buildings of Palladio (Figs. 736, 737), whose *Four Books on Architecture* (1570) served as his guide to Roman antiquities. Returning with a full understanding of the classical architectural vocabulary, he created strong, lucid compositions in which all details were carefully related to the whole. Isolated from the mainstreams of both Europe and England, Jones' classicism summed up the Renaissance while his vigorous massing and deeply carved detail anticipated the French Baroque (see Chap. 22). Much of his work has been lost, but something of his style survives in the main salon at Coleshill, designed as a double cube by Roger Pratt, a friend and follower of Jones (Fig. 752). The sumptuously carved ceiling orders the long interior, articulating the placement of fireplace and windows. Urns, scrolls, and a bust give added prominence to the marble fireplace.

Inigo Jones survived the beheading of his patron, King Charles, but Cromwell's Commonwealth brought architecture to a halt. As a result, Jones had no real artistic successors in England until his work attracted the fresh enthusiasm of the Anglo-Palladian architects of the early 18th century (see p. 541).

752. The influence of Inigo Jones may be seen in the monumental proportions and lush decoration of the main salon at Coleshill, Berkshire, built by Roger Pratt about 1650. Most of the furniture, however, dates from the second half of the 18th century. (*Copyright Country Life*)

Baroque and Rococo

The 17th century in Europe was a period of consolidation, during which the constant warfare of the 15th and 16th centuries gave way to a political stability imposed by absolute monarchy. Great wealth poured into Europe from international and transatlantic trade and accumulated in the hands of a few rulers (especially the French king), whose power to shape the lives of their subjects was enormous. The church recovered from the political in-fighting of the previous century, and a strong Papacy, supported by the Spanish crown, directed the Counter-Reformation as a militant attack against the Protestant movement. Intellectual and scientific achievements of the Renaissance were synthesized, while the telescope and other discoveries opened new avenues of knowledge.

Art and architecture in the 17th century gave visual expression to this age of power. The *Baroque* style originated in Italy as an expression of papal dominion and religious fervor; the style then spread to France, where it became the symbol of royal grandeur.

Unlike the Renaissance, the Baroque age did not name itself. The term, derived from the Portugese *barocco,* for imperfect pearl, was first used in a derogatory sense by later Neoclassical critics of the style (see Chap. 24). Yet the movement's widespread acceptance, however colored by national interpretations, made the Baroque the first truly European style in all the arts.

Baroque architecture, like that of the Renaissance, employed the classical orders and aimed at unity and balance, but there the resemblance ended. The Renaissance created unified designs from the balanced arrangement of separate parts; by contrast, Baroque compositions subordinated all parts to a dynamic movement experienced as a totality. In the Renaissance, a neutral, even light revealed clearly defined, tectonic forms; in Baroque designs, selective lighting gave dramatic emphasis to a fluid intermingling of varied forms. Renaissance balance had an intellectual appeal; Baroque movement and climax appealed directly to the senses. And where Renaissance architects designed a simple structure and then applied the ornament, Baroque architects often tailored structure to meet the requirements of a comprehensive decorative program.

Baroque architects carefully planned the effects of space and light in order to shape the spectator's experience as he walked through a building. Time and motion thus became active ingredients in architectural design, and for this reason the full impact of the Baroque style cannot be recorded except by motion pictures.

The persuasive monumental character of Baroque architecture made it best suited to the churches and public monuments commissioned by powerful prelates and rulers. Great palaces were the only dwellings to make full use of the style (Fig. 753). In more modest homes, the Baroque spirit expressed itself in furniture and in the ornament applied to doors, fireplaces, and staircases.

In summary, the Baroque style affected interior design in these directions:

☐ **Aims**—movement, climax; immediate impact
☐ **Character**—energetic, aggressive, monumental
☐ **Design**—fluid forms in both structure and ornament; great variety marshalled into compelling unity; symmetrical balance; strong, sweeping rhythms
☐ **Scale**—very large
☐ **Shapes**—animated, fluid; compound curves, especially S-scrolls; classical forms stretched, compressed, twisted, clustered
☐ **Ornament**—thickly applied to all surfaces; organic and figural decoration prominent; structural forms animated; heavy build-up and projection of ornaments
☐ **Colors**—deep, rich, closely harmonized; much gold leaf; emphasis on contrast between highlights and shadows

The Baroque style underwent changes as it spread from Italy to other countries. A distinctive version, conceived on a grandiose scale, emerged in France under Louis XIV. The *Rococo* developed as a reaction to, and refinement of, the style of Louis XIV. Although it influenced Italian, English, and especially German architecture, the Rococo was essentially a French style concerned primarily with the decoration of interiors (see p. 536).

In England, furniture designers of the 17th and early 18th centuries accepted many features of the Baroque and Rococo styles, but native preferences fostered the creation of a distinctive national style in architecture.

	Italy	France	Germany	England	
			Baroque and Rococo		
	Italy	France	Germany	England	
1600	**Baroque 1580–1750**	**Baroque** Henry IV (1589–1610) Louis XIII (1610–43)	Thirty Years' War 1618–48	**Early Stuart 1603–49 Commonwealth 1649–60**	
		Louis XIV (1643–1715)	**Baroque 1660–1710**	**Baroque Influences 1660–1725**	**Late Stuart** Charles II (1660–85) James II (1685–88)
1700		**Rococo 1700–50**			**William & Mary (1688–1702) Queen Anne (1702–14)**
		Louis XV (1715–75)	**Rococo 1710–60**		**Early Georgian** George I (1714–27)
				Anglo-Palladian Style, 1725–60	George II (1727–60)
1760				**Rococo Influences 1735–60**	

The Baroque in Italy: c. 1580–1750

Italy remained politically divided from the 16th until the 19th century. The South belonged to the Spanish-held Kingdom of Naples; the central part of the peninsula formed the Papal States; and in the North numerous smaller states either remained independent or passed from one foreign rule to another. Originating in Rome, the Baroque style rapidly spread elsewhere through the competition among rulers to acquire the best and latest in artistic fashion.

Palaces and villas were seldom constructed with the undulating walls characteristic of church façades. Relatively stable and compact exteriors served several purposes: to offset the rich decoration of windows, doors, and rooflines; to crown elaborate hillside gardens filled with fountains and grottoes; and to assure the visitor's surprise at the fluid shapes and dense concentration of ornament inside.

Interiors   Most rooms remained rectangular, but curved shapes and diagonal alignments added variety. Series of rooms were arranged for sequential contrasts in size, shape, and amount of light. Baroque imagination ran free in the design of staircases. In the Palazzo Carignano in Turin (Fig. 753), the curving path of the staircase invites the spectator to climb to a concealed destination, while the contrast between shadowed steps and a brightly lit landing dramatizes the action.

Individual rooms were conceived on a lofty scale, decorated in sumptuous display of architectural ornament, and organized around a central focus of interest. We may contrast, for example, the treatment of fireplaces in interiors of the High Renaissance and of the middle Baroque period (Figs. 735, 754). The Renaissance fireplace is painted to blend into the wall, as if the designer wished to deny its existence; by contrast, the Baroque example is an elaborate marble structure towering as high as the cornice and dominating the entire room. A comparison of the two ceilings further reveals the Baroque love of dramatic effects. Instead

left: 753. A twisting stairway of marble and stucco invites immediate exploration in the Palazzo Carignano, built in Turin between 1679 and 1692 by Italian architect Guarino Guarini. See also Fig. 730. *(Photograph: Aschieri)*

right: 754. A monumental marble fireplace dominates an interior of about 1640 in the Palazzo Terzi in Bergamo, Italy. *(Photograph: Foto Da-Re Bergamo-Art Reference Bureau)*

right: 755. A walnut credenza from the first half of the 17th century has a strong, clearly evident, basic design. The contorted figures of children, exuberant scrolls at the back, and the busts of three women unexpectedly half-emerging from the panels break free of the rectilinear framework in typically Baroque fashion. (*M. H. de Young Memorial Museum, San Francisco* [*gift of William Randolph Hearst*])

below right: 756. The back of a late Baroque wood bench (1718) from northern Italy is painted with an opulent profusion of human figures and animals engulfed in swirling draperies. Vigorous S-curves appear below in consoles, scrolls, and the marine tails of winged unicorns. (*M. H. de Young Memorial Museum, San Francisco* [*gift of Mrs. Robert A. Magowan*])

of simple coffers, the Baroque ceiling has a heavy cornice resting on thinly tapered brackets, between which over-lifesize figures threaten to topple downward.

Baroque interiors retained the classical orders, as well as the Renaissance preference for symmetry, but all elements, including furniture, were enlarged in scale and animated with energy and movement.

Furnishings　　The basically rectilinear framework of Renaissance furniture persisted, while a profusion of figural ornament contributed broken and curved silhouettes (Fig. 755). Bold projections, deep undercutting, swirling curves, and bright colors produced dramatic contrasts between highlights and shadows. In some cases, the abundant decoration all but obscured the underlying structure in the interest of sculptural plasticity (Fig. 756). Out of context, much Baroque furniture seems overemphatic, but the pieces are handsomely appropriate when seen in the monumental settings for which they were designed.

Chairs of the period boasted more flowing outlines than those of the Renaissance. Heavily carved and often gilded, they were upholstered in large-patterned velvets, silks, and stamped leather, often with nailheads arranged decoratively. Typical tables were of the *console* type, set against the wall with marble tops supported by bases carved as cherubim, mermaids, or dolphins. Tall cabinets, broken or undulating in outline, had profuse decoration; a variety of beds included four-posters and those with large painted headboards. Mirrors became larger than before and had rich, heavy frames.

Textiles and decorative accessories increased in scale and became freer in design. A wide range of colors, with emphasis on strong, contrasting hues, added to the general splendor of the interiors.

The Baroque style persisted in Italy into the 18th century. There were also notable developments in the Rococo and Neoclassical styles, but by then artistic leadership had passed to France.

757. The Salon de la Paix (Hall of Peace) in Louis XIV's chateau at Versailles was designed by court painter Charles LeBrun and completed in 1686. Different colored marbles, mirrors, paintings, gilded decorations, and a monumental glass chandelier create a sumptuous but highly ordered setting for acts of state. (*Photograph: Alinari-Giraudon*)

above: **758.** A stately cabinet by André Boulle features luxurious ornamentation in marble, lacquered wood, ormolu, pewter, and tortoise shell. This rich profusion, however, is contained by a tectonic overall design—a combination characteristic of the French Baroque. (*Victoria & Albert Museum, London [Crown Copyright]*)

right **759.** French furnishings of the late 17th century, arranged as in a state bedroom, illustrate the lavishness of the period of Louis XIV. The great carpet was made for the Louvre at the Savonnerie Manufactory. An upholstered chair, recalling Italian examples (Fig. 754), stands in front of a restrained ebony and ivory cabinet (c. 1640–50) and an exuberantly carved candlestand. (*Metropolitan Museum of Art, New York*)

Baroque and Rococo in France

French fashion determined international taste from the middle of the 17th century until the early 20th. This cultural leadership began with the French Baroque style of Louis XIV, which was imitated in all the capitals of Europe. Arising on the fringes of Louis XIV's court, the Rococo style became equally influential as the highest standard of interior design in the first half of the 18th century.

The French Baroque: Louis XIV (1643–1715)

Assuming personal rule in 1661, Louis XIV ruled France at a time when that nation led the rest of Europe. Finance minister Jean Baptiste Colbert (1619–83) helped to concentrate the country's wealth in the hands of the King, who directed his absolute power toward the domination of European affairs. The arts were organized as an instrument of royal prestige, and to that end Colbert instituted Academies of Architecture, Fine Arts, and Music, as well as royal factories for the production of furniture, tapestries, and luxurious accessories.

Under the general supervision of the painter Charles LeBrun (1619–90), the French Baroque evolved as a national style devoted to the glorification of France and her master, the "Sun-King." Above all else, the Louis XIV style aimed at grandeur. The products of Louis' reign revealed a consistency of purpose in all the arts: imposing scale, a strong sense of tectonic structure, and a profuse display of luxurious ornament. Formal restraint and decorative splendor combined to express the pomp and formality of court life during the *grand siècle*.

The King set the standards of domestic architecture in his palaces—the Louvre, Versailles, and others. In their vast scale and their integration with expansive, formally planned gardens, these structures revealed a thoroughly Baroque sensibility, though exterior façades generally displayed simple, rectilinear outlines and a restrained treatment of the classical orders.

Interiors   Each part of the King's daily routine, from his rising to his retiring, was a state event witnessed by courtiers. Every room in the palace thus became a public space, formalized by lofty proportions and lavish decoration (Fig. 757). Walls and ceilings formed a unified composition employing a variety of media: marble panels and carving, paintings, tapestries, mirrors, and glass. Wood walls were normally painted in light colors to offset gilded carving. Furniture, pushed back against the walls, remained secondary to the massive enclosing surfaces.

Furnishings   French Baroque furniture combined monumentality and ornateness. Straight lines provided the framework for a free play of boldly projecting ornament. The variety of motifs ranged from abstract swirls and foliate patterns to nymphs, wreaths, shells, and sphinxes. Veneers of different woods, colored lacquers, and inlays enriched surfaces, while sculptural accents came from mounts made of brass and *ormolu,* an alloy of copper and zinc with the luster of gold. André Boulle (1642–1732), the leading furniture maker of the period, created cabinets of dazzling elegance through inlays of semitransparent tortoise-shell, pewter, and brass (Fig. 758).

Seating became a part of courtly ritual: a throne was reserved for the king, armchairs for princes, and other chairs and stools for the nobility and lesser ranks. Large, broad-backed chairs were upholstered in velvet, silk, or tapestry, their arms and stretchers often carved in flowing S-curves (Fig. 759). The sofa and chaise longue were introduced to give additional seating.

Tables came in a variety of shapes for special purposes, including the writing desk. Specialized cabinets provided storage for books, hats, and clothing. The ancestor of the modern chest of drawers appeared in the *commode,* composed of two or more drawers supported by legs.

The splendor of royal interiors was completed by tapestries woven at the Gobelin factory in Paris or at another in Beauvais, and by carpets made in the Savonnerie works at Chaillot (Fig. 759). Hanging tapestries, many designed under the guidance of LeBrun, combined pictorial scenes with dense floral, vegetable, and other ornamentation well suited to the medium. The fabric also served as upholstery and as coverings and canopies for beds. Equally rich pile carpets, tightly packed with scrolls and foliage, were conceived to harmonize with the interiors, often echoing the design of the ceiling.

The Rococo: Louis XV (1715–74)

When Louis XIV reached the age of 62 in 1700, his enthusiasm for courtly spectacle had begun to wane. French social life shifted from the court to the houses of the nobility and wealthy bourgeoisie, where private conversation, however artfully cultivated, required a setting for which the ponderous dignity of Versailles seemed inappropriate. Born of the desire for elegant but less pretentious surroundings, the Rococo style became identified with the reign of the new king, Louis XV (1715–74), who preferred the Rococo even after the rise of Neoclassicism (see Chap. 24).

Probably derived from the French *rocaille* ("rock-work"), the term *rococo* was coined by later critics of the style's fanciful treatment of ornament. More than a style of decoration, however, the Rococo offered a new approach to interior design. Convenience and intimacy, qualities conspicuously lacking in grand Baroque palaces, became a major concern in the planning and furnishing of stately Parisian houses. Plans were compactly arranged for easy access to rooms, in contrast to the Baroque emphasis on axial sequences. Hollow walls and false ceilings, constructed in light materials, reduced the scale of individual rooms, while rounded corners encouraged a more informal arrangement of furniture (Fig. 760). Armchairs, sofas and other furnishings provided genuine comfort while contributing to the overall decor.

Rococo decoration retained the Baroque dependence on flowing curvilinear forms, as well as the sense of structural framework in the treatment of walls, but the Louis XV style applied ornament in smaller units of greater variety and largely eliminated classical pilasters and entablatures. An emphasis on continuity and smooth transition prevailed over the articulation of structure. Inspired by silks and ceramics imported from China, the Rococo also introduced asymmetry, achieving balance in subtler ways than before.

Although similar to the Baroque in some respects, the Rococo formed a distinct style whose characteristics can be summarized as follows:

- **Aims**—comfort, luxury, beauty
- **Character**—delicate; intimate and inviting; lighthearted
- **Design**—unified by decoration spread over all surfaces; curved forms, fluidly intermingled; rhythms resembling rippling water, flickering flames, and vinelike plants; basically symmetrical, but with asymmetrical details
- **Scale**—small
- **Shapes**—curving, intricate, free-flowing, especially the **C**-shape with compound curve; graceful transitions from one shape to another
- **Ornament**—the Baroque repertory, plus many other motifs; lace, ribbon, vinelike tendrils; rocks, shells, leaves, flowers, fruit; more stylized than in Baroque works
- **Colors**—soft, light; generally of high value and low intensity

The Rococo was essentially an interior style. Exteriors actually became simpler, with larger windows and less emphasis on columnar schemes than before. Inside, differences of scale distinguished rooms according to function, while private and social spaces were segregated and grouped for convenience. The Rococo period also developed mechanical aids, such as the prandial elevator or "dumb-waiter," by which food could be lifted quickly from the kitchen to the upper rooms.

Interiors   Compared to Versailles, Rococo interiors had a lighthearted atmosphere perfectly suited to the polite conversation that dominated the social life of the period. Callers were received in the salon or the *boudoir* (a private reception room for the lady of the house).

Rococo designers gave equal attention to minute detail and unified overall effect. Slender moldings, changing into foliate swirls at the top and bottom, divided

the walls into rich diversity of paintings, tapestries, mirrors, and gilded carving (Fig. 761). Wall ornament, however, often broke through boundaries to continue on the ceiling, while corners disappeared behind a continuous enclosing surface (Fig. 760). The close collaboration of architects, wood and plaster workers, gilders, and the weavers of tapestries, upholstery, and carpets resulted in stunningly unified interiors. A preference for asymmetrical patterns—found on wall decorations, furniture, and textiles—expressed the freedom and subtlety of Rococo design. Finally, the knowing selection of gay, light colors, such as pale rose, light green, and many yellows, contributed much to the cheerful ambience of the whole interior.

Furnishings   Rococo designers gradually modified the Baroque style by lightening projecting ornaments and emphasizing curved forms. Structural parts were made to flow smoothly into one another, as in the legs and seats of chairs (Fig. 762). Fully developed Rococo furniture avoided right angles and simple geometric shapes as avidly as the Renaissance had sought them. Seating was dimensioned,

shaped, and softened with loose down cushions to put the occupants luxuriously at ease. Chaise longues, sofas, and ottomans aided cordiality and comfort. Tables and cabinets, invariably supported by graceful cabriole legs, continued in great variety for specialized purposes. Fluidly shaped metal appliqués enriched the swelling surfaces of larger pieces (Fig. 763).

In the trend toward lightness, walnut and ebony were partially superseded by a variety of domestic and imported woods, including rosewood, mahogany, satinwood, and many fruit woods. Marquetry was used to decorate many of the surfaces, but painted furniture became common by the middle of the century.

Textiles were asymmetrical but subtly balanced (Fig. 762). Flowing patterns of flowers, foliage, ribbons, and shells wandered with a deceptive air of nonchalance over smooth, finely woven silks, as well as on the heavier needlepoints, tapestries, and velours. Printed cottons, known as *toiles de Jouy,* provided monochromatic pictures for those who could not afford silk, while wallpaper appeared as a substitute for hanging tapestries.

German Baroque and Rococo

Some of the most imaginative achievements of Baroque and Rococo design occurred in Germany and Austria. German countries had been receptive to Renaissance influences from Italy, France, and the Low Countries during the 16th century, but the Thirty Years' War (1619–48) and the threat of invasion from both Louis XIV and the Turkish sultan all but halted architecture in the 17th century. A flood of construction followed in the 18th century, however, as palaces, churches, and hundreds of monasteries took shape under the influence of the Baroque and Rococo. German architects never really distinguished the two styles, but they extended Rococo principles to the design of whole buildings. German furniture of the period followed French models rather closely.

One of the most impressive interiors in Europe is the central hall of the Amalienburg, a pavilion built between 1734 and 1739 in the park of Nymphenburg Palace

near Munich (Fig. 764). This unique mixture of Rococo fluidity of form and Baroque grandeur was the product of close collaboration between Flemish architect François de Cuvilliés, wood carver Joachim Dietrich, and stucco worker Johann Zimmermann. Here the Rococo trends toward the dissolution of structure and the fusion of all the decorative arts reached its peak. The dense, fluid movement of ornament over all surfaces destroys distinctions between wall and ceiling, as between each wall panel and its neighbor, while the room itself seems to expand and turn back on itself through complex reflections in the mirrors. All individual parts are fused into a continuous, unbroken membrane of glittering silver and glass.

765. Chatsworth House in Derbyshire, England, was begun in 1686 by William Talman, a follower of Sir Christopher Wren. In the State Drawing Room, the composition of the richly carved overmantel recalls the French Baroque (Fig. 757), while Italian influence appears in the coved ceiling, painted by an Italian artist, and in tapestries based on High Renaissance designs. Strongly patterned upholstery and heavy cabriole legs add to the Baroque splendor. (*Photograph: National Monuments Record* [*Crown Copyright*])

England in the Baroque Age: 1660–1760

Cromwell's Commonwealth ended with the Restoration of monarchy in 1660, when Charles II returned from ten years' exile in Holland to assume the English crown. Throughout his reign, Charles sought to duplicate in England the autocratic power that his first cousin, Louis XIV, enjoyed in France. The continuation of Charles' policy by his son and successor James II (1685–88) provoked the English nobility to offer the crown to William of Orange, the Dutch leader who had married James' daughter Mary. This "Glorious Revolution" (1688) assured the limitation of royal power by an aristocratic Parliament, which forced further concessions from the first Hanoverian king, George I (1714–25). England's parliamentary form of government set her apart from all other European countries, and this isolation soon found visual expression.

Turbulent politics gave rise to conflicting trends in the architecture of this period. A long stay in Holland had exposed Charles II to the Baroque trends current there, and his French sympathies led him to admire the style of Louis XIV. Baroque design thus became transplanted to England, especially in the houses of the King's aristocratic supporters, who returned from exile with a taste for foreign fashions. At the same time, however, the concept of royal absolutism associated with the French Baroque made the style repugnant to the "Whig" nobility, who favored constitutional limitations on monarchic power. Thus, while a few great architects employed a Baroque idiom in churches, public buildings, and some houses (Fig. 765), the style was generally resisted in most domestic design. Vague

above: 767. Large, simple wall panels, restrained plasterwork on the ceiling, and a compact fireplace with small-scale ornament create an unobtrusive, all-white setting in an early 18th-century English room. The tall cabinet with Oriental lacquer decorations and the upholstered wing chair are contemporary with the room, while the chair near the tripod-base tea table dates from about 1750. The firescreen is covered in a Rococo fabric, and the marble console tables, supported by dolphins, are Baroque in character. (*Nelson Gallery-Atkins Museum, Kansas City* [*Nelson Fund*])

above: 766. The gallery of Chiswick House in London, one of the earliest examples of the Anglo-Palladian style, was built by its owner, Lord Burlington, between 1725 and 1729. At the left is a "Palladian" window characteristic of the English style: a central arched window is flanked by smaller, rectangular openings framed by columns and pilasters. (*Photograph: Department of the Environment* [*Crown Copyright Reserved*])

right: 768. This room from Kirtlington Park in Oxfordshire, England, was completed in 1748. Rococo swags of fruit and foliage, as well as C-shape scrolls and ribbons, appear in the marble fireplace, wood-carved door and console table, a bronze chandelier, and especially in the delicate plasterwork of the walls and ceiling. The furniture of the period includes a pair of fine Chippendale chairs. (*Metropolitan Museum of Art, New York* [*Fletcher Fund*])

opposition to foreign modes of architecture turned into the positive search for a national style in the early Georgian period, when a younger generation of professional and "gentleman" architects looked back to Inigo Jones and Palladio as the models of propriety. The result, culminating under George II (1727–60), was a uniquely English style of architecture.

Furniture, on the other hand, showed strong Baroque influences, which came chiefly from Holland. A rapid change in fashions gave rise to distinctive styles during the reigns of the late Stuarts (1660–88), William and Mary (1688–1702), and Queen Anne (1702–14). The French Rococo began to affect English furniture during the 1730s, but the style was soon adapted to native tastes.

The leading architect of his day, Sir Christopher Wren (1632–1723) designed dozens of churches in a vigorous Baroque style but found little time for domestic architecture. Ambitious dwellings of the period generally had simple rectangular shapes, with pitched roofs and dormer windows. Restrained exteriors, built in red brick with stone pilasters and details, reflected current trends in Holland. English gardens at this time imitated on a smaller scale the formality and axial symmetry of French examples.

Interiors

The Baroque Style   Still the preferred treatment for walls, wood paneling usually extended to the ceiling. Oak was finished naturally, but pine was painted white or green and accented with gilt. Swags of fruit and leaves often decorated woodwork as well as plaster ceilings. Baroque influences appeared in elaborately carved fireplaces and doors, dense overall ornament, and elaborate ceilings painted with illusionistic effects (Fig. 765).

The Baroque style reached its apogee between 1690 and 1725 in the enormous, sprawling houses of John Vanbrugh (1664–1724), whose interiors were correspondingly large and ornate. Even at their most Baroque, however, English interiors never had the dramatic climax of Italian examples (Fig. 754) or the ponderous formality of Versailles (Fig. 757).

The Anglo-Palladian Style   Even as Vanbrugh's mansions reached completion, Colin Campbell (d. 1729), a professional architect, and the Earl of Burlington (1694–1753) initiated a new movement, inspired by the architecture of Palladio and Inigo Jones. In 1725, Lord Burlington designed Chiswick House, a prime example of the "Anglo-Palladian" style (Fig. 766). The square, symmetrical plan, with a circular hall in the center, was based directly on Palladio's Villa Rotonda (Fig. 736), while the richly decorated ceilings and fireplaces had native precedents in the work of Jones (Fig. 752). The gallery, illustrated here, reveals Baroque influences in the broken pediment over the door, the general richness of the ornament, and the elaborate marble console tables beneath the mirrors. At the same time, large areas of plain surface and the precious care with which all elements are balanced against each other anticipate the Neoclassical styles that arose during the second half of the 18th century (see Chap. 24).

A more representative Georgian interior appears in Figure 767. The wood paneling is painted white to match the plaster ceiling, whose decoration is molded simply. Baroque exuberance appears only in the marble console tables and the broken pediments of the fireplace. Interiors of this period were sometimes enlivened by fabrics, French wallpapers—especially *flock* papers with textured surfaces imitating fabrics—and scenic wallpapers imported from East Asia.

Even the addition of Rococo ornament did little to change the elegant sobriety of Georgian interiors (Fig. 768). A few English patrons ordered complete rooms in a thoroughly French style, but normally the foliate swags and floral patterns provided light, decorative accents without disturbing the restrained and dignified quality of the interior.

left: 769. Exuberant, dynamic curves permeate the design of an English walnut armchair with caned seat and back, made in the period of Charles II (1660–85). In England, the Baroque and Rococo had greater impact on furniture and decorative arts than in architecture. (*Metropolitan Museum of Art, New York [Kennedy Fund, 1918]*)

right: 770. A walnut cabinet exemplifies the lively furniture style prevailing under William and Mary (1688–1702). Most conspicuous are the jaunty, broken-S-curve supports, which rest on curving stretchers and ball feet. Closer inspection reveals intricate, wispy decorations in marquetry covering the simple, rectangular body as well as the drawer, legs, and stretchers. (*Metropolitan Museum of Art, New York [bequest of Annie C. Kane, 1926]*)

Furnishings

English craftsmen of the late 17th and early 18th centuries developed quickly, absorbing a wide variety of influences. The furnishings of the period can be divided into distinct phases roughly corresponding with the succession of monarchs.

The Late Stuart Period (1660–88)   Walnut supplanted oak in the late Stuart period, as Baroque exuberance replaced the simpler, more structural designs of the earlier period. Deep, robust carving created dynamic, flowing patterns. Spiral turnings, fluid C- and S-curves, and much openwork decorated tables and the high-back chairs of the period (Fig. 769). Important additions included chests of drawers on stands and elongated chairs or "daybeds."

William and Mary (1688–1702)   Under William and Mary the basic trends of the preceding period were reinforced, but with modifications and some innovations. A new series of case pieces included writing and dressing tables. Furniture became smaller and more comfortable, while Baroque details were accepted and adapted to English tastes. Veneers and marquetry embellished flat and curving surfaces with intricate, interlacing patterns (Fig. 770).

Queen Anne (1702–14)   English craftsmen of the early 1700s continued to consider comfort as well as elegance in the design of chairs. The cabriole leg and other Baroque-inspired curving shapes gave Queen Anne furniture a sense of sturdy gracefulness. Chairs, with flowing silhouettes and little applied ornament, were especially elegant (Fig. 771). The custom of serving tea at social gatherings caused the development of small, low tables, while the vogue for collecting Oriental

ceramics brought the introduction of china cabinets. Fully upholstered wing chairs, often brilliantly colored, also appeared at this time (Fig. 772).

The Early Georgian Period (1714–60)   Baroque design reached its final flourish in the marble console tables supported by exuberant scrolls or animal forms, as designed by Vanbrugh and others to fit a large-scale architectural setting (Fig. 767). Other designers continued in the handsome Queen Anne tradition. A thorough adaptation of the French Rococo began with the reign of George II (1727–60), and walnut was largely superseded by West Indian mahogany, whose strength and ease of carving permitted greater delicacy and slenderness.

The foremost furniture maker of the Early Georgian period was Thomas Chippendale (1718–79). In 1754 he published *The Gentleman and Cabinet-Maker's Director,* an influential compendium of designs that connected his name with much that he never saw. Rather than creating wholly original designs, he combined French Baroque and Rococo curves, Gothic linearity and pointed arches, genteel Queen Anne work, and complicated Chinese fretwork. Chippendale's chair designs, wedding sturdiness to lightness and grace, were especially popular (Fig. 773). Later he produced furniture for houses where the Adam brothers worked and was strongly influenced by their restrained, unified interpretation of Neoclassical form and decoration (see pp. 561–562).

The Baroque-Rococo period in England was a prosperous age, when many ideas were tried and assimilated with varying degrees of success. A bewildering variety of influences found their way into Early Georgian houses. Perhaps it is this homelike gathering of many things that still gives these interiors, and their American counterparts, wide appeal.

Colonial
North America

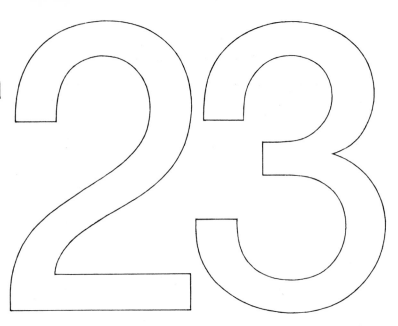

The earliest European settlers of North America came from a variety of national, social, and economic backgrounds, but they were largely lower- and middle-class people of modest means. Adapting to the necessities of a new environment, the colonists built modified versions of the simple, unpretentious houses they had left behind in their homelands.

The colonies in New England and farther south along the Atlantic coast were the most important for the history of American architecture and interior design. Unlike the French fur traders and Spanish missionaries, the predominantly English settlers of these areas immediately established permanent societies, which grew with each generation and thus required a full range of domestic amenities. The primacy of English models in the development of American homes was sealed by the restriction of trade from countries other than England after the Navigation Acts (1651) and by the eventual defeat of Spanish and French colonial powers.

Our concentration on the mainstream, however, should not obscure the contributions of other nationalities. The Spaniards, settling in Florida and the Southwest in the later 16th century, built thick-walled houses around open courts in the native style of their homeland. French settlements along the St. Lawrence River, the Great Lakes, and the Mississippi were usually trading posts with simple buildings based on medieval practices. In Louisiana, however, the French constructed houses with raised ground floors because of the dense underbrush and damp climate. Roofed outdoor galleries, which offered protection from rain and heat, became essential features of later Southern plantation houses. In Pennsylvania, the Germans developed a distinctive building tradition using local types of stone. And in New York, or New Amsterdam as it was then called, the Dutch built townhouses with stepped gables and dormers adorning high-pitched roofs that shed snow easily. Dutch farmhouses, whose sloping roofs extended beyond the walls to cover long front porches, differed considerably from English work.

The Early Colonial Style: c. 1630–1720

The Pilgrims arrived in New England two centuries after the Renaissance had begun in Florence. Stern, hardworking people of modest origins, the earliest settlers often endured their first winters living in caves, dugouts, or crude shelters made of branches and mud. As soon as possible, they built permanent structures whose

Colonial North America and the English Sources of Its Furniture			
	England	**North America**	
		Architecture	Furniture
1600	**Early Stuart** 1603–49		
	Commonwealth 1649–60	**Early Colonial** **1630–1720**	based on medieval, Elizabethan, and Early Stuart models 1630–90
	Late Stuart 1660–85		
	William & Mary **1688–1702**		"William & Mary" 1690–1720
1700	**Queen Anne** **1702–14**		
	Georgian George I (1714–27) George II (1727–60) George III (1760–1820)	**Colonial Georgian** **1720–90**	"Queen Anne" 1720–40 "Chippendale" 1740–90
1800			

functional character was dictated by the necessity of physical survival in a harsh climate. When conditions stabilized, the colonists began to erect houses on the model of those they had left behind—not the palaces and villas of the court and aristocracy, but rural, middle-class dwellings largely untouched by Renaissance or Baroque fashions. These factors, together with the limitations imposed by available materials and the scarcity of skilled craftsmen, gave Early Colonial houses and furnishings the following characteristics:

- **Aims**—use and economy
- **Character**—plain, sturdy, with little emphasis on comfort
- **Design**—dictated by function; straightforward solution of problems; highly unified, due to lack of variety
- **Scale**—no larger than necessary for basic needs and durability
- **Shapes**—simple, rectangular; curves limited to turnings and a few other parts of furniture
- **Ornament**—natural surfaces exposed; enrichment growing directly out of materials and tools; applied ornament based on a variety of European models, primarily English
- **Colors**—natural to materials: wood, brick, stone, metal; wool dyed in a few strong colors

The typical early house consisted of a simple rectangular room, where the family lived, ate, and slept, with a large fireplace used for heating and cooking (Fig. 774). Attached to the chimney near a small entrance, a tiny staircase led to a low attic, providing additional sleeping and storage space.

As prosperity came to New England, this basic plan was elaborated by the addition of a second room with its own fireplace on the other side of the central chimney. Economy of means thus led to a simple, symmetrical plan in the two-room house. A second story provided additional bedrooms, and the sloping roof could be extended over a "lean-to" area in the rear, which usually housed a separate kitchen. This "saltbox" house persisted into the late 18th century and was later revived in the 20th century. Heavy timber posts and beams provided the structural frame for houses in the northern colonies. The remaining parts of the walls were filled at first with mortared twigs and clay, later with bricks or stone. The combi-

774. A typical Early Colonial hall, from a house built about 1684 in Essex, Massachusetts, served for living, cooking, eating, and sleeping. Natural, unfinished oak and maple are used in the wide-planked floor, fireplace wall, exposed ceiling rafters, all the furniture, and even in bowls and utensils. The painted chest of drawers was made about 1700 in the colorful style typical of the Connecticut River Valley. At the rear is a built-in storage cabinet attached to the plaster-covered wall. (*Henry Francis du Pont Winterthur Museum, Winterthur, Del.*)

nation of exposed wood and whitewash created picturesque *half-timbered* exteriors, but the need for insulation led builders increasingly to cover outer walls in *clapboard* siding (overlapping horizontal boards), which the weather turned to a silver-gray tone. Later, clapboards were painted brown or red, and still later white or another light color.

In Maryland, Virginia, and the Carolinas, the availability of lime and good clay made brick the chief building material. Chimneys, instead of being enclosed by surrounding rooms, projected from the end walls at opposite sides of the house. Southern colonists imitated English fashions more closely than did the settlers of New England, but otherwise the two areas developed along similar lines.

Interiors   The rooms in Early Colonial houses were small, rectangular spaces with low ceilings (Fig. 775). Ceiling beams and structural supports in the walls were left exposed and unpainted, while the spaces between them were plastered and painted white. Floors consisted of wide oak planks, left bare at first but later given color and greater warmth by the addition of rugs. Small, shuttered windows, glazed in little diamond-shape panes, admitted daylight with a minimum amount of outside exposure.

The dominant feature of every room was the thick-walled brick fireplace, which had to be large enough to permit the preparation of food (Fig. 774). The fireplace also provided heat—essential to survival during the winter months—and evening light, but the large flue also drew continual draughts of cold air through the poorly insulated house. Plain vertical boards often sheathed the wall on either side of the fireplace (Fig. 774). Toward the end of the 17th century, this sheathing developed into carved paneling, which was sometimes left natural but more often painted brown, green, red, or yellow.

Furnishings   The multiple uses of interior space kept furnishings sparse, but the pieces themselves were solidly constructed with heavy proportions. Combining medieval, Elizabethan, and Early Stuart influences, local craftsmen created fresh interpretations of imported models. Renaissance architectural motifs, turned posts and spindles, and inventive floral designs relieved the four-square severity of most designs.

Different woods met a variety of special requirements: oak was the standard material, but ash and hickory also served for strong supports; the close grain of maple invited its use for turned carving; and pine, easy to work but durable, provided an ideal medium for simple decorative relief. Walnut became popular late in the 17th century and remained in favor long after the introduction of mahogany about 1700.

Richly carved cabinets and chests were especially typical of the Early Colonial period. Reaching a peak of elaboration in the 17th century, the "court cupboard" had open shelves above and below for the display of household plate, pewter, and ceramics (Figs. 775, 776). The blocky proportions and "melon bulb" turnings of the larger pieces recall Elizabethan precedents (Fig. 749). Low chests of drawers with paneled fronts sometimes carried delightful floral decorations carved in low

below: 775. A room from the Thomas Hart house, built between 1640 and 1670 in Ipswich, Massachusetts, is arranged as a typically multipurpose room. A heavy, centered "summer beam" supports the lighter ones running across the ceiling. Except for the bulky, vigorously turned gateleg table from Pennsylvania, all of the furniture is from New England. (*Henry Francis du Pont Winterthur Museum, Winterthur, Del.*)

right: 776. Massachusetts craftsmen carved this oak court cupboard between 1660 and 1680. The robust forms and chunky proportions reveal the influence of Elizabethan models (see Fig. 749). A similar but lighter example appears in Figure 775. (*Metropolitan Museum of Art, New York* [*gift of Mrs. Russell Sage, 1909*])

relief or painted in red, black, and yellow (Fig. 777). The common placement of a chest on a waist-high stand with drawers led to the development of the high, one-piece chest or *highboy* (Fig. 788). Special cases evolved for the storage of spices and books, the latter type often designed with a slanted top to hold the all-important Bible.

The typical chair of the period, similar to those made throughout Europe, had simple cylindrical legs and arms, a stick back, and a cane seat. Turned carving in the supports and back provided restrained elaboration, as in the *Carver* chair shown in Figure 778. A related type of "stick" chair boasted a profusion of turned posts and spindles, while another employed horizontal slats for the back. Less common was the heavy, panel-back *wainscot* chair (Fig. 779), which reflected the elaborate English furniture of the late 16th and early 17th centuries (Figs. 747, 750). The flat, decorative carving of these pieces offered charming simplifications of Renaissance ornament, such as pilasters, vine scrolls, the *guilloche* (a linear braid of interlaced circles), and rosettes.

Tables followed a variety of functional designs: the board and braced trestle could be separated and easily moved (Fig. 774); the gateleg table expanded to provide space for meals and retracted conveniently afterwards (Fig. 775); and the "chair table" offered a hinged top that could be lifted up to form the high back of an armchair! Beds were of simple frames with slats or ropes holding straw or feather mattresses (Figs. 774, 775). Bed hangings often supplied warmth and a measure of privacy.

Increased trade at the end of the 17th century brought closer contact with European fashions, and Baroque influences entered America through the William and Mary style and contemporary work from Holland and Spain. Walnut replaced oak as the preferred wood, while veneers, marquetry, and painted decoration became more popular, as in the chest of drawers in Figure 774. Crude cabriole legs, shells, and pediments began a repertory that the 18th century refined and expanded. Chairs acquired elaborate scrolls and other curvilinear forms; seats and backs were made of cane or occasionally padded with simple upholstery (Fig. 780).

Throughout the 17th century, textiles and accessories were limited in number. Window and bed curtains, of homespun wool or sometimes linen, were left their natural color or dyed indigo or reddish brown. Wooden dishes gave way to glazed ceramics, but wealthier colonists imported fine pewter and silver products. The

777. An oak and pine chest with drawers, dated "April 15th 1704," is of a type often found in 17th-century Connecticut homes. Horizontal moldings and vertical balusters emphasize the rectilinear shape, but the low-relief carving and painted decorations on the panels introduce an unexpected playfulness. (*Art Institute of Chicago* [*Wirt D. Walker Fund*])

end of the century witnessed the introduction of checkered weaves, India prints, and "Turkey work" (imitating Oriental carpets). Small rugs, first used as table coverings, were supplemented by larger carpets laid on the floor.

The Colonial Georgian Style: c. 1720–90

Prosperity and a flood of immigrations brought social stratification to the American colonies. The emerging upper classes and wealthy merchants looked to the English aristocracy for models of "good taste" in all aspects of culture, including the design and decoration of houses. In order to satisfy the demand for new fashions, colonial craftsmen depended heavily on the dozens of illustrated books on architecture and design published in England during the 18th century. For example, Colin Campbell's *Vitruvius Brittanicus* (1715–25) offered engravings of English country houses, while Chippendale's *The Gentleman and Cabinet-Maker's Director* (1754) and Abraham Swan's *Collection of Designs in Architecture* (1757) provided explicit, detailed designs that were widely copied in the colonies.

Most middle-class houses of the 18th century followed the patterns established in the previous period, with decor and furnishings improving as expenses permitted (Fig. 781). But the more ambitious houses of the wealthy, built in major cities and on large southern estates, imitated the stately Georgian mansions of England.

The architecture of each region had its own special character. New England architects, after some initially awkward experiments in translating masonry forms into wood construction, developed a crisp, dignified style. English influence gradually displaced Dutch traditions in the stone architecture of New York. Brick was the preferred material along the southern seaboard, where estates sometimes grew into large complexes; and the houses of Philadelphia boasted the richest assimilation of the European decorative vocabulary.

Despite regional variations, however, architects of the Colonial Georgian period pursued consistent aims. Symmetrical plans, with four or five rooms contained in

781. This interior from the Samuel Wentworth house in Portsmouth, New Hampshire, was built in 1671 and paneled in 1710. The room reveals a greater emphasis on comfort, spaciousness, and refinement than was true in the Early Colonial period (Figs. 774, 775). The early 18th-century furniture includes two brightly patterned wing chairs, a leather-padded armchair, and a round gateleg table of light proportions. Chinese-style lacquer decorations embellish the highboy in the rear. (*Metropolitan Museum of Art, New York*)

a simple rectangle, rose to a height of two or three stories. Each room had a fireplace, and the proliferation of chimneys freed the center of the house for a spacious hall or large staircase. Centered on a symmetrical façade, the front door received discreet emphasis from pilasters and a pediment, or a small porch. Projecting cornices accented rooflines, and gently sloping roofs gradually became flatter, eventually disappearing behind a balustrade. Large, double-sash windows, evenly spaced on the outside, made for bright interiors.

Interiors   The rooms shown in Figures 781 to 784 suggest the diversity of Colonial Georgian interiors. The low ceiling and exposed beams in the parlor of the Wentworth house date from its construction in 1671 (Fig. 781), but the paneling, installed in 1710, articulates the wall and emphasizes the fireplace in a new spirit of restrained architectural embellishment. In most houses, the fireplace wall was the first to be paneled; the remaining walls were painted in a light color, as in the Wentworth house, or covered in paper or fabric above a waist-high paneled dado. In the parlor of Vauxhall Gardens (Fig. 782), unpainted wood surrounds a fireplace framed by imported Delft tiles, while the other walls are covered in flock canvas (whose green and yellow pattern echoes the upholstered seats of the chairs). This room also reflects the 18th-century preference for higher ceilings with beams concealed by a flat plaster surface.

High proportions and generously scaled doors and windows gave fully developed Colonial Georgian interiors an effect of airy spaciousness. Paneling was painted white and sometimes extended to the ceiling on all four sides of a room (Fig. 783). Architectural elements, taken from a medley of Renaissance, Baroque, and Rococo sources, accented doors, walls, and ceilings. Mantels and overmantels received the greatest elaboration, but fireplaces themselves, needed only for heat after the development of separate kitchens, became smaller than before.

above: 782. The parlor from Vauxhall Gardens, a house built in southern New Jersey between 1700 and 1725, illustrates the richness and elegance attained in the Colonial Georgian period. Delft tiles around the fireplace, a large Oriental carpet, and patterned fabrics on the walls and in upholstery serve as decorative foils to the plain plaster ceiling, simply paneled fireplace wall, and the restrained elegance of American furniture in Queen Anne style. (*Henry Francis du Pont Winterthur Museum, Winterthur, Del.*)

left: 783. A bed-sitting room from Patuxent Manor, Maryland (1744) is entirely paneled and painted a light yellow-gray. Chairs, chest, and card tables follow Chippendale designs, and the tea table is set with English porcelain and a pewter kettle from Connecticut. The imposing bed has crewel embroidery curtains. (*Henry Francis du Pont Winterthur Museum, Winterthur, Del.*)

Colonial North America **551**

above: 784. A room from the Samuel Powell house in Philadelphia was furnished about 1768. The paneled fireplace wall, painted off-white, is a formal, highly ordered composition embellished with free-flowing details that echo the delicate Rococo plasterwork of the ceiling. The paneling and crisply framed door stand out against the landscapes, buildings, birds, and plants of the Oriental wallpaper. (*Metropolitan Museum of Art, New York*)

left: 785. A braced comb-back Windsor chair, made about 1760 of maple, oak, and pine, combines lightness and strength in a lean, functional design. Based on the traditional "everyday" furniture of unpretentious homes in England, the Windsor chair became a standard form of seating throughout North America. Arms, back, and braces are supported by the seat, which is saddle-shaped for comfort. (*Museum of Fine Arts, Boston*)

The cosmopolitan influences that contributed to the American Georgian style are especially evident in the house furnished by Samuel Powell in 1768, two years before he became the mayor of Philadelphia (Fig. 784). White walls and ceiling offset the strong asymmetrical pattern of the Chinese-style wallpaper and the glittering, cut-glass chandelier, both of which Powell brought back from his extensive travels in Europe. The projecting brackets and broken pediment above the fireplace (framed by imported blue marble) derive from Baroque sources, while the delicate tendrils lightly molded on the plaster ceiling reveal the influence of the Rococo. The overall effect is a pleasing combination of logic and fancy.

Furnishings   Reverse curves and deep carving began in the Colonial furniture of the late 17th century. In the 18th century, proportions became lighter, curves longer, and transitions smoother, as American designers relied increasingly on restrained English interpretations of Rococo design. By 1750, distinctive characteristics could be discerned in the furniture of the major centers of production: lightness and delicacy in Boston, simple profiles and restrained ornament in

Newport, heavier proportions and decoration in New York, and exuberant detailing in Philadelphia. All colonial products, however, relied more on shape and silhouette than on rich materials or applied ornament. Walnut and mahogany were the preferred woods, but maple and pine served as less expensive substitutes.

Seats were varied in form but generally shaped to fit the human body. Colonial craftsmen of the early decades created some excellent variations of the Queen Anne chair, whose cabriole legs and curved, solid-splat back joined sturdiness with elegance (Fig. 782). Upholstered chairs and couches, including the comfortable wing chair, became increasingly popular (Figs. 781, 784). By 1760, Chippendale's influence brought chairs with bow backs and pierced splats (Fig. 783), and the straight leg began to compete with the cabriole form. The Windsor chair, arriving from England around 1725, was by 1760 one of the most typical features of modest homes throughout the colonies (Fig. 785). Embellished only by turnings in supports and back, the all-wood design offered a combination of strength, lightness, ease of construction, and comfort. The Windsor chair typically had a saddle seat and high back, but variations included chairs with headrests or writing arms, double settles, and highchairs.

Tables of the gateleg type gave way to oval-topped designs with cabriole legs and drop leaves (Fig. 782). Rectangular side tables facilitated service in the dining room. The parlor and bedroom acquired tea tables with piecrust rims and tripod supports, as well as card tables, sometimes with folding legs (Figs. 783, 784).

Cabinets and chests continued as the greatest strength of American furniture design. A multipurpose unit based on English precedents, the *secretary* incorporated drawers for storage, a hinged writing surface, and a set of shelves behind inlaid or mirrored doors (Fig. 786). Newport craftsmen produced impressive cabinets of substantial proportions and elegant shapes. The example in Figure 787, a dressing table composed of a "kneehole" between two projecting sets of drawers, displays the popular shell motif in two forms: as a convex projection and as a concave depression. Brass handles and shaped surfaces provided the only other decoration.

The most elegant storage pieces were chests of drawers on legs: the short *lowboy*, which doubled as a dressing or side table (Fig. 783), and the tall *highboy*. Beginning with simple lines and tall, straight legs, the highboy soon acquired graceful cabriole legs and a wealth of elaborate decoration, especially in the scrolled pediments, finials, and busts at the top (Fig. 788). The origin of the piece, in the placement of one chest atop another, left traces in the narrow molding separating a lower, wider pair of drawers from a narrower but taller set above. Free-flowing Rococo carving and elegant brass attachments embellished the most splendid examples.

above: 786. Mirrored doors surmount the slanting drop front of a black-walnut secretary, made in Pennsylvania in the first quarter of the 18th century. The severe design is enhanced only by simple finials, ball feet, and a few small accents in brass. (*Philadelphia Museum of Art; photograph: A. J. Wyatt*)

left: 787. A solidly proportioned mahogany dressing table reveals Chippendale influence. The knee-hole form, popular in England, seldom appeared in America outside of Newport, Rhode Island, where this piece was made between 1750 and 1775. The stylized shell, here employed in both convex and concave forms, is another characteristic of Newport workshops. (*Metropolitan Museum of Art, New York* [*gift of Mrs. Russell Sage, 1909*])

Large, imposing beds with fabric hangings dominated the bedrooms of the period (Fig. 783). After the middle of the century, hangings diminished in size and eventually disappeared, leaving four tall posts as vestiges with no function other than decoration.

Textiles of great diversity ranged from luxurious silk damask, brocade draperies and upholstery, and Oriental rugs (Fig. 782) to the more serviceable wool, linen, and cotton curtains and upholstery, and to the hooked or braided rugs that made humble dwellings as cheerful, if not as luxurious, as the larger homes.

Imported and locally made accessories contributed to the sparkle and richness of interiors. "China" came from the Orient by way of European trade; but local artisans created glassware, pewter, and silver of high quality. Mirrors became larger, with carved and gilded frames. Lighting after dark improved with better candles, whale-oil lamps, and chandeliers of metal or glass (Figs. 782–784).

The Colonial period was an age of assimilation in the United States. European modes of architectural and furniture design were copied from handbooks and imported exemplars, but American interpretations were often fresh and original. Despite "incorrect" proportions and "impure" ornament, Colonial furnishings derived a special charm from their direct, uncomplicated approach to structure and decoration. Compared to those of 18th-century France, American interiors look provincial and awkward, but they also seem accessible and inviting through the combination of diverse elements.

The social and economic turbulence of the American Revolution inhibited new construction during the 1770s and 1780s. When conditions stabilized by around 1790, statesmen and artists were faced with the task of finding a style of architecture that would express the independence of the new republic as well as its European heritage. By this time, however, European art had turned in the direction of Neoclassicism, which American design followed in a search for authority among the styles of the past.

788. An elegant mahogany highboy of about 1765 demonstrates the high caliber of Philadelphia craftsmanship in the period before the American Revolution. The foliate carving on the legs and skirt bears favorable comparison with English work (Fig. 773) associated with Chippendale's workshop. (*Metropolitan Museum of Art, New York* [*Kennedy Fund, 1918*])

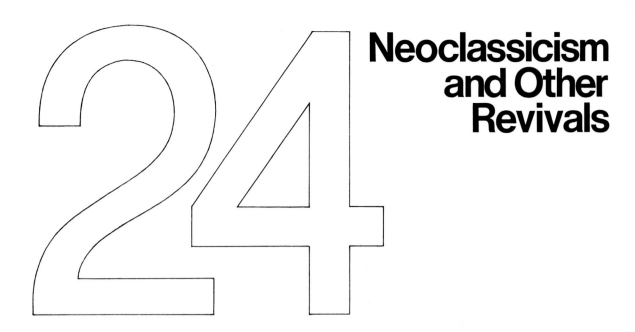

Neoclassicism and Other Revivals

An age of rationalism, revolution, and industrialization, the period spanning the late 18th century and the 19th gave the modern world its essential character. Rationalism created the experimental method and systematically challenged earlier ideas of religion, philosophy, science, and politics. Radical political thought denied the legitimacy of colonial rule in America (1776) and hereditary, divine-right monarchy in France (1789), initiating a series of revolutions extending to the middle of the 19th century. During the same period, the progress of scientific discovery and its economic exploitation culminated in the "Industrial Revolution."

The arts responded to the dawn of the modern age by reviving the styles of the past. *Neoclassicism,* or *Romantic Classicism* as the movement is often called, began around 1750 as a reaction against the Baroque and Rococo styles, and the emulation of classical antiquity remained the predominant mode of architectural design until the end of the 19th century. At the same time, the Gothic and other styles of the European past were also newly appreciated and imitated, as were the arts of China and the Near East. The revival of historic styles and the imitation of exotic modes reached a climax in the middle of the 19th century.

Neoclassicism

The imitation of classical architecture in the 18th and early 19th centuries became increasingly accurate as antiquity became better known. No longer content with the summaries given in Renaissance treatises, architects and amateurs traveled to the actual monuments and published accurate, measured drawings of both Greek and Roman buildings in Italy, Greece, Turkey, and Syria. Archaeology, the objective study of the past through its physical remains, arose dramatically with the excavation of Herculaneum and Pompeii. These small Roman towns, preserved intact under the lava of Vesuvius since A.D. 79, contained dozens of moderately scaled, livable houses, whose furnishings and colorful decoration had a strong impact on interior design in the second half of the 18th century.

The growth of archaeological knowledge gradually enabled 18th-century architects to distinguish Renaissance from ancient—and Greek from Roman—modes of building. The later phase of Neoclassicism, during the late 18th and early 19th centuries, developed strong preferences for Greek over Roman architecture, and for the literal imitation of specific monuments.

Neoclassicism and Other Revivals		
	France	England	United States
1750	**Early Neoclassicism 1750–1804** Louis XVI (1774–92) Directoire (1793–1804)	**Early Neoclassicism, or Adam Style 1760–1800** George III (1760–1820)	**Colonial Georgian 1720–90** **Early Neoclassicism, or Federal Style 1790–1820**
1800	**Late Neoclassicism, or Empire 1804–15**	**Late Neoclassicism, or Regency 1800–37** George IV (1820–30)	**Late Neoclassicism, Greek Revival, or Empire 1820–60**
	1815–90: continuation of Empire; revival of Gothic, Louis XIV, Rococo, & Renaissance	**Eclectic Revivals** Gothic 1750–1900 Oriental 1750–1900 Elizabethan 1820–50 Rococo 1825–50 **High Victorian 1850–80**	**Eclectic Revivals** Gothic 1830–1900 Oriental 1870–1900 Rococo 1840–60 **High Victorian 1870–90**

The classical revival of the 18th century was more self-conscious than that of the Renaissance. Awareness of a contemporary age distinct from both antiquity and the Renaissance gave rise to a sense of isolation from the past and nostalgia for ways of life that were no longer possible. This emotional response to the past formed an integral part of *Romanticism,* a movement loosely defined by its passion for the irregular, surprising, and awe-inspiring qualities of unspoiled nature. Interest in the exotic and in individual expression eventually led Romanticism to revolt against the increasing rigidity of Neoclassicism, but in the 18th century the two

789. The principal room of the Hôtel de Tessé, built in Paris about 1770, illustrates the aristocratic refinement of early French Neoclassicism. Tall windows and white walls trimmed with gold leaf create a light, spacious atmosphere. Embroidered satin and rich velvet upholstery enhances furnishings of the period. (*Metropolitan Museum of Art, New York* [*gift of Mrs. Herbert N. Straus, 1943*])

movements developed together. The union of reason and nature was most conspicuous in the carefully planned informality of the English garden, where wandering paths in rustic groves opened suddenly to reveal picturesque views of an artificial ruin or miniature Greek temple.

As a whole, Neoclassicism tended toward simplicity, stability, and a predominance of straight lines and right angles. Although readily accepted throughout Europe, the style assumed different forms in various countries, and its development in domestic design can be divided into distinct early and late phases. *Early Neoclassicism*, inspired by the small-scale decoration of Pompeian houses, was essentially a revision of earlier styles along lines of restraint and dignity. This phase is known as the *Louis XVI* style in France, the *Late Georgian* or *Adam* style in England, and the *Federal* style in the United States. *Late Neoclassicism*, beginning around 1790, revealed an imposing solidity of form and a more literal dependence on Roman and especially Greek architecture and furnishings. The initiative set by Napoleon's *Empire* was followed in the English *Regency* and American *Greek Revival* or *Empire* styles. The characteristics that unite and distinguish the two phases of Neoclassicism can be summarized as follows:

	Early Neoclassicism	Late Neoclassicism
☐ **aims**	dignity, repose, stability, comprehensive unity	
☐ **character**	restrained elegance	imposing monumentality
☐ **design**	straight lines and right angles, relieved by simple geometric curves; comparatively plain, flat surfaces; strict symmetry	
☐ **scale**	moderate	large
☐ **shapes**	precise, linear, geometrical	massive, architectonic, three-dimensional
☐ **ornament**	small-scale, light; floral and foliate motifs	heavy, sculptural; architectural motifs and animal parts
☐ **colors**	pastels	strong, resonant colors

Neoclassicism emerged quite rapidly in the second half of the 18th century in France and England, where it lasted between fifty and seventy-five years, crossing the ocean to the United States before 1800. Despite its effects on churches and public buildings, Neoclassicism changed the interiors of houses more than their exteriors, and the Empire and Regency styles found clearest expression in furniture.

French Neoclassicism: 1750–1850

The reaction against the Rococo style began in the 1750s and was firmly established even before the reign of Louis XVI (1774–92), whose name is often applied to the early phase of French Neoclassicism. The French Revolution initiated a period of general turmoil, and the only stable political entity, the Directoire (1793–1804) gave its name to an austere style that led directly into the Late Neoclassical Empire style fostered by Napoleon I (1804–15).

The Louis XVI Style: c. 1750–92

Interiors   Neoclassical architects retained some aspects of Rococo houses, such as the convenient arrangement of rooms and the restrained treatment of exteriors, but interiors became larger again, with high ceilings and tall windows and doors (Fig. 789). A preponderance of straight lines and right angles created a sense of dignity without the density of colored marble that had embellished Baroque interiors. Emphasized cornices returned to make a clear distinction between walls and ceiling. Walls were paneled in slender rectangles framed by thin, finely detailed, gilded moldings. The paneling was usually painted white, cream, or gray, while subdued pastels colored tapestries and upholstery. Fireplaces had simple rectangular shapes, with horizontal mantels supported by little columns or bundles of reeds; mirrors, larger than before, were crowned by semicircular arches.

Furnishings   While retaining many full-bodied curves, Louis XVI furniture developed a distinctive emphasis on slender, straight lines. Chairs and tables typically had thin vertical legs enriched by straight or spiral channels. Chair backs acquired simple shapes: rectangles, circles, and ovals. Strict symmetry and the clear separation of one part from another characterized all Neoclassical furniture.

Cabinets and chests of all sorts relied on smooth, flat planes of dark mahogany or ebony, enlivened by marquetry in restrained, geometric patterns (Fig. 790). Bronze and ormolu attachments were applied sparingly, in low relief, to accent the basic design. Other furniture was painted grayish-white, gray-green, and other soft tones. Upholstery conformed in character, with delicately colored brocades, embroidered satins, and stamped velvet in small floral patterns, feather motifs, ribbons, or simple stripes.

The Empire Style: 1804–15

A growing sensitivity to archaeological correctness led to the stricter imitation of classical sources in the late 18th century. This spirit of revival was given the legitimacy of a national cause by Napoleon, who believed that his own empire required a monumental style like that of ancient Rome. Napoleon's expedition to Egypt in 1798 inspired much borrowing from ancient Egyptian designs as well.

Interiors   Large-scale, clear-cut shapes and an emphasis on flat planes marked interiors of the Empire style (Fig. 791). Walls, articulated by flat pilasters (as during the Renaissance) or rectangular panels, were often painted in strong Pompeian colors, such as hot reds and yellows, harsh greens, and deep blues. Pompeian houses also inspired painted decoration in the form of stylized vegetable motifs arranged in geometric patterns on walls and ceilings. Mirrors, shaped in simple rectangles, became larger and wider. Windows had elaborate curtains, and this fondness for curtains extended to complex hangings across entire walls and in tentlike canopies over beds (Fig. 792). Strong color contrasts, bulky proportions, and simple, large-scale ornament gave interiors a grandiose, stable effect.

Furnishings   Empire interiors took much of their character from the heavy, solid furniture of the period. The wide exposure of flat surfaces and the conspicuous separation of individual parts gave all pieces a studied air of permanence. Dark mahogany, ebony, and "ebonized" fruitwoods received accents of sharp contrast from widely spaced attachments in gilded brass. Ornamental motifs were derived directly and explicitly from Greek vases, Roman houses, and Etruscan tombs. Case pieces and larger tables had strictly rectilinear outlines, though supports often took the form of sphinxes, herms, winged figures, eagles, and swans. Circular tables with inlaid marble tops stood on elaborate pedestal bases. Chairs and sofas, combining gentle curves with straight, thick lines, were often uncomfortable, because designers sometimes concerned themselves more with antique motifs than with human anatomy. Beds and couches reached an unparalleled monumentality, as elaborate scrolled headrests and footrests graced massive platforms that today seem like river barges (Fig. 792). Carpets, woven in strong rectilinear patterns, completed the static richness of Empire interiors.

English Neoclassicism: 1760–1830

The Anglo-Palladian movement had already revealed the relative independence of English architecture from the prevailing Baroque and Rococo fashions of France.

790. A French secretary of about 1780 features inlays of various woods, restrained mountings of gilt bronze, and a marble top. Strict symmetry and geometric order predominate in the severe profile and rectilinear marquetry patterns. (*M. H. de Young Memorial Museum, San Francisco* [*Roscoe and Margaret Oakes Collection*])

above: 791. This room in the Fontainebleau palace, erected during the Renaissance, was remodeled in the Empire style for Napoleon I. Imperial symbols are repeated on the walls, in the upholstery, and in applied metal ornaments of the furniture. (*Photograph: H. Roger Viollet*)

left: 792. A bedroom in the chateau of Malmaison, near Paris, was refurnished in 1810 for the Empress Josephine, whose initial appears in the chair backs and on the base of the bed. The monumental canopied bed, the tripod washstand, and the backdrop of spindly columns and spreading draperies recall the furnishings of the Greeks, Romans, and ancient Egyptians. (*Photograph: Musées Nationaux*)

Neoclassicism and Other Revivals   **559**

English Neoclassicism acquired an equally distinctive character under the leadership of Robert Adam, who freely interpreted classical sources in a light and graceful style of decoration. Adam dominated English design until the 1790s, when renewed French influence fostered a preference for heavier proportions and literal dependence on ancient models, culminating in the Regency style.

above left: 793. Robert Adam, the arbiter of English Neoclassical taste, designed the dining room of Saltram House, Devonshire, in about 1768. The oval-back chairs, of Hepplewhite design, harmonize with the delicate play of straight and curved lines that governs the entire room. (*Photograph: A. F. Kersting*)

above right: 794. A fine bow-front commode is one of a pair designed by Adam in 1773 for the drawing room at Osterly Park in Middlesex, England. Decorative motifs inlaid in various woods reappear in the carved marble fireplace reflected in the mirror. (*Photograph: Victoria & Albert Museum [Crown Copyright]*)

right: 795. Two designs for shield-back chairs by George Hepplewhite are taken from his *Cabinet-Maker and Upholsterer's Guide* (1788). Hepplewhite's book popularized the delicate Adam style on both sides of the Atlantic.

The Late Georgian Style: 1760–1800

The leading architect during the early reign of George III (1760–1820) was a Scotsman, Robert Adam (1728–92). Although he designed several impressive houses and introduced innovative variety in room shapes and sequences, Adam's primary importance lay in his style of interior decoration. Before beginning his career, Adam traveled to Italy, where he met French and Italian architects who were developing the theories of Neoclassicism and visited the monuments of Rome as well as the newly excavated houses at Pompeii and Herculaneum. Returning to England in 1758, he began remodeling and completing older or unfinished country houses for the aristocracy. Adam's distinctive style, while indebted to native Anglo-Palladian traditions and contemporary French design, grew primarily from personal and highly inventive interpretation of Pompeian interiors, decorative paintings of the Italian Renaissance, and current publications on Greek and Roman architecture.

Interiors   Adam rejected heavy architectural features in favor of small-scale ornament applied in low relief over planar surfaces (Fig. 793). Straight lines, simple curves, and strict symmetry created an impression of orderly refinement. Larger units were subdivided into smaller ones, so that the whole remained coherent while details invited continually closer inspection. Instead of the white paneling of the Early Georgian period. Adam preferred plaster walls painted in pastel colors to bring out the finely molded stucco relief, painted white. Doors and mantels became less monumental, while profuse decoration focused interest on the ceiling. Adam developed a personal vocabulary of ornament, comprised of attenuated classical orders, wispy swags and garlands, medallions, delicate scrolls of acanthus, and other plant motifs.

Often given complete control of a house and everything in it, Adam brought a comprehensive unity to interior spaces through a controlled range of harmonizing colors and the repetition of motifs in various parts of the room. The carpet woven for the dining room at Saltram House, for example, repeats the design of the ceiling (Fig. 793). Both surfaces are decorated with a large circle, filled by a central medallion and four segments, which is related to a rectangular frame through circular rosettes and symmetrical acanthus scrolls in the corners. The repetition is enlivened by differences in detail, which take full advantage of the colorful texture of weaving and the delicacy of stucco relief.

Furnishings   Robert Adam's concern for the unity of his interiors led him to design furniture that would harmonize in scale and decoration with the architectural setting. His pieces combined simple outlines, rectilinear structure, and tapered straight legs with a variety of simple curves and delicate relief-carved, inlaid, or painted ornament.

The motifs adorning Adam's interiors reappeared on his furniture. The commode illustrated in Figure 794, a bow-front design popularized by Adam, has a satinwood frieze across the top, with acanthus and urns interrupted by a plaque showing griffins flanking a portrait medallion. The same frieze reappears above the doors and fireplace of the room for which the commode was intended. Adam also designed elaborate side tables flanked by pedestals supporting large urns, as well as fully developed sideboards, settees, window seats, and a variety of mirrors.

The Adam style quickly transformed English furniture, notably in the late works of Chippendale. Its influence spread beyond English shores through publications by Adam and his followers.

George Hepplewhite (d. 1786), after initial Rococo experiments, followed Adam's lead in the preference for straight lines and geometric curves. A book of furniture designs published by his widow in 1788 assured Hepplewhite an international reputation. Especially influential were his chair designs, with straight legs of round or square sections tapering toward "spade" or "thimble" feet (Fig. 795).

Oval-, shield-, and heart-shape backs had pierced, lightly carved splats with curvilinear contours. Continuous, serpentine curves united the whole design. Adam's elaborate side tables with flanking pedestals for storage became compressed into a single unit in the tripartite sideboard—a design quickly adopted from Hepplewhite's book by American craftsmen (Fig. 800).

Thomas Sheraton (1751–1806) similarly established his reputation by a four-volume book of designs published in 1791–94. Sheraton's designs resembled Hepplewhite's in their moderate scale, slender forms, straight legs, and the use of marquetry or painted decoration. Sheraton, however, placed greater emphasis on the straight line, the right angle, and short, simple curves (Fig. 796). This rectilinear quality, as best seen in Sheraton's chair backs, brought with it a greater complexity of surface detail. Sheraton's later work, published in two additional books (1803–06), became much heavier and led directly into the Regency style.

The Regency Style: c. 1800–37

The English Regency style takes its name from the rule of the Prince of Wales from 1811 to 1820 during the illness of George III, but the style began with the Prince's earliest commissions at Brighton soon after 1800 and continued even beyond his reign as George IV (1820–30).

Interiors   The delicacy of Early Neoclassicism yielded to bold simplicity and large-scale compositions in the Regency style. Interiors became plainer, with an emphasis on flat surfaces and isolated rich ornaments. Walls were often painted in strong colors, against which white pilasters or gilded fixtures stood out in deliberate contrast.

The Regency style received its fullest popular expression from Thomas Hope, a well-traveled amateur who decorated and furnished his own house and then published the results in a book entitled *Household Furniture and Interior Decoration* (1807). Hope designed one room with couches covering three sides, in the manner

above: 796. A side chair and armchair reveal the rectilinear emphasis and surface enrichment of the furniture designs published by Thomas Sheraton in his *Cabinet-Maker and Upholsterer's Drawing Book* (1791–94).

right 797. The late Neoclassicism of the English Regency period appears in a room from the home of Thomas Hope, who illustrated his design in *Household Furniture and Interior Decoration* (1807). Massive furnishings, strong colors, and a profusion of gold ornament gave the actual room a heavier appearance than is suggested by the dry, crisp style of Hope's drawing.

798. Solid proportions and an emphatic profile lend dignity to a mahogany "Grecian" sofa, made in England about 1820. The strongly patterned wallpaper also belongs to the Regency period. (*Royal Pavilion, Brighton*)

of ancient Roman dining rooms, and installed a set of landscape paintings on the walls—a decorative program recalling that of Pompeian houses (Fig. 797). The landscapes, however, represented "buildings of India," and to harmonize with them Hope laid Persian carpets on the floor and treated the ceiling—"imitated from those prevailing in Turkish palaces"—as a canopy-shape trellis of reeds. The author adds that the colors of the room are "everywhere very vivid, and very strongly contrasted." The Regency preference for flatness and sharp silhouettes found clear expression in the precise and arid drawing style of Hope's illustrations.

Furnishings   Strong design and large scale made Regency furniture dominate the space it occupied. A spirit of archaeological correctness stimulated the literal imitation of specific Greek, Roman, and Egyptian forms and ornaments. Classical X-shape supports, for example, were especially popular for chairs and stools. Boldly scaled animal forms, such as lions, sphinxes, and chimaeras, created arresting designs but sometimes detracted from the unity of the whole table or chair (Fig. 797). Case pieces, invariably heavy, were adorned with architectural supports and moldings. One of the most successful adaptations of classical design, the "Grecian" sofa had scroll-shape head- and footrests, lion's-paw feet, and an emphatic silhouette of straight lines joined with a few strong curves (Fig. 798). Most Regency furniture consisted of severely rectilinear shapes with long, plain surfaces in dark mahogany, sparsely relieved by projecting gilded metal attachments. Its heavy proportions led directly to the bulkier furniture of the Victorian age.

American Neoclassicism: c. 1790–1860

Neoclassicism in the United States is sometimes dated from 1769. In that year the young Thomas Jefferson (1743–1826) designed Monticello, his home in Virginia, with a freestanding portico, central domed hall, and strictly symmetrical plan. The movement gained general currency, however, around 1790, when Jefferson and other patrons and architects looked to ancient Roman buildings and contemporary French and English neoclassicism for models of a "natural" and "rational" style of architecture for the new Republic.

The *Federal* style—the early phase of American Neoclassicism—flourished in the decades between 1790 and 1820, the same period in which national leaders developed the institutions of centralized government. Public buildings of the Federal style were given a new formality based on Roman, Renaissance, and contemporary European sources, while domestic interiors and furniture revealed a strong dependence on the restrained Neoclassicism of Adam and his followers.

left: 799. A room from the Derby house (1799), built by Samuel MacIntire in Salem, Massachusetts, illustrates the Neoclassicism of the Federal style. The influence of Robert Adam appears in the delicate, low-relief decorations of the ceiling, fireplace, and door, while the chairs derive from designs by Hepplewhite and Sheraton. Compare Figs. 795, 796. (*Philadelphia Museum of Art* [*given by George Horace Lorimer*])

above: 800. This elegant mahogany sideboard was made in New York City in 1793 for Oliver Wolcott, the first governor of Connecticut. The refined simplicity of the design may be contrasted with the elaborate sideboards of the Victorian period, as in Figure 809. (*Collection Mrs. Walter B. Robb* [*reproduced by permission of The Magazine* Antiques])

801. The taut elegance of Duncan Phyfe's finely crafted furniture sets the tone of a room assembled as a New York interior of the early 19th century. Thin, unobtrusive moldings accent the walls and ceiling, which are otherwise left bare to offset the freely draped curtains and sparkling glass chandeliers and sconces. (*Henry Francis du Pont Winterthur Museum, Winterthur, Del.*)

After 1820, monumental architecture turned from Roman to Greek models as the authority of true classical design. This *Greek Revival* movement had its counterpart in the American Empire style of interior and furniture design, which was strongly influenced by the French Empire and English Regency styles.

The Federal Style: c. 1790–1820

Interiors   Simple rectangular rooms were governed by a rectilinear emphasis and embellished by light, delicate ornament (Fig. 799). The influence of Robert Adam's small-scale foliate patterns appeared in plaster ceiling decorations and in shallow carving over doors and fireplaces, which became less monumental than in the Colonial Georgian period. Walls were typically left in plaster, painted white or a pastel shade, with woodwork restricted to a base molding, chair rail, and thin cornice (Figs. 799, 801). High ceilings and large windows, their frames covered by ample curtains, contributed to the restful dignity of Federal houses.

Furnishings   The trend initiated by Adam toward light construction and straight lines reached America around 1790, primarily through the pattern books of Hepplewhite and Sheraton. A room from the Derby house in Salem, for example, contains both a Hepplewhite-style shield-back chair and a square-back armchair of the type published by Sheraton (Fig. 799; compare Figs. 795, 796). In the same room a mirror, framed by spindly little columns, hangs on the wall above a side table, whose gently swelling front is inlaid with satinwood.

The sideboard, introduced by Hepplewhite's *Guide* of 1788, became extremely popular during the Federal period. The example illustrated in Figure 800, built of mahogany with marquetry in lightly colored woods, has storage space below the central section as well as in the pedestal cabinets. Its high quality and the individual character of its decoration—especially the unique swags of cloth represented on the doors—reveal the originality with which American craftsmen adapted English designs.

Duncan Phyfe, the most accomplished American furniture designer of his day, operated a shop in New York from 1795 until his death in 1845. Beginning with free variations on Sheraton designs, Phyfe's furniture imitated European fashions in a gradual assimilation of Directoire, Empire, and Regency characteristics, with proportions becoming heavier as the Victorian taste emerged. Throughout his long career, however, Phyfe never copied slavishly, and many of his pieces achieved greater elegance and unity of design than their published models.

Examples of Phyfe's earlier work have been assembled in a typical room of the period (Fig. 801). The elegant simplicity of the square-back chairs, executed in 1807, betrays Sheraton's influence while hinting at the severity of newer trends, but the harmonious unity of the overall design shows the sure touch of an individual master. Other Sheraton variations appear in the straight-back sofas, one upholstered and the other with a cane back, and the "sofa table," with drawers for writing materials, resting on a pair of tripod legs. The folding-leaf card tables against the wall recall the more curvilinear designs of the Colonial Georgian period.

The Empire Style: c. 1820–60

Interiors   While Greek Revival houses often acquired freestanding Doric porticoes two stories high, interiors tended toward imposing scale and weighty architectural decoration (Fig. 802). Plain walls were painted in strong colors, while doors and windows of monumental scale were emphasized by wide, flat frames or classical pilasters and entablatures. The spirit of archaeological revival appears in the fireplace of the King house in Albany, illustrated here; figured herms support a mantel adorned with shallow reliefs imitating classical Greek tombstones. Hanging from the ceiling is a heavy chandelier, in which cut glass is subordinated to prominent metal parts, including lyre-shaped chain links and classical acanthus-scroll brackets holding the candles.

Furnishings   The spacious interiors of Empire-style homes were filled with heavily proportioned furnishings. Marble-top tables of dark mahogany rested on thick supports embellished by gilded metal attachments. Isolated ornaments carved in high relief, including the favorite lion's-paw foot, stood out against smooth, plain surfaces and abrupt right angles. Monumental wardrobes regained the popularity they had lost during the 18th century. Side tables, case pieces, and seats were often massively proportioned and decorated with architectural features. Chairs of a lighter design, however, were based on those shown in classical painting, as reflected in the continuous curve joining back and seat of the chair in the foreground of Figure 802. Geometric designs and vivid, contrasting colors in curtains, carpets, and upholstery added a sense of plush richness to American Empire interiors.

Other Revivals: 1750–1900

The historical perspective that Neoclassicism brought to the study of Greek and Roman antiquity inevitably gave rise to an appreciation of other periods and cultures. If classical art, properly understood, could be adapted to the needs of the modern age, the same principle could be applied to the Gothic and Renaissance styles and the art of the Orient. The revival and imitation of historic and foreign

styles began at the same time as Neoclassicism—around 1750—and continued as the accepted practice throughout the 19th century. Eclecticism, the selective use and combination of elements taken from a variety of unrelated sources, rested on the theory that every style had its own vocabulary and standards of excellence. Posing as an alternative to the narrow Neoclassicism dictated by the academies, eclecticism offered artists a variety of styles, whose evocations of the distant past or exotic lands had an irresistable appeal to Romantic artists.

The scope, sources, and accuracy of stylistic revival varied considerably. Gothic, Chinese, Islamic, Renaissance, and even the Baroque and Rococo styles were employed for whole buildings, separate interiors, or individual pieces of furniture. Chinese pagodas and brand-new Gothic "ruins" appeared in picturesque gardens in England and elsewhere. An otherwise Neoclassical house might have a Gothic study and Chinese bedroom, or an Elizabethan dining room and Rococo parlor. Originality counted for more than archaeological accuracy, and motifs of disparate sources often appeared in the same room and on the same piece of furniture. This tendency culminated in the High Victorian period, when a distinctive style emerged out of a thorough mixture of the styles of the past.

The Chinese Taste

Porcelain, fabrics, wallpaper, and other decorative objects from China had been imported to Europe since the Renaissance, but they were usually appreciated merely as curiosities. In the 18th century, however, Oriental art inspired much of Rococo decoration. After 1750, as East Asia became better known through detailed accounts and illustrated travel books, whole buildings—usually garden pavilions—and interiors were designed in an Oriental style. It was especially fashionable to have a bedroom in "the Chinese taste," and bedroom furniture naturally followed. Like all European beds of the mid-18th century, the example in Figure 803 is raised above the floor and has a canopy supported by posts; but here the tall headboard is decorated in Oriental fretwork, and the canopy resembles the roof of a Chinese pagoda. Fretwork and other Chinese motifs appeared on chairs and mirrors of the period, while cabinets were often lacquered ("japanned") in Oriental style throughout the 18th century.

opposite: 802. The parlor of the Rufus King house (1830–40) in Albany, New York, illustrates the heavy richness of Greek Revival interiors and Empire furniture. The emphasis on massive solidity extends even to the chandelier and curtains, which differ markedly from those in Figure 801. (*Henry Francis du Pont Winterthur Museum, Winterthur, Del.*)

right: 803. The exotic appeal of the Orient is expressed in a black and gold bed, made about 1750 for Badminton house in Gloucestershire, England. The gilded mirror on the wall reveals a mingling of Chinese with Rococo motifs. (*Victoria & Albert Museum, London [Crown Copyright]*)

Chinese-style interiors in the Royal Pavilion at Brighton (1802, 1815–21) contained furniture made of bamboo, or beechwood simulating bamboo; this vaguely Oriental style remained popular in England and America until the end of the 19th century. Interest in the exotic shifted somewhat from China to the Islamic Near East, but toward the end of the century Chinese and Japanese art served as inspiration for several progressive architects and designers (see Chap. 25).

The Gothic Revival

Much maligned by the Renaissance, the Gothic style nevertheless survived in occasional new constructions in northern Europe during the 17th and early 18th centuries. The deliberate, conscious revival of Gothic forms, however, began in England after 1750 and continued, dominating church architecture everywhere, throughout the 19th century.

The earlier manifestations of the movement were essentially light-hearted, Romantic conceits created by cultivated amateurs such as Horace Walpole, son of England's first Prime Minister. From about 1750, Walpole and a series of collaborators refurbished and gradually enlarged his own house, Strawberry Hill. The deliberately assymetrical plan of the house seemed to reflect its piecemeal growth, and the resulting irregularity of its exterior anticipated the picturesque sham castles popular in England and Scotland in the early 19th century.

The interiors of Walpole's house initiated the Gothic Revival in domestic architecture (Fig. 804). The walls of the library, added in 1754, are sheathed in a series of wide pointed arches, divided by buttresslike vertical posts, with tall pinnacles reaching toward the ceiling. Although a few details were based on authentic English Gothic monuments, the horizontal emphasis of the woodwork and flat ceiling betrays an 18th-century taste, and the skeletal Gothic screen seems easily detachable from its setting in solid masonry. The result is a charming, antiquarian essay on Gothic, appropriate for the library of a gentleman-scholar.

By the middle of the 19th century, Gothic interiors could be found throughout Europe, England, and the United States. Carved wooden paneling reappeared in major rooms, and tall, narrow windows were often filled with tracery and colored glass. The original Gothic style had never taken hold in medieval Italy, but the Gothic Revival met with greater success. The eclecticism that resulted can be seen in a room in Trieste, where a mixture of Gothic and Renaissance motifs decorates a coved ceiling of Baroque type (Fig. 805).

Furniture posed problems for the Gothic Revival, because the Middle Ages provided few models beyond choir stalls, altar tables, and the like. One solution was to substitute Renaissance designs, as in the "Elizabethan" revival (see below). Another was to take the pointed arches, complex piers, and spiky pinnacles of the great cathedrals, as well as the tracery patterns of their windows, and simply apply them to chairs and tables whose proportions and other details reflected contemporary fashion (Fig. 805). Hoping to improve on the awkwardness of such combinations, A. W. Pugin (1812–52), whose writing popularized the Gothic Revival everywhere, created several furniture designs of outstanding quality. In the chair illustrated here (Fig. 806), Pugin avoids explicitly architectural forms and employs Gothic moldings and foliate motifs in a way that enhances a straightforward structure of Regency derivation.

During the course of its long history (1750–1900), the Gothic Revival embraced a variety of divergent trends. Picturesque "ruins" set in garden landscapes evoked Romantic visions of the past. Thanks to Pugin's influential writings and the religious reform movements, Gothic was identified with Christianity and became the proper style for churches throughout the western world. Gothic imitations in homes and furnishings were often clumsy and impractical, yet the same interest in medieval architecture and crafts inspired progressive thinkers, whose theories laid the foundations of modern design (see Chap. 25).

806. The sensitive reworking of Gothic forms distinguishes an upholstered mahogany armchair designed about 1840 by A. W. N. Pugin for Scarisbricke Hall in Lancashire, England. (*Victoria & Albert Museum, London* [*Crown Copyright*])

The "Elizabethan" Revival

In England, the Romantic glorification of the native past stimulated an "Elizabethan" revival, which in fact drew upon English sources ranging from Tudor to Late Stuart. Interiors featured geometrical wall paneling and carved ceilings, while furniture displayed a wealth of turned carving. An upholstered mahogany chair of the "Elizabethan" style (Fig. 807) offers a simplified version of designs from the period of Charles II (Fig. 769).

The Rococo Revival

French styles, from Louis XIV to Empire, reappeared or lingered on in France and other countries, but a Victorian version of the Rococo became especially popular around the middle of the 19th century in England and the United States. A good American example is the parlor of the Milligan house, whose exterior was designed to imitate an Italian Renaissance villa (Fig. 808). The furniture exhibits the continuous curving shapes and characteristic cabriole legs of the Rococo style, but the proportions have changed. Short, thin legs support heavy, thickly upholstered chairs, while the marble-top table has S- and C-scrolled legs with an

above: 807. An Elizabethan Revival chair features elaborate turnings that recall Restoration furniture (Fig. 769), but the wide, solid proportions and naturalistic embroidery betray a mid-19th-century date. (*Victoria & Albert Museum, London* [*Crown Copyright*])

right: 808. The Rococo Revival thrives in a parlor of about 1853 from the home of Robert J. Milligan in Saratoga, New York. Thickly stuffed upholstery, heavy proportions, and dark colors clearly distinguish the 19th-century revival from the 18th-century Rococo. (*Brooklyn Museum*)

809. Themes of hunting and natural abundance cover every available surface of a monumental sideboard that would seem more at home in a Baroque cathedral than a middle-class dining room. Although exhibited in Manchester in 1857, the showpiece was made in 1853 for Alscot Park, a private home in Warwickshire, England. (*Photograph: A. F. Kersting*)

undisciplined life of their own. Elaborately carved, gilded mirror and picture frames, thick curtains, and a heavy chandelier all compete for individual attention. A vivid, large-scale floral pattern in the carpet (and on the walls in most houses) adds to the atmosphere of crowded richness.

In the 19th century, furniture was no longer produced by individual masters for well-informed, demanding patrons. Machine construction and mass production allowed large firms to sell their wares in quantity to middle-class customers who wanted the trappings of luxury as quickly and as cheaply as possible. The shift in patronage and change in technology seldom resulted in work of high quality. One exception, however, was the work of John Henry Belter (1804–63), who produced vigorously inventive Rococo Revival furniture in New York during the 1840s and 1850s. Belter also invented a process for bending and steaming layers of wood into curved shapes—a technique that led to important innovations in the later 19th and 20th centuries.

The High Victorian Style: c. 1850–80

At no time during the long reign of Queen Victoria (1837–1901) did a single vocabulary of forms achieve the widespread and consistent acceptance that had characterized earlier historic styles. Nevertheless, the elements of past styles were adopted in a manner that makes Victorian products recognizable as such. The taste that informed and permeated that wide variety of borrowings came into clearest focus in the third quarter of the 19th century, beginning around 1850 in England and two decades later in the United States. High Victorian design characteristically sought massive proportions, generally dark colors, and a dense ornamentation of all surfaces.

The pivotal event in Victorian design was the Great Exhibition held in London in 1851. Within the "Crystal Palace," a prefabricated iron-and-glass structure prophetic of 20th-century architecture, exhibitions of art, crafts, and machines celebrated industrial prosperity. Many other such exhibitions, especially in England and the United States, followed during the second half of the century.

The furniture shown at these trade fairs, although made solely for display, reflected and determined popular taste. A mammoth sideboard, made in 1853 and displayed at the Manchester Art Treasures Exhibition of 1857, reveals an eclecticism so instinctive that specific sources become elusive (Fig. 809). Gothic moldings and

finials, Renaissance allegorical figures, and Baroque scale and composition all fuse in an article whose function derives from the dining-room ensembles of Robert Adam! Yet distinctive Victorian preferences appear in the bulky proportions, broken silhouette, rich density of decoration, and the extremely naturalistic treatment of foliage.

The translation of the "exhibition style" into the homes and furnishings of the wealthy middle class can be seen in a bedroom from the Stanford mansion in San Francisco (Fig. 810). Strong, individual patterns cover the ceiling, wallpaper, carpet, curtains, and other fabrics. The large scale of all furnishings, including an elaborate chandelier, complete the impression of plush magnificence.

The furniture in this room, especially the monumental, canopied bed, reveals the Victorian taste for massiveness combined with profuse decoration of all surfaces. A generalized and synthetic eclecticism here seems to favor English Renaissance and Baroque sources, though Neoclassical elements appear in the X-shape supports of a small table and in the "Grecian" sofa. Following the dominant trend of the 1870s and 1880s, chairs and sofa are almost entirely covered with well-padded, embroidered upholstery.

The thorough dependence on older historic styles during the 19th century contrasted sharply with the contemporary development of new materials and mass-production techniques. Victorians were especially fond of simulating one material in another, as in Rococo chairs made of papier-mâché, "bamboo" furniture of beechwood, or the "cane" seat of an outdoor garden settee made entirely of cast iron (Fig. 811). This example reveals a related tendency in the literal naturalism of the vines, leaves, and grapes that make up the rest of the chair. The designer, while inventively exploiting the plasticity and tensile strength of the new medium, seems to do everything he can to transform it into something else.

Despite their whimsical appeal, such pieces had a duality of purpose that left little room for further development. Reacting with moral outrage, progressive designers of the later 19th century urged the thorough reform of taste in the applied arts through an emphasis on honest craftsmanship. Although resisting the inevitable progress of industrialization, these critics laid the theoretical foundation for later accomplishments. It was only in the 20th century that architecture, and with it all other aspects of design, finally came to terms with the machine age.

below: 810. A High Victorian bedroom from the Stanford house in San Francisco was furnished for comfort, solidity, and richness in 1878. A similar but more ornate bed of the same period appears in Figure 178. (*Photograph: Eadweard Muybridge; print made from a negative in the Stanford University Archives*)

above: 811. Vine leaves and grapes act as the legs and back of a cast-iron garden seat made about 1880 by E. T. Barnum in Detroit, Michigan. Manufactured in England from the 1830s and in the United States from the 1840s, such cast-iron furniture served primarily for outdoor use. (*Greenfield Village and the Henry Ford Museum, Dearborn, Mich.*)

Modern Traditions

The appearance of today's homes reflects an evolution in architecture and design that began in the late 19th century, reached a critical turning point in the early 20th, and has been refined and elaborated since then.

During these two centuries, western civilization underwent a transformation more rapid and comprehensive than any that had occurred in its previous history. Scientific discoveries and the theories of evolution and relativity challenged fundamental concepts of humanity and the universe. Conflicts between classes, nations, and ideologies culminated in the Russian Revolution and two World Wars. Perhaps the most important factor was the Industrial Revolution, which, in creating vast new sources of wealth and power, destroyed the old order of society, shifted international relations, and profoundly affected the lives of people everywhere. Transportation by railroad, steamship, automobile, and airplane, as well as communication by telegraph, telephone, radio, and the visual media brought individuals throughout the world into closer contact with each other, important events, and commercial products. In prosperous nations, improved material conditions changed living patterns and social structure, and the middle class became the predominant consumers of the products of industry.

The arts of the home naturally reflected these fundamental changes in culture and society. The domestic styles of the late 19th and 20th centuries exhibit a broad variety of aims and achievements that cannot easily be summarized in diagrammatic form. In general, however, both architecture and furnishings gradually abandoned the imitation of past styles, whether in the form of archaeological reproduction, eclectic mixture, or free variation on past modes. Together with this development, both areas of design evolved a new formal language that took full advantage of the materials and methods introduced by industry. The aesthetic principle that the form of any object should express its function, materials, and process of construction became predominant, but this did not prevent architects and designers from creating distinct personal styles.

Perhaps the single most important innovation in house design during this period was the rejection of the enclosed box in favor of the fluid interpenetration of spaces expressed in the open plan. The strength of new materials, such as iron, steel, and concrete, facilitated the distinction between structural support and the devices used to separate interior spaces, while the development of central heating eliminated the need to contain heat in closed-off rooms.

Modern Traditions	
Europe	United States

1860	**Arts and Crafts Movement: 1860–1900**
1890	**Art Nouveau: 1890–1905**
1900	**Frank Lloyd Wright:** Prairie style (1900-10)
1910	**De Stijl: 1917–31** (Holland)
1920	**International Style, I: 1919–33** The Bauhaus (Germany) Mies van der Rohe (Germany) Le Corbusier (France)
1930	**Art Deco: 1925–40**
1940	**Post-World War II Styles** (continuing to the present day)
	Scandinavian design: 1930– Frank Lloyd Wright: later career (1935-59) and followers
	International Style, II: 1940–
	Le Corbusier: late style (1945–65) and followers

Progressive Trends in the 19th Century

The beginning stages of the modern movement took the form of a conscious revolt against popular taste, as expressed in the poor quality and stylistic confusion found in household objects mass-produced for commercial distribution. This reaction began in England, where early and rapid industrial progress had affected the crafts sooner than elsewhere. As early as the 1840s, John Ruskin (1819–1900), popularizer of the Middle Ages and the undisputed arbiter of Victorian taste, condemned machine-made ornaments and the use of one material to simulate another as immoral "deceits." Similar sentiments were expressed by A. W. N. Pugin (1812–52), who wrote in *Contrasts* (1836) that "the great test of beauty is the fitness of the design for the purpose for which it was intended." The contemporary validity of the statement contrasts with the "dated" quality of his Gothic Revival buildings and furniture (Fig. 806).

William Morris

Like Ruskin and Pugin, William Morris (1834–96) identified art with morality, hated modern civilization, and looked to the Middle Ages as a model for society and art. Ruskin and Morris both held that machine production destroyed the "joy in work" that had led medieval craftsmen to create objects of true beauty. Condemning both industry and the capitalistic system, Morris advocated a thorough reform of both art and society on a Utopian medieval model. Household furnishings, he argued, should offer honesty of construction and genuineness of materials, rather than stylistic imitation, applied details, and illusionistic effects.

Morris went beyond his predecessors, however, by putting his theories to the test of reality. In 1861 he established a firm, later renamed "Morris & Co.," which produced textiles, wallpaper, and furnishings. Morris was aided by a number of artists and craftsmen in the design and execution of the firm's products.

The results of this collaboration appear in a room created in 1867 (Fig. 812). Architect Philip Webb designed the walls and ceiling with their painted and molded-plaster decorations, while painter Edward Burne-Jones provided stained-glass windows and the small painted panels in the wainscoting. Morris himself

812. William Morris and Philip Webb designed the "Green Room" in 1867 as a refreshment area for the South Kensington (now Victoria & Albert) Museum in London. The interior contains several furnishings designed and decorated at various times by Morris, Webb, and others. (*Victoria & Albert Museum, London* [*Crown Copyright*])

designed the carpet, and, with his wife, painted the folding screen with figures from a tale by Chaucer. Morris & Co. produced all the furnishings, including a grand piano and several massively proportioned cabinets, whose sturdy construction and hand-painted, elegantly stylized decorations clearly identify each piece as the unique product of individual craftsmanship.

The Arts and Crafts Movement

Morris dedicated much of his later life to the promulgation of his ideas in books and lectures, as well as through the example of his own pattern designs and the production of his firm. Unfortunately, the firm's handcrafted wares were inevitably more expensive than the debased products of industry and therefore failed to effect the broad reform on all levels of society that Morris had hoped to achieve. Nevertheless, he attracted a wide following among artists, architects, and critics, including Charles Eastlake, whose *Hints on Household Taste* (1868) was especially influential in America. A number of guilds and associations were formed in the 1880s to consolidate the efforts of likeminded designers and attract public interest in their work. The Arts and Crafts Exhibition Society, founded in 1888, gave its name to the entire reform movement.

The general trend during the later 19th century brought furnishings and interiors away from the heavy, rather medieval forms of Morris' circle toward lighter, simpler shapes with fewer historic references. A major factor in this development was the liberating influence of Japanese art, which became widely known, especially in the 1880s, through illustrated travel books and imported prints, scrolls, and pottery. Japanese homes typically contained no furniture as we know it (Fig. 3), but their uncluttered spaciousness and refined detailing seemed like a breath of fresh air next to the dense clutter of the Victorian drawing room. The elegant linear patterns of Japanese prints contributed to the flatter, more stylized decorations applied to the later examples of Arts and Crafts furniture (Fig. 815).

Charles F. A. Voysey (1857–1941) claims distinction as the most important of Morris' successors before the end of the 19th century. The houses he designed in the 1890s featured bright, uncluttered interiors, and his designs for wallpaper and textiles were the best of the day. Japanese influence contributed to the fresh, airy

quality of Voysey's furniture (Fig. 813). Voysey hated ostentation, but the elegant flat patterns of his hinges and plaques revealed a unique talent for linear design.

Arts and Crafts in America

The theories and achievements of the Arts and Crafts movement had a profound effect on the Continent by the turn of the century, but their earliest and most fruitful influence was in the United States.

Henry Hobson Richardson (1838–86) developed a personal style of architecture using rough blocks of stone in thick courses, round arches, and towers recalling the Romanesque churches of medieval Europe. His houses featured exteriors in local stone or weathered wooden shingles that harmonized with the natural setting. The size and placement of windows accommodated internal need rather than external regularity, and interiors followed an asymmetrical plan with a free flow of space around the entrance hall and stairway (Fig. 814). The example illustrated here reveals an emphasis on the warm attraction of expertly crafted woodwork in the supporting posts, framed wall panels, exposed ceiling beams, and vertical screens and balustrades. The interpenetration of spaces, as well as the built-in furniture, anticipates the work of Frank Lloyd Wright (see p. 580).

Honesty of construction and a simple, rectilinear outline characterize the drop-front desk produced about 1880 by the Herter Brothers of New York (Fig. 815). The flat surface pattern of stylized flowers, framed in rectangular panels, achieves the elegance and sophistication sought by later designers of the reform movement. Like the work of Morris and his associates, Herter Brothers' furniture emphasized qualities that could result only from individual handcrafting.

The reform movement in America gained widespread popularity among the middle classes through the designs and publications of Gustav Stickley (1848–1942). After a trip to Europe and England, where he met Voysey, Stickley introduced a line of "Craftsman" furniture, whose severely rectilinear construction out of thick pieces of wood, usually oak, emphasized honest joinery, simplicity, and massive solidity (Fig. 197). From 1901 until 1916, Stickley published *The Craftsman*, a magazine that served as the forum of progressive design and gave its name to the American reform movement.

Currents Outside the Mainstream

Even while Ruskin and Morris assailed the decline of quality in the household arts, at least two independent developments were taking place that in some degree fulfilled the ideals of the Arts and Crafts movement.

Shaker Homes   The Shakers, a radical offshoot of the Quakers, came from England to the United States in the second half of the 18th century in order to pursue a communal, religious lifestyle. A strict but cheerful work ethic, a passion for cleanliness and order, and a compulsion for efficiency all contributed to an austere approach to design. Shaker homes were characteristically clean and uncluttered—especially through the use of built-in cabinets and strips of pegs, on which not only coats but also chairs and other pieces of furniture were hung when not in use (Fig. 816). The Shakers frowned on the luxury of superficial embellishments, preferring economy of means and fitness of purpose as the standards of design. Furniture designs were those of the 18th century, modified and pared down to their essentials to achieve maximum efficiency and lightness. Every piece was fabricated with utmost care by craftsmen who saw their task as a religious exercise.

The Shaker experience bears a surprising resemblance to Morris' Utopian vision of communal handcraft villages, and yet the results were very different—and in fact more modern in appearance than the solid furniture and densely patterned interiors created by Morris and Webb. The functional but personal quality of Shaker homes continues to inspire the design of contemporary interiors (Fig. 285).

Michael Thonet   In his zeal to correct the vulgarities of most furnishings produced by industry, Morris condemned the entire system. Yet during his lifetime the principles of honest construction and genuine materials—if not handcraftsmanship—had already been reconciled with mass production in the elegantly functional designs of Michael Thonet (1796–1871), the inventor of the bentwood chair. Born in a small town on the Rhine, Thonet moved to Vienna hoping to make cabinets for great palaces. Instead, in the 1830s, he invented a process for steaming and bending solid lengths of beechwood into gently curved shapes. The result was a type of sturdy, lightweight, and inexpensive furniture whose unprecedented popularity brought it to cafés, ice cream parlors, and homes of all social and economic levels throughout Europe and the United States (Fig. 817). The Prague chair, introduced in 1851, featured rectangular lines with rounded corners, arms, and a cane seat. Slightly modified versions are still in production 125 years later (Fig.

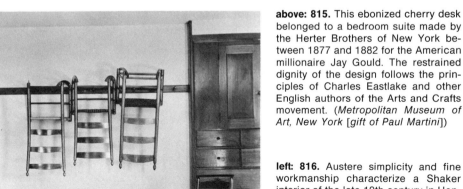

above: 815. This ebonized cherry desk belonged to a bedroom suite made by the Herter Brothers of New York between 1877 and 1882 for the American millionaire Jay Gould. The restrained dignity of the design follows the principles of Charles Eastlake and other English authors of the Arts and Crafts movement. (*Metropolitan Museum of Art, New York* [*gift of Paul Martini*])

left: 816. Austere simplicity and fine workmanship characterize a Shaker interior of the late 19th century in Hancock, Massachusetts. Ladder-back rocking chairs recall the furniture of the Early Colonial period. (*Photograph: William Winter; courtesy Shaker Museum, Old Chatham, N.Y.*)

817. Michael Thonet first mass-produced this version of the Vienna café chair in 1876. A single section of bent wood forms the back and rear legs. With minor variations, it is still in production today. (*Museum of Modern Art, New York*)

536). The desk armchair, mass-produced from 1870, was selected in 1925 to furnish an exhibition pavillion by the architect Le Corbusier (see p. 584), who declared that "this chair possesses nobility" (Fig. 47). Thonet's rockers fared less well with modern functionalists, who objected to the swirling arabesques that now seem wonderfully suited to the chair's swaying motion (Fig. 189). Thonet's firm and others have produced numerous variations on all of the originals, but these 19th-century designs have stood up remarkably well and still grace many contemporary homes (Figs. 4, 357, 452).

Art Nouveau: 1890–1905

The first truly original style since the Rococo, Art Nouveau appeared almost simultaneously throughout Europe during the 1890s. Although it formed a transition between the 19th and 20th centuries, the "Style 1900" bore little resemblance to the work that preceded or followed its brief popularity.

The explicit aim of Art Nouveau was to create a totally new formal language from which all traces of the past had been eliminated. The characteristic motif became the sinuous line, ending in a whiplash curve like the bud of a plant. Abstract but not geometric, the stylized forms expressed the process of natural growth without depending on literal representation.

All of these features appear in the Tassel house in Brussels, designed by the Belgian architect Victor Horta (1861–1947) and built between 1892 and 1893 (Fig. 818). Although probably influenced by Japanese prints and certain forward-looking English textile and book designs, Horta essentially created the style, in fully developed form, in a single building. In the stair-hall, a slender iron column, sprouting leaflike tendrils, supports arched ceiling beams pierced by openwork. Sinuous, meandering ribbons in asymmetrical patterns appear everywhere: painted on walls, inlaid in floor mosaics, and molded in the iron handrail. Until now, iron had never been so frankly exposed except in bridges and engineering works. In Horta's hands, Art Nouveau combined industrial materials with handcraft uniqueness, and functional expression with rampant decoration.

Like the Rococo, Art Nouveau was primarily a style of interior decoration, which its leading practitioners extended to everything in the house, including furniture, fixtures, lamps, and doorknobs. Hector Guimard (1867–1942), the leading Art Nouveau architect in France, even designed special nail heads as part of a totally unified environment. Long, sinuous lines, interrupted by bulbous knots, flow over Guimard's furniture, creating a dynamic unity out of deliberately asymmetrical designs (Fig. 819).

Although unaware of developments in Brussels and Paris, Antoni Gaudí (1852–1926) independently evolved a similar style of greater power and individuality (Fig. 820). Gaudí's style is more plastic and sculptural than the linear elegance of his French and Belgian contemporaries. The swelling masses of Gaudí's exteriors seem to be in constant motion, pulling interior spaces askew and leaving strange kidney-shaped, round-cornered windows that seem hollowed out by the wind. The same fluid shapes reappear in furnishings and fixtures, but not always for purely aesthetic reasons: the saddle-seated chairs of the Casa Battló are molded for human comfort, and the "ears" projecting from the chair backs provide convenient, if quite unnecessary, handles for moving them about.

The most prophetic exponent of Art Nouveau—and the only major one in Britain—was Charles Rennie Macintosh (1868–1928), a Scottish architect whose early interiors in Glasgow in the 1890s paralleled the work of Horta. With Macintosh, however, the delicate swirls of linear pattern are held in place by a framework of slender verticals and a few tempering horizontals, resulting in light, airy interiors with surfaces enlivened by evocative accents (Fig. 821). His furniture was often built in, but even his freestanding chairs defined spatial volumes through their tall, straight backs and lean, rectilinear shapes.

left: 818. A profusion of dynamic curvilinear patterns overwhelms the stair-hall of the Hôtel Tassel in Brussels (1892–93), designed by Victor Horta. The earliest Art Nouveau building was also the first private residence to make use of iron, both as a structural material and as decoration. (*Photograph: Museum of Modern Art*)

below left: 819. An angled cupboard of triangular section (1904–07) illustrates Hector Guimard's talent for asymmetrical designs united by flowing, continuous lines. The pear-wood cupboard formed part of Guimard's total design of a house for Léon Nozal in Paris. (*Musée des Arts Décoratifs, Paris*)

below right: 820. Bulging, slippery forms abound in the dining room and furnishings of the Casa Battló, built in Barcelona from 1904 to 1906 by Catalan architect Antoni Gaudí. (*Photograph: MAS*)

bottom right: 821. Charles Rennie Macintosh collaborated with his wife in designing the drawing room of their own Glasgow apartment in 1900. The light, airy quality and rectilinear discipline of the interior recalls the work of Voysey (see Fig. 813) and distinguishes Scottish Art Nouveau from the Continental movement. (*Photograph: T & R Annan & Sons, Ltd.*)

Art Nouveau had only two major practitioners in the United States. One was Louis Sullivan (1856–1924), the pioneer Chicago architect who developed a lush, florid brand of stylized naturalism in the ornament he applied to commercial structures. The other was Louis Comfort Tiffany (1848–1933). A leading designer and manufacturer of decorative art in metal and glass, Tiffany combined vibrant colors and asymmetrical decorative patterns in the lush trees and flowers of his lampshades and stained-glass windows (Fig. 822), but he is equally well known for his exquisite "Favrile" glassware, whose graceful, tapering shapes, translucent colors, and swirling forms seemed to arise naturally from the glass-blowing process. Tiffany also produced glass lighting fixtures and bronze lamps and candlesticks.

Frank Lloyd Wright, 1900–10

The series of houses built by Frank Lloyd Wright (1867–1959) during the first decade of the 20th century represent the culmination of the craftsman movement as well as the beginning of modern home design. Wright's "Prairie" houses, as he called them, incorporated many features of Richardson's and contemporary craftsman-style homes—opening one room off another, for example, and the use of unpretentious materials, as well as covered verandas placed around the house—but he expanded, refined, and integrated these elements into a coherent, powerful style. Contrary to his denials, the influence of Japanese architecture also contributed to the architect's masterful handling of materials and space, as well as his articulation of surfaces in strong vertical and horizontal lines.

Trained in Chicago under Louis Sullivan, Wright developed the theory that architecture should be "organic," that a building should "grow" from the inside out, as determined by function, materials, and site. Thus the fireplace, traditionally the focus of family life, became the central feature around which interior spaces were planned informally to allow free circulation within the house and between the interior and the outdoors (Fig. 823). Unexpected light sources and variations in ceiling height—reaching two stories at least once in most of Wright's houses—gave each area a distinct atmosphere without interrupting the continuous flow of space (Fig. 824). Voids and solid elements interacted to create a dynamic sense of movement throughout the interior. In addition to skylights and clerestories (often partially concealed), windows appeared in continuous horizontal bands held firmly in place between the ceiling and a common sill. Contrasting materials, the accentuation of structural features, and geometric detailing provided a decorative scheme fully integrated with the architecture. Much of the furniture was built in, but Wright specially designed even the freestanding pieces of each house.

The dynamic interaction between solid mass and fluid space found equally forceful expression in Wright's exteriors, of which the Robie house in Chicago is a distinguished example (Fig. 823, 825). A massive chimney, rising from the center, provides the visual and structural anchor for deeply cantilevered, low-pitched roofs, which spread outward like wings to claim areas of open space as part of the home's territory. Yet this sense of movement is tied firmly to the ground by a succession of parallel planes in the balconies and ground-level parapets. Together, these broad horizontals seem to respond to the flat site and echo the distant horizon. The bold geometric forms act as a foil to the natural landscape, whose colors, however, are repeated in the materials of brick, stone and wood. The overhanging eaves also protect the terraces that extend the house into the landscape. Interior and exterior thus formed a single entity in the Prairie house, with which Wright hoped to express the freedom of movement and wide, open spaces of the American Midwest.

Wright's position as the bridge between the 19th-century reform movement and the 20th-century acceptance of industrial technology was best expressed by the architect himself in the title of a lecture he delivered in 1901: "The Art and Craft of the Machine." Wright told his audience: "The machine is here to stay. There is no more important work before the architect now than to use this normal tool of civilization to the best advantage." Unlike the Bauhaus leaders of the 1920s and 1930s, however, Wright never *celebrated* the machine. Throughout his long career, which continued with great vitality and new innovations until his death

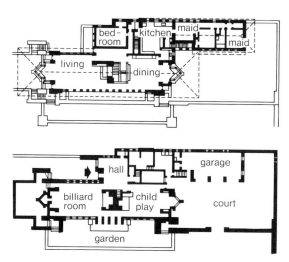

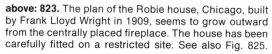

above: 823. The plan of the Robie house, Chicago, built by Frank Lloyd Wright in 1909, seems to grow outward from the centrally placed fireplace. The house has been carefully fitted on a restricted site. See also Fig. 825.

above right: 824. Architectural features are exploited for richly decorative effects in the hallway of the Coonley house, erected by Frank Lloyd Wright in 1908 in Riverside, Illinois. The corridor space flows freely into and beyond the living room, which is distinguished by a higher ceiling and a flood of light. (*Photograph: Chicago Architectural Photographing Company*)

below right: 825. The exterior of the Robie house springs outward from its massive chimney, expressing the centrality of the hearth inside (see Fig. 823). The broad, sweeping horizontals and interlocking masses and voids epitomize the "Prairie" style of Wright's early career. (*Photograph: Hedrich-Blessing*)

below: 826. Gerrit Rietveld, of the De Stijl group in Holland, created the Red-Blue Chair in 1917 as a deliberate break with traditional furniture design. The back is painted red, the seat blue, and the remaining pieces black with white ends. (*Museum of Modern Art, New York [gift of Philip Johnson]*)

bottom: 827. The first tubular steel chair was designed in 1925 by Marcel Breuer, then the 23-year-old master of the Bauhaus furniture workshop. Breuer's tubular armchair remains one of the most popular furnishings of contemporary homes. (*Museum of Modern Art, New York [gift of Edgar J. Kaufmann, Jr.]*)

in 1959, Wright maintained a romantic love of nature as strong as his hatred of the city. Even when responding to the Bauhaus-born International Style, he continued to exploit the varied colors and textures of natural materials and to integrate his houses with the contours of their natural settings (Fig. 636).

Design for the Machine Age: 1900–30

The maturity of modern architecture in the 1920s grew directly from the functionalist trend that emerged in Europe, partly in reaction to Art Nouveau, during the early years of the 20th century. This trend began in Austria, where Viennese architect Adolph Loos (1870–1933) succinctly expressed his attitude toward decoration in the title of his essay "Ornament and Crime" (1908). Other architects in France and Germany pioneered in the structural and expressive use of reinforced concrete, steel, and glass, creating several exteriors free of historic reminiscences.

De Stijl

A decisive contribution to modern design issued from a group of Dutch artists and architects associated with the magazine *De Stijl* (*Style*), founded in 1917. Promising a "radical renewal of art," the painters of the group developed a totally nonrepresentational mode, restricting the elements of painting to an abstract arrangement of lines and geometric shapes on a flat surface, using only black, white, and the primary colors of red, blue, and yellow. Gerrit Rietveld (1888–1964), a furniture designer turned architect, translated these principles into three-dimensional form as early as 1917 in his "Red-Blue Chair" (Fig. 826). The chair's rectilinear structure, flat planes of wood, and simple joinery recall the furniture of Macintosh and Wright, but the emphasis here is very different. Paint and varnish conceal the natural grain of the wooden members, whose sharp edges suggest a machine aesthetic rather than the individual craftsmanship that actually produced the chair. Intersecting elements almost always continue beyond the point of intersection, as if they could be extended infinitely into the surrounding space. The slanting planes of the seat and back seem to be the only concession to human comfort. Yet for all its freshness and absolute renunciation of past modes, the Red-Blue Chair remains an overinvolved exercise—a rigid demonstration of an aesthetic doctrine. It was left to the Bauhaus to create a modern mode of design flexible enough to meet the needs of complex, technological society.

The Bauhaus: 1919–33

Certainly the single most influential force in shaping all of modern architecture was the Bauhaus, the German state school of design. Walter Gropius (1883–1969) founded the school in Weimar in 1919 and later moved it to a new building complex of his own design in Dessau. Initially devoted to arts and crafts in the tradition of the English reform movement, the Bauhaus curriculum was soon revised to place an emphasis on working with the machine in the design of buildings, furniture, textiles, and household articles. The chief aesthetic principle was to simplify the design of any object, so that no unnecessary elements would distract from the pure statement of function, material, and the process of industrial fabrication. Attracting to its faculty artists, architects, craftsmen, industrial designers, and leaders of industry itself, the Bauhaus remained the center of European innovation until the Nazi regime forced its closing in 1933. After two generations of reform and debate, "Arts and Crafts" at last gave way to the "new unity" of art and technology.

One of the earliest expressions of this aim appeared in the invention of chairs made of tubular steel by the Hungarian architect-designer, Marcel Breuer (b. 1902). Breuer's tubular armchair of 1925 (Fig. 827) reflects its inspiration in the handlebars of a bicycle as much as in the formal precedents of De Stijl (Fig. 826), but its wholehearted exploitation of resilient, lightweight steel marks a pivotal moment in the history of design. Canvas or leather straps stretched across the metal tubes provide seat, back, and armrests; the wide stance of the chair ensures a stability surprising in a piece so easy to move. Chromium plating creates a gleaming, smooth surface that celebrates the precision of industrial production.

Breuer also designed a much simpler stool—an inverted U in tubular steel surmounted by stretched canvas or a block of wood—which was mass-produced in 1926 for Gropius' new Bauhaus buildings in Dessau. In the same year, another Bauhaus member, Ludwig Miës van der Rohe (see below) adopted Breuer's use of tubular steel in the first "cantilever chair," in which a single, continuous length of steel was arched upward from the floor to provide resilient support in a simple, graceful design (Fig. 828). The excessive springiness of Miës' chair had to be corrected in later versions, however, and the leather or woven-cane seat and back could not be attached by machine. Breuer's more practical version of the cantilever chair appeared in 1928 (Fig. 195). The rectilinear S-shape of the tubular support offered less bounce and did not encumber the sitter's legs, while the separate attachment of seat and back allowed efficient mass-production and clearly expressed a distinction between the parts. The lightness, clarity, and comfort of Breuer's chairs have ensured their popularity to this day (Figs. 547, 581).

Miës van der Rohe

The most innovative German architect of the 1920s was Ludwig Miës van der Rohe (1886–1969), who succeeded Gropius as director of the Bauhaus from 1930 to 1933. More than any other individual, Miës crystalized the machine-oriented aesthetic of the Bauhaus and spread its ideals throughout Europe and America in what came to be recognized as the "International Style." As early as 1919, Miës designed a project for a thirty-story skyscraper with floors cantilevered from a central core and enclosed entirely in glass—a scheme boldly forecasting buildings of the 1950s.

Miës van der Rohe's famous statement that "less is more" epitomized the architect's working method of reducing an object to its essentials and then refining the design through fastidious attention to every detail. Thus the expression of structure became the focus of Miës' architecture, with steel columns, slablike roofs, and nonsupporting walls all clearly distinguished and arranged on a rectangular grid plan. Miës' early masterpiece was an exhibition pavilion in Barcelona (1929), which he adapted as a model house shown in Berlin in 1931 (Figs. 829,

828. Slow, graceful curves and wide proportions characterize the earliest cantilever chair, designed by Ludwig Miës van der Rohe in 1926. The forthright clarity and refined elegance of the design are paralled in Miës' buildings. (*Museum of Modern Art, New York* [*gift of Edgar J. Kaufmann, Jr.*])

829–830. Miës van der Rohe summed up his architectural principles in a model home, erected for a building exhibition held in Berlin under his own direction in 1931.

above right: 829. The plan is extremely open but zoned for different activities.

right: 830. Inside the exhibition house, living and dining areas are discreetly defined within the continuous flow of open space. The furniture, all designed by Miës, includes a Barcelona chair (1929), a low glass-top table, two "Tugendhat" chairs (1929) similar to the Barcelona, and four cantilever chairs (1926) grouped around a circular dining table. (*Photograph: Museum of Modern Art* [*Miës van der Rohe Archive*])

830). Under a low, flat roof resting on thin steel columns, freestanding walls divide the interior space into loosely defined areas. Those walls, parallel and perpendicular to each other, extend onto the flat site in an abstract arrangement recalling the compositions of De Stijl. The open plan also recalls Wright, but Miës strove to give his interiors a sense of static, classical repose rather than dynamic contrasts. The structure was meant to recede from view, to act as the neutral enclosure of a strictly ordered volume. Steel construction allowed supporting posts to be widely separated, so that interior spaces became broad, uncluttered, and infinitely adjustable. Wide, expansive windows, reaching to the logical boundaries of floor and ceiling, divided interior from exterior space with minimal emphasis. Living functions were sparsely defined by a single wall or a strategically placed carpet.

Miës designed every detail of his houses, including all the chairs and tables visible in Figure 830. In the foreground is his "Barcelona" chair, produced for the Barcelona pavillion of 1929. One meter square in plan, the chair's large scale reflects the ample proportions of Miës himself, but the gentle curves of its X-shape supports are a perfect expression of luxurious comfort. The two pieces cannot be joined mechanically, which unfortunately increases the cost of production. Yet no other chair designed since the Empire period rivals the Barcelona's monumental dignity (Fig. 23, 25), and it continues to hold a place of honor in today's homes.

Le Corbusier

Charles Edouard Jeanneret-Gris (1888–1965), commonly known as Le Corbusier or by the nickname "Corbu," had the benefit of broad exposure to the work of many early 20th-century masters. Although never a member of the Bauhaus, Le Corbusier participated directly in the creation of the "International Style" during the 1920s. Corbu possessed Gropius' and Miës' vision of the architect as a designer for all of society, as well as their concern for incorporating industrial technology in a new architecture. Moreover, he brought a painter's sense of abstract visual form to the creation of a monumental style of building.

In 1919 and 1920, contemporary with Miës' projects for glass skyscrapers, Le Corbusier developed a program for domestic architecture in what he called the "Citrohan" house, a prototype single-family dwelling planned as part of an urban settlement. The prototype had several specifications, including a two-story living area, lit by a tall "window-wall" and backed by a lower room under a balcony. As we have seen, this use of vertical space has returned to prominence in many contemporary homes (Fig. 27; Pl. 22, p. 162).

Except for this feature, the salient characteristics of the Citrohan prototype appeared in the masterpiece of Corbu's early career, the Villa Savoye, built between 1929 and 1930 in the Paris suburb of Poissy (Fig. 831). Constructed of reinforced concrete, the house is raised off the ground on stilts or "pilotis," freeing the ground for circulation—Corbu explains—while a roof garden "recaptures" the open space covered by the structure. Frame construction frees the enclosing walls to be treated as geometric shapes dominated by long, horizontal "ribbon" windows. The wide spacing of concrete structural supports also allows for an open plan in the interior, here treated with living areas grouped around a sunken patio.

Le Corbusier called the modern house a "machine for living in" and stated that functional considerations necessitated his commitment to "pilotis," roof gardens, the "free façade," ribbon windows, and the open plan. Yet Corbu's functionalism often yielded to an equally strong aesthetic stance. Thus we see that on one side of the Savoye house, the ribbon window is continued unglazed across the open patio, simply in order to preserve the similarity of all four façades and the clarity of the rectangular, prismatic exterior. Similarly, the practical utility of the windscreen on the roof in no way dictates its wonderfully sculptural form.

Equally opposed to Wright's romantic integration of house and landscape and Miës' rationalist ideal of neutral, reticulated space, Le Corbusier saw architecture as a heroic statement—an assertion of human will on the indifference of nature. The "pilotis" raised the house and its occupants to a commanding position above the landscape, whose diverse colors, textures, and contours served only as a foil for the smooth, white surfaces and sharp, pristine shapes of Corbu's architecture.

Le Corbusier's interiors were like hollow cubes, enclosed by geometric solids and sometimes enlivened by pastel colors and protruding sculptural shapes, such as the cylindrical staircase in the Savoye house. Corbu furnished several interiors with the aid of his brother, Pierre Jeanneret, and furniture designer Charlotte Perriand. Together they designed the elegant built-in storage walls and three very different chairs installed in a remodeled home (Fig. 832). The "Basculant" armchair (right) and formfitting chaise longue (left) both had tension springs to provide resiliency, while the cube chair (rear) consisted entirely of stuffed leather pillows contained in a steel cage. Though less rational and more expensive than the chairs of Breuer and Miës, this sophisticated furniture remains perfectly at home in the most contemporary surroundings (Fig. 482).

Art Deco

The popularization of modern trends in design took the form of the *Art Deco* or *Paris moderne* style of the later 1920s and 1930s. Named after the Exposition Internationale des Arts Decoratifs, held in Paris in 1925, Art Deco quickly reached the general public through the efforts of department stores in Europe and America. On the whole, this "modernistic" style applied new materials and geometric decorations to traditional forms more acceptable to popular taste than the austere designs of the Bauhaus. Shiny metals, glossy lacquered woods, polished stone, glass, and some of the newly invented plastics were used in various, usually contrasting combinations. Geometric shapes, especially the triangle, appeared in dynamic patterns, including zig-zags, thunderbolts, and sunbursts (Fig. 833). During the 1930s, "airflow" patterns and "streamlining," suggesting the speed and power of modern machines, covered not only automobiles but everything from skyscrapers to easy chairs (Fig. 508). Essentially a symbolic style, Art Deco celebrated mechanistic progress in much the same way that Art Nouveau had expressed organic growth. Although responsible for several stunning creations, the style lacked the theoretical foundation that allowed Bauhaus and later designers to integrate function, materials, and process in designs of more lasting value. The spread of "modernistic styling" also coincided with the introduction of planned obsolescence in the design of automobiles and home appliances.

833. Ceramic tile, glass, and gold plate create a dazzling display of Art Deco modernism in a private office bathroom, designed by Jacques Delamarre, in the Chanin Building, New York City (1929). A sunburst appears above the shower doors, which present a dynamic pattern of triangles, quadrants, and semicircles. (*Photograph: Angelo Hornak*)

Homes and Furnishings after 1930

The achievements of the early 20th century were gradually refined, expanded, and popularized during the period after 1930. Despite the persistence of revivalistic modes, industrial materials, simple forms without applied ornament, and direct functional expression became standard features of architecture and household furnishings. Nevertheless, as modern concepts of design gained wider currency, the Bauhaus approach was moderated and made more flexible. Thus, in both architecture and furnishings, less geometrical shapes and traditional materials such as wood and brick became accepted alongside the polished chrome and machinelike severity of the 1920s. The development of plastics provided new materials whose potentials were slow to be exploited and are still being explored today.

Furnishings

Renewed interest in wood and in less rectilinear shapes characterized furniture design after 1930. The persistence of strong craft traditions and the late arrival of industrialization contributed to the high quality of Scandinavian furniture, which became extremely popular throughout the world during the thirties, forties, and fifties. From the outset, first-rate designers collaborated with industry to create mass-produced furniture of almost handcrafted quality. Finnish architect Alvar Aalto (b. 1898) combined simplicity and lightness with the natural grain and color of laminated birch in a series of chairs and stacking stools designed from 1933 (Fig. 834). Native design traditions inspired new variations by a number of other designers in Denmark and Sweden.

The polished metal frames and geometric forms of the Bauhaus lost their supremacy in other countries, too. Even Marcel Breuer (Fig. 827) turned to form-fitting bent plywood in a chair he designed in 1935 (Fig. 148).

American furniture design rose to prominence through the work of Charles Eames (b. 1907) and Eero Saarinen (1910–61), who collaborated in a prize-winning chair design of 1940, in which back, seat, and arms formed a single, multicurved shell of bent plywood. Though produced only in a modified version, this prototype formed the basis for the later work of each individual. Eames' side chair of 1946 combined the best qualities of industrial and natural materials (Fig. 281). Metal rods provide a strong, lightweight support, while seat and back are molded to human comfort in walnut plywood. Rubber disks joining the two elements add resilience. A similar combination of materials, together with thick upholstery, appeared in Eames' more recent lounge chair and ottoman (Fig. 527).

Saarinen developed his and Eames' original scheme into a set of single-pedestal tables and chairs, in which the seat, back, arms, and support all formed part of a unified, curving shape (Fig. 835). As we have seen elsewhere (see Chap. 7), the almost infinite flexibility of plastic has made this material a major focus of contemporary design innovation.

Domestic Architecture

Architecture in the period after 1930 was largely shaped by the early accomplishments and continuing careers of the three leading masters: Wright, Miës van der Rohe, and Le Corbusier. The emphasis on volume, lightness, and severity shared by Miës and Corbu in the early period gradually reached an almost universal currency, and some of the best examples of the International Style were built in the forties and fifties by Miës and his followers. Yet from the mid-1930s, Frank Lloyd Wright repeatedly challenged the assumptions of the International Style in houses and other buildings that gave new life to the romantic, "organic" approach he had created in the first decade of the century. The styles of both camps were imitated and widely popularized, and the rigid distinction between

above: 834. Finland's Alvar Aalto employed both solid and laminated wood in his crisply designed chairs and stacking stools of the 1930s. Legs of solid wood divide into layers at the knee to form strong, resilient supports. (*Courtesy ARTEK*)

below: 835. A graceful continuity of line enhances the single-pedestal chair designed in 1958 by Eero Saarinen, an American born in Finland. Seat, back, and arms, made of molded plastic reinforced with fiberglass, rest on a base of cast aluminum. (*Courtesy Knoll International*)

the two approaches broke down in favor of a more flexible interaction. During the same period, Le Corbusier translated his original mode into more sculptural and monumental terms. Throughout the past decades, younger architects of considerable talent have built on the work of the masters and explored new approaches, contributing to the variety of contemporary architecture.

Wright and His Influence Frank Lloyd Wright had already turned to a new but characteristically individual style in the 1920s. His California houses of that period featured simpler compositions than before, invisible flat roofs, and a new building material, concrete blocks, which were decoratively stamped to create dense optical patterns on all surfaces.

Wright condemned the International Style as so many "boxes on stilts," but he responded to the European challenge with the Kaufmann house, built in the late thirties (Fig. 636). The use of reinforced concrete in the boldly cantilevered terraces, the avoidance of ornament throughout, and the spacious interiors with floor-to-ceiling windows all reflect European influence; but the dramatic massing of forms, close relationship to the site, and use of roughly textured local stone in the chimney-core recall features of Wright's early "Prairie" houses. Supported by cantilevers instead of stilts, the balconies are nevertheless suspended above the ground like Le Corbusier's buildings. Yet the broad, massive terraces echo the rock ledge and waterfall below, while the rest of the house is firmly anchored to the hillside, from which an outcropping of natural rock reaches into the interior as part of the central fireplace.

From the 1930s until his death in 1959, Wright continued to expand his vocabulary in a number of domestic and other structures. He frequently articulated interior spaces by means of different floor levels, and in the forties and fifties he built a number of houses with inventive plans based on angular shapes and on circles of different sizes (Fig. 836).

Wright was too individualistic to become a teacher in the usual sense, but he trained many capable assistants who continued his principles in careers of their own, particularly in California and the Midwest. Followers and imitators spread the master's influence far and wide—and sometimes rather thin, as in the "ranch style" homes built by developers in the fifties and sixties. Many aspects of the "Prairie" houses passed into general currency during this period. Wright's influence is clear, for example, in the low, horizontal proportions, deep roof overhangs, natural materials, and free indoor-outdoor communication of a California house built in 1950 (Fig. 837).

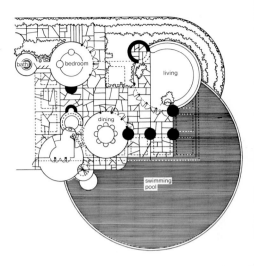

836. Each living function is housed in a separate plywood cylinder in a project that Frank Lloyd Wright proposed first in 1938 for the Ralph Jester house in southern California and again in 1940 for the Martin Pence house in Hawaii. The circular rooms open onto a terrace under a broad, flat roof, supported by thick columns and smaller cylinders made of stone. Wright continued to experiment with circular plans during the 1940s and 50s.

below left: 837. Architect Gordon Drake and landscape designer Douglas Baylis hoped to encourage casual indoor-outdoor living in their "Unit House," erected in San Francisco in 1950. Planned on a three-foot module, the dwelling was designed to expand with the changing needs of a growing household. (*Photograph: Julius Shulman*)

The International Style

The closing of the Bauhaus in 1933 marked the end of the "classic" or definitive phase of the International Style. Of its creators, Corbu developed along different lines, while the former leaders of the Bauhaus were dispersed and temporarily cut off from major commissions. In the late thirties, Miës, Gropius, and Breuer came to the United States, where they assumed academic positions and resumed their active careers. This artistic emigration from Germany accelerated the diffusion of the International Style throughout the world and contributed to the shift in architectural leadership from Europe to the New World after World War II. By the 1950s, transparent cubes of lightweight steel and glass could be found everywhere from Tokyo to Rio De Janeiro.

At the same time, the adoption of the new mode by increasing numbers of architects naturally led to greater diversity. The almost dogmatic unity of the 1920s gave way increasingly to personal and regional variations. And just as Wright and his followers responded to the European achievement, the International Style came to admit textured surfaces, natural materials, and greater variety in planning. This trend can be seen in the work of Richard Neutra (1892–1970), a Vienna-born architect who had worked briefly with Wright before establishing a practice in California. Neutra's houses of the 1940s exhibit the lean steel-frame construction, glass walls, and geometric composition of the International Style, but they also feature the warm textures of wood and brick, as well as an open, informal integration with the immediate landscape (Fig. 838). Similar combinations appeared in the buildings of Alvar Aalto and Marcel Breuer.

The sleek, technological emphasis of the 1920s by no means disappeared, however. From 1940 until his death in 1969, Miës van der Rohe simplified and refined his basic concern with the metal frame and neutral, reticulated volumes. Perhaps the ultimate expression of his principles in domestic architecture was the Glass House designed in 1949 by Miës' foremost disciple, Philip Johnson (b. 1906; Figs. 24, 25). Except for an enclosed circular bathroom, the house is entirely surrounded by glass walls, which all but eliminate the distinction between interior space and the carefully landscaped setting. Reduced to barest essentials, the structure has an obvious, self-evident quality that belies its originality.

Le Corbusier and his Influence

Beginning in the 1930s, Le Corbusier turned away from the taut, white, planar surfaces of the Villa Savoye (Fig. 831) toward a more sculptural conception of architectural form, with an increasing interest in the plastic moldability and rough textures of exposed reinforced concrete. Although primarily concerned with city planning and large-scale projects, Corbu built a few smaller houses, in which vigorously shaped spaces and masses were enlivened by contrasting surfaces of concrete, brick, tile, and stone (Fig. 839). Yet he did not

abandon his original "heroic" approach in favor of a Wrightian integration with nature. Le Corbusier's exteriors emphasized the weight and mass of concrete in thick, heavy rectangles, protruding geometric shapes, and a balanced contrast between solids and voids that turned buildings into giant abstract sculptures.

Le Corbusier's sculptural manipulation of reinforced concrete represented an essential departure from the International Style of his earlier years, and this new approach was soon taken up by other architects. Among them was Paul Rudolph (b. 1918), a former student of Gropius and Breuer, who in 1960 designed a striking house in Florida using concrete-block construction (Fig. 840). The exterior façade features an asymmetrical arrangement of open, thick-membered rectangles, whose extension beyond the walls and roofline indicates a relaxation of strict Bauhaus functionalism. Continuous interior spaces are related through changing floor and ceiling levels, with an upstairs balcony overlooking a two-story entertainment area. This type of vertical space, expressed in general terms on the exterior, recalls earlier concepts of Wright and Corbu while clearly relating to the homes of today.

In 1950 the history of modern architecture and design was seen in terms of a unitary progression, beginning with the reforming struggle of William Morris and culminating in the final mastery of technology in the machine style of the Bauhaus— whose enlightened gospel, the International Style, gradually reached to the farthest corners of the earth. Today's perspective is less doctrinaire. In a sense, we live in a new age of eclecticism, but the sources are not the historic modes of a remote past; inspiration lies rather in the immediate heritage of the post-industrial era.

Thus we find that the various phases of the modern period are all accessible to contemporary restatement, without the need for pointlessly literal imitation. The Arts and Crafts tradition lives on in the individual workmanship of handmade houses and the general emphasis on personality in the home environment (Fig. 655). Distant echoes of Art Nouveau reverberate in the fluid curves of houses built of plastic foam or poured concrete (Fig. 382). The International Style certainly retains validity for its adaptability, economy, and elegance (Fig. 319). The lesson of Frank Lloyd Wright is particularly relevant today, when ecological arguments bolster those of aesthetics for an integration of house and landscape (Fig. 708). Both the smooth, white surfaces of Le Corbusier's early work and the sculptural plasticity of his later style reappear in contemporary homes (Figs. 628, 639, 640).

The modern period thus provides not a single development of quickly outdated fashions but rather a rich and varied range of choices. No one approach can be accepted without question or without rethinking its suitability to the present day. Yet an awareness of the modern heritage enriches our experience and enables us to respond more effectively to contemporary life.

840. Designed by Paul Rudolph, the Milam residence was built in 1960–62 on the shore of St. John's County, Florida. The bold, white rectangles dominating the rear facade create a partial sunscreen for the large areas of glass. (*Photograph: Joseph W. Molitor*)

Bibliography

DESIGN

Art Today. Ray Faulkner and Edwin Ziegfeld. 5th ed., New York: Holt, Rinehart & Winston, 1969, reprint 1974.
Basic Design: The Dynamics of Visual Form. Maurice de Sausmarez. New York: Van Nostrand Reinhold, 1964.
Design and Form: The Basic Course at the Bauhaus. Johannes Itten. New York: Van Nostrand Reinhold, 1964.
Design Awareness. Robert Sommer. New York: Holt, Rinehart & Winston, 1972.
Design Collection, The. New York: Museum of Modern Art, 1970.
Design: Sources and Resources. Louise Ballinger and T. Vroman. New York: Van Nostrand Reinhold, 1965.
Design Through Discovery. Marjorie E. Bevlin. 2nd ed. New York: Holt, Rinehart & Winston.
Elements of Design. Donald M. Anderson. New York: Holt, Rinehart & Winston, 1961.
Index of American Design, The. Erwin O. Christensen. New York: Macmillan, 1950.
Man-Made Object, The. Gyorgy Kepes, ed. New York: Braziller, 1966.
Measure of Man, The: Human Factors in Design. Henry Dreyfuss. Rev. ed., New York: Watson-Guptill, 1967.
On Designing. Anni Albers. Middletown, Conn.: Wesleyan U., 1971.

COLOR

Art of Color, The. Johannes Itten. 1961. Reprint, New York: Van Nostrand Reinhold, 1973.
Color: Origin, Systems, Uses. Harald Küppers. New York: Van Nostrand Reinhold, 1973.
Color Primer: A Basic Treatise on the Color System of Wilhelm Ostwald. Faber Birren, ed. New York: Van Nostrand Reinhold, 1969.
Grammar of Color, A: A Basic Treatise on the Color System of Albert H. Munsell. Albert H. Munsell. Faber Birren, ed. New York: Van Nostrand Reinhold, 1969.
Interaction of Color. Josef Albers. 1963. Abr. ed., New Haven: Yale U., 1971.
Light, Color and Environment. Faber Birren. New York: Van Nostrand Reinhold, 1969.
Munsell System of Color Notation, The. Baltimore: Munsell Color Co.
Student Handbook of Color. Charles N. Smith. New York: Van Nostrand Reinhold, 1965.

INTERIOR DESIGN

American Interior Design. Meyric R. Rogers. New York: Norton, 1947.
Color in Decoration. Jose Wilson and Arthur Leaman. New York: Van Nostrand Reinhold, 1971.

Decoration Defined. Jose Wilson and Arthur Leaman. New York: Simon & Schuster, 1973.
Decorative Art in Modern Interiors. Ella Moody, ed. New York: Viking, yearly 1971–73.
Decorative Art in Modern Interiors 1974/75. Maria Schofield, ed. New York: Viking, 1974.
Design Guide for Home Safety, A. Washington, D.C.: U.S. Government Printing Office, 1972.
Designing and Decorating Interiors. David B. Van Dommelen. New York: Wiley, 1965.
Homes Are for People. Satenig S. St. Marie. New York: Wiley, 1973.
Humanscale 1/2/3. Niels Diffrient, et al. Cambridge, Mass.: M.I.T., 1974.
I.E.S. Lighting Handbook. John E Kaufman and Jack F. Christensen, eds. 5th ed. New York: Illuminating Engineering Society, 1972.
Interior Design: An Introduction to Architectural Interiors. Arnold Friedman, et al. New York: American Elsevier, 1970.
Interior Design and Decoration. Sherrill Whiton. Rev. ed. of *Elements of Interior Decoration,* 1937. New York: Lippincott, 1974.
Interior Designer's Drapery Sketchfile, The. Marjorie B. Helsel, ed. New York: Watson-Gutpill, 1969.
Interior Space—Interior Design: Livability and Function with Flair. Virginia Frankel. Garden City, N.Y.: Doubleday, 1973.
Interiors for Old Houses. Jacques Debaigts. New York: Van Nostrand Reinhold, 1973.
Japanese Interiors. Editorial Board, Gakuyo Shobo. San Francisco: Japan Publications Trading Co., 1970.
Kitchen in History, The. Molly Harrison. New York: Scribner, 1973.
Living for Today. Karen Fisher. New York: Viking, 1972.
Living with Books: 116 Designs for Homes and Offices. Rita Reif. New York: Quadrangle, 1973.
Money Saver's Guide to Decorating, The. Ellen Liman. New York: Macmillan, 1972.
1601 Decorating Ideas for Modern Living. Gerd Hatje and Peter Kaspar. New York: Abrams, 1974.
Personal House, The: Homes of Artists and Writers. Betty Alswang and Ambur Hiken. Cincinnati: Whitney Library of Design, 1961.
Personal Space: The Behavioral Basis of Design. Robert Sommer. Englewood Cliffs N.J.: Prentice-Hall, 1969.
Style for Living. Alexandra Stoddard. Garden City, N.Y.: Doubleday, 1974.
Use of Color in Interiors, The. Albert O. Halse. New York: McGraw-Hill, 1968.
Young Designs in Color. Barbara Plumb. New York: Viking, 1972.
Young Designs in Living. Barbara Plumb. New York: Viking, 1969.

FURNITURE
General

Art of Furniture, The. Ole Wanacher. New York: Van Nostrand Reinhold, 1967.
Encyclopedia of Furniture, The. Joseph Aronson. 3rd ed., New York: Crown, 1965.
Modern Chairs, 1918–1970. London: Whitechapel Art Gallery, Victoria & Albert Museum, 1970.
Modern Furniture and Decoration. Robert Harling, ed. New York: Viking, 1971.
New Furniture 10. Gerd Hatje and Elke Kaspar, eds. New York: Praeger, 1971.
Nomadic Furniture. James Hennessey and Victor Papanek. New York: Random, 1973.

Antiques

American Furniture: A Complete Guide to 17th, 18th & Early 19th Century Styles. Helen Comstock. New York: Viking, 1962.
American Furniture of the Federal Period, 1788–1825. Charles Montgomery. New York: Viking, 1966.
American Furniture, Queen Anne and Chippendale Periods, 1725–1788. Joseph Downs. Rev. ed., New York: Viking, 1967.
American Heritage History of Antiques from the Civil War to World War I, The. Marshall B. Davidson and the eds. of *American Heritage.* New York: American Heritage, 1969.
Antique Furniture: The Guide for Collectors, Investors and Dealers. L. G. G. Ramsey and Helen Comstock, eds. New York: Hawthorn, 1969.
Cabinetmakers and Furniture Designers. Hugh Honour. New York: Putnam, 1969.
Complete Guide to Furniture Styles. Louise Ade Boger. Rev. ed., New York: Scribner, 1969.
Concise Encyclopedia of American Antiques, The. Helen Comstock, ed. New York: Hawthorn, 1965.
Dictionary of Antiques. George Savage. New York: Praeger, 1970.
Dictionary of English Antique Furniture. David Ash. Levittown, N.Y.: Transatlantic Arts, 1971.
Early American Furniture Makers. Thomas H. Ormsby. New York: Archer, 1957.
Furniture in England. S. W. Wolsey and R. W. P. Luff. New York: Praeger, 1969.
Furniture Past and Present. Louise Ade Boger. Garden City, N.Y.: Doubleday, 1966.
People and Furniture: The Social Background of the English Home. Molly Harrison. Totowa, N.J.: Rowman & Littlefield, 1971.

CRAFTS
General and Miscellaneous

Craft of the Silversmith, The. Geoffrey Holden. New York: Viking, 1954.

Crafts Design. Spencer Moseley, et al. Belmont, Calif.: Wadsworth, 1962.

Crafts of the Modern World. Rose Slivka, et al. New York: Horizon, 1968.

In Praise of Hands: Contemporary Crafts of the World. Octavio Paz and the World Crafts Council. Greenwich, Conn.: New York Graphic, 1974.

Modern Silver Throughout the World: 1880–1967. Graham Hughes. New York: Viking, 1967.

Organic Design in Home Furnishings. Eliot F. Noyes. 1941. Reprint, New York: Arno, 1970.

Plastics as an Art Form. Thelma R. Newman. Philadelphia: Chilton, 1964.

Ceramics

Ceramics: A Potter's Handbook. Glenn C. Nelson. 3rd ed., New York: Holt, Rinehart & Winston, 1971.

World Ceramics. Robert J. Charleston. New York: McGraw-Hill, 1968.

Glass

Glass. George Savage. New York: Putnam, 1965.

Glass: Handblown, Sculptured, Colored: Philosophy and Methods. John Burton. Philadelphia: Chilton, 1968.

200 Years of American Blown Glass. George McKearin and Helen S. McKearin. Rev. ed. New York: Crown, 1966.

Visual Art in Glass. Dominick Labino. Dubuque, Iowa: Wm. C. Brown, 1968.

Textiles

Beyond Craft: The Art Fabric. Mildred Constantine and Jack Lenor Larsen. New York: Van Nostrand Reinhold, 1972.

Carpets from the Orient. J. M. Con. New York: Universe, 1966.

Fabric Almanac II. Marvin Klapper. 2nd ed., New York: Fairchild, 1971.

Fabric Decoration Book, The. Patricia Ellisor Gaines. New York: Morrow, 1975.

Indian Blankets and Their Makers. George Wharton James. 1914. Reprint, New York: Dover, 1974.

Introductory Textile Science. Marjory L. Joseph. 2nd ed., New York: Holt, Rinehart & Winston, 1972.

Navajo and His Blanket, The. Uriah S. Hollister. 1903. Reprint, Glorieta, N. M.: Rio Grande, 1974.

Navajo Blanket, The. Mary Hunt Kahlenberg and Anthony Berlant. New York: Praeger, 1972.

Oriental Rugs: A Comprehensive Study. Murray L. Eiland. Greenwich, Conn.: New York Graphic, 1973.

Oriental Rugs and Carpets. Fabio Formenton. New York: McGraw-Hill, 1972.

Rugs and Wall Hangings. Jean Scobey. New York: Dial, 1974.

Textile Fabrics and Their Selection. Isabel Wingate. 6th ed., Englewood Cliffs, N.J.: Prentice-Hall, 1970.

Textile Handbook. 4th ed., Washington, D.C.: American Home Economics Assoc., 1970.

Weaving: A Handbook for Fiber Craftsmen. Shirley E. Held. New York: Holt, Rinehart & Winston, 1973.

ARCHITECTURE

General

Architecture Observed. Alan Dunn. Hightstown, N.J.: Architectural Record, 1973.

Experiencing Architecture. Steen Eiler Rasmussen. 1959. Reprint, Cambridge, Mass.: M.I.T., 1962.

People and Buildings. Robert Gutman, ed. New York: Basic Books, 1972.

Houses

Architectural Record Book of Vacation Houses, The. Herbert Smith. Hightstown, N.J.: Architectural Record, 1970.

Architecture Without Architects: A Short Introduction to Non-Pedigreed Architecture. Bernard Rudofsky. New York: Museum of Modern Art, 1965.

Beautiful Homes and Gardens in California. Herbert Weisskamp. New York: Abrams, 1964.

Handmade Houses: A Guide to the Woodbutcher's Art. Art Boericke and Barry Shapiro. San Francisco: Scrimshaw, 1973.

House in the City, A: A Guide to Buying and Renovating Old Row Houses. H. Dickson McKenna. New York: Van Nostrand Reinhold, 1971.

Houses Architects Design for Themselves. Walter F. Wagner, Jr., and Karin Schlegel, eds. New York: McGraw-Hill, 1974.

Houses Around the World. Louise L. Floethe. New York: Scribner, 1973.

Modern Japanese House, The: Inside and Outside. Hiroshi Sasaki, ed. San Francisco: Japan Publications Trading, 1970.

Place of Houses, The. Charles Moore, et al. New York: Holt, Rinehart & Winston, 1974.

Record Houses of 19—. Architectural Record. New York: McGraw-Hill, yearly.

Shelter. Shelter Publications. New York: Random, 1973.

Shelter and Society. Paul Oliver, ed. New York: Praeger, 1969.

They Chose To Be Different: Unusual California Homes. Chuck Crandall. San Francisco: Chronicle, 1972.

Varieties of Human Habitation. R. Martin Helick. Cambridge, Mass.: M.I.T., 1970.

ENVIRONMENTAL AND URBAN DESIGN

American Building 2: The Environmental Forces That Shape It. James Marston Fitch. Boston: Houghton Mifflin, 1972.

Architecture: City Sense. Theo Crosby. New York: Van Nostrand Reinhold, 1965.

Arts of the Environment. Gyorgy Kepes, ed. New York: Braziller, 1972.

Bucket of Oil, A: The Humanistic Approach to Building Design for Energy Conservation. William W. Caudill, et al. Boston: Cahners, 1974.

Cluster Development. Wilston H. White. New York: American Conservation Assn., 1964.

Complexity and Contradiction in Architecture. Robert Venturi. New York: Museum of Modern Art, 1966.

Death and Life of Great American Cities, The. Jane Jacobs. New York: Random, 1961.

Design for the Real World: Human Ecology and Social Change. Victor Papanek. New York: Bantam, 1973.

Design with Nature. Ian L. McHarg. Garden City, N.Y.: Natural History, 1969.

For Everyone a Garden. Moshe Safdie. Cambridge, Mass.: M.I.T., 1973.

Future of the City, The: New Directions in Urban Planning. Peter Wolf. New York: Watson-Guptill, 1974.

God's Own Junkyard: The Planned Deterioration of America's Landscape. Peter Blake. New York: Holt, Rinehart & Winston, 1964.

Handbook of Urban Landscape. Cliff Tandy, ed. New York: Crane-Russak, 1972.

Housing and Society. Glenn H. Beyer. New York: Macmillan, 1965.

Image of the City. Kevin Lynch. Cambridge, Mass.: M.I.T., 1968.

Matrix of Man: An Illustrated History of Urban Environment. Sibyl Moholy-Nagy. New York: Praeger, 1968.

New Towns in America: The Design and Development Process. James Bailey, ed., with American Institute of Architects. New York: Wiley, 1973.

PUD: A Better Way for the Suburbs. Maxwell C. Huntoon, Jr. Washington, D.C.: Urban Land Institute, 1971.

Row Houses and Cluster Houses: An International Survey. Hubert Hoffmann. New York: Praeger, 1967.

Urban Design as Public Policy. Jonathan Barnett. Hightstown, N.J.: Architectural Record, 1974.

Wasteland: Building the American Dream. Stephen A. Kurtz. New York: Praeger, 1973.

LANDSCAPE DESIGN AND HORTICULTURE

ABC of Indoor Plants, The. Jocelyn Baines and Katherine Hey. New York: Knopf, 1973.

Beginner's Kitchen Garden, The. Jan Riemer. New York: Morrow, 1975.

Bringing the Outdoors In. Peter Loewer. New York: Walker, 1974.

Budget Landscaping. Carlton B. Lees. New York: Holt, Rinehart and Winston, 1960.

Fruits for the Home Garden. Ken and Pat Kraft. New York: Morrow, 1975.

Garden, The: An Illustrated History. Julia S. Berrall. New York: Viking, 1966.

Handbook for the Home. Department of Agriculture. Washington, D.C.: U.S. Government Printing Office, 1973.

History of Gardens and Gardening, A. Edward Hyams. New York: Praeger, 1971.

Houseplants Are For Pleasure: How to Grow Healthy Plants of Home Decoration. Helen Van Pelt Wilson. Garden City, N.Y.: Doubleday, 1973.

Japanese Garden, The: An Approach to Nature. Teiji Ito. New Haven, Conn.: Yale U., 1972.

Landscape Gardening. James Underwood Crockett and eds. of Time-Life Books. New York: Time-Life, 1971.

Landscaping and the Small Garden. Marjorie J. Dietz. Garden City, N.Y.: Doubleday, 1973.

HISTORY

General

Concise History of Interior Decoration, A. George Savage. New York: Grosset & Dunlap, 1966.

History of the House. E. Camesasca, ed. New York: Putnam, 1971.

Illustrated History of Furnishing, An. Mario Praz. New York: Braziller, 1964.

Europe: Renaissance to Revivals

Architecture of the Italian Renaissance. Peter Murray. New York: Schocken, 1963.

Baroque Architecture. Christian Norberg Schulz. New York: Abrams, 1971.

English Country House, The. Olive Cook. New York: Putnam, 1974.

French Decorative Art 1638–1793. George Savage. New York: Praeger, 1969.

Outline of European Architecture, An. Nikolaus Pevsner. Rev. ed., Baltimore: Penguin, 1960.

Victorian Comfort: A Social History of Design from 1830–1900. John Gloag. New York: St. Martin, 1974.

American: Colonial to Revivals

American Architecture and Urbanism: A Historical Essay. Vince J. Scully, Jr. New York: Praeger, 1969.

American Woman's Home: Or Principles of Domestic Science. Catherine Beecher and Harriet Beecher Stowe. 1869. Reprint, New York: Arno, 1972.

Art and Life in America. Oliver Larkin. Rev. ed., New York: Holt, Rinehart & Winston, 1960.

Arts and Crafts in New England 1704–1775, The. Francis Dow. New York: DaCapo, 1967.

Arts in America, The: The Colonial Period. Louis B. Wright, et al. New York: Scribner, 1966.

Arts in America, The: The 19th Century. Wendell D. Barrett, et al. New York: Scribner, 1969.

Colonial Craftsman, The. Carl Bridenbaugh. Chicago: U. of Chicago, 1966.

Dwellings of Colonial America. Thomas Waterman. Chapel Hill, N.C.: U. of North Carolina, 1950.

Gingerbread Age, The. John Maass. New York: Bramhall, 1957.

Great Houses of America. Henry Lionel Williams and O. K. Williams. New York: Putnam, 1966.

History of American Art, A. Daniel M. Mendelowitz. New York: Holt, Rinehart & Winston, 1970.

Treatise on Domestic Economy. Catherine Beecher. Boston: Thomas Webb, 1842.

Victorian Home in America, The. John Maass. New York: Hawthorn, 1972.

Modern

Architecture: Nineteenth and Twentieth Centuries. Henry Russell Hitchcock, et al. 2nd ed., Baltimore: Penguin, 1963.

Art Nouveau. S. T. Madsen. New York: McGraw-Hill, 1967.

Arts and Crafts Movement in America 1876–1916, The. Robert Judson Clark, ed. Princeton, N.J.: Princeton U., 1972.

Craftsman Homes. Gustav Stickley. New York: Craftsman, 1909.

Encyclopedia of Modern Architecture. Wolfgang Pehnt, ed. New York: Abrams, 1964.

Frank Lloyd Wright. Peter Blake. Baltimore: Penguin, 1964.

International Style, The. Henry Russell Hitchcock and Philip Johnson. 1932. Reprint, New York: Norton, 1966.

Le Corbusier and the Tragic View of Architecture. Charles Jencks. Cambridge, Mass.: Harvard U., 1974.

Louis C. Tiffany, Rebel in Glass. Robert Koch. New York: Crown, 1964.

Miës van der Rohe. Peter Blake. Baltimore: Penguin, 1964.

Modern Architecture. Vincent J. Scully, Jr. Rev. ed., New York: Braziller, 1974.

Richard Neutra. Esther McCoy. New York: Braziller, 1960.

Walter Gropius. James Marsten Fitch. New York: Braziller, 1960.

Work of William Morris, The. P. Thompson, ed. London: Heinemann, 1967.

Notes to the Text

CHAPTER 1

1. Edward T. Hall, *The Hidden Dimension* (New York: Anchor, 1969), pp. 68–69.
2. Margaret Mead, *Blackberry Winter: My Earlier Years* (New York: Morrow, 1972), p. 143.
3. Paul Bohannan, *Social Anthropology* (New York: Holt, Rinehart and Winston, 1963), p. 86.

CHAPTER 4

1. Glenn H. Beyer, ed., *The Cornell Kitchen. Product Design Through Research* (Ithaca, N.Y.: Cornell University, College of Human Ecology, 1952); Rose E. Steidl, *Functional Kitchens*, Cornell Extension Bulletin 1166 (Ithaca, N.Y.: Cornell University, College of Human Ecology, 1969); *Beltsville Energy-Saving Kitchen, Design No. 2,* U.S. Department of Agriculture Bulletin No. 463 (Washington, D.C.: U.S. Government Printing Office, 1961).
2. *Beltsville Energy-Saving Kitchen, Design No. 1,* U.S. Department of Agriculture Bulletin No. 418 (Washington, D.C.: U.S. Government Printing Office, 1957); *Beltsville Energy-Saving Kitchen, Design No. 2,* U.S. Department of Agriculture Bulletin No. 463 (Washington, D.C.: U.S. Government Printing Office, 1961).

CHAPTER 5

1. James Marston Fitch, *American Building 2: The Environmental Forces That Shape It* (Boston: Houghton Mifflin, 1972).

CHAPTER 7

1. Emilio Ambasz, ed., *Italy: The New Domestic Landscape: Achievements and Problems of Italian Design* (New York: Museum of Modern Art, 1972), p. 163.

CHAPTER 9

1. The Munsell system of color notation is accepted by the United States of America Standards Institute for color identification.
2. The Ostwald system of color notation is used as the basis for the Color Harmony Manual and Descriptive Color Names Dictionary, Published by the Container Corporation of America (Chicago, 1948).

CHAPTER 16

1. Robert Sommer, *Personal Space: The Behavioral Basis of Design* (Englewood Cliffs, N.J.: Prentice-Hall, 1969), p. 66.

CHAPTER 18

1. Joseph Carreiro and Steven Mensch, *Building Blocks: Design Potentials and Constraints* (Ithaca, N.Y.: Cornell University, Office of Regional Resources and Development, Center for Urban Development Research, 1971), p. 12.

CHAPTER 20

1. Ian McHarg, *Design with Nature* (Garden City, N.Y.: Natural History Press, 1969), p. 29.
2. James Bailey, ed., *New Towns in America: The Design and Development Process* (Washington, D.C. and New York: American Institute of Architects and Wiley, 1973), p. 74.
3. William Wayne Caudill, Frank D. Lawyer, and Thomas A. Bullock, *A Bucket of Oil: The Humanist Approach to Building Design for Energy Conservation* (Boston: Cahners, 1974), p. 70.
4. Arthur J. Pulos, "The Universal Object,: *Industrial Design*, XX:1 (January-February 1973), pp. 43, 46.
5. John Morris Dixon, "Job Site for Utopia," *Progressive Architecture*, LIV:3 (April 1973), p. 79.

Terms italicized within definitions are themselves defined in the glossary.

ABS (acrylonitrile, butadiene, styrene) A tough, lightweight, highly moldable *plastic* compound especially suited to fitted parts and interlocking components; major uses include *modular* furniture, luggage, plumbing systems.

acoustics A science dealing with sound as it is produced, transmitted, and controlled. Often refers specifically to the optimum perception of musical sounds.

acrylics Rigid, durable *plastics* that are very clear and transparent and have the unique ability to "pipe" light. Common trade names include Lucite, Plexiglas, and Perspex.

adobe brick *Brick* composed of sun-dried clay with a *cement* or asphalt stabilizer; a traditional building material in the southwestern United States and other hot, dry climates.

area The two-dimensional measure of a surface; in home design, usually the square measure of large planar elements—walls, floors, or the whole enclosure.

ASA (acrylonitrile, styrene, acrylic elastomer) A *plastic* compound with properties similar to those of *ABS*.

ashlar *Masonry* construction in rectangular stones or *bricks*.

atrium plan An architectural *plan* in which all major rooms open directly upon an atrium or central courtyard, which may be glass-enclosed.

awning windows Windows hinged at the top or occasionally at the bottom that swing in or out to open.

ballon frame See *skeletal frame construction*.

bay window A window set in a frame projecting outward from a wall to create an interior recess. Usually of fixed glass, the window may have movable sections.

beam The horizontal member of a structure's support skeleton resting on vertical *posts*; usually a heavy timber or metal bar.

bi-nuclear plan An architectural *plan* that divides a structure into two separated *wings*. In home design, such a plan often sets aside one wing for group living, the other for bedrooms.

board-and-batten construction A type of wall surfacing in which wide vertical boards are sealed at their junctures by narrow strips of wood, the battens.

bow window A *bay window* taking the form of an unbroken curve.

braced frame See *skeletal frame construction*.

brick A clay block hardened by heat, often used as a building material. See also *adobe brick, firebrick*.

broadloom Floor *textiles* woven on looms more than 36 inches wide.

cabriole A furniture leg of double curvature, tapering gradually to an ornamental foot, often in the form of an animal's paw.

cantilever In architecture, any horizontal member—a *beam,* floor, or other surface—projecting beyond its support.

carpet A soft-surface floor covering available by the yard and blanketing the entire floor. Increasingly, the term is used to embrace partial floor coverings or *rugs*.

casement window A window hinged at one side to swing inward or outward.

cast To mold a substance while it is in a maleable, usually liquid state, allowing it afterward to set or harden. Also, the result of such a process.

cavity-wall construction A building technique that provides hollow space within a wall to afford room for pipe and wiring as well as *insulation* in the form of thermal materials or simply trapped air.

cement A finely powdered composition of alumina, silica, lime, iron oxide, and magnesia which, when combined with water, sets to a hard, durable mass; the binding agent for *concrete*.

ceramics Objects shaped from clay and heated (fired) in a kiln to make them hard and durable.

chaise longue An elongated seat for reclining with a raised backrest and sometimes with arms.

china Fine white *ceramic* ware fired at a very high temperature; the material of figurines and much expensive dinnerware.

clapboard A wood *siding* composed of narrow boards each with one thinner edge to facilitate horizontal overlapping; also, an individual board of this type.

clerestory A window or bank of windows inserted between two roof levels to bring light high into a room.

closed plan An architectural *plan* that divides the internal space of a structure into separate, discrete rooms.

cluster planning The arrangement of dwelling units (usually attached, low-rise structures) in concentrated groupings in order to create larger communally shared open spaces than are possible in conventional *tract development*.

commode A low chest of two or more drawers resting on legs.

concrete A material consisting of *cement* mixed in varying proportions with sand and gravel or other aggregates. With the addition of water, the mixture becomes moldable, capable of assuming almost any shape. Concrete dries to a heavy, stonelike mass of great strength. Pre*cast* blocks and slabs offer particular convenience for building. See also *reinforced concrete*.

concrete blocks Large, generally hollow, brick-like blocks composed of *concrete*. They are widely used in building, especially for walls.

condominium A multiunit living complex—usually of the apartment-house type but sometimes organized as a group of separate dwellings—in which residents own their individual units. Services and maintenance are provided by a management company, which charges a fee to residents.

conduction A heating system whereby radiators circulating hot water or steam warm the air in an enclosure.

console table A table placed against, or whose top is affixed to, a wall.

convection A heating system whereby air warmed in a furnace is blown out through registers.

cornice The topmost horizontal member of any structure. In interior design, a horizontal band at a window top or ceiling that conceals curtain or *drapery* tops and rods.

coved ceiling A ceiling that curves into the supporting walls, rather than meeting them at right angles.

crystal In common usage, *glass* of superior quality containing lead.

dado The specially finished lower portion of an interior wall defined by a continuous horizontal *molding* that is normally waist-high; also, the molding itself.

daybed An elongated chair or *chaise longue;* more generally, a convertible couch in which the mattresses serve as the seating surface.

dead storage Holding space either beyond unaided human reach or otherwise inconveniently situated.

dome A hemispherical roof or vault. In theory, the result of rotating an arch about its vertical axis.

dormer A window structure projecting outward from a sloped roof.

double-glazing The process of providing windows with two thin sheets of *glass* hermetically sealed together and trapping air between them; often used for window walls because of the superior cold insulation.

double-hung windows Windows having two vertically movable *sashes*.

draperies Loosely hung, often heavy *fabric* curtains.

drop-leaf table A table whose top has one or more hinged "leaves" that can be folded down.

dropped ceiling That portion of a ceiling lowered below the actual functional level or below other sections of the ceiling within the same space. Often, a dropped ceiling serves to articulate specific segments of a room, such as a dining area.

earthenware A relatively coarse red or brown *ceramic* ware fired at a low temperature; typically brittle and fragile, porous if *unglazed*.

ell A right-angled building extension.

fabric Cloth; more specifically, a construction of *fibers*, not necessarily woven.

fiber A material of natural or synthetic derivation capable of forming a continuous filament such as *yarn* or thread.

fiberglass Any number of *plastic* resins, such as polyesters, polypropylene, or *nylon* reinforced with segments of *glass fibers*.

figure As applied to wood, the overall pattern and character, including all irregularities of *grain*, burls, knots, and so forth.

film As applied to *textiles*, an extremely thin sheet of *plastic* produced by extrusion, *casting*, or calendering (compression between rollers or plates). Films are used as *fabrics* or as bonding *laminates*.

firebrick Very hard *brick* capable of withstanding the intense heat of a kiln or fireplace interior.

flatware The implements of eating and serving food—knives, forks, and spoons.

fluorescent lighting Artificial lighting that results when electrical current activates a gaseous mixture of mercury and argon within a sealed *glass* tube to create invisible radiation which is then absorbed by the tube's interior surface coating of fluorescent material to yield visible luminescence.

fretwork Ornamental openwork or relief arranged as a network of small, usually straight bars; often carved.

FRP *Fiberglass*-reinforced *plastics* in thin, translucent sheets; often used for patio roofs, light-transmitting walls and ceilings, and furniture.

gabled roof A double-pitched roof; a roof that comes to a point and forms a triangle; also describes the interior ceiling.

galvanized iron Iron coated with zinc or paint to retard rust.

gateleg table A *drop-leaf* table with legs that rotate outward to support collapsible leaves.

geodesic dome Developed by R. Buckminster Fuller, a self-supporting rigid network of steel or paper rods joined in triangular patterns and covered with a membrane of *glass, plastic,* or other material.

glass A mixture of silicates, alkalies, and lime that is extremely moldable when heated to high temperatures—permitting blown, molded, pressed, and stretched forms—and cools to a rigid, nonabsorbent, transparent or translucent substance.

glass blocks Hollow, bricklike forms of *glass* available in a variety of shapes and sizes. They can be set together or joined to other materials with *mortar*.

glaze A protective and/or decorative glassy coating bonded to a *ceramic* piece by firing.

grain Disposition of the vertical *fibers* and pores in a piece of wood. More generally, *texture*, from fine to coarse, resulting from the particle composition of the material. See also *hardwood, softwood*.

gypsum board Also known as wallboard or plasterboard, an interior wall surfacing consisting of thin panels of a *plaster*like material. The boards are not decorative, so they must be painted, wallpapered, or covered with another material.

half-timbered Constructed of exposed wood *beams* and *posts* with remaining spaces filled by *masonry, brick,* or wattle and daub.

hardwood Finely *grained* wood types from broad-leaf, deciduous trees such as maple, oak, and walnut. Hardwoods are for the most part (although not always) harder than *softwoods;* they are also more expensive and accept fine finishes and intricate shapes more readily.

highboy A tall chest of drawers, usually divided to simulate a chest-on-chest, with the lower section most often resting on short legs.

incandescent lighting Artificial radiant lighting created by heating a filament—usually of tungsten in common house bulbs—to a temperature at which it glows.

inlay A general term for techniques of decoration whereby pieces of wood, metal, ivory, or shell combine in patterns of contrasting color and/or *texture,* either as insertions in a background material or applications to a solid backing, to result in a continuous surface. See also *intarsia, marquetry, parquetry*.

insulation The prevention, by means of certain materials, of an excessive transfer of electricity, cold, heat, or sound between the inside and the outside of a structure or between portions of a structure; also, the materials themselves.

intarsia A type of *inlay* in which shaped pieces (usually of wood) are fitted and glued into a flat surface of solid wood.

jalousie windows Louvered window units of narrow, adjustable *glass, plastic,* or wood strips, most often arranged horizontally.

lamination The process of bonding together, generally with glue, thin sheets or small pieces of material to create a substance having properties the material would not otherwise possess, such as strength, durability, or intricate form.

lath A framework of thin wood or metal ribs integral with a building skeleton for the support of *tiles, plaster, reinforced concrete, plastic* foams, or the like.

line Technically, the extension of a point in a single dimension. More generally, the outline of a form or shape. In the language of design, the general disposition and dominant direction of elements.

load-bearing wall construction A structural system in which thick, solid walls of stone, *brick, adobe, concrete-block masonry,* or poured *concrete* carry the weight of the roof to the foundations.

loft An upper floor, normally of a commercial building or warehouse, converted into a spacious home or studio. Also, a raised platform or projecting balcony used for sleeping.

lowboy A low chest of drawers resting on short legs; the Colonial American term for a *commode*.

luminescence Visible light produced by friction or by electrical or chemical action, as opposed to *incadescence* produced by heat.

mansard roof A roof sloped in two planes, the lower slope being the steeper. A mansard roof provides more attic space than a conventional pitched or *gabled* roof.

marquetry An elaborate *inlay* technique in which pieces of wood, shell, and ivory are set in a wood *veneer,* which is then glued to a firm backing.

masonry Architectural construction of stones, *bricks, tiles, concrete blocks,* or *glass blocks* joined together with *mortar.* In broader usage, construction, as of a wall, from *plaster* or *concrete.*

megastructure A very large building usually intended to enclose an entire self-sufficient community.

melamines High-melting, transparent-to-translucent *plastics* noted for the exceptional durability they bring to *laminated* counters and tabletops and molded dinnerware. Common trade names are Formica, Micarta, and Melmac.

mobile home Originally, a small, compact dwelling capable of being towed by an automobile or truck. Today the term applies to any *prefabricated* home equipped with axles. The basic *module* can be no more than 12 feet wide, although frequently two sections are bolted together.

modular Built of *modules* or according to standardized sets of measurements.

module One of a series of units designed and scaled to integrate with each other in many different combinations to form, for example, a set of furnishings, a system of construction, or whole buildings. In current usage, the term is most often applied to *prefabricated,* mass-produced units.

molding An ornamental strip of wood or plaster that protrudes from a ceiling or wall surface.

monolithic construction A building system in which the major part of the structure consists of a single, self-supporting mass, usually of *reinforced concrete, plastic,* or *fiberglass.*

mortar *Cement,* lime, or *plaster* combined with sand and water. When wet, the substance is moldable; it hardens to form the binding agent of *masonry* construction.

new town An integrally designed, self-contained community with planned growth patterns, population size, and land-use distribution. A new-town-in-town is constructed within an existing city.

nylon The generic term (as well as trade name) for a family of *plastics* exhibiting high tensile strength in *fiber* or sheet form.

open plan An architectural *plan* organized with few fixed partitions to provide maximum flexibility in the use of interior space.

paneling Thin, flat wood boards or other similarly rectangular pieces of construction material joined side by side to form the interior and usually decorative surface for walls or ceilings.

panelized housing Dwelling structures assembled from *modular, prefabricated* panels or sheets that serve as walls, floors, and ceilings.

parquetry *Inlay* of wood that takes the form of geometric patterns; used primarily for floors and sometimes for tabletops.

plan The configuration of spaces and rooms,

walls and openings in an architectural structure; also, the graphic representation of such an arrangement.

plane A two-dimensional expanse; a flat surface.

Planned Unit Development (PUD) An integrally designed, high-density community planned for optimum land usage and composed predominantly of clustered dwelling units (*townhouses* and apartments) combined with some commercial development. See also *new town.*

plaster A paste, usually of lime, sand, and water, which hardens as it dries. Often used as a finish for interior wall and ceiling surfaces.

plastic Describing a maleable, ductile material. More specifically, a member of any of the several families of synthetic polymer substances.

plate glass Ground and polished *glass* sheets formed by spreading molten material upon an iron table mold with rollers.

plugmold strips Long tracks with numerous electrical outlets that permit flexible spacing of lighting fixtures and bulbs.

plywood A composite sheet of *laminated veneers,* some or all made of wood, with the *grain* of adjacent strata arranged at different angles to each other for increased strength.

polyethylenes A group of lightweight, flexible *plastics* characterized by a waxy surface and resistance to chemicals and moisture but not high temperatures; popular for household containers.

polystyrenes A family of rigid, transparent-to-opaque *plastics* that are durable, capable of accepting varied finishes, and possessed of good *insulation* properties.

polyurethanes See *urethanes.*

porcelain High-grade, translucent white *ceramic* ware fired at extremely high temperatures; most familiar in fine dishes and ornaments, but with many industrial applications, such as plumbing fixtures and electrical *insulators.*

post In architecture, a vertical member that supports horizontal *beams* to create a structure framework.

prefabricate To mass-produce standardized construction parts or *modules* for later assembly and/or combination.

printing As applied to *textiles,* the application of dyes according to a selective pattern to create a design by such methods as woodcut, silk screen, and tie-dye.

proportion The relation in terms of magnitude, quantity, or degree of parts to each other or to the whole. See also *scale.*

radiation A type of heating in which the heat is transmitted by radiant panels—installed in the architectural shell and warmed by air or water heated in a furnace or by electrical current—to solid masses within the area.

ranch style Descriptive of a single-story dwelling often of *open plan* and having a low-pitched roof.

reinforced concrete Concrete embedded before hardening with steel rods, which lend the material a tensile strength far beyond its original capacity.

rubble masonry *Masonry* construction of rough, irregularly shaped stones joined with *mortar.*

rug A heavy *fabric* floor covering made or cut to standard sizes; also, a floor covering that covers only a portion of the surface. See also *carpeting.*

salt box A *skeletal-frame,* two-story dwelling with a double-pitched roof whose rear slope is continued over a one-story extension at the rear.

sash A window frame holding panes of glass; the movable part of the window.

scale Size relative to a standard or to a familiar size.

secretary A tall writing desk with drawers for storage below and a set of shelves enclosed by doors above a hinged writing surface.

shape The measurable, identifiable contours of an object.

shed ceiling A single-slope, lean-to type ceiling.

shingle A thin slab of wood or other material, slightly thinner at one end. Laid in overlapping rows, shingles form a building's *siding* or roof covering.

siding The exterior surfacing of a building; boards, metal slabs, *shingles,* or other materials providing protective covering for the exposed outer walls of frame buildings.

site The actual ground space on which a house is constructed.

skeletal frame construction A building system consisting of a supporting framework of *posts* and *beams,* to which walls and roof are attached as a shell or skin. If junctures of the support skeleton are strengthened by diagonal cross-pieces, the arrangement is termed a braced frame or, in small wooden-frame homes, a balloon frame.

skylight A window in a roof admitting natural light through reinforced *glass* or some other transparent or translucent material.

softwood Coarse-*grained,* fibrous wood primarily from trees with needle-type leaves that they do not shed, such as pine, cedar, and redwood. Although they may actually be harder than some *hardwoods,* softwoods are less expensive and cannot be given as high a finish.

split-level A house in which the floor level of one portion lies approximately midway between floors of the adjoining two-story section.

spur wall A freestanding wall projecting from an adjoining wall at one end.

stainless steel Durable, blue-gray steel made rust- and stain-resistant by the inclusion of chromium.

stoneware A relatively fine, durable, and waterproof *ceramic* ware made from gray or light brown clays fired at medium temperatures, often used for medium-price dinnerware.

stressed skin construction A building system in which geometrically shaped panels are arranged to form a self-supporting structure.

stucco A weather-resistant *plaster* for exterior use.

studio A one-room apartment; a combined living/working space.

suspension A variation of *skeletal frame construction* in which horizontal *beams,* floors, or roofs are hung from the supporting vertical *posts.*

terra cotta Fired clay, usually low-fire *earthenware;* also, the reddish-brown color associated with this ware.

textile A *fiber* construction; technically, a woven *fabric.*

texture Tactile surface quality, perceived directly through touch, or indirectly through vision.

tile Stone, *concrete,* or *ceramic* pieces, flattened and/or curved, used for roofing and as wall and floor covering. Also, thin slabs of cork, linoleum, or other resilient material used primarily to protect and enhance interior walls, floors, and ceilings.

townhouse Once termed a "row house," a structure two to five stories high that directly abuts the buildings adjacent on either side. Interior space tends to be long and narrow, with doors and windows only at the front and back.

tract development A residential community planned with detached, single-family dwellings, each on its own plot of land. Lots and houses typically are arranged in a tight grid pattern. Compare *cluster planning.*

turning The art of shaping decorative wooden cylindrical forms—furniture parts, columns, utensils—through the cutting action of a fixed tool upon a piece of wood as it rotates rapidly on a lathe. Also, the result of this technique.

upholstery A soft covering of *fabric* on seating units, sometimes but not necessarily over padding, stuffing, and possibly springs.

urethanes Lightweight, cellular *plastics* capable of assuming nearly any density and thus any hardness from resilient to rigid. Urethane foams can be sprayed as surface coating or preformed as cushioning and *insulation.*

utility core A central space or a unit, sometimes *prefabricated,* that contains all a home's service elements, including bathrooms, heating, air-conditioning, and the like.

valance A wide *cornice* of rigid material or *fabric.*

veneer A thin facing of decorative or protective material attached to another material, which is usually of inferior quality.

vinyls A versatile family of strong, lightweight *plastics* available in flexible and rigid, molded and *film,* foam and cellular forms.

wallboard See *gypsum board.*

weaving The process of interlacing two or more sets of *yarns,* usually set at right angles to each other, to make *textiles.*

wing A building portion that extends from or is subordinate to the major central area.

yarn A long strand, either of *fibers* twisted together or of extruded synthetic material, used in *fabric* construction.

Index

Georgian style, Colonial, 549–554; English, 557, 561–562

glass, 248–255, 585; architectural, 249 (Fig. 319), 253 (Fig. 326), 254, 266 (Pl. 38), 352 (Figs. 465, 466), 465 (Fig. 822); crystal, 176 (Fig. 227), 249, 253 (Fig. 324); cut, 252, 253 (Fig. 324); drawn, 252; enameled, 252; engraved, 252; etched, 252, 253 (Fig. 325); handblown, 155 (Fig. 199), 251 (Fig. 321); gilded, 252; *latticino*, 253 (Fig. 323); leaded, 252, 254, 352 (Figs. 465, 466), 253 (Fig. 326); molded, 251 (Fig. 322); for pictures, 443; pressed, 251; rolled, 252; stained, 252, 254, 266 (Pl. 38); see also *glassware, mirrors, windows*

glass blocks, 237 (Fig. 298), 307 (Fig. 405)

Glass House (Johnson), 20 (Figs. 24, 25), 588

glassware, 435–436

Gothic Revival, 568 (Figs. 804, 805), 569 (Fig. 806)

Greek Revival style, 557, 565, 567 (Fig. 802)

grilles, 341; window, 339; wooden, 336 (Pl. 50)

Gropius, Walter, 582, 583

Guarini, Guarino, 517 (Fig. 730), 533 (Fig. 753)

guest house, 61 (Fig. 73)

guest room, 62 (Fig. 74)

Guimard, Hector, 578, 579 (Fig. 819)

Gwathmey & Siegel, 161 (Pl. 21), 390 (Fig. 522)

handmade houses, 469 (Fig. 655)

heating, 104–106

hedges, 487

Hepplewhite, George, 560 (Fig. 794), 561–562; influence of, 562, 564 (Fig. 799), 565

Herter Brothers, furniture, 576, 577 (Fig. 815)

highboy, 550 (Fig. 781), 551 (Fig. 782), 553, 554 (Fig. 788)

high-rise housing, 495

High Victorian style, 571–572

Hope, Thomas, 562 (Fig. 797), 563

Horta, Victor, 578, 579 (Fig. 818)

hue, 192–194, 200–202

indoor-outdoor communication, 479–481

Industrial Revolution, 143, 151–153, 156–158, 555, 573

inlay, wood, 226 (Fig. 288), 227

insulation, 104–105

intarsia, 227

International style, 19 (Fig. 22), 582–584, 586–589

Italian design, 145

Japanese house, 349 (Fig. 460), 575

Johnson, Philip, 19 (Figs. 22, 23), 20 (Figs. 24, 25, 26), 21, 504 (Fig. 714), 588

Jones, Inigo, 529 (Fig. 752), 541

kitchens, 66–81 (Figs. 80–83), 349 (Fig. 459); appliances, 68 (Table 4.1); colors in, 77 (Pl. 13), 178 (Pl. 26); design of, 73–81; dimensions, 68 (Fig. 84); lighting for, 101; location of, 75 (Fig. 158); prototype, 143; requirements, 69–71; work areas, 143 (Fig. 182)

knitting, 275–276

Knodel, Gerhardt, 170 (Fig. 218)

lamps, see lighting

landscape design, 476–491, 498–500

Larsen, Jack Lenor, 151, 167 (Fig. 213), 273 (Fig. 351), 281 (Fig. 366), 313 (Fig. 412), 382 (Fig. 369), 455 (Fig. 631)

laundry facilities, 81–82

Le Brun, Charles, 534 (Fig. 757), 535

Le Corbusier, 115, 578, 584 (Figs. 831, 832), 585, 586, 588 (Fig. 839), 589; influence of, 588–589

Lewis Wharf, Boston, 506 (Figs. 717, 718)

light, 88–103; color of, 96, 112 (Pl. 19); brightness needed, 94–95; reflection, 97 (Table 5.3); see also *lighting*

lighting, 88–103; artificial, 90–97; bathroom, 57

(Fig. 69), 101; bedroom, 49, 101; colored, 112 (Pl. 19); daylight, 89–90; dining, 39, 101; entrance, 100 (Fig. 127), 101; exterior, 101–102 (Fig. 128); fixtures 97–100 (Figs. 121–125, 127); as furniture, 100 (Fig. 126), 250 (Fig. 320); kitchen, 78–81, 101; lamps, 100, 248 (Fig. 318), 429 (Figs. 592–594); plugmold, 98 (Fig. 123), 446 (Fig. 623); recessed, 112 (Pl. 18); spotlights, 98 (Fig. 122); types of, 91–95; see also *light, skylights*

living rooms, 417 (Table 16.1), 418 (Fig. 579); lighting for, 101; view, 177 (Pl. 24)

Louis XIV style, 531, 535

Louis XV style, 536

Louis XVI style, 557–558

louvers, 339; wooden, 338 (Fig. 443)

low-rise housing, 497

Lucite, 261, 406; chair, 406 (Fig. 555); dining table and chairs, 266 (Pl. 39); in furniture design, 260 (Fig. 341)

MacIntire, Samuel, 564 (Fig. 799)

Macintosh, Charles Rennie, 578, 579 (Fig. 821)

macramé, 197 (Pl. 28), 276 (Fig. 351)

Mannerist style, 518, 522

marquetry, 227, 519 (Fig. 731), 538, 542 (Fig. 770), 548, 558 (Fig. 790), 562

masonry, 229–241, 306; block materials, 233, 235 (Pl. 60); floors, 355, 358; form in, 240–241; moldable materials, 235; rubble, 232 (Pl. 34), 233 (Fig. 291); walls, 232 (Pl. 34), 294–295

mattresses, 389–390; sizes, 415 (Fig. 577)

McHarg, Ian, quoted, 500

medium-rise housing, 496

megastructures, 509–510 (Figs. 723–725); ecological, 512–513 (Figs. 726, 727)

Meier, Richard, 139 (Fig. 176), 161 (Pl. 20), 178 (Pl. 26), 333 (Fig. 439), 335 (Pl. 48), 343 (Fig. 453), 460 (Figs. 639, 640)

metal, 255–259; form in, 258; as furniture material, 395 (Figs. 534, 535), 406; ornament in, 258–259; resistance of, 258 (Fig. 335); stove, 318 (Pl. 47)

metalwork, 445

Miës van der Rohe, Ludwig, 77 (Pl. 13), 115, 583 (Figs. 828–830), 586, 588

mirrors, 254–255; gilded, 567 (Fig. 803); as wall material, 254 (Fig. 327), 307

mixing center, kitchen, 67 (Figs. 82, 83), 69 (Figs. 86, 87)

mobile homes, 13, 131 (Fig. 169), 474, 475 (Figs. 668, 669); communities, 507–508

modular design, 158 (Fig. 202); bathroom units, 473; furniture, 385 (Fig. 512), 389 (Fig. 519), 392 (Fig. 525); housing, 130–131 (Fig. 168), 163 (Figs. 205–207), 472–474 (Figs. 662–667), 507 (Fig. 720)

monolithic construction, 465

Moore, Charles, 98 (Fig. 123), 115 (Fig. 140), 178 (Pl. 27), 284 (Pl. 42), 294 (Fig. 383), 338 (Fig. 442), 422, 423 (Fig. 583), 446 (Fig. 623)

Moore & Turnbull, 239 (Fig. 299), 368 (Fig. 489), 388 (Fig. 516), 427 (Fig. 590)

Morris, William, 155, 574–575 (Fig. 812), 589

motor homes, 474, 475 (Fig. 670)

multiple-family plans, 125

multiunit housing, 493–498, 500 (Fig. 708)

Munsell, Albert, color system, 202 (Fig. 252), 203

music, settings for, 33–34

Neoclassicism, 555–566; American Federal style, 565; American Empire style, 565–566; Early, 557; English Late Georgian style, 561–562; English Regency style, 562–563; French Louis XVI style, 557–558; French Empire style, 558; Late, 557

Neutra, Richard, 588 (Fig. 838); quoted, 29

new towns, 471–472, 501–504; Columbia, Md., 471 (Fig. 661), 503 (Figs. 712–713), 504; Reston, Va., 501–503 (Figs. 709–711)

new-towns-in-town, 504–505 (Figs. 714–716)

Noyes, Eliot, 123 (Fig. 155), 294–295 (Figs. 384–387)

Ostwald, Wilhelm, 202; color system, 203 (Fig. 254), 204

outlets, electrical, 102–103

paint, 297 (Figs. 390, 391), 308–309 (Fig. 406)

Palladio, Andrea, 521 (Figs. 736–737), 522, 529; *Four Books on Architecture*, 541; Anglo-Palladian style, 541

paneling, plywood, 223 (Fig. 280), 307 (Fig. 404), 349 (Fig. 461); wood, 220 (Fig. 272), 304 (Fig. 396)

panelized housing, 130 (Figs. 166, 167), 472–473 (Figs. 662–666)

Panton, Verner, 146 (Fig. 186), 147

parquetry, 227; floors, 360 (Fig. 477), 361 (Fig. 480)

patchwork, 281; quilt, 59 (Pl. 9), 282 (Fig. 368)

patios, interior, 486 (Fig. 687); lighting for, 101–102

Peruzzi, Baldassare, 521 (Fig. 735)

pewter, 259 (Fig. 336); flatware, 435 (Fig. 604)

Phyfe, Duncan, 564 (Fig. 801), 565

pillows, 439 (Fig. 613)

plans, 124–132; Beecher, 144 (Fig. 183); bi-nuclear, 120–212; closed, 114–115 (Fig. 139); expanable, 129 (Fig. 165); industrialized, 130–132; multifamily, 125; multiple-story, 124; open, 114–115 (Fig. 138); selection of, 132–136

planned communities, 500–510

Planned Unit Development (PUD), 504–506 (Figs. 714–718)

plants, as design elements, 440 (Figs. 614–616), 441; garden, 489; potted, 483; as window treatment, 342

plaster, 240

plastics, 260–267; environmental problems of, 264; families of, 311–312; foamed, 260 (Fig. 339), 262 (Fig. 343); 406, 466 (Fig. 652), 467; form in, 264–267; as furniture material, 406, 586; in Italian design, 145; ornament in, 264–267; resins, 261; tables, 385 (Fig. 513); wall coverings, 311–312

Plateresque style, 525 (Fig. 744)

Platner, Warren, 150 (Fig. 194), 151, 326 (Fig. 428), 440 (Fig. 614)

play areas, 36, 47 (Fig. 53), 384, 483–485 (Figs. 682–685)

Plexiglas, 261, 406; "Infinity" table, 100 (Fig. 126)

plumbing, 122

plywood, 222 (Figs. 277–279); lumber-core, 222 (Fig. 278); particle-board, 222 (Fig. 279); veneer-core, 222 (Fig. 277)

"Poker" table, 398 (Fig. 544)

polyester, 267 (Fig. 345)

polyethylenes, 262

polystyrenes, 262–263

polyurethane foam, 145, 466 (Fig. 652), 467

pool house, 178 (Pl. 27)

pools, swimming, 483 (Fig. 682), 484 (Figs. 683, 684), 489 (Fig. 692)

porches, 480 (Fig. 677), 481

Port la Galère, France, 508 (Fig. 722), 509

prefabrication, of houses, 163 (Figs. 205–207), 239 (Fig. 301), 472–475 (Figs. 662–670), 507 (Fig. 720), of window units, 327 (Fig. 430)

Pugin, A. W. N., 569 (Fig. 806), 574

Queen Anne style, 542–543 (Figs. 771, 772), 553; American (Fig. 782)

rattan, 403 (Fig. 549), 407 (Figs. 556, 557)

refrigerator center, 69 (Fig. 85)

Regency style, 557, 562 (Fig. 797), 563 (Fig. 798)

remodeling, of houses, 470–471 (Figs. 657–660)

Renaissance, 517–529; English, 526–529; French, 522–524; Italian, 518–522; Spanish, 524–526

LITTLE HOUSE
Laura Ingalls Wilder

MY FIRST LITTLE HOUSE BOOKS

CHRISTMAS
IN THE
BIG WOODS

ADAPTED FROM THE LITTLE HOUSE BOOKS

By Laura Ingalls Wilder

Illustrated by Renée Graef

HARPERCOLLINS PUBLISHERS

For my Dad
—R.G.

Christmas in the Big Woods Text adapted from Little House in the Big Woods, *copyright 1932 by Laura Ingalls Wilder, renewed 1959 by Roger Lea MacBride. Illustrations copyright © 1995 by Renée Graef. Printed in the U.S.A. All rights reserved. Library of Congress Cataloging-in-Publication Data Wilder, Laura Ingalls, 1867–1957. Christmas in the Big Woods / adapted from the Little house books by Laura Ingalls Wilder ; illustrated by Renée Graef. p. cm. — (My first Little house books) Summary: A young pioneer girl and her family celebrate Christmas in their cabin in the Wisconsin woods. ISBN 0-06-024752-5. — ISBN 0-06-024753-3 (lib. bdg.) — ISBN 0-06-443400-1 (pbk.). [1. Christmas—Fiction. 2. Frontier and pioneer life—Wisconsin— Fiction. 3. Family life—Wisconsin—Fiction. 4. Wisconsin—Fiction] I. Graef, Renée, ill. II. Series. PZ7.W6461Ch 1995 E—dc20 94-14478 CIP AC Typography by Christine Kettner 3 4 5 6 7 8 9 10 HarperCollins®, ☰®, and Little House® are trademarks of HarperCollins Publishers Inc.*

Illustrations for the My First Little House Books are inspired by the work of Garth Williams with his permission, which we gratefully acknowledge.

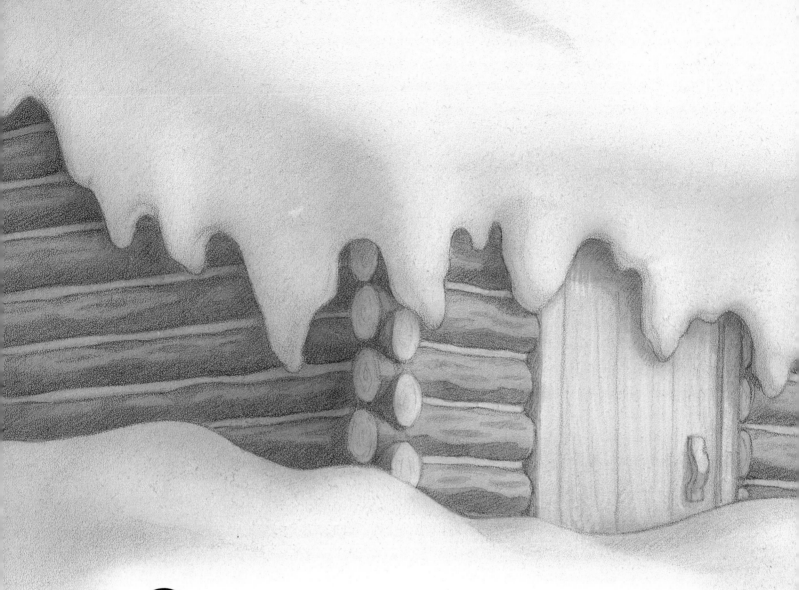

Once upon a time, a little girl named Laura lived in the Big Woods of Wisconsin in a little house made of logs.

Laura lived in the little house with her Pa, her Ma, her big sister Mary, her little sister Carrie, and their good old bulldog Jack.

Christmas was coming, and the little house
was covered with snow. When Pa came in from
shoveling, he caught Laura up in a big bear hug
against his cold winter coat. His mustache was
covered with melting snowflakes.

Ma was busy all day long cooking good things for Christmas. She baked bread and apple pies, and filled a big jar with cookies. Laura and Mary got to lick the spoon.

Pa and Ma showed Laura and Mary how to make
molasses candy by pouring hot sugar-and-molasses
syrup into pans of snow. The syrup hardened at
once and turned into candy! Laura and Mary
could eat one piece each, but the rest was saved
for Christmas Day.

The day before Christmas, Aunt Eliza, Uncle Peter, and cousins Peter, Alice, and Ella came to visit. Laura and Mary heard sleigh bells ringing, and then a big bobsled came out of the woods. Aunt Eliza, Uncle Peter, and the cousins were inside covered up with blankets.

When everyone came inside, the little house was filled to the seams. Jack ran around in circles, barking happily. Now there were lots of children to play with!

Laura and Mary and the cousins put on their warm coats and mittens and scarves and went outside to make pictures in the soft, deep snow.

They played so hard that when night came, they were too excited to sleep. But they knew they must, or Santa Claus would not come. So they hung their stockings by the fireplace, put on their red flannel nightgowns, and went to bed.

In the morning they all woke up almost at the same moment and ran to see what was in their stockings. In every stocking was a pair of bright red mittens and a stick of red-and-white-striped peppermint candy. They were so happy they could hardly speak.

But Laura was the happiest of all. In her stocking was a beautiful rag doll with black button eyes and a pink-and-blue calico dress. Laura named her doll Charlotte, and she let all the other children hold her.

For Christmas breakfast Ma made each child a pancake man. All the children held their plates next to the stove and watched while Ma made the pancake men one by one out of pancake batter. Peter ate his up right away, but the girls ate theirs slowly to make them last.

It was too cold to go outside, so the children
played quietly inside. They ate their candy,
admired their mittens, and looked at the pictures
in Pa's big green book until it was time for the
cousins to go home. Laura held Charlotte in her
arms the whole time.

At last Aunt Eliza, Uncle Peter, and the cousins bundled up in their coats and blankets and got into the bobsled. "Good-by!" they called, and off they went into the woods. In a little while the happy sound of sleigh bells was gone, and Christmas was over. But what a happy Christmas it had been!

DATE DUE			
DEC 4 '01			

E
WAT

Watson, Mary.

The butterfly seeds

30000100107022

659976 01720   01160C

Mary Watson

The BUTTERFLY SEEDS

TAMBOURINE BOOKS NEW YORK

Library of Congress Cataloging in Publication Data
Watson, Mary, 1953–
The butterfly seeds / by Mary Watson. — 1st ed.   p. cm.
Summary: When his family comes to America,
Jake brings special seeds that produce
a wonderful reminder of his grandfather.
[1. Emigration and immigration—Fiction.
2. Grandfathers—Fiction.]   I. Title.
PZ7.W3278Bu 1995 [E]—dc20 95-13250 CIP AC
ISBN 0-688-14132-3 (tr). — ISBN 0-688-14133-1 (le)

1 3 5 7 9 10 8 6 4 2
First edition

*In memory of my grandfather,
and the many happy hours I spent with him
in his greenhouse.*

Jake's house was empty, except for the overstuffed trunk in the middle of the floor.

"Sit on it, Mama," Papa instructed.

His sisters giggled as they watched Mama bounce up and down while Papa tried to close the latch.

But Jake just stared out the window. He kept thinking about how much he would miss Grandpa.

When Grandpa came to say good-bye, he brought presents for everyone. But he gave Jake something special.

"They're butterfly seeds," Grandpa said, poking around in the little tin box. "Just plant them in your new garden, and, like magic, you'll have hundreds of butterflies."

"Are you sure they will grow in America, Grandpa?" Jake asked sadly. Grandpa pressed the little box tightly into Jake's hand and nodded.

That evening, Jake's family crowded
onto the deck of the great S.S. *Celtic.* Many
of the passengers were carrying balls of yarn
with the ends trailing over the side of the
boat.

When the ship pulled away from the
dock, those left behind held the ends and
watched the lines stretch out across the
ocean. Jake could barely see Grandpa when
his yarn-line was pulled from his hand. He
reached into his pocket to make sure
Grandpa's seeds were safe.

That night, the ship tossed, rolling the
passengers back and forth in their narrow
bunk beds. Jake couldn't sleep. He reached
over and slipped his hand into his jacket
pocket.

"What do you have there?" Benny asked.
The boys moved closer to the dim cabin
light.

"They're butterfly seeds," Jake said,
opening the tin.

"What kind of seeds?" a few sleepy-eyed
children asked as they crawled down from
their bunk.

Then Jake told them about Grandpa's
seeds, and the beautiful butterfly garden
he would plant in America.

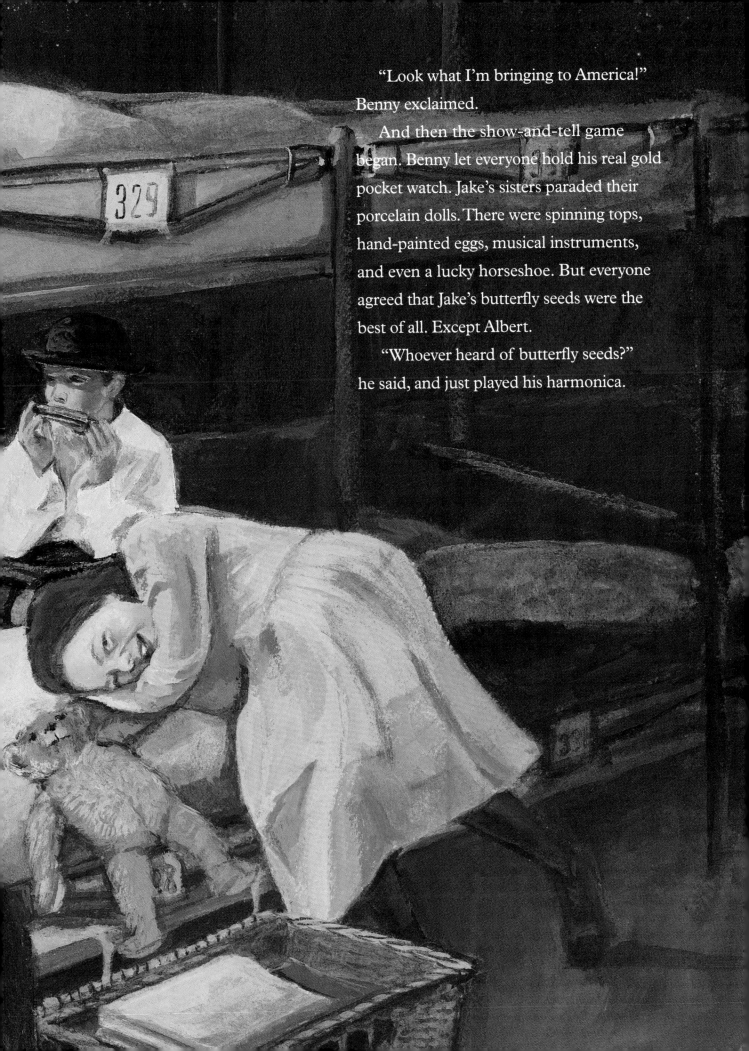

"Look what I'm bringing to America!"
Benny exclaimed.

And then the show-and-tell game
began. Benny let everyone hold his real gold
pocket watch. Jake's sisters paraded their
porcelain dolls. There were spinning tops,
hand-painted eggs, musical instruments,
and even a lucky horseshoe. But everyone
agreed that Jake's butterfly seeds were the
best of all. Except Albert.

"Whoever heard of butterfly seeds?"
he said, and just played his harmonica.

After two long weeks, the ship docked in New York. Papa held tightly to Mama and the children as everyone was herded onto the waiting ferryboats.

When the ferries reached Ellis Island, the passengers were shuffled into long lines to be inspected. Jake's heart raced, as he slowly inched up in line. He wondered if they would take away his seeds. The inspectors looked in Jake's ears and eyes—but not in his pockets. Grandpa's seeds were safe!

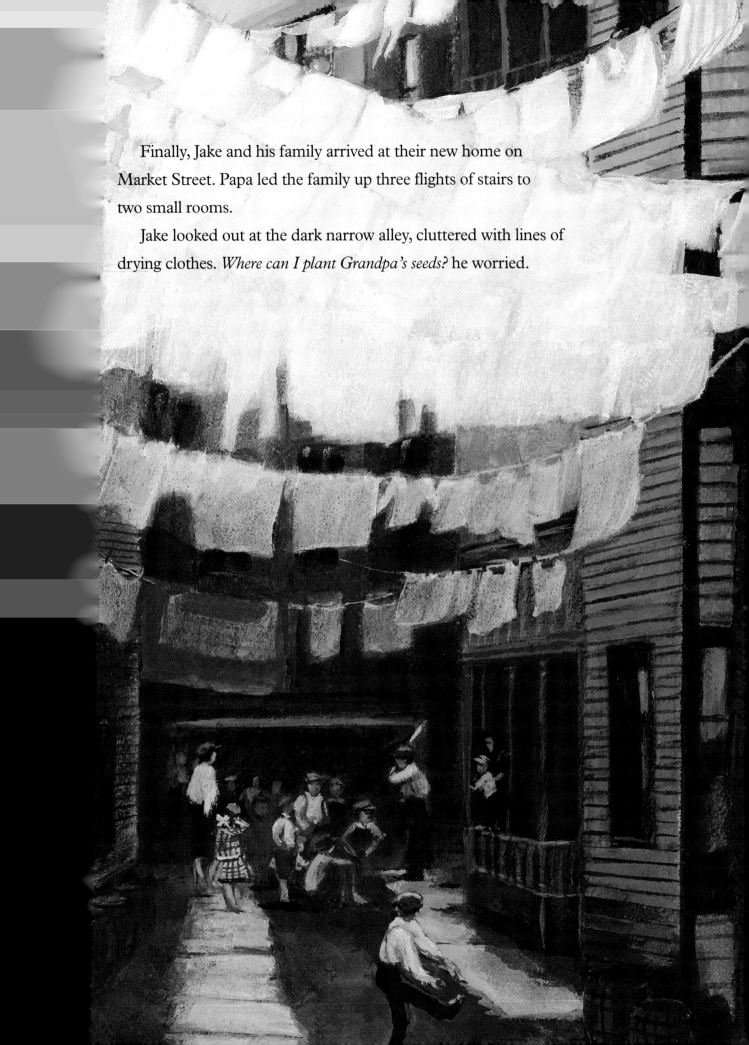

Finally, Jake and his family arrived at their new home on
Market Street. Papa led the family up three flights of stairs to
two small rooms.

Jake looked out at the dark narrow alley, cluttered with lines of
drying clothes. *Where can I plant Grandpa's seeds?* he worried.

The next morning, Jake was up early. Below, he spotted a fruit vendor emptying a crate of apples into his cart.

"Could I have that empty crate, sir?" he yelled down.

Before Mr. Gargiulo could figure out where the question had come from, Jake was standing breathlessly beside him.

"I'm going to make a window box . . . so I can plant my grandpa's seeds in it . . . and that's why I need the crate," he blurted out.

"You can have the crate, boy, but I don't think it's any good for planting seeds." Mr. Gargiulo wiggled his fingers between the slats.

"All you need is a piece of burlap to fix that," called Mr. Lingchow, the fish peddler.

He emptied his catch into an icy bin and handed Jake the empty bag. Jake opened the seam with his pocketknife and spread the burlap evenly inside the crate.

Jake hurried across the street to
the blacksmith shop to show Papa. It
was Papa's first day at his new job, and
he didn't pay much attention when Jake
asked for his advice.

"I need a way to keep this crate from
falling off our windowsill," Jake shouted over
the ring of the anvil.

"Maybe I can help you," someone
hollered. It was Mr. O'Malley, the shop
owner. He knew just what Jake needed. He
hammered two bars of red-hot metal into a
strong pair of window-box hangers.

After work, Papa nailed the box into place. Jake rigged up a clothesline and a pulley to hoist up buckets of dirt from the alley. All of the neighborhood children wanted to help. All except for Albert, who played his harmonica instead.

It was a hot summer. Jake and his new friends climbed the fire escape every day to check the window box. They would hang over the railing and search through the bushy plants for butterflies.

"Maybe your silly old grandpa got the seeds mixed up," Albert would mutter.

Jake began to wonder if Grandpa's seeds were magic or just a story made up for a homesick boy.

Then one day the sky rumbled, and a sudden shower drenched the hot, steaming streets.

When the sun reappeared, merchants and shoppers filled the street once more. The children went back to their play.

Suddenly, Mr. Gargiulo called out, "Look at that beautiful butterfly."

The children chased the butterfly through the crowded street until it flew up to Jake's window box.

"Look at them all!" Albert shouted.

Jake heard Albert's yell and opened his window.

"They're finally here, Grandpa!" Jake whispered, as if Grandpa
were listening. "Your butterflies are here . . . and they like
America too."